BATMAN

GOTHAM KNIGHTS: TRANSFERENCE

BA

writers
DEVIN K. GRAYSON   JEN VAN
METER

pencillers
DALE EAGLESHAM   ROGER ROBINSON
PAUL RYAN   COY TURNBULL

inkers
JOHN FLOYD   JOHN LOWE   PAUL RYAN

colorists
DIGITAL CHAMELEON   PAMELA RAMBO
JEAN SEGARRA   WILDSTORM FX

letterers
SEAN KONOT   BILL OAKLEY

collection cover artist
BRIAN BOLLAND

BATMAN created by
BOB KANE with BILL FINGER

GOTHAM KNIGHTS:

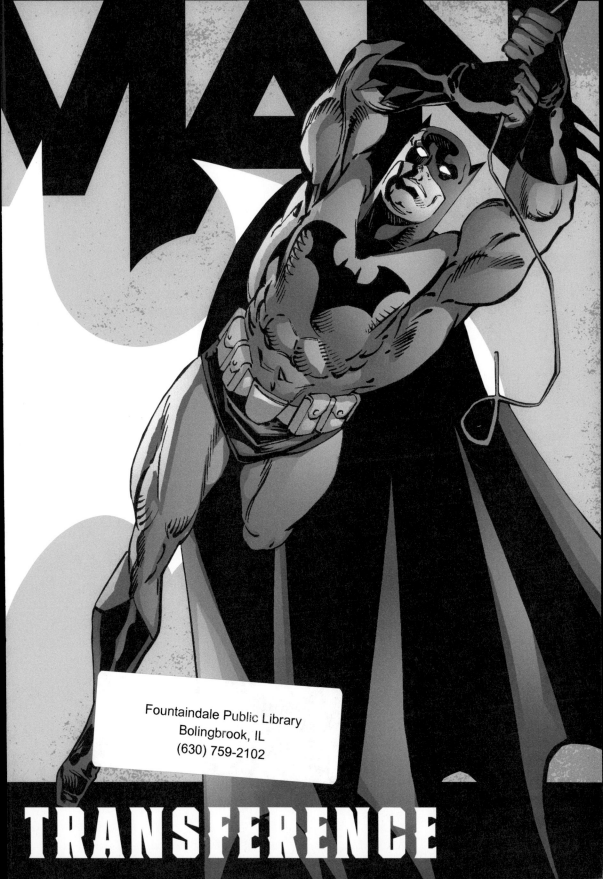

TRANSFERENCE

DENNY O'NEIL, BOB SCHRECK Editors - Original Series

JOSEPH ILLIDGE Associate Editor - Original Series

FRANK BERRIOS Assistant Editor - Original Series

JEB WOODARD Group Editor - Collected Editions

STEVE COOK Design Director - Books

MEGEN BELLERSEN Publication Design

CHRISTY SAWYER Publication Production

BOB HARRAS Senior VP - Editor-in-Chief, DC Comics

PAT McCALLUM Executive Editor, DC Comics

DAN DiDIO Publisher

JIM LEE Publisher & Chief Creative Officer

BOBBIE CHASE VP - New Publishing Initiatives & Talent Development

DON FALLETTI VP - Manufacturing Operations & Workflow Management

LAWRENCE GANEM VP - Talent Services

ALISON GILL Senior VP - Manufacturing & Operations

HANK KANALZ Senior VP - Publishing Strategy & Support Services

DAN MIRON VP - Publishing Operations

NICK J. NAPOLITANO VP - Manufacturing Administration & Design

NANCY SPEARS VP - Sales

MICHELE R. WELLS VP & Executive Editor, Young Reader

BATMAN: GOTHAM KNIGHTS: TRANSFERENCE

Published by DC Comics. Compilation and all new material Copyright © 2019 DC Comics. All Rights Reserved.
Originally published in single magazine form in *Batman: Gotham Knights* 1-12. Copyright © 2000, 2001 DC Comics.
All Rights Reserved. All characters, their distinctive likenesses, and related elements featured in this publication
are trademarks of DC Comics. The stories, characters, and incidents featured in this publication are entirely
fictional. DC Comics does not read or accept unsolicited submissions of ideas, stories, or artwork.
DC - a WarnerMedia Company.

DC Comics, 2900 West Alameda Ave., Burbank, CA 91505
Printed by LSC Communications, Owensville, MO, USA. 11/29/19. First Printing.
ISBN: 978-1-4012-9407-6

Library of Congress Cataloging-in-Publication Data is available.

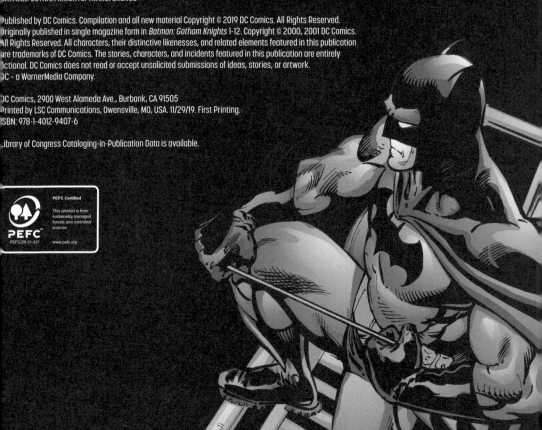

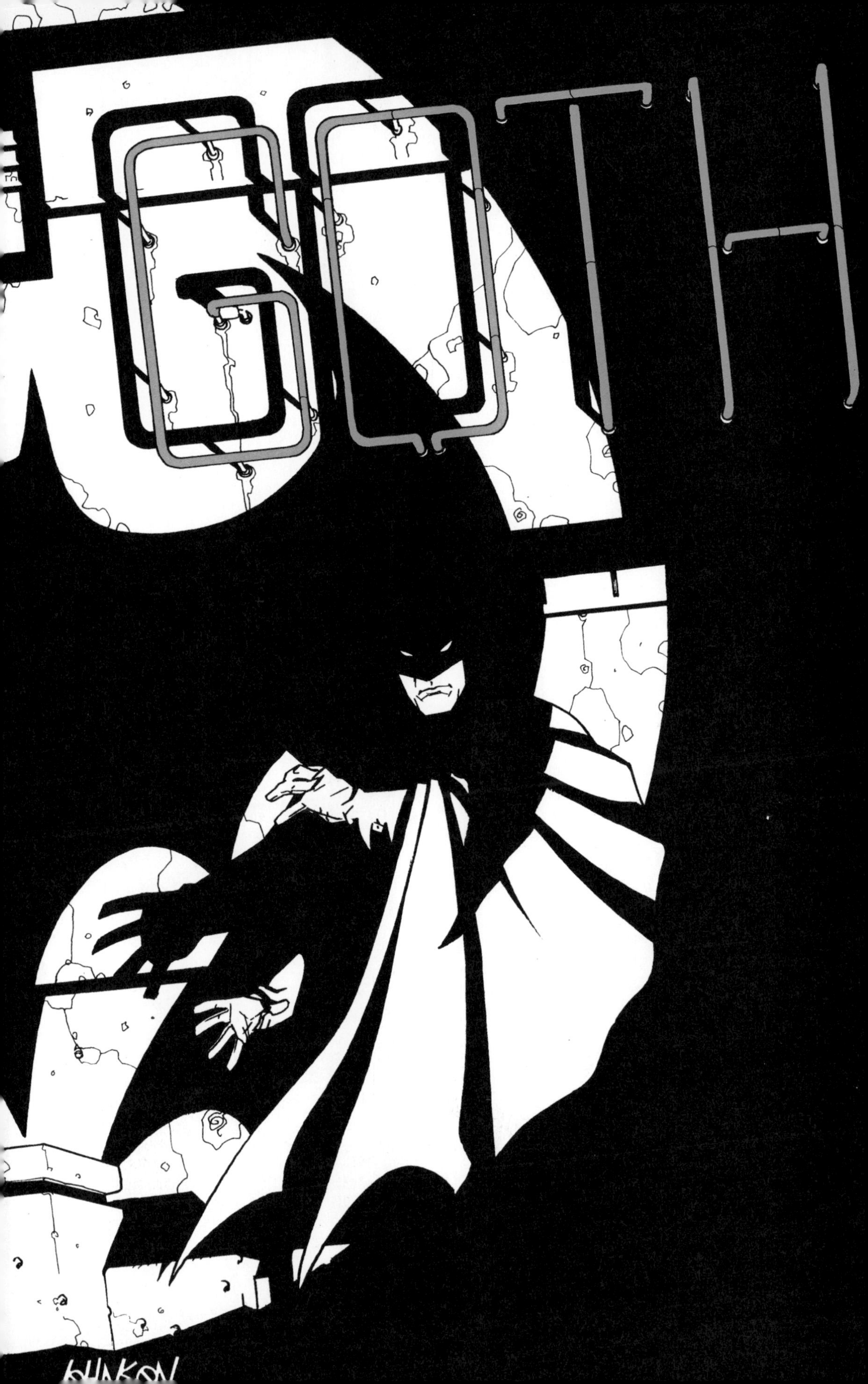
GOTH

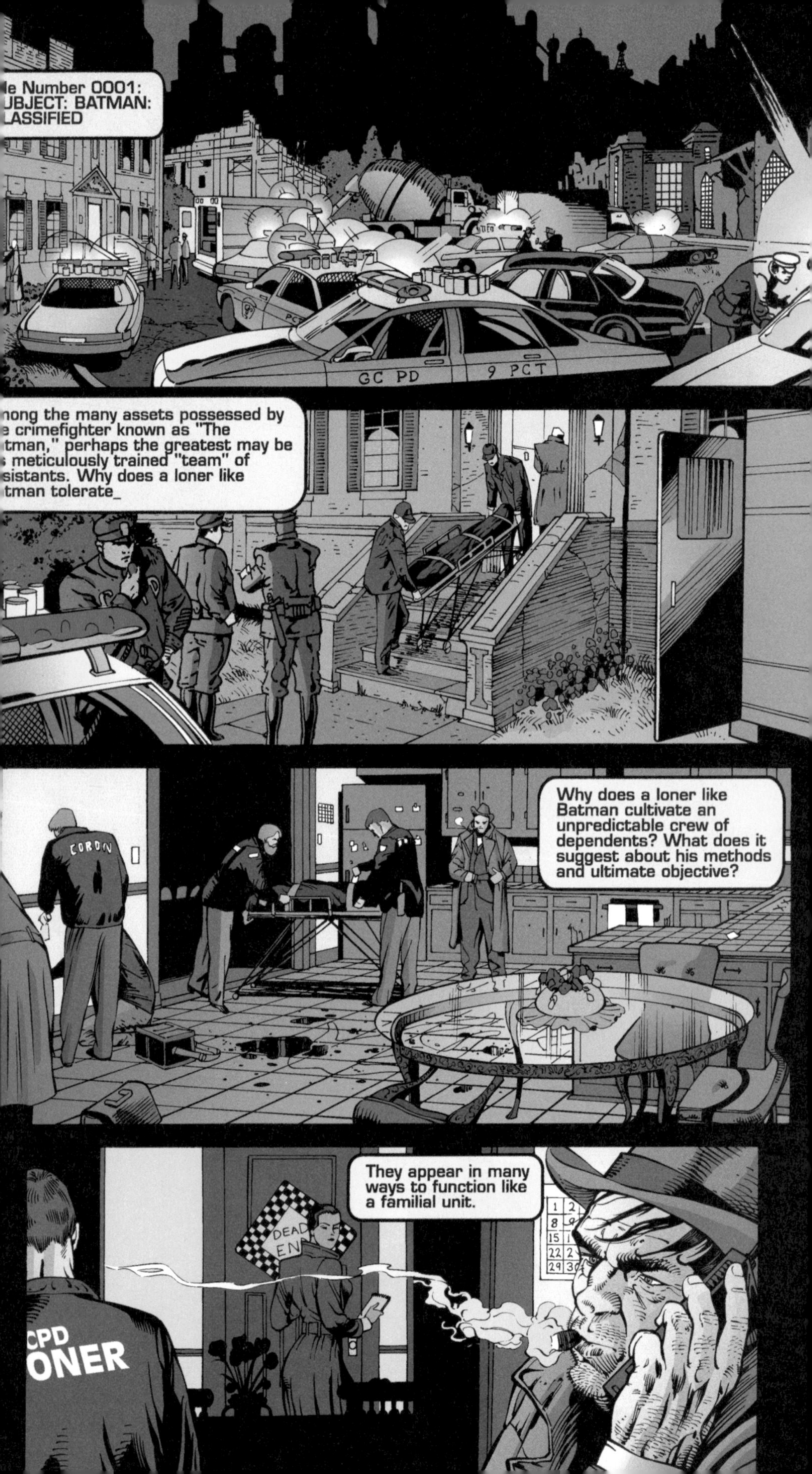
le Number 0001:
UBJECT: BATMAN:
LASSIFIED
GC PD 9 PCT
nong the many assets possessed by e crimefighter known as "The tman," perhaps the greatest may be s meticulously trained "team" of sistants. Why does a loner like tman tolerate_
Why does a loner like Batman cultivate an unpredictable crew of dependents? What does it suggest about his methods and ultimate objective?
They appear in many ways to function like a familial unit.
DEAD END
CPD
ONER

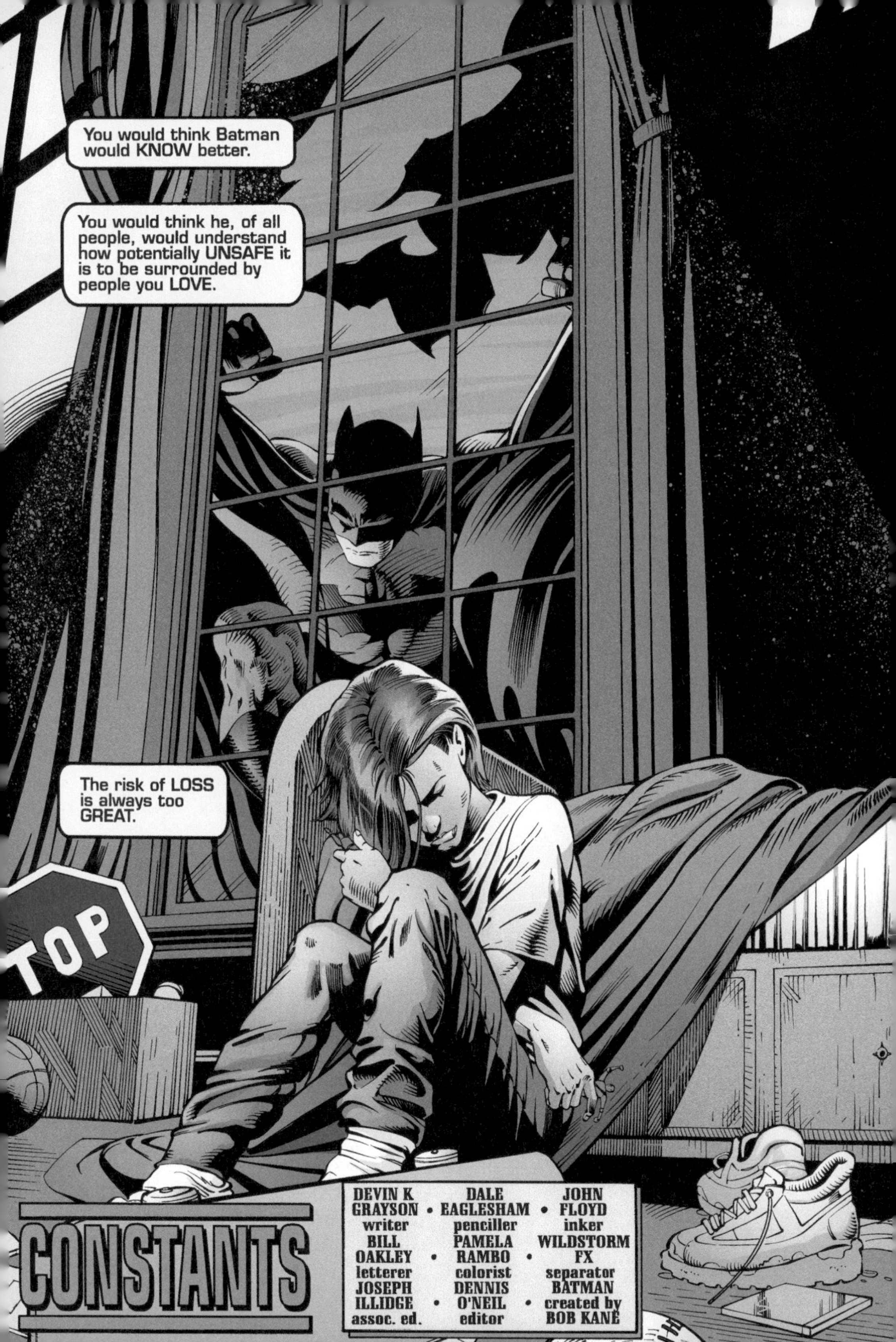

You would think Batman would KNOW better.
You would think he, of all people, would understand how potentially UNSAFE it is to be surrounded by people you LOVE.
The risk of LOSS is always too GREAT.
TOP
CONSTANTS
DEVIN K GRAYSON • DALE EAGLESHAM • JOHN FLOYD
writer penciller inker
BILL OAKLEY • PAMELA RAMBO • WILDSTORM FX
letterer colorist separator
JOSEPH ILLIDGE • DENNIS O'NEIL • BATMAN created by BOB KANE
assoc. ed. editor

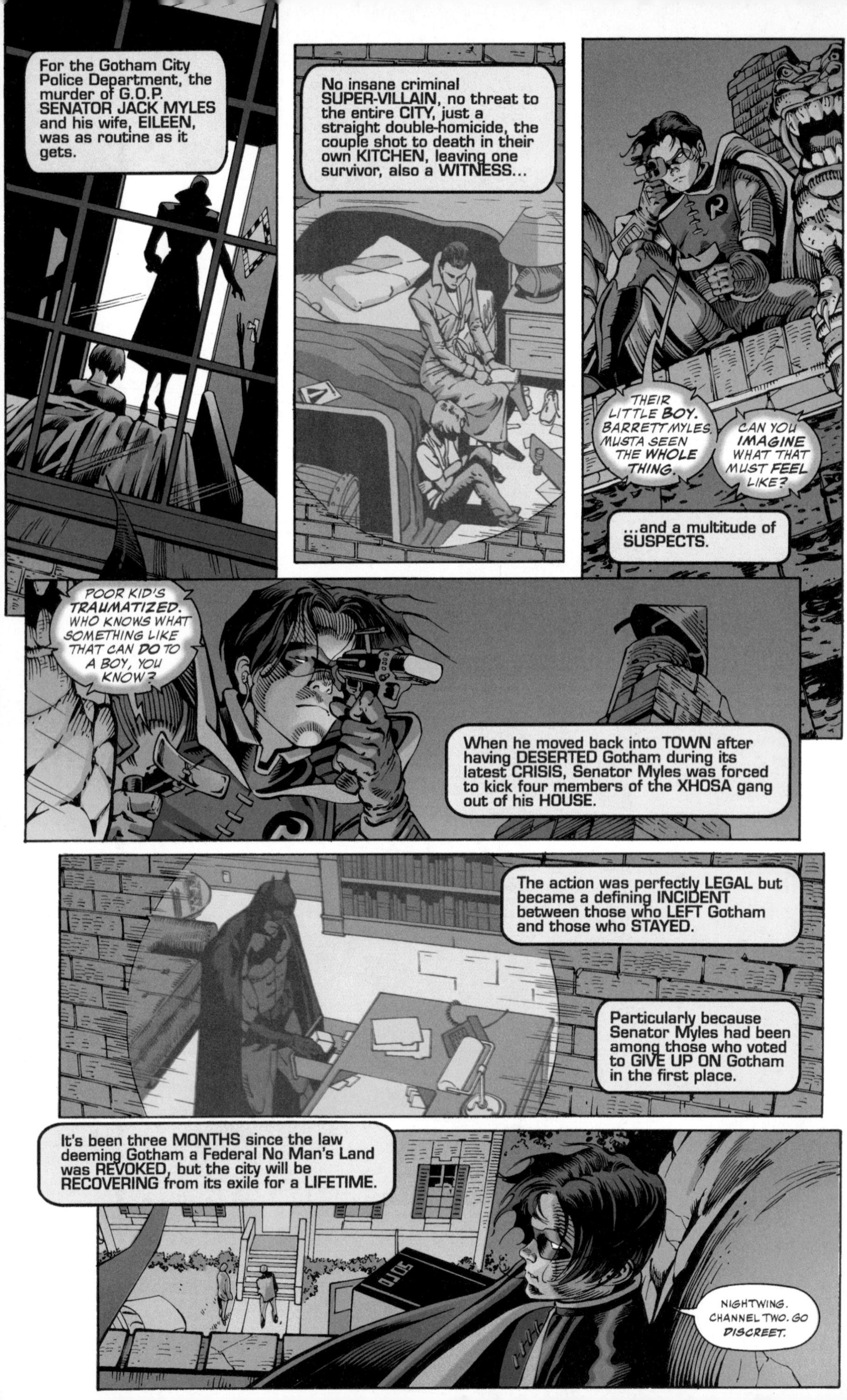
For the Gotham City Police Department, the murder of G.O.P. SENATOR JACK MYLES and his wife, EILEEN, was as routine as it gets.
No insane criminal SUPER-VILLAIN, no threat to the entire CITY, just a straight double-homicide, the couple shot to death in their own KITCHEN, leaving one survivor, also a WITNESS...
THEIR LITTLE BOY. BARRETT MYLES. MUSTA SEEN THE WHOLE THING.
CAN YOU IMAGINE WHAT THAT MUST FEEL LIKE?
...and a multitude of SUSPECTS.
POOR KID'S TRAUMATIZED. WHO KNOWS WHAT SOMETHING LIKE THAT CAN DO TO A BOY, YOU KNOW?
When he moved back into TOWN after having DESERTED Gotham during its latest CRISIS, Senator Myles was forced to kick four members of the XHOSA gang out of his HOUSE.
The action was perfectly LEGAL but became a defining INCIDENT between those who LEFT Gotham and those who STAYED.
Particularly because Senator Myles had been among those who voted to GIVE UP ON Gotham in the first place.
It's been three MONTHS since the law deeming Gotham a Federal No Man's Land was REVOKED, but the city will be RECOVERING from its exile for a LIFETIME.
NIGHTWING. CHANNEL TWO. GO DISCREET.

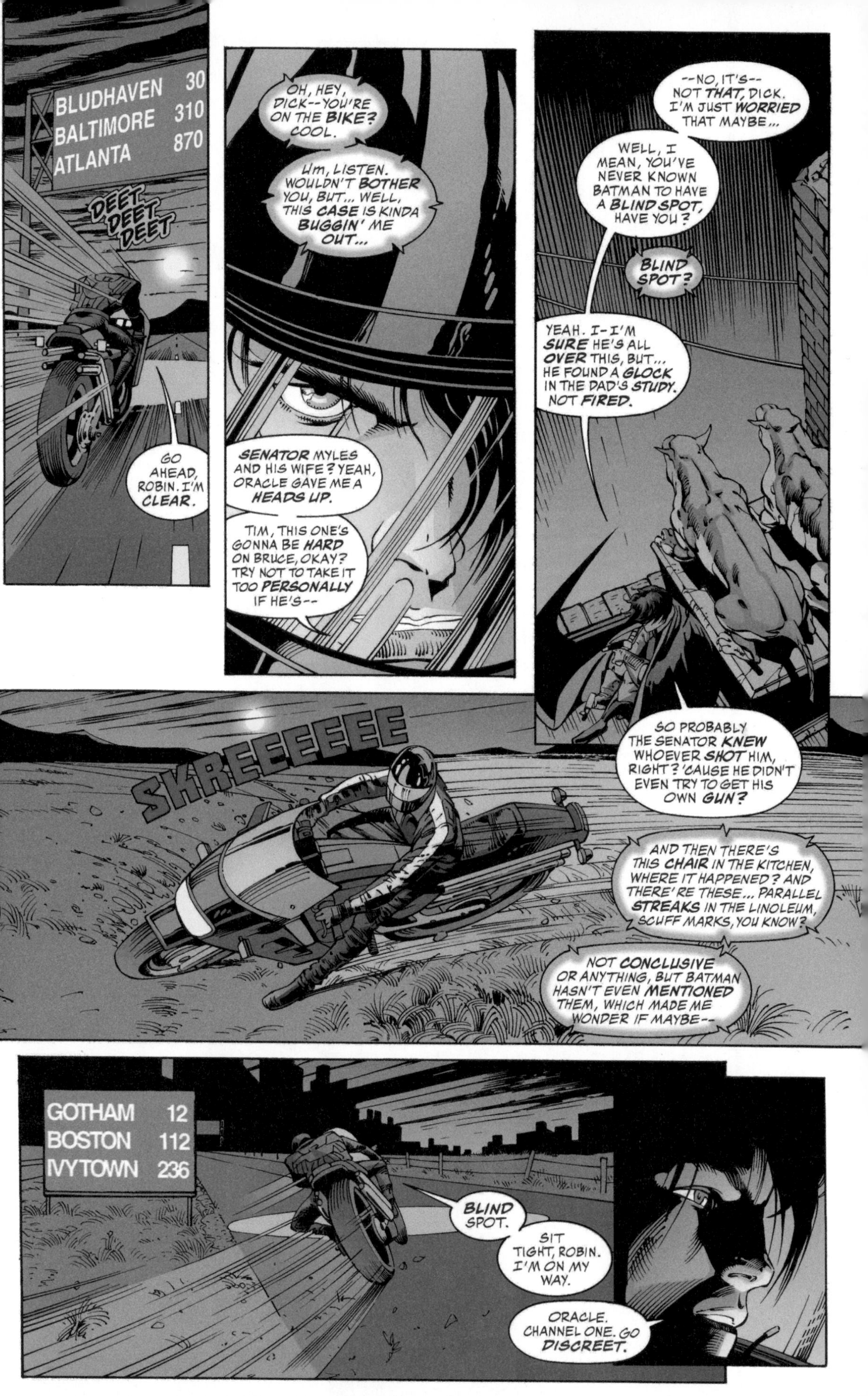
BLUDHAVEN 30
BALTIMORE 310
ATLANTA 870
DEET DEET DEET
GO AHEAD, ROBIN. I'M CLEAR.
OH, HEY, DICK--YOU'RE ON THE BIKE? COOL.
UM, LISTEN. WOULDN'T BOTHER YOU, BUT... WELL, THIS CASE IS KINDA BUGGIN' ME OUT...
SENATOR MYLES AND HIS WIFE? YEAH, ORACLE GAVE ME A HEADS UP.
TIM, THIS ONE'S GONNA BE HARD ON BRUCE, OKAY? TRY NOT TO TAKE IT TOO PERSONALLY IF HE'S--
--NO, IT'S-- NOT THAT, DICK. I'M JUST WORRIED THAT MAYBE...
WELL, I MEAN, YOU'VE NEVER KNOWN BATMAN TO HAVE A BLIND SPOT, HAVE YOU?
BLIND SPOT?
YEAH. I-I'M SURE HE'S ALL OVER THIS, BUT... HE FOUND A GLOCK IN THE DAD'S STUDY. NOT FIRED.
SKREEEEEEE
SO PROBABLY THE SENATOR KNEW WHOEVER SHOT HIM, RIGHT? 'CAUSE HE DIDN'T EVEN TRY TO GET HIS OWN GUN?
AND THEN THERE'S THIS CHAIR IN THE KITCHEN, WHERE IT HAPPENED? AND THERE'RE THESE... PARALLEL STREAKS IN THE LINOLEUM, SCUFF MARKS, YOU KNOW?
NOT CONCLUSIVE OR ANYTHING, BUT BATMAN HASN'T EVEN MENTIONED THEM, WHICH MADE ME WONDER IF MAYBE--
GOTHAM 12
BOSTON 112
IVYTOWN 236
BLIND SPOT.
SIT TIGHT, ROBIN. I'M ON MY WAY.
ORACLE. CHANNEL ONE. GO DISCREET.

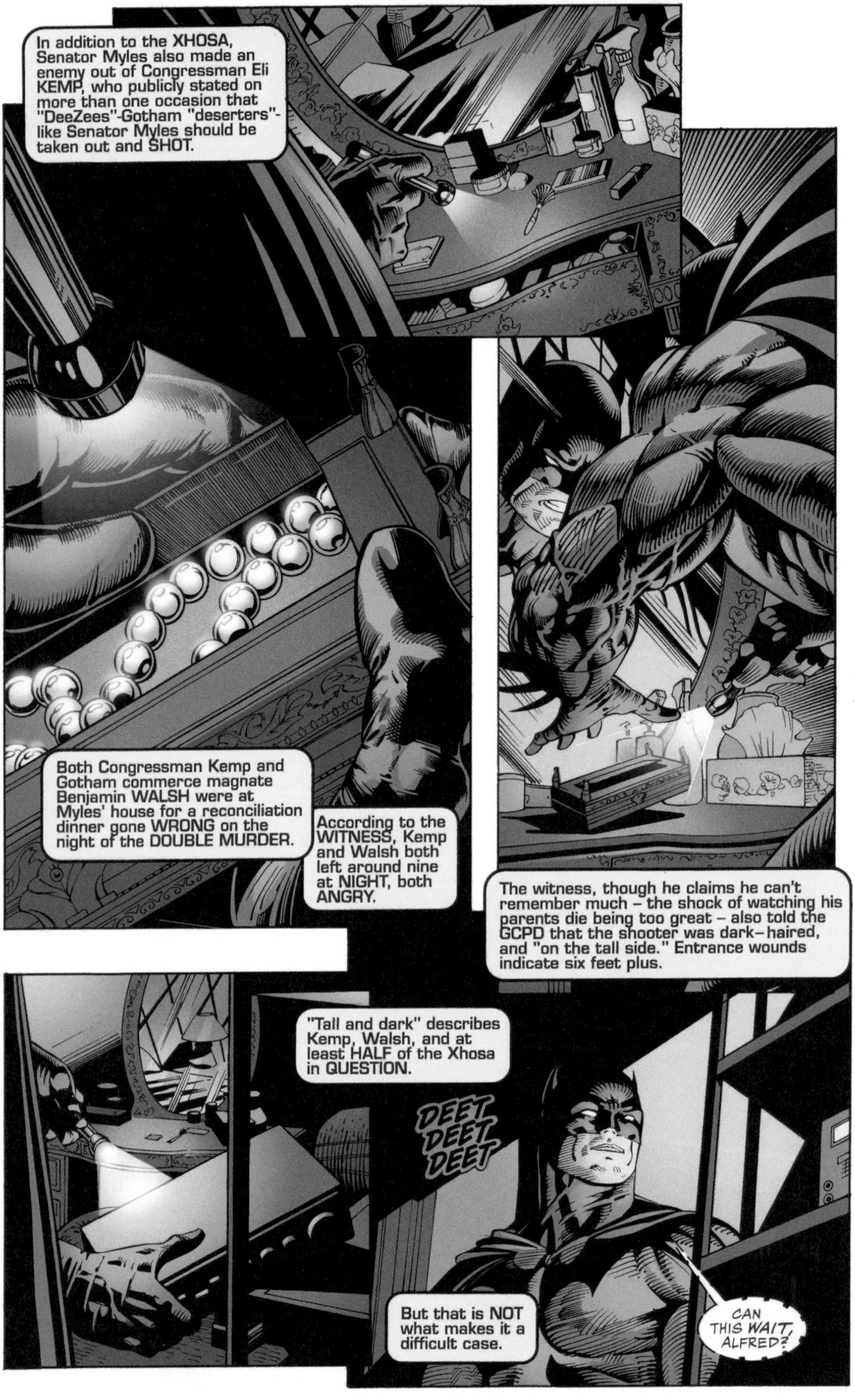
In addition to the XHOSA, Senator Myles also made an enemy out of Congressman Eli KEMP, who publicly stated on more than one occasion that "DeeZees"-Gotham "deserters"-like Senator Myles should be taken out and SHOT.
Both Congressman Kemp and Gotham commerce magnate Benjamin WALSH were at Myles' house for a reconciliation dinner gone WRONG on the night of the DOUBLE MURDER.
According to the WITNESS, Kemp and Walsh both left around nine at NIGHT, both ANGRY.
The witness, though he claims he can't remember much – the shock of watching his parents die being too great – also told the GCPD that the shooter was dark–haired, and "on the tall side." Entrance wounds indicate six feet plus.
"Tall and dark" describes Kemp, Walsh, and at least HALF of the Xhosa in QUESTION.
DEET DEET DEET
But that is NOT what makes it a difficult case.
CAN THIS WAIT, ALFRED?

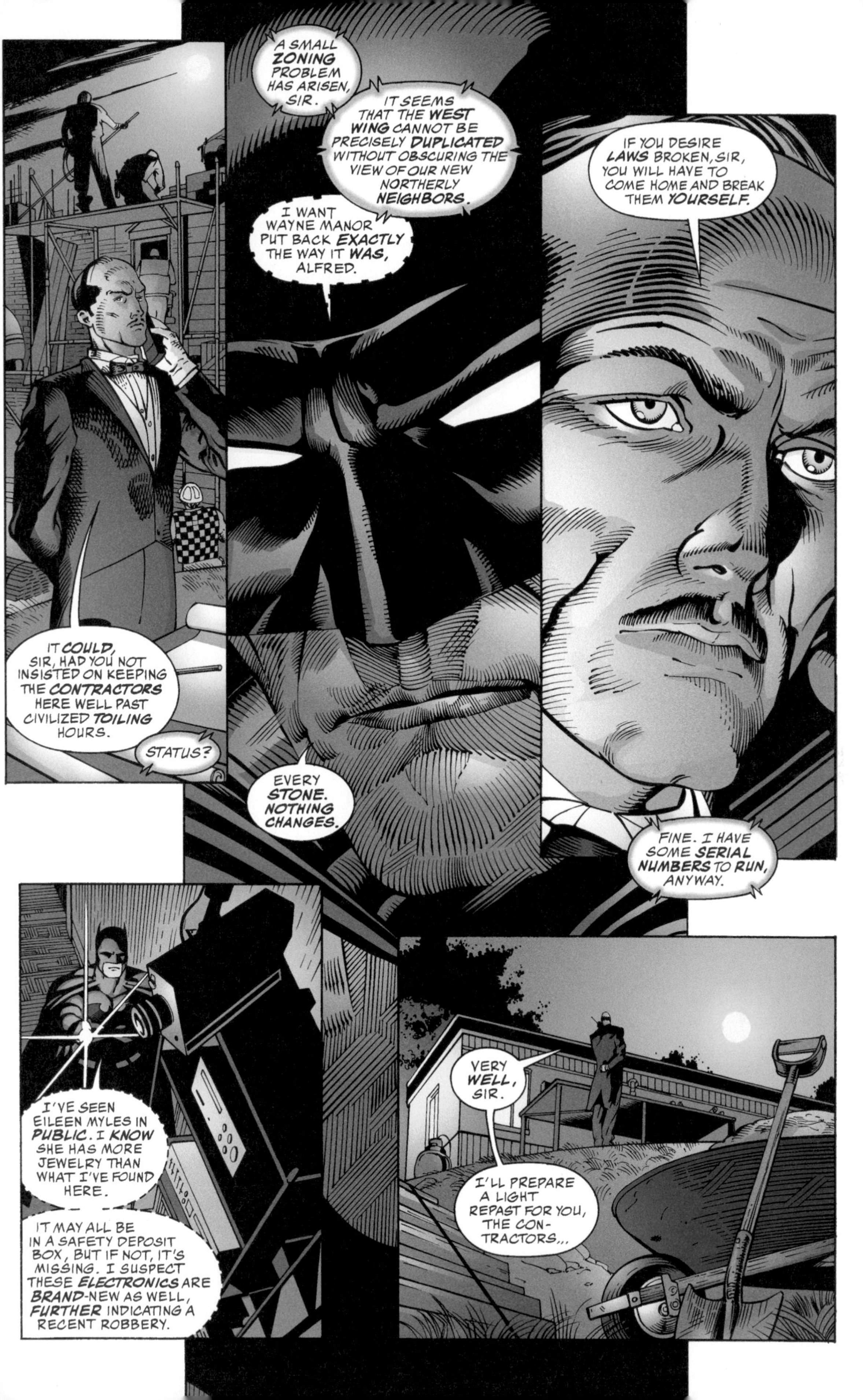

A SMALL ZONING PROBLEM HAS ARISEN, SIR.
IT SEEMS THAT THE WEST WING CANNOT BE PRECISELY DUPLICATED WITHOUT OBSCURING THE VIEW OF OUR NEW NORTHERLY NEIGHBORS.
I WANT WAYNE MANOR PUT BACK EXACTLY THE WAY IT WAS, ALFRED.
IF YOU DESIRE LAWS BROKEN, SIR, YOU WILL HAVE TO COME HOME AND BREAK THEM YOURSELF.
STATUS?
IT COULD, SIR, HAD YOU NOT INSISTED ON KEEPING THE CONTRACTORS HERE WELL PAST CIVILIZED TOILING HOURS.
EVERY STONE. NOTHING CHANGES.
FINE. I HAVE SOME SERIAL NUMBERS TO RUN, ANYWAY.
I'VE SEEN EILEEN MYLES IN PUBLIC. I KNOW SHE HAS MORE JEWELRY THAN WHAT I'VE FOUND HERE.
IT MAY ALL BE IN A SAFETY DEPOSIT BOX, BUT IF NOT, IT'S MISSING. I SUSPECT THESE ELECTRONICS ARE BRAND-NEW AS WELL, FURTHER INDICATING A RECENT ROBBERY.
VERY WELL, SIR.
I'LL PREPARE A LIGHT REPAST FOR YOU, THE CON-TRACTORS...

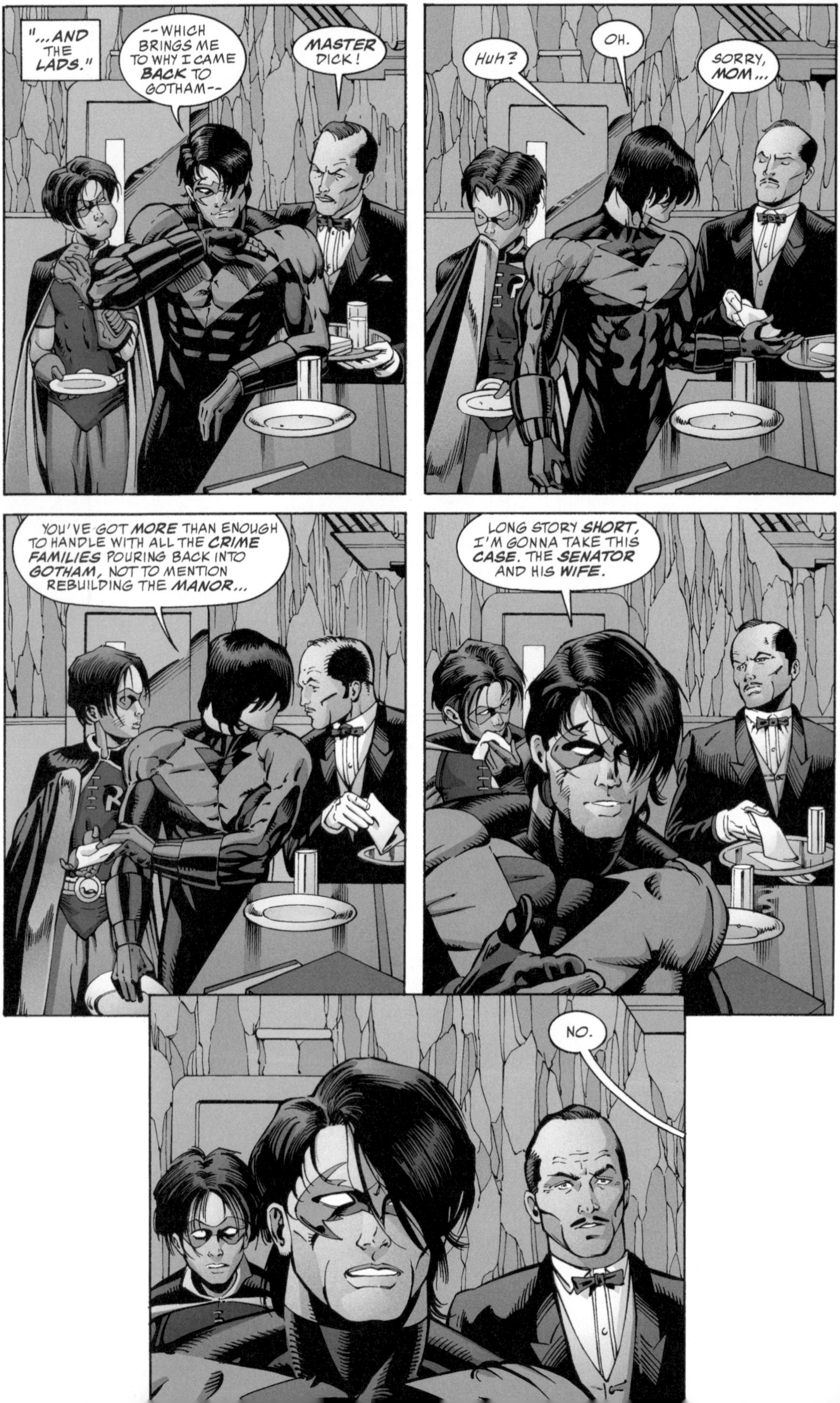
"...AND THE LADS."
--WHICH BRINGS ME TO WHY I CAME BACK TO GOTHAM--
MASTER DICK!
HUH?
OH.
SORRY, MOM...
YOU'VE GOT MORE THAN ENOUGH TO HANDLE WITH ALL THE CRIME FAMILIES POURING BACK INTO GOTHAM, NOT TO MENTION REBUILDING THE MANOR...
LONG STORY SHORT, I'M GONNA TAKE THIS CASE. THE SENATOR AND HIS WIFE.
NO.

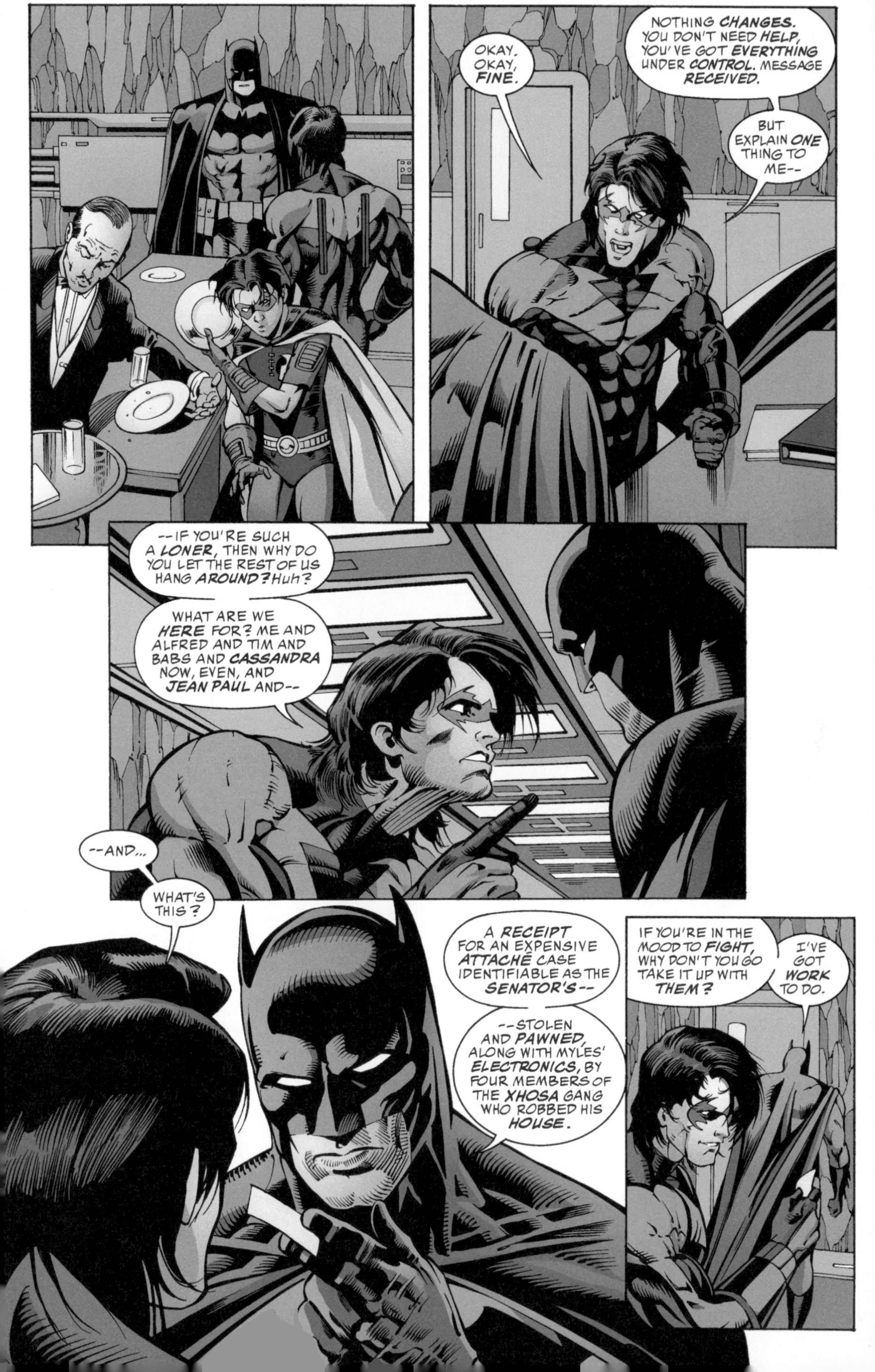
OKAY. OKAY, FINE.
NOTHING CHANGES. YOU DON'T NEED HELP, YOU'VE GOT EVERYTHING UNDER CONTROL. MESSAGE RECEIVED.
BUT EXPLAIN ONE THING TO ME--
--IF YOU'RE SUCH A LONER, THEN WHY DO YOU LET THE REST OF US HANG AROUND? Huh?
WHAT ARE WE HERE FOR? ME AND ALFRED AND TIM AND BABS AND CASSANDRA NOW, EVEN, AND JEAN PAUL AND--
--AND...
WHAT'S THIS?
A RECEIPT FOR AN EXPENSIVE ATTACHÊ CASE IDENTIFIABLE AS THE SENATOR'S--
--STOLEN AND PAWNED, ALONG WITH MYLES' ELECTRONICS, BY FOUR MEMBERS OF THE XHOSA GANG WHO ROBBED HIS HOUSE.
IF YOU'RE IN THE MOOD TO FIGHT, WHY DON'T YOU GO TAKE IT UP WITH THEM?
I'VE GOT WORK TO DO.

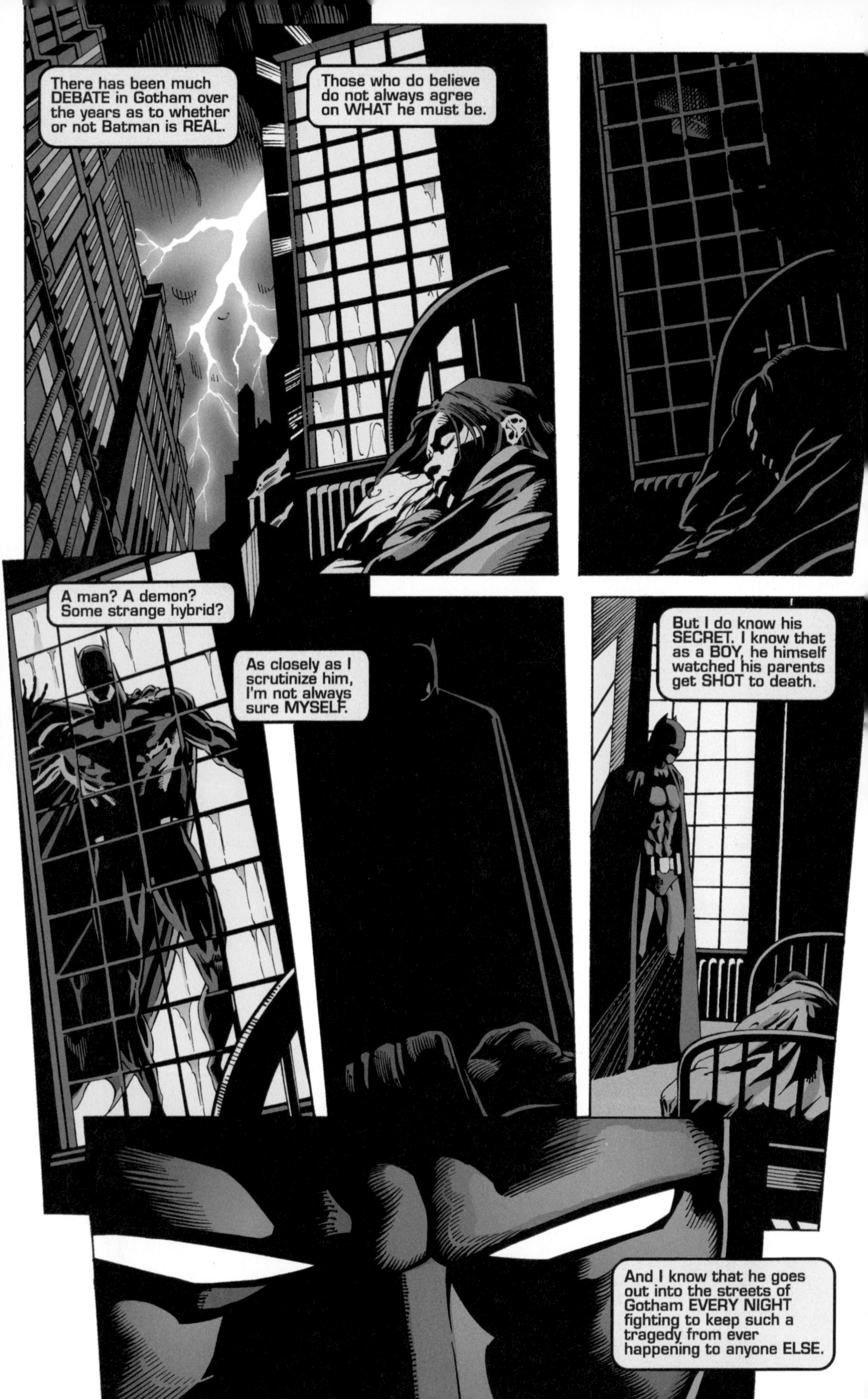
There has been much DEBATE in Gotham over the years as to whether or not Batman is REAL.
Those who do believe do not always agree on WHAT he must be.
A man? A demon? Some strange hybrid?
As closely as I scrutinize him, I'm not always sure MYSELF.
But I do know his SECRET. I know that as a BOY, he himself watched his parents get SHOT to death.
And I know that he goes out into the streets of Gotham EVERY NIGHT fighting to keep such a tragedy from ever happening to anyone ELSE.

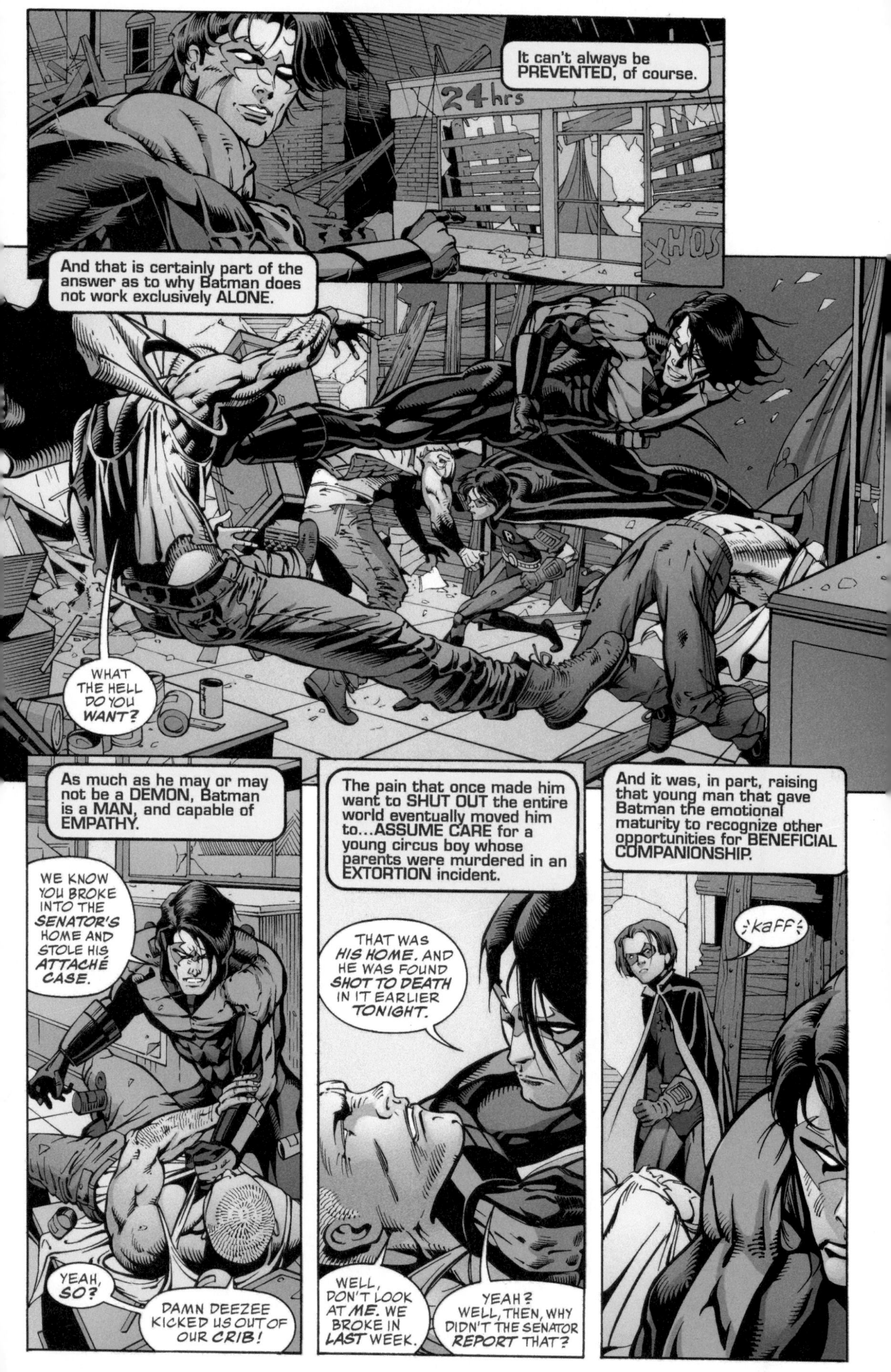

It can't always be PREVENTED, of course.
24 hrs
And that is certainly part of the answer as to why Batman does not work exclusively ALONE.
WHAT THE HELL DO YOU WANT?
As much as he may or may not be a DEMON, Batman is a MAN, and capable of EMPATHY.
WE KNOW YOU BROKE INTO THE SENATOR'S HOME AND STOLE HIS ATTACHÉ CASE.
YEAH, SO?
DAMN DEEZEE KICKED US OUT OF OUR CRIB!
The pain that once made him want to SHUT OUT the entire world eventually moved him to...ASSUME CARE for a young circus boy whose parents were murdered in an EXTORTION incident.
THAT WAS HIS HOME. AND HE WAS FOUND SHOT TO DEATH IN IT EARLIER TONIGHT.
WELL, DON'T LOOK AT ME. WE BROKE IN LAST WEEK.
YEAH? WELL, THEN, WHY DIDN'T THE SENATOR REPORT THAT?
And it was, in part, raising that young man that gave Batman the emotional maturity to recognize other opportunities for BENEFICIAL COMPANIONSHIP.
kaff

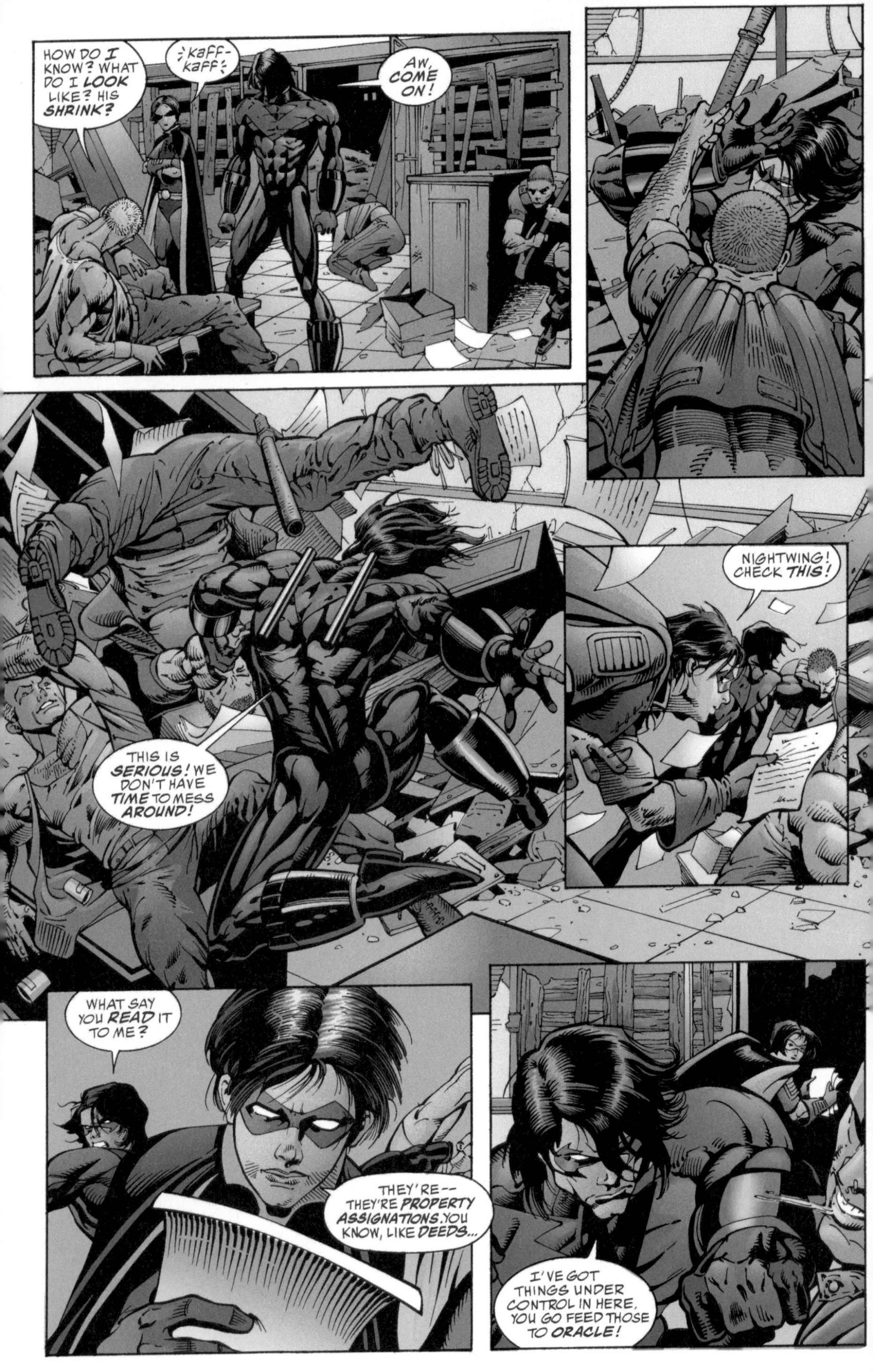
HOW DO I KNOW? WHAT DO I LOOK LIKE? HIS SHRINK?
kaff-kaff
AW, COME ON!
THIS IS SERIOUS! WE DON'T HAVE TIME TO MESS AROUND!
NIGHTWING! CHECK THIS!
WHAT SAY YOU READ IT TO ME?
THEY'RE-- THEY'RE PROPERTY ASSIGNATIONS. YOU KNOW, LIKE DEEDS...
I'VE GOT THINGS UNDER CONTROL IN HERE, YOU GO FEED THOSE TO ORACLE!

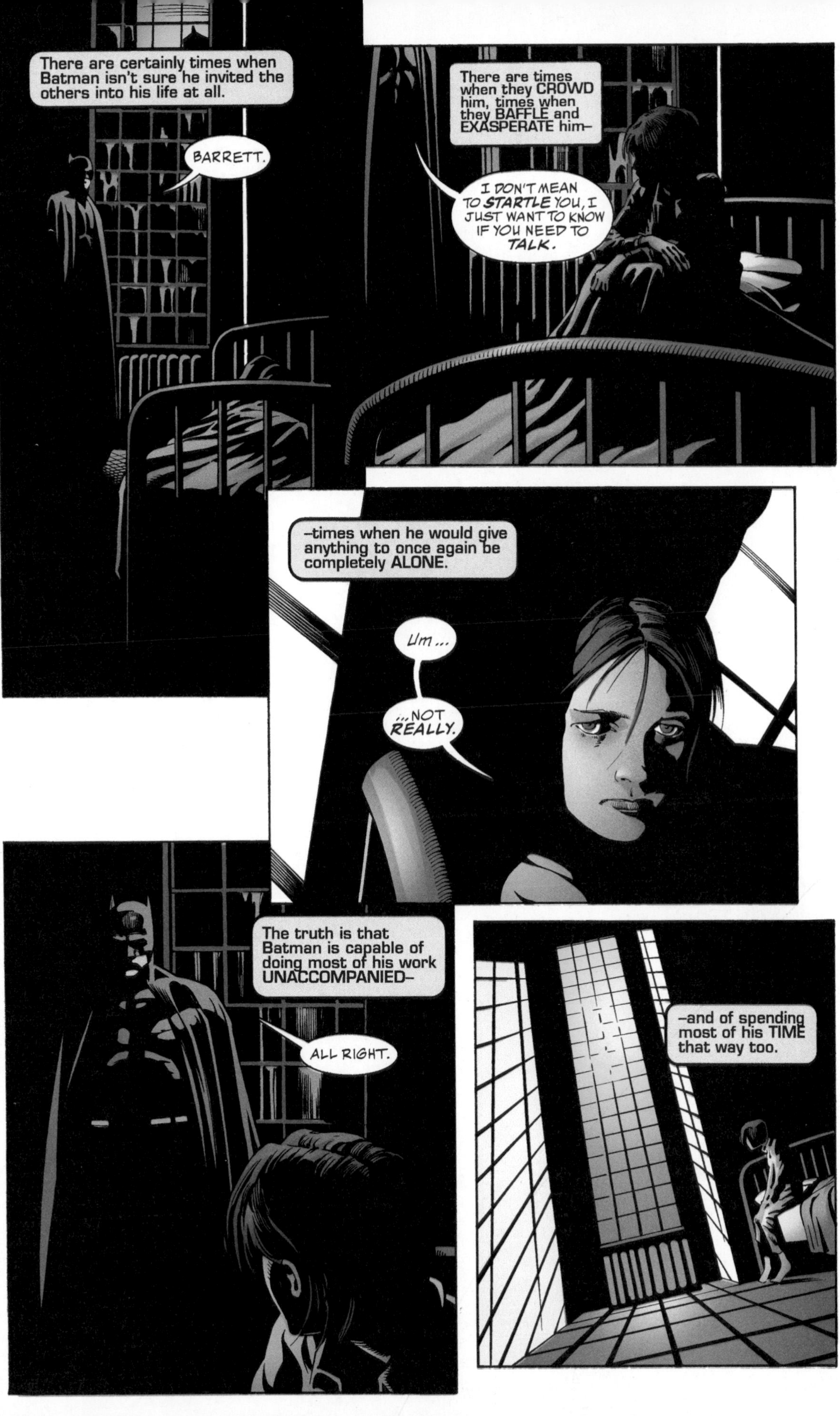

There are certainly times when Batman isn't sure he invited the others into his life at all.
BARRETT.
There are times when they CROWD him, times when they BAFFLE and EXASPERATE him–
I DON'T MEAN TO STARTLE YOU, I JUST WANT TO KNOW IF YOU NEED TO TALK.
–times when he would give anything to once again be completely ALONE.
Um...
...NOT REALLY.
The truth is that Batman is capable of doing most of his work UNACCOMPANIED–
ALL RIGHT.
–and of spending most of his TIME that way too.

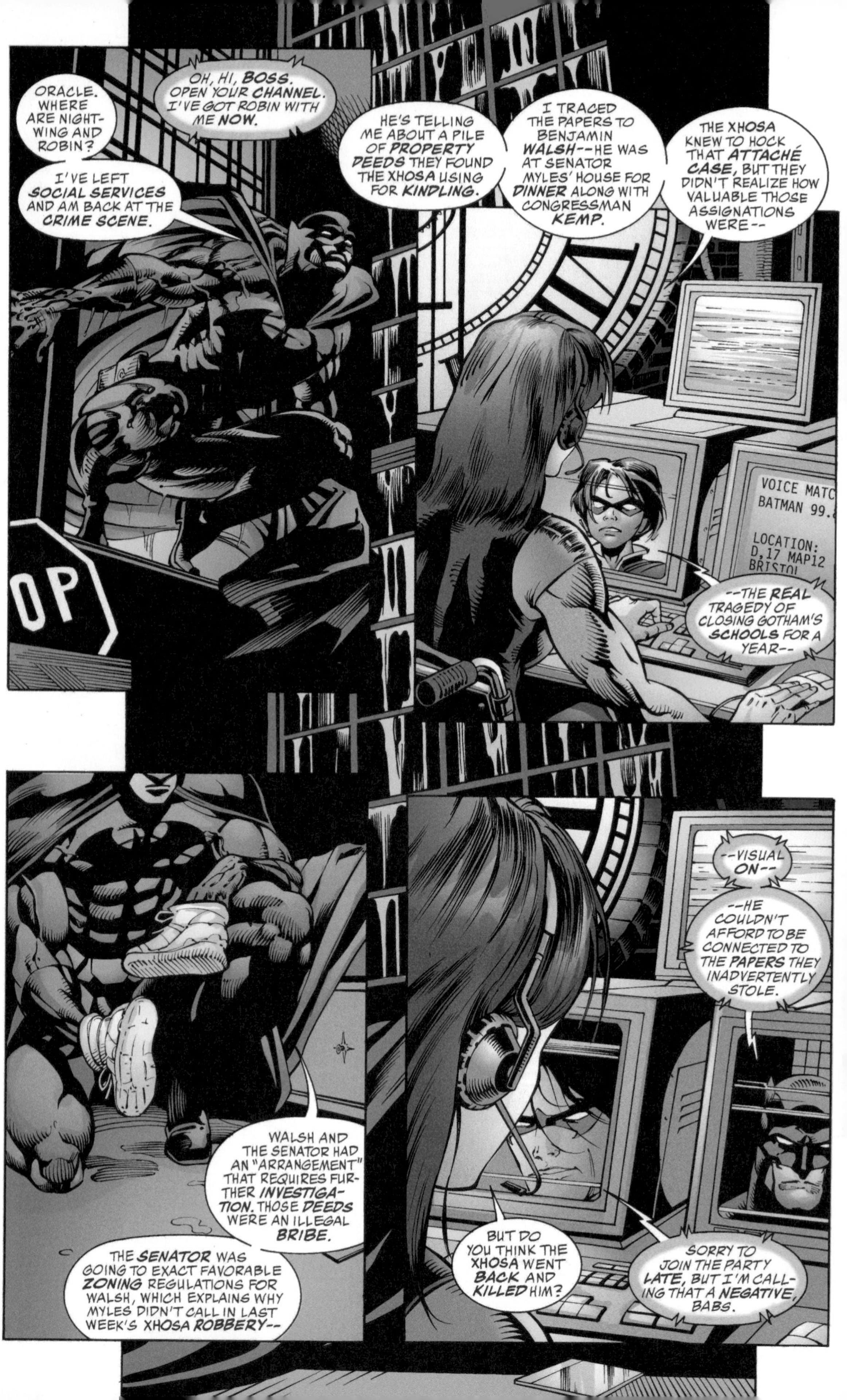
ORACLE. WHERE ARE NIGHTWING AND ROBIN?
OH, HI, BOSS. OPEN YOUR CHANNEL. I'VE GOT ROBIN WITH ME NOW.
I'VE LEFT SOCIAL SERVICES AND AM BACK AT THE CRIME SCENE.
OP
HE'S TELLING ME ABOUT A PILE OF PROPERTY DEEDS THEY FOUND THE XHOSA USING FOR KINDLING.
I TRACED THE PAPERS TO BENJAMIN WALSH--HE WAS AT SENATOR MYLES' HOUSE FOR DINNER ALONG WITH CONGRESSMAN KEMP.
THE XHOSA KNEW TO HOCK THAT ATTACHÉ CASE, BUT THEY DIDN'T REALIZE HOW VALUABLE THOSE ASSIGNATIONS WERE--
VOICE MATC
BATMAN 99.
LOCATION:
D,17 MAP12
BRISTOL
--THE REAL TRAGEDY OF CLOSING GOTHAM'S SCHOOLS FOR A YEAR--
WALSH AND THE SENATOR HAD AN "ARRANGEMENT" THAT REQUIRES FURTHER INVESTIGATION. THOSE DEEDS WERE AN ILLEGAL BRIBE.
THE SENATOR WAS GOING TO EXACT FAVORABLE ZONING REGULATIONS FOR WALSH, WHICH EXPLAINS WHY MYLES DIDN'T CALL IN LAST WEEK'S XHOSA ROBBERY--
--VISUAL ON--
--HE COULDN'T AFFORD TO BE CONNECTED TO THE PAPERS THEY INADVERTENTLY STOLE.
BUT DO YOU THINK THE XHOSA WENT BACK AND KILLED HIM?
SORRY TO JOIN THE PARTY LATE, BUT I'M CALLING THAT A NEGATIVE, BABS.

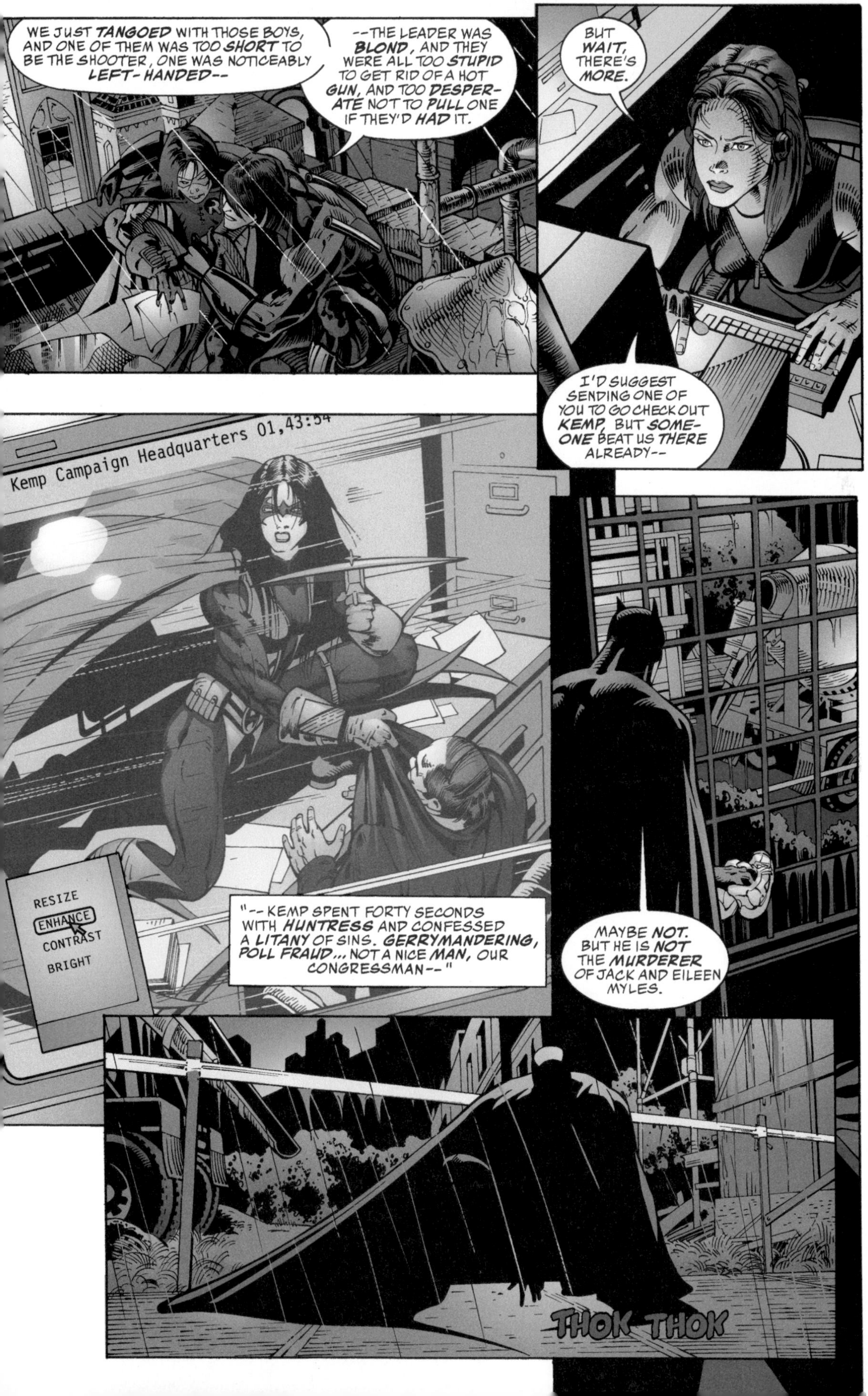
WE JUST TANGOED WITH THOSE BOYS, AND ONE OF THEM WAS TOO SHORT TO BE THE SHOOTER, ONE WAS NOTICEABLY LEFT-HANDED--
--THE LEADER WAS BLOND, AND THEY WERE ALL TOO STUPID TO GET RID OF A HOT GUN, AND TOO DESPERATE NOT TO PULL ONE IF THEY'D HAD IT.
BUT WAIT, THERE'S MORE.
I'D SUGGEST SENDING ONE OF YOU TO GO CHECK OUT KEMP, BUT SOMEONE BEAT US THERE ALREADY--
Kemp Campaign Headquarters 01,43:54
RESIZE
ENHANCE
CONTRAST
BRIGHT
"--KEMP SPENT FORTY SECONDS WITH HUNTRESS AND CONFESSED A LITANY OF SINS. GERRYMANDERING, POLL FRAUD... NOT A NICE MAN, OUR CONGRESSMAN--"
MAYBE NOT. BUT HE IS NOT THE MURDERER OF JACK AND EILEEN MYLES.
THOK THOK

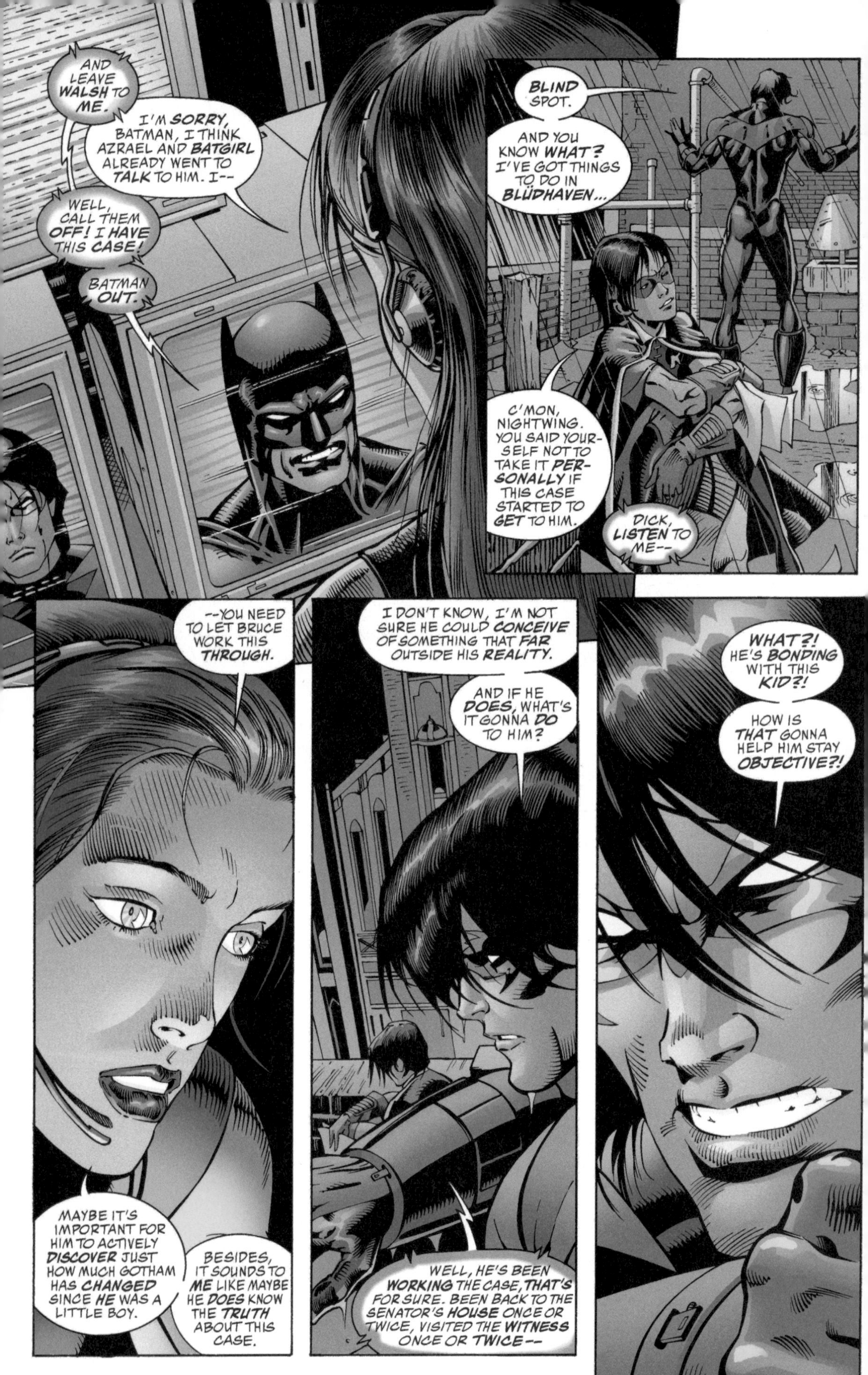
AND LEAVE WALSH TO ME.
I'M SORRY, BATMAN, I THINK AZRAEL AND BATGIRL ALREADY WENT TO TALK TO HIM. I--
WELL, CALL THEM OFF! I HAVE THIS CASE!
BATMAN OUT.
BLIND SPOT.
AND YOU KNOW WHAT? I'VE GOT THINGS TO DO IN BLÜDHAVEN...
C'MON, NIGHTWING. YOU SAID YOURSELF NOT TO TAKE IT PERSONALLY IF THIS CASE STARTED TO GET TO HIM.
DICK, LISTEN TO ME--
--YOU NEED TO LET BRUCE WORK THIS THROUGH.
MAYBE IT'S IMPORTANT FOR HIM TO ACTIVELY DISCOVER JUST HOW MUCH GOTHAM HAS CHANGED SINCE HE WAS A LITTLE BOY.
BESIDES, IT SOUNDS TO ME LIKE MAYBE HE DOES KNOW THE TRUTH ABOUT THIS CASE.
I DON'T KNOW, I'M NOT SURE HE COULD CONCEIVE OF SOMETHING THAT FAR OUTSIDE HIS REALITY.
AND IF HE DOES, WHAT'S IT GONNA DO TO HIM?
WELL, HE'S BEEN WORKING THE CASE, THAT'S FOR SURE. BEEN BACK TO THE SENATOR'S HOUSE ONCE OR TWICE, VISITED THE WITNESS ONCE OR TWICE--
WHAT?! HE'S BONDING WITH THIS KID?!
HOW IS THAT GONNA HELP HIM STAY OBJECTIVE?!

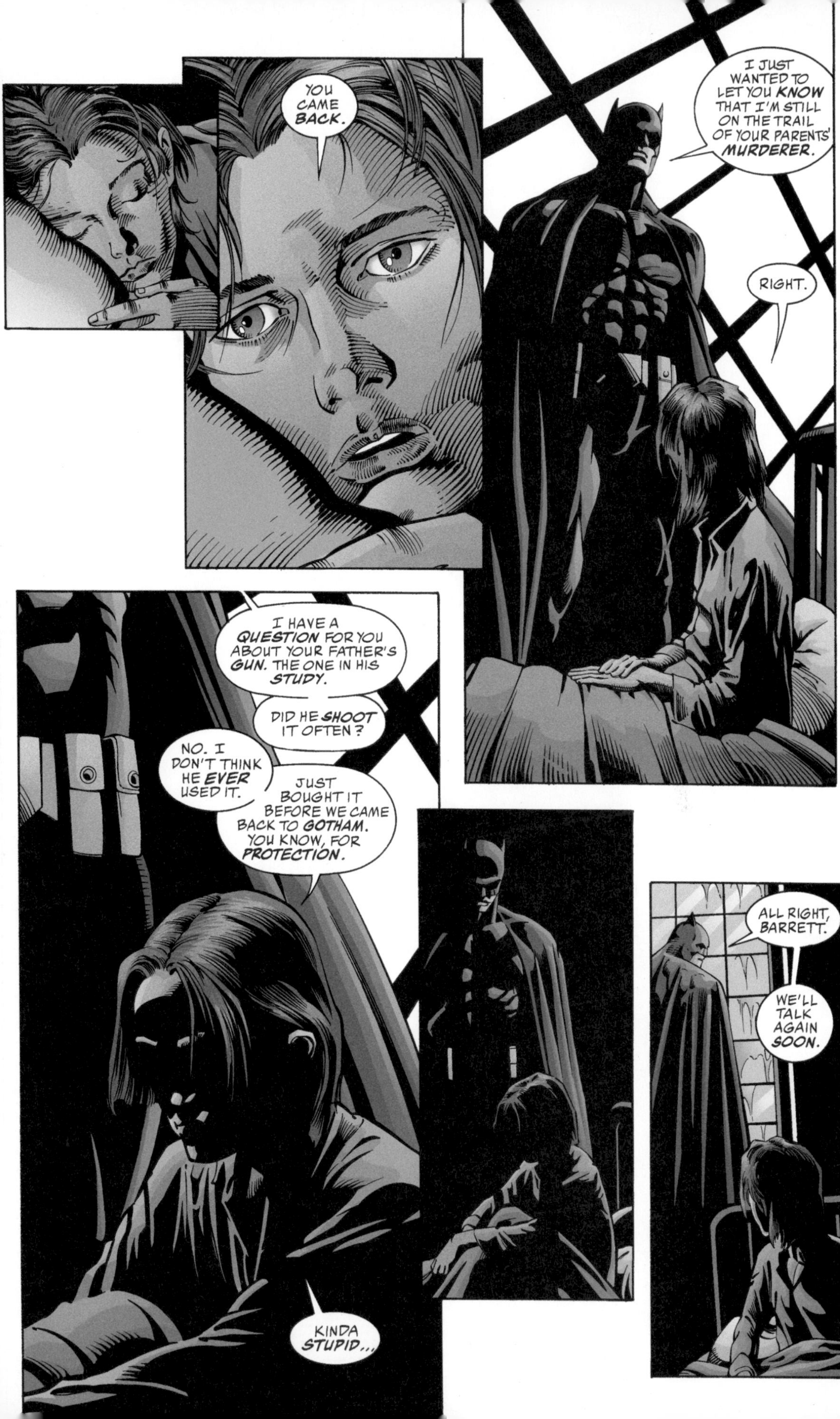
YOU CAME BACK.
I JUST WANTED TO LET YOU KNOW THAT I'M STILL ON THE TRAIL OF YOUR PARENTS' MURDERER.
RIGHT.
I HAVE A QUESTION FOR YOU ABOUT YOUR FATHER'S GUN. THE ONE IN HIS STUDY.
DID HE SHOOT IT OFTEN?
NO. I DON'T THINK HE EVER USED IT.
JUST BOUGHT IT BEFORE WE CAME BACK TO GOTHAM. YOU KNOW, FOR PROTECTION.
KINDA STUPID...
ALL RIGHT, BARRETT.
WE'LL TALK AGAIN SOON.

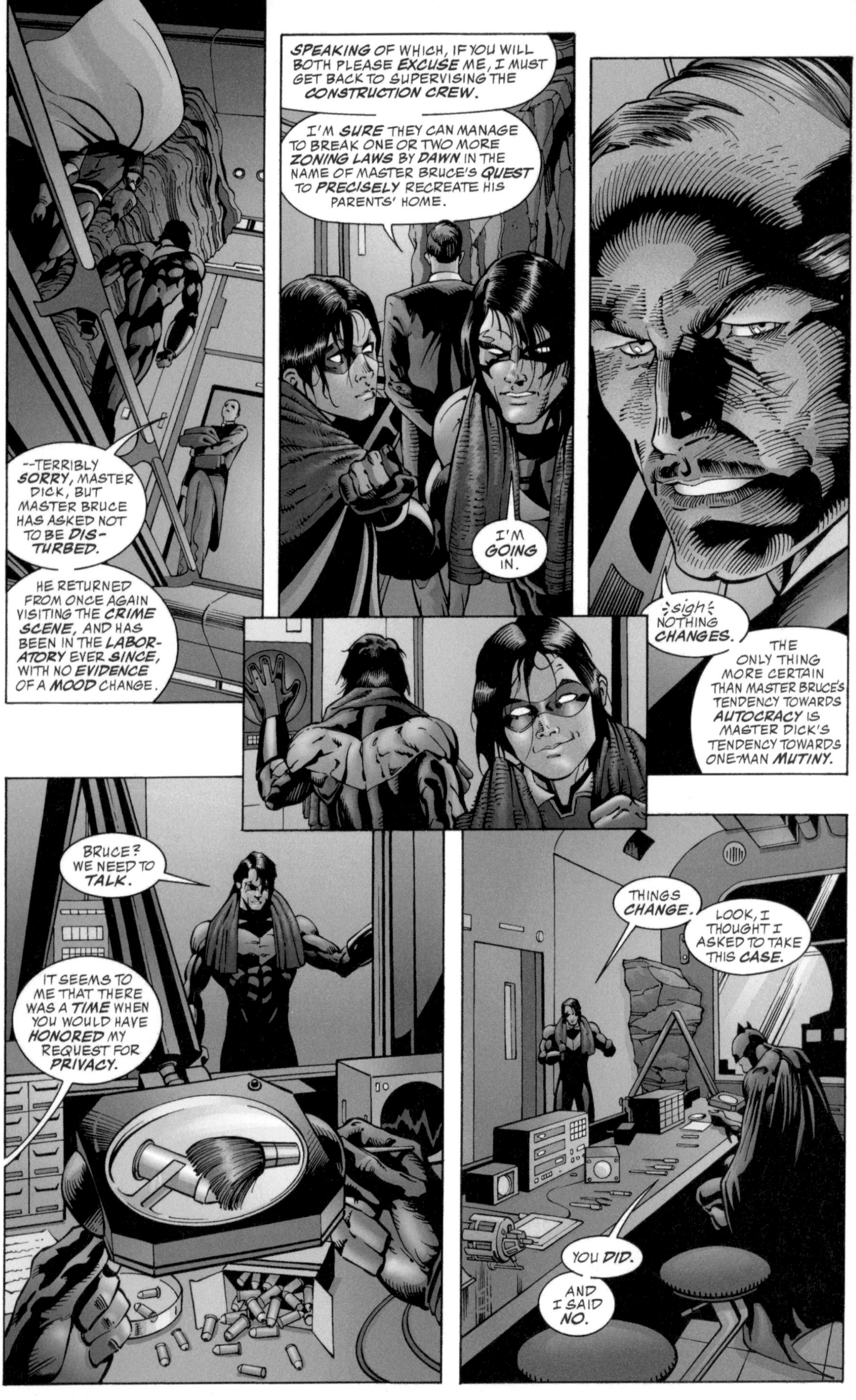
--TERRIBLY SORRY, MASTER DICK, BUT MASTER BRUCE HAS ASKED NOT TO BE DISTURBED.
HE RETURNED FROM ONCE AGAIN VISITING THE CRIME SCENE, AND HAS BEEN IN THE LABORATORY EVER SINCE, WITH NO EVIDENCE OF A MOOD CHANGE.
SPEAKING OF WHICH, IF YOU WILL BOTH PLEASE EXCUSE ME, I MUST GET BACK TO SUPERVISING THE CONSTRUCTION CREW.
I'M SURE THEY CAN MANAGE TO BREAK ONE OR TWO MORE ZONING LAWS BY DAWN IN THE NAME OF MASTER BRUCE'S QUEST TO PRECISELY RECREATE HIS PARENTS' HOME.
I'M GOING IN.
sigh NOTHING CHANGES.
THE ONLY THING MORE CERTAIN THAN MASTER BRUCE'S TENDENCY TOWARDS AUTOCRACY IS MASTER DICK'S TENDENCY TOWARDS ONE-MAN MUTINY.
BRUCE? WE NEED TO TALK.
IT SEEMS TO ME THAT THERE WAS A TIME WHEN YOU WOULD HAVE HONORED MY REQUEST FOR PRIVACY.
THINGS CHANGE.
LOOK, I THOUGHT I ASKED TO TAKE THIS CASE.
YOU DID.
AND I SAID NO.

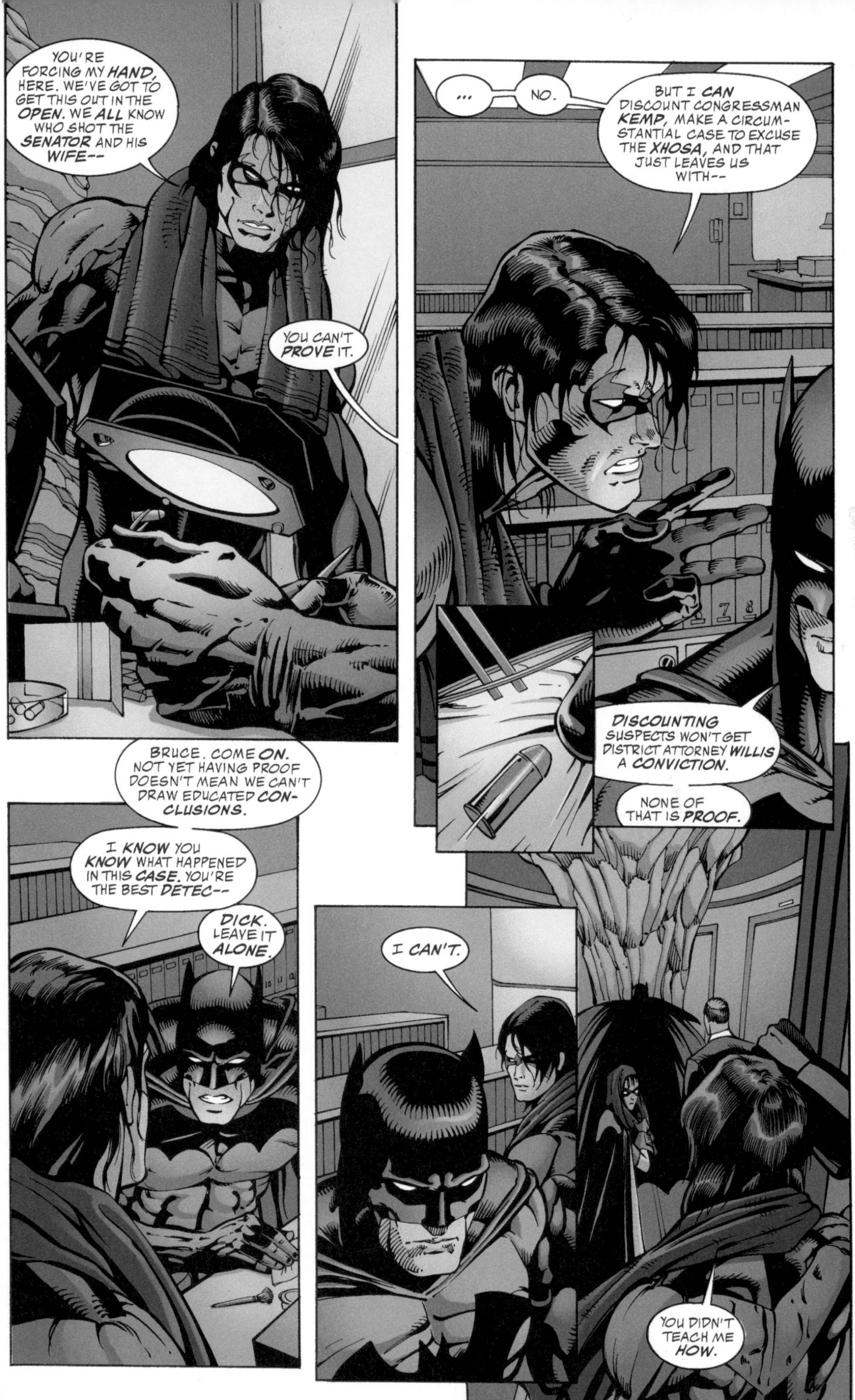
YOU'RE FORCING MY HAND, HERE. WE'VE GOT TO GET THIS OUT IN THE OPEN. WE ALL KNOW WHO SHOT THE SENATOR AND HIS WIFE--
YOU CAN'T PROVE IT.
...
NO.
BUT I CAN DISCOUNT CONGRESSMAN KEMP, MAKE A CIRCUM-STANTIAL CASE TO EXCUSE THE XHOSA, AND THAT JUST LEAVES US WITH--
DISCOUNTING SUSPECTS WON'T GET DISTRICT ATTORNEY WILLIS A CONVICTION.
NONE OF THAT IS PROOF.
BRUCE. COME ON. NOT YET HAVING PROOF DOESN'T MEAN WE CAN'T DRAW EDUCATED CON-CLUSIONS.
I KNOW YOU KNOW WHAT HAPPENED IN THIS CASE. YOU'RE THE BEST DETEC--
DICK. LEAVE IT ALONE.
I CAN'T.
YOU DIDN'T TEACH ME HOW.

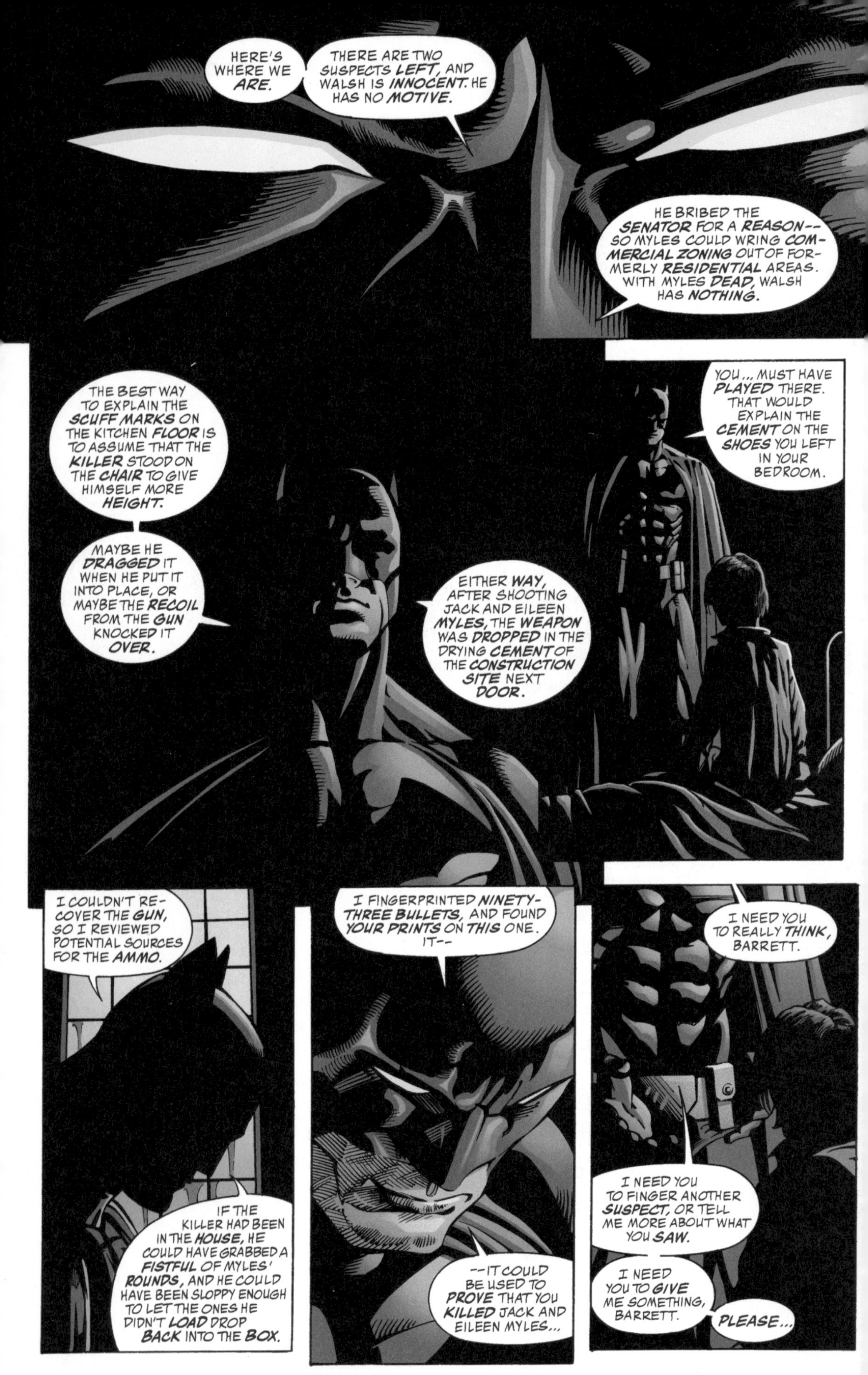
HERE'S WHERE WE ARE.
THERE ARE TWO SUSPECTS LEFT, AND WALSH IS INNOCENT. HE HAS NO MOTIVE.
HE BRIBED THE SENATOR FOR A REASON-- SO MYLES COULD WRING COMMERCIAL ZONING OUT OF FORMERLY RESIDENTIAL AREAS. WITH MYLES DEAD, WALSH HAS NOTHING.
THE BEST WAY TO EXPLAIN THE SCUFF MARKS ON THE KITCHEN FLOOR IS TO ASSUME THAT THE KILLER STOOD ON THE CHAIR TO GIVE HIMSELF MORE HEIGHT.
MAYBE HE DRAGGED IT WHEN HE PUT IT INTO PLACE, OR MAYBE THE RECOIL FROM THE GUN KNOCKED IT OVER.
EITHER WAY, AFTER SHOOTING JACK AND EILEEN MYLES, THE WEAPON WAS DROPPED IN THE DRYING CEMENT OF THE CONSTRUCTION SITE NEXT DOOR.
YOU... MUST HAVE PLAYED THERE. THAT WOULD EXPLAIN THE CEMENT ON THE SHOES YOU LEFT IN YOUR BEDROOM.
I COULDN'T RECOVER THE GUN, SO I REVIEWED POTENTIAL SOURCES FOR THE AMMO.
IF THE KILLER HAD BEEN IN THE HOUSE, HE COULD HAVE GRABBED A FISTFUL OF MYLES' ROUNDS, AND HE COULD HAVE BEEN SLOPPY ENOUGH TO LET THE ONES HE DIDN'T LOAD DROP BACK INTO THE BOX.
I FINGERPRINTED NINETY-THREE BULLETS, AND FOUND YOUR PRINTS ON THIS ONE. IT--
--IT COULD BE USED TO PROVE THAT YOU KILLED JACK AND EILEEN MYLES...
I NEED YOU TO REALLY THINK, BARRETT.
I NEED YOU TO FINGER ANOTHER SUSPECT, OR TELL ME MORE ABOUT WHAT YOU SAW.
I NEED YOU TO GIVE ME SOMETHING, BARRETT.
PLEASE...

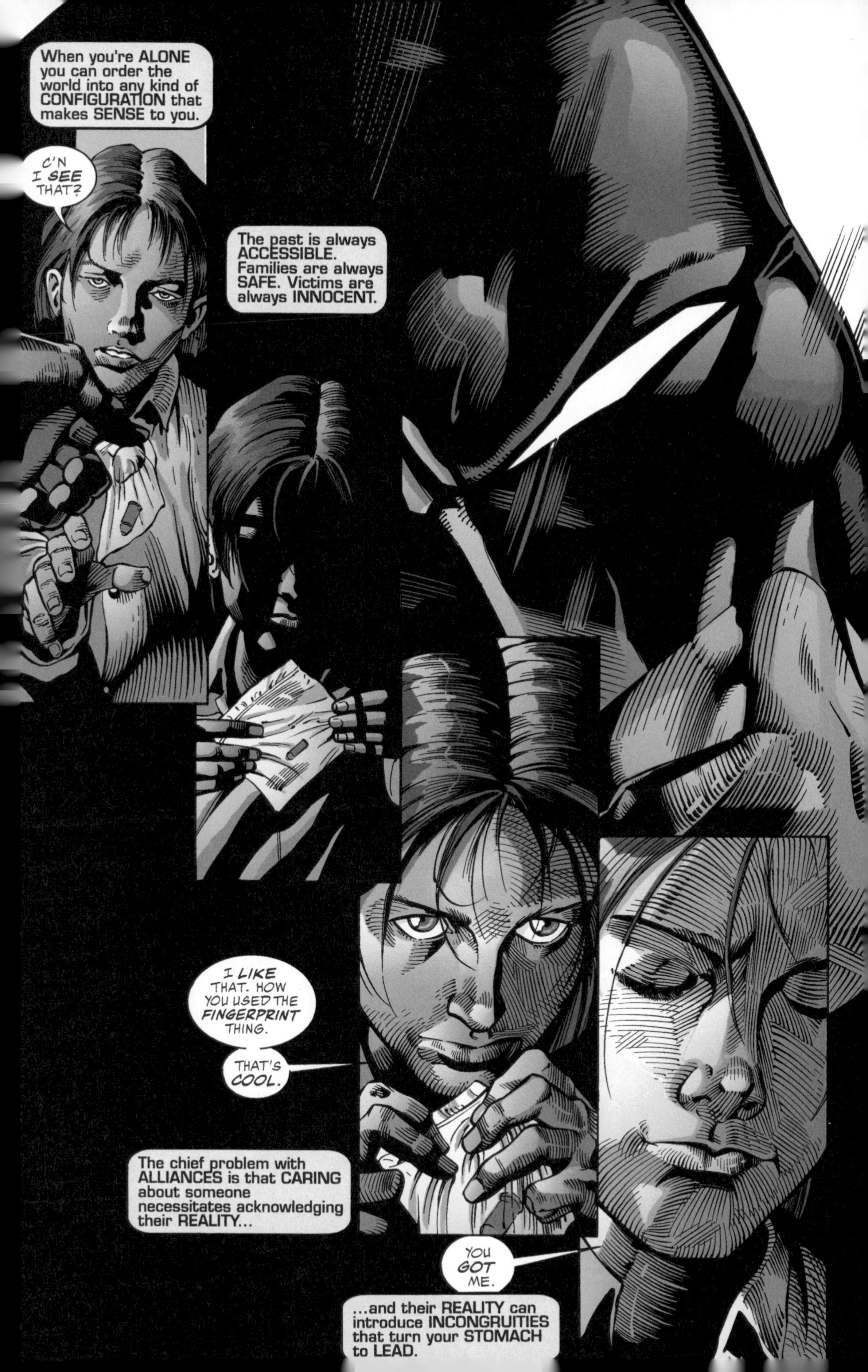
When you're ALONE you can order the world into any kind of CONFIGURATION that makes SENSE to you.
C'N I SEE THAT?
The past is always ACCESSIBLE. Families are always SAFE. Victims are always INNOCENT.
I LIKE THAT. HOW YOU USED THE FINGERPRINT THING.
THAT'S COOL.
The chief problem with ALLIANCES is that CARING about someone necessitates acknowledging their REALITY...
YOU GOT ME.
...and their REALITY can introduce INCONGRUITIES that turn your STOMACH to LEAD.

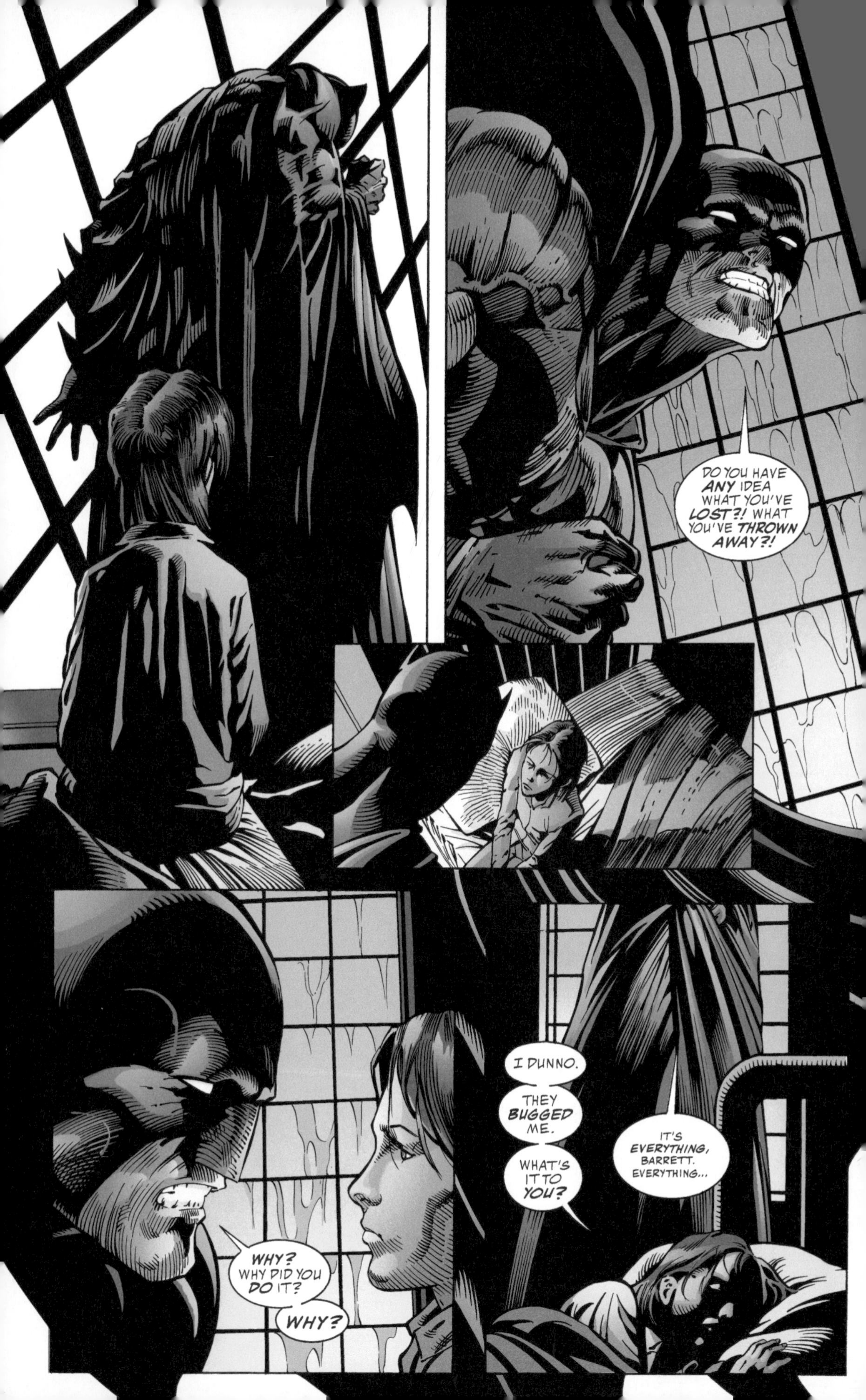
DO YOU HAVE ANY IDEA WHAT YOU'VE LOST?! WHAT YOU'VE THROWN AWAY?!
WHY? WHY DID YOU DO IT?
WHY?
I DUNNO.
THEY BUGGED ME.
WHAT'S IT TO YOU?
IT'S EVERYTHING, BARRETT. EVERYTHING...

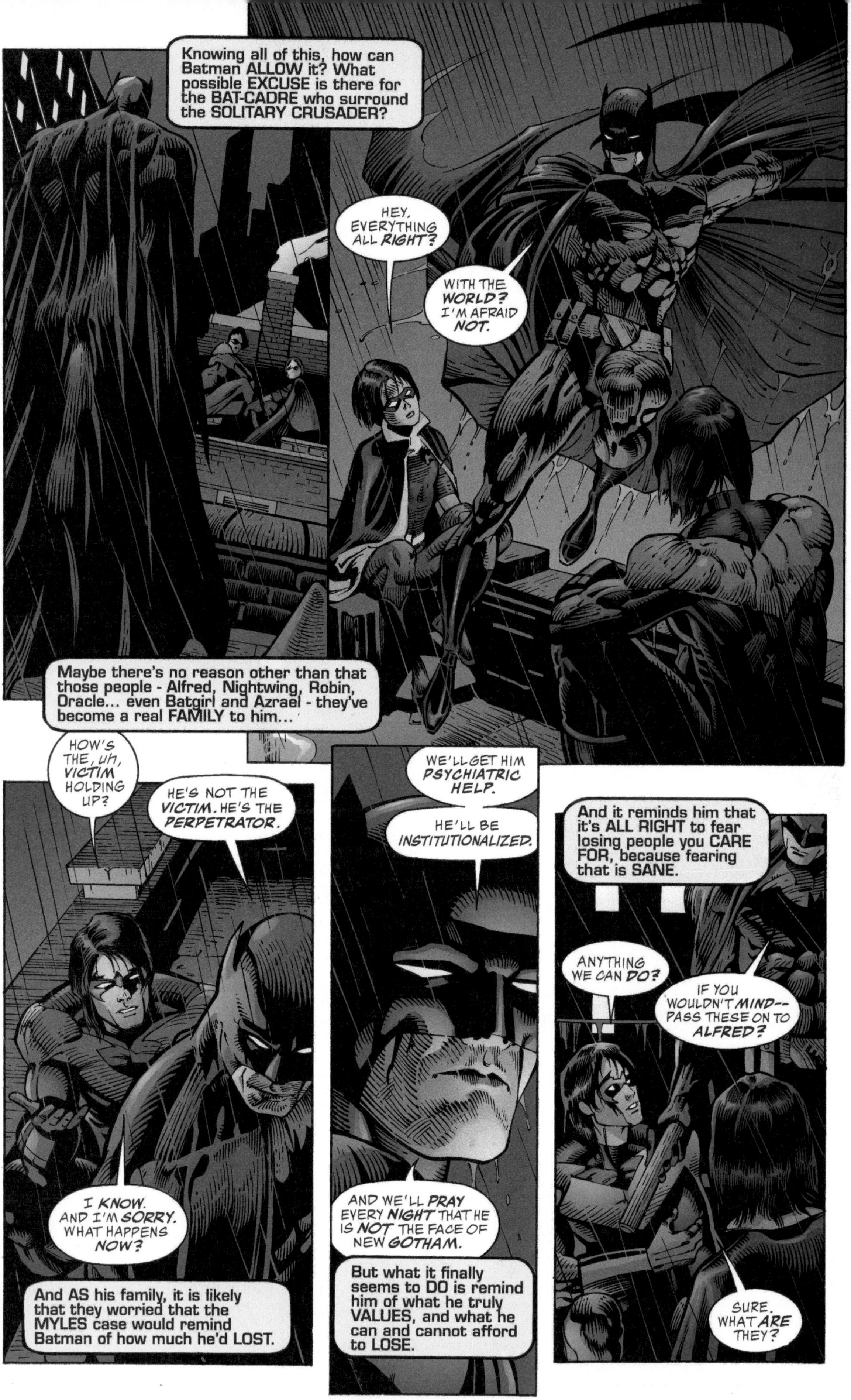
Knowing all of this, how can Batman ALLOW it? What possible EXCUSE is there for the BAT-CADRE who surround the SOLITARY CRUSADER?
HEY. EVERYTHING ALL RIGHT?
WITH THE WORLD? I'M AFRAID NOT.
Maybe there's no reason other than that those people - Alfred, Nightwing, Robin, Oracle... even Batgirl and Azrael - they've become a real FAMILY to him...
HOW'S THE, uh, VICTIM HOLDING UP?
HE'S NOT THE VICTIM. HE'S THE PERPETRATOR.
I KNOW. AND I'M SORRY. WHAT HAPPENS NOW?
And AS his family, it is likely that they worried that the MYLES case would remind Batman of how much he'd LOST.
WE'LL GET HIM PSYCHIATRIC HELP.
HE'LL BE INSTITUTIONALIZED.
AND WE'LL PRAY EVERY NIGHT THAT HE IS NOT THE FACE OF NEW GOTHAM.
But what it finally seems to DO is remind him of what he truly VALUES, and what he can and cannot afford to LOSE.
And it reminds him that it's ALL RIGHT to fear losing people you CARE FOR, because fearing that is SANE.
ANYTHING WE CAN DO?
IF YOU WOULDN'T MIND-- PASS THESE ON TO ALFRED?
SURE. WHAT ARE THEY?

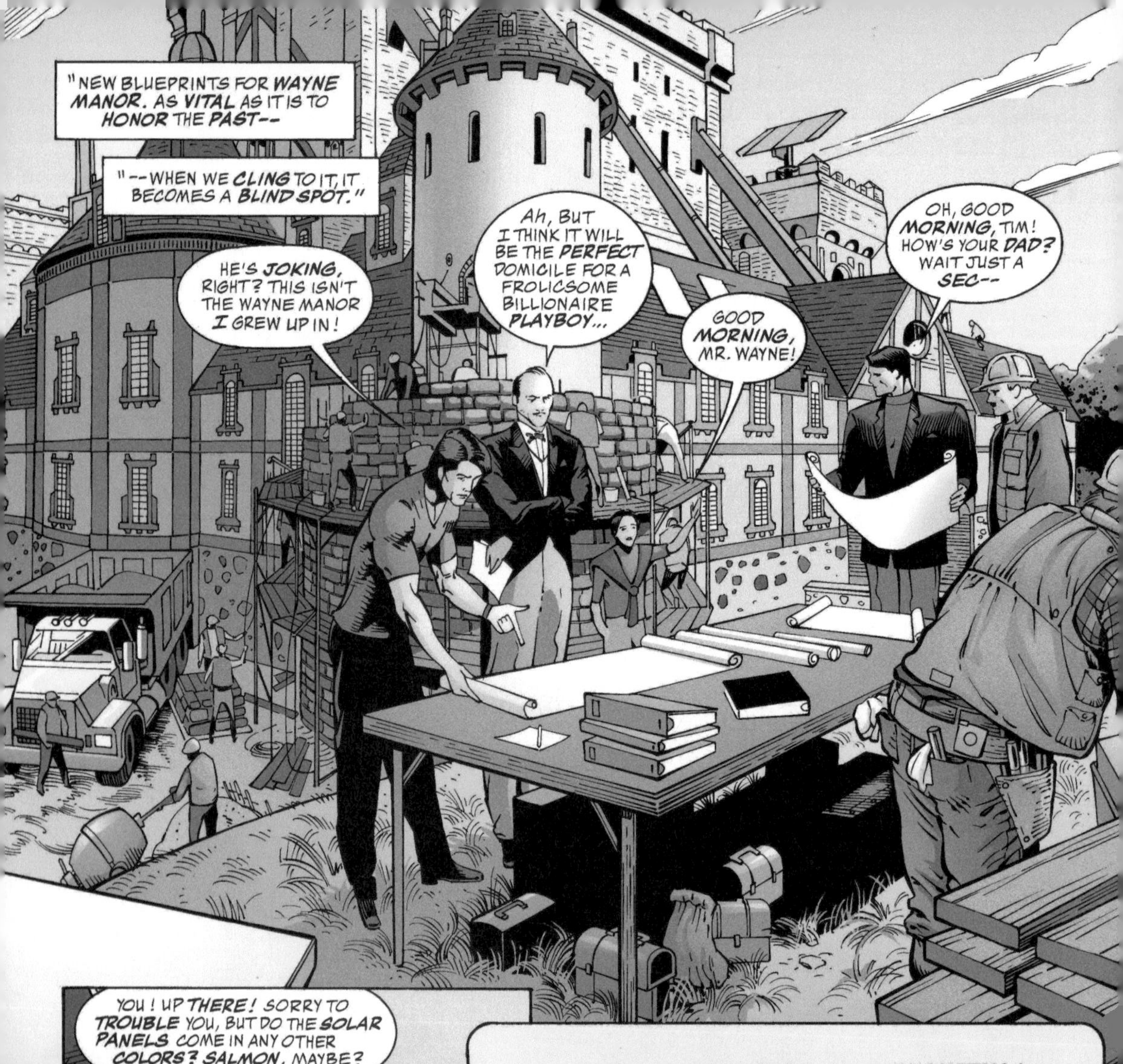
"NEW BLUEPRINTS FOR WAYNE MANOR. AS VITAL AS IT IS TO HONOR THE PAST--
"--WHEN WE CLING TO IT, IT BECOMES A BLIND SPOT."
HE'S JOKING, RIGHT? THIS ISN'T THE WAYNE MANOR I GREW UP IN!
Ah, BUT I THINK IT WILL BE THE PERFECT DOMICILE FOR A FROLICSOME BILLIONAIRE PLAYBOY...
GOOD MORNING, MR. WAYNE!
OH, GOOD MORNING, TIM! HOW'S YOUR DAD? WAIT JUST A SEC--

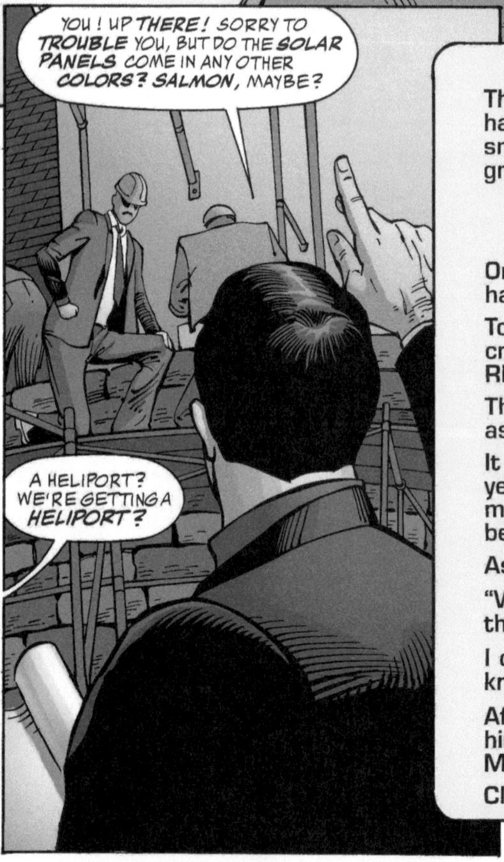
YOU! UP THERE! SORRY TO TROUBLE YOU, BUT DO THE SOLAR PANELS COME IN ANY OTHER COLORS? SALMON, MAYBE?
A HELIPORT? WE'RE GETTING A HELIPORT?

Though Batman's CRUSADE began PRIVATELY, he has come to have great IMPACT, both on his own small circle of CONFIDANTS, and also on the greater crimefighting community.

Or perhaps, more to the point, they have come to have great impact on HIM.

To really understand him as a man and as a crimefighter, detailed analysis of these RELATIONSHIPS is undoubtedly in order.

The proposed examination will, at any rate, serve as one attempt to bring him into sharper focus.

It has certainly becom clear over the past ten years that Batman is an entity worthy of the most meticulous scrutiny I can possibly bring to bear upon him,

As Zen scholar Shunryu put it:

"When you understand one thing through and through, you understand everything."

I don't pretend to be that ambitious, but I WILL know Batman.

After all. in the END, the final hour of RETIRING him PERMANENTLY will almost certainly fall to ME.

Close file 0001.

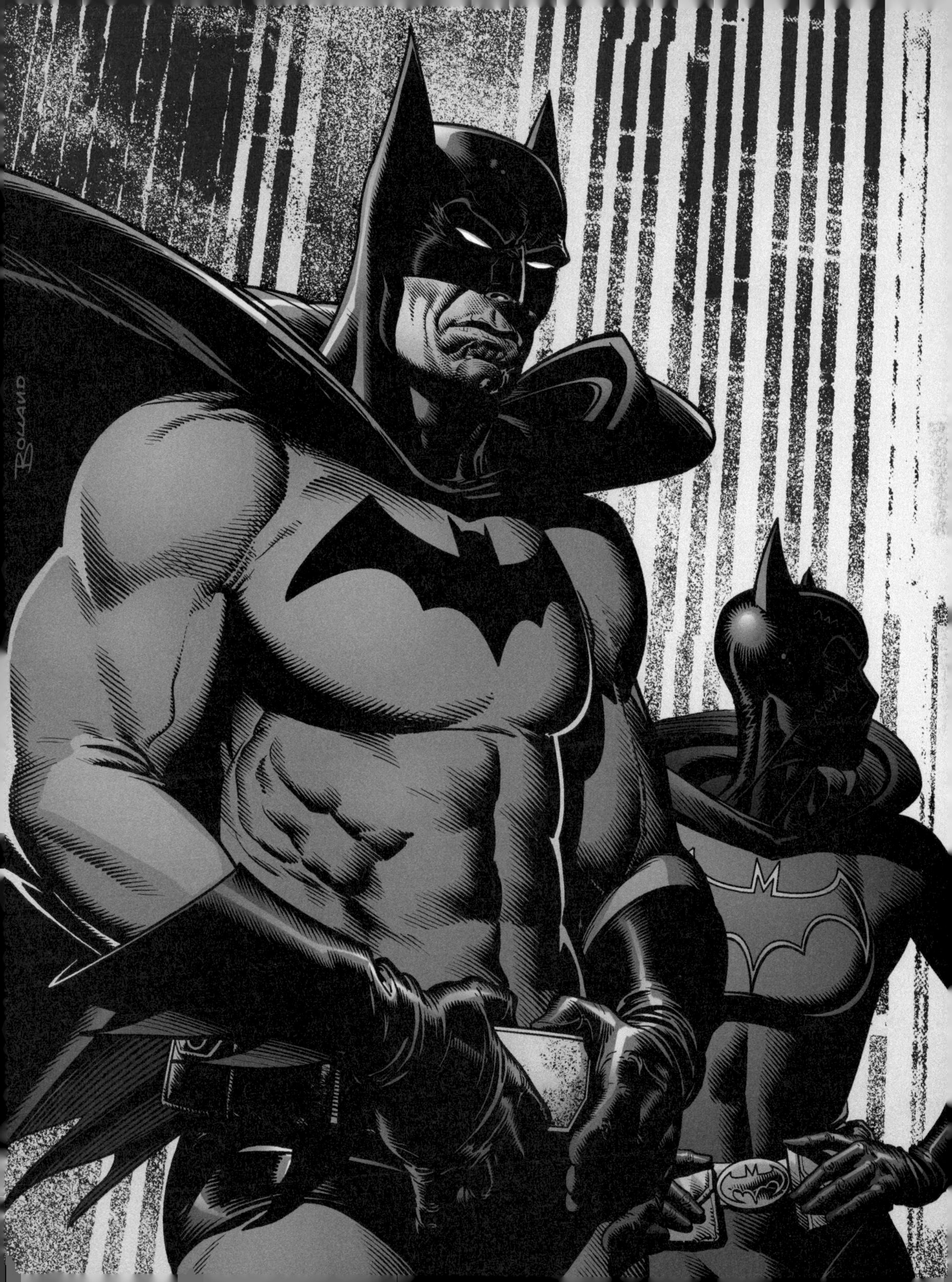
BOLLAND

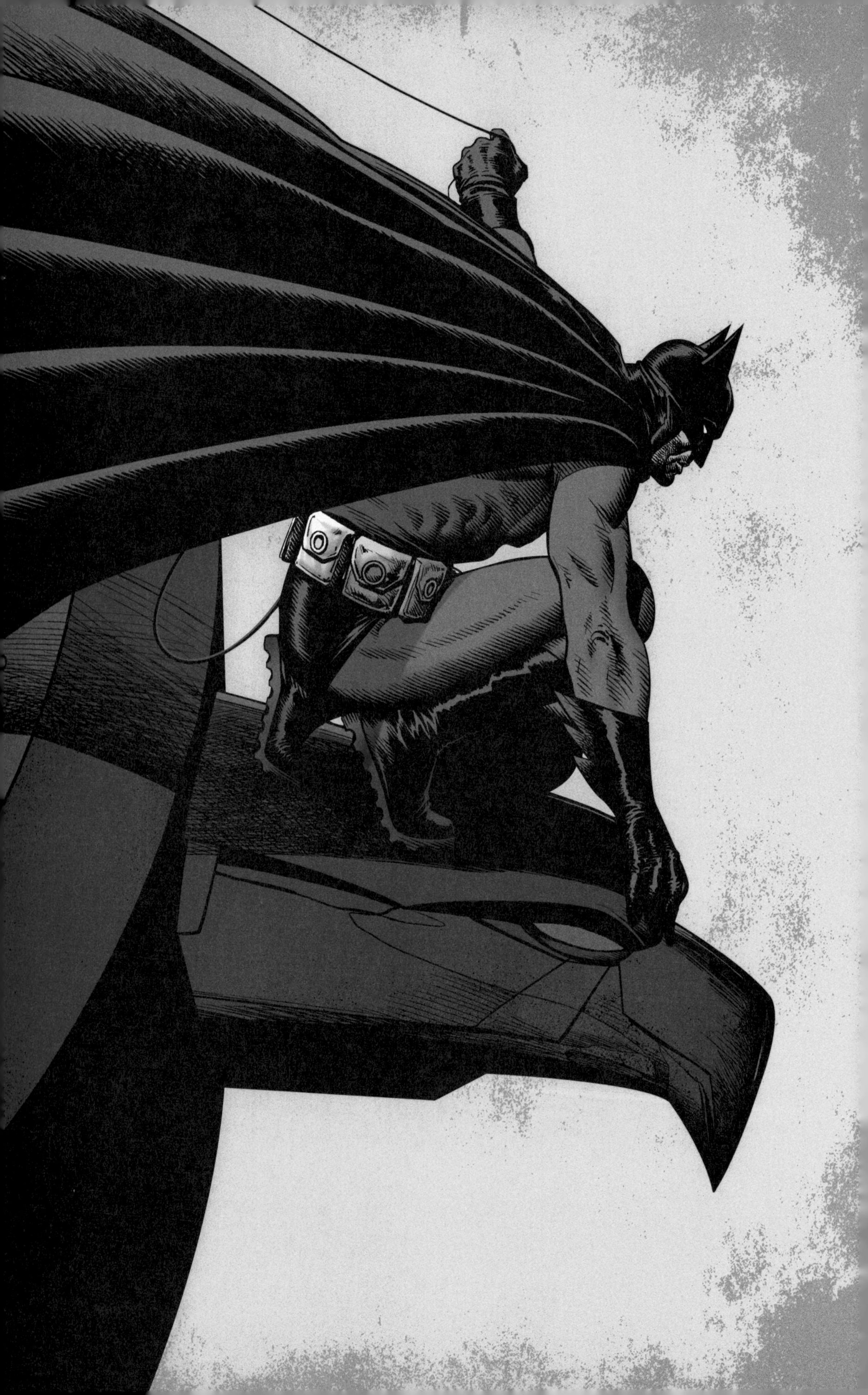

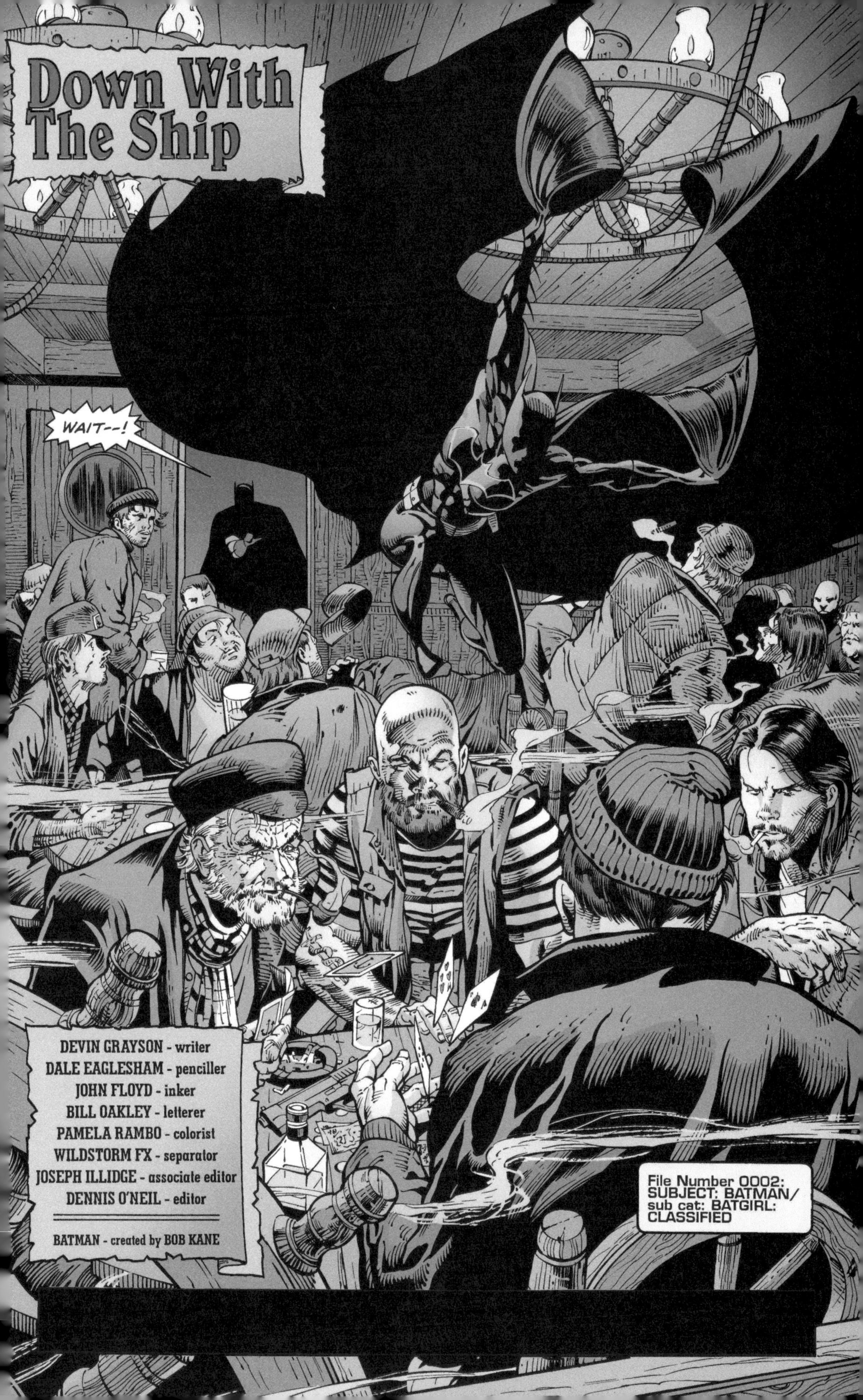
Down With The Ship
WAIT--!
DEVIN GRAYSON - writer
DALE EAGLESHAM - penciller
JOHN FLOYD - inker
BILL OAKLEY - letterer
PAMELA RAMBO - colorist
WILDSTORM FX - separator
JOSEPH ILLIDGE - associate editor
DENNIS O'NEIL - editor
BATMAN - created by BOB KANE
File Number 0002:
SUBJECT: BATMAN/
sub cat: BATGIRL:
CLASSIFIED

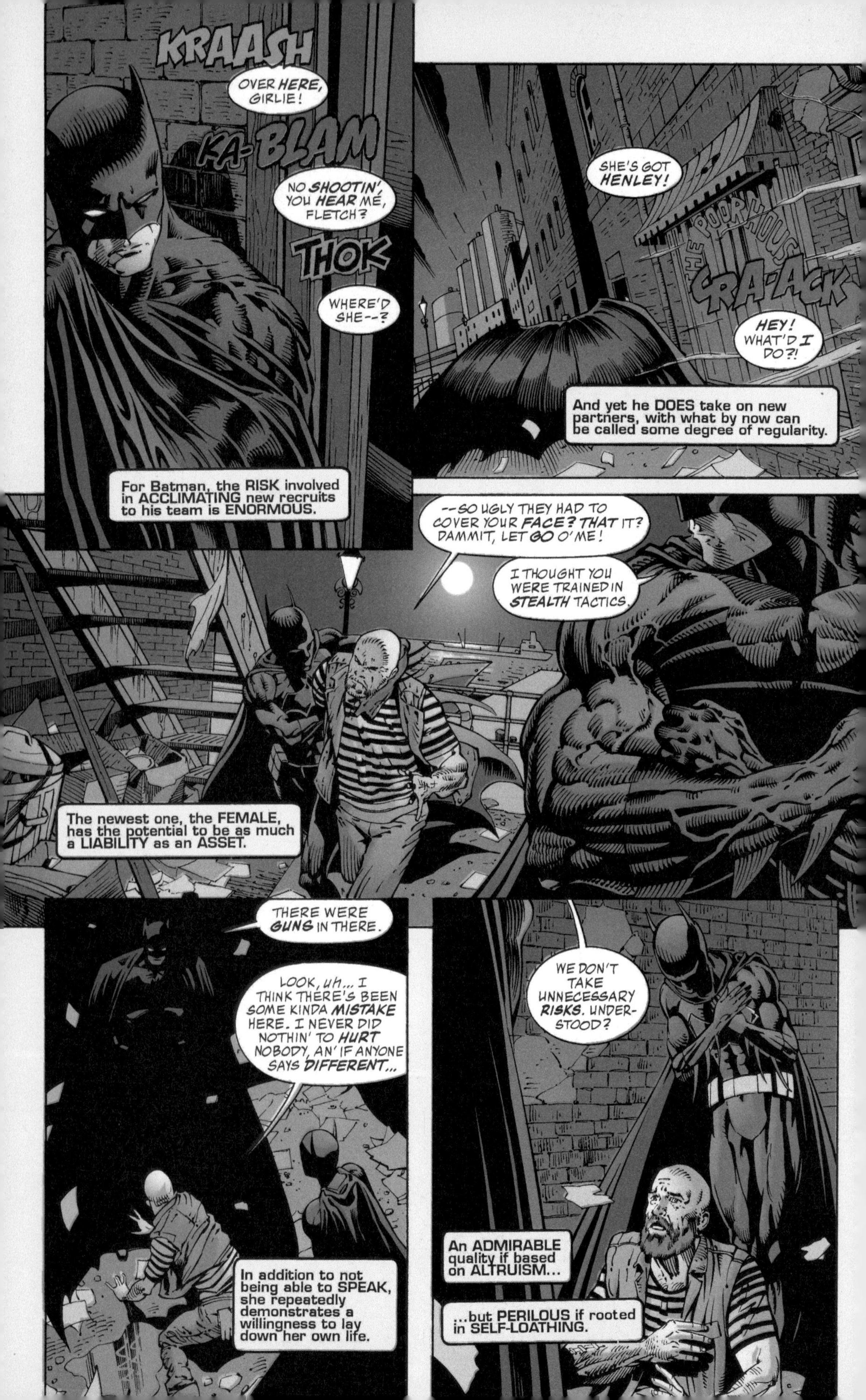
KRAASH
OVER HERE, GIRLIE!
KA-BLAM
NO SHOOTIN', YOU HEAR ME, FLETCH?
THOK
WHERE'D SHE--?
For Batman, the RISK involved in ACCLIMATING new recruits to his team is ENORMOUS.
SHE'S GOT HENLEY!
THE POORHOUSE
CRA-ACK
HEY! WHAT'D I DO?!
And yet he DOES take on new partners, with what by now can be called some degree of regularity.
--SO UGLY THEY HAD TO COVER YOUR FACE? THAT IT? DAMMIT, LET GO O'ME!
I THOUGHT YOU WERE TRAINED IN STEALTH TACTICS.
The newest one, the FEMALE, has the potential to be as much a LIABILITY as an ASSET.
THERE WERE GUNS IN THERE.
LOOK, uh... I THINK THERE'S BEEN SOME KINDA MISTAKE HERE. I NEVER DID NOTHIN' TO HURT NOBODY, AN' IF ANYONE SAYS DIFFERENT...
In addition to not being able to SPEAK, she repeatedly demonstrates a willingness to lay down her own life.
WE DON'T TAKE UNNECESSARY RISKS. UNDERSTOOD?
An ADMIRABLE quality if based on ALTRUISM...
...but PERILOUS if rooted in SELF-LOATHING.

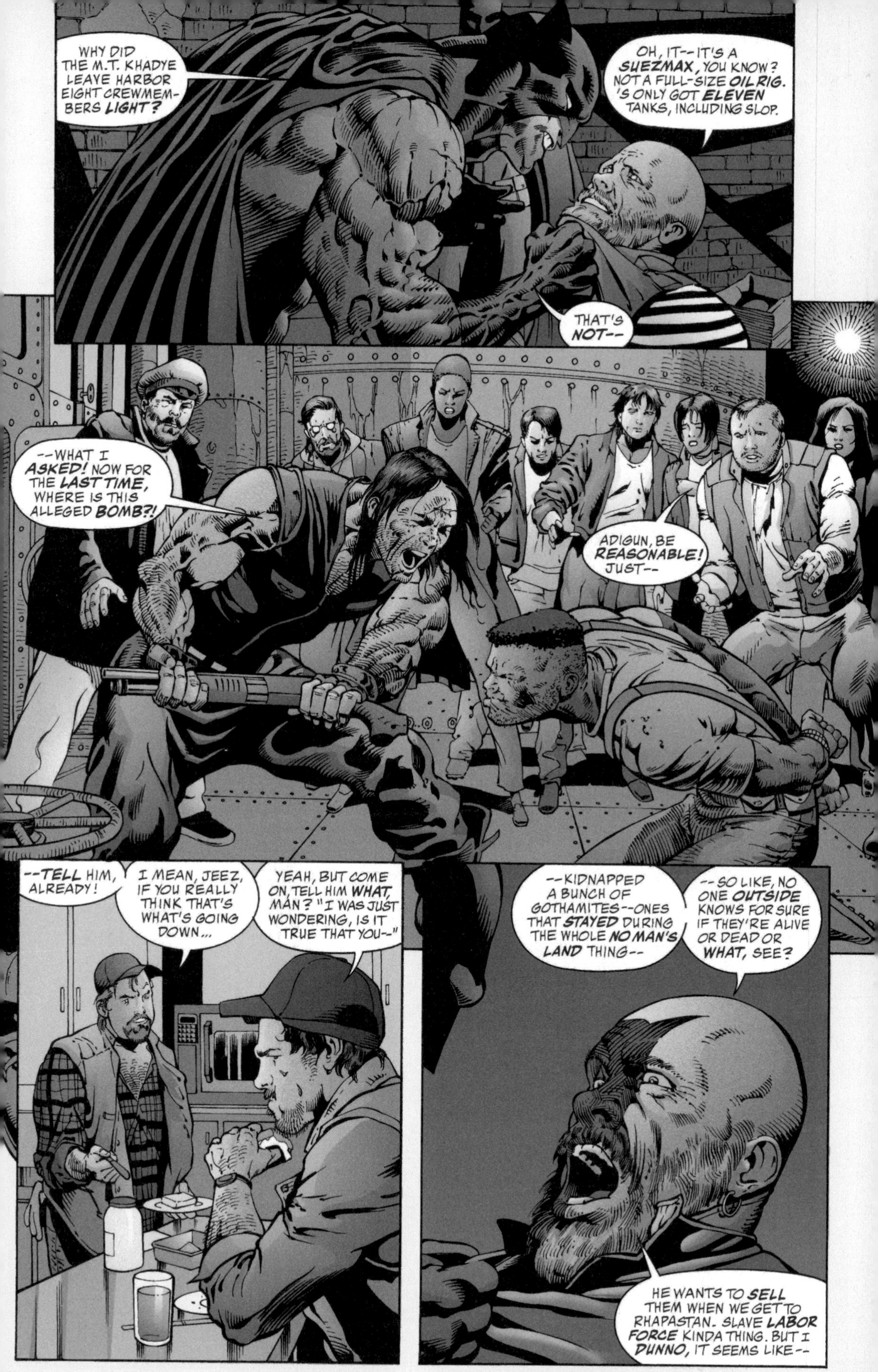
WHY DID THE M.T. KHADYE LEAVE HARBOR EIGHT CREWMEMBERS LIGHT?
OH, IT--IT'S A SUEZMAX, YOU KNOW? NOT A FULL-SIZE OIL RIG. 'S ONLY GOT ELEVEN TANKS, INCLUDING SLOP.
THAT'S NOT--
--WHAT I ASKED! NOW FOR THE LAST TIME, WHERE IS THIS ALLEGED BOMB?!
ADIGUN, BE REASONABLE! JUST--
--TELL HIM, ALREADY!
I MEAN, JEEZ, IF YOU REALLY THINK THAT'S WHAT'S GOING DOWN...
YEAH, BUT COME ON, TELL HIM WHAT, MAN? "I WAS JUST WONDERING, IS IT TRUE THAT YOU--"
--KIDNAPPED A BUNCH OF GOTHAMITES--ONES THAT STAYED DURING THE WHOLE NO MAN'S LAND THING--
--SO LIKE, NO ONE OUTSIDE KNOWS FOR SURE IF THEY'RE ALIVE OR DEAD OR WHAT, SEE?
HE WANTS TO SELL THEM WHEN WE GET TO RHAPASTAN. SLAVE LABOR FORCE KINDA THING. BUT I DUNNO, IT SEEMS LIKE--

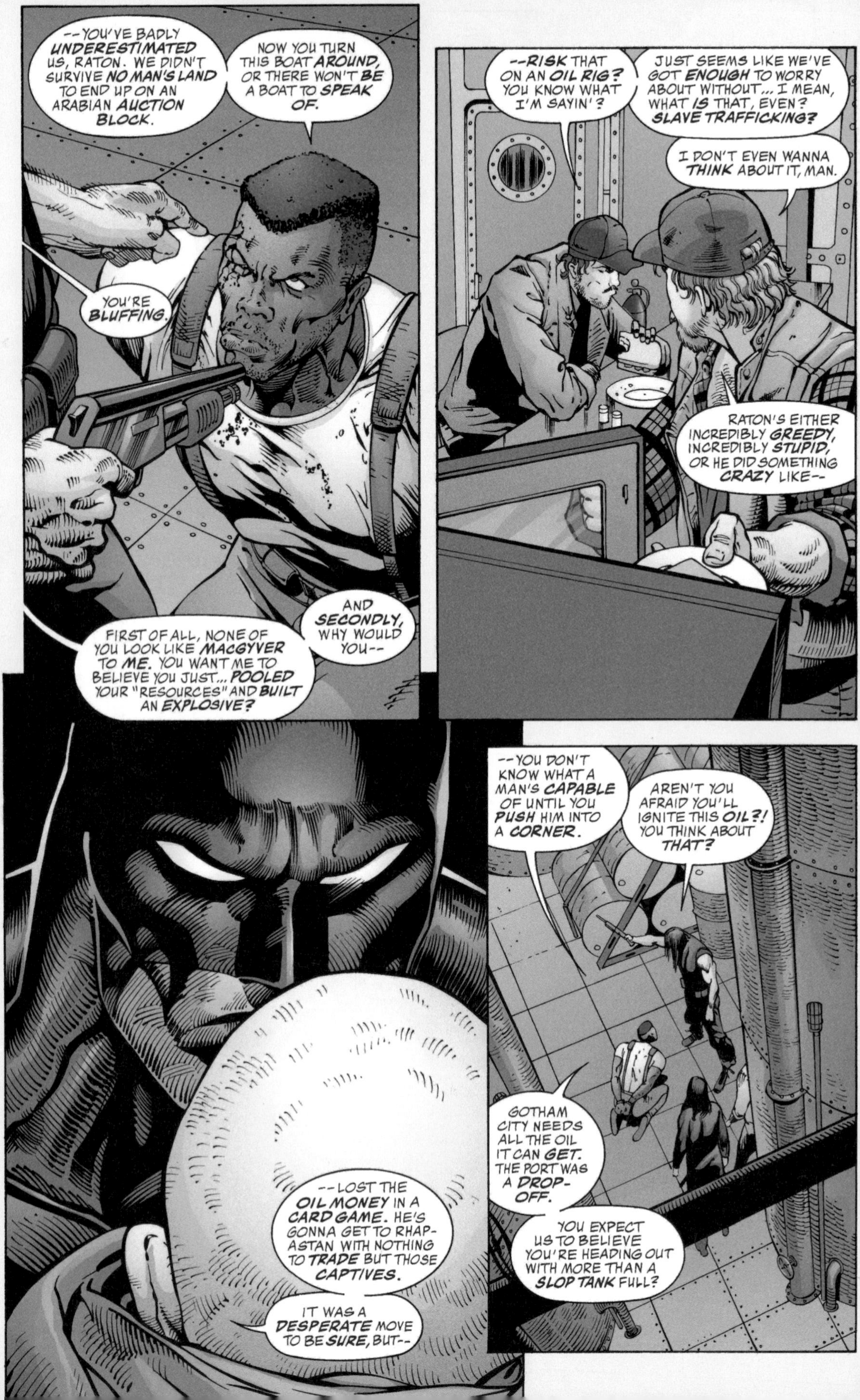
--YOU'VE BADLY UNDERESTIMATED US, RATON. WE DIDN'T SURVIVE NO MAN'S LAND TO END UP ON AN ARABIAN AUCTION BLOCK.
NOW YOU TURN THIS BOAT AROUND, OR THERE WON'T BE A BOAT TO SPEAK OF.
YOU'RE BLUFFING.
FIRST OF ALL, NONE OF YOU LOOK LIKE MACGYVER TO ME. YOU WANT ME TO BELIEVE YOU JUST... POOLED YOUR "RESOURCES" AND BUILT AN EXPLOSIVE?
AND SECONDLY, WHY WOULD YOU--
--RISK THAT ON AN OIL RIG? YOU KNOW WHAT I'M SAYIN'?
JUST SEEMS LIKE WE'VE GOT ENOUGH TO WORRY ABOUT WITHOUT... I MEAN, WHAT IS THAT, EVEN? SLAVE TRAFFICKING?
I DON'T EVEN WANNA THINK ABOUT IT, MAN.
RATON'S EITHER INCREDIBLY GREEDY, INCREDIBLY STUPID, OR HE DID SOMETHING CRAZY LIKE--
--LOST THE OIL MONEY IN A CARD GAME. HE'S GONNA GET TO RHAP-ASTAN WITH NOTHING TO TRADE BUT THOSE CAPTIVES.
IT WAS A DESPERATE MOVE TO BE SURE, BUT--
--YOU DON'T KNOW WHAT A MAN'S CAPABLE OF UNTIL YOU PUSH HIM INTO A CORNER.
AREN'T YOU AFRAID YOU'LL IGNITE THIS OIL?! YOU THINK ABOUT THAT?
GOTHAM CITY NEEDS ALL THE OIL IT CAN GET. THE PORT WAS A DROP-OFF.
YOU EXPECT US TO BELIEVE YOU'RE HEADING OUT WITH MORE THAN A SLOP TANK FULL?

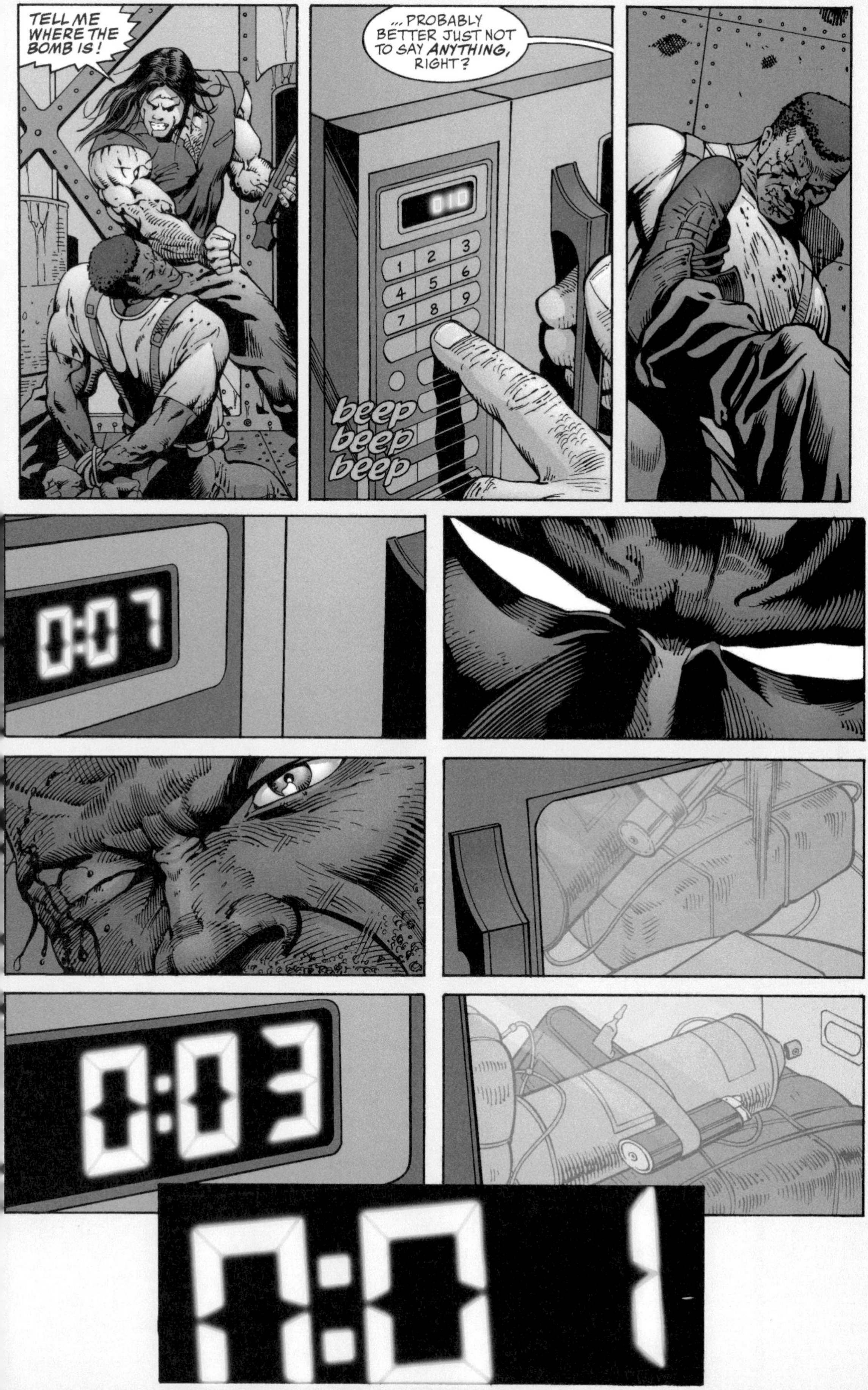
TELL ME WHERE THE BOMB IS!
...PROBABLY BETTER JUST NOT TO SAY ANYTHING, RIGHT?
beep beep beep
0:07
0:03

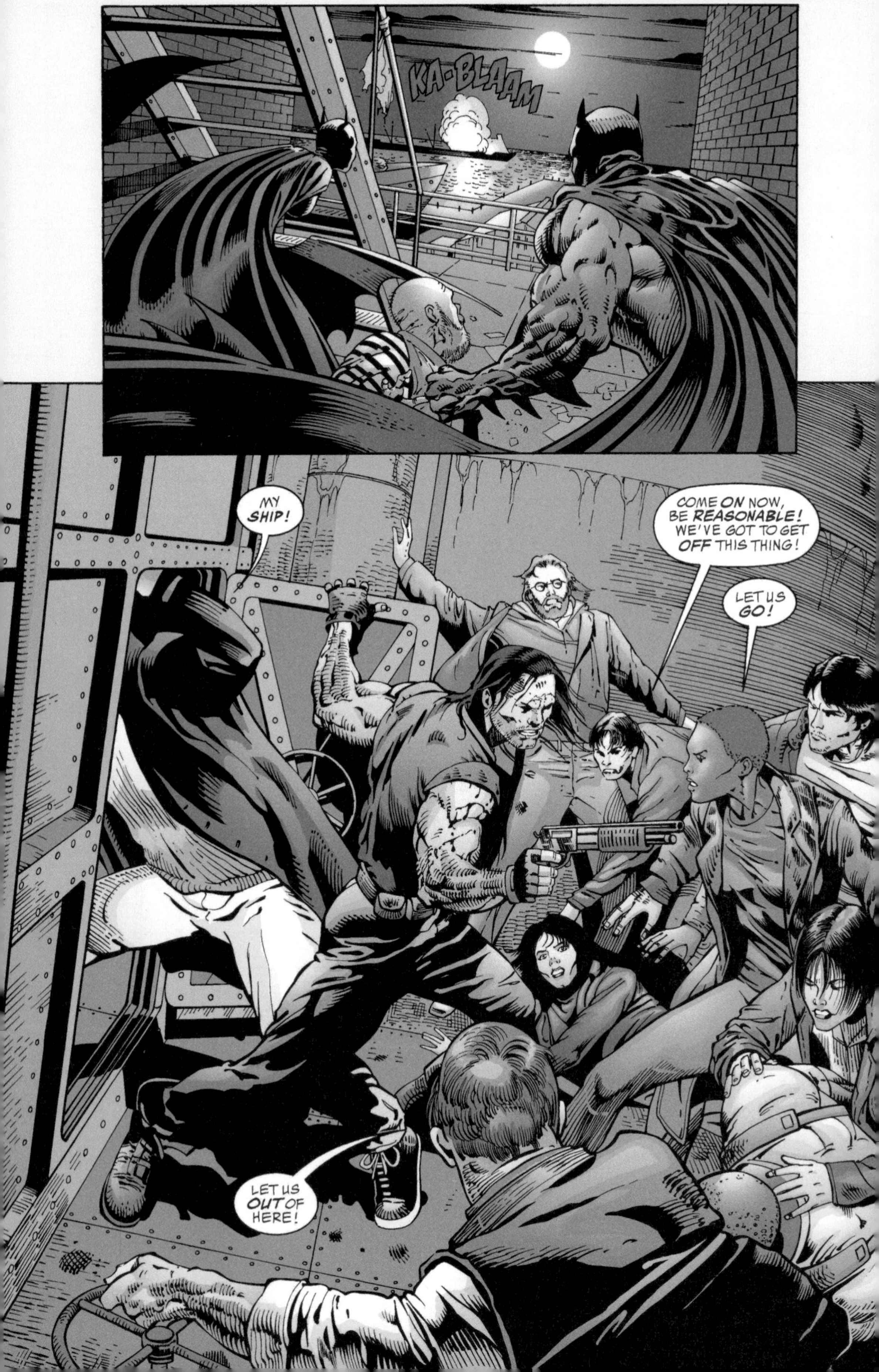
KA-BLAAM
MY SHIP!
COME ON NOW, BE REASONABLE! WE'VE GOT TO GET OFF THIS THING!
LET US GO!
LET US OUT OF HERE!

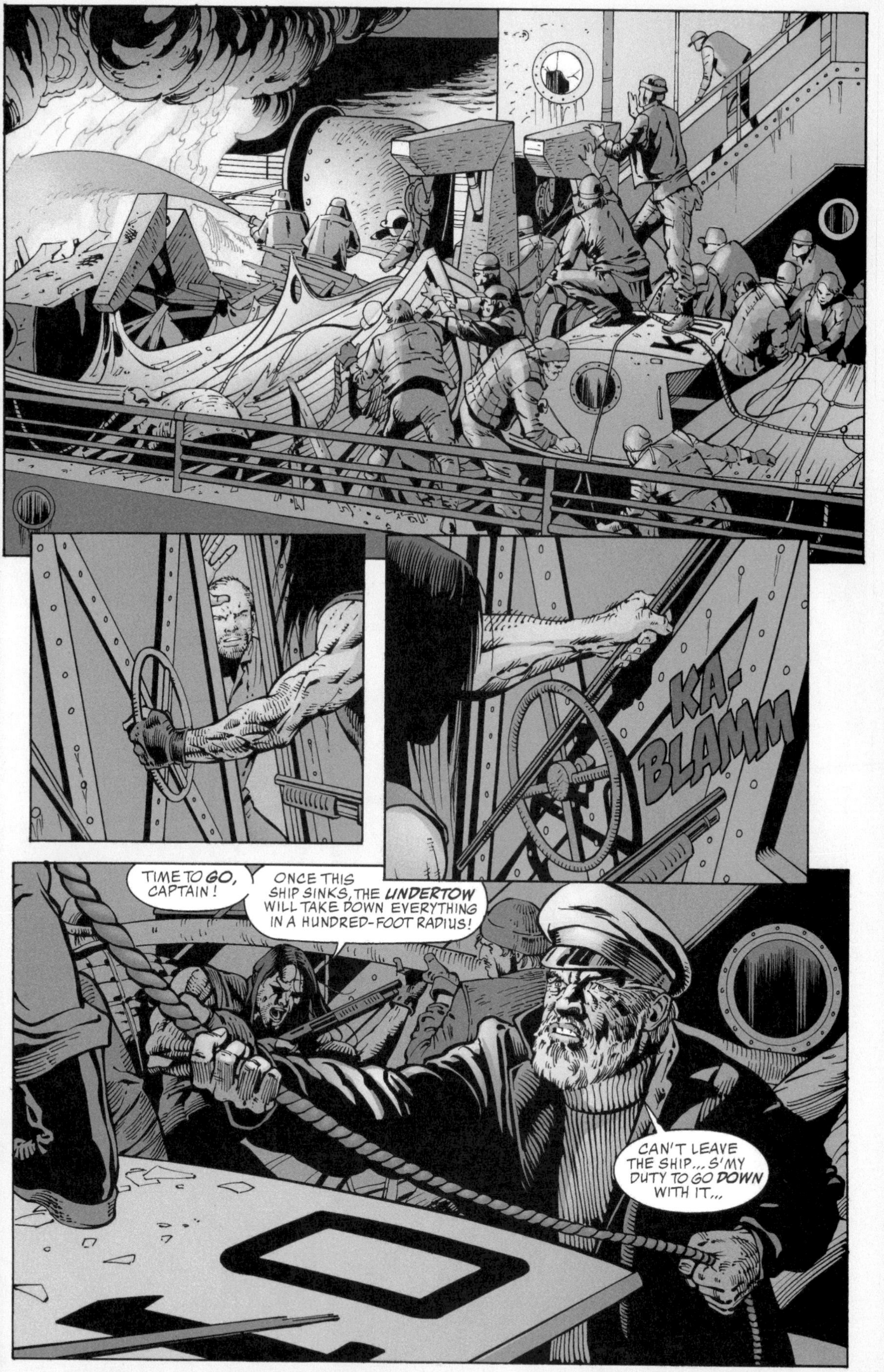
KA-
BLAMM
TIME TO GO, CAPTAIN!
ONCE THIS SHIP SINKS, THE UNDERTOW WILL TAKE DOWN EVERYTHING IN A HUNDRED-FOOT RADIUS!
CAN'T LEAVE THE SHIP... S'MY DUTY TO GO DOWN WITH IT...

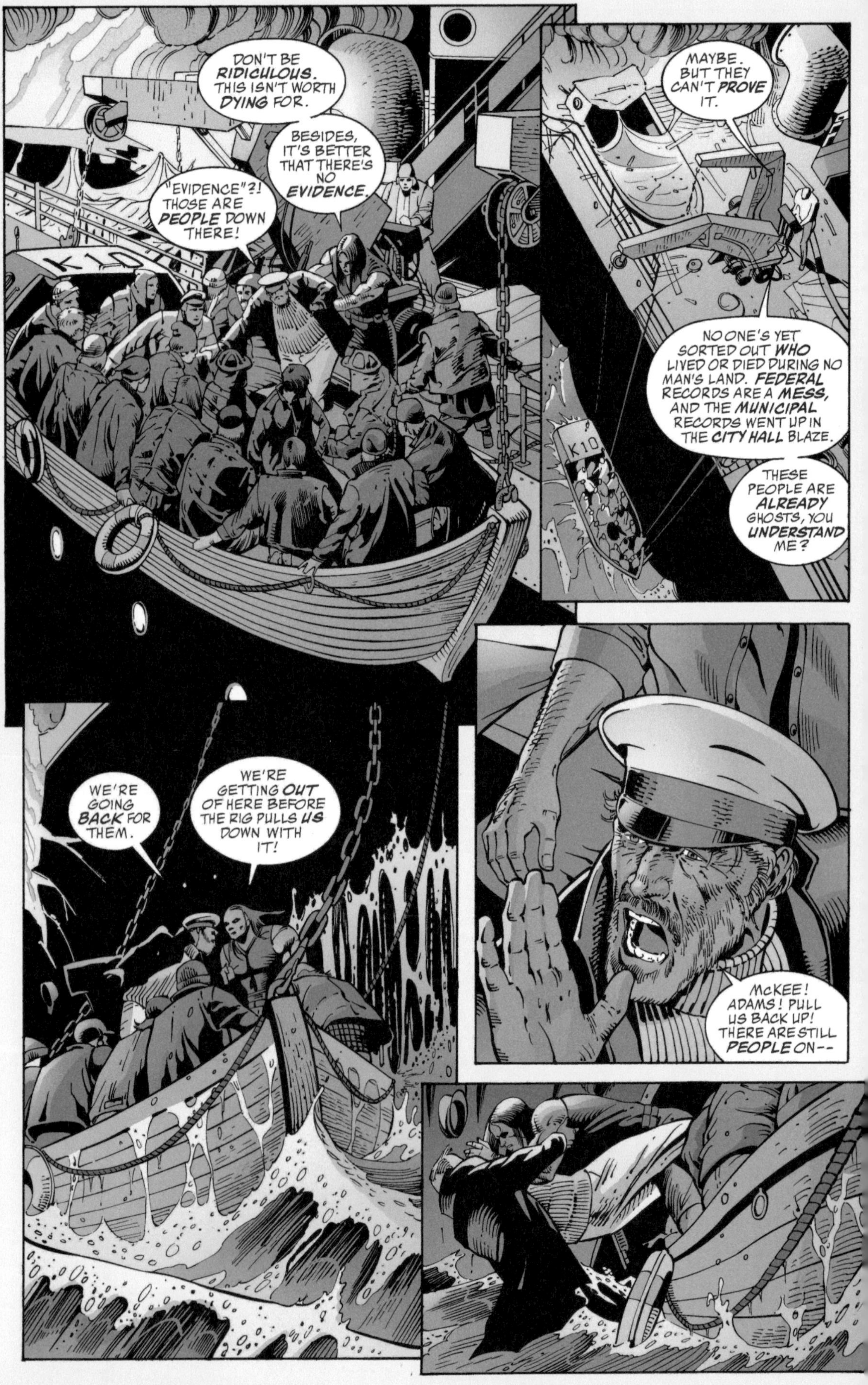

DON'T BE RIDICULOUS. THIS ISN'T WORTH DYING FOR.
BESIDES, IT'S BETTER THAT THERE'S NO EVIDENCE.
"EVIDENCE"?! THOSE ARE PEOPLE DOWN THERE!
K10
MAYBE. BUT THEY CAN'T PROVE IT.
NO ONE'S YET SORTED OUT WHO LIVED OR DIED DURING NO MAN'S LAND. FEDERAL RECORDS ARE A MESS, AND THE MUNICIPAL RECORDS WENT UP IN THE CITY HALL BLAZE.
K10
THESE PEOPLE ARE ALREADY GHOSTS, YOU UNDERSTAND ME?
WE'RE GOING BACK FOR THEM.
WE'RE GETTING OUT OF HERE BEFORE THE RIG PULLS US DOWN WITH IT!
McKEE! ADAMS! PULL US BACK UP! THERE ARE STILL PEOPLE ON--

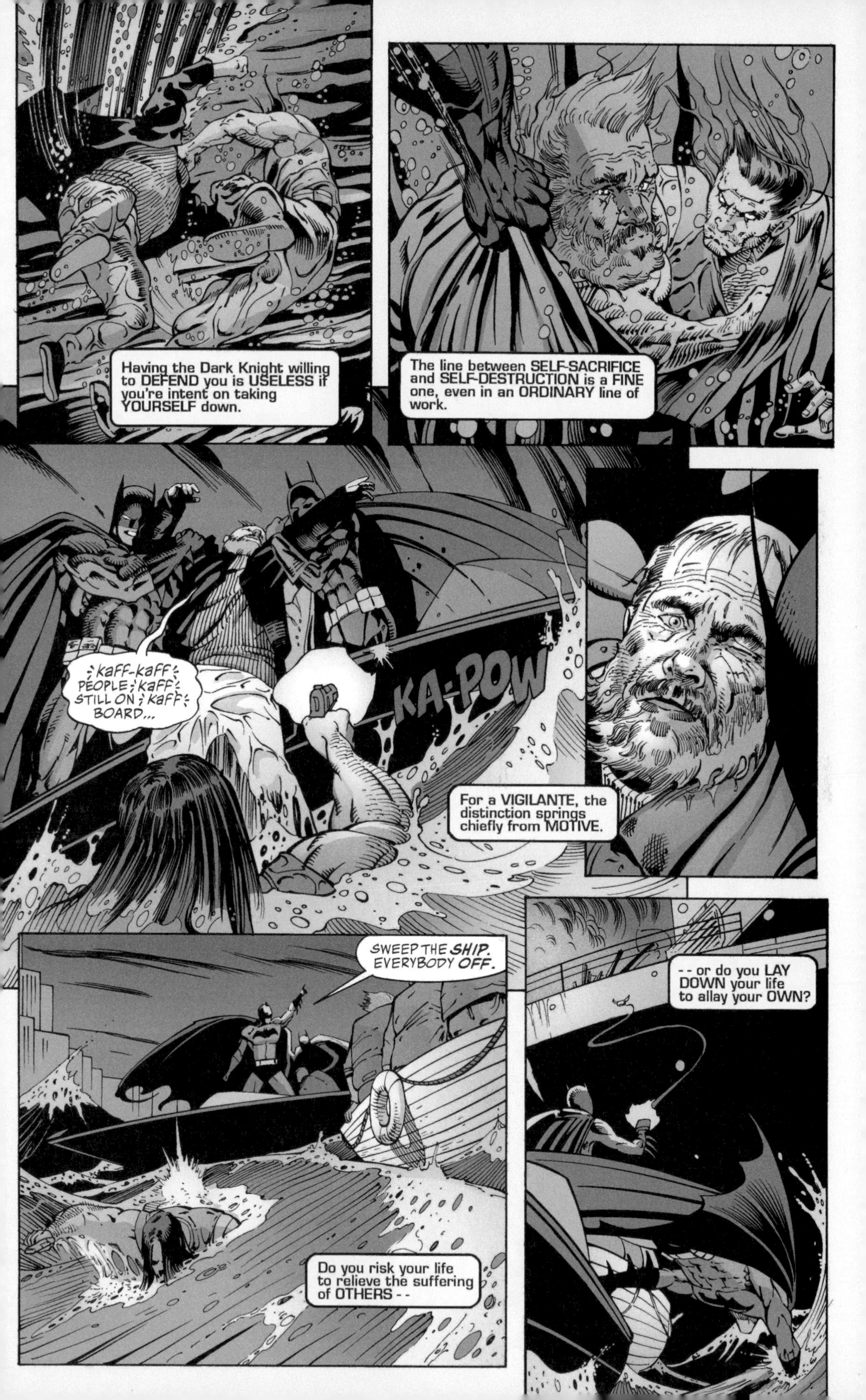
Having the Dark Knight willing to DEFEND you is USELESS if you're intent on taking YOURSELF down.
The line between SELF-SACRIFICE and SELF-DESTRUCTION is a FINE one, even in an ORDINARY line of work.
;KAFF-KAFF; PEOPLE ;KAFF; STILL ON ;KAFF; BOARD...
KA-POW
For a VIGILANTE, the distinction springs chiefly from MOTIVE.
SWEEP THE SHIP. EVERYBODY OFF.
Do you risk your life to relieve the suffering of OTHERS --
-- or do you LAY DOWN your life to allay your OWN?

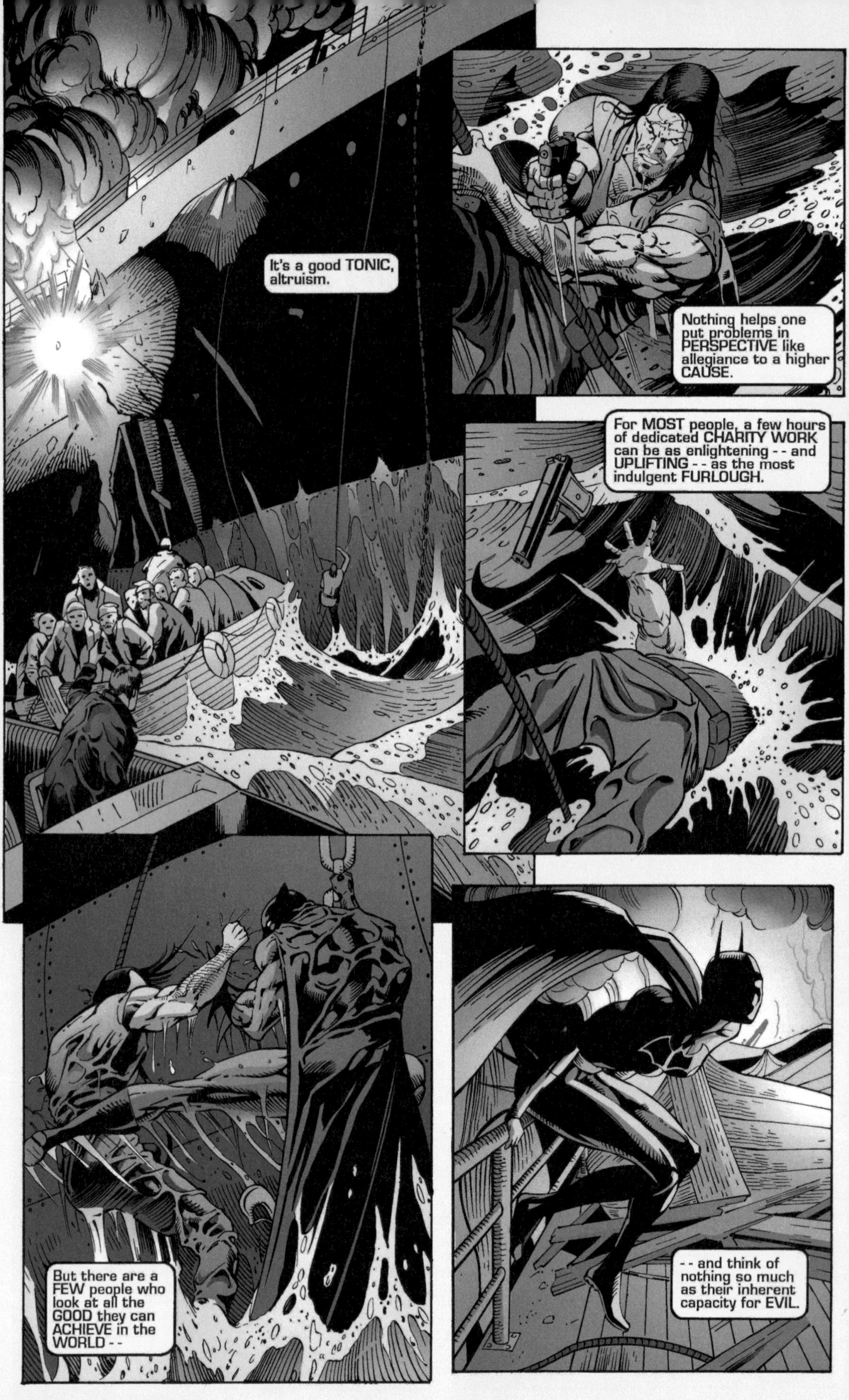
It's a good TONIC, altruism.
Nothing helps one put problems in PERSPECTIVE like allegiance to a higher CAUSE.
For MOST people, a few hours of dedicated CHARITY WORK can be as enlightening - - and UPLIFTING - - as the most indulgent FURLOUGH.
But there are a FEW people who look at all the GOOD they can ACHIEVE in the WORLD - -
- - and think of nothing so much as their inherent capacity for EVIL.

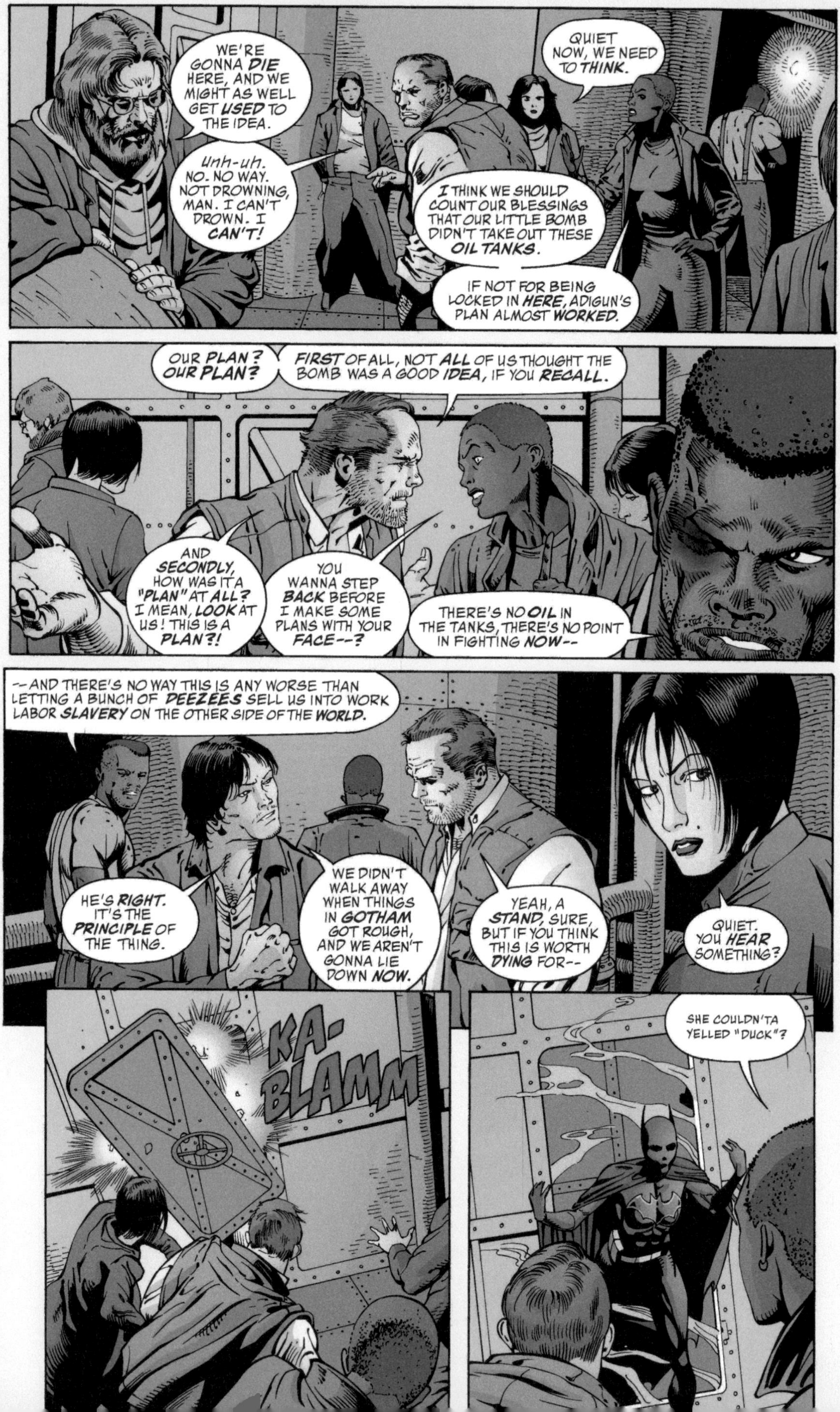
WE'RE GONNA DIE HERE, AND WE MIGHT AS WELL GET USED TO THE IDEA.
unh-uh. NO. NO WAY. NOT DROWNING, MAN. I CAN'T DROWN. I CAN'T!
QUIET NOW, WE NEED TO THINK.
I THINK WE SHOULD COUNT OUR BLESSINGS THAT OUR LITTLE BOMB DIDN'T TAKE OUT THESE OIL TANKS.
IF NOT FOR BEING LOCKED IN HERE, ADIGUN'S PLAN ALMOST WORKED.
OUR PLAN? OUR PLAN?
FIRST OF ALL, NOT ALL OF US THOUGHT THE BOMB WAS A GOOD IDEA, IF YOU RECALL.
AND SECONDLY, HOW WAS IT A "PLAN" AT ALL? I MEAN, LOOK AT US! THIS IS A PLAN?!
YOU WANNA STEP BACK BEFORE I MAKE SOME PLANS WITH YOUR FACE--?
THERE'S NO OIL IN THE TANKS, THERE'S NO POINT IN FIGHTING NOW--
--AND THERE'S NO WAY THIS IS ANY WORSE THAN LETTING A BUNCH OF DEEZEES SELL US INTO WORK LABOR SLAVERY ON THE OTHER SIDE OF THE WORLD.
HE'S RIGHT. IT'S THE PRINCIPLE OF THE THING.
WE DIDN'T WALK AWAY WHEN THINGS IN GOTHAM GOT ROUGH, AND WE AREN'T GONNA LIE DOWN NOW.
YEAH, A STAND, SURE, BUT IF YOU THINK THIS IS WORTH DYING FOR--
QUIET. YOU HEAR SOMETHING?
KA-BLAMM
SHE COULDN'TA YELLED "DUCK"?

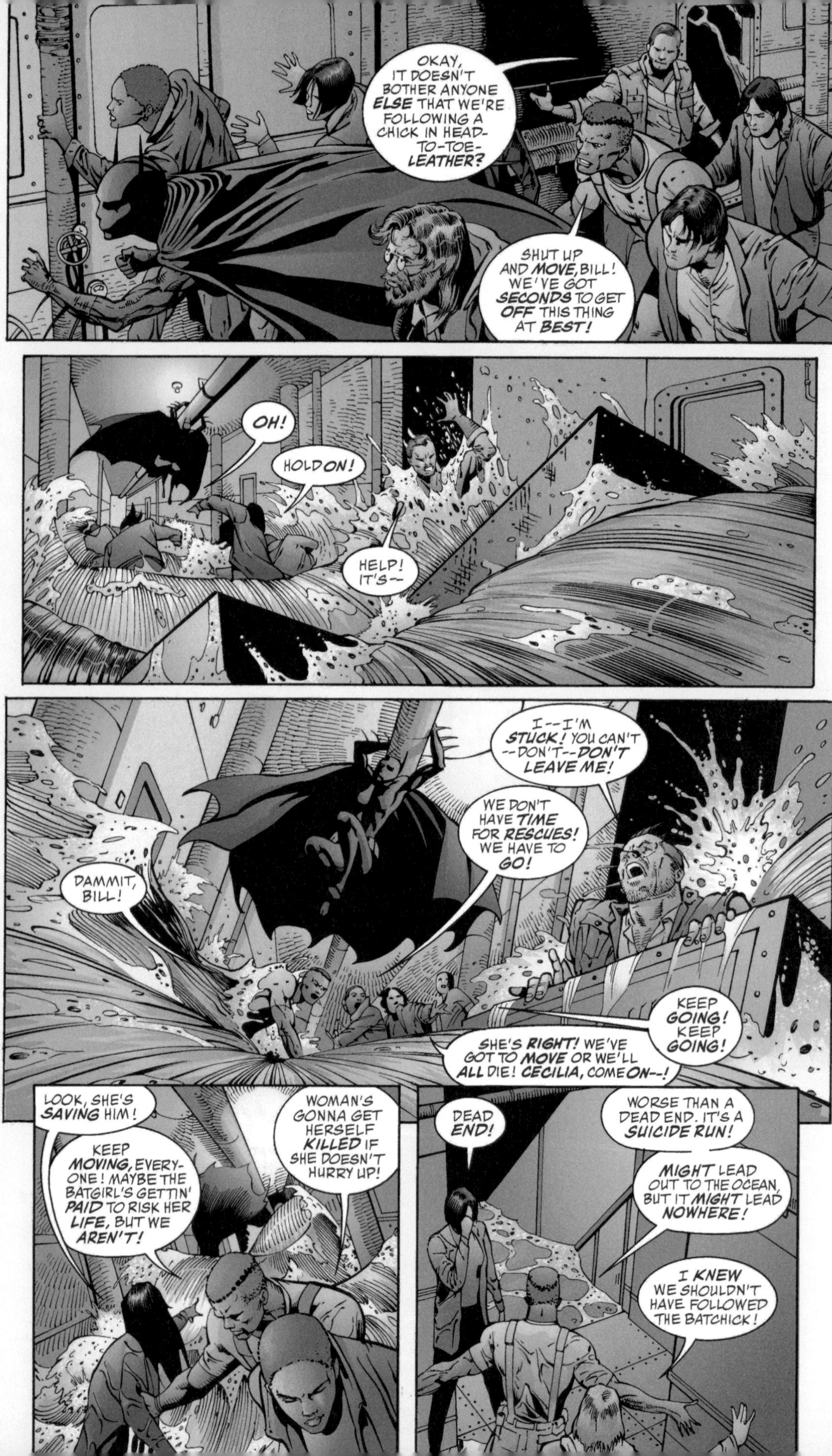

OKAY, IT DOESN'T BOTHER ANYONE ELSE THAT WE'RE FOLLOWING A CHICK IN HEAD-TO-TOE-LEATHER?
SHUT UP AND MOVE, BILL! WE'VE GOT SECONDS TO GET OFF THIS THING AT BEST!
OH!
HOLD ON!
HELP! IT'S--
I--I'M STUCK! YOU CAN'T --DON'T--DON'T LEAVE ME!
WE DON'T HAVE TIME FOR RESCUES! WE HAVE TO GO!
DAMMIT, BILL!
KEEP GOING! KEEP GOING!
SHE'S RIGHT! WE'VE GOT TO MOVE OR WE'LL ALL DIE! CECILIA, COME ON--!
LOOK, SHE'S SAVING HIM!
KEEP MOVING, EVERY-ONE! MAYBE THE BATGIRL'S GETTIN' PAID TO RISK HER LIFE, BUT WE AREN'T!
WOMAN'S GONNA GET HERSELF KILLED IF SHE DOESN'T HURRY UP!
DEAD END!
WORSE THAN A DEAD END. IT'S A SUICIDE RUN!
MIGHT LEAD OUT TO THE OCEAN, BUT IT MIGHT LEAD NOWHERE!
I KNEW WE SHOULDN'T HAVE FOLLOWED THE BATCHICK!

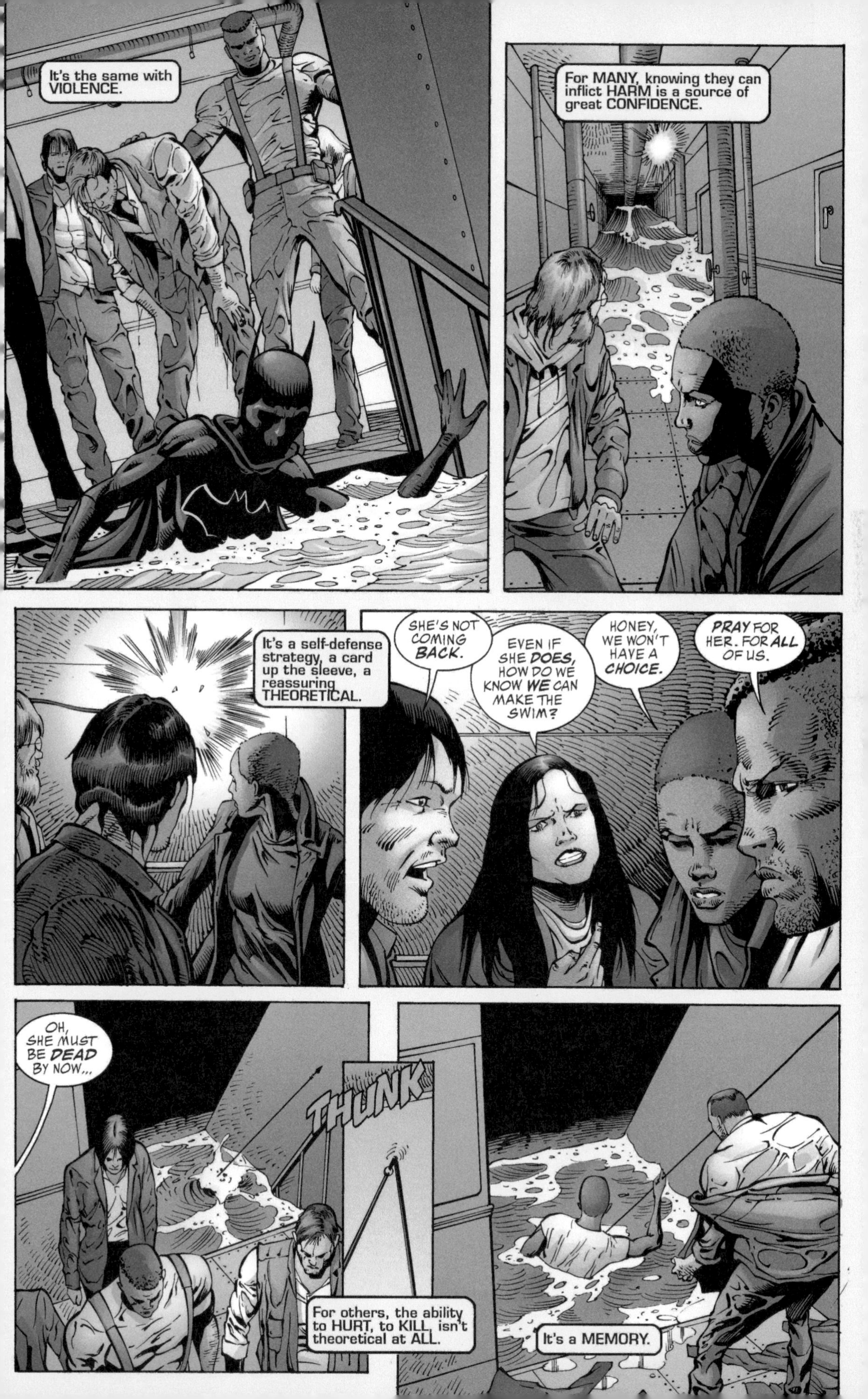
It's the same with VIOLENCE.
For MANY, knowing they can inflict HARM is a source of great CONFIDENCE.
It's a self-defense strategy, a card up the sleeve, a reassuring THEORETICAL.
SHE'S NOT COMING BACK.
EVEN IF SHE DOES, HOW DO WE KNOW WE CAN MAKE THE SWIM?
HONEY, WE WON'T HAVE A CHOICE.
PRAY FOR HER. FOR ALL OF US.
OH, SHE MUST BE DEAD BY NOW...
THUNK
For others, the ability to HURT, to KILL, isn't theoretical at ALL.
It's a MEMORY.

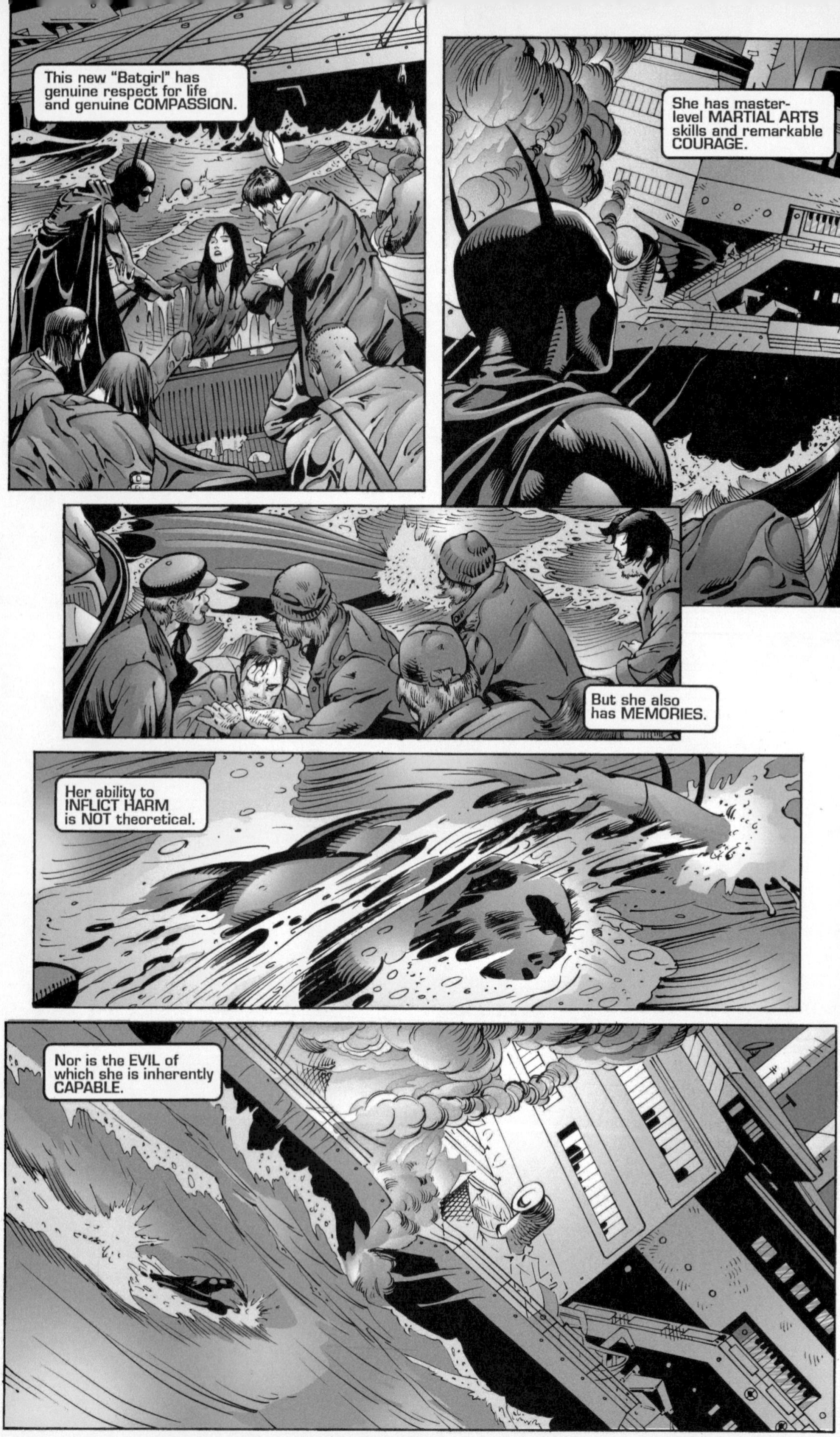
This new "Batgirl" has genuine respect for life and genuine COMPASSION.
She has master-level MARTIAL ARTS skills and remarkable COURAGE.
But she also has MEMORIES.
Her ability to INFLICT HARM is NOT theoretical.
Nor is the EVIL of which she is inherently CAPABLE.

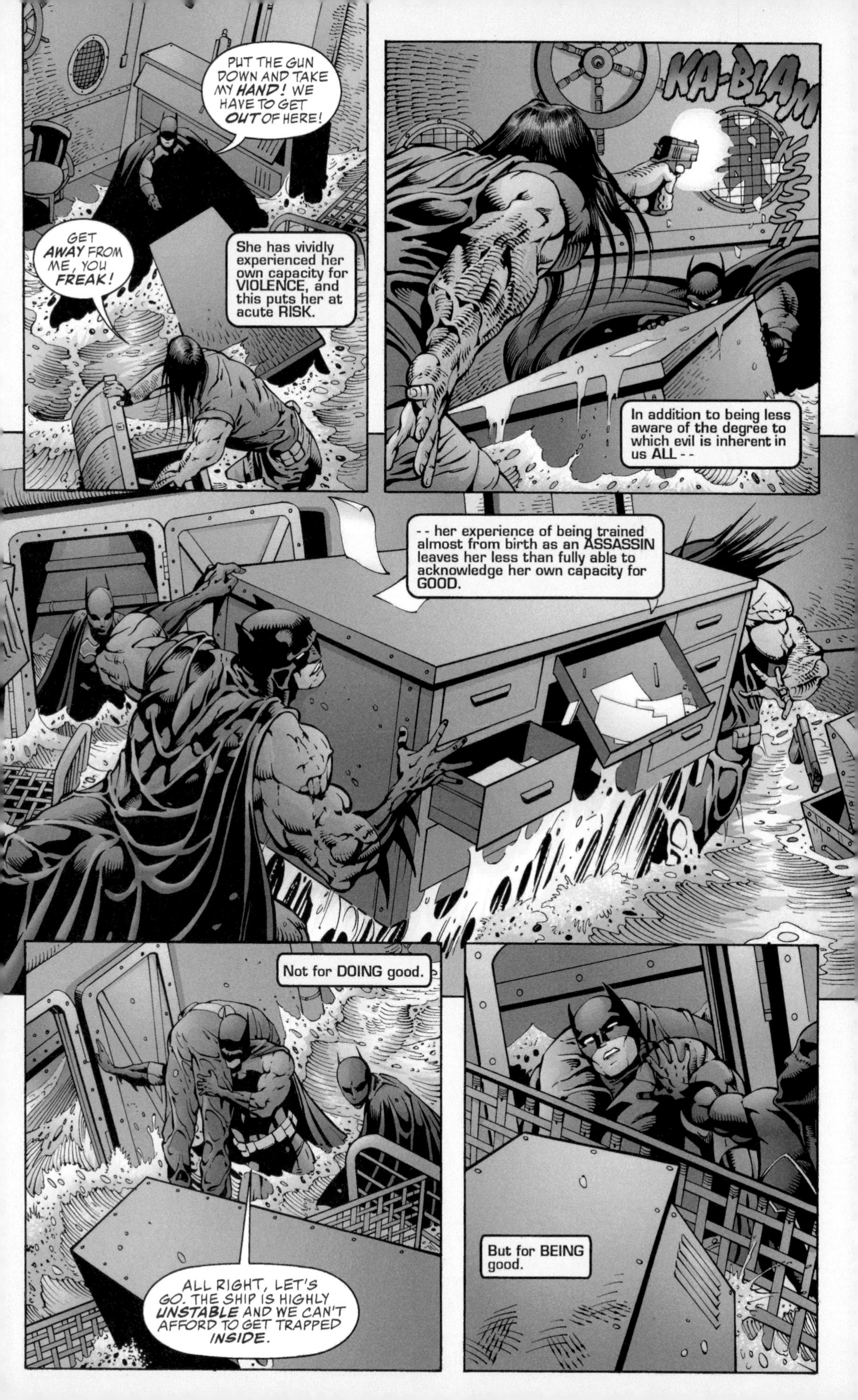
PUT THE GUN DOWN AND TAKE MY HAND! WE HAVE TO GET OUT OF HERE!
GET AWAY FROM ME, YOU FREAK!
She has vividly experienced her own capacity for VIOLENCE, and this puts her at acute RISK.
KA-BLAM
KSSSH
In addition to being less aware of the degree to which evil is inherent in us ALL --
-- her experience of being trained almost from birth as an ASSASSIN leaves her less than fully able to acknowledge her own capacity for GOOD.
Not for DOING good.
ALL RIGHT, LET'S GO. THE SHIP IS HIGHLY UNSTABLE AND WE CAN'T AFFORD TO GET TRAPPED INSIDE.
But for BEING good.

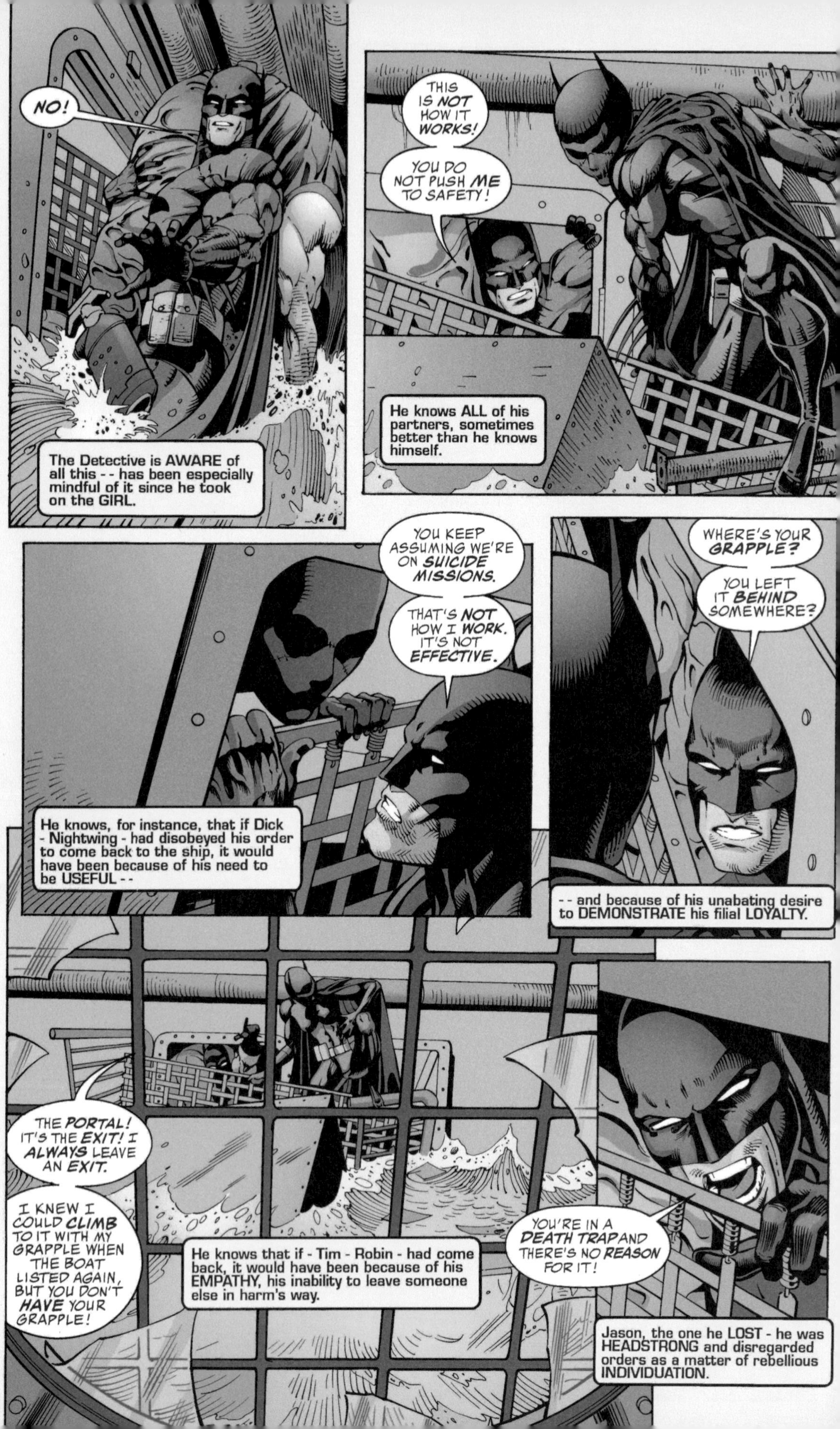
NO!
The Detective is AWARE of all this - - has been especially mindful of it since he took on the GIRL.
THIS IS NOT HOW IT WORKS!
YOU DO NOT PUSH ME TO SAFETY!
He knows ALL of his partners, sometimes better than he knows himself.
YOU KEEP ASSUMING WE'RE ON SUICIDE MISSIONS.
THAT'S NOT HOW I WORK. IT'S NOT EFFECTIVE.
He knows, for instance, that if Dick - Nightwing - had disobeyed his order to come back to the ship, it would have been because of his need to be USEFUL - -
WHERE'S YOUR GRAPPLE?
YOU LEFT IT BEHIND SOMEWHERE?
- - and because of his unabating desire to DEMONSTRATE his filial LOYALTY.
THE PORTAL! IT'S THE EXIT! I ALWAYS LEAVE AN EXIT.
I KNEW I COULD CLIMB TO IT WITH MY GRAPPLE WHEN THE BOAT LISTED AGAIN, BUT YOU DON'T HAVE YOUR GRAPPLE!
He knows that if - Tim - Robin - had come back, it would have been because of his EMPATHY, his inability to leave someone else in harm's way.
YOU'RE IN A DEATH TRAP AND THERE'S NO REASON FOR IT!
Jason, the one he LOST - he was HEADSTRONG and disregarded orders as a matter of rebellious INDIVIDUATION.

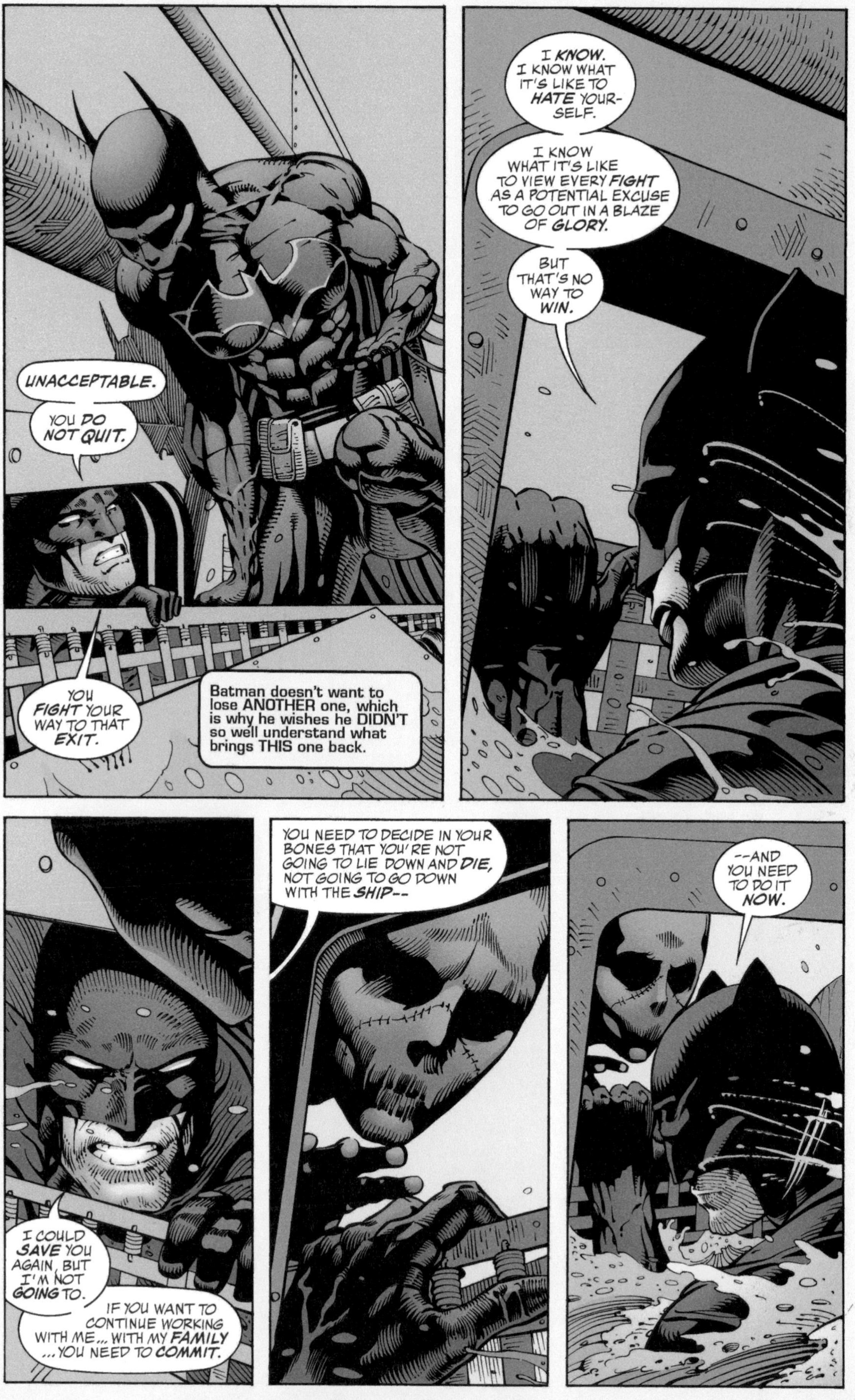

UNACCEPTABLE.
YOU DO NOT QUIT.
YOU FIGHT YOUR WAY TO THAT EXIT.
Batman doesn't want to lose ANOTHER one, which is why he wishes he DIDN'T so well understand what brings THIS one back.
I KNOW. I KNOW WHAT IT'S LIKE TO HATE YOURSELF.
I KNOW WHAT IT'S LIKE TO VIEW EVERY FIGHT AS A POTENTIAL EXCUSE TO GO OUT IN A BLAZE OF GLORY.
BUT THAT'S NO WAY TO WIN.
I COULD SAVE YOU AGAIN, BUT I'M NOT GOING TO.
IF YOU WANT TO CONTINUE WORKING WITH ME... WITH MY FAMILY ...YOU NEED TO COMMIT.
YOU NEED TO DECIDE IN YOUR BONES THAT YOU'RE NOT GOING TO LIE DOWN AND DIE, NOT GOING TO GO DOWN WITH THE SHIP--
--AND YOU NEED TO DO IT NOW.

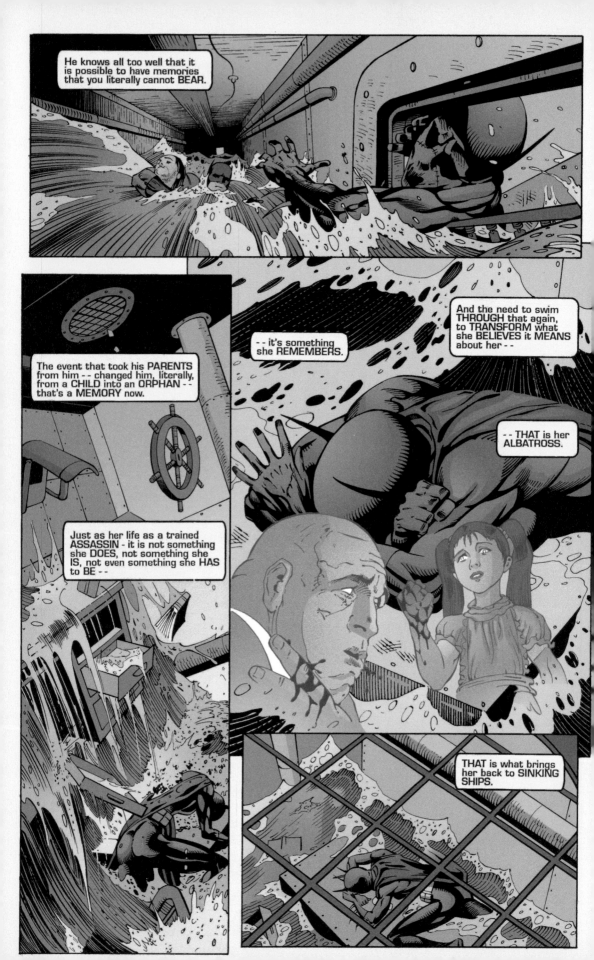

He knows all too well that it is possible to have memories that you literally cannot BEAR.

The event that took his PARENTS from him -- changed him, literally, from a CHILD into an ORPHAN -- that's a MEMORY now.

Just as her life as a trained ASSASSIN - it is not something she DOES, not something she IS, not even something she HAS to BE --

-- it's something she REMEMBERS.

And the need to swim THROUGH that again, to TRANSFORM what she BELIEVES it MEANS about her --

-- THAT is her ALBATROSS.

THAT is what brings her back to SINKING SHIPS.

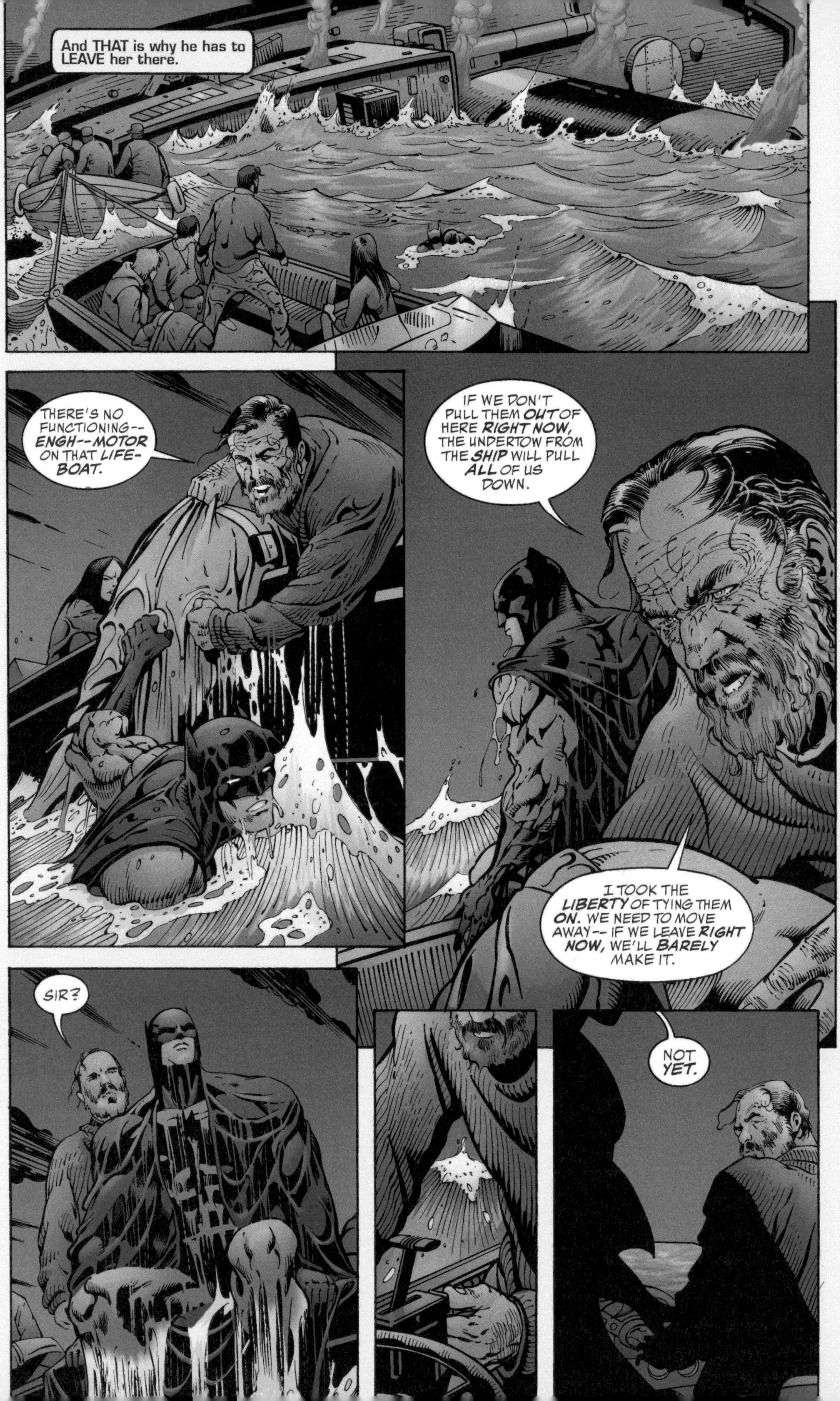
And THAT is why he has to LEAVE her there.
THERE'S NO FUNCTIONING-- ENGH--MOTOR ON THAT LIFE-BOAT.
IF WE DON'T PULL THEM OUT OF HERE RIGHT NOW, THE UNDERTOW FROM THE SHIP WILL PULL ALL OF US DOWN.
I TOOK THE LIBERTY OF TYING THEM ON. WE NEED TO MOVE AWAY-- IF WE LEAVE RIGHT NOW, WE'LL BARELY MAKE IT.
SIR?
NOT YET.

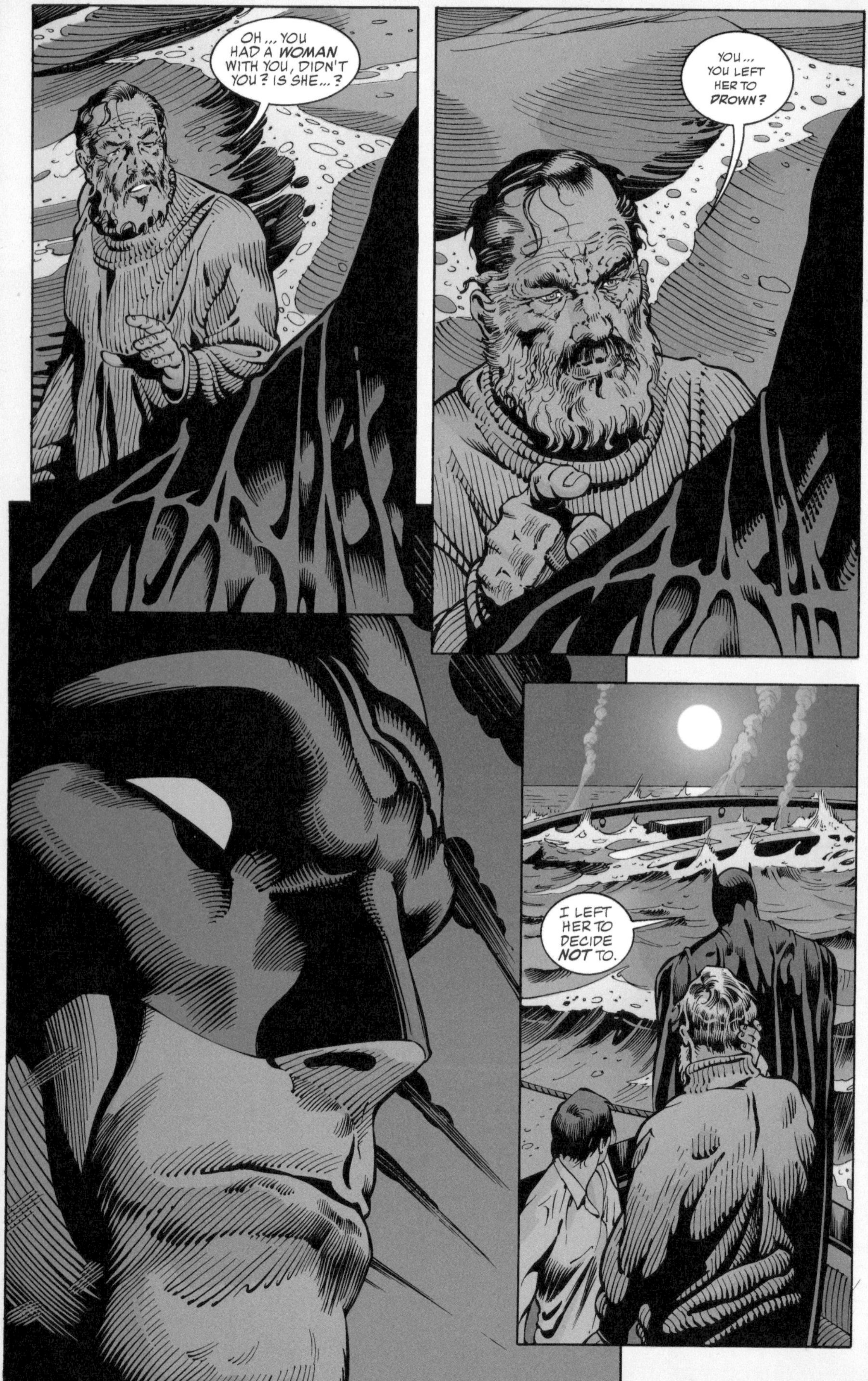
OH... YOU HAD A **WOMAN** WITH YOU, DIDN'T YOU? IS SHE...?
YOU... YOU LEFT HER TO **DROWN?**
I LEFT HER TO DECIDE **NOT** TO.

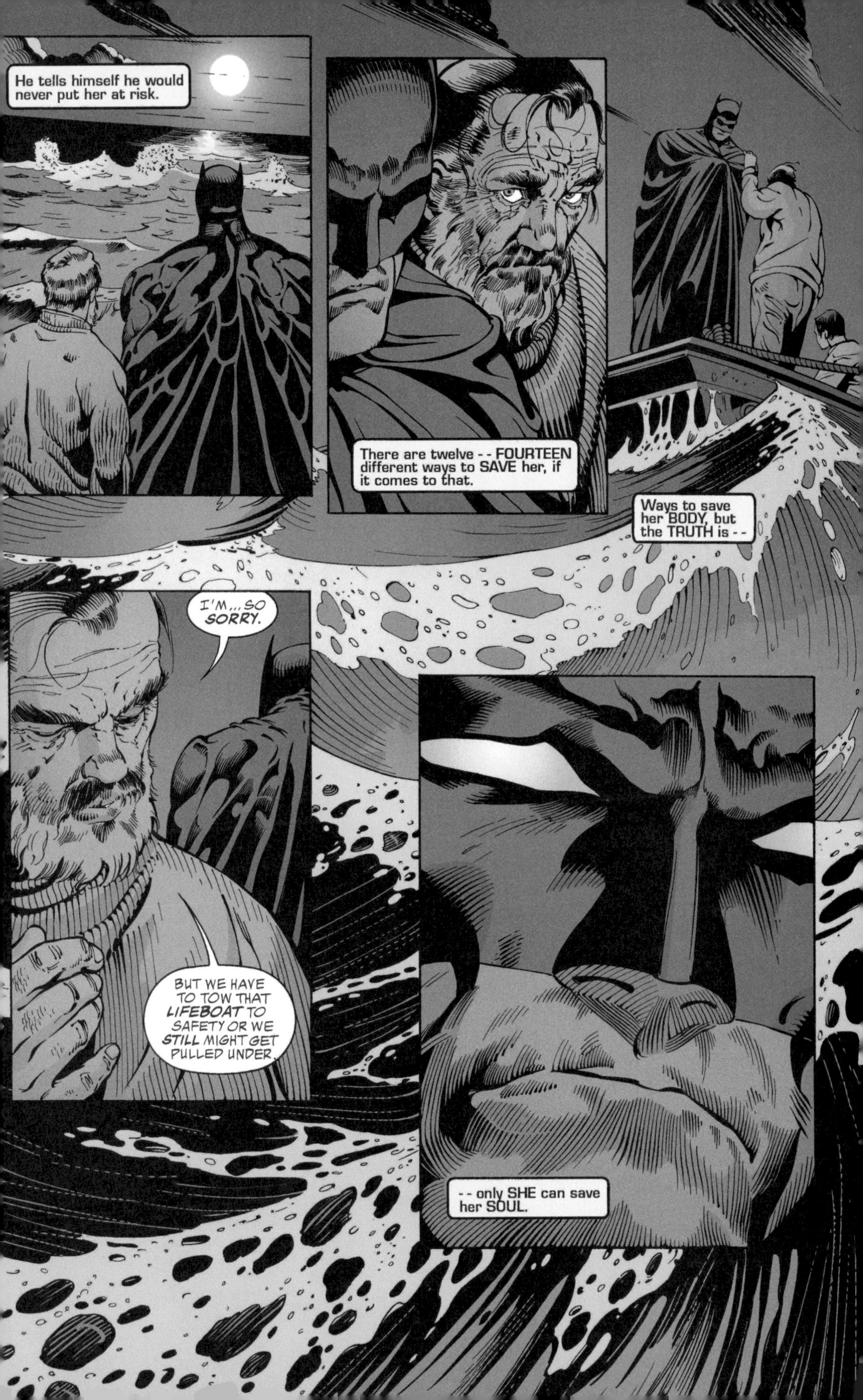
He tells himself he would never put her at risk.
There are twelve - - FOURTEEN different ways to SAVE her, if it comes to that.
Ways to save her BODY, but the TRUTH is - -
I'M... SO SORRY.
BUT WE HAVE TO TOW THAT LIFEBOAT TO SAFETY OR WE STILL MIGHT GET PULLED UNDER.
- - only SHE can save her SOUL.

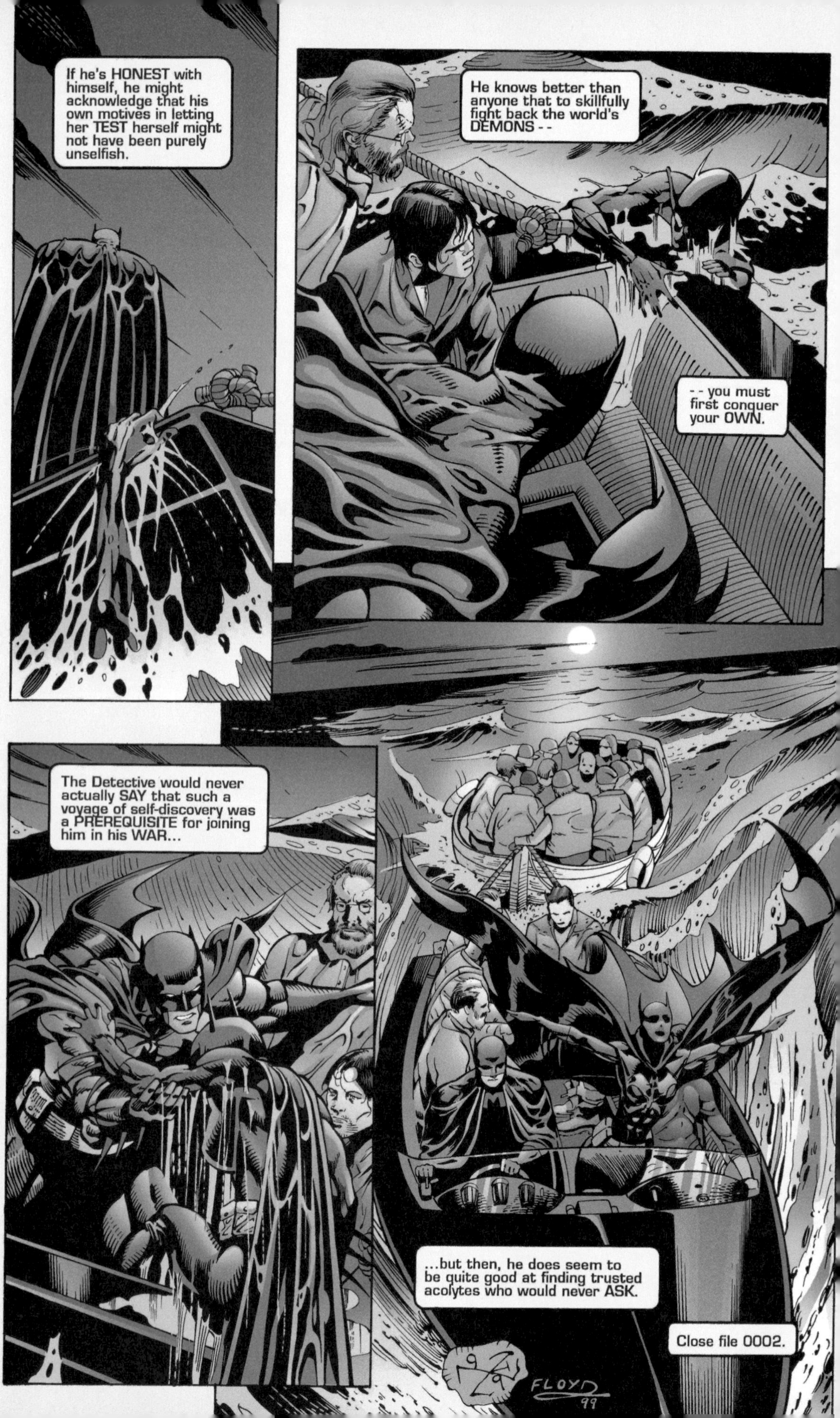
If he's HONEST with himself, he might acknowledge that his own motives in letting her TEST herself might not have been purely unselfish.
He knows better than anyone that to skillfully fight back the world's DEMONS - -
- - you must first conquer your OWN.
The Detective would never actually SAY that such a voyage of self-discovery was a PREREQUISITE for joining him in his WAR...
...but then, he does seem to be quite good at finding trusted acolytes who would never ASK.
Close file 0002.
FLOYD 99

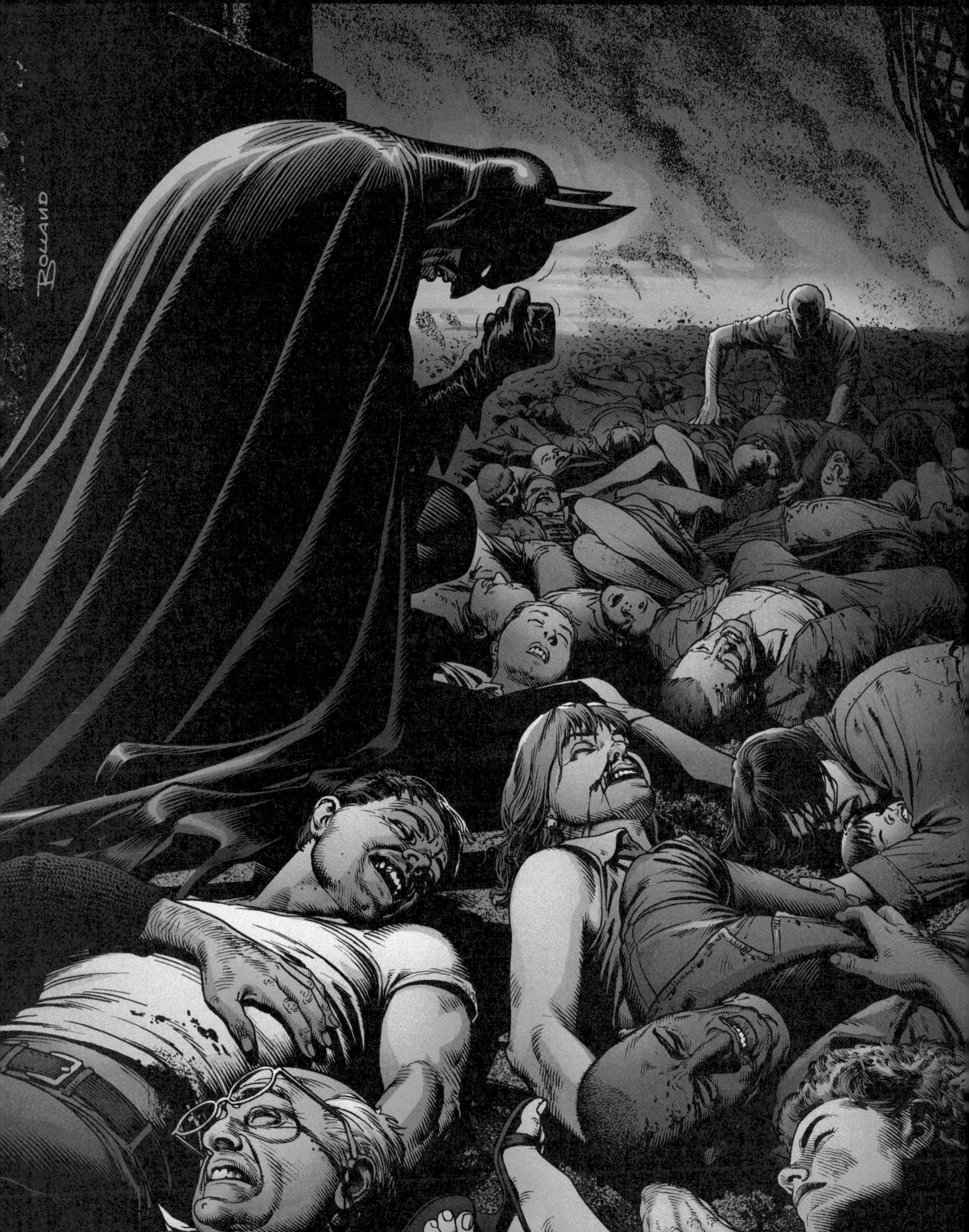
BOLLAND

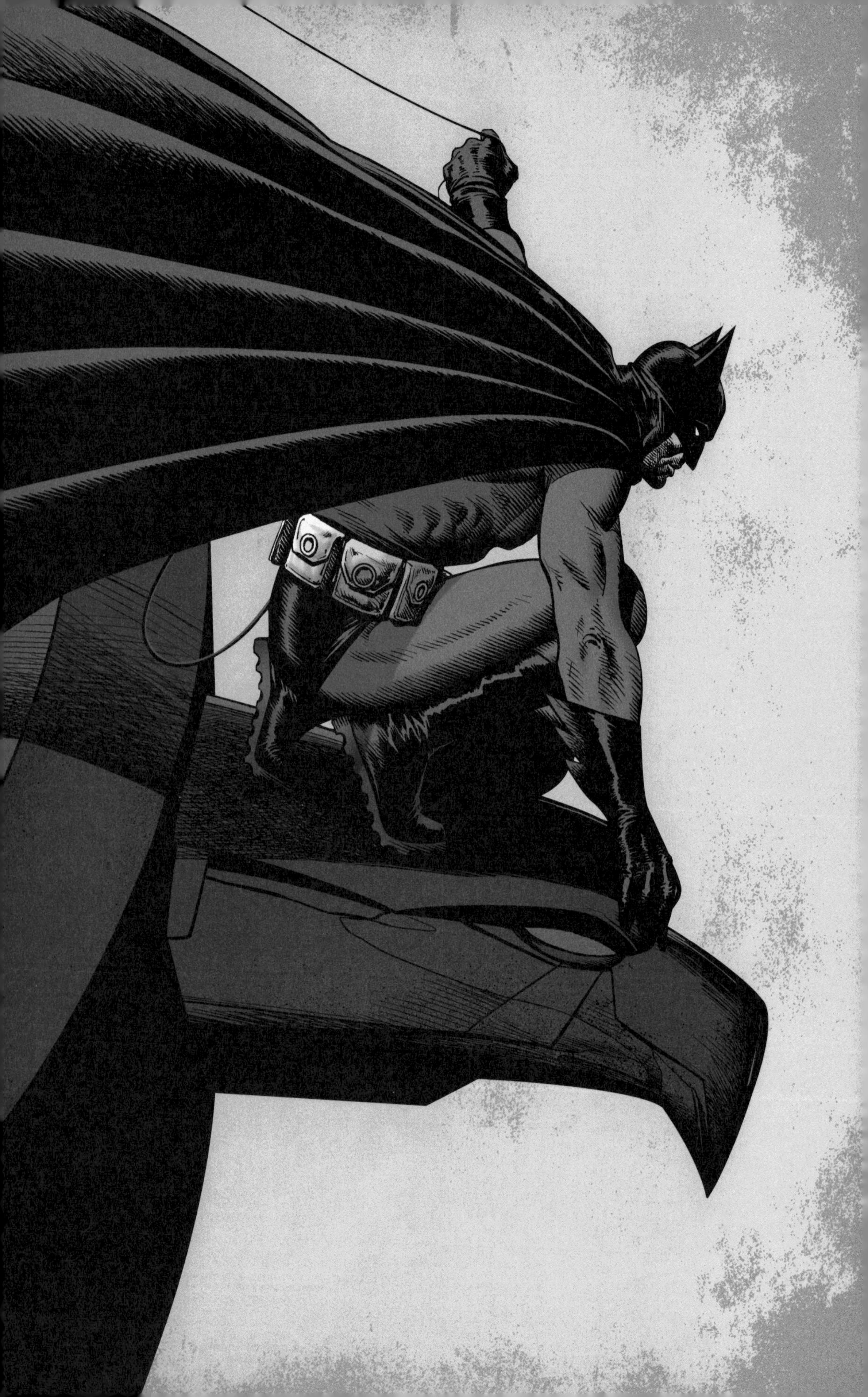

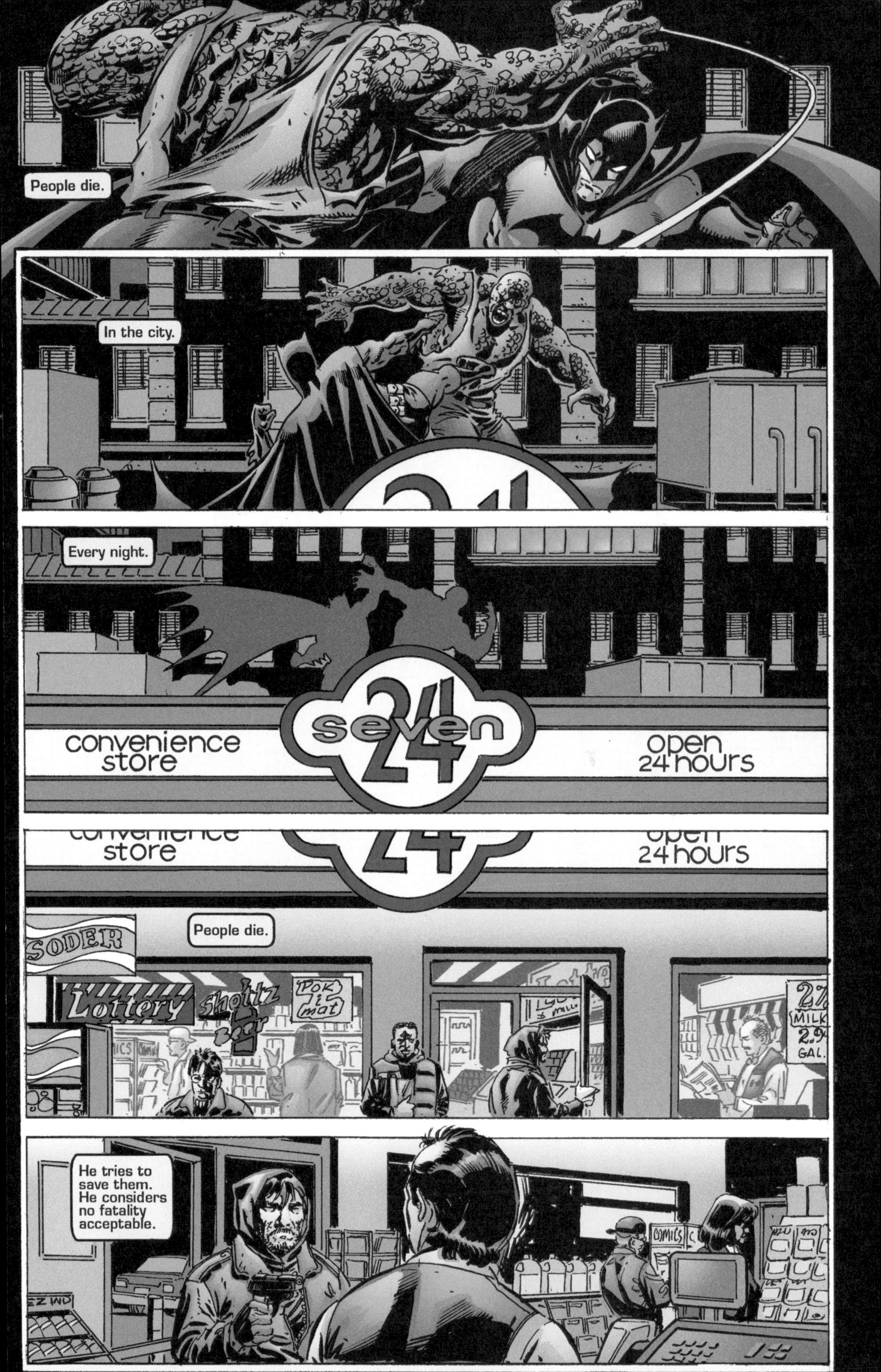

People die.
In the city.
Every night.
seven 24
convenience store
open 24 hours
convenience store
open 24 hours
People die.
SODER
Lottery
Shottz Beer
Pok i mat
2% MILK 2.9 GAL.
He tries to save them. He considers no fatality acceptable.
COMICS

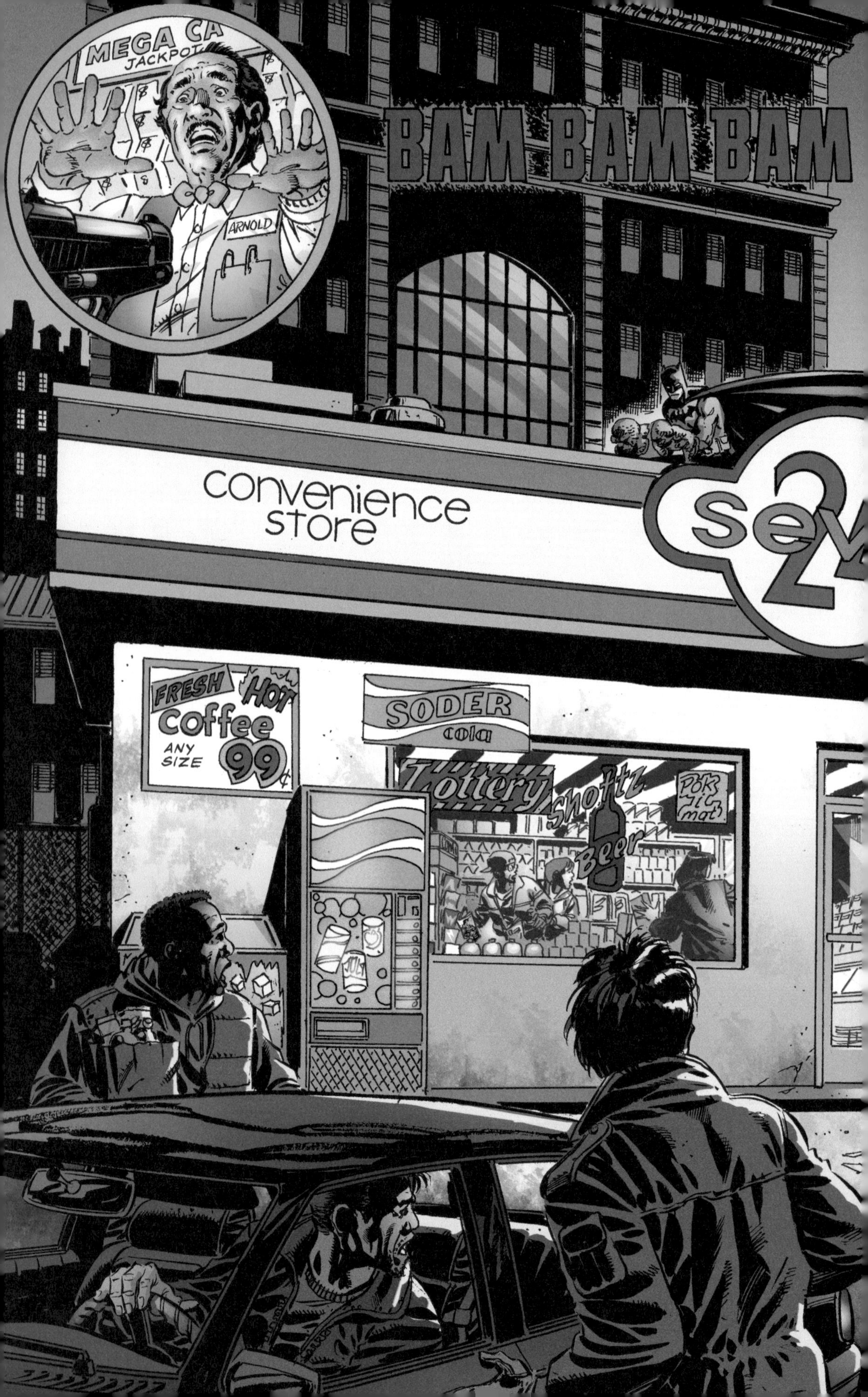
MEGA CA
JACKPOT
ARNOLD
BAM BAM BAM
convenience store
sev 24
FRESH HOT Coffee ANY SIZE 99¢
SODER cola
Lottery
Shoftz Beer
Pok it mat

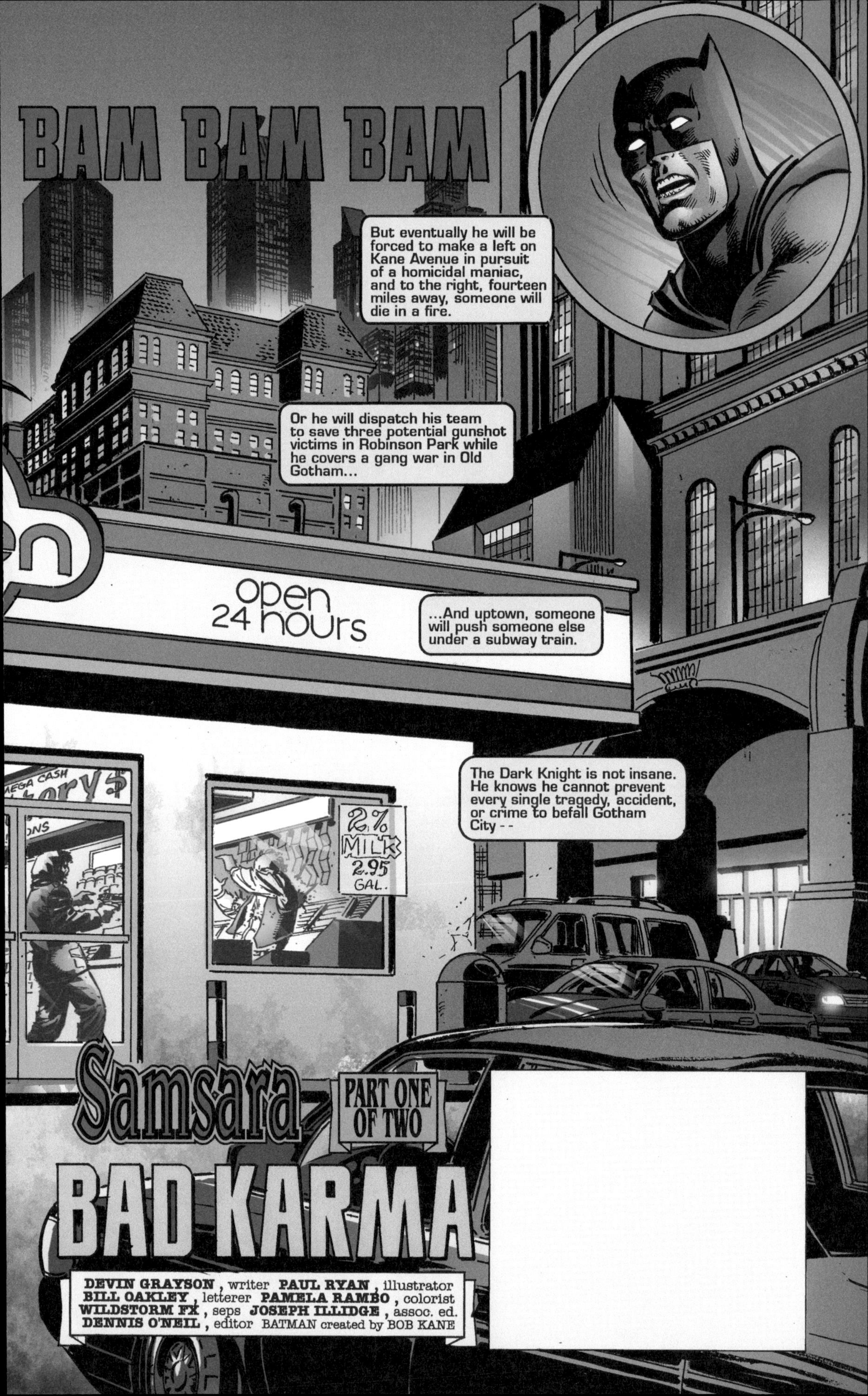
BAM BAM BAM
But eventually he will be forced to make a left on Kane Avenue in pursuit of a homicidal maniac, and to the right, fourteen miles away, someone will die in a fire.
Or he will dispatch his team to save three potential gunshot victims in Robinson Park while he covers a gang war in Old Gotham...
open 24 hours
...And uptown, someone will push someone else under a subway train.
The Dark Knight is not insane. He knows he cannot prevent every single tragedy, accident, or crime to befall Gotham City --
2% MILK 2.95 GAL.
Samsara
PART ONE OF TWO
BAD KARMA
DEVIN GRAYSON, writer PAUL RYAN, illustrator
BILL OAKLEY, letterer PAMELA RAMBO, colorist
WILDSTORM FX, seps JOSEPH ILLIDGE, assoc. ed.
DENNIS O'NEIL, editor BATMAN created by BOB KANE

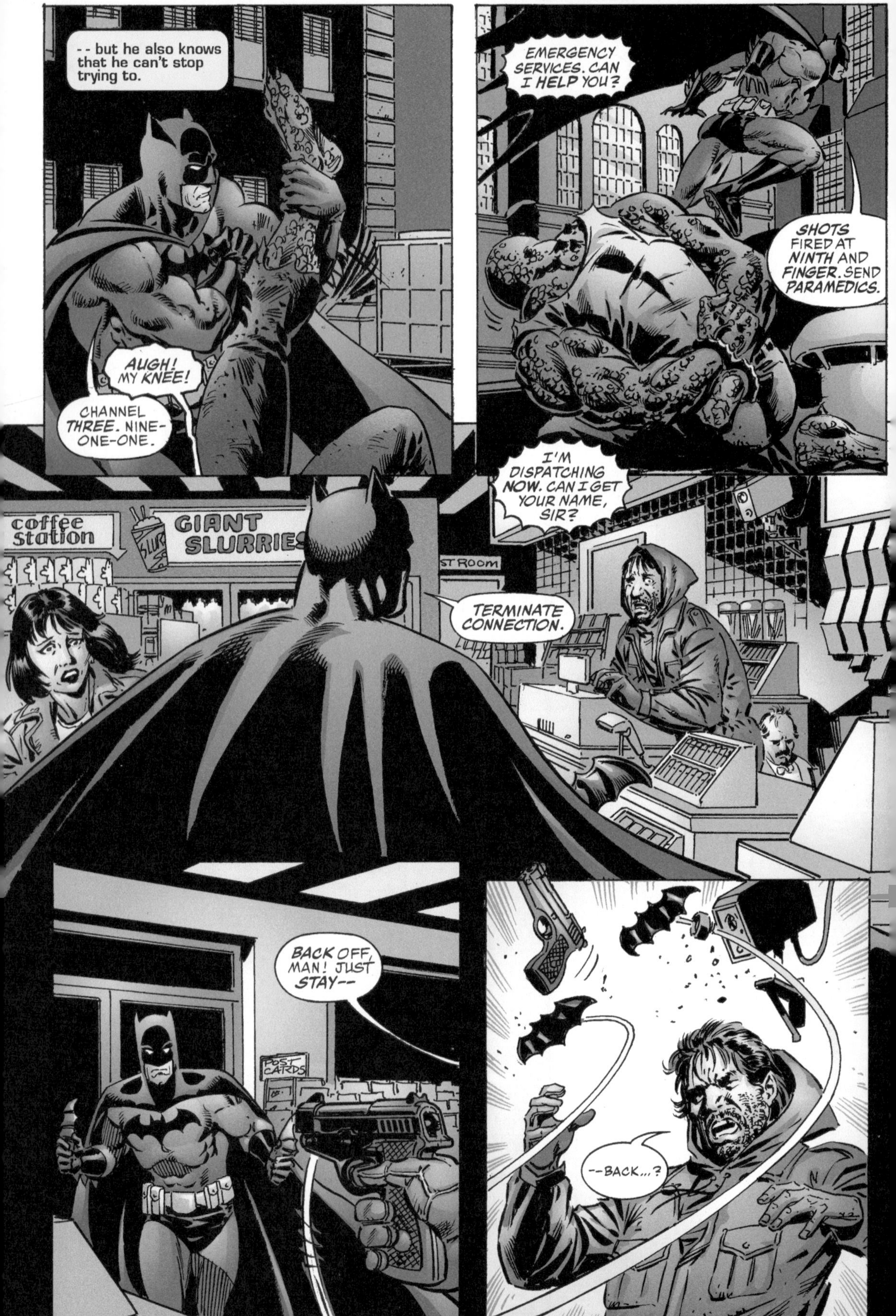

-- but he also knows that he can't stop trying to.
AUGH! MY KNEE!
CHANNEL THREE. NINE-ONE-ONE.
EMERGENCY SERVICES. CAN I HELP YOU?
SHOTS FIRED AT NINTH AND FINGER. SEND PARAMEDICS.
coffee station
GIANT SLURRIES
I'M DISPATCHING NOW. CAN I GET YOUR NAME, SIR?
TERMINATE CONNECTION.
BACK OFF, MAN! JUST STAY--
POST CARDS
--BACK...?

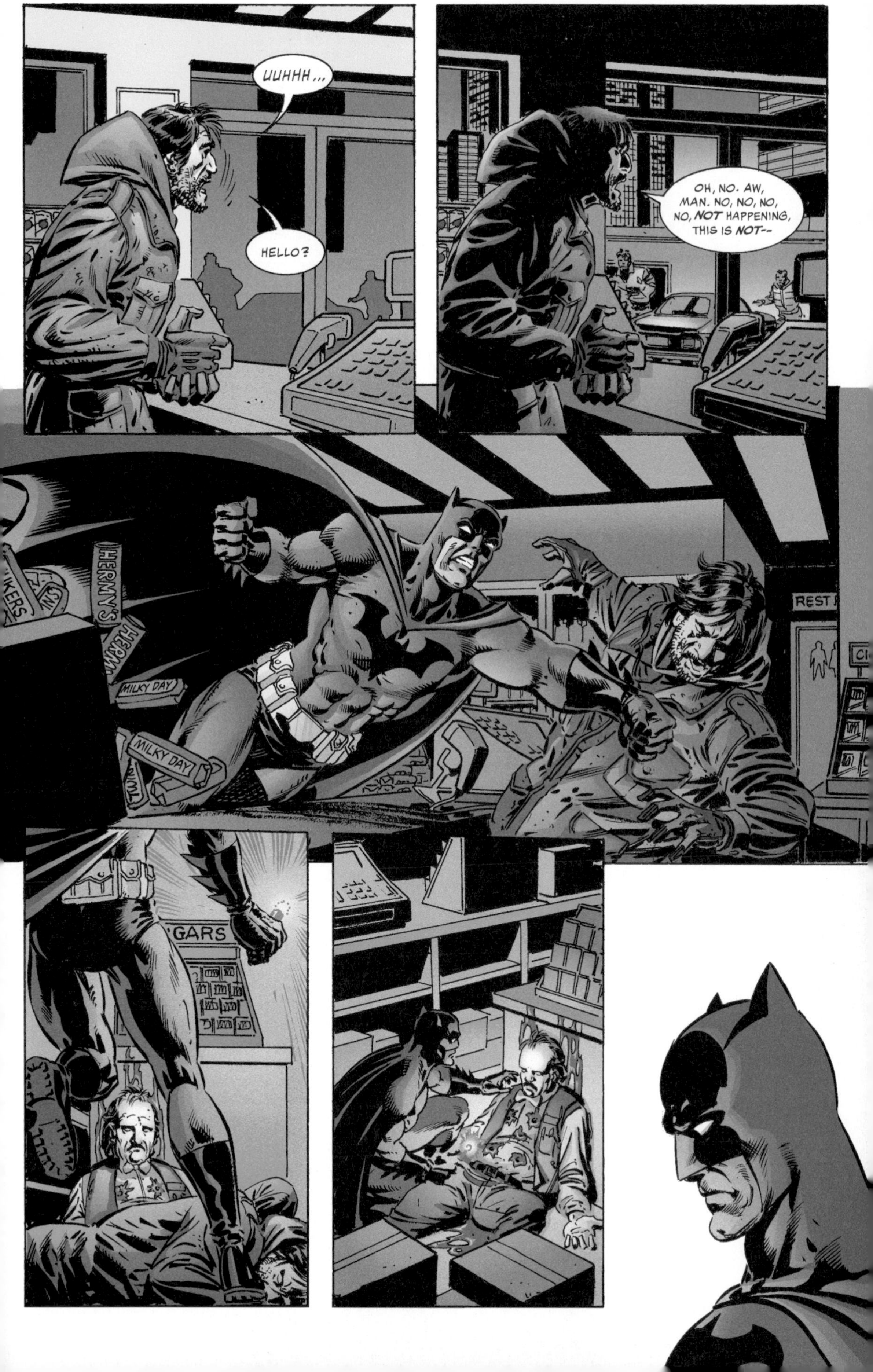
UUHHH...
HELLO?
OH, NO. AW, MAN. NO, NO, NO, NO, NOT HAPPENING, THIS IS NOT--
HERMY'S
MILKY DAY
MILKY DAY
REST
GARS

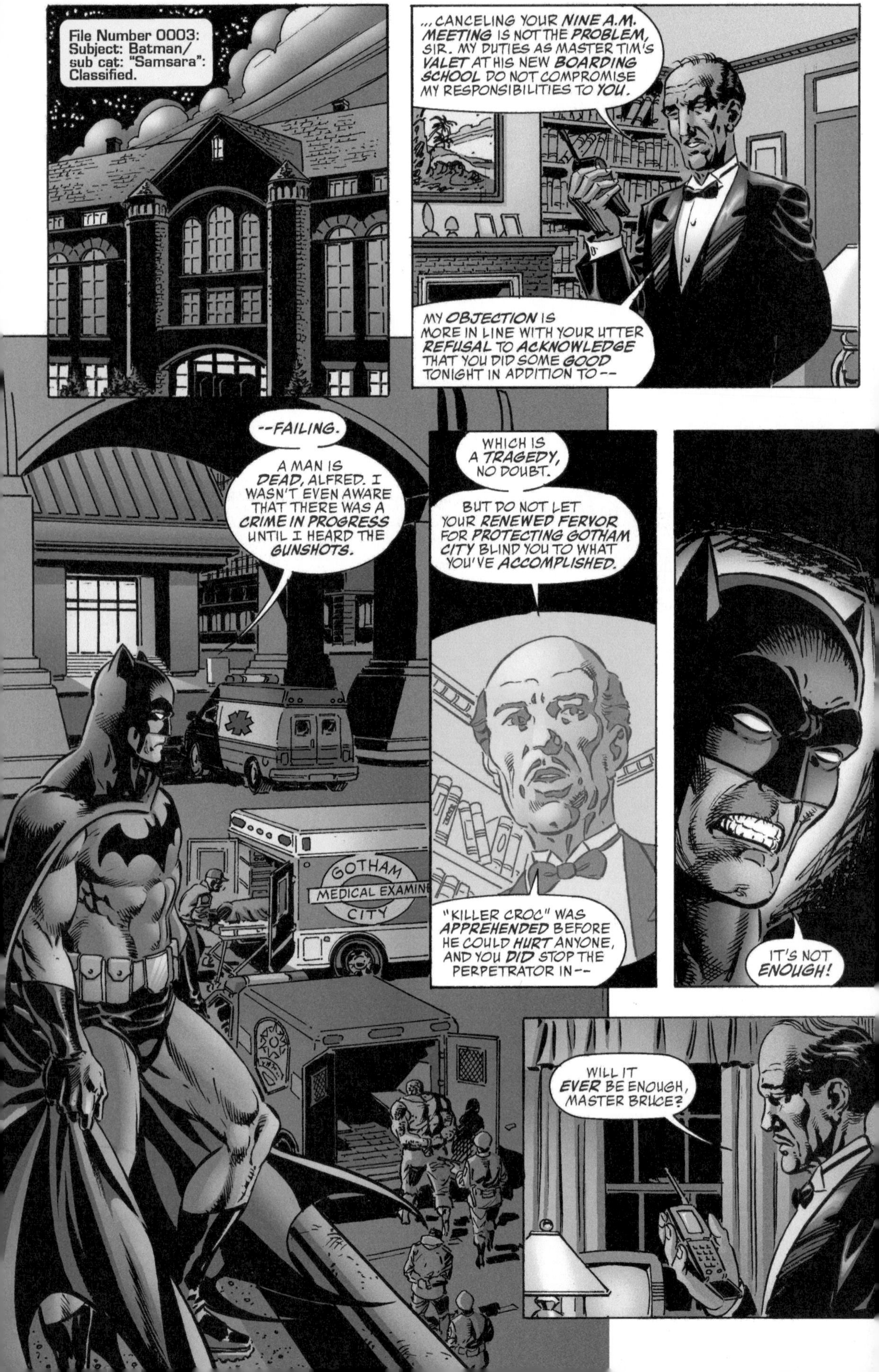
File Number 0003:
Subject: Batman/
sub cat: "Samsara":
Classified.
...CANCELING YOUR NINE A.M. MEETING IS NOT THE PROBLEM, SIR. MY DUTIES AS MASTER TIM'S VALET AT HIS NEW BOARDING SCHOOL DO NOT COMPROMISE MY RESPONSIBILITIES TO YOU.
MY OBJECTION IS MORE IN LINE WITH YOUR UTTER REFUSAL TO ACKNOWLEDGE THAT YOU DID SOME GOOD TONIGHT IN ADDITION TO--
--FAILING.
A MAN IS DEAD, ALFRED. I WASN'T EVEN AWARE THAT THERE WAS A CRIME IN PROGRESS UNTIL I HEARD THE GUNSHOTS.
GOTHAM
MEDICAL EXAMINE
CITY
WHICH IS A TRAGEDY, NO DOUBT.
BUT DO NOT LET YOUR RENEWED FERVOR FOR PROTECTING GOTHAM CITY BLIND YOU TO WHAT YOU'VE ACCOMPLISHED.
"KILLER CROC" WAS APPREHENDED BEFORE HE COULD HURT ANYONE, AND YOU DID STOP THE PERPETRATOR IN--
IT'S NOT ENOUGH!
WILL IT EVER BE ENOUGH, MASTER BRUCE?

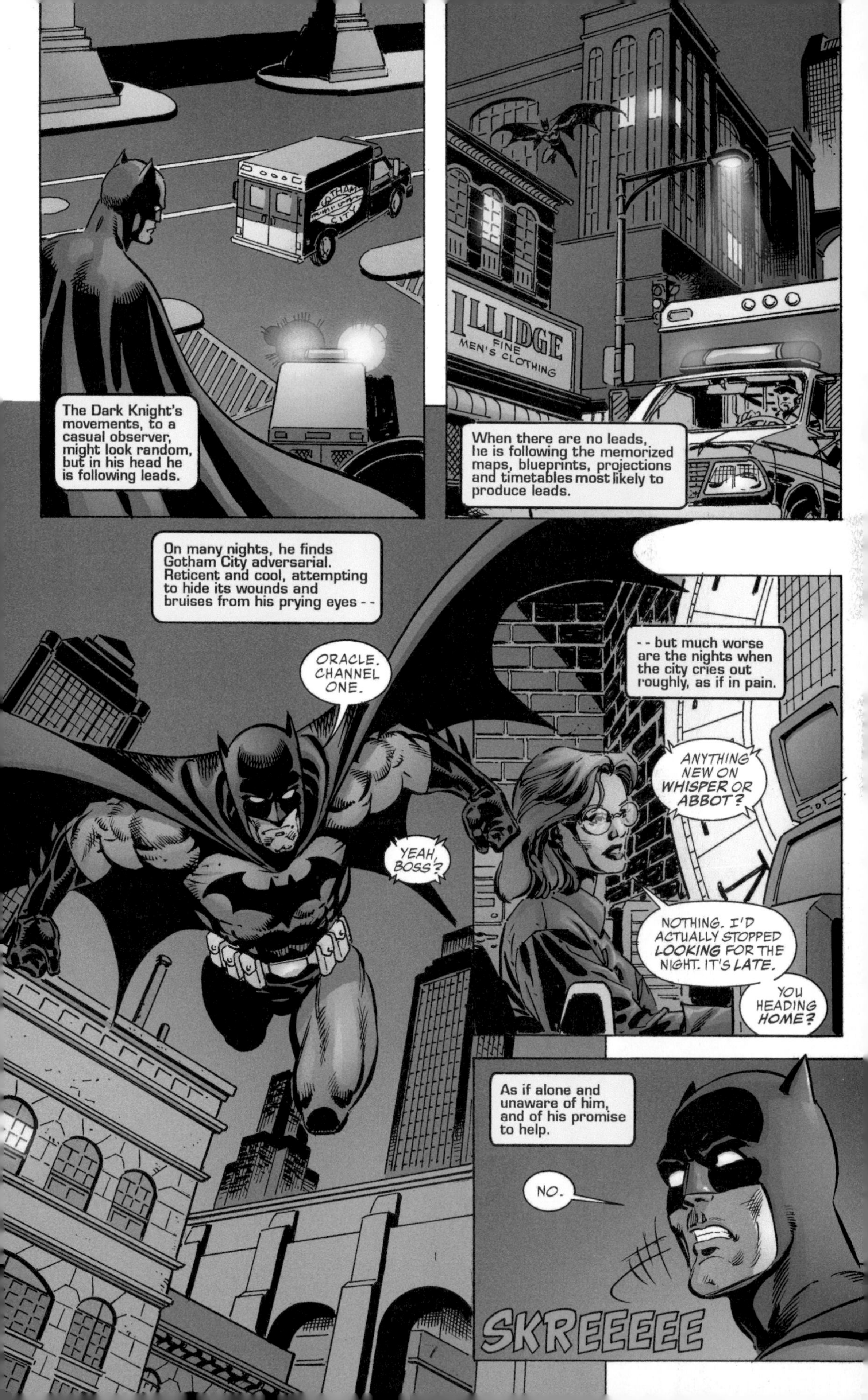
The Dark Knight's movements, to a casual observer, might look random, but in his head he is following leads.
ILLIDGE FINE MEN'S CLOTHING
When there are no leads, he is following the memorized maps, blueprints, projections and timetables most likely to produce leads.
On many nights, he finds Gotham City adversarial. Reticent and cool, attempting to hide its wounds and bruises from his prying eyes - -
- - but much worse are the nights when the city cries out roughly, as if in pain.
ORACLE. CHANNEL ONE.
YEAH, BOSS?
ANYTHING NEW ON WHISPER OR ABBOT?
NOTHING. I'D ACTUALLY STOPPED LOOKING FOR THE NIGHT. IT'S LATE.
YOU HEADING HOME?
As if alone and unaware of him, and of his promise to help.
NO.
SKREEEEEE

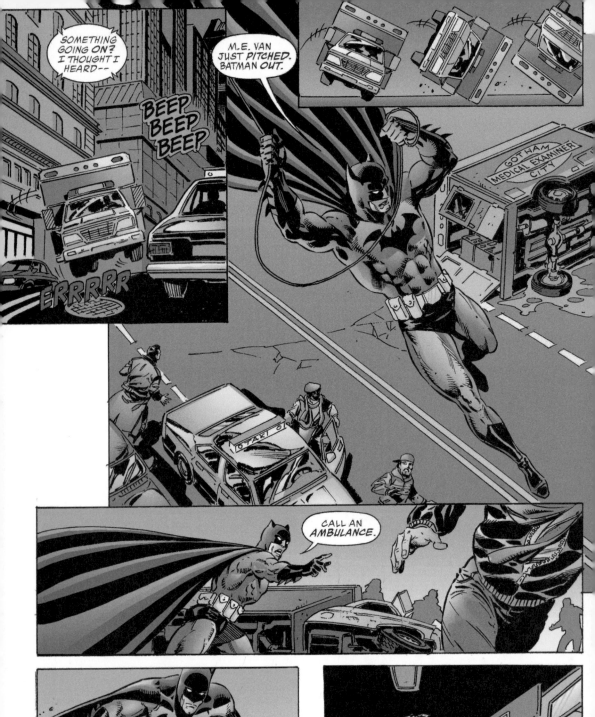

SOMETHING GOING ON? I THOUGHT I HEARD--

BEEP BEEP BEEP

ERRRRR

M.E. VAN JUST *PITCHED* BATMAN *OUT*.

GOTHAM MEDICAL EXAMINER CITY

CALL AN AMBULANCE.

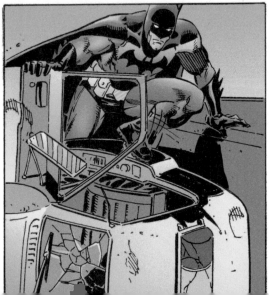

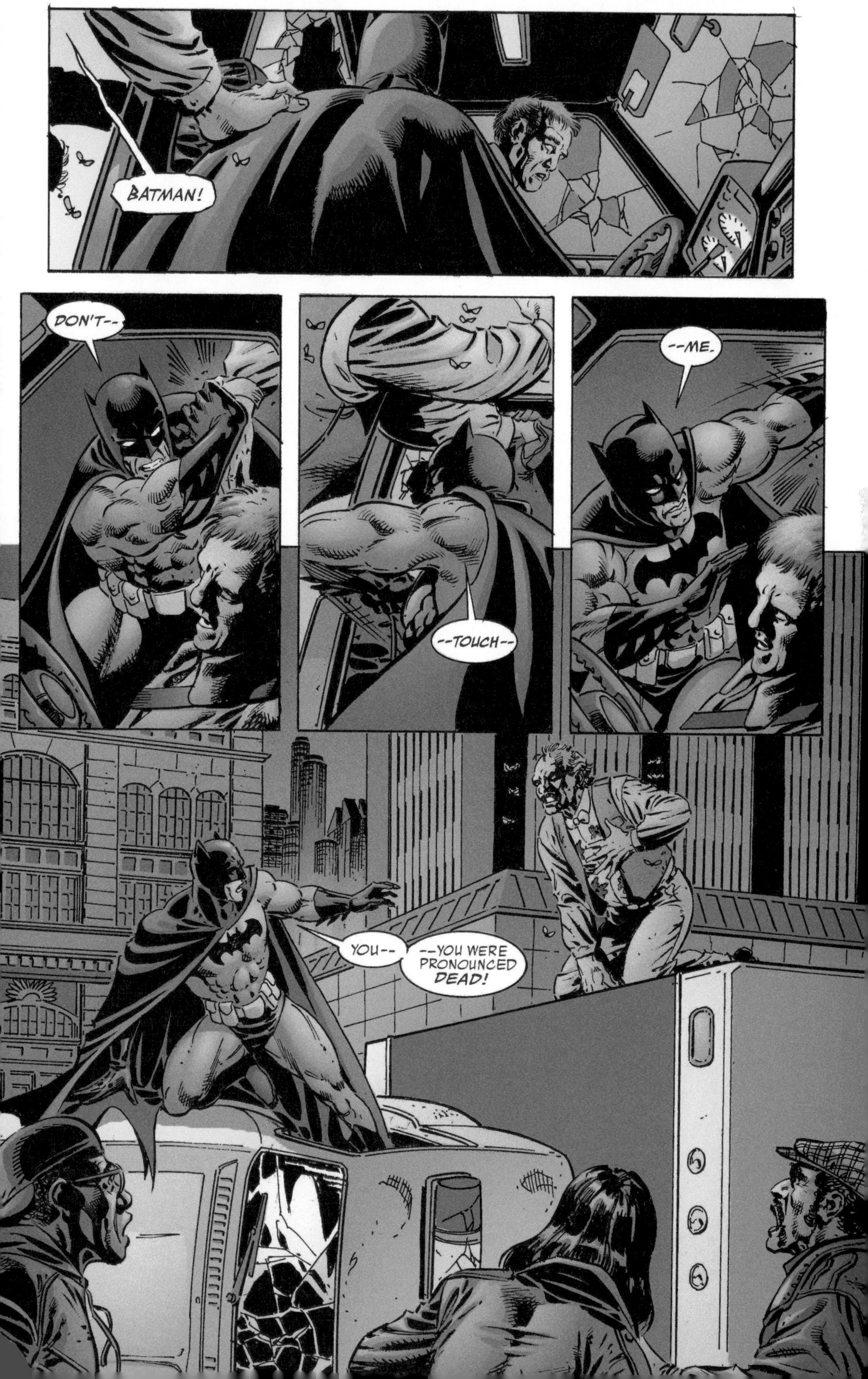
BATMAN!
DON'T--
--TOUCH--
--ME.
YOU--
--YOU WERE PRONOUNCED DEAD!

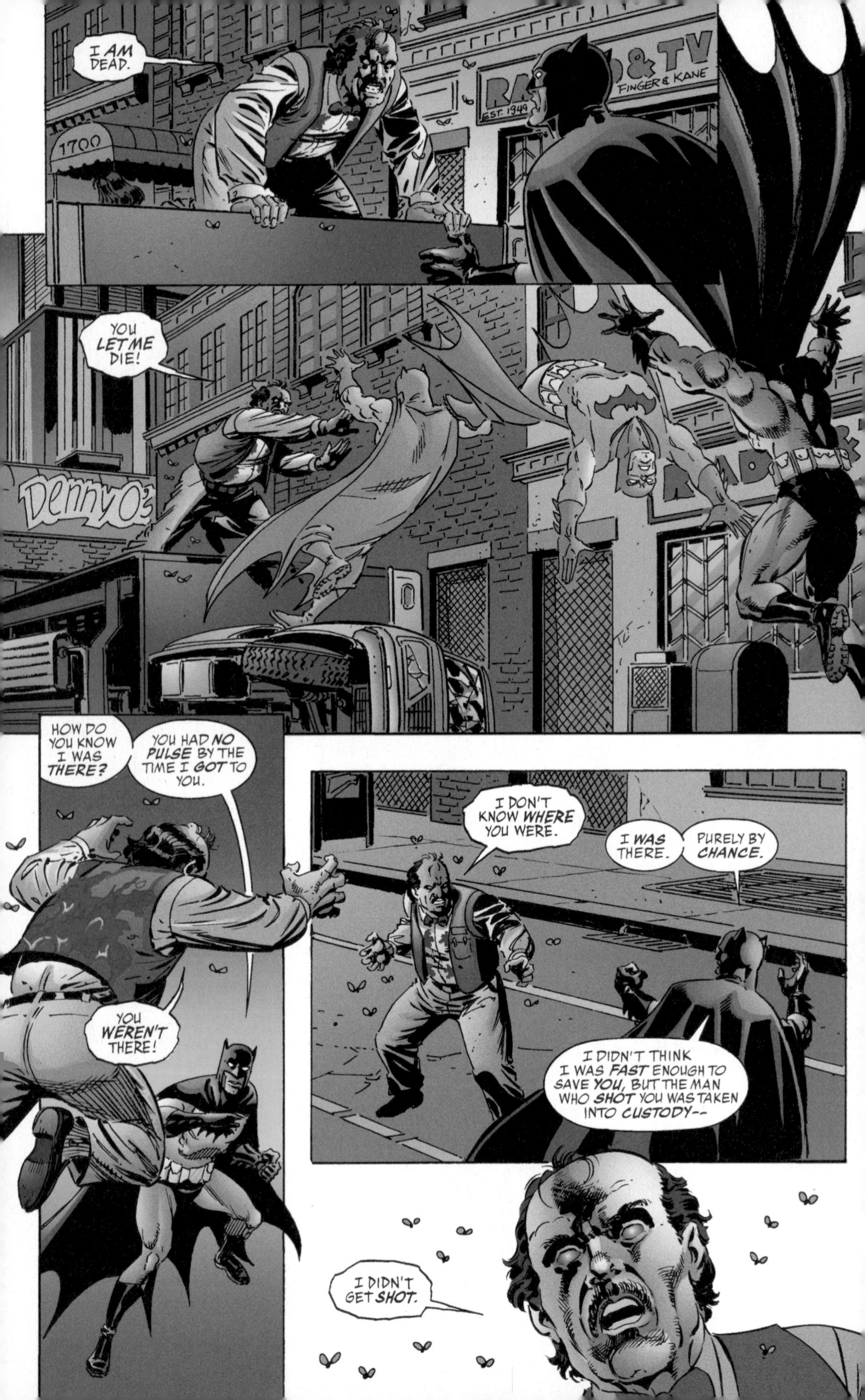
I AM DEAD.
RA[..] & TV
FINGER & KANE
EST. 1949
1700
YOU LET ME DIE!
Denny O's
HOW DO YOU KNOW I WAS THERE?
YOU HAD NO PULSE BY THE TIME I GOT TO YOU.
YOU WEREN'T THERE!
I DON'T KNOW WHERE YOU WERE.
I WAS THERE.
PURELY BY CHANCE.
I DIDN'T THINK I WAS FAST ENOUGH TO SAVE YOU, BUT THE MAN WHO SHOT YOU WAS TAKEN INTO CUSTODY--
I DIDN'T GET SHOT.

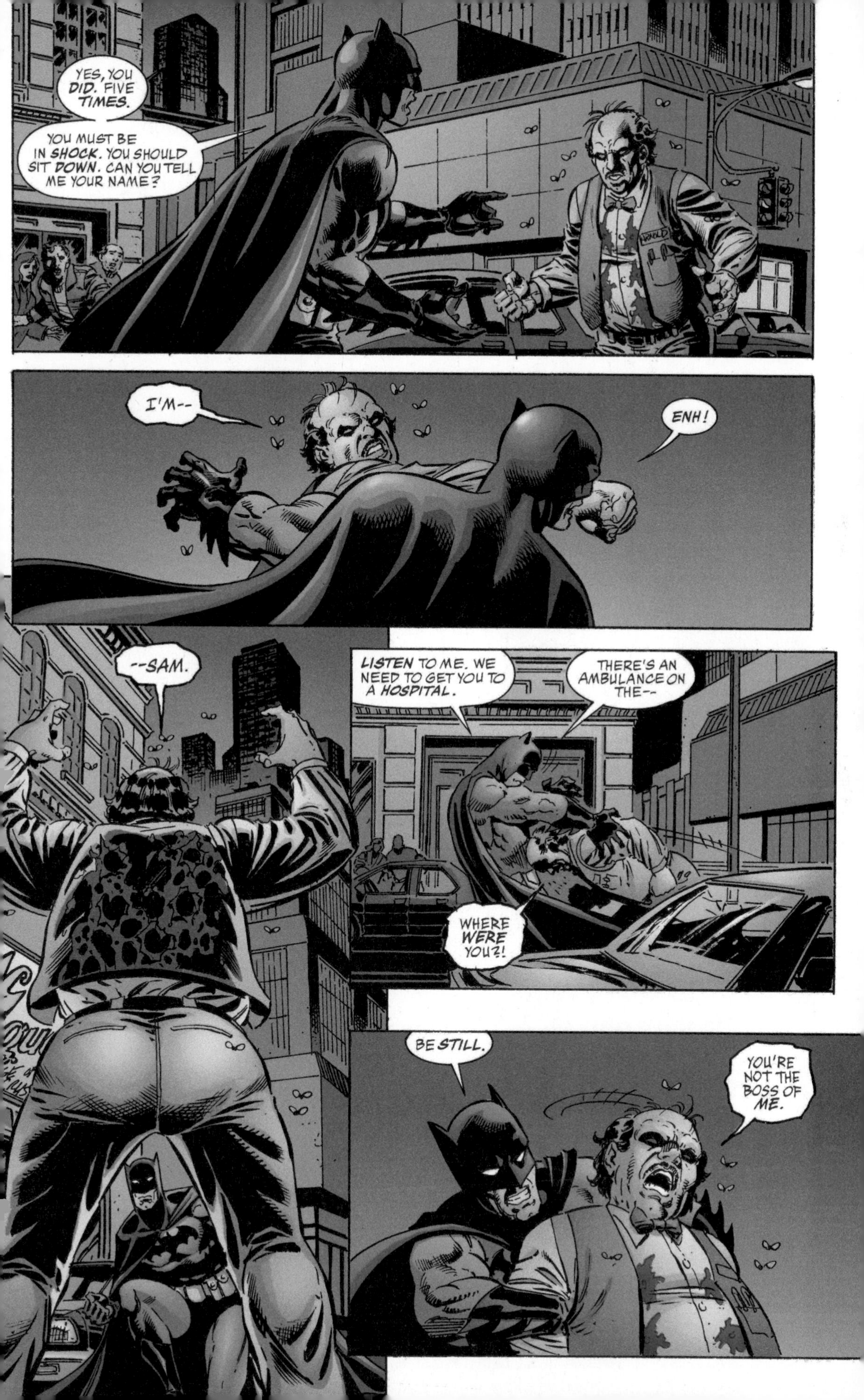
YES, YOU DID. FIVE TIMES.
YOU MUST BE IN SHOCK. YOU SHOULD SIT DOWN. CAN YOU TELL ME YOUR NAME?
I'M--
ENH!
--SAM.
LISTEN TO ME. WE NEED TO GET YOU TO A HOSPITAL.
THERE'S AN AMBULANCE ON THE--
WHERE WERE YOU?!
BE STILL.
YOU'RE NOT THE BOSS OF ME.

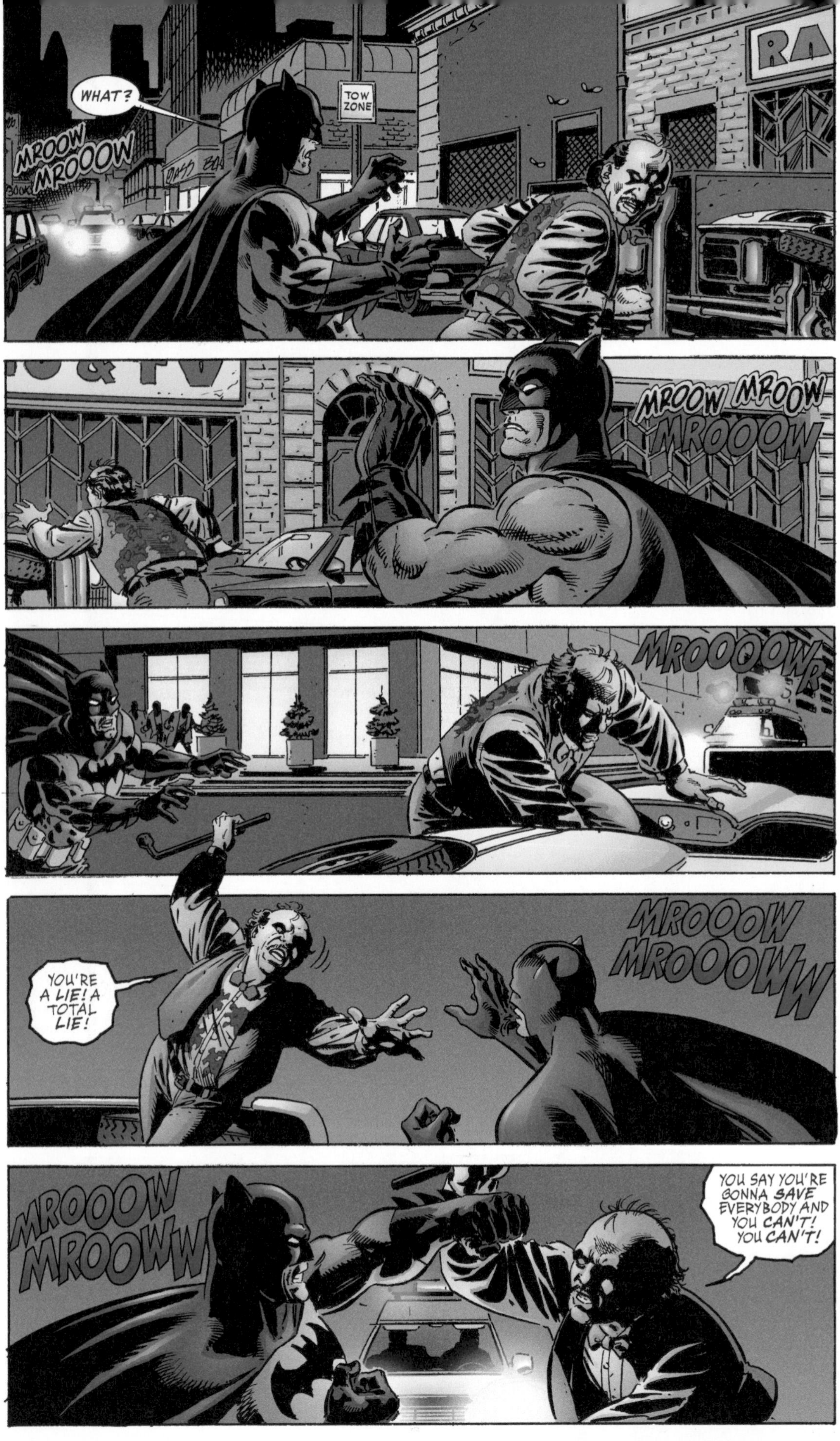
MROOW MROOOW
WHAT?
TOW ZONE
MROOW MROOW MROOOW
MROOOOWR
YOU'RE A **LIE**! A TOTAL **LIE**!
MROOOW MROOOWW
MROOOW MROOWW
YOU SAY YOU'RE GONNA **SAVE** EVERYBODY AND YOU **CAN'T**! YOU **CAN'T**!

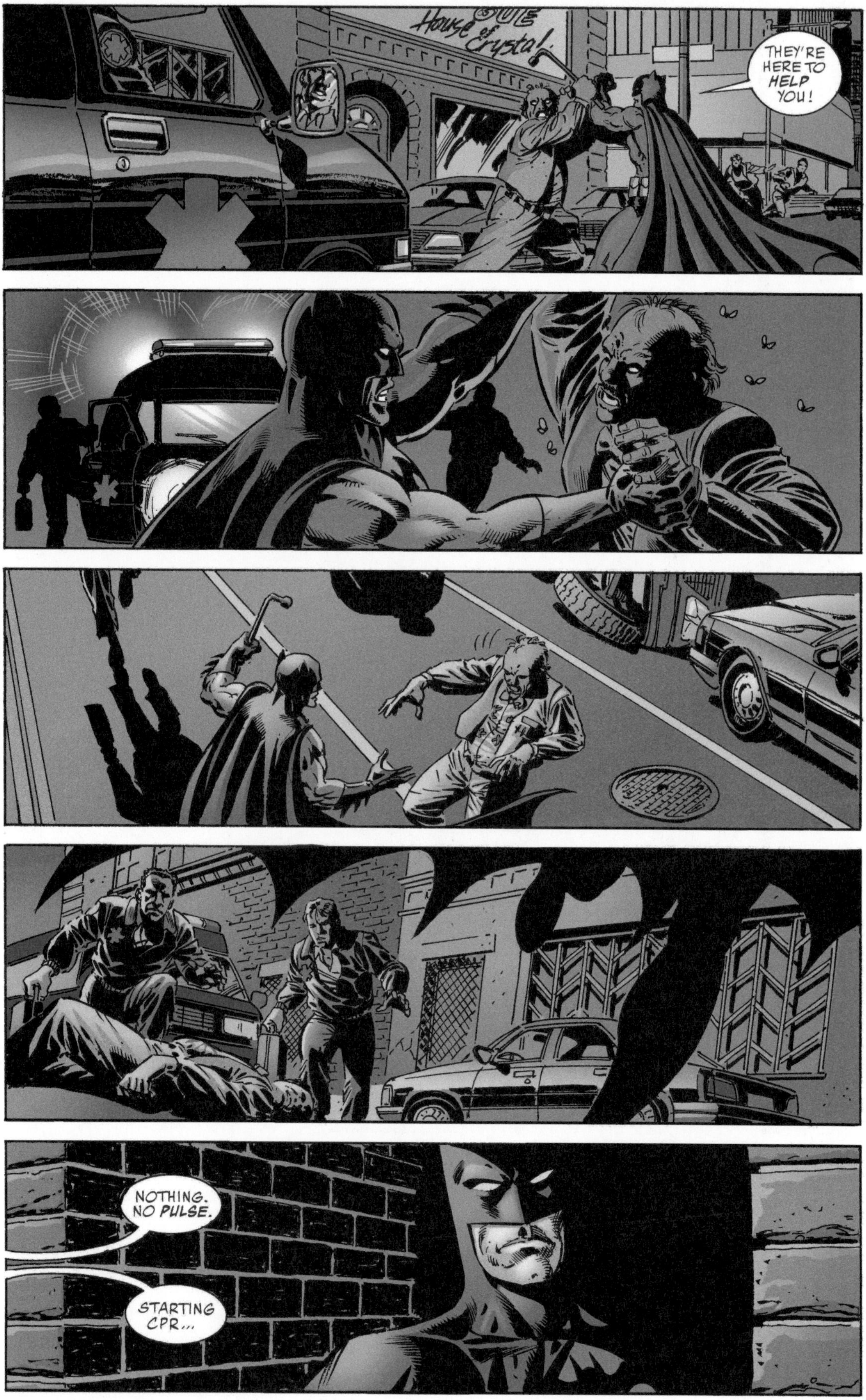
House of Crystal
THEY'RE HERE TO HELP YOU!
NOTHING. NO PULSE.
STARTING CPR...

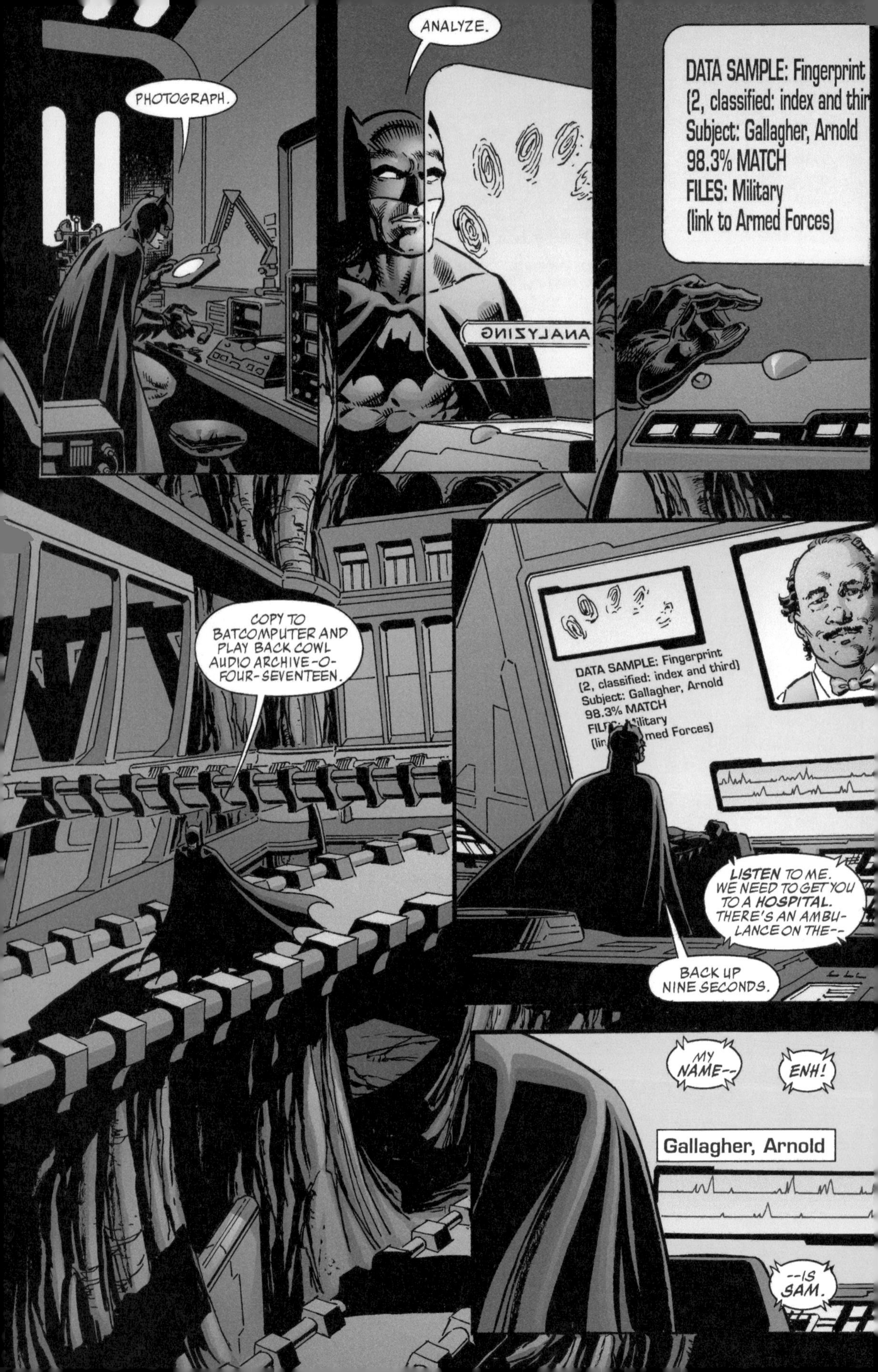
PHOTOGRAPH.
ANALYZE.
ANALYZING
DATA SAMPLE: Fingerprint
(2, classified: index and thir
Subject: Gallagher, Arnold
98.3% MATCH
FILES: Military
(link to Armed Forces)
COPY TO BATCOMPUTER AND PLAY BACK COWL AUDIO ARCHIVE-O-FOUR-SEVENTEEN.
LISTEN TO ME. WE NEED TO GET YOU TO A HOSPITAL. THERE'S AN AMBULANCE ON THE--
BACK UP NINE SECONDS.
MY NAME--
ENH!
Gallagher, Arnold
--IS SAM.

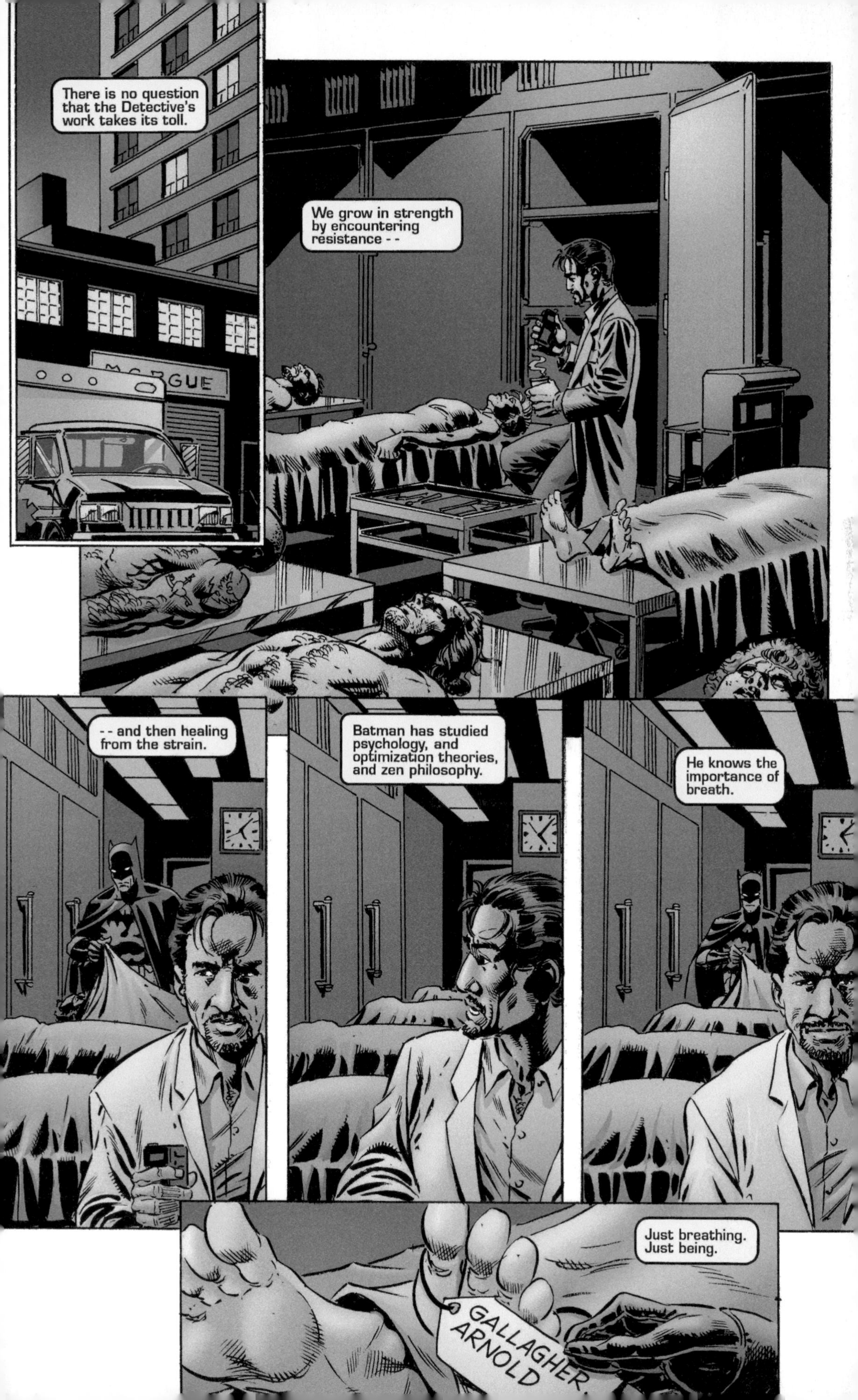
There is no question that the Detective's work takes its toll.
MORGUE
We grow in strength by encountering resistance - -
- - and then healing from the strain.
Batman has studied psychology, and optimization theories, and zen philosophy.
He knows the importance of breath.
Just breathing. Just being.
GALLAGHER, ARNOLD

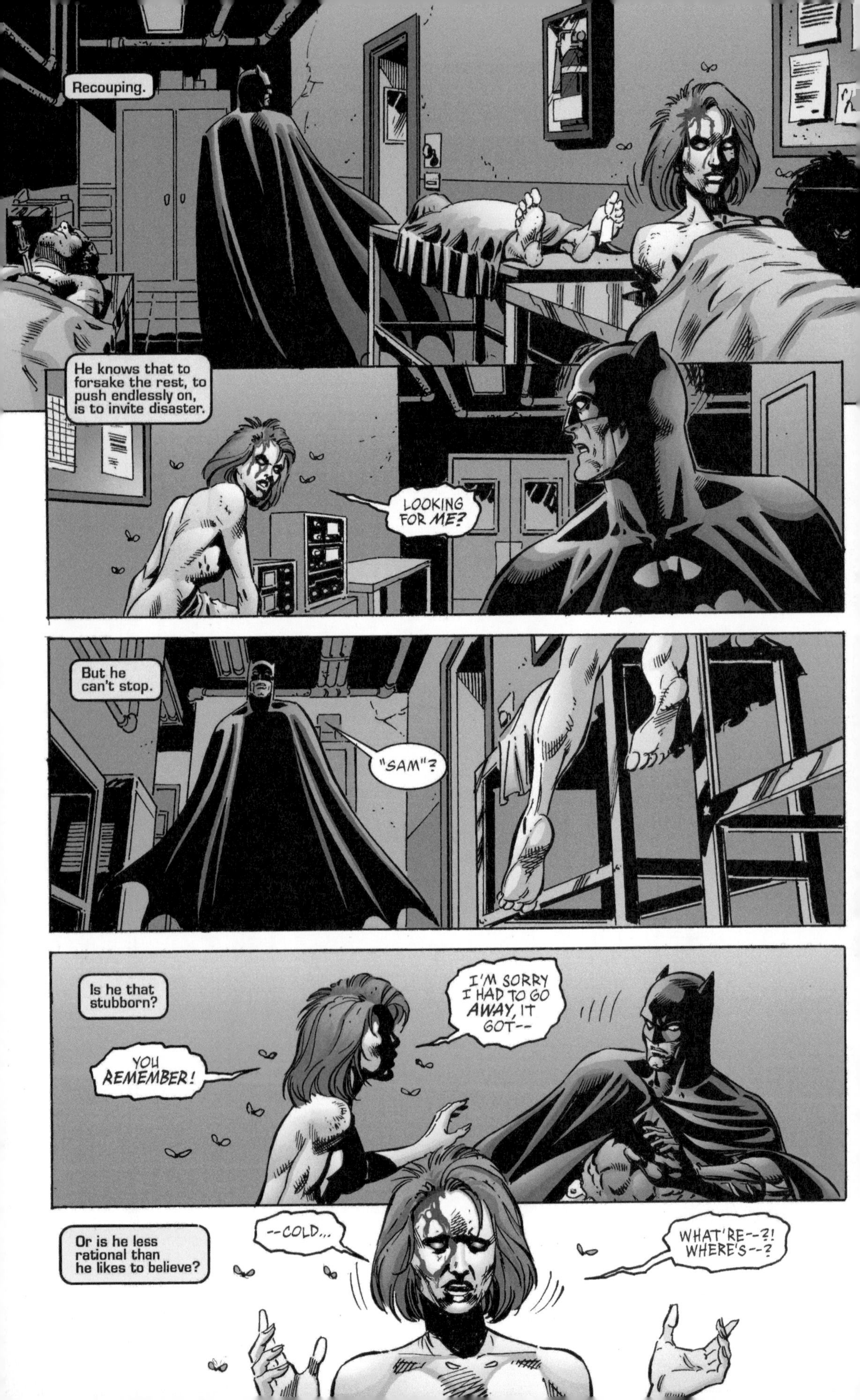
Recouping.
He knows that to forsake the rest, to push endlessly on, is to invite disaster.
LOOKING FOR ME?
But he can't stop.
"SAM"?
Is he that stubborn?
I'M SORRY I HAD TO GO AWAY, IT GOT--
YOU REMEMBER!
Or is he less rational than he likes to believe?
--COLD...
WHAT'RE--?! WHERE'S--?

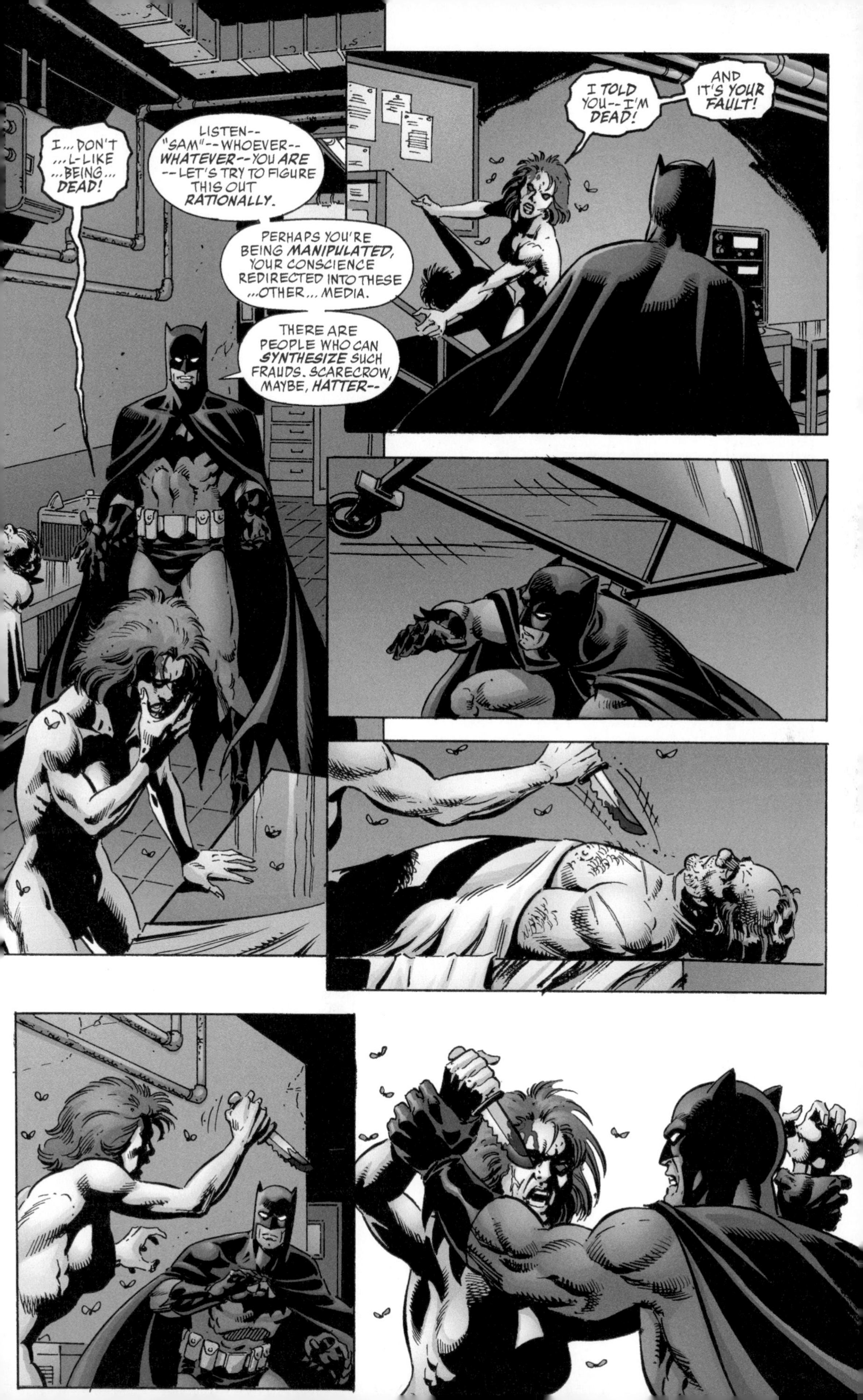
I... DON'T ...L-LIKE ...BEING... DEAD!
LISTEN-- "SAM"--WHOEVER-- WHATEVER--YOU ARE --LET'S TRY TO FIGURE THIS OUT RATIONALLY.
PERHAPS YOU'RE BEING MANIPULATED, YOUR CONSCIENCE REDIRECTED INTO THESE ...OTHER... MEDIA.
THERE ARE PEOPLE WHO CAN SYNTHESIZE SUCH FRAUDS. SCARECROW, MAYBE, HATTER--
I TOLD YOU--I'M DEAD!
AND IT'S YOUR FAULT!

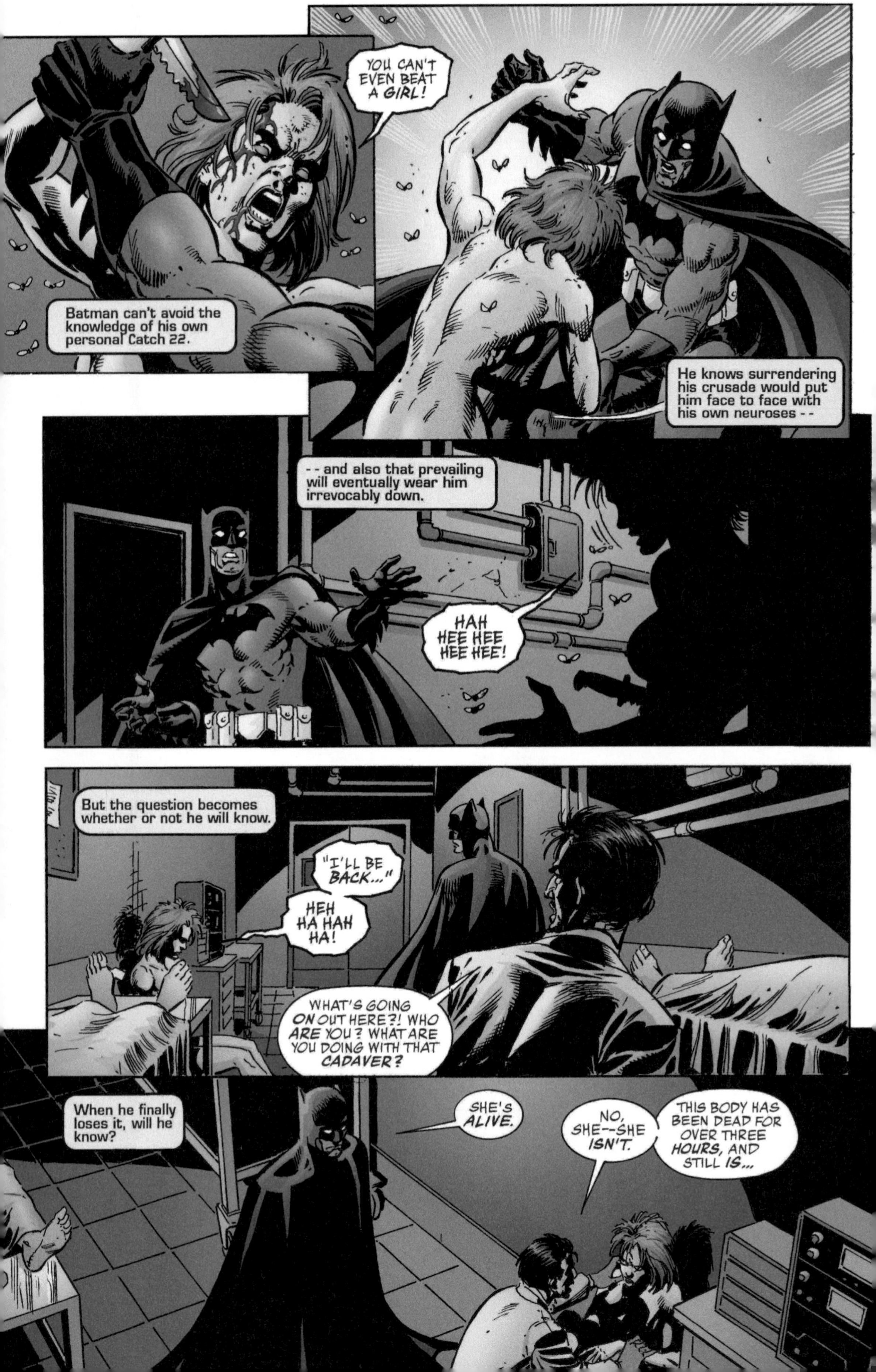
YOU CAN'T EVEN BEAT A GIRL!
Batman can't avoid the knowledge of his own personal Catch 22.
He knows surrendering his crusade would put him face to face with his own neuroses --
-- and also that prevailing will eventually wear him irrevocably down.
HAH HEE HEE HEE HEE!
But the question becomes whether or not he will know.
"I'LL BE BACK..."
HEH HA HAH HA!
WHAT'S GOING ON OUT HERE?! WHO ARE YOU? WHAT ARE YOU DOING WITH THAT CADAVER?
When he finally loses it, will he know?
SHE'S ALIVE.
NO, SHE--SHE ISN'T.
THIS BODY HAS BEEN DEAD FOR OVER THREE HOURS, AND STILL IS...

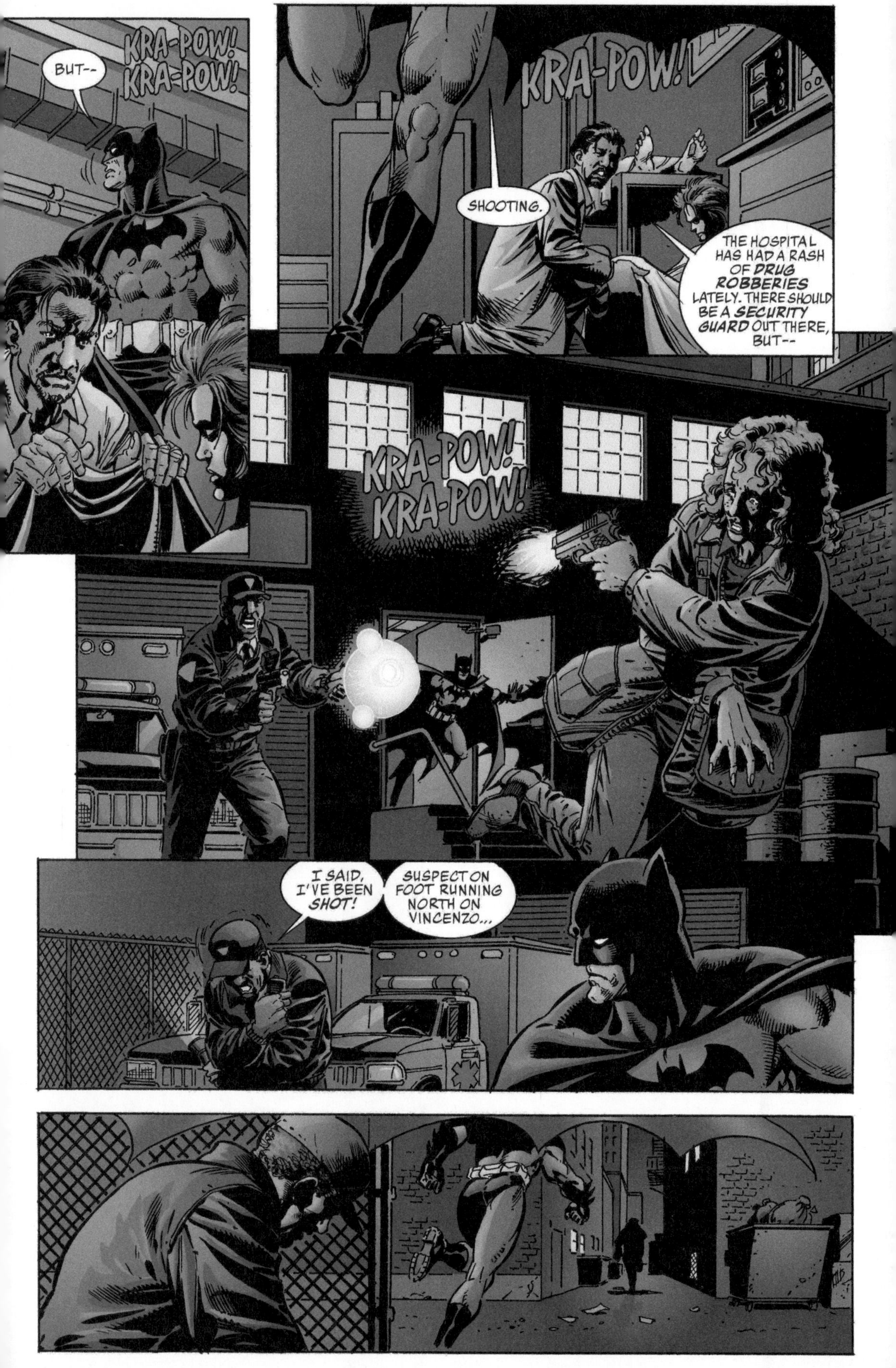
KRA-POW! KRA-POW!
BUT--
KRA-POW!
SHOOTING.
THE HOSPITAL HAS HAD A RASH OF DRUG ROBBERIES LATELY. THERE SHOULD BE A SECURITY GUARD OUT THERE, BUT--
KRA-POW! KRA-POW!
I SAID, I'VE BEEN SHOT!
SUSPECT ON FOOT RUNNING NORTH ON VINCENZO...

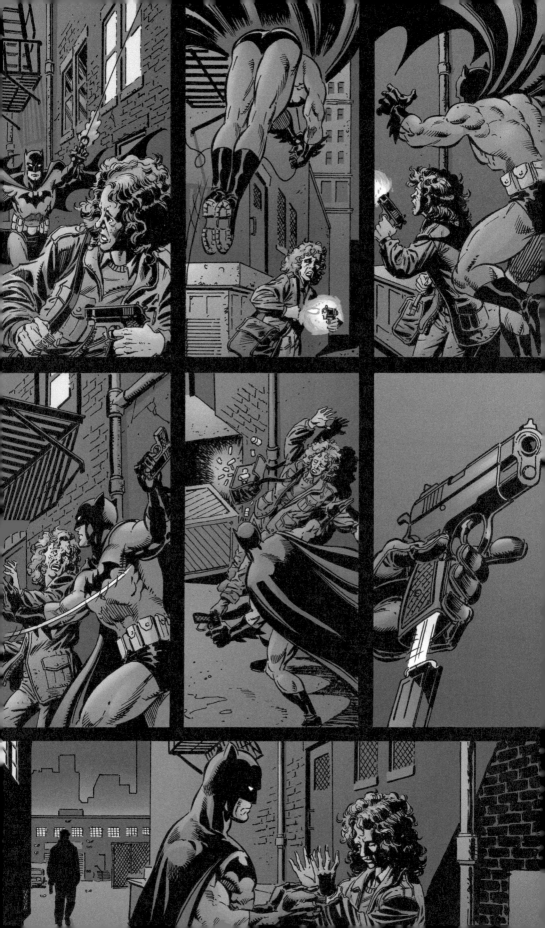

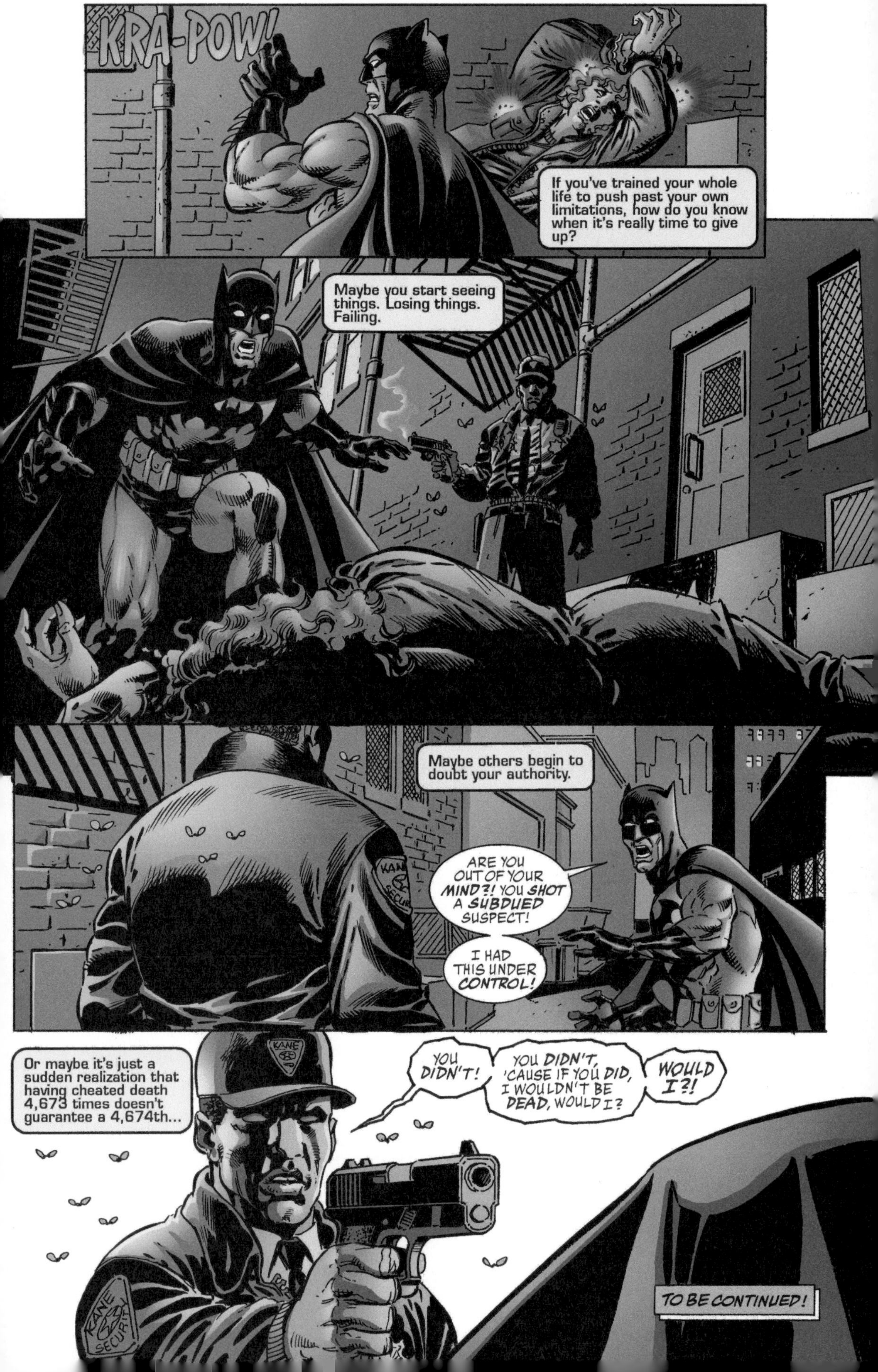
KRA-POW!
If you've trained your whole life to push past your own limitations, how do you know when it's really time to give up?
Maybe you start seeing things. Losing things. Failing.
Maybe others begin to doubt your authority.
ARE YOU OUT OF YOUR MIND?! YOU SHOT A SUBDUED SUSPECT!
I HAD THIS UNDER CONTROL!
Or maybe it's just a sudden realization that having cheated death 4,673 times doesn't guarantee a 4,674th...
YOU DIDN'T!
YOU DIDN'T, 'CAUSE IF YOU DID, I WOULDN'T BE DEAD, WOULD I?
WOULD I?!
TO BE CONTINUED!

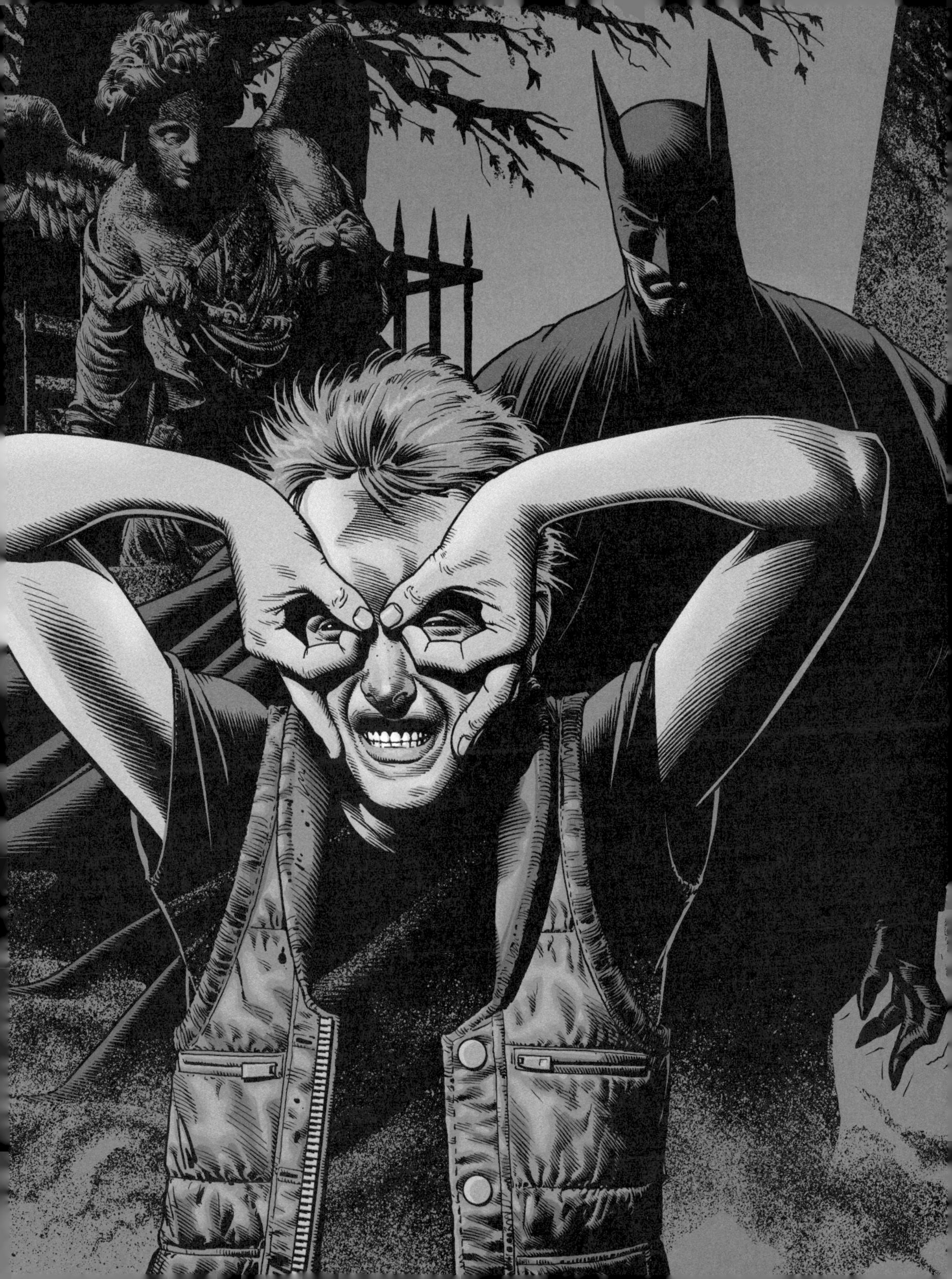

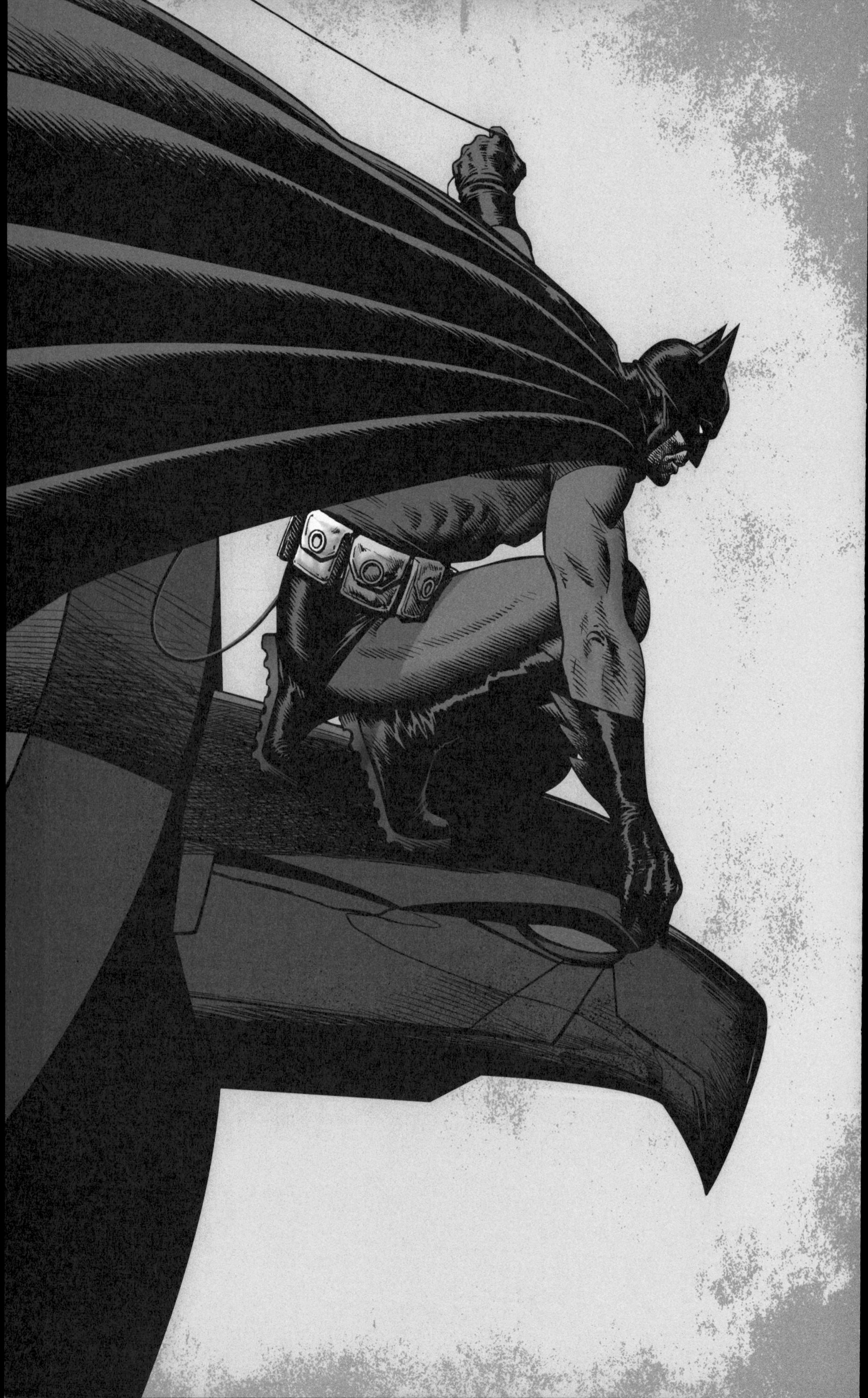

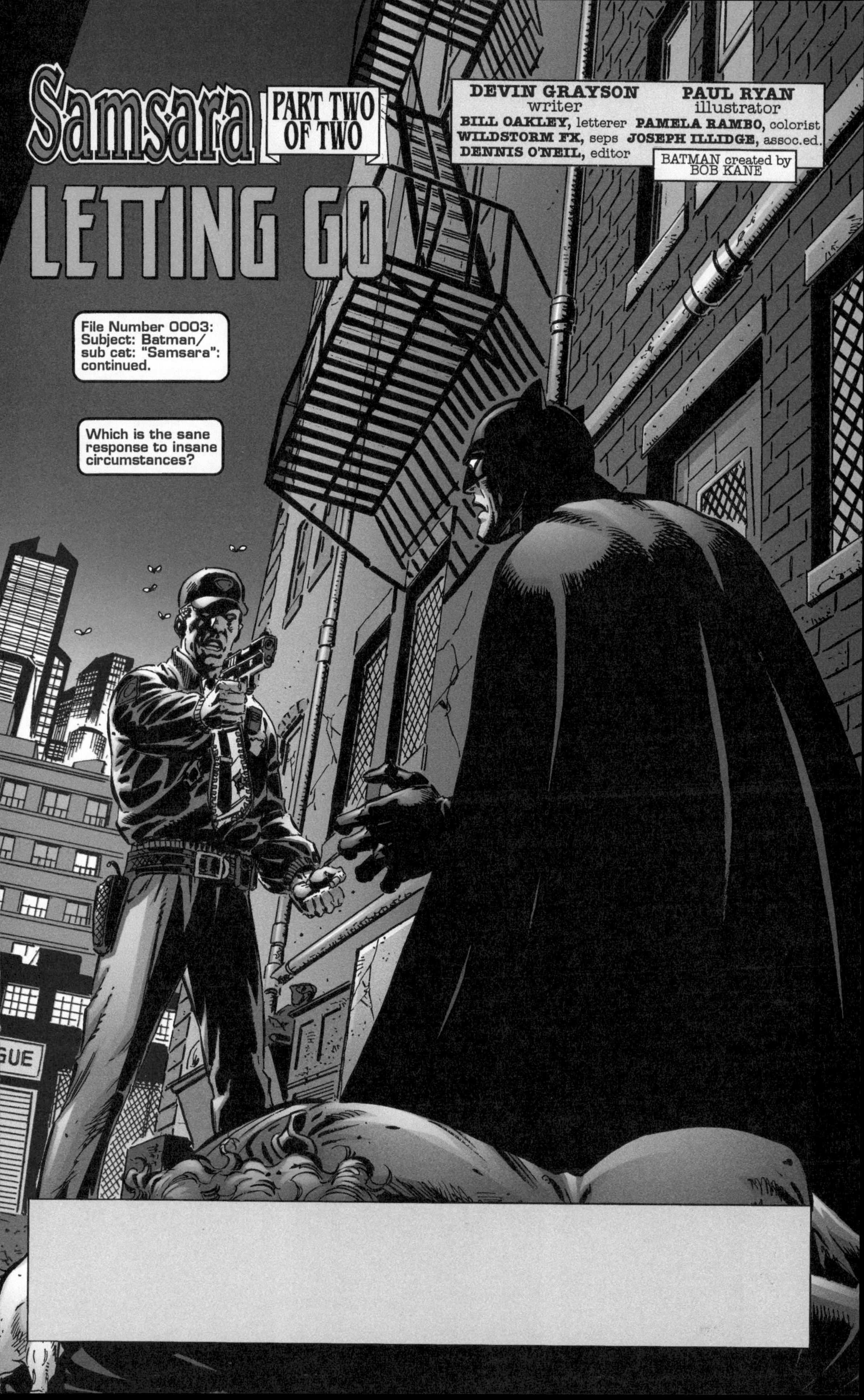
Samsara
PART TWO OF TWO
LETTING GO
DEVIN GRAYSON writer
PAUL RYAN illustrator
BILL OAKLEY, letterer
PAMELA RAMBO, colorist
WILDSTORM FX, seps
JOSEPH ILLIDGE, assoc.ed.
DENNIS O'NEIL, editor
BATMAN created by BOB KANE
File Number 0003: Subject: Batman/ sub cat: "Samsara": continued.
Which is the sane response to insane circumstances?
GUE

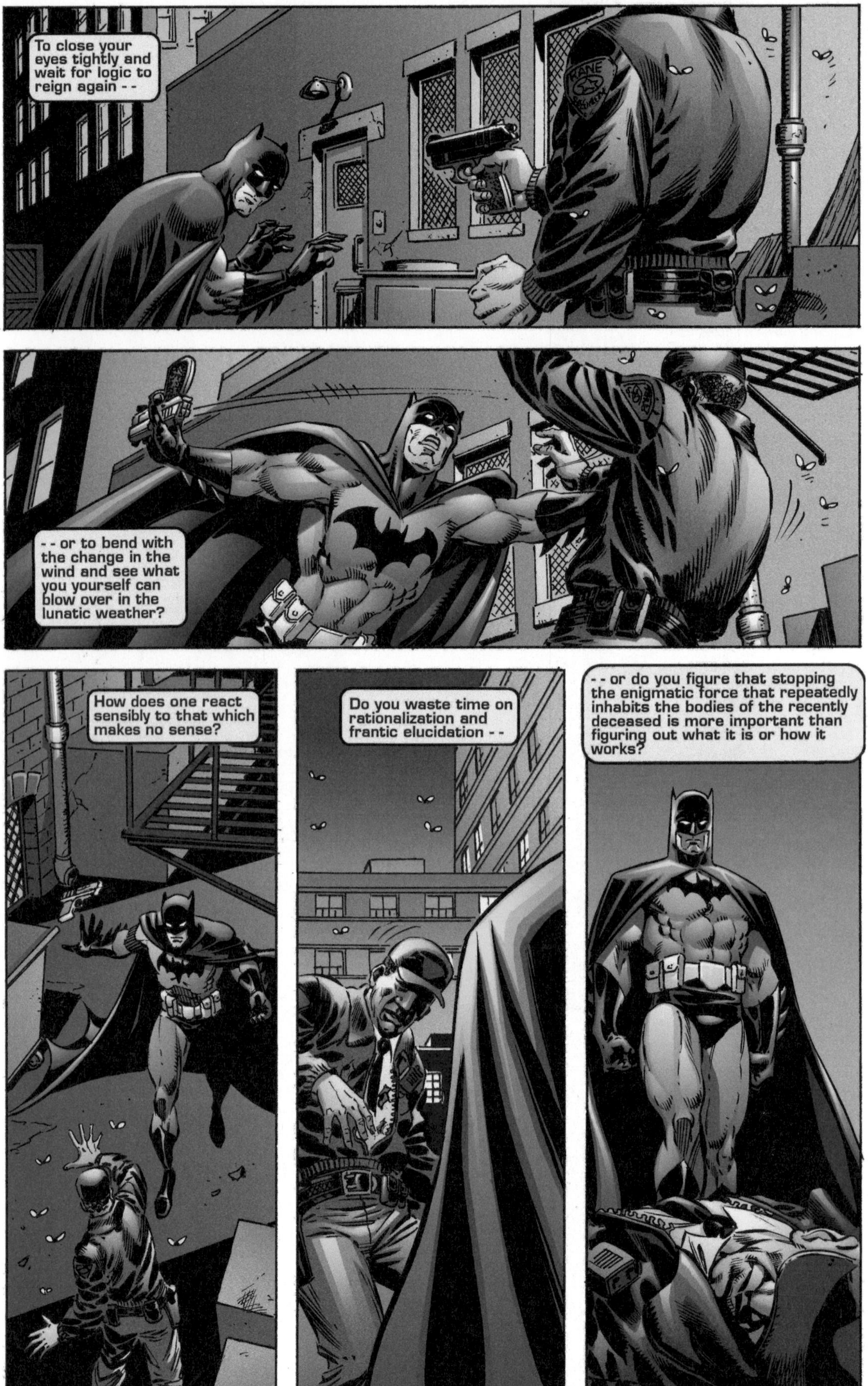
To close your eyes tightly and wait for logic to reign again - -
KANE
- - or to bend with the change in the wind and see what you yourself can blow over in the lunatic weather?
How does one react sensibly to that which makes no sense?
Do you waste time on rationalization and frantic elucidation - -
- - or do you figure that stopping the enigmatic force that repeatedly inhabits the bodies of the recently deceased is more important than figuring out what it is or how it works?

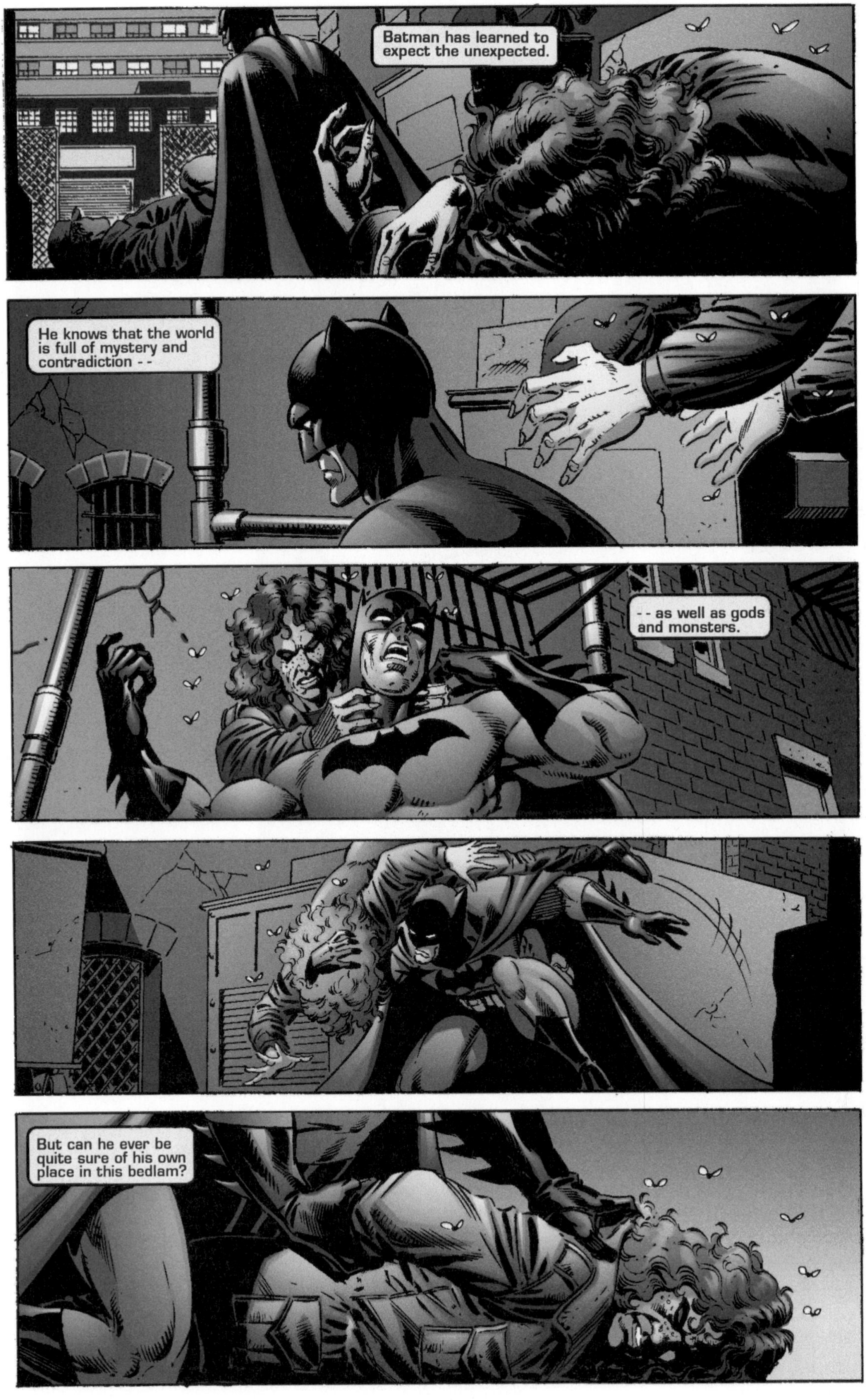
Batman has learned to expect the unexpected.
He knows that the world is full of mystery and contradiction - -
- - as well as gods and monsters.
But can he ever be quite sure of his own place in this bedlam?

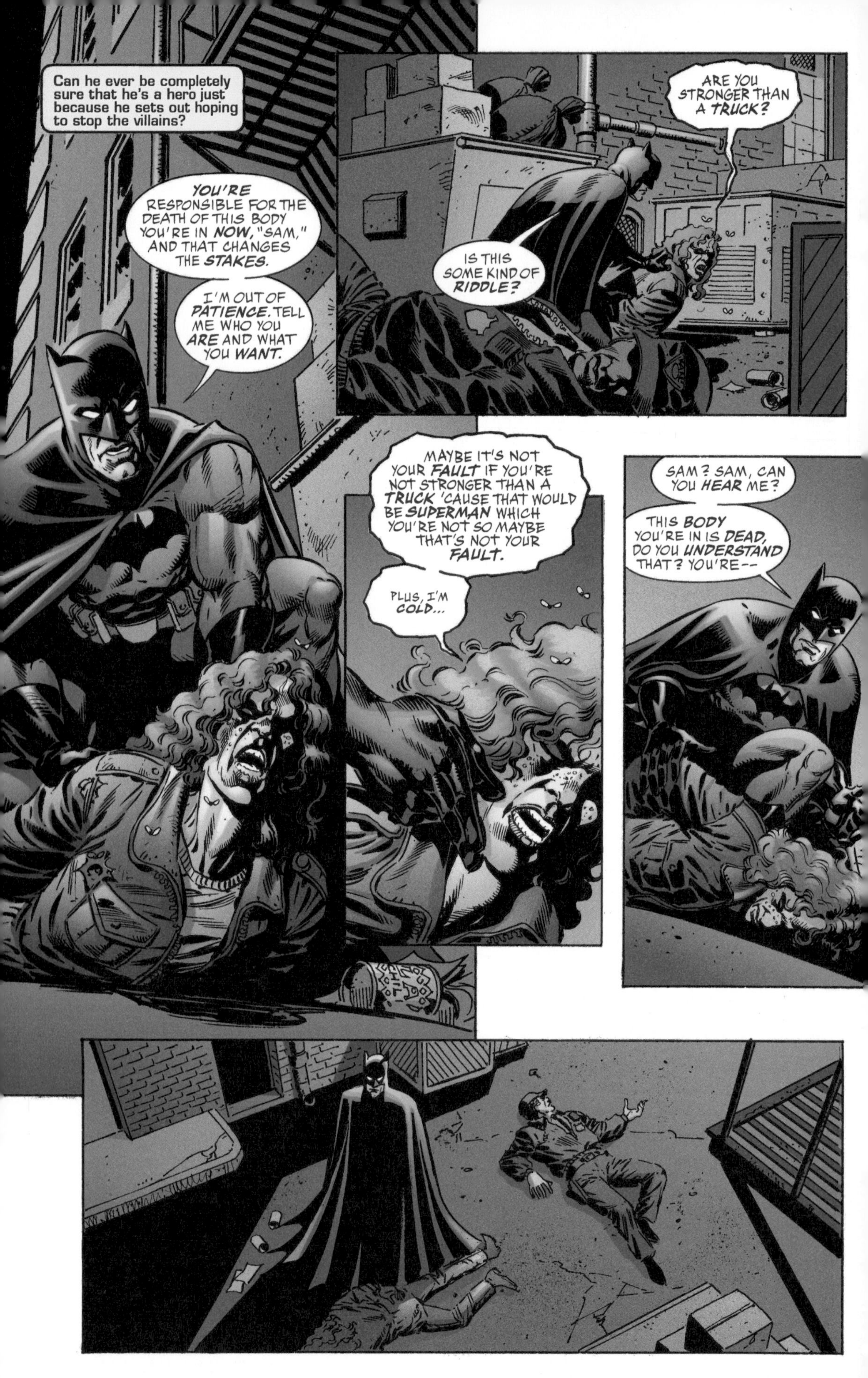

Can he ever be completely sure that he's a hero just because he sets out hoping to stop the villains?
ARE YOU STRONGER THAN A TRUCK?
IS THIS SOME KIND OF RIDDLE?
YOU'RE RESPONSIBLE FOR THE DEATH OF THIS BODY YOU'RE IN NOW, "SAM," AND THAT CHANGES THE STAKES.
I'M OUT OF PATIENCE. TELL ME WHO YOU ARE AND WHAT YOU WANT.
MAYBE IT'S NOT YOUR FAULT IF YOU'RE NOT STRONGER THAN A TRUCK 'CAUSE THAT WOULD BE SUPERMAN WHICH YOU'RE NOT SO MAYBE THAT'S NOT YOUR FAULT.
PLUS, I'M COLD...
SAM? SAM, CAN YOU HEAR ME?
THIS BODY YOU'RE IN IS DEAD, DO YOU UNDERSTAND THAT? YOU'RE--

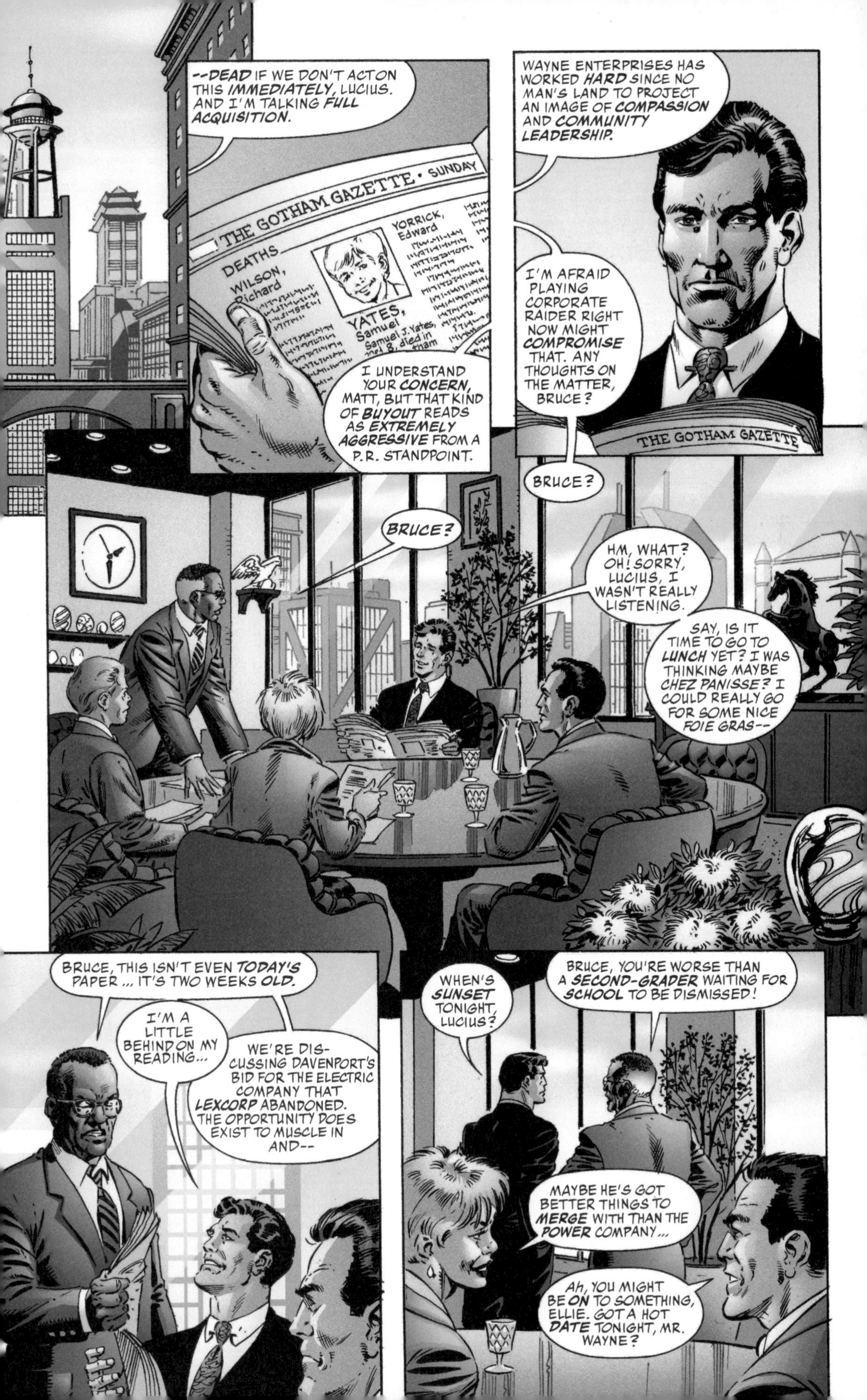
--DEAD IF WE DON'T ACT ON THIS IMMEDIATELY, LUCIUS. AND I'M TALKING FULL ACQUISITION.
THE GOTHAM GAZETTE • SUNDAY
DEATHS
WILSON, Richard
YORRICK, Edward
YATES, Samuel
I UNDERSTAND YOUR CONCERN, MATT, BUT THAT KIND OF BUYOUT READS AS EXTREMELY AGGRESSIVE FROM A P.R. STANDPOINT.
WAYNE ENTERPRISES HAS WORKED HARD SINCE NO MAN'S LAND TO PROJECT AN IMAGE OF COMPASSION AND COMMUNITY LEADERSHIP.
I'M AFRAID PLAYING CORPORATE RAIDER RIGHT NOW MIGHT COMPROMISE THAT. ANY THOUGHTS ON THE MATTER, BRUCE?
THE GOTHAM GAZETTE
BRUCE?
BRUCE?
HM, WHAT? OH! SORRY, LUCIUS, I WASN'T REALLY LISTENING.
SAY, IS IT TIME TO GO TO LUNCH YET? I WAS THINKING MAYBE CHEZ PANISSE? I COULD REALLY GO FOR SOME NICE FOIE GRAS--
BRUCE, THIS ISN'T EVEN TODAY'S PAPER ... IT'S TWO WEEKS OLD.
I'M A LITTLE BEHIND ON MY READING...
WE'RE DISCUSSING DAVENPORT'S BID FOR THE ELECTRIC COMPANY THAT LEXCORP ABANDONED. THE OPPORTUNITY DOES EXIST TO MUSCLE IN AND--
WHEN'S SUNSET TONIGHT, LUCIUS?
BRUCE, YOU'RE WORSE THAN A SECOND-GRADER WAITING FOR SCHOOL TO BE DISMISSED!
MAYBE HE'S GOT BETTER THINGS TO MERGE WITH THAN THE POWER COMPANY...
Ah, YOU MIGHT BE ON TO SOMETHING, ELLIE. GOT A HOT DATE TONIGHT, MR. WAYNE?

To honor life -- to wish for and work towards an end to unnecessary loss and suffering -- is that enough?

As long as his actions are just, does it matter what he believes?

Is Batman justified in acknowledging the inevitability of mortality while guarding the life of even his greatest foe?

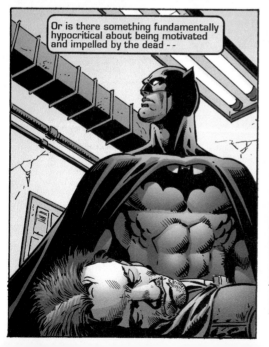

Or is there something fundamentally hypocritical about being motivated and impelled by the dead --

-- while working every moment with every fiber of your being to stay alive?

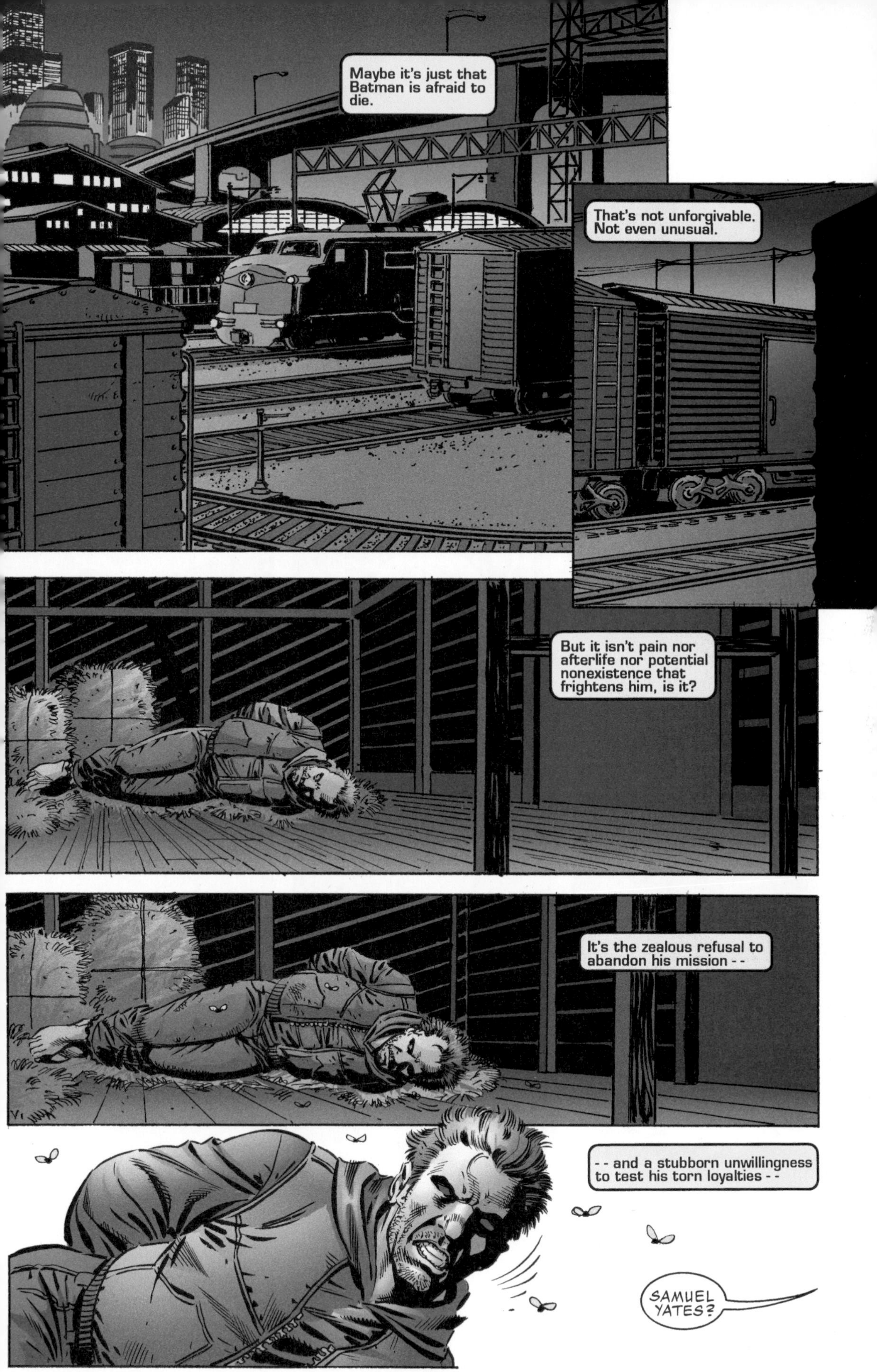
Maybe it's just that Batman is afraid to die.
That's not unforgivable. Not even unusual.
But it isn't pain nor afterlife nor potential nonexistence that frightens him, is it?
It's the zealous refusal to abandon his mission - -
- - and a stubborn unwillingness to test his torn loyalties - -
SAMUEL YATES?

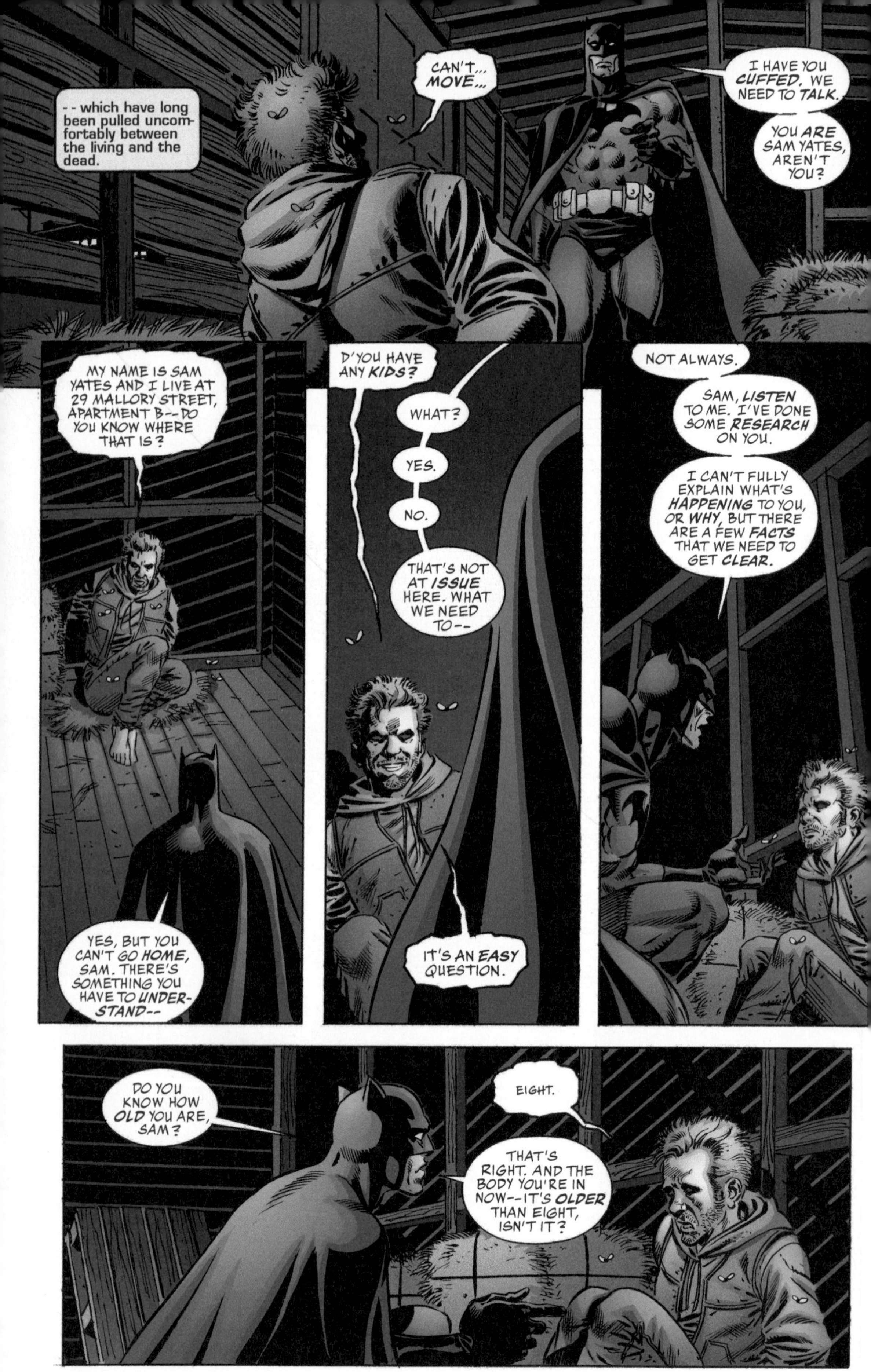

-- which have long been pulled uncomfortably between the living and the dead.
CAN'T... MOVE...
I HAVE YOU CUFFED. WE NEED TO TALK.
YOU ARE SAM YATES, AREN'T YOU?
MY NAME IS SAM YATES AND I LIVE AT 29 MALLORY STREET, APARTMENT B--DO YOU KNOW WHERE THAT IS?
YES, BUT YOU CAN'T GO HOME, SAM. THERE'S SOMETHING YOU HAVE TO UNDERSTAND--
D'YOU HAVE ANY KIDS?
WHAT?
YES.
NO.
THAT'S NOT AT ISSUE HERE. WHAT WE NEED TO--
IT'S AN EASY QUESTION.
NOT ALWAYS.
SAM, LISTEN TO ME. I'VE DONE SOME RESEARCH ON YOU.
I CAN'T FULLY EXPLAIN WHAT'S HAPPENING TO YOU, OR WHY, BUT THERE ARE A FEW FACTS THAT WE NEED TO GET CLEAR.
DO YOU KNOW HOW OLD YOU ARE, SAM?
EIGHT.
THAT'S RIGHT. AND THE BODY YOU'RE IN NOW--IT'S OLDER THAN EIGHT, ISN'T IT?

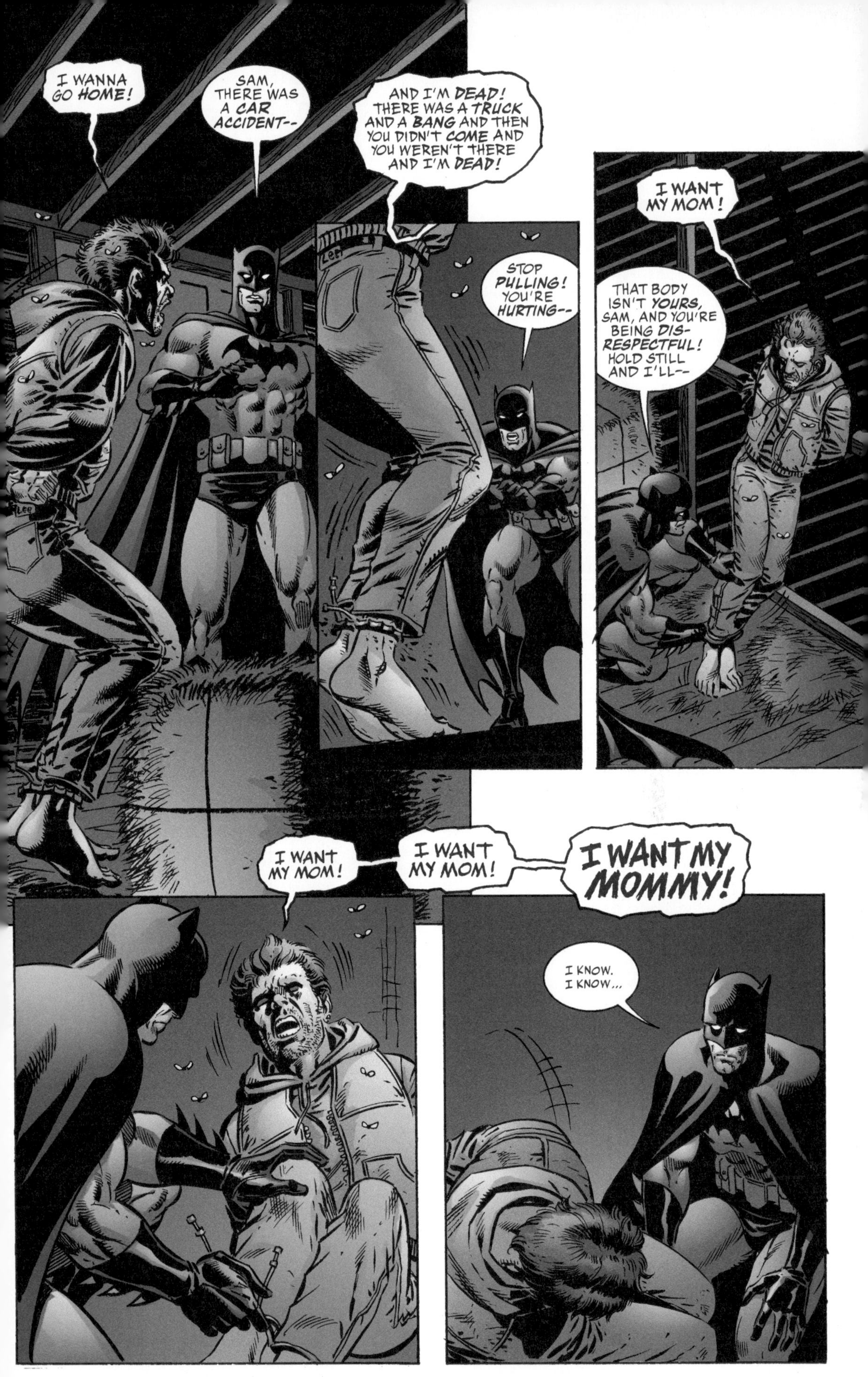
I WANNA GO HOME!
SAM, THERE WAS A CAR ACCIDENT--
AND I'M DEAD! THERE WAS A TRUCK AND A BANG AND THEN YOU DIDN'T COME AND YOU WEREN'T THERE AND I'M DEAD!
STOP PULLING! YOU'RE HURTING--
I WANT MY MOM!
THAT BODY ISN'T YOURS, SAM, AND YOU'RE BEING DIS-RESPECTFUL! HOLD STILL AND I'LL--
I WANT MY MOM!
I WANT MY MOM!
I WANT MY MOMMY!
I KNOW. I KNOW...

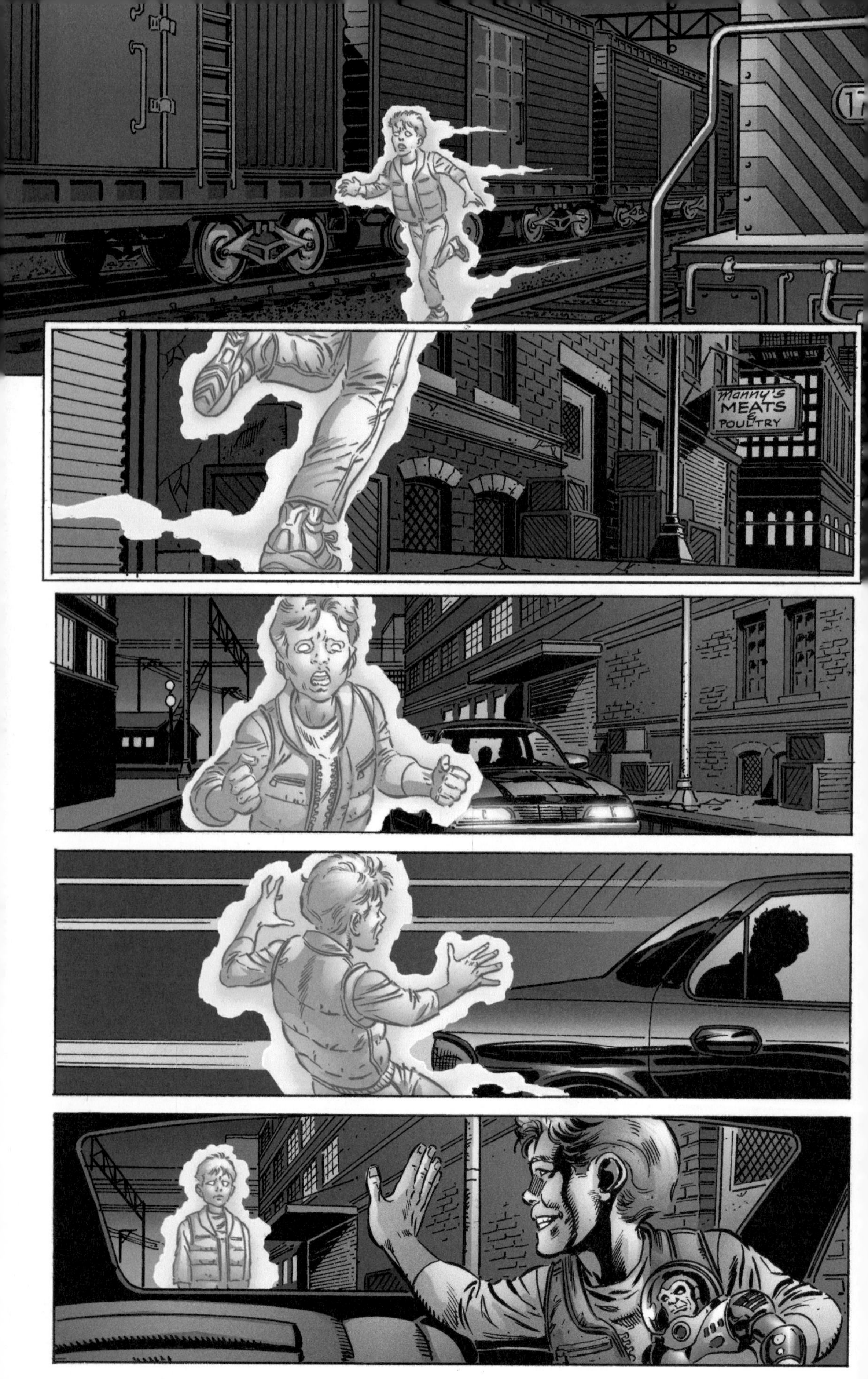
Manny's
MEATS
&
POULTRY

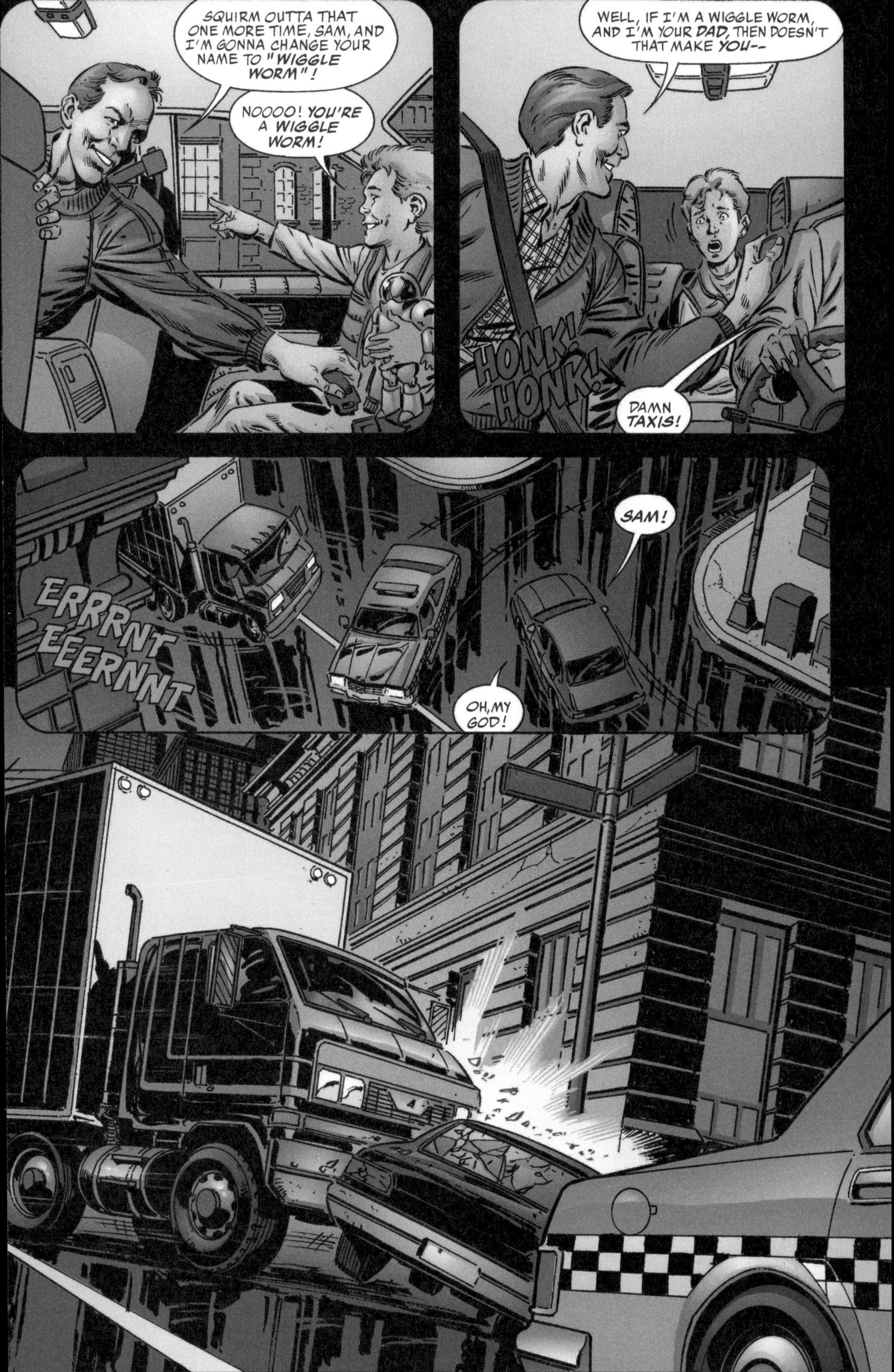
SQUIRM OUTTA THAT ONE MORE TIME, SAM, AND I'M GONNA CHANGE YOUR NAME TO "WIGGLE WORM"!
NOOOO! YOU'RE A WIGGLE WORM!
WELL, IF I'M A WIGGLE WORM, AND I'M YOUR DAD, THEN DOESN'T THAT MAKE YOU--
HONK! HONK!
DAMN TAXIS!
ERRRNT EEERNNT
SAM!
OH, MY GOD!

YES?

Um, MR. YATES?

THAT'S RIGHT.

IS THIS ABOUT MYRA? I CHECKED ON HER JUST TWENTY MINUTES AGO AND SHE WASN'T *BOTHERING* ANYONE...

MYRA?

MY *WIFE.*

WHO ARE *YOU?*

OH, I-- I'M SORRY, HAVE I PROPERLY INTRODUCED MYSELF? MY NAME'S BRUCE WAYNE, AND I RUN A SERVICE CALLED V.I.P.-- THE VICTIMS, INCORPORATED PROGRAM. MAYBE YOU'VE--

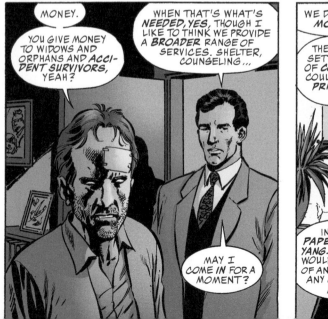

MONEY.

YOU GIVE MONEY TO WIDOWS AND ORPHANS AND *ACCIDENT SURVIVORS,* YEAH?

WHEN THAT'S WHAT'S *NEEDED,* YES, THOUGH I LIKE TO THINK WE PROVIDE A *BROADER* RANGE OF SERVICES. SHELTER, COUNSELING...

MAY I COME *IN* FOR A MOMENT?

WE DON'T NEED *MONEY.*

THE *CAR COMPANY* SETTLED WITH US OUT OF *COURT.* AS IF THEY COULD ACTUALLY PUT A *PRICE* ON MY SON'S *HEAD...*

YES, YOUR *SON--* SAM. PLEASE ALLOW ME TO EXPRESS MY *CONDOLENCES.* IT'S A TERRIBLE TRAGEDY.

INTERESTING *PAPERWEIGHT. YIN* AND *YANG.* YOU-- *uh*-- YOU WOULDN'T BE A PRACTITIONER OF AN *EASTERN* RELIGION BY ANY CHANCE, WOULD YOU, MR. YATES?

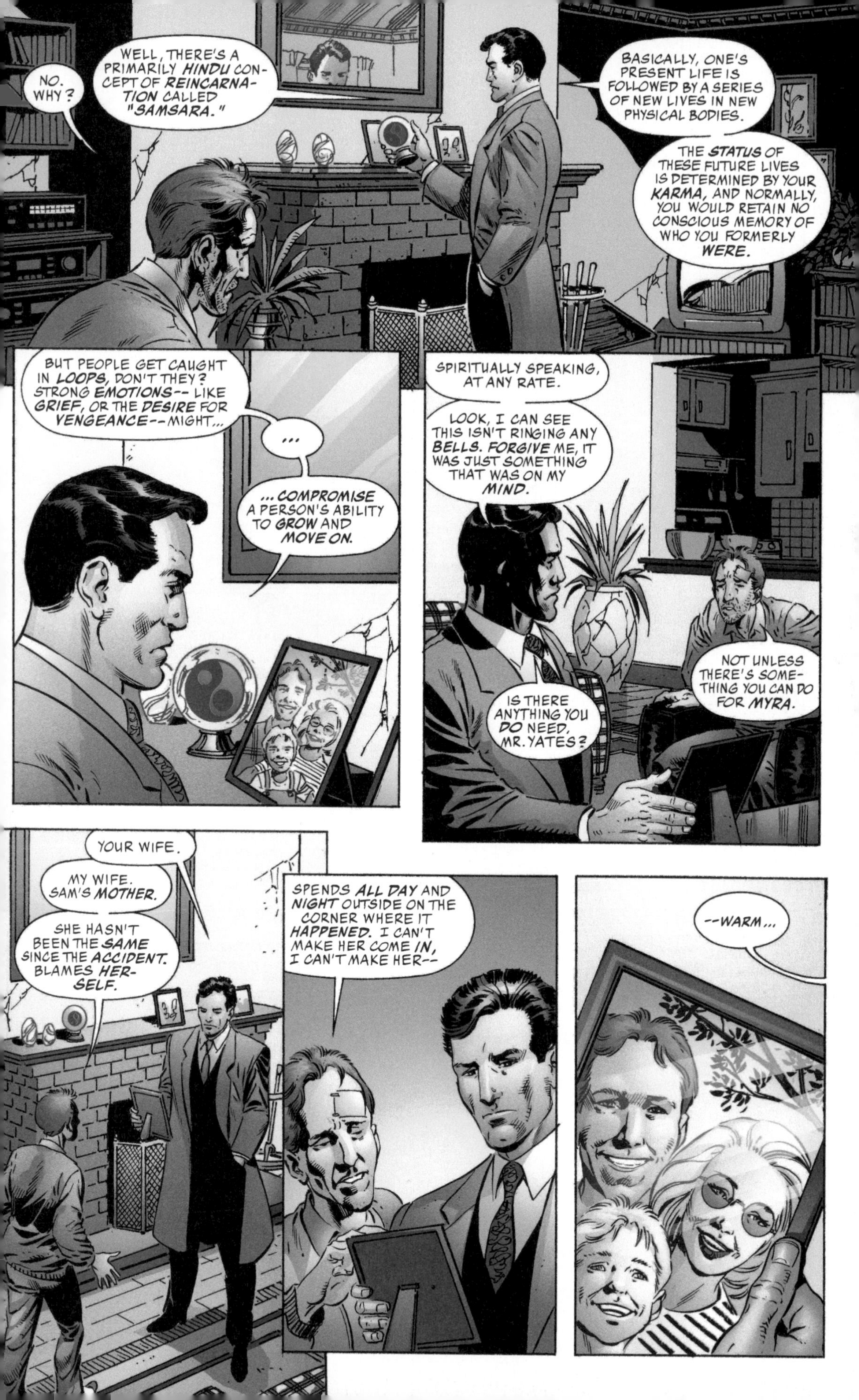
NO. WHY?
WELL, THERE'S A PRIMARILY HINDU CONCEPT OF REINCARNATION CALLED "SAMSARA."
BASICALLY, ONE'S PRESENT LIFE IS FOLLOWED BY A SERIES OF NEW LIVES IN NEW PHYSICAL BODIES.
THE STATUS OF THESE FUTURE LIVES IS DETERMINED BY YOUR KARMA, AND NORMALLY, YOU WOULD RETAIN NO CONSCIOUS MEMORY OF WHO YOU FORMERLY WERE.
BUT PEOPLE GET CAUGHT IN LOOPS, DON'T THEY? STRONG EMOTIONS-- LIKE GRIEF, OR THE DESIRE FOR VENGEANCE--MIGHT...
...
...COMPROMISE A PERSON'S ABILITY TO GROW AND MOVE ON.
SPIRITUALLY SPEAKING, AT ANY RATE.
LOOK, I CAN SEE THIS ISN'T RINGING ANY BELLS. FORGIVE ME, IT WAS JUST SOMETHING THAT WAS ON MY MIND.
IS THERE ANYTHING YOU DO NEED, MR. YATES?
NOT UNLESS THERE'S SOMETHING YOU CAN DO FOR MYRA.
YOUR WIFE.
MY WIFE. SAM'S MOTHER.
SHE HASN'T BEEN THE SAME SINCE THE ACCIDENT. BLAMES HERSELF.
SPENDS ALL DAY AND NIGHT OUTSIDE ON THE CORNER WHERE IT HAPPENED. I CAN'T MAKE HER COME IN, I CAN'T MAKE HER--
--WARM...

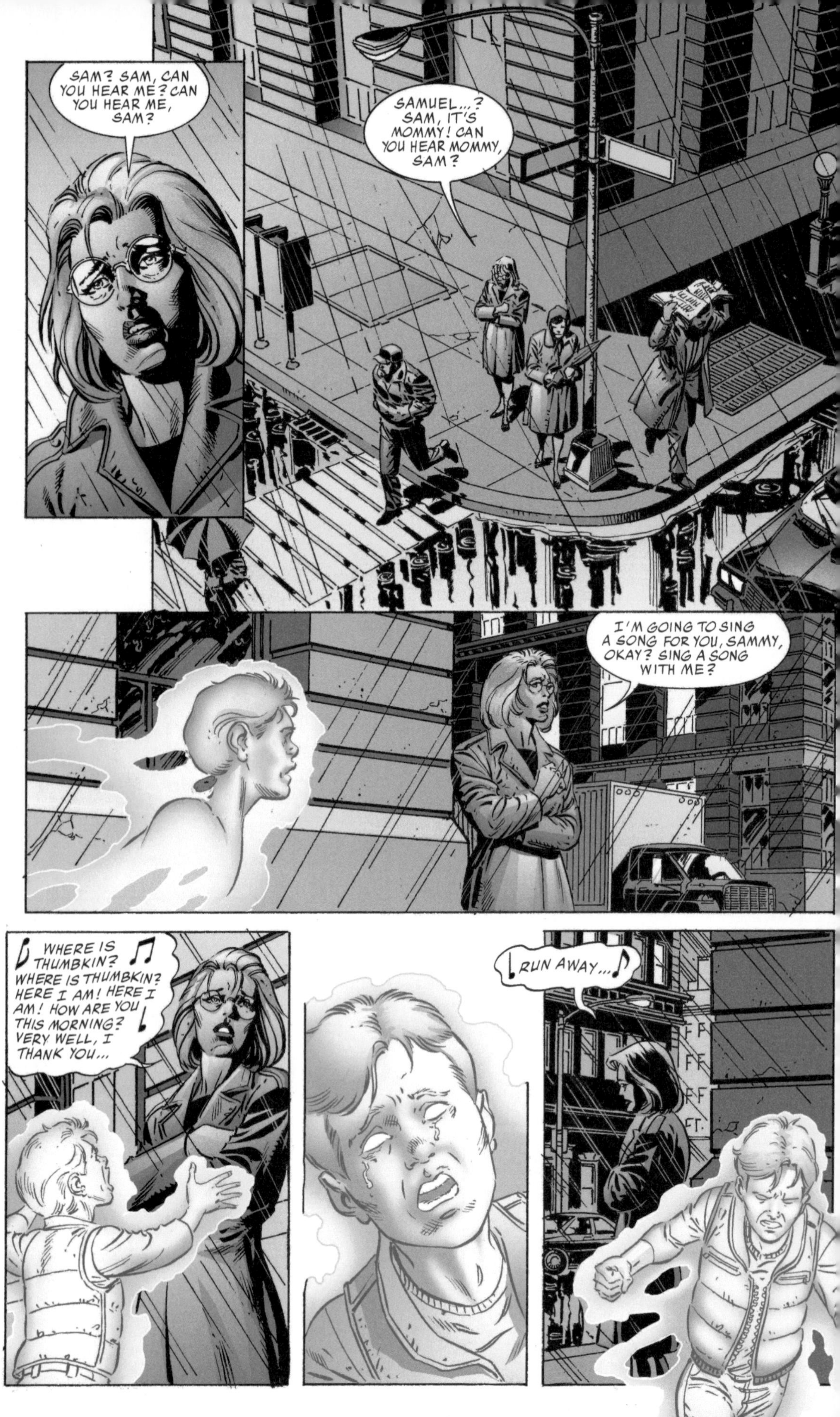
SAM? SAM, CAN YOU HEAR ME? CAN YOU HEAR ME, SAM?
SAMUEL...? SAM, IT'S MOMMY! CAN YOU HEAR MOMMY, SAM?
I'M GOING TO SING A SONG FOR YOU, SAMMY, OKAY? SING A SONG WITH ME?
WHERE IS THUMBKIN? WHERE IS THUMBKIN? HERE I AM! HERE I AM! HOW ARE YOU THIS MORNING? VERY WELL, I THANK YOU...
RUN AWAY...

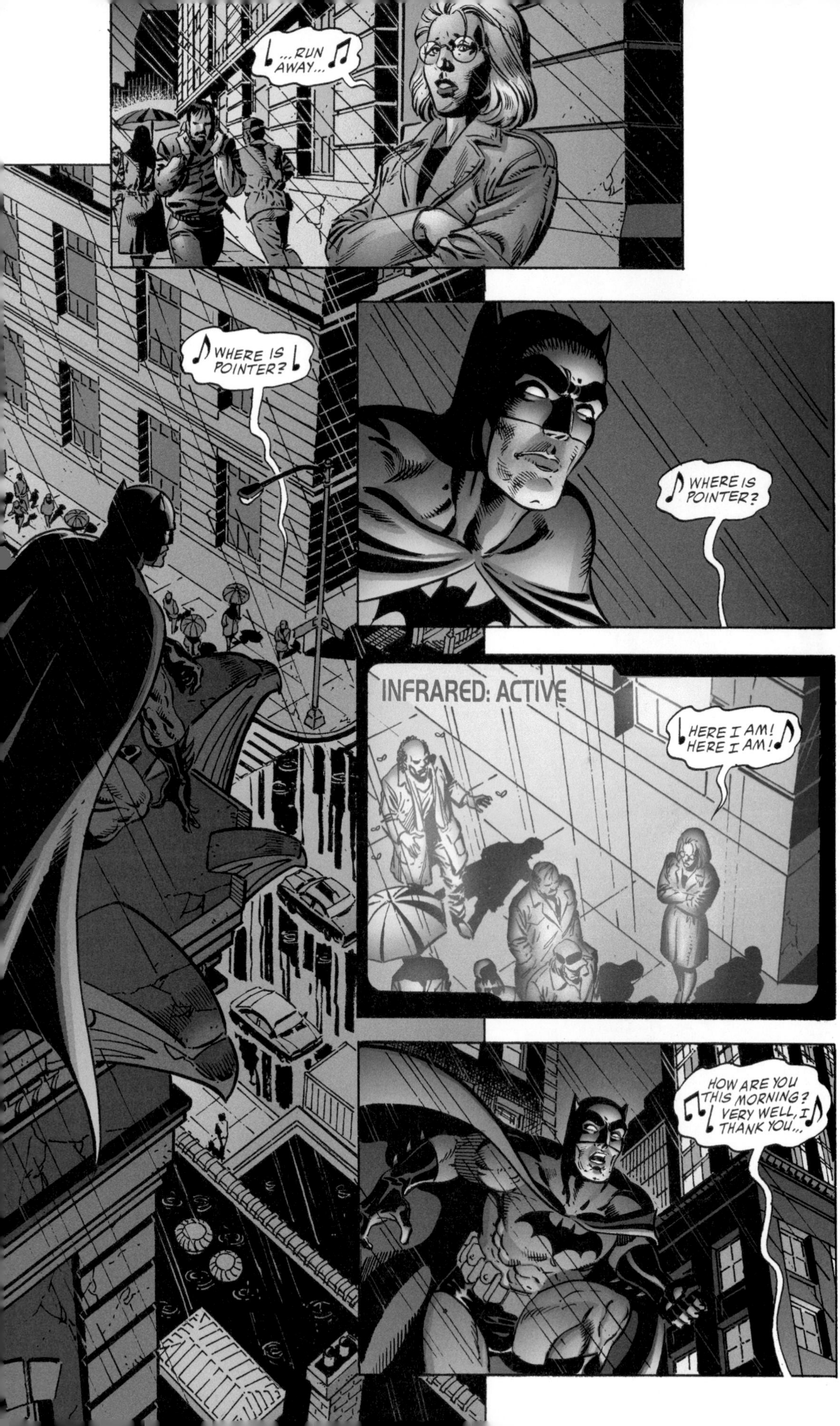
...RUN AWAY...
WHERE IS POINTER?
WHERE IS POINTER?
INFRARED: ACTIVE
HERE I AM! HERE I AM!
HOW ARE YOU THIS MORNING? VERY WELL, I THANK YOU...

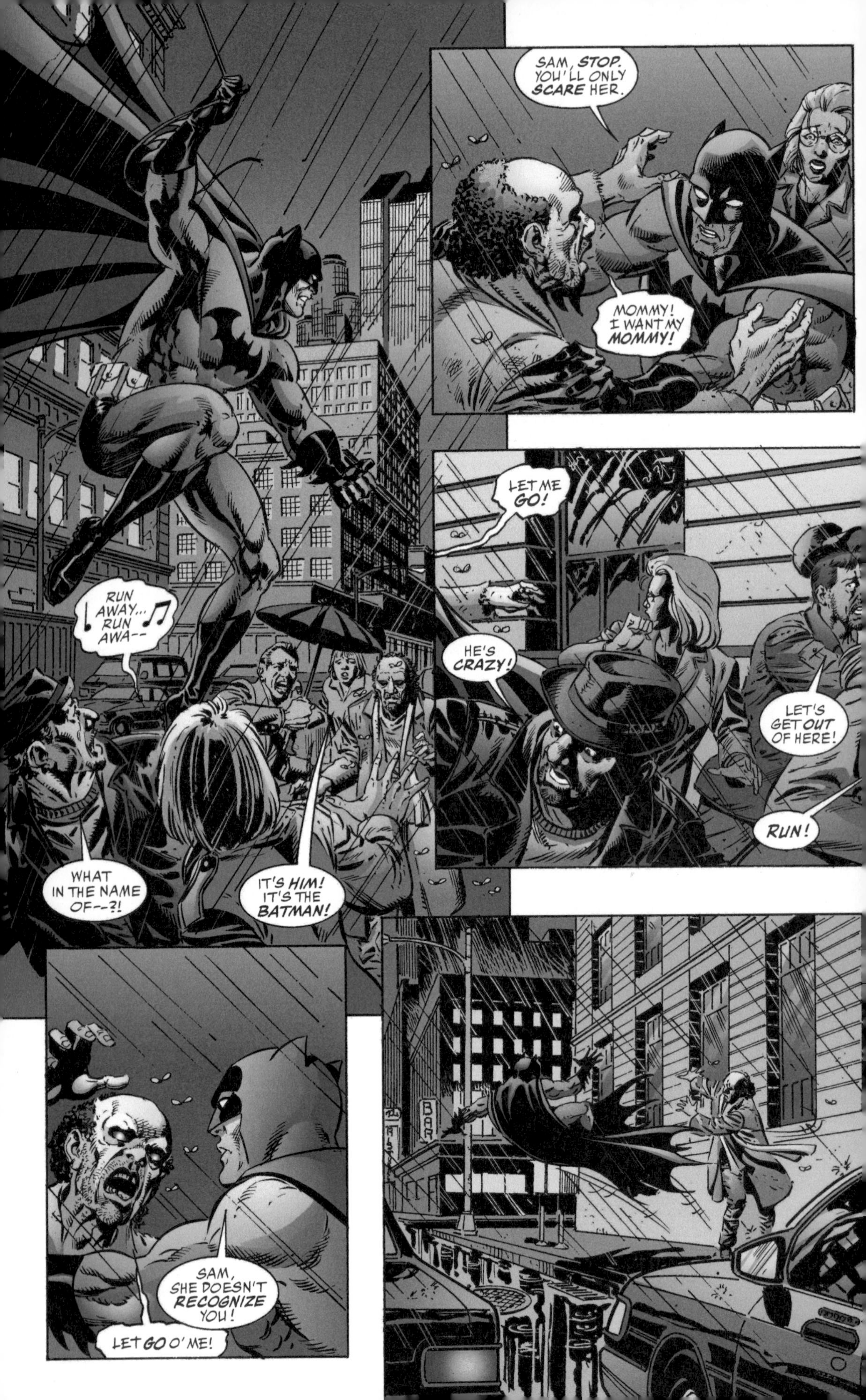
RUN AWAY... RUN AWA--
WHAT IN THE NAME OF--?!
IT'S HIM! IT'S THE BATMAN!
SAM, STOP. YOU'LL ONLY SCARE HER.
MOMMY! I WANT MY MOMMY!
LET ME GO!
HE'S CRAZY!
LET'S GET OUT OF HERE!
RUN!
SAM, SHE DOESN'T RECOGNIZE YOU!
LET GO O' ME!
BAR

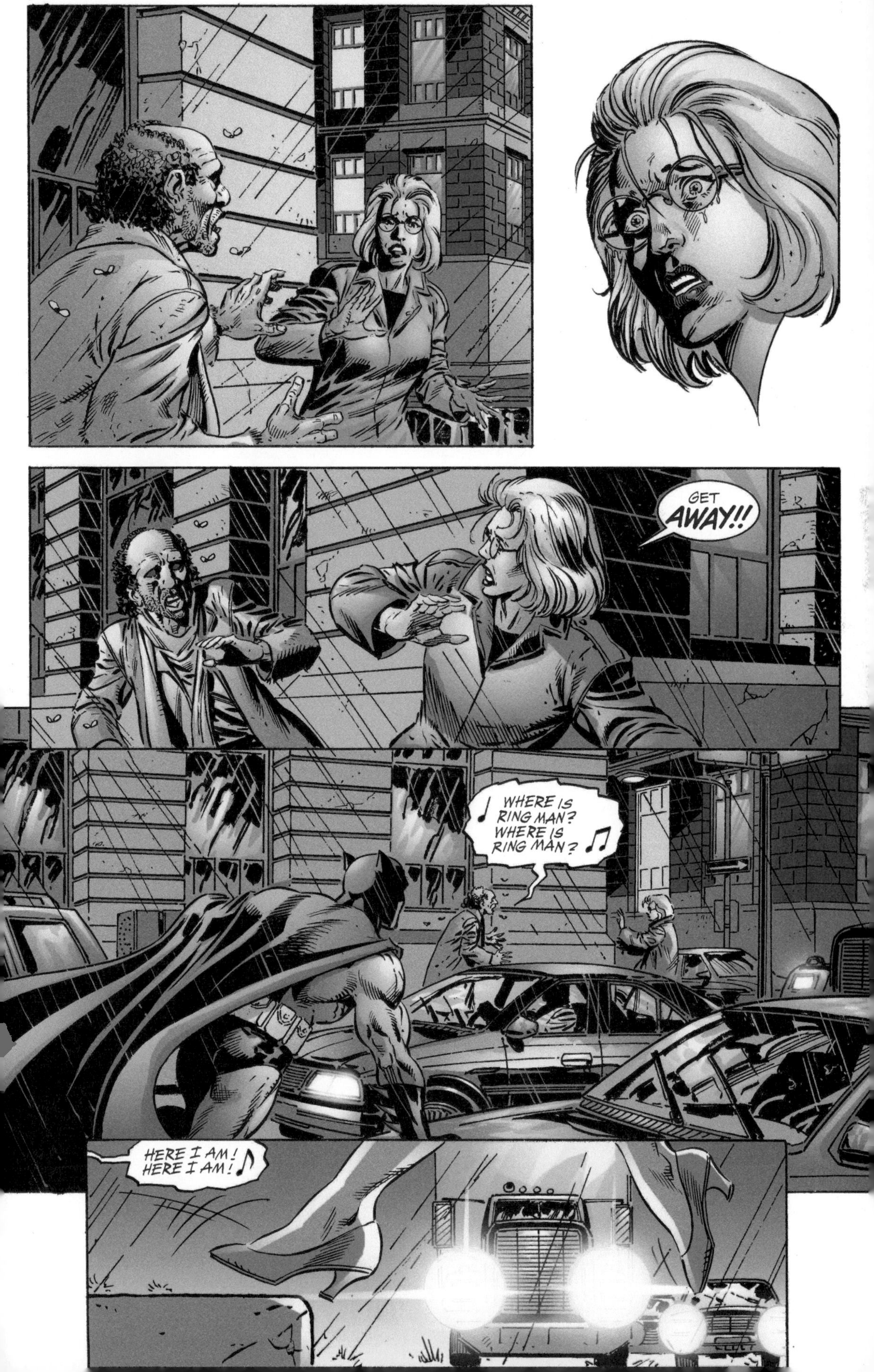
GET AWAY!!
WHERE IS RING MAN? WHERE IS RING MAN?
HERE I AM! HERE I AM!

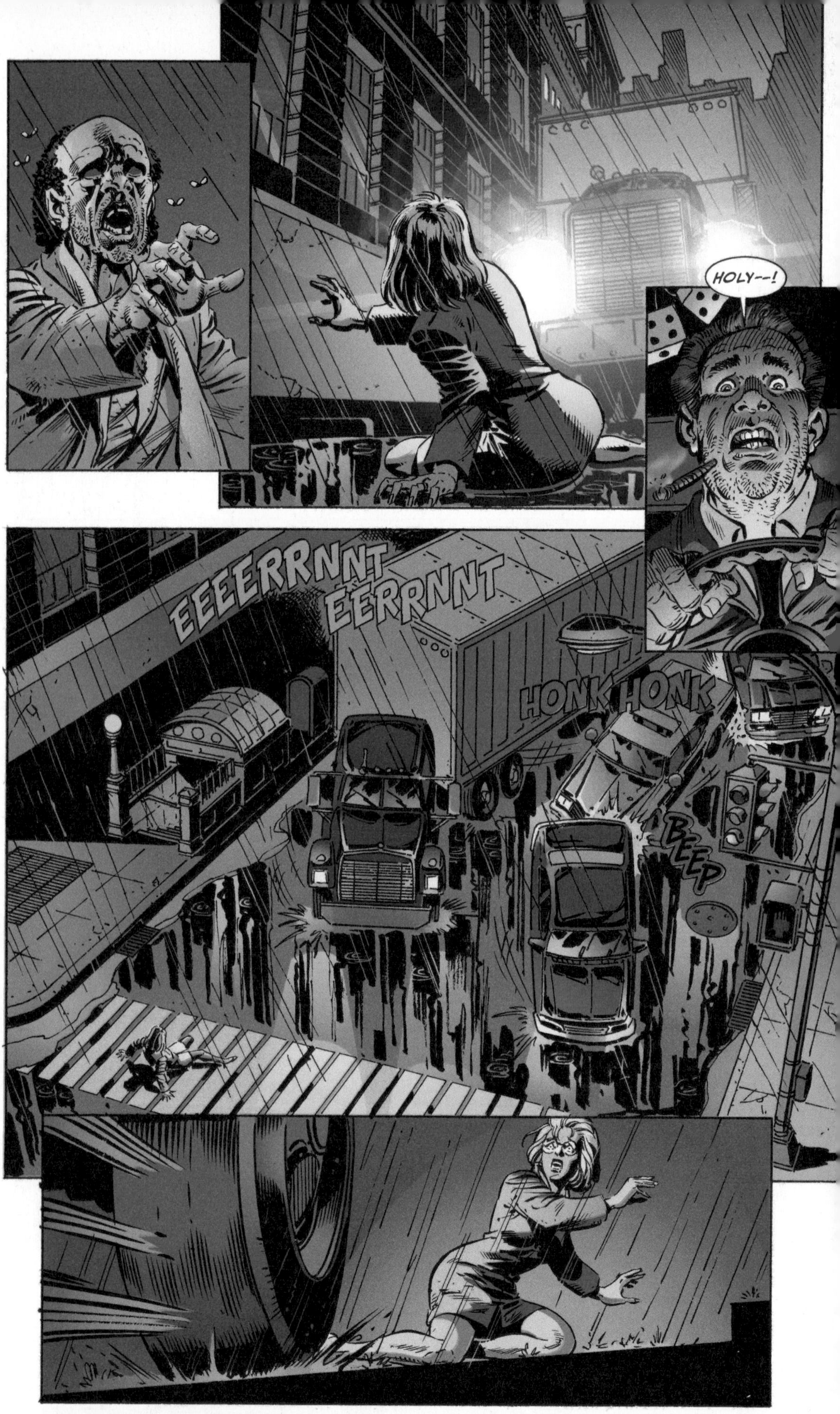
HOLY--!
EEEERRRNNT
EERRNNT
HONK HONK
BEEP

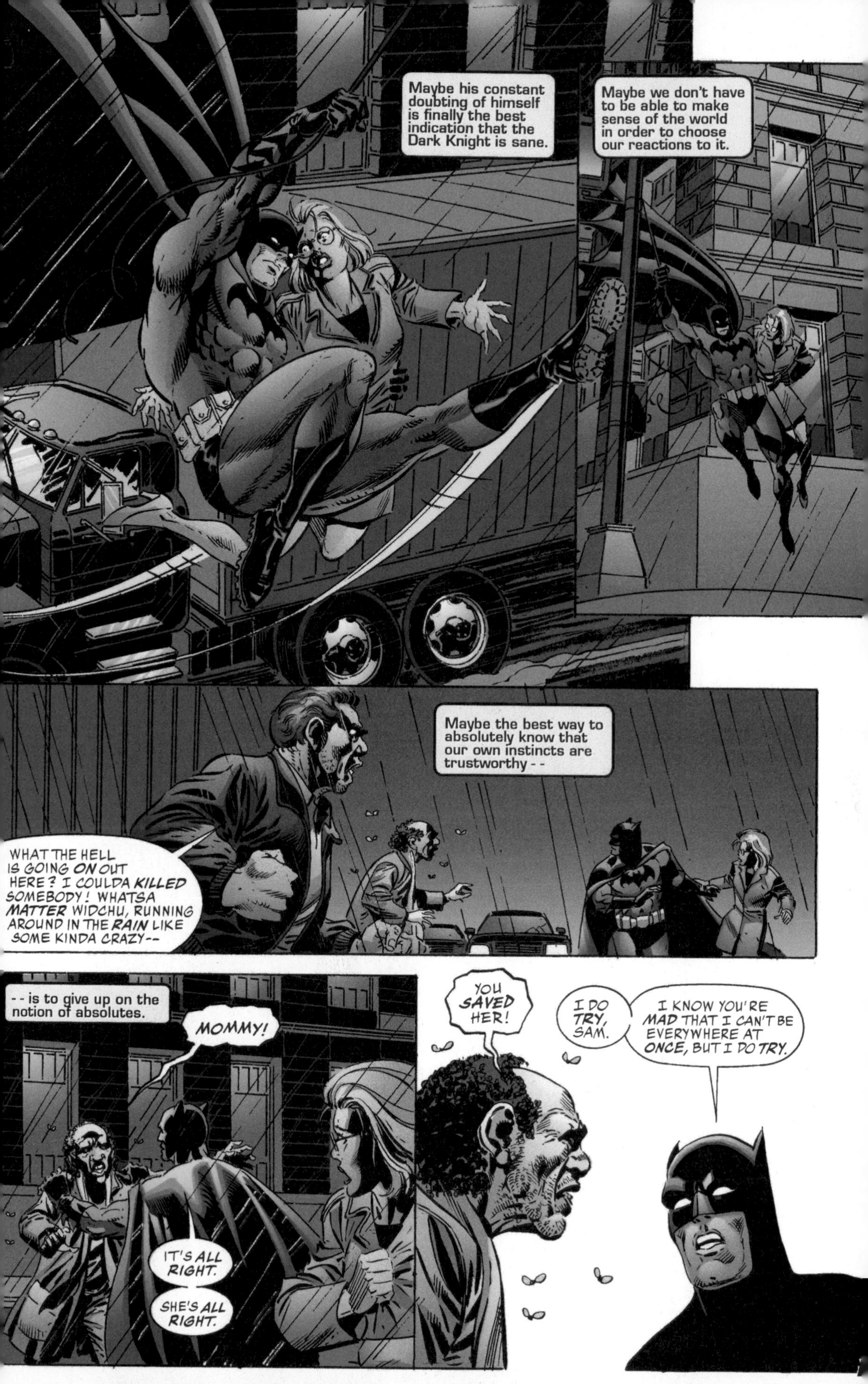
Maybe his constant doubting of himself is finally the best indication that the Dark Knight is sane.
Maybe we don't have to be able to make sense of the world in order to choose our reactions to it.
Maybe the best way to absolutely know that our own instincts are trustworthy - -
WHAT THE HELL IS GOING ON OUT HERE? I COULDA KILLED SOMEBODY! WHATSA MATTER WIDCHU, RUNNING AROUND IN THE RAIN LIKE SOME KINDA CRAZY--
- - is to give up on the notion of absolutes.
MOMMY!
IT'S ALL RIGHT.
SHE'S ALL RIGHT.
YOU SAVED HER!
I DO TRY, SAM.
I KNOW YOU'RE MAD THAT I CAN'T BE EVERYWHERE AT ONCE, BUT I DO TRY.

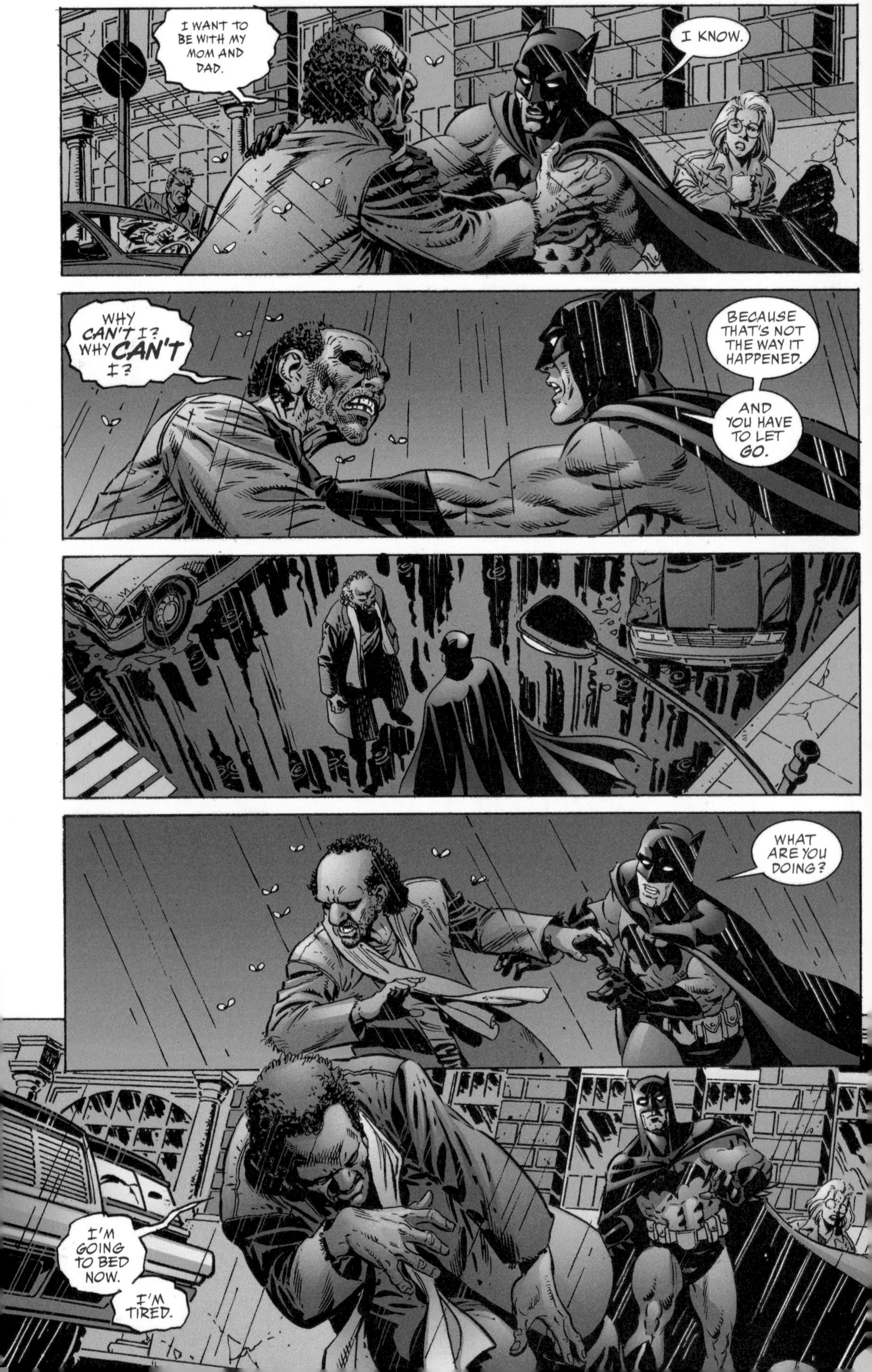
I WANT TO BE WITH MY MOM AND DAD.
I KNOW.
WHY CAN'T I? WHY CAN'T I?
BECAUSE THAT'S NOT THE WAY IT HAPPENED.
AND YOU HAVE TO LET GO.
WHAT ARE YOU DOING?
I'M GOING TO BED NOW.
I'M TIRED.

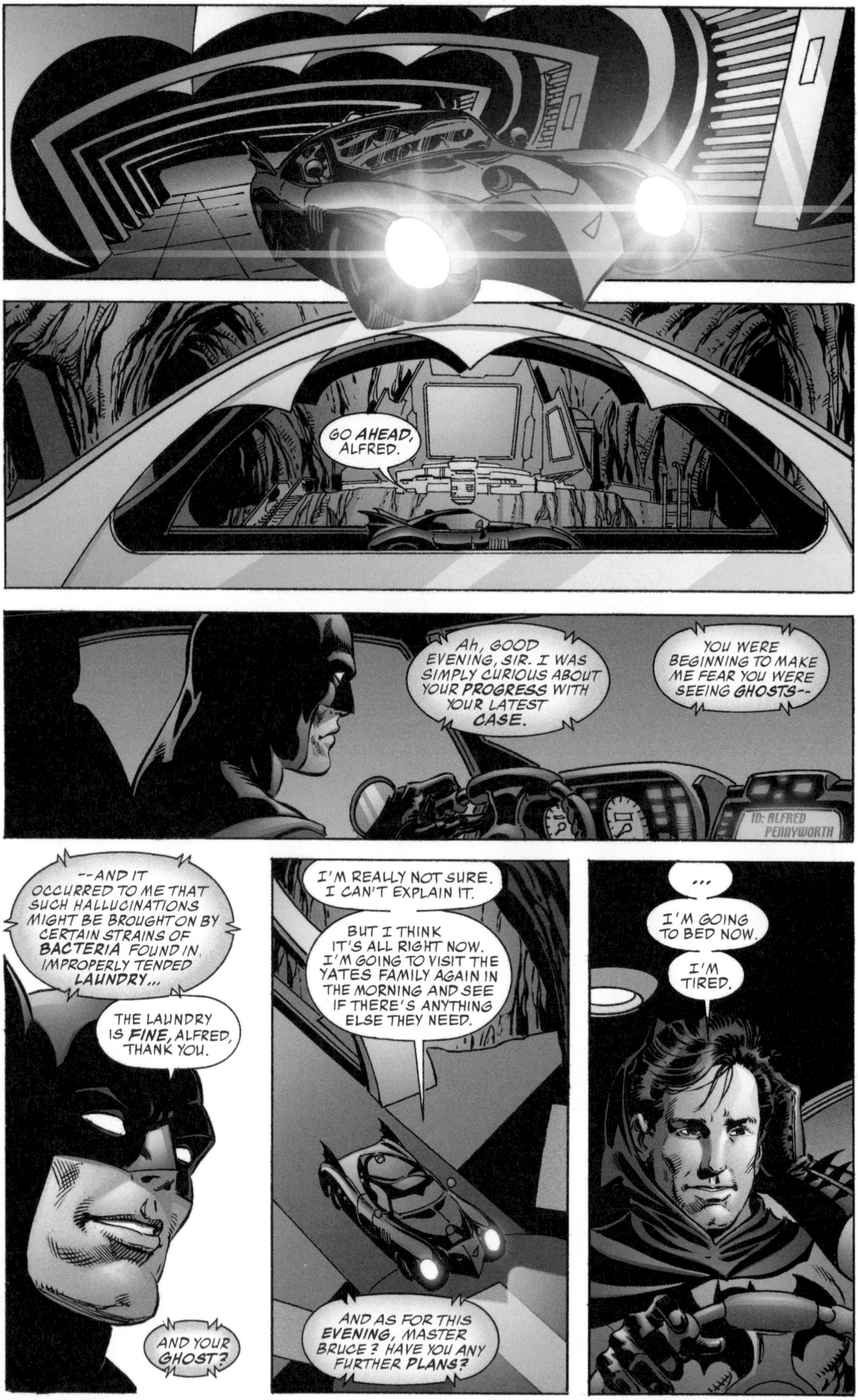
GO AHEAD, ALFRED.
Ah, GOOD EVENING, SIR. I WAS SIMPLY CURIOUS ABOUT YOUR PROGRESS WITH YOUR LATEST CASE.
YOU WERE BEGINNING TO MAKE ME FEAR YOU WERE SEEING GHOSTS--
ID: ALFRED PENNYWORTH
--AND IT OCCURRED TO ME THAT SUCH HALLUCINATIONS MIGHT BE BROUGHT ON BY CERTAIN STRAINS OF BACTERIA FOUND IN IMPROPERLY TENDED LAUNDRY...
THE LAUNDRY IS FINE, ALFRED, THANK YOU.
AND YOUR GHOST?
I'M REALLY NOT SURE. I CAN'T EXPLAIN IT.
BUT I THINK IT'S ALL RIGHT NOW. I'M GOING TO VISIT THE YATES FAMILY AGAIN IN THE MORNING AND SEE IF THERE'S ANYTHING ELSE THEY NEED.
AND AS FOR THIS EVENING, MASTER BRUCE? HAVE YOU ANY FURTHER PLANS?
...
I'M GOING TO BED NOW.
I'M TIRED.

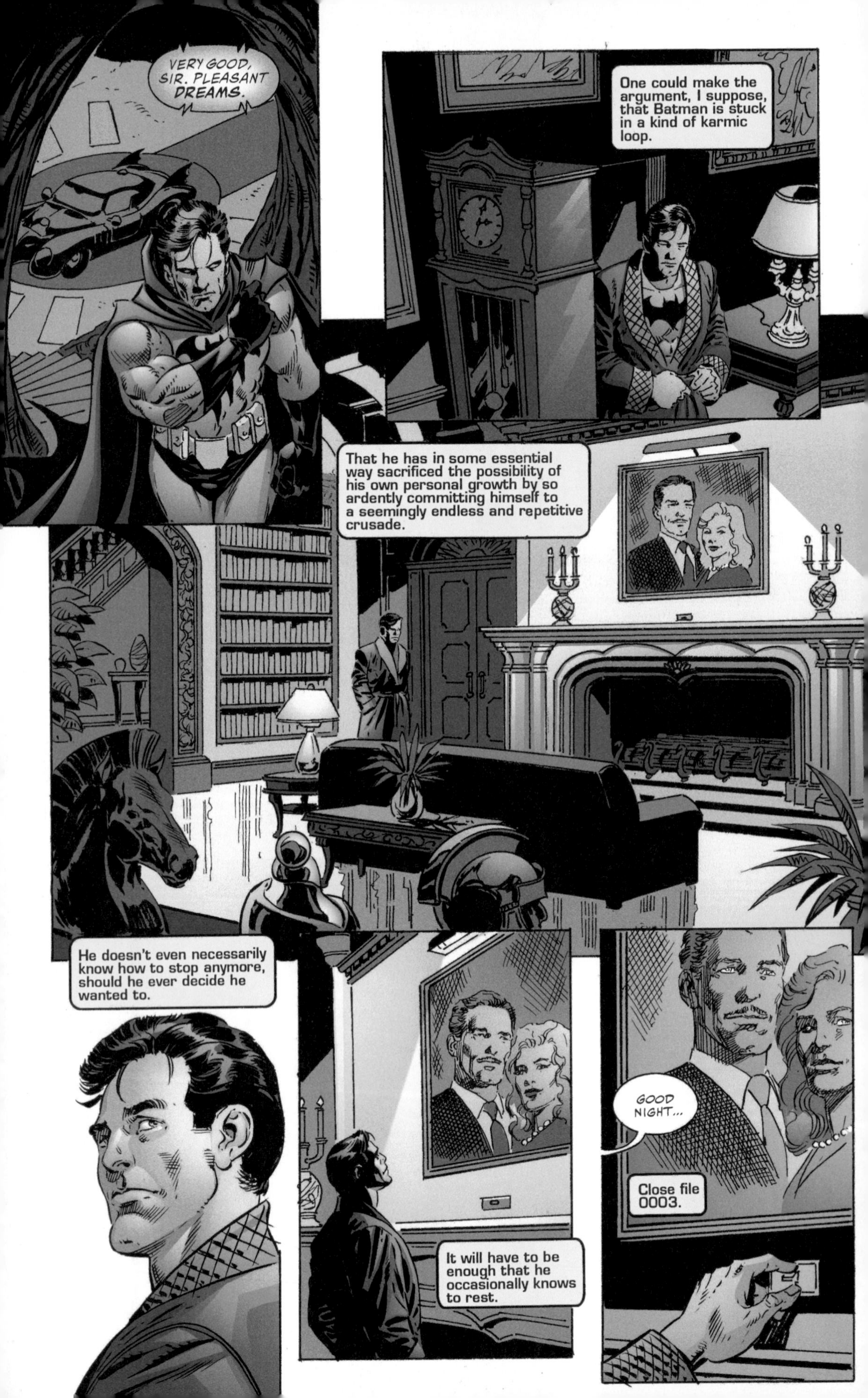
VERY GOOD, SIR. PLEASANT DREAMS.
One could make the argument, I suppose, that Batman is stuck in a kind of karmic loop.
That he has in some essential way sacrificed the possibility of his own personal growth by so ardently committing himself to a seemingly endless and repetitive crusade.
He doesn't even necessarily know how to stop anymore, should he ever decide he wanted to.
It will have to be enough that he occasionally knows to rest.
GOOD NIGHT...
Close file 0003.

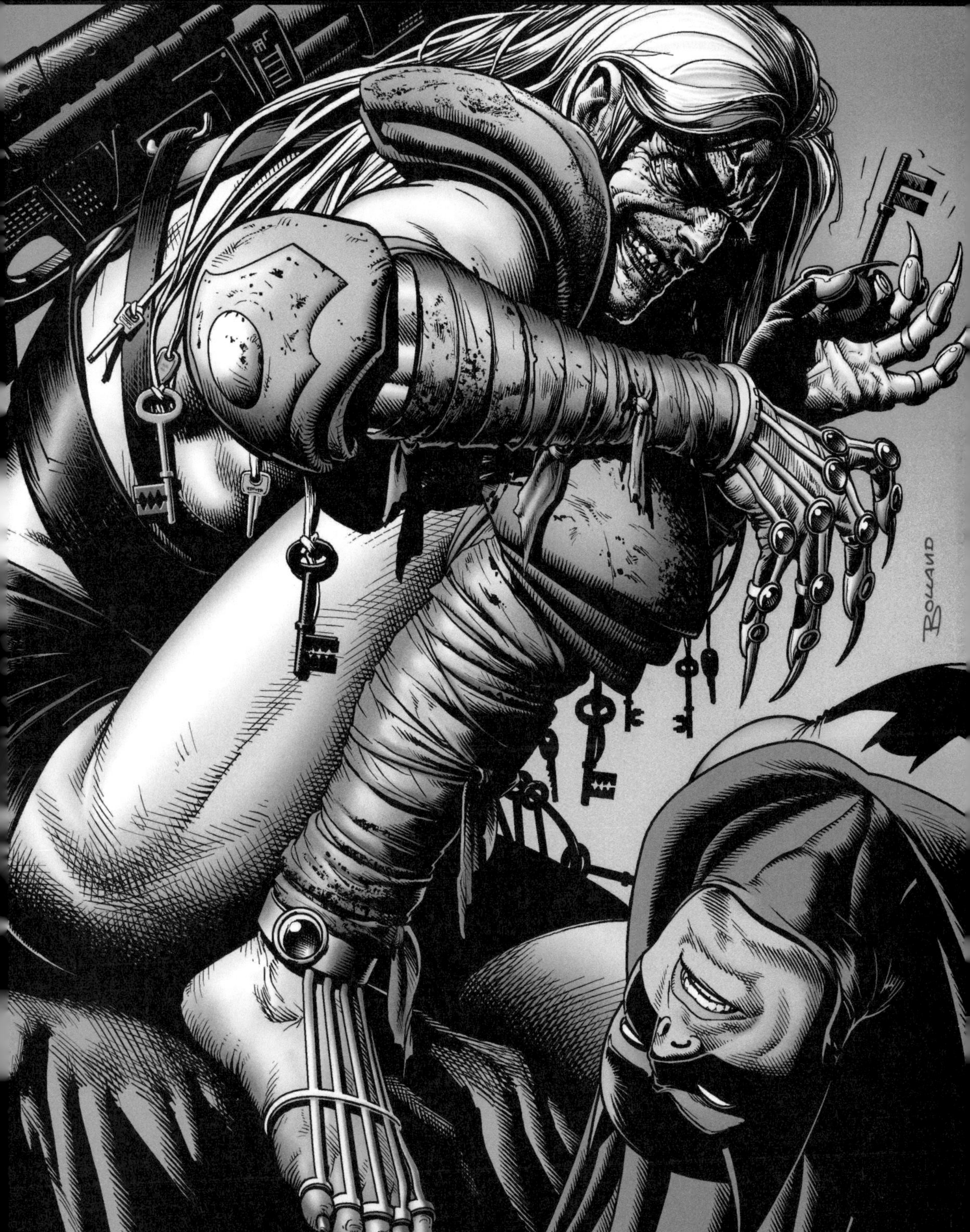
BOLLAND

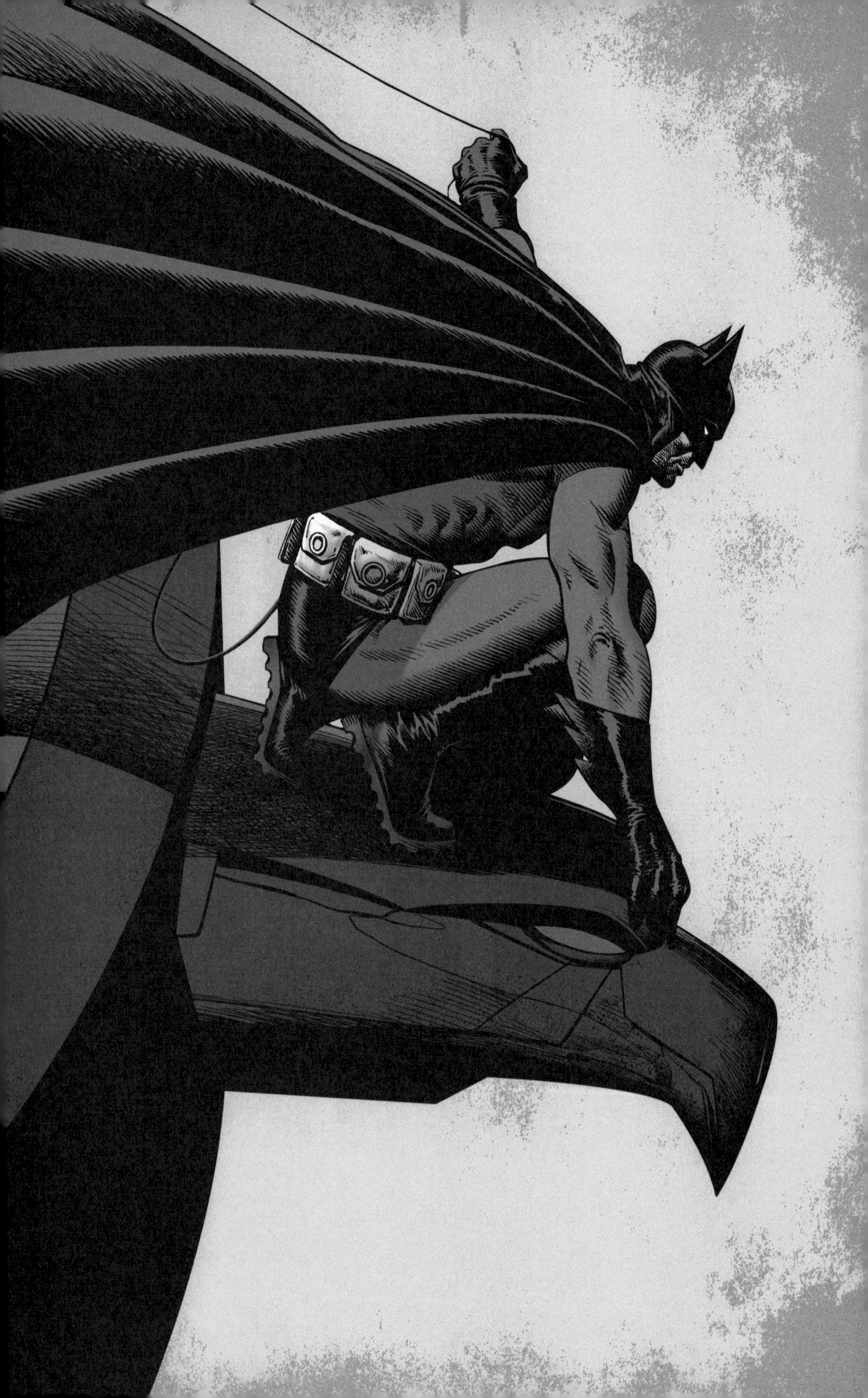

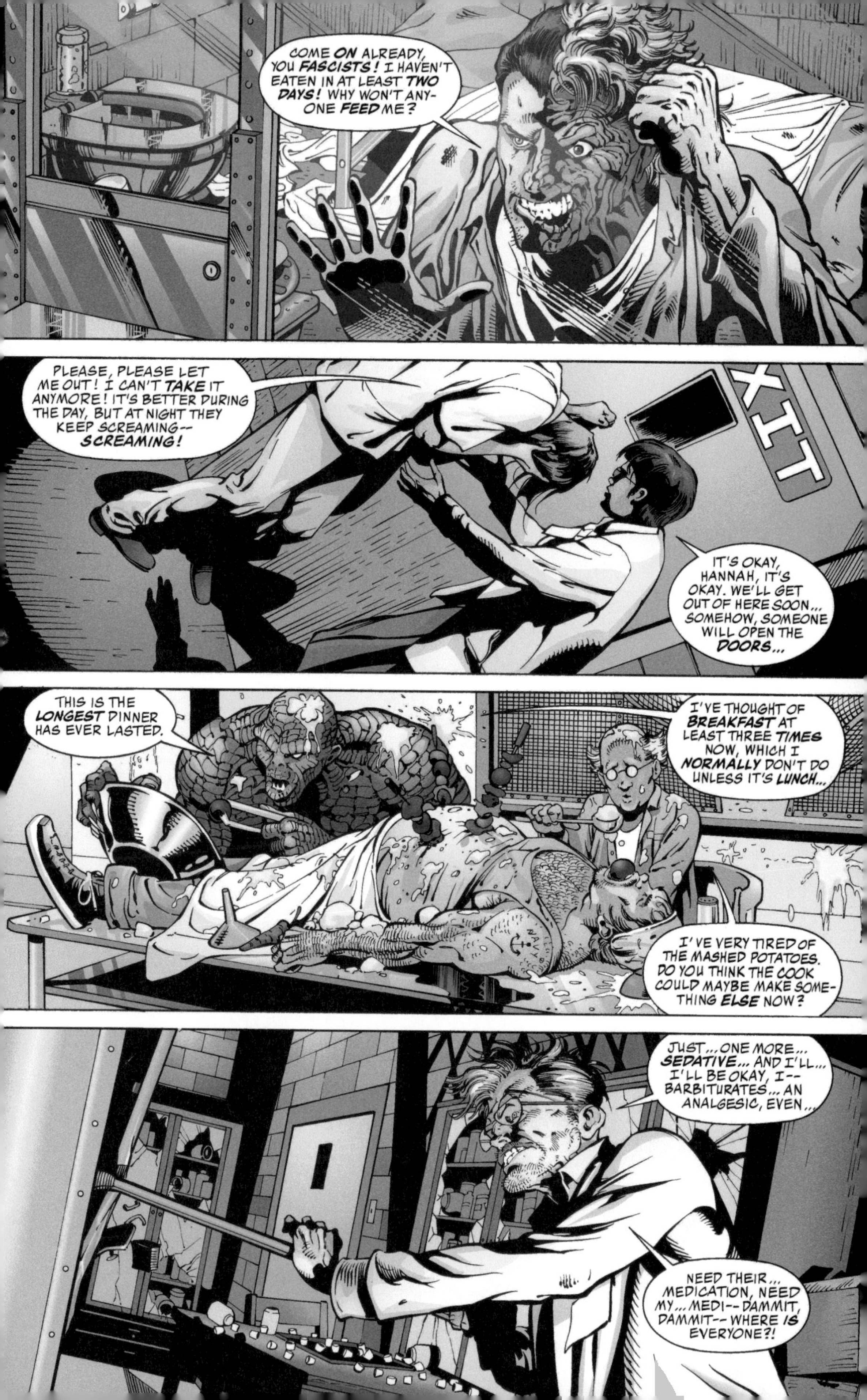
COME ON ALREADY, YOU FASCISTS! I HAVEN'T EATEN IN AT LEAST TWO DAYS! WHY WON'T ANY-ONE FEED ME?
PLEASE, PLEASE LET ME OUT! I CAN'T TAKE IT ANYMORE! IT'S BETTER DURING THE DAY, BUT AT NIGHT THEY KEEP SCREAMING-- SCREAMING!
XIT
IT'S OKAY, HANNAH, IT'S OKAY. WE'LL GET OUT OF HERE SOON... SOMEHOW, SOMEONE WILL OPEN THE DOORS...
THIS IS THE LONGEST DINNER HAS EVER LASTED.
I'VE THOUGHT OF BREAKFAST AT LEAST THREE TIMES NOW, WHICH I NORMALLY DON'T DO UNLESS IT'S LUNCH...
NAVY
I'VE VERY TIRED OF THE MASHED POTATOES. DO YOU THINK THE COOK COULD MAYBE MAKE SOME-THING ELSE NOW?
JUST... ONE MORE... SEDATIVE... AND I'LL... I'LL BE OKAY, I-- BARBITURATES... AN ANALGESIC, EVEN...
NEED THEIR... MEDICATION, NEED MY... MEDI-- DAMMIT, DAMMIT-- WHERE IS EVERYONE?!

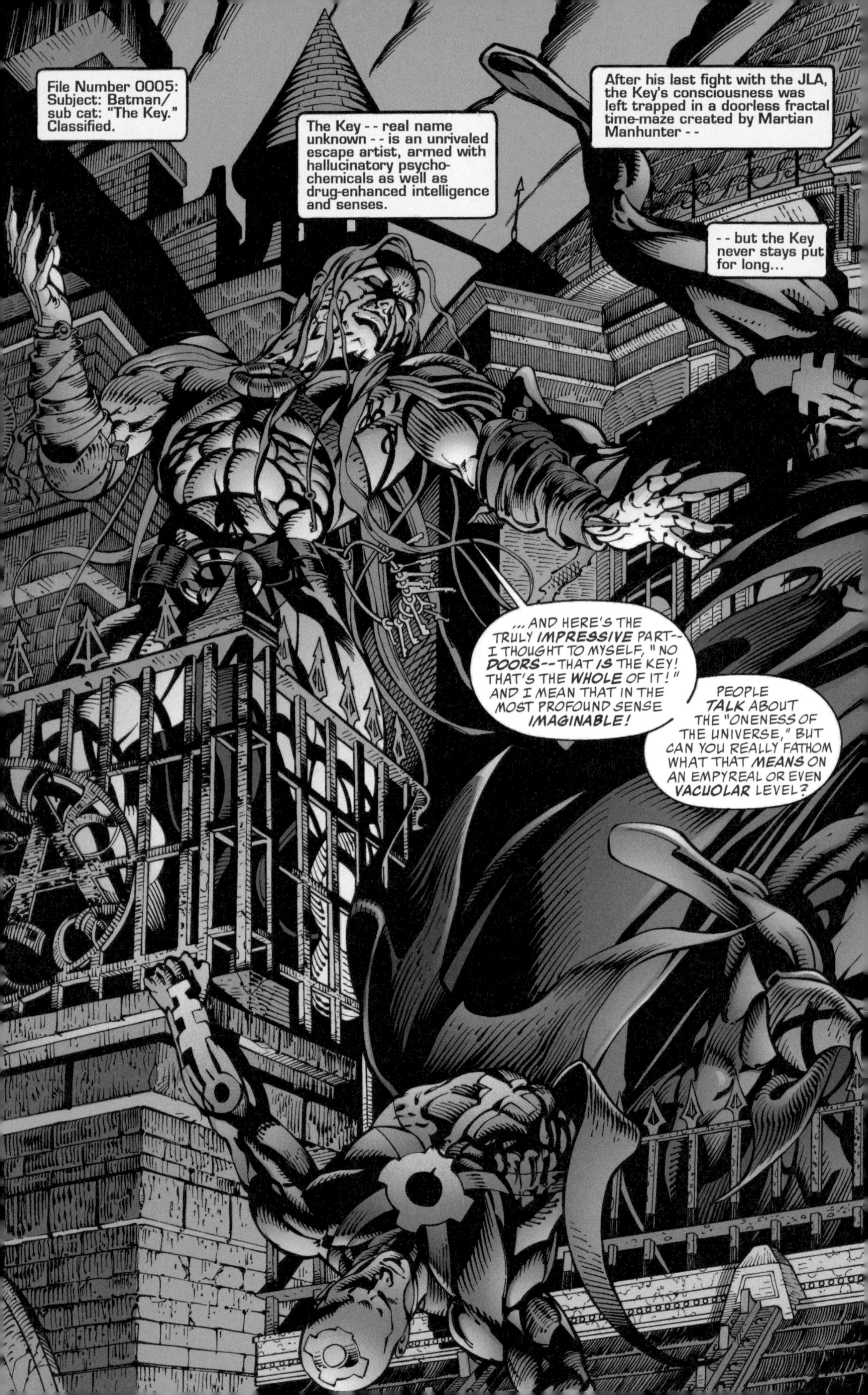
File Number 0005:
Subject: Batman/
sub cat: "The Key."
Classified.
The Key - - real name unknown - - is an unrivaled escape artist, armed with hallucinatory psycho-chemicals as well as drug-enhanced intelligence and senses.
After his last fight with the JLA, the Key's consciousness was left trapped in a doorless fractal time-maze created by Martian Manhunter - -
- - but the Key never stays put for long...
...AND HERE'S THE TRULY IMPRESSIVE PART-- I THOUGHT TO MYSELF, "NO DOORS-- THAT IS THE KEY! THAT'S THE WHOLE OF IT!" AND I MEAN THAT IN THE MOST PROFOUND SENSE IMAGINABLE!
PEOPLE TALK ABOUT THE "ONENESS OF THE UNIVERSE," BUT CAN YOU REALLY FATHOM WHAT THAT MEANS ON AN EMPYREAL OR EVEN VACUOLAR LEVEL?

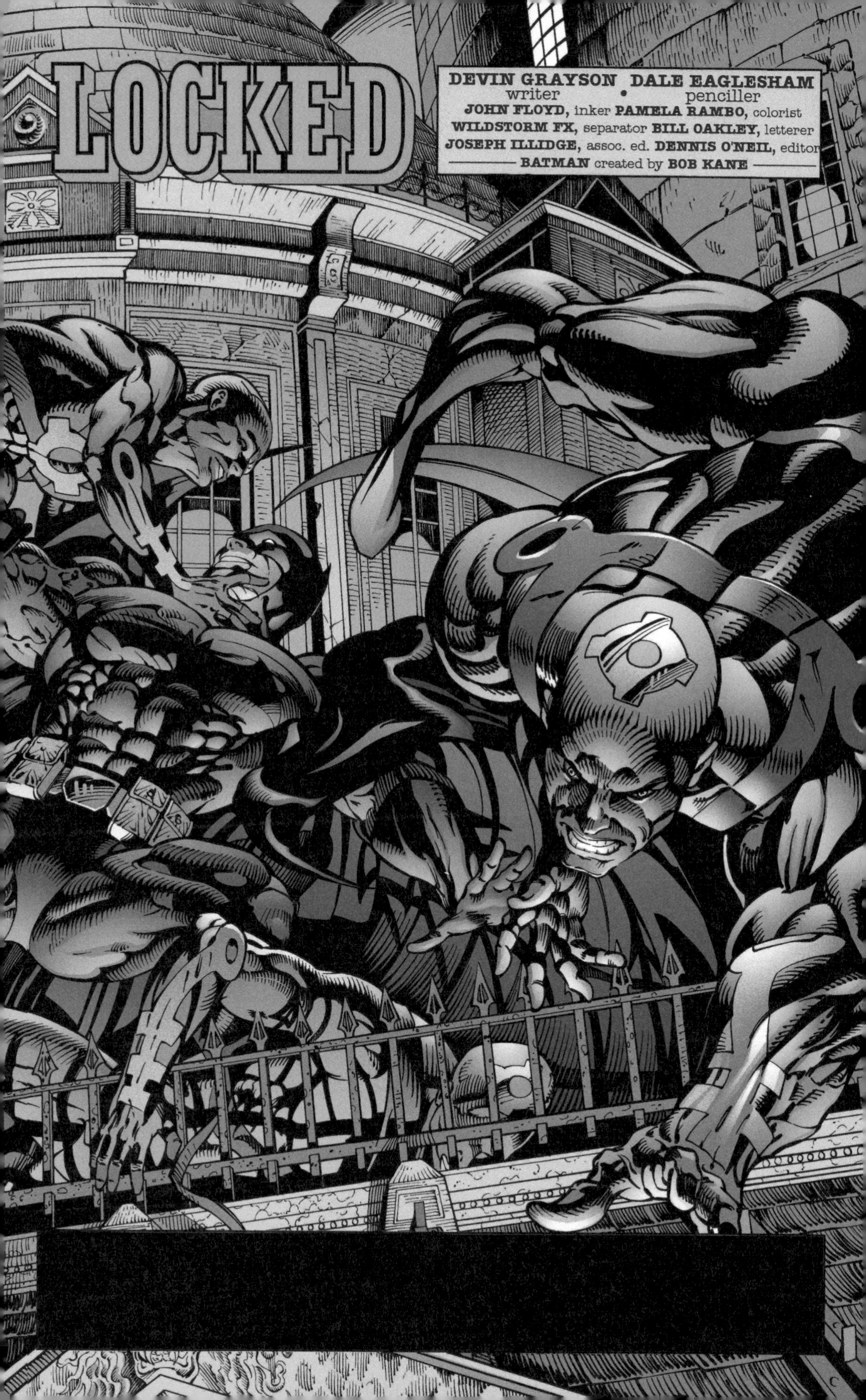
LOCKED
DEVIN GRAYSON writer • DALE EAGLESHAM penciller
JOHN FLOYD, inker PAMELA RAMBO, colorist
WILDSTORM FX, separator BILL OAKLEY, letterer
JOSEPH ILLIDGE, assoc. ed. DENNIS O'NEIL, editor
BATMAN created by BOB KANE

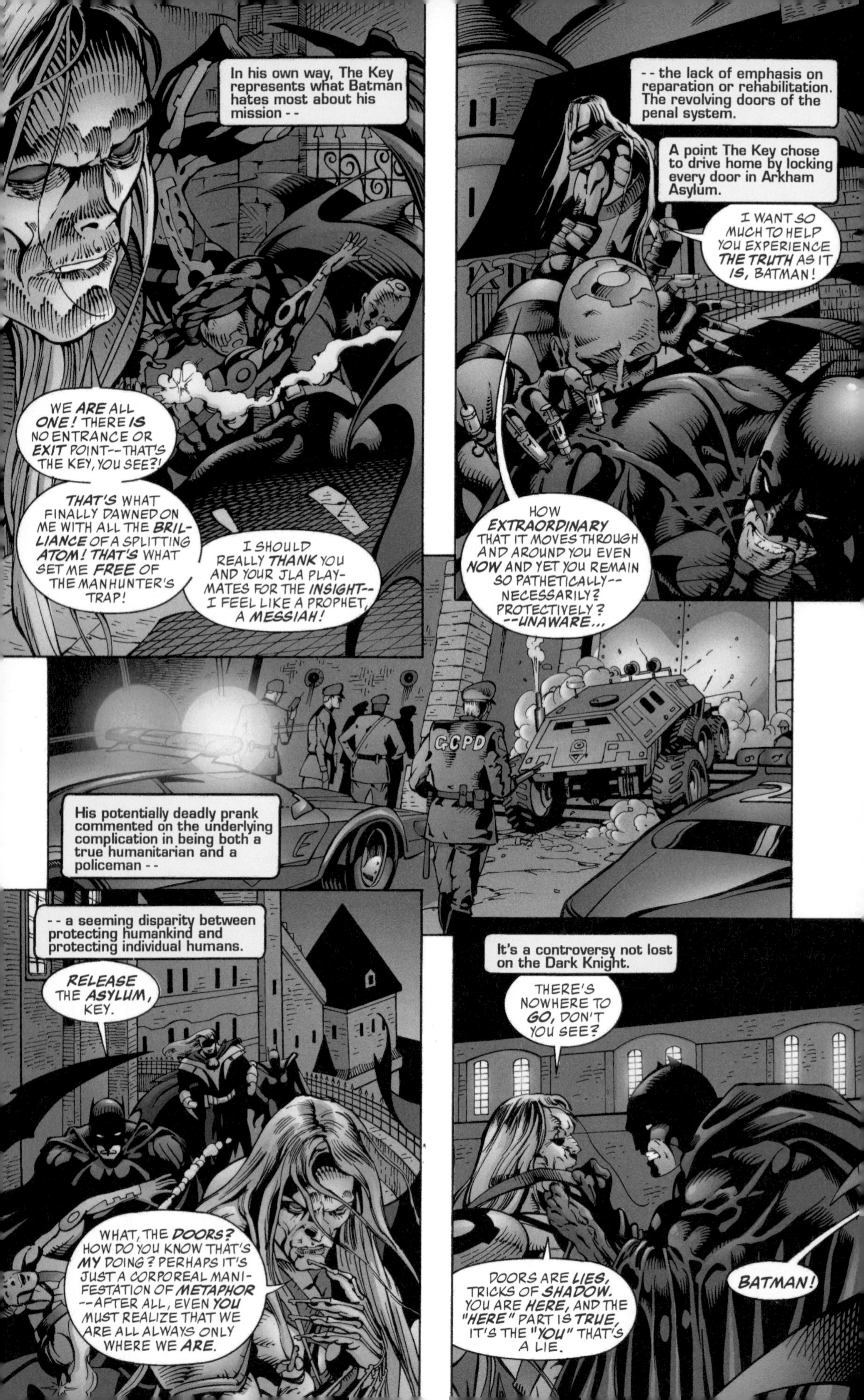
In his own way, The Key represents what Batman hates most about his mission - -
- - the lack of emphasis on reparation or rehabilitation. The revolving doors of the penal system.
A point The Key chose to drive home by locking every door in Arkham Asylum.
I WANT SO MUCH TO HELP YOU EXPERIENCE THE TRUTH AS IT IS, BATMAN!
WE ARE ALL ONE! THERE IS NO ENTRANCE OR EXIT POINT--THAT'S THE KEY, YOU SEE?!
THAT'S WHAT FINALLY DAWNED ON ME WITH ALL THE BRILLIANCE OF A SPLITTING ATOM! THAT'S WHAT SET ME FREE OF THE MANHUNTER'S TRAP!
I SHOULD REALLY THANK YOU AND YOUR JLA PLAYMATES FOR THE INSIGHT-- I FEEL LIKE A PROPHET, A MESSIAH!
HOW EXTRAORDINARY THAT IT MOVES THROUGH AND AROUND YOU EVEN NOW AND YET YOU REMAIN SO PATHETICALLY-- NECESSARILY? PROTECTIVELY? --UNAWARE...
GCPD
His potentially deadly prank commented on the underlying complication in being both a true humanitarian and a policeman - -
- - a seeming disparity between protecting humankind and protecting individual humans.
RELEASE THE ASYLUM, KEY.
WHAT, THE DOORS? HOW DO YOU KNOW THAT'S MY DOING? PERHAPS IT'S JUST A CORPOREAL MANIFESTATION OF METAPHOR --AFTER ALL, EVEN YOU MUST REALIZE THAT WE ARE ALL ALWAYS ONLY WHERE WE ARE.
It's a controversy not lost on the Dark Knight.
THERE'S NOWHERE TO GO, DON'T YOU SEE?
DOORS ARE LIES, TRICKS OF SHADOW. YOU ARE HERE, AND THE "HERE" PART IS TRUE, IT'S THE "YOU" THAT'S A LIE.
BATMAN!

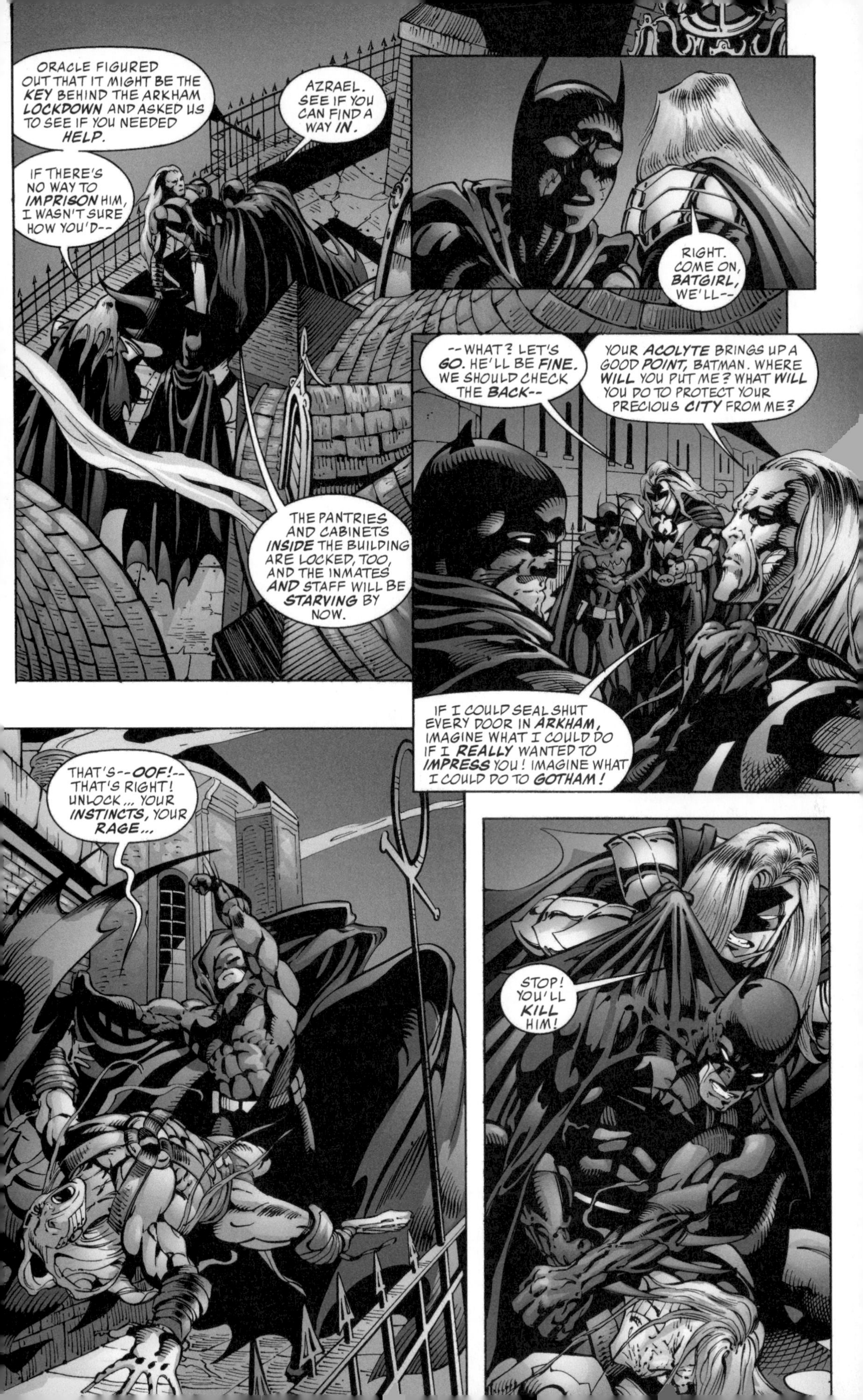
ORACLE FIGURED OUT THAT IT MIGHT BE THE KEY BEHIND THE ARKHAM LOCKDOWN AND ASKED US TO SEE IF YOU NEEDED HELP.
IF THERE'S NO WAY TO IMPRISON HIM, I WASN'T SURE HOW YOU'D--
AZRAEL. SEE IF YOU CAN FIND A WAY IN.
THE PANTRIES AND CABINETS INSIDE THE BUILDING ARE LOCKED, TOO, AND THE INMATES AND STAFF WILL BE STARVING BY NOW.
RIGHT. COME ON, BATGIRL, WE'LL--
--WHAT? LET'S GO. HE'LL BE FINE. WE SHOULD CHECK THE BACK--
YOUR ACOLYTE BRINGS UP A GOOD POINT, BATMAN. WHERE WILL YOU PUT ME? WHAT WILL YOU DO TO PROTECT YOUR PRECIOUS CITY FROM ME?
IF I COULD SEAL SHUT EVERY DOOR IN ARKHAM, IMAGINE WHAT I COULD DO IF I REALLY WANTED TO IMPRESS YOU! IMAGINE WHAT I COULD DO TO GOTHAM!
THAT'S--OOF!--THAT'S RIGHT! UNLOCK... YOUR INSTINCTS, YOUR RAGE...
STOP! YOU'LL KILL HIM!

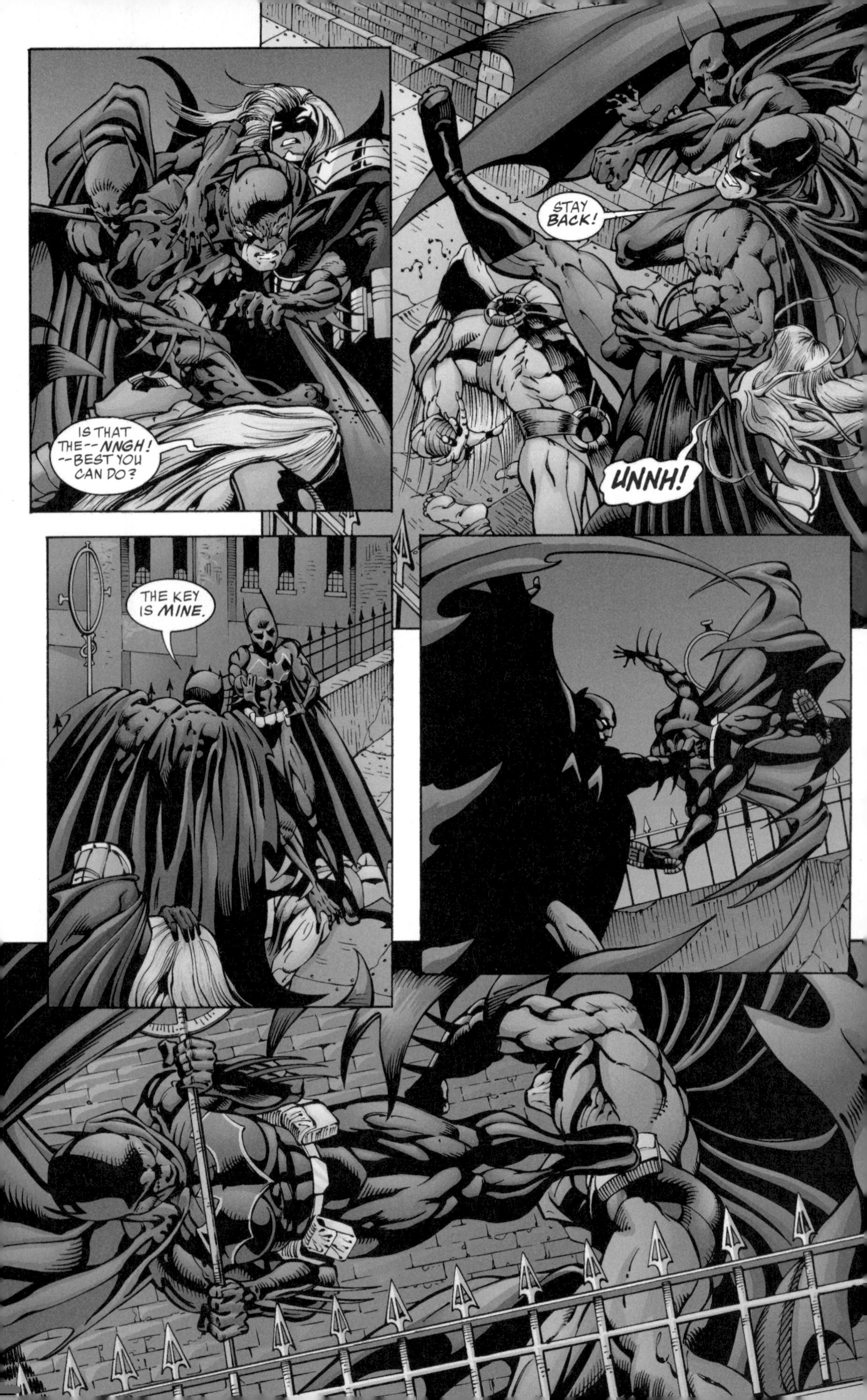
IS THAT THE--NNGH! --BEST YOU CAN DO?
STAY BACK!
UNNH!
THE KEY IS MINE.

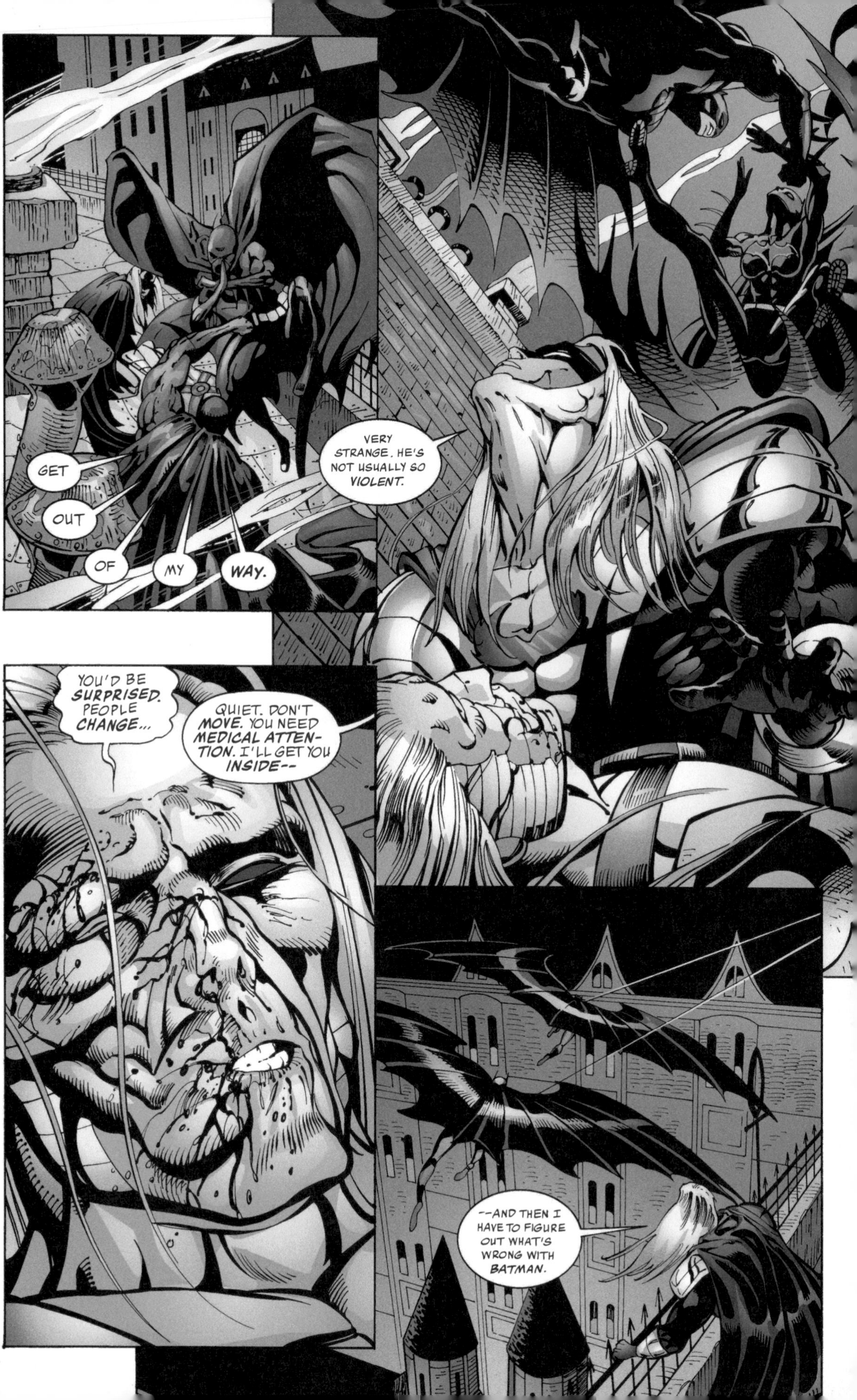
GET
OUT
OF
MY
WAY.
VERY STRANGE. HE'S NOT USUALLY SO VIOLENT.
YOU'D BE SURPRISED. PEOPLE CHANGE...
QUIET. DON'T MOVE. YOU NEED MEDICAL ATTENTION. I'LL GET YOU INSIDE--
--AND THEN I HAVE TO FIGURE OUT WHAT'S WRONG WITH BATMAN.

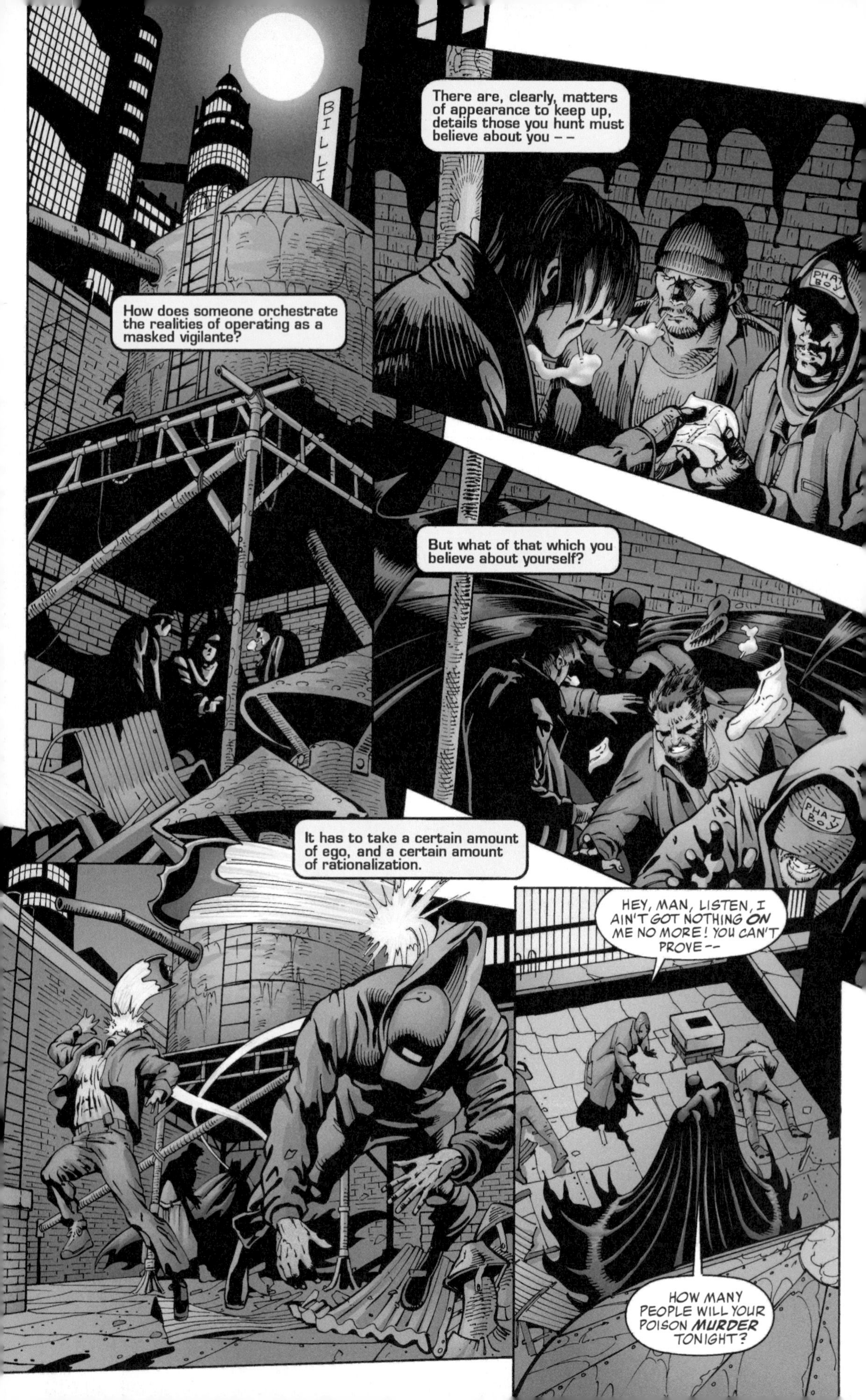
BILLIA
How does someone orchestrate the realities of operating as a masked vigilante?
There are, clearly, matters of appearance to keep up, details those you hunt must believe about you --
PHAT BOY
But what of that which you believe about yourself?
PHAT BOY
It has to take a certain amount of ego, and a certain amount of rationalization.
HEY, MAN, LISTEN, I AIN'T GOT NOTHING ON ME NO MORE! YOU CAN'T PROVE--
HOW MANY PEOPLE WILL YOUR POISON MURDER TONIGHT?

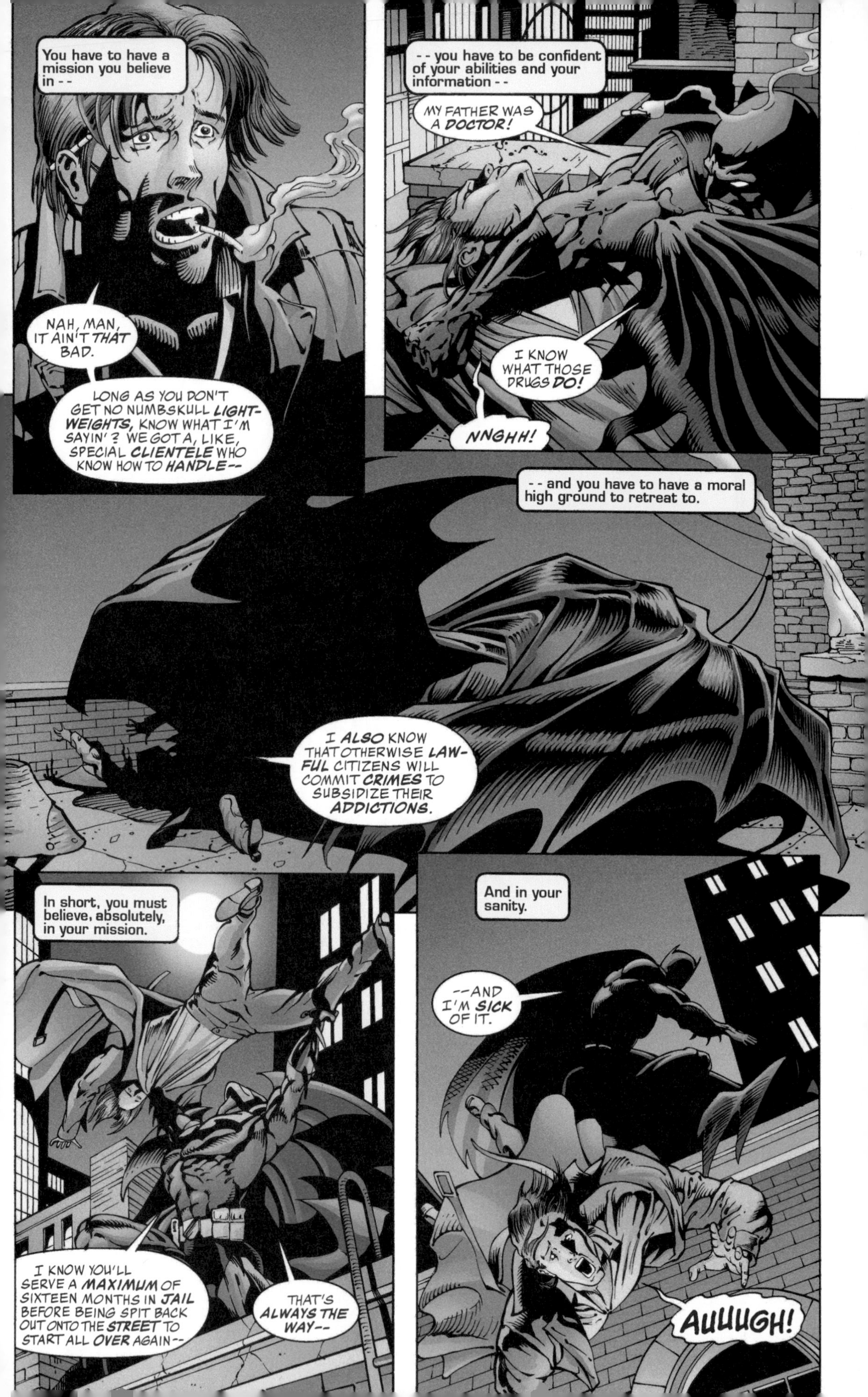
You have to have a mission you believe in - -
NAH, MAN, IT AIN'T THAT BAD.
LONG AS YOU DON'T GET NO NUMBSKULL LIGHT-WEIGHTS, KNOW WHAT I'M SAYIN'? WE GOT A, LIKE, SPECIAL CLIENTELE WHO KNOW HOW TO HANDLE--
- - you have to be confident of your abilities and your information - -
MY FATHER WAS A DOCTOR!
I KNOW WHAT THOSE DRUGS DO!
NNGHH!
- - and you have to have a moral high ground to retreat to.
I ALSO KNOW THAT OTHERWISE LAW-FUL CITIZENS WILL COMMIT CRIMES TO SUBSIDIZE THEIR ADDICTIONS.
In short, you must believe, absolutely, in your mission.
I KNOW YOU'LL SERVE A MAXIMUM OF SIXTEEN MONTHS IN JAIL BEFORE BEING SPIT BACK OUT ONTO THE STREET TO START ALL OVER AGAIN--
THAT'S ALWAYS THE WAY--
And in your sanity.
--AND I'M SICK OF IT.
AUUUGH!

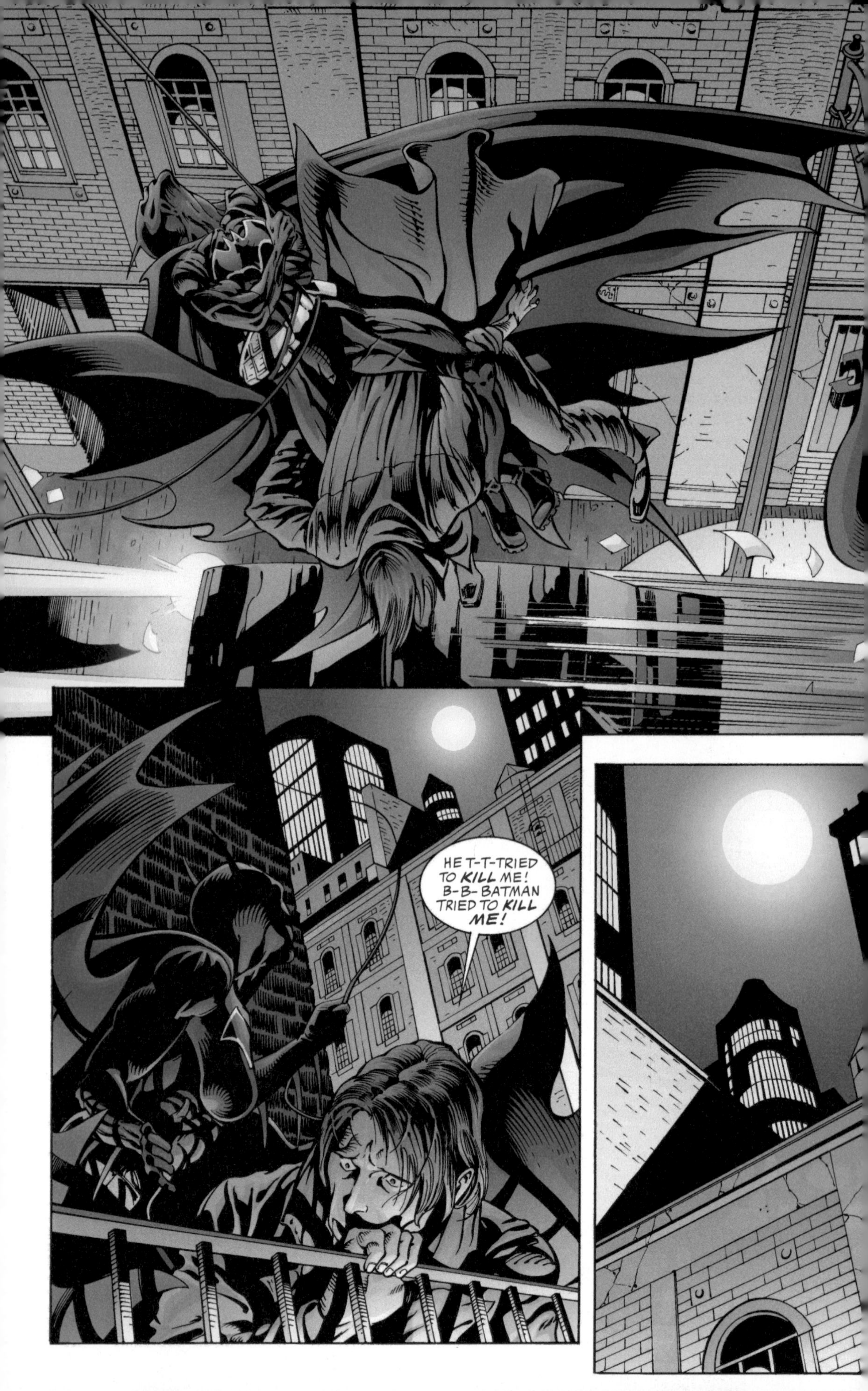
HE T-T-TRIED TO KILL ME! B-B- BATMAN TRIED TO KILL ME!

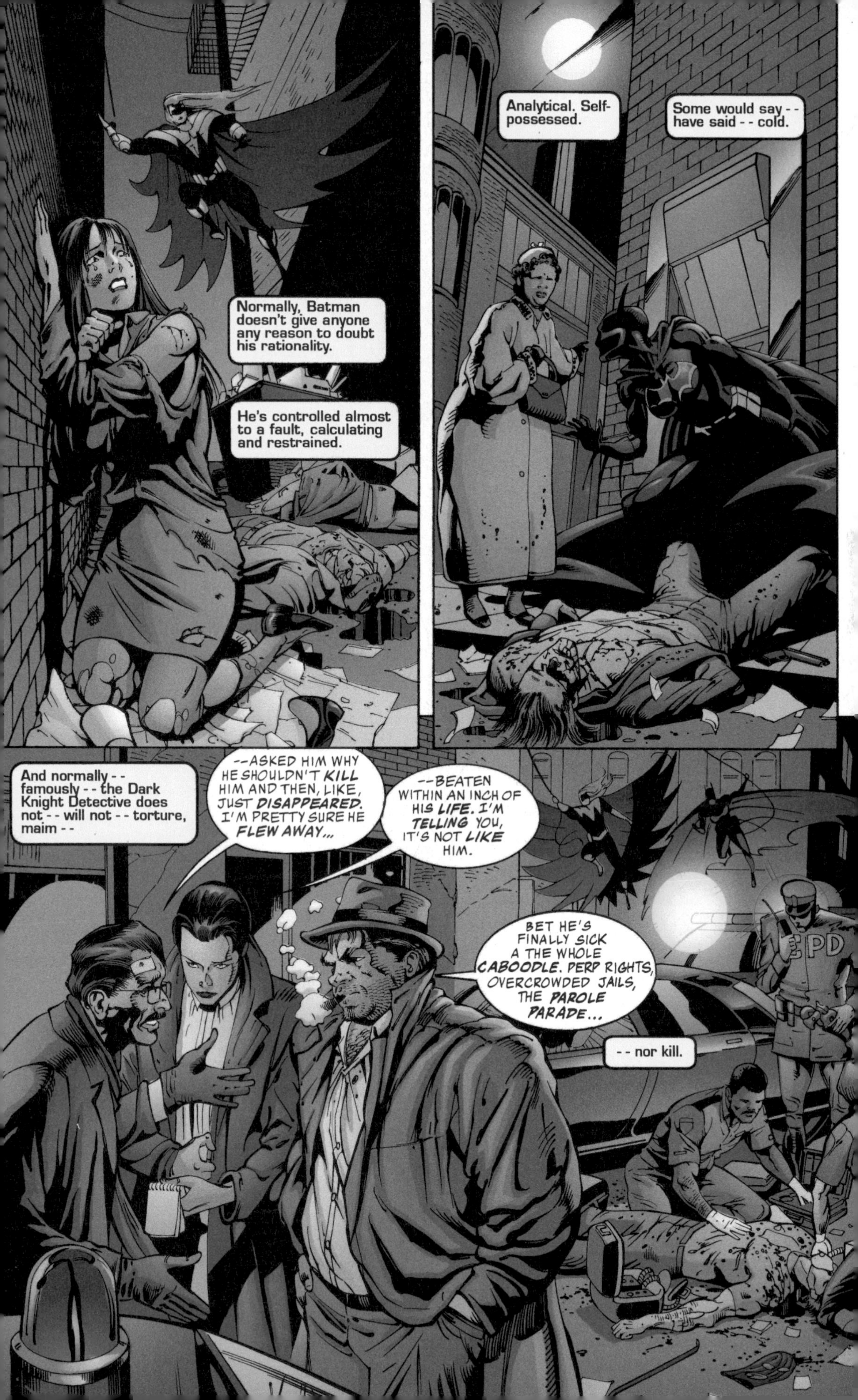
Normally, Batman doesn't give anyone any reason to doubt his rationality.
He's controlled almost to a fault, calculating and restrained.
Analytical. Self-possessed.
Some would say - - have said - - cold.
And normally - - famously - - the Dark Knight Detective does not - - will not - - torture, maim - -
--ASKED HIM WHY HE SHOULDN'T KILL HIM AND THEN, LIKE, JUST DISAPPEARED. I'M PRETTY SURE HE FLEW AWAY...
--BEATEN WITHIN AN INCH OF HIS LIFE. I'M TELLING YOU, IT'S NOT LIKE HIM.
BET HE'S FINALLY SICK A THE WHOLE CABOODLE. PERP RIGHTS, OVERCROWDED JAILS, THE PAROLE PARADE...
- - nor kill.
GCPD

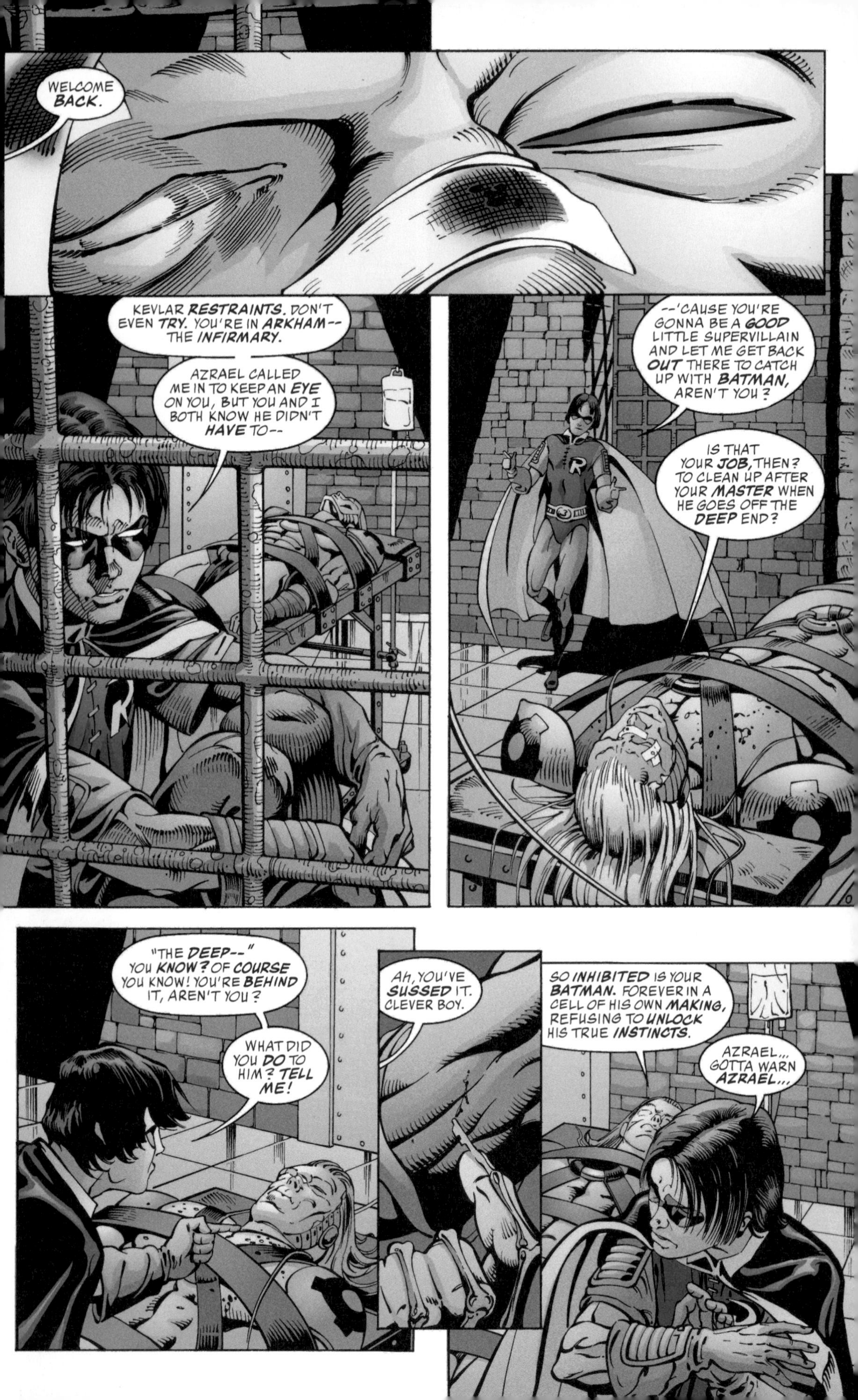
WELCOME BACK.
KEVLAR RESTRAINTS. DON'T EVEN TRY. YOU'RE IN ARKHAM-- THE INFIRMARY.
AZRAEL CALLED ME IN TO KEEP AN EYE ON YOU, BUT YOU AND I BOTH KNOW HE DIDN'T HAVE TO--
--'CAUSE YOU'RE GONNA BE A GOOD LITTLE SUPERVILLAIN AND LET ME GET BACK OUT THERE TO CATCH UP WITH BATMAN, AREN'T YOU?
IS THAT YOUR JOB, THEN? TO CLEAN UP AFTER YOUR MASTER WHEN HE GOES OFF THE DEEP END?
"THE DEEP--" YOU KNOW? OF COURSE YOU KNOW! YOU'RE BEHIND IT, AREN'T YOU?
WHAT DID YOU DO TO HIM? TELL ME!
Ah, YOU'VE SUSSED IT. CLEVER BOY.
SO INHIBITED IS YOUR BATMAN. FOREVER IN A CELL OF HIS OWN MAKING, REFUSING TO UNLOCK HIS TRUE INSTINCTS.
AZRAEL... GOTTA WARN AZRAEL...

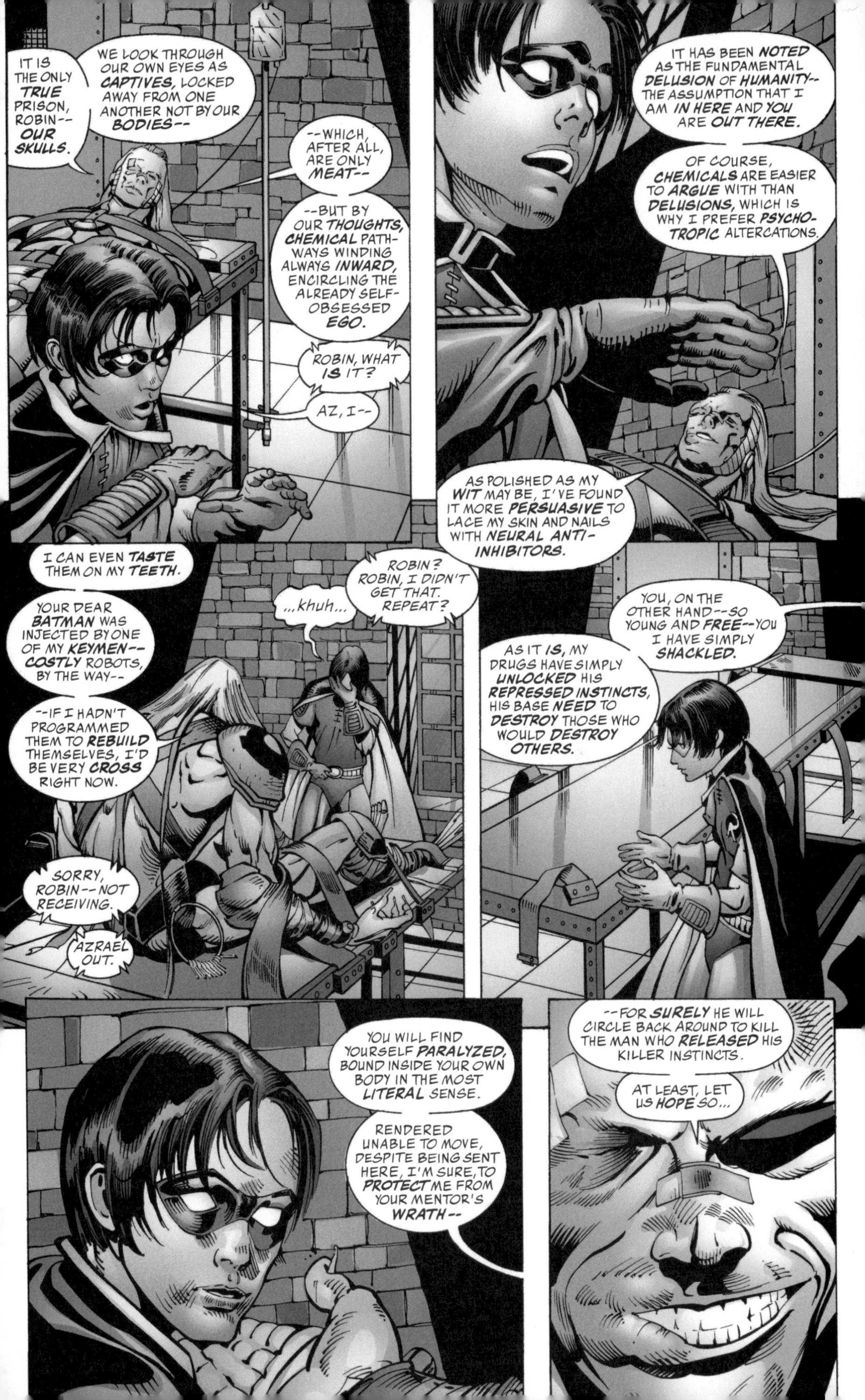
IT IS THE ONLY TRUE PRISON, ROBIN-- OUR SKULLS.
WE LOOK THROUGH OUR OWN EYES AS CAPTIVES, LOCKED AWAY FROM ONE ANOTHER NOT BY OUR BODIES--
--WHICH, AFTER ALL, ARE ONLY MEAT--
--BUT BY OUR THOUGHTS, CHEMICAL PATHWAYS WINDING ALWAYS INWARD, ENCIRCLING THE ALREADY SELF-OBSESSED EGO.
ROBIN, WHAT IS IT?
AZ, I--
IT HAS BEEN NOTED AS THE FUNDAMENTAL DELUSION OF HUMANITY-- THE ASSUMPTION THAT I AM IN HERE AND YOU ARE OUT THERE.
OF COURSE, CHEMICALS ARE EASIER TO ARGUE WITH THAN DELUSIONS, WHICH IS WHY I PREFER PSYCHOTROPIC ALTERCATIONS.
AS POLISHED AS MY WIT MAY BE, I'VE FOUND IT MORE PERSUASIVE TO LACE MY SKIN AND NAILS WITH NEURAL ANTI-INHIBITORS.
I CAN EVEN TASTE THEM ON MY TEETH.
YOUR DEAR BATMAN WAS INJECTED BY ONE OF MY KEYMEN-- COSTLY ROBOTS, BY THE WAY--
--IF I HADN'T PROGRAMMED THEM TO REBUILD THEMSELVES, I'D BE VERY CROSS RIGHT NOW.
...khuh...
ROBIN? ROBIN, I DIDN'T GET THAT. REPEAT?
SORRY, ROBIN-- NOT RECEIVING.
AZRAEL OUT.
AS IT IS, MY DRUGS HAVE SIMPLY UNLOCKED HIS REPRESSED INSTINCTS, HIS BASE NEED TO DESTROY THOSE WHO WOULD DESTROY OTHERS.
YOU, ON THE OTHER HAND--SO YOUNG AND FREE--YOU I HAVE SIMPLY SHACKLED.
YOU WILL FIND YOURSELF PARALYZED, BOUND INSIDE YOUR OWN BODY IN THE MOST LITERAL SENSE.
RENDERED UNABLE TO MOVE, DESPITE BEING SENT HERE, I'M SURE, TO PROTECT ME FROM YOUR MENTOR'S WRATH--
--FOR SURELY HE WILL CIRCLE BACK AROUND TO KILL THE MAN WHO RELEASED HIS KILLER INSTINCTS.
AT LEAST, LET US HOPE SO...

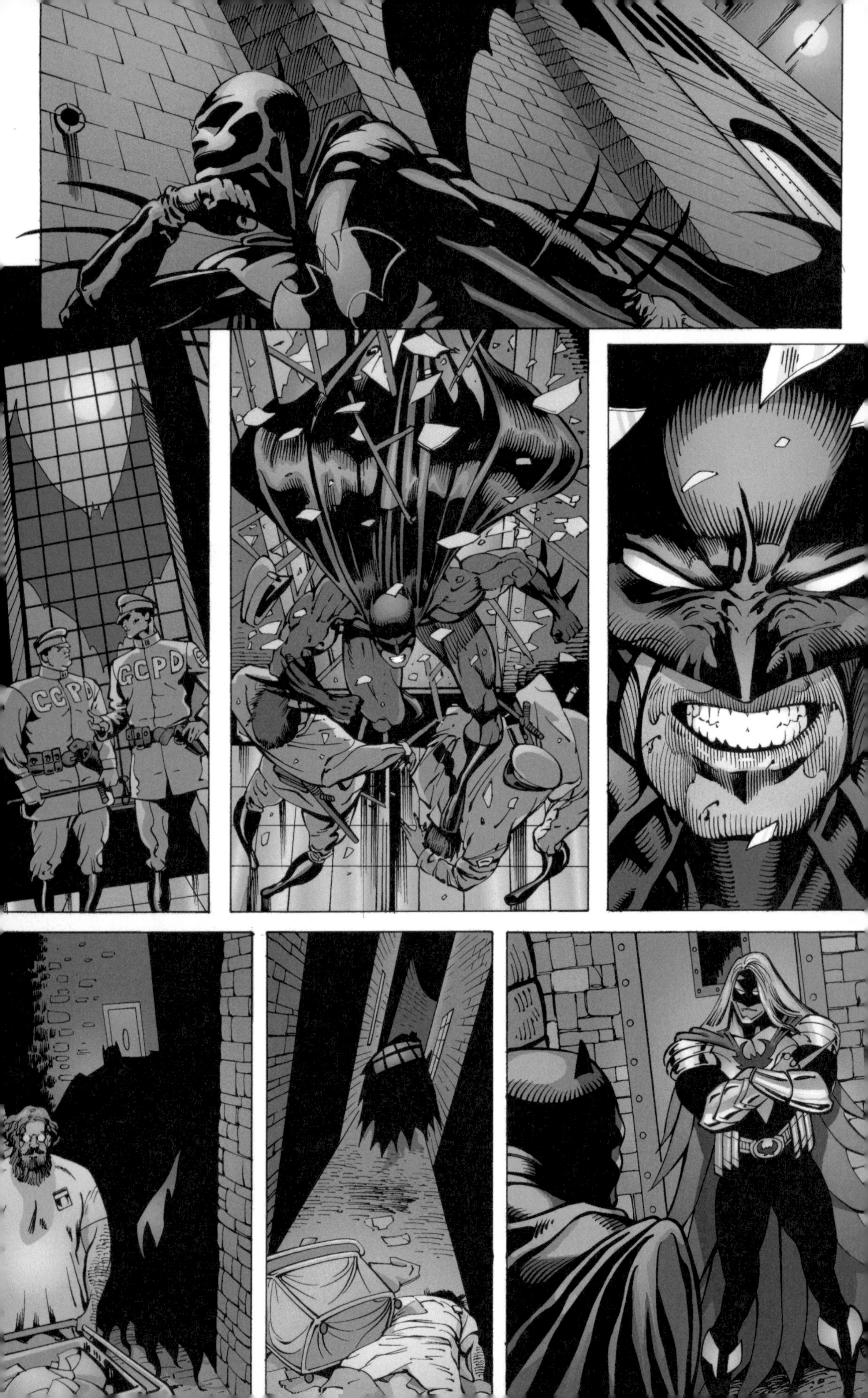
GCPD
GCPD

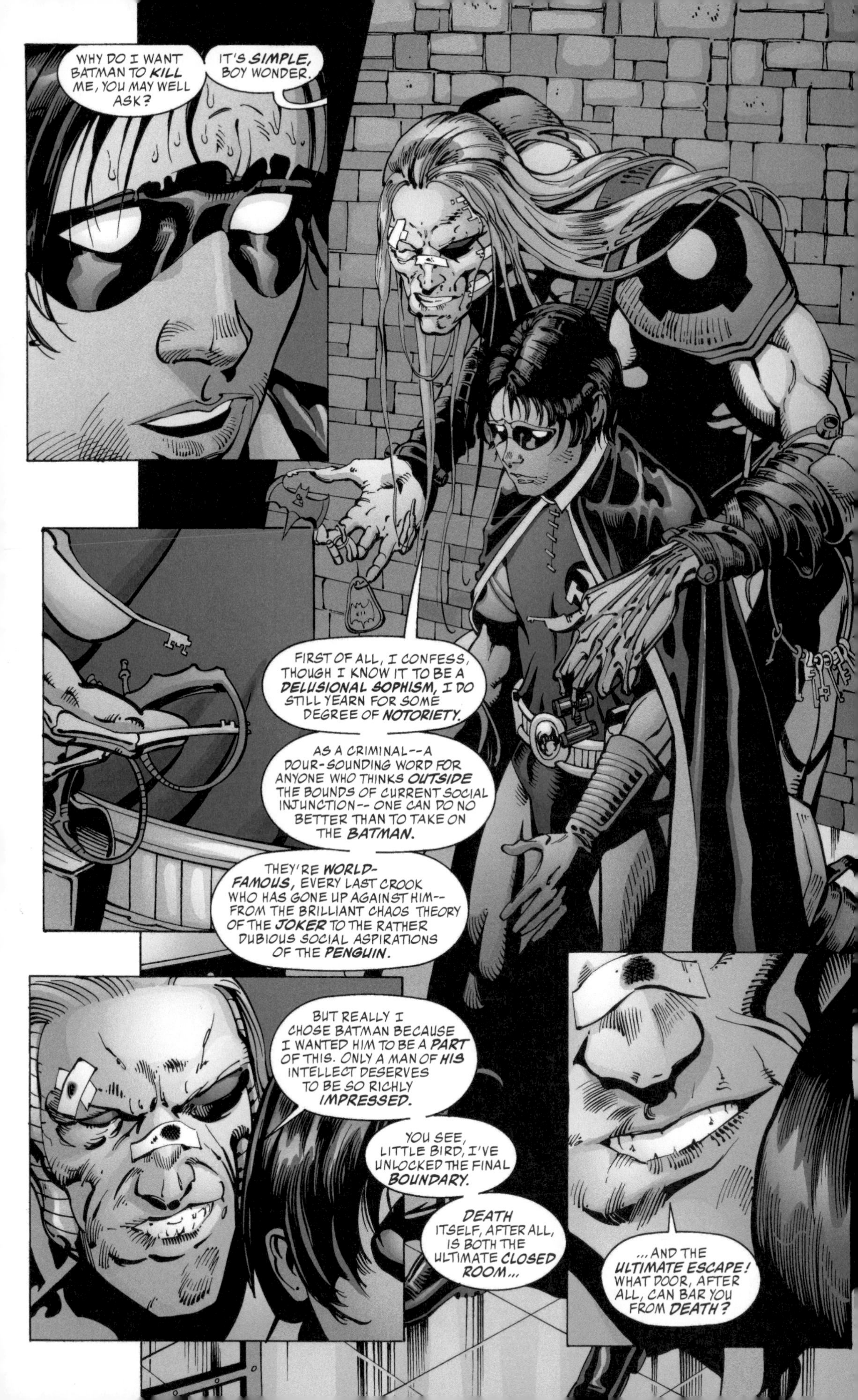

WHY DO I WANT BATMAN TO KILL ME, YOU MAY WELL ASK?
IT'S SIMPLE, BOY WONDER.
FIRST OF ALL, I CONFESS, THOUGH I KNOW IT TO BE A DELUSIONAL SOPHISM, I DO STILL YEARN FOR SOME DEGREE OF NOTORIETY.
AS A CRIMINAL--A DOUR-SOUNDING WORD FOR ANYONE WHO THINKS OUTSIDE THE BOUNDS OF CURRENT SOCIAL INJUNCTION-- ONE CAN DO NO BETTER THAN TO TAKE ON THE BATMAN.
THEY'RE WORLD-FAMOUS, EVERY LAST CROOK WHO HAS GONE UP AGAINST HIM--FROM THE BRILLIANT CHAOS THEORY OF THE JOKER TO THE RATHER DUBIOUS SOCIAL ASPIRATIONS OF THE PENGUIN.
BUT REALLY I CHOSE BATMAN BECAUSE I WANTED HIM TO BE A PART OF THIS. ONLY A MAN OF HIS INTELLECT DESERVES TO BE SO RICHLY IMPRESSED.
YOU SEE, LITTLE BIRD, I'VE UNLOCKED THE FINAL BOUNDARY.
DEATH ITSELF, AFTER ALL, IS BOTH THE ULTIMATE CLOSED ROOM...
...AND THE ULTIMATE ESCAPE! WHAT DOOR, AFTER ALL, CAN BAR YOU FROM DEATH?

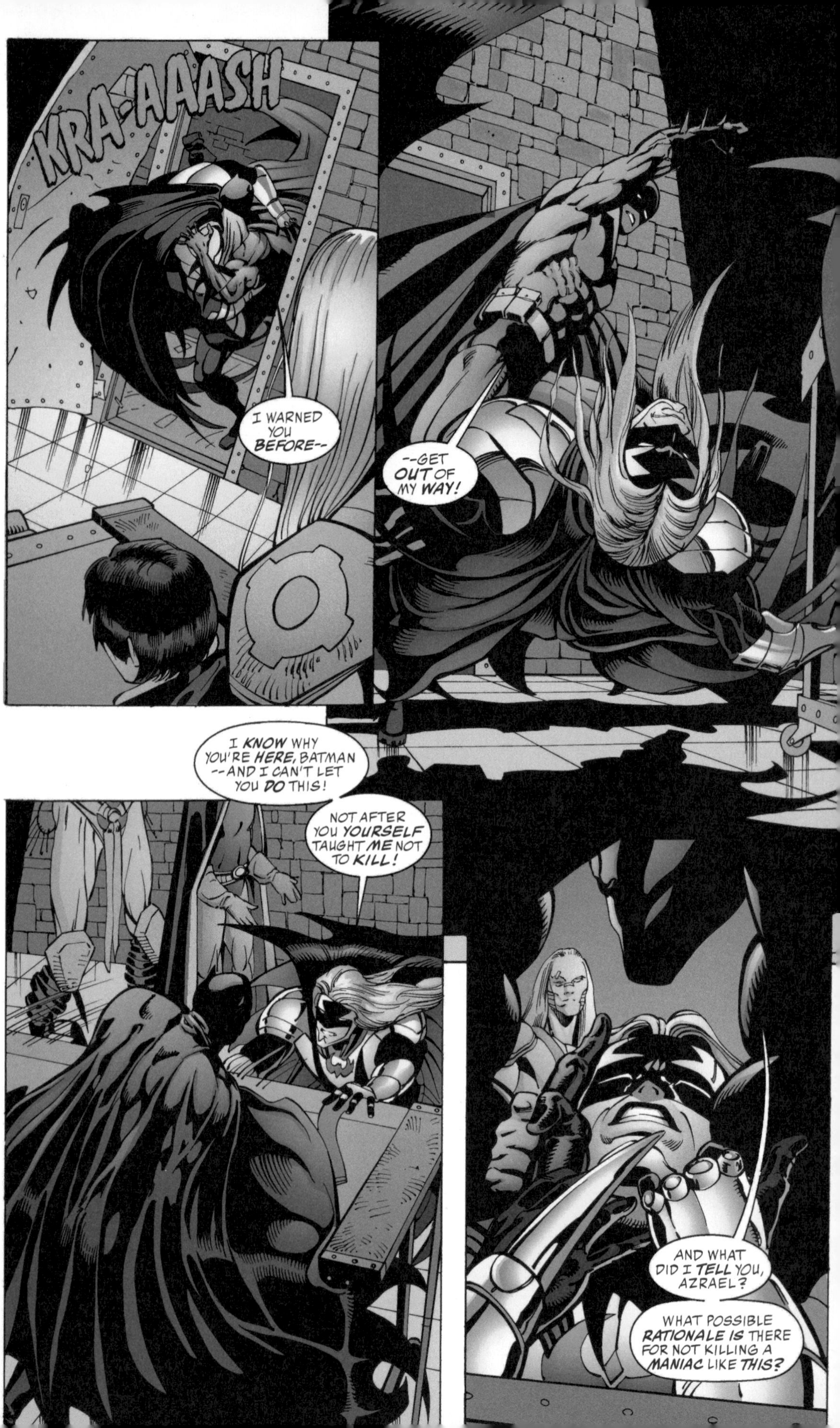
KRA-AAASH
I WARNED YOU BEFORE--
--GET OUT OF MY WAY!
I KNOW WHY YOU'RE HERE, BATMAN --AND I CAN'T LET YOU DO THIS!
NOT AFTER YOU YOURSELF TAUGHT ME NOT TO KILL!
AND WHAT DID I TELL YOU, AZRAEL?
WHAT POSSIBLE RATIONALE IS THERE FOR NOT KILLING A MANIAC LIKE THIS?

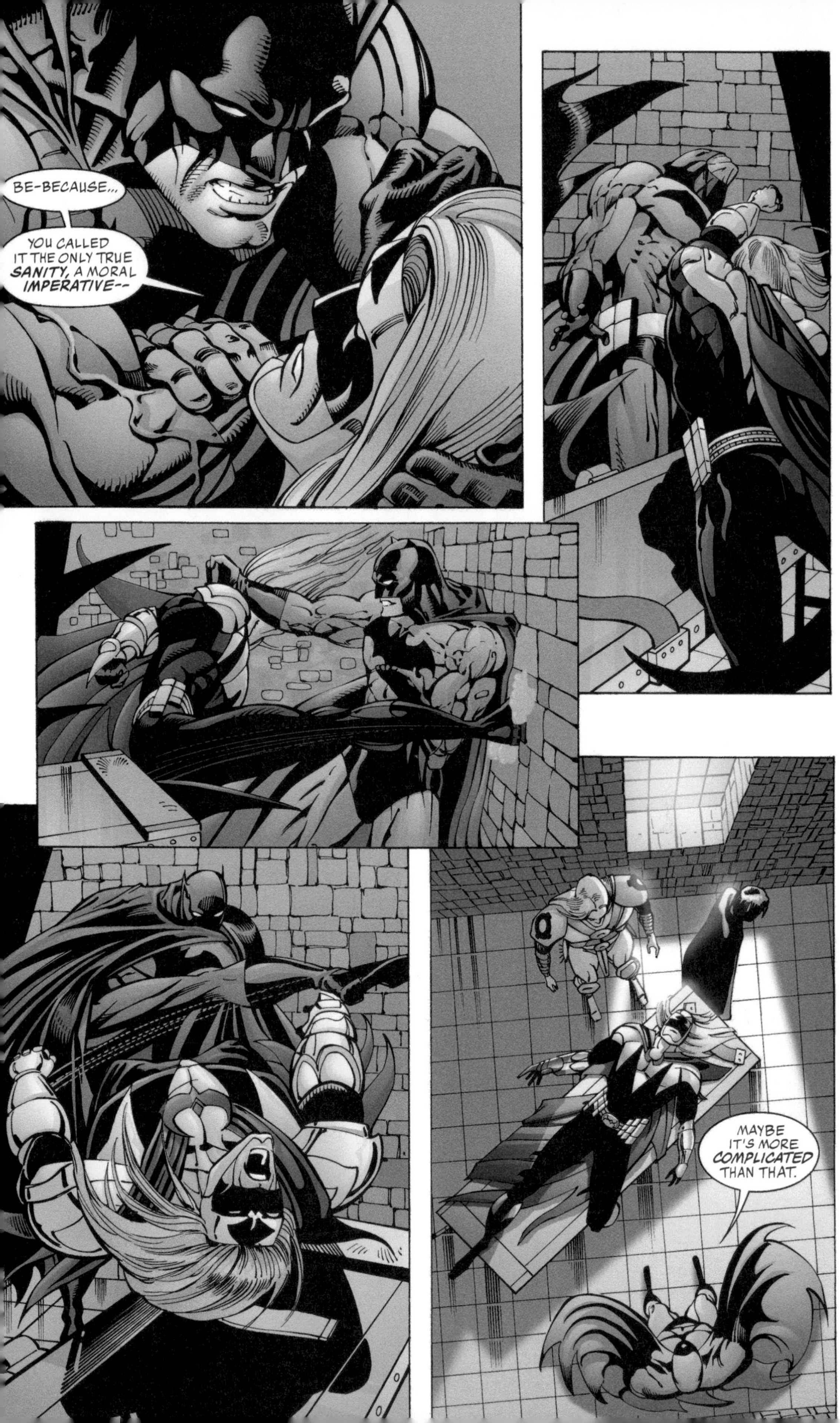
BE-BECAUSE...
YOU CALLED IT THE ONLY TRUE SANITY, A MORAL IMPERATIVE--
MAYBE IT'S MORE COMPLICATED THAN THAT.

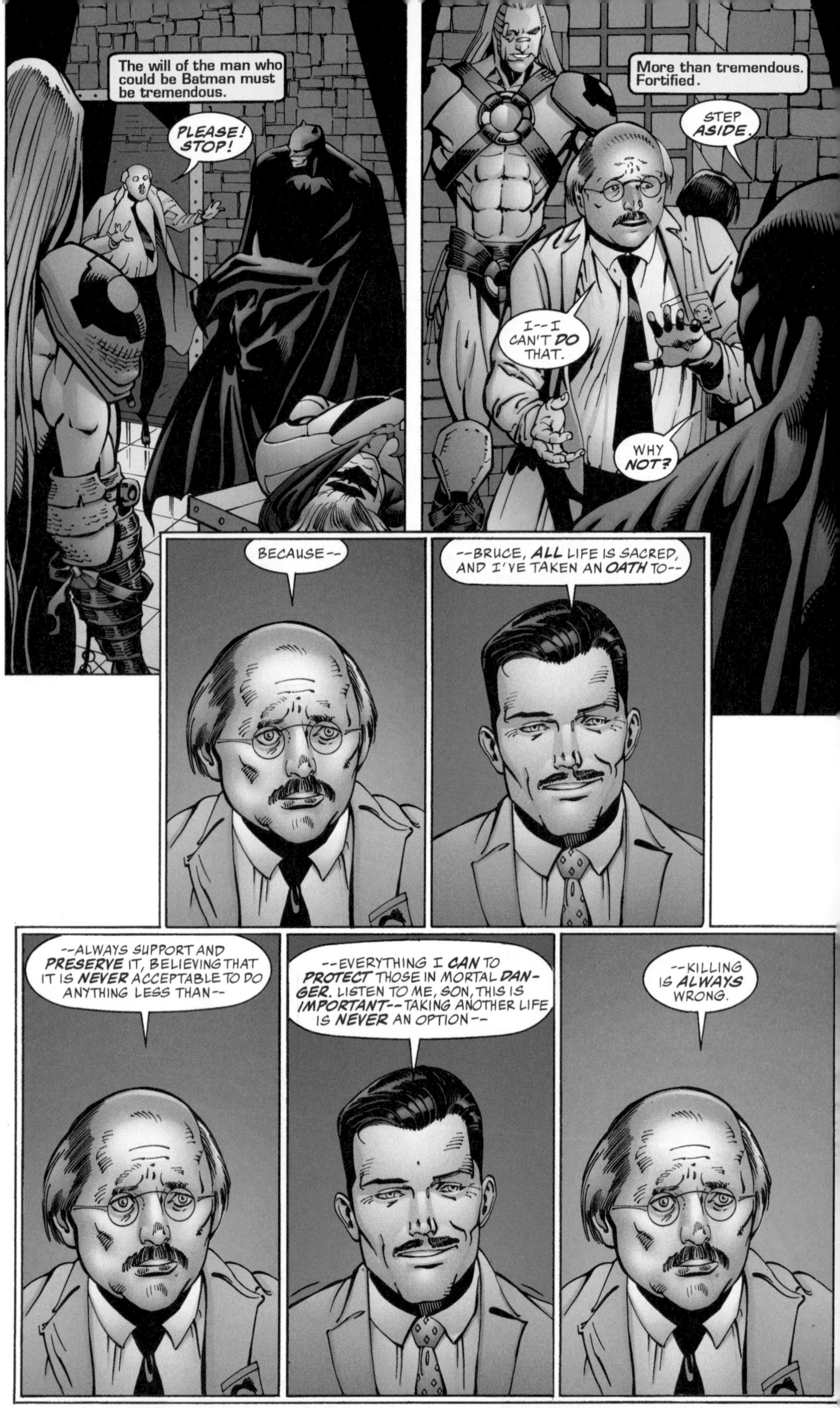
The will of the man who could be Batman must be tremendous.
PLEASE! STOP!
More than tremendous. Fortified.
STEP ASIDE.
I--I CAN'T DO THAT.
WHY NOT?
BECAUSE--
--BRUCE, ALL LIFE IS SACRED, AND I'VE TAKEN AN OATH TO--
--ALWAYS SUPPORT AND PRESERVE IT, BELIEVING THAT IT IS NEVER ACCEPTABLE TO DO ANYTHING LESS THAN--
--EVERYTHING I CAN TO PROTECT THOSE IN MORTAL DANGER. LISTEN TO ME, SON, THIS IS IMPORTANT--TAKING ANOTHER LIFE IS NEVER AN OPTION--
--KILLING IS ALWAYS WRONG.

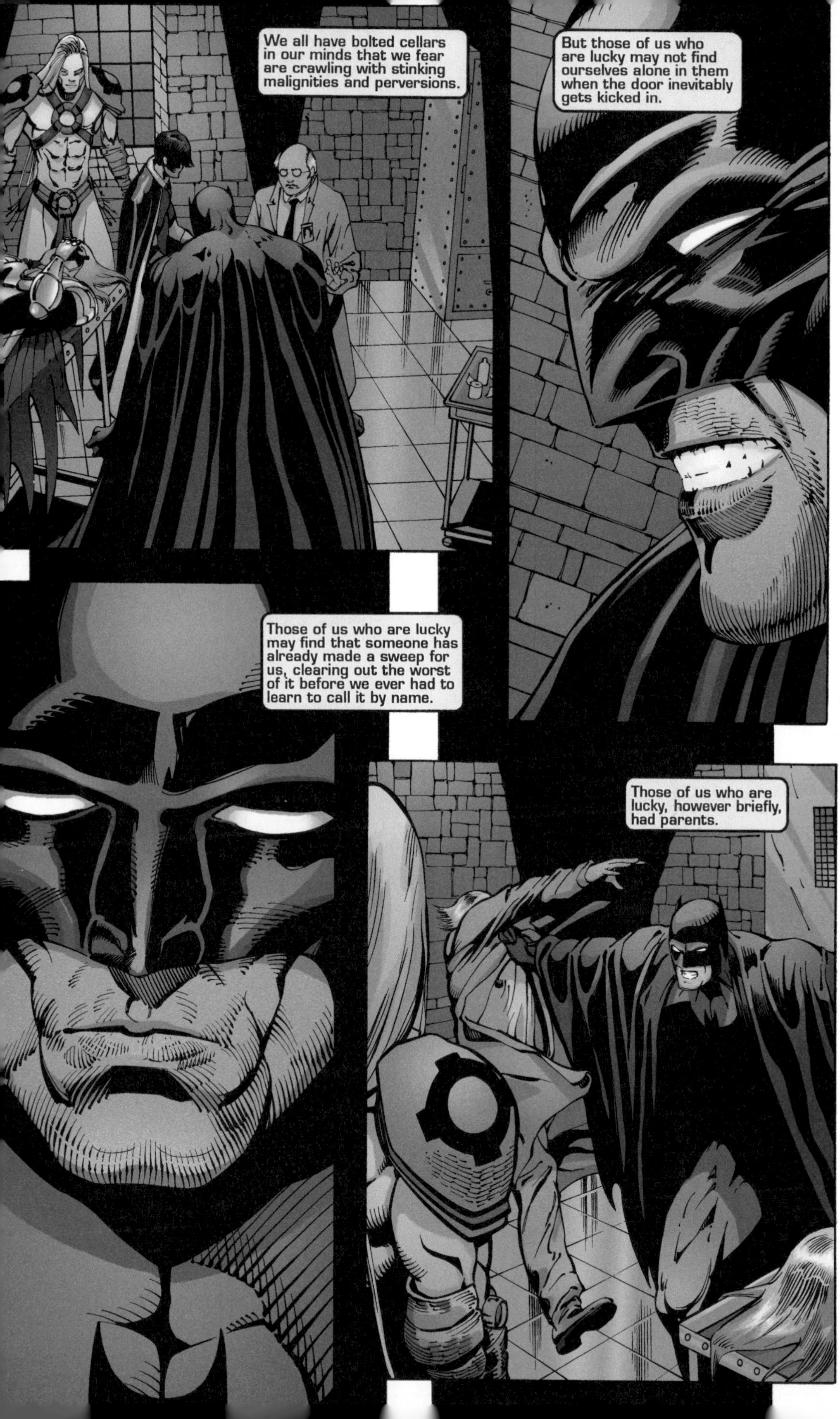
We all have bolted cellars in our minds that we fear are crawling with stinking malignities and perversions.
But those of us who are lucky may not find ourselves alone in them when the door inevitably gets kicked in.
Those of us who are lucky may find that someone has already made a sweep for us, clearing out the worst of it before we ever had to learn to call it by name.
Those of us who are lucky, however briefly, had parents.

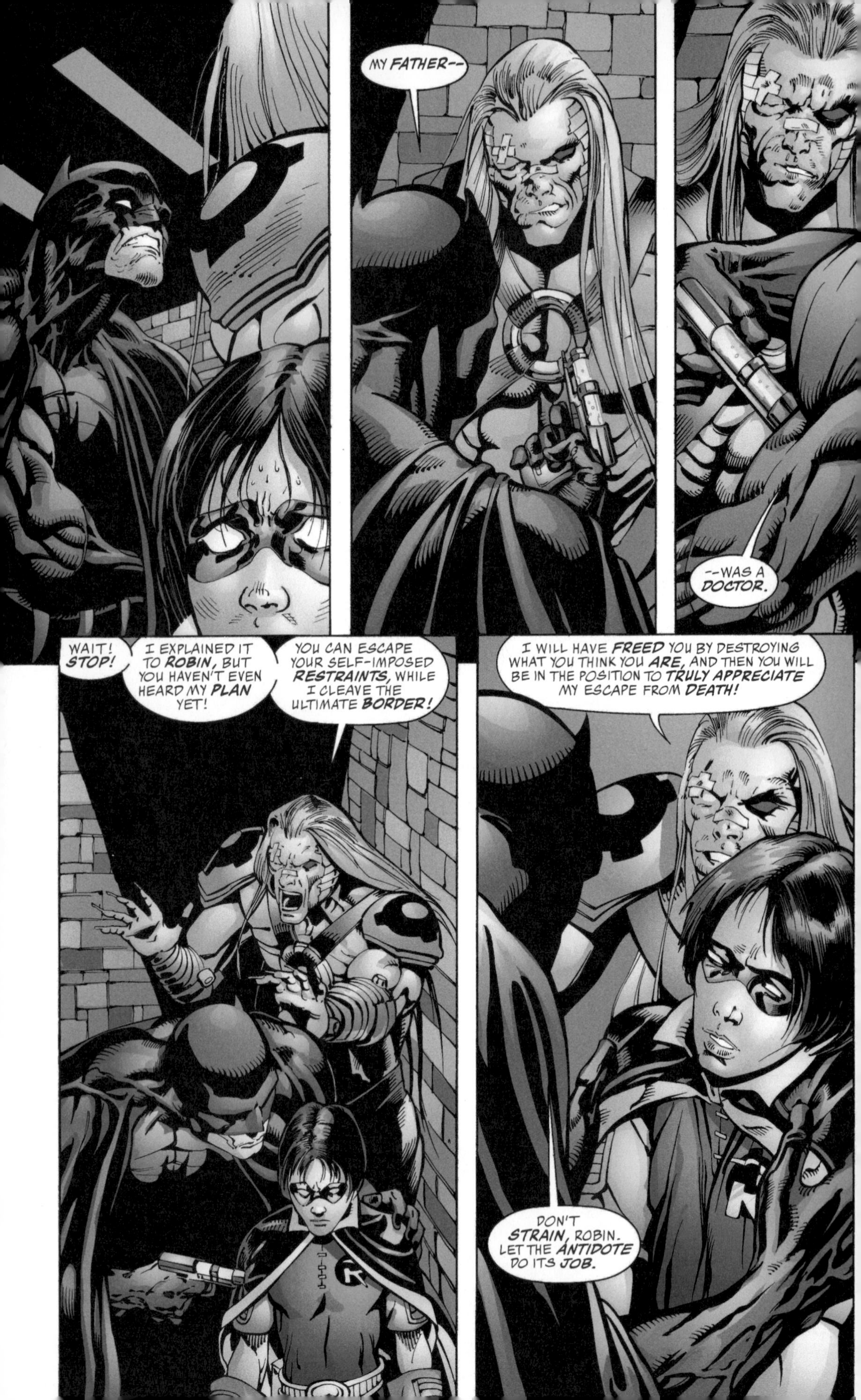
MY FATHER--
--WAS A DOCTOR.
WAIT! STOP!
I EXPLAINED IT TO ROBIN, BUT YOU HAVEN'T EVEN HEARD MY PLAN YET!
YOU CAN ESCAPE YOUR SELF-IMPOSED RESTRAINTS, WHILE I CLEAVE THE ULTIMATE BORDER!
I WILL HAVE FREED YOU BY DESTROYING WHAT YOU THINK YOU ARE, AND THEN YOU WILL BE IN THE POSITION TO TRULY APPRECIATE MY ESCAPE FROM DEATH!
DON'T STRAIN, ROBIN. LET THE ANTIDOTE DO ITS JOB.

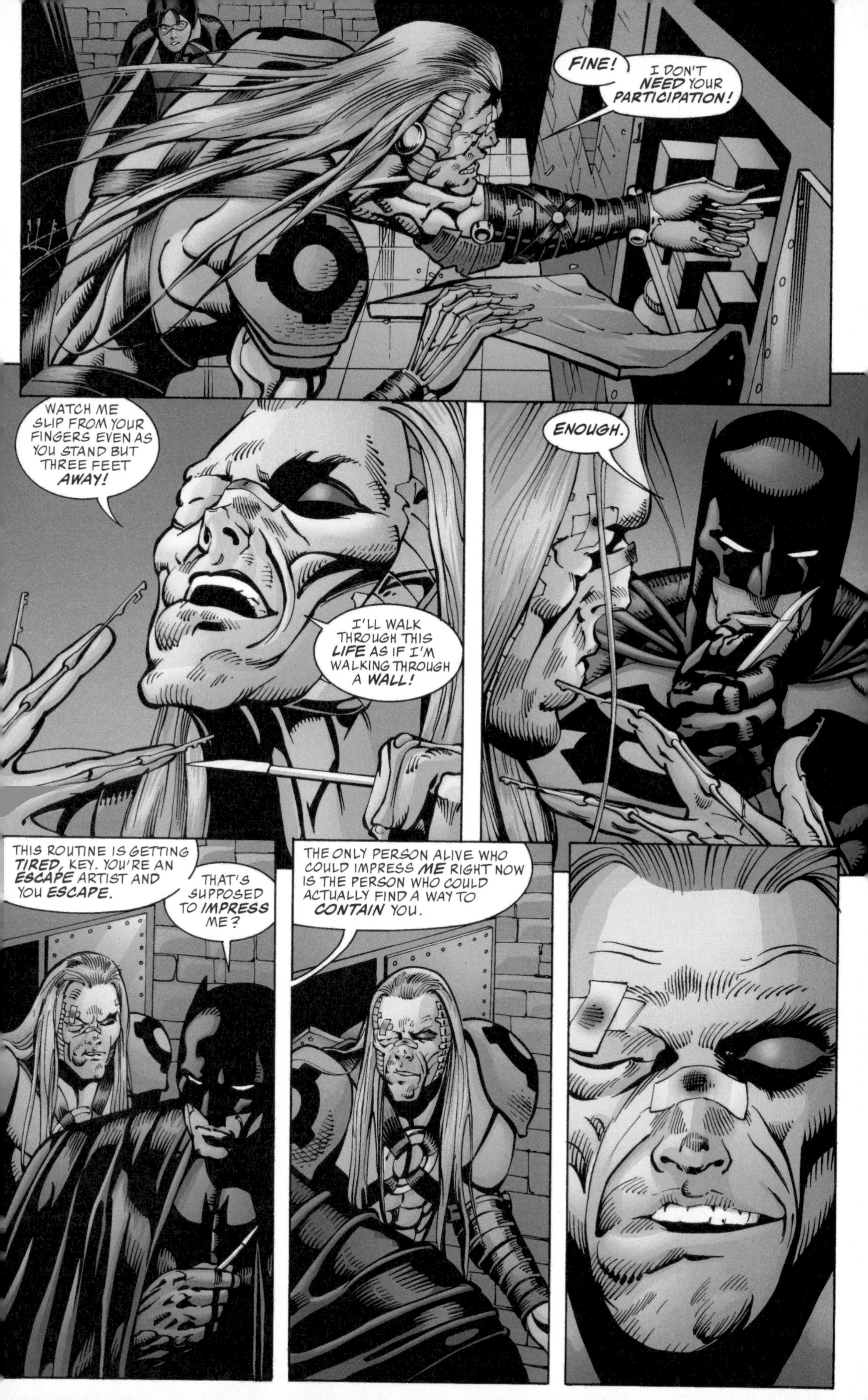
FINE!
I DON'T NEED YOUR PARTICIPATION!
WATCH ME SLIP FROM YOUR FINGERS EVEN AS YOU STAND BUT THREE FEET AWAY!
I'LL WALK THROUGH THIS LIFE AS IF I'M WALKING THROUGH A WALL!
ENOUGH.
THIS ROUTINE IS GETTING TIRED, KEY. YOU'RE AN ESCAPE ARTIST AND YOU ESCAPE.
THAT'S SUPPOSED TO IMPRESS ME?
THE ONLY PERSON ALIVE WHO COULD IMPRESS ME RIGHT NOW IS THE PERSON WHO COULD ACTUALLY FIND A WAY TO CONTAIN YOU.

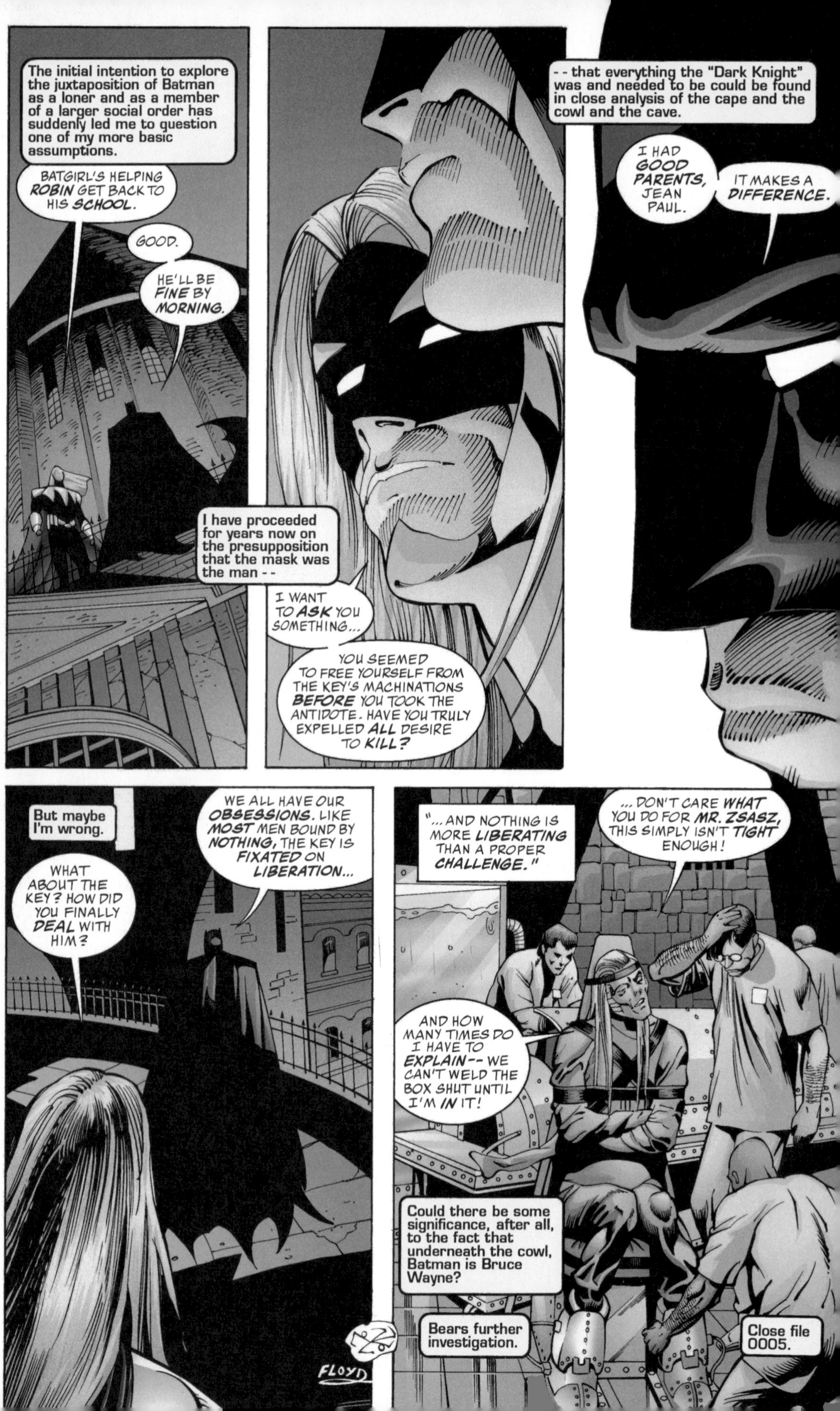

The initial intention to explore the juxtaposition of Batman as a loner and as a member of a larger social order has suddenly led me to question one of my more basic assumptions.
BATGIRL'S HELPING ROBIN GET BACK TO HIS SCHOOL.
GOOD.
HE'LL BE FINE BY MORNING.
I have proceeded for years now on the presupposition that the mask was the man - -
I WANT TO ASK YOU SOMETHING...
YOU SEEMED TO FREE YOURSELF FROM THE KEY'S MACHINATIONS BEFORE YOU TOOK THE ANTIDOTE. HAVE YOU TRULY EXPELLED ALL DESIRE TO KILL?
- - that everything the "Dark Knight" was and needed to be could be found in close analysis of the cape and the cowl and the cave.
I HAD GOOD PARENTS, JEAN PAUL.
IT MAKES A DIFFERENCE.
But maybe I'm wrong.
WHAT ABOUT THE KEY? HOW DID YOU FINALLY DEAL WITH HIM?
WE ALL HAVE OUR OBSESSIONS. LIKE MOST MEN BOUND BY NOTHING, THE KEY IS FIXATED ON LIBERATION...
"...AND NOTHING IS MORE LIBERATING THAN A PROPER CHALLENGE."
...DON'T CARE WHAT YOU DO FOR MR. ZSASZ, THIS SIMPLY ISN'T TIGHT ENOUGH!
AND HOW MANY TIMES DO I HAVE TO EXPLAIN-- WE CAN'T WELD THE BOX SHUT UNTIL I'M IN IT!
Could there be some significance, after all, to the fact that underneath the cowl, Batman is Bruce Wayne?
Bears further investigation.
Close file 0005.
FLOYD

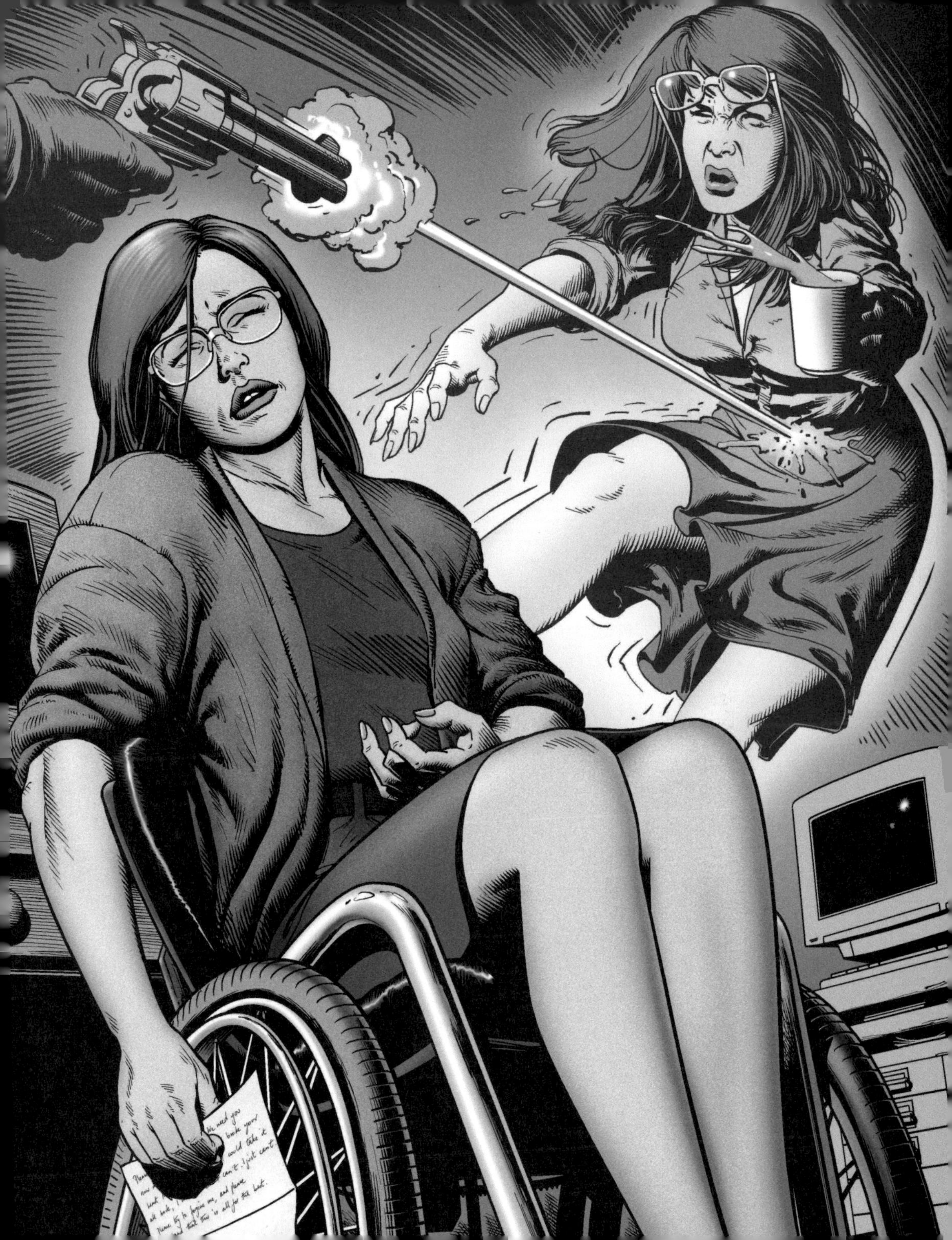
We need you
broke your
could take it
can't. I just can't.
Please try to forgive me, and please
and that this is all for the best.

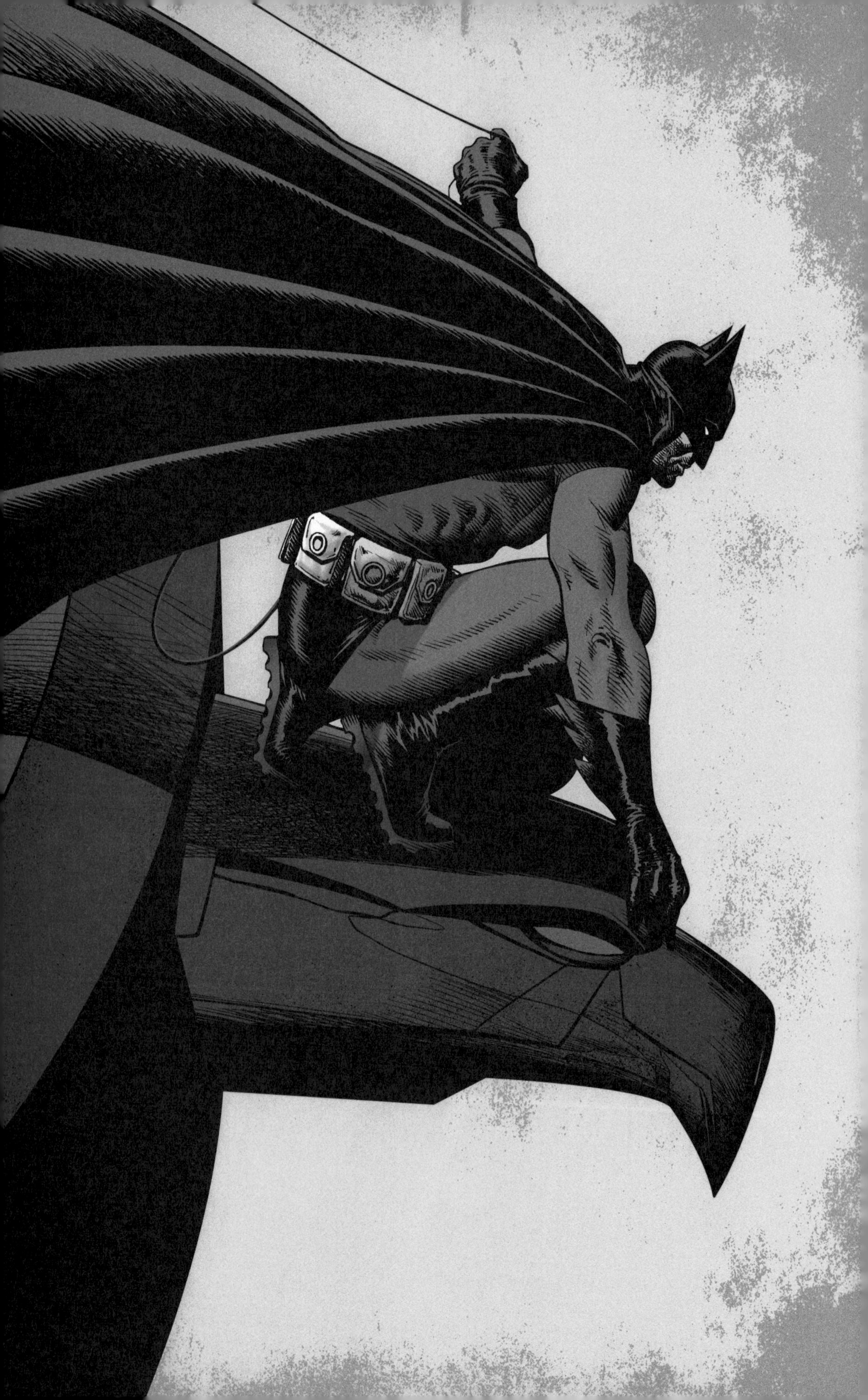

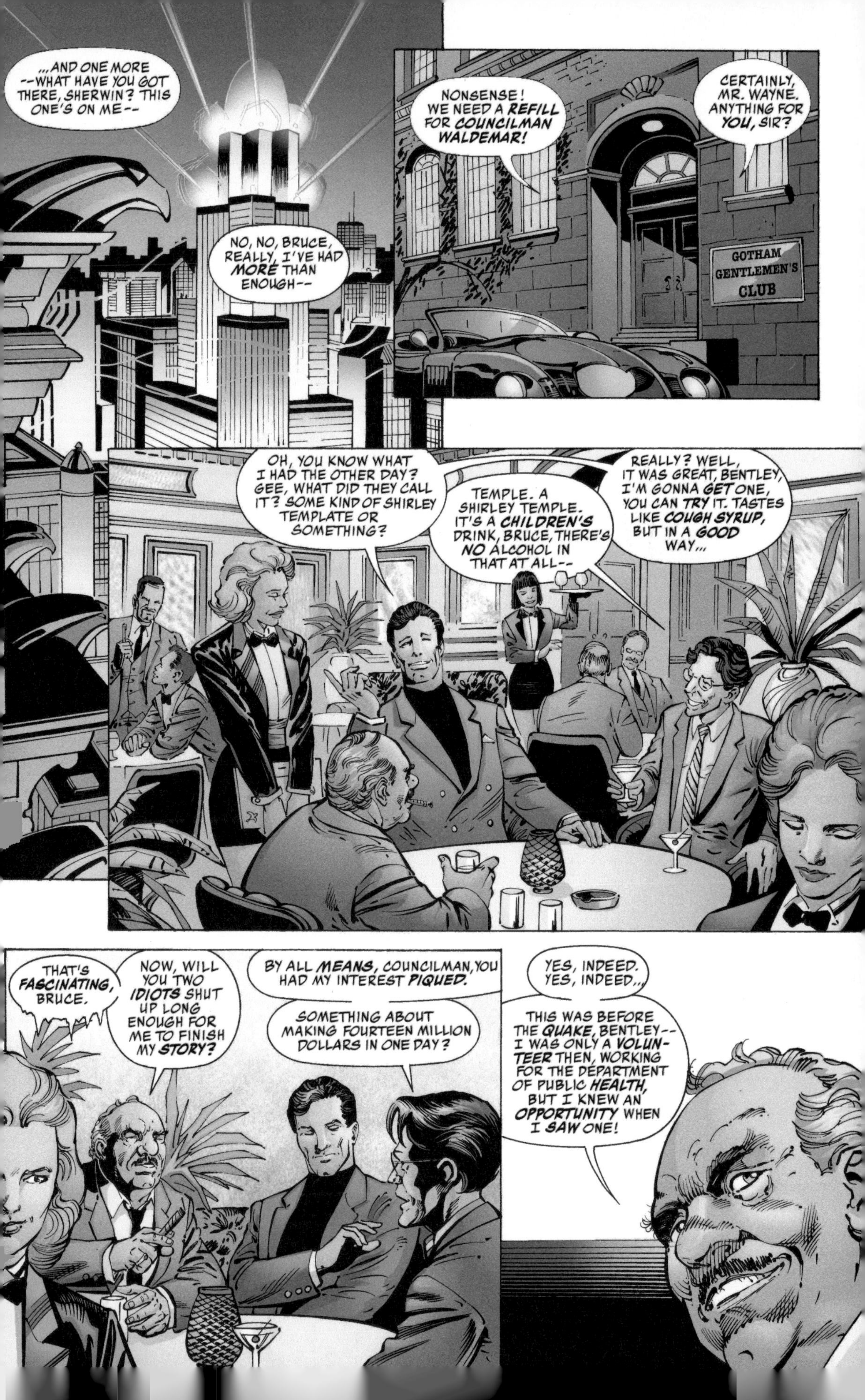

...AND ONE MORE --WHAT HAVE YOU GOT THERE, SHERWIN? THIS ONE'S ON ME--
NO, NO, BRUCE, REALLY, I'VE HAD MORE THAN ENOUGH--
NONSENSE! WE NEED A REFILL FOR COUNCILMAN WALDEMAR!
CERTAINLY, MR. WAYNE. ANYTHING FOR YOU, SIR?
GOTHAM GENTLEMEN'S CLUB
OH, YOU KNOW WHAT I HAD THE OTHER DAY? GEE, WHAT DID THEY CALL IT? SOME KIND OF SHIRLEY TEMPLATE OR SOMETHING?
TEMPLE. A SHIRLEY TEMPLE. IT'S A CHILDREN'S DRINK, BRUCE, THERE'S NO ALCOHOL IN THAT AT ALL--
REALLY? WELL, IT WAS GREAT, BENTLEY, I'M GONNA GET ONE, YOU CAN TRY IT. TASTES LIKE COUGH SYRUP, BUT IN A GOOD WAY...
THAT'S FASCINATING, BRUCE.
NOW, WILL YOU TWO IDIOTS SHUT UP LONG ENOUGH FOR ME TO FINISH MY STORY?
BY ALL MEANS, COUNCILMAN, YOU HAD MY INTEREST PIQUED.
SOMETHING ABOUT MAKING FOURTEEN MILLION DOLLARS IN ONE DAY?
YES, INDEED. YES, INDEED...
THIS WAS BEFORE THE QUAKE, BENTLEY-- I WAS ONLY A VOLUNTEER THEN, WORKING FOR THE DEPARTMENT OF PUBLIC HEALTH, BUT I KNEW AN OPPORTUNITY WHEN I SAW ONE!

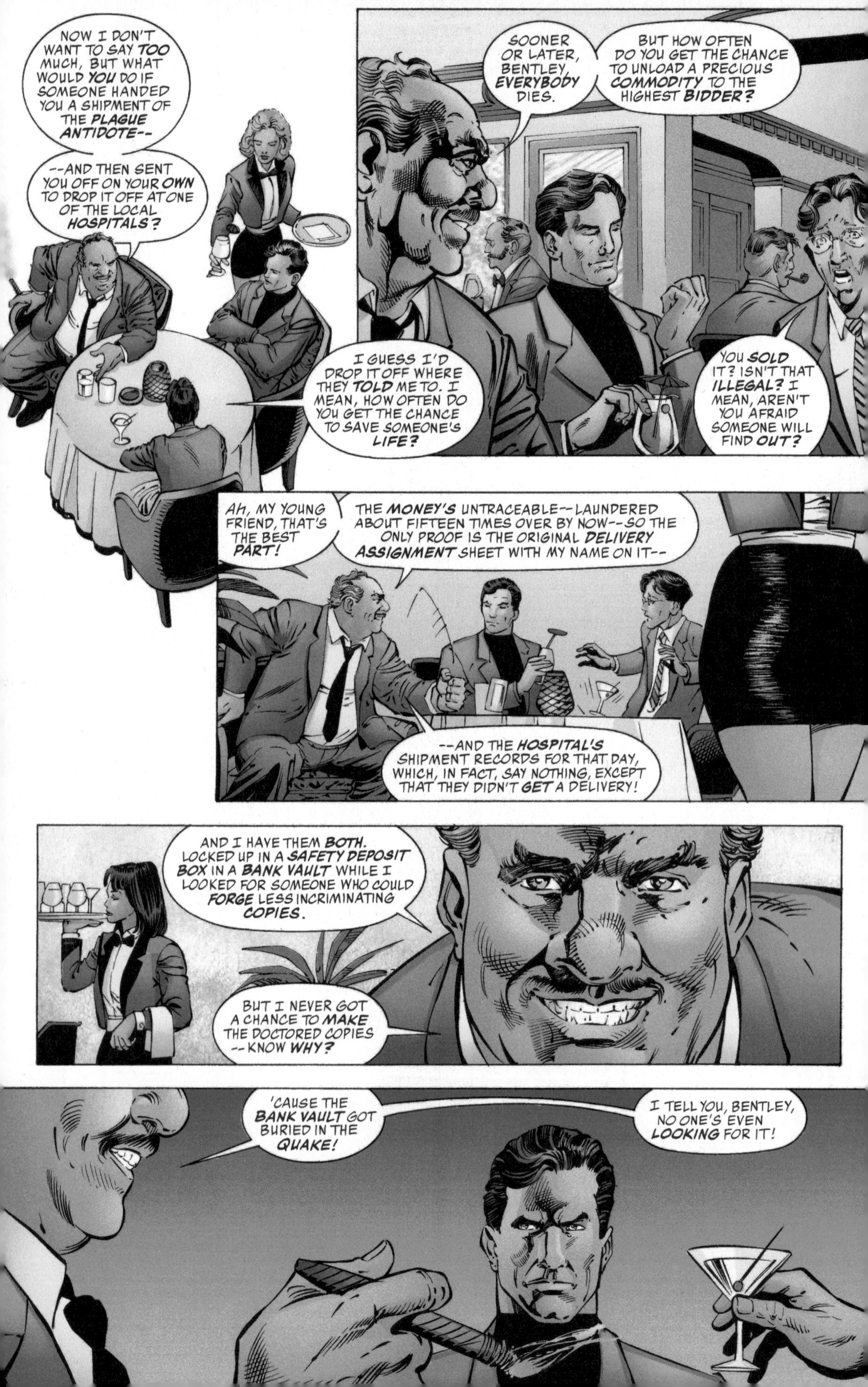
NOW I DON'T WANT TO SAY TOO MUCH, BUT WHAT WOULD YOU DO IF SOMEONE HANDED YOU A SHIPMENT OF THE PLAGUE ANTIDOTE--
--AND THEN SENT YOU OFF ON YOUR OWN TO DROP IT OFF AT ONE OF THE LOCAL HOSPITALS?
I GUESS I'D DROP IT OFF WHERE THEY TOLD ME TO. I MEAN, HOW OFTEN DO YOU GET THE CHANCE TO SAVE SOMEONE'S LIFE?
SOONER OR LATER, BENTLEY, EVERYBODY DIES.
BUT HOW OFTEN DO YOU GET THE CHANCE TO UNLOAD A PRECIOUS COMMODITY TO THE HIGHEST BIDDER?
YOU SOLD IT? ISN'T THAT ILLEGAL? I MEAN, AREN'T YOU AFRAID SOMEONE WILL FIND OUT?
AH, MY YOUNG FRIEND, THAT'S THE BEST PART!
THE MONEY'S UNTRACEABLE-- LAUNDERED ABOUT FIFTEEN TIMES OVER BY NOW-- SO THE ONLY PROOF IS THE ORIGINAL DELIVERY ASSIGNMENT SHEET WITH MY NAME ON IT--
--AND THE HOSPITAL'S SHIPMENT RECORDS FOR THAT DAY, WHICH, IN FACT, SAY NOTHING, EXCEPT THAT THEY DIDN'T GET A DELIVERY!
AND I HAVE THEM BOTH. LOCKED UP IN A SAFETY DEPOSIT BOX IN A BANK VAULT WHILE I LOOKED FOR SOMEONE WHO COULD FORGE LESS INCRIMINATING COPIES.
BUT I NEVER GOT A CHANCE TO MAKE THE DOCTORED COPIES --KNOW WHY?
'CAUSE THE BANK VAULT GOT BURIED IN THE QUAKE!
I TELL YOU, BENTLEY, NO ONE'S EVEN LOOKING FOR IT!

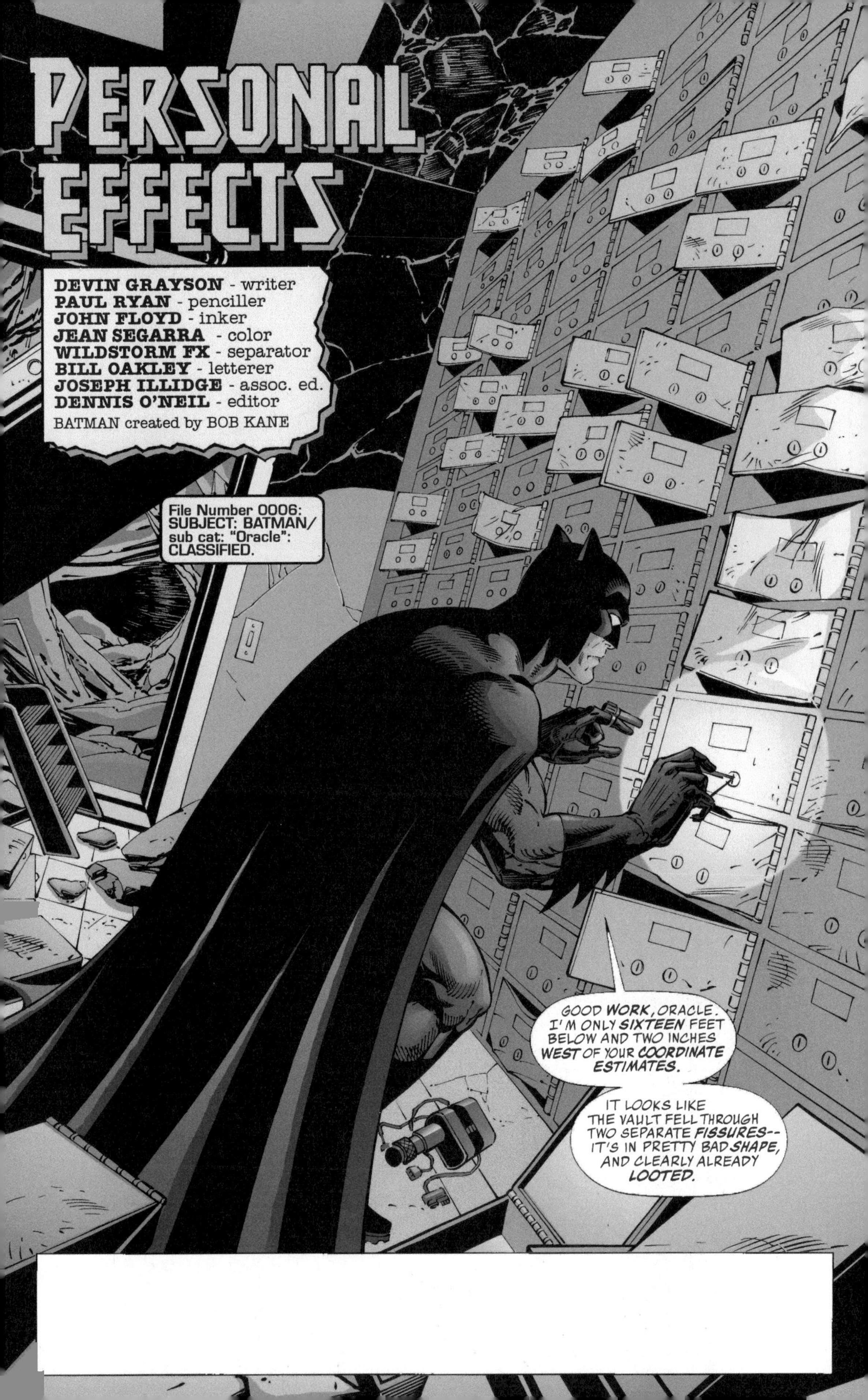
PERSONAL EFFECTS
DEVIN GRAYSON - writer
PAUL RYAN - penciller
JOHN FLOYD - inker
JEAN SEGARRA - color
WILDSTORM FX - separator
BILL OAKLEY - letterer
JOSEPH ILLIDGE - assoc. ed.
DENNIS O'NEIL - editor
BATMAN created by BOB KANE
File Number 0006: SUBJECT: BATMAN/ sub cat: "Oracle": CLASSIFIED.
GOOD WORK, ORACLE. I'M ONLY SIXTEEN FEET BELOW AND TWO INCHES WEST OF YOUR COORDINATE ESTIMATES.
IT LOOKS LIKE THE VAULT FELL THROUGH TWO SEPARATE FISSURES-- IT'S IN PRETTY BAD SHAPE, AND CLEARLY ALREADY LOOTED.

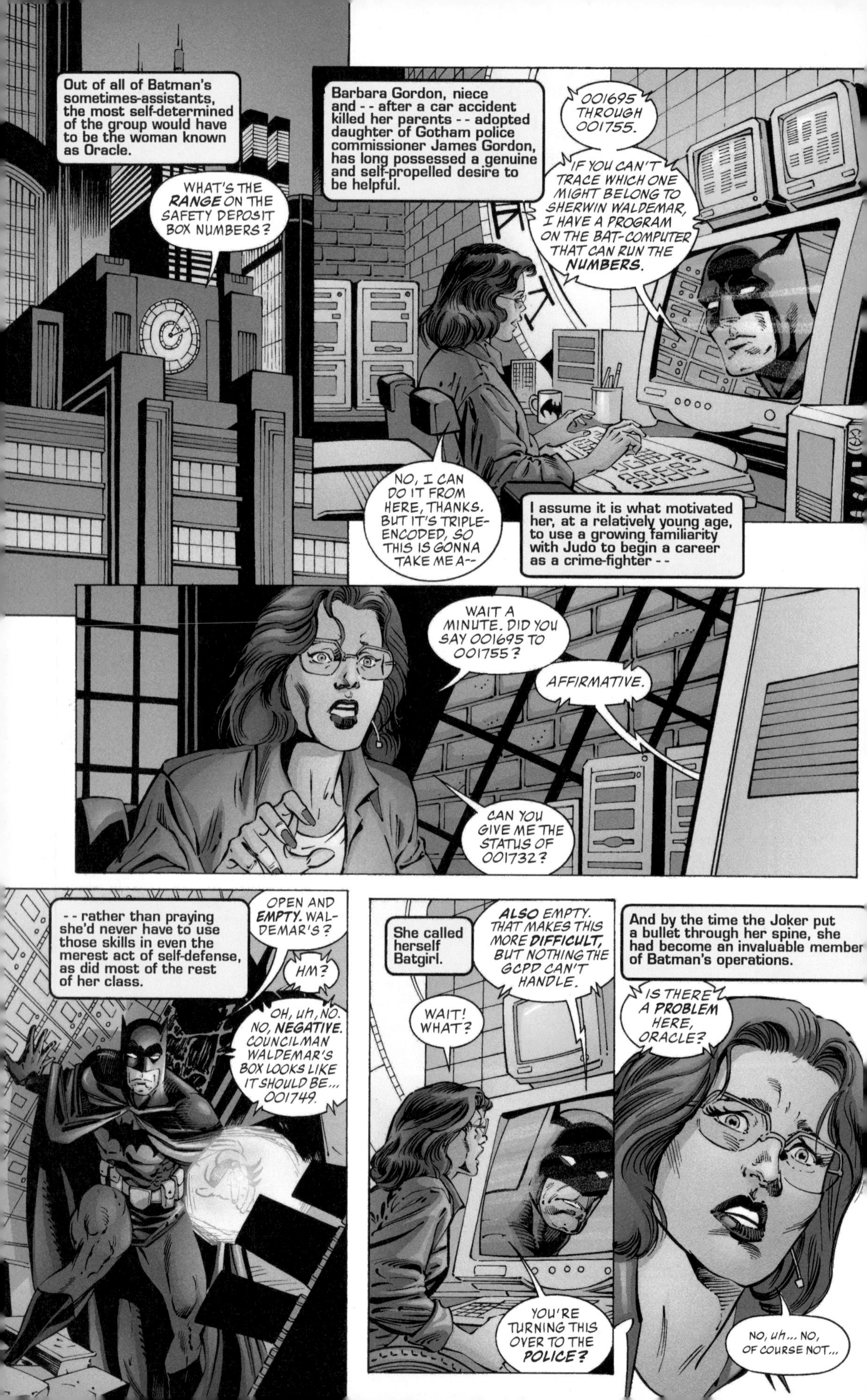
Out of all of Batman's sometimes-assistants, the most self-determined of the group would have to be the woman known as Oracle.
WHAT'S THE RANGE ON THE SAFETY DEPOSIT BOX NUMBERS?
Barbara Gordon, niece and - - after a car accident killed her parents - - adopted daughter of Gotham police commissioner James Gordon, has long possessed a genuine and self-propelled desire to be helpful.
001695 THROUGH 001755.
IF YOU CAN'T TRACE WHICH ONE MIGHT BELONG TO SHERWIN WALDEMAR, I HAVE A PROGRAM ON THE BAT-COMPUTER THAT CAN RUN THE NUMBERS.
NO, I CAN DO IT FROM HERE, THANKS. BUT IT'S TRIPLE-ENCODED, SO THIS IS GONNA TAKE ME A--
I assume it is what motivated her, at a relatively young age, to use a growing familiarity with Judo to begin a career as a crime-fighter - -
WAIT A MINUTE. DID YOU SAY 001695 TO 001755?
AFFIRMATIVE.
CAN YOU GIVE ME THE STATUS OF 001732?
- - rather than praying she'd never have to use those skills in even the merest act of self-defense, as did most of the rest of her class.
OPEN AND EMPTY. WALDEMAR'S?
HM?
OH, uh, NO. NO, NEGATIVE. COUNCILMAN WALDEMAR'S BOX LOOKS LIKE IT SHOULD BE... 001749.
She called herself Batgirl.
ALSO EMPTY. THAT MAKES THIS MORE DIFFICULT, BUT NOTHING THE GCPD CAN'T HANDLE.
WAIT! WHAT?
YOU'RE TURNING THIS OVER TO THE POLICE?
And by the time the Joker put a bullet through her spine, she had become an invaluable member of Batman's operations.
IS THERE A PROBLEM HERE, ORACLE?
NO, uh... NO, OF COURSE NOT...

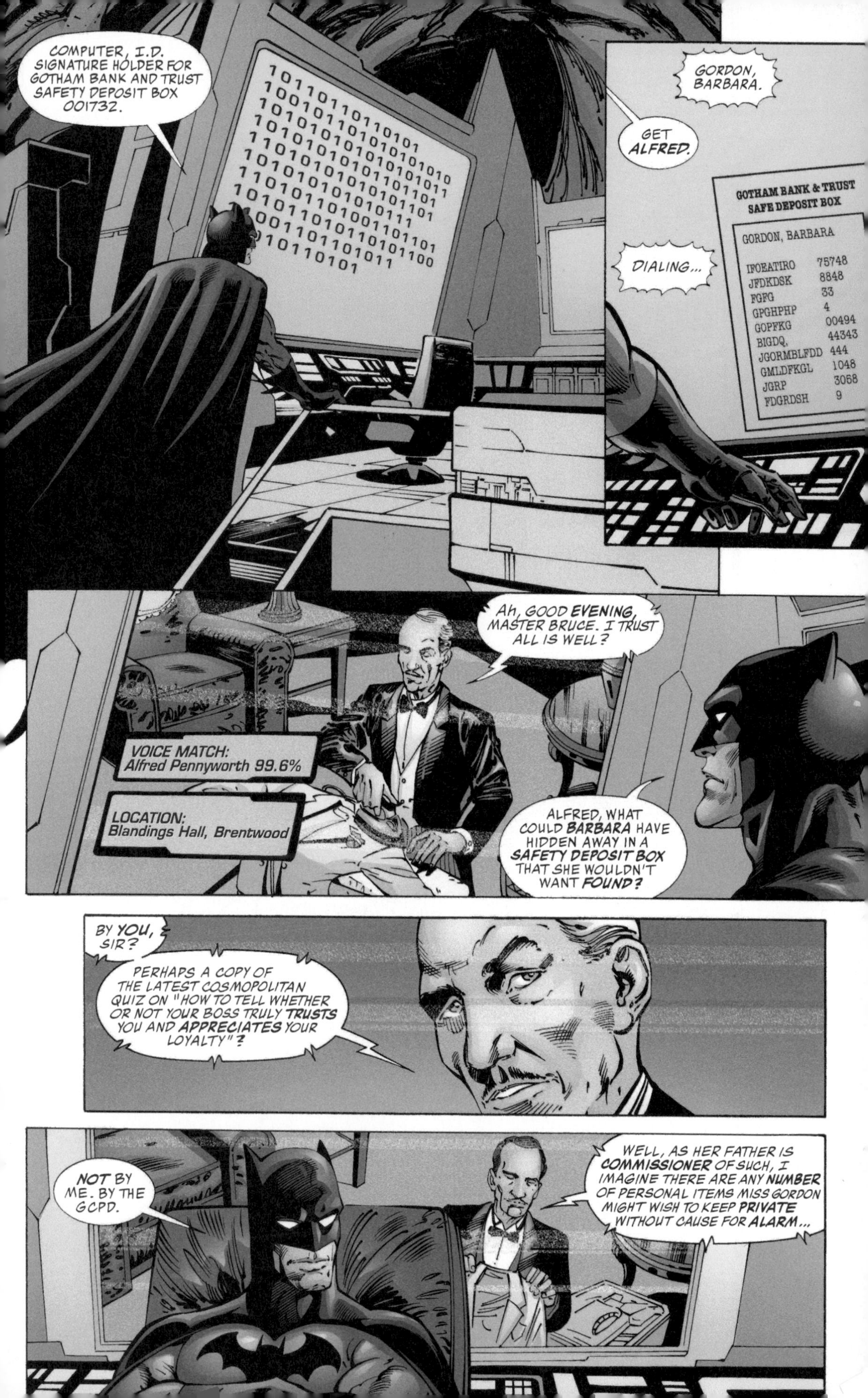
COMPUTER, I.D. SIGNATURE HOLDER FOR GOTHAM BANK AND TRUST SAFETY DEPOSIT BOX 001732.
GORDON, BARBARA.
GET ALFRED.
GOTHAM BANK & TRUST
SAFE DEPOSIT BOX
GORDON, BARBARA
IFOEATIRO 75748
JFDKDSK 8848
FGFG 33
GPGHPHP 4
GOPFKG 00494
BIGDQ. 44343
JGORMBLFDD 444
GMLDFKGL 1048
JGRP 3068
FDGRDSH 9
DIALING...
Ah, GOOD EVENING, MASTER BRUCE. I TRUST ALL IS WELL?
VOICE MATCH: Alfred Pennyworth 99.6%
LOCATION: Blandings Hall, Brentwood
ALFRED, WHAT COULD BARBARA HAVE HIDDEN AWAY IN A SAFETY DEPOSIT BOX THAT SHE WOULDN'T WANT FOUND?
BY YOU, SIR?
PERHAPS A COPY OF THE LATEST COSMOPOLITAN QUIZ ON "HOW TO TELL WHETHER OR NOT YOUR BOSS TRULY TRUSTS YOU AND APPRECIATES YOUR LOYALTY"?
NOT BY ME. BY THE GCPD.
WELL, AS HER FATHER IS COMMISSIONER OF SUCH, I IMAGINE THERE ARE ANY NUMBER OF PERSONAL ITEMS MISS GORDON MIGHT WISH TO KEEP PRIVATE WITHOUT CAUSE FOR ALARM...

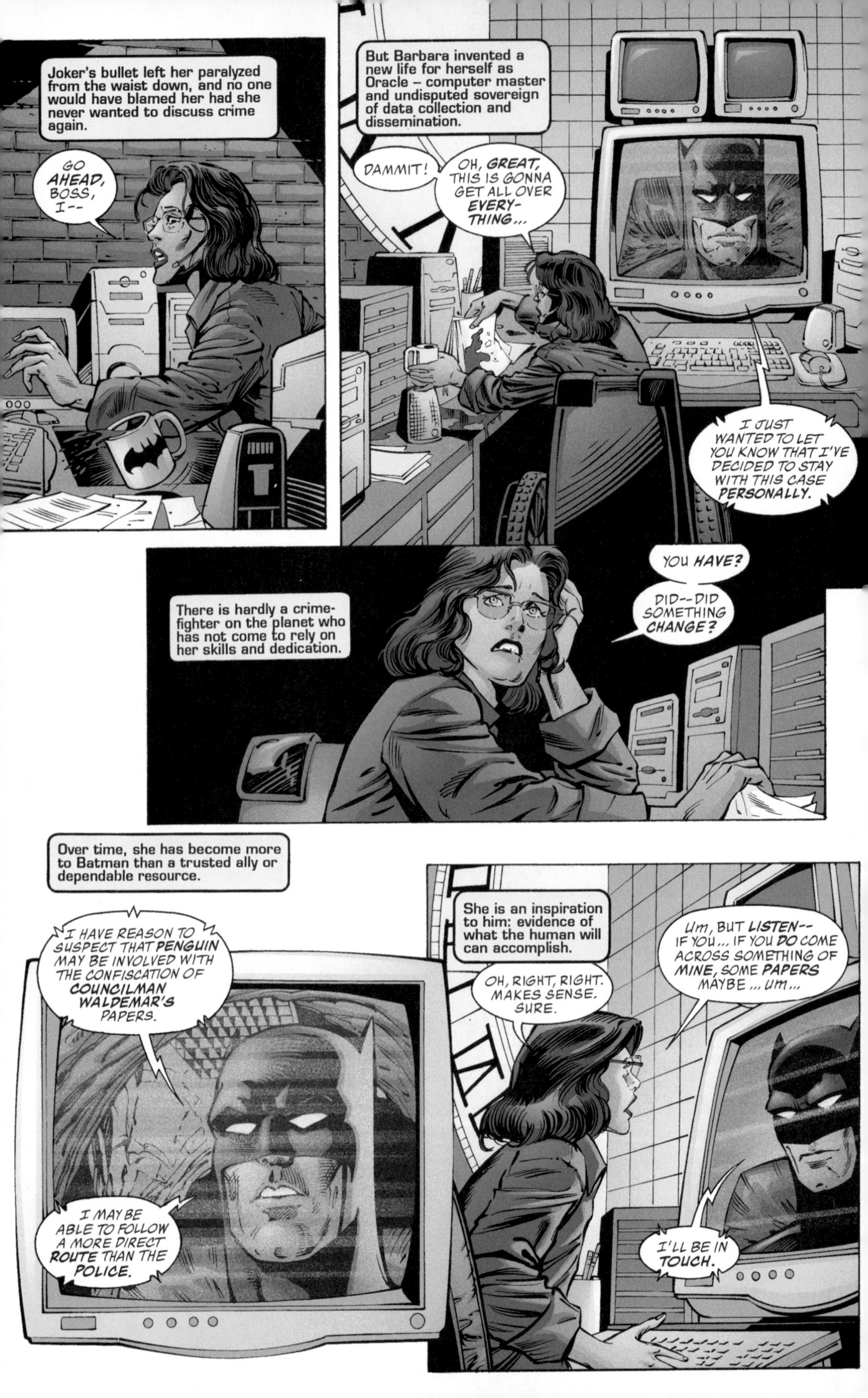
Joker's bullet left her paralyzed from the waist down, and no one would have blamed her had she never wanted to discuss crime again.
GO AHEAD, BOSS, I--
But Barbara invented a new life for herself as Oracle – computer master and undisputed sovereign of data collection and dissemination.
DAMMIT!
OH, GREAT, THIS IS GONNA GET ALL OVER EVERY-THING...
I JUST WANTED TO LET YOU KNOW THAT I'VE DECIDED TO STAY WITH THIS CASE PERSONALLY.
There is hardly a crime-fighter on the planet who has not come to rely on her skills and dedication.
YOU HAVE?
DID--DID SOMETHING CHANGE?
Over time, she has become more to Batman than a trusted ally or dependable resource.
I HAVE REASON TO SUSPECT THAT PENGUIN MAY BE INVOLVED WITH THE CONFISCATION OF COUNCILMAN WALDEMAR'S PAPERS.
I MAY BE ABLE TO FOLLOW A MORE DIRECT ROUTE THAN THE POLICE.
She is an inspiration to him: evidence of what the human will can accomplish.
OH, RIGHT, RIGHT. MAKES SENSE. SURE.
UM, BUT LISTEN-- IF YOU... IF YOU DO COME ACROSS SOMETHING OF MINE, SOME PAPERS MAYBE ... UM...
I'LL BE IN TOUCH.

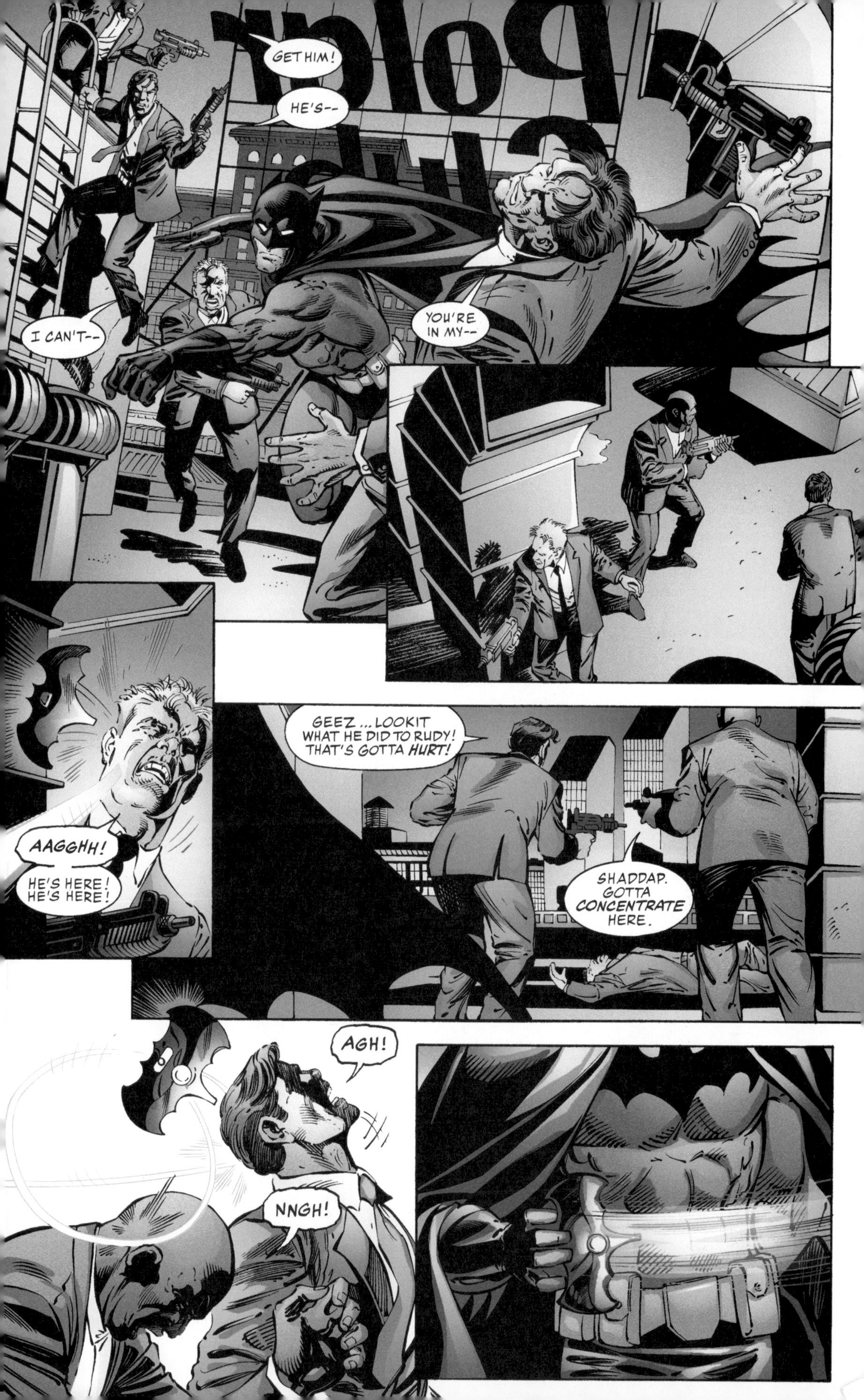
GET HIM!
HE'S--
I CAN'T--
YOU'RE IN MY--
AAGGHH!
HE'S HERE! HE'S HERE!
GEEZ ... LOOKIT WHAT HE DID TO RUDY! THAT'S GOTTA HURT!
SHADDAP. GOTTA CONCENTRATE HERE.
AGH!
NNGH!

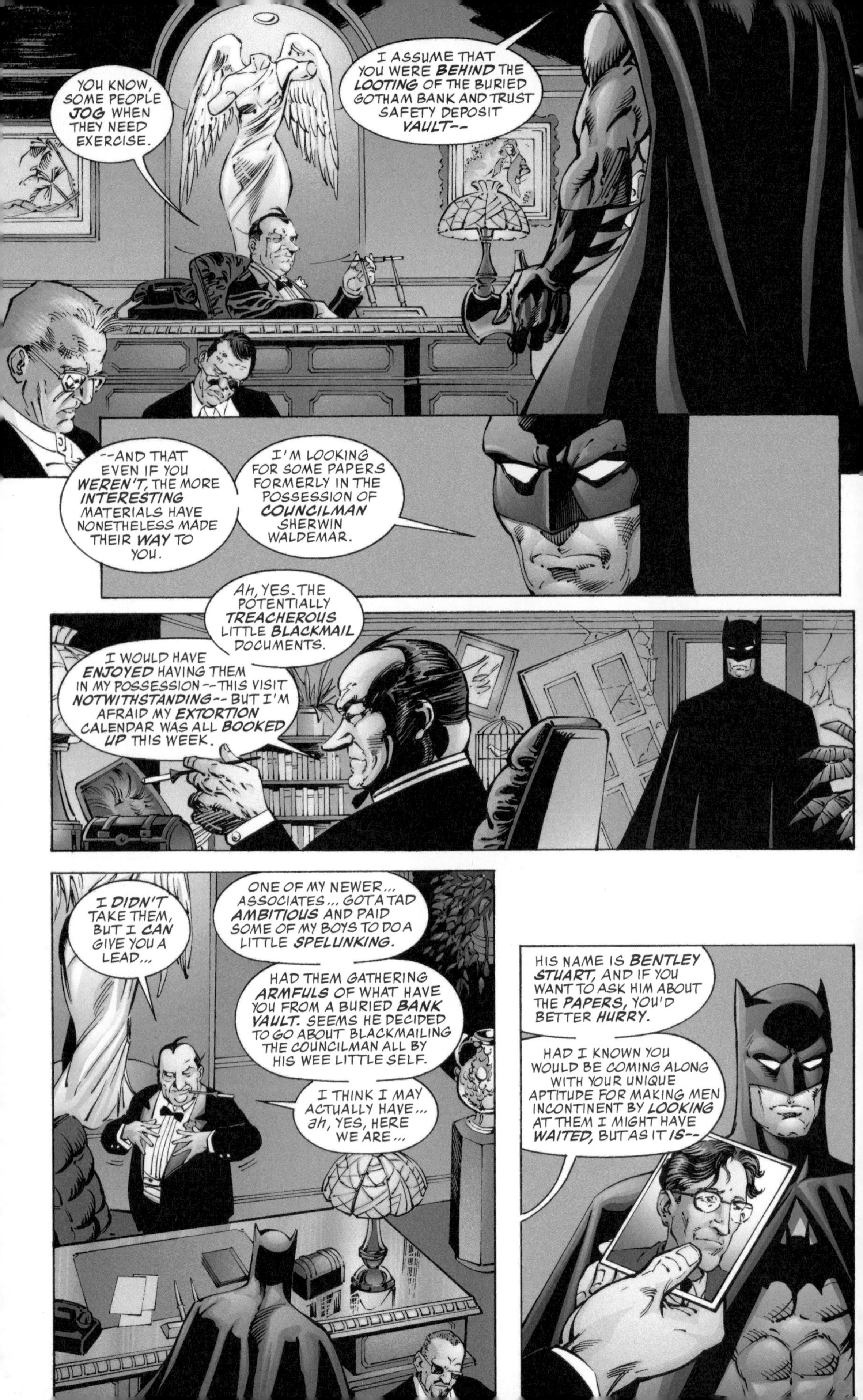
YOU KNOW, SOME PEOPLE JOG WHEN THEY NEED EXERCISE.
I ASSUME THAT YOU WERE BEHIND THE LOOTING OF THE BURIED GOTHAM BANK AND TRUST SAFETY DEPOSIT VAULT--
--AND THAT EVEN IF YOU WEREN'T, THE MORE INTERESTING MATERIALS HAVE NONETHELESS MADE THEIR WAY TO YOU.
I'M LOOKING FOR SOME PAPERS FORMERLY IN THE POSSESSION OF COUNCILMAN SHERWIN WALDEMAR.
Ah, YES. THE POTENTIALLY TREACHEROUS LITTLE BLACKMAIL DOCUMENTS.
I WOULD HAVE ENJOYED HAVING THEM IN MY POSSESSION--THIS VISIT NOTWITHSTANDING-- BUT I'M AFRAID MY EXTORTION CALENDAR WAS ALL BOOKED UP THIS WEEK.
I DIDN'T TAKE THEM, BUT I CAN GIVE YOU A LEAD...
ONE OF MY NEWER... ASSOCIATES... GOT A TAD AMBITIOUS AND PAID SOME OF MY BOYS TO DO A LITTLE SPELUNKING.
HAD THEM GATHERING ARMFULS OF WHAT HAVE YOU FROM A BURIED BANK VAULT. SEEMS HE DECIDED TO GO ABOUT BLACKMAILING THE COUNCILMAN ALL BY HIS WEE LITTLE SELF.
I THINK I MAY ACTUALLY HAVE... ah, YES, HERE WE ARE...
HIS NAME IS BENTLEY STUART, AND IF YOU WANT TO ASK HIM ABOUT THE PAPERS, YOU'D BETTER HURRY.
HAD I KNOWN YOU WOULD BE COMING ALONG WITH YOUR UNIQUE APTITUDE FOR MAKING MEN INCONTINENT BY LOOKING AT THEM I MIGHT HAVE WAITED, BUT AS IT IS--

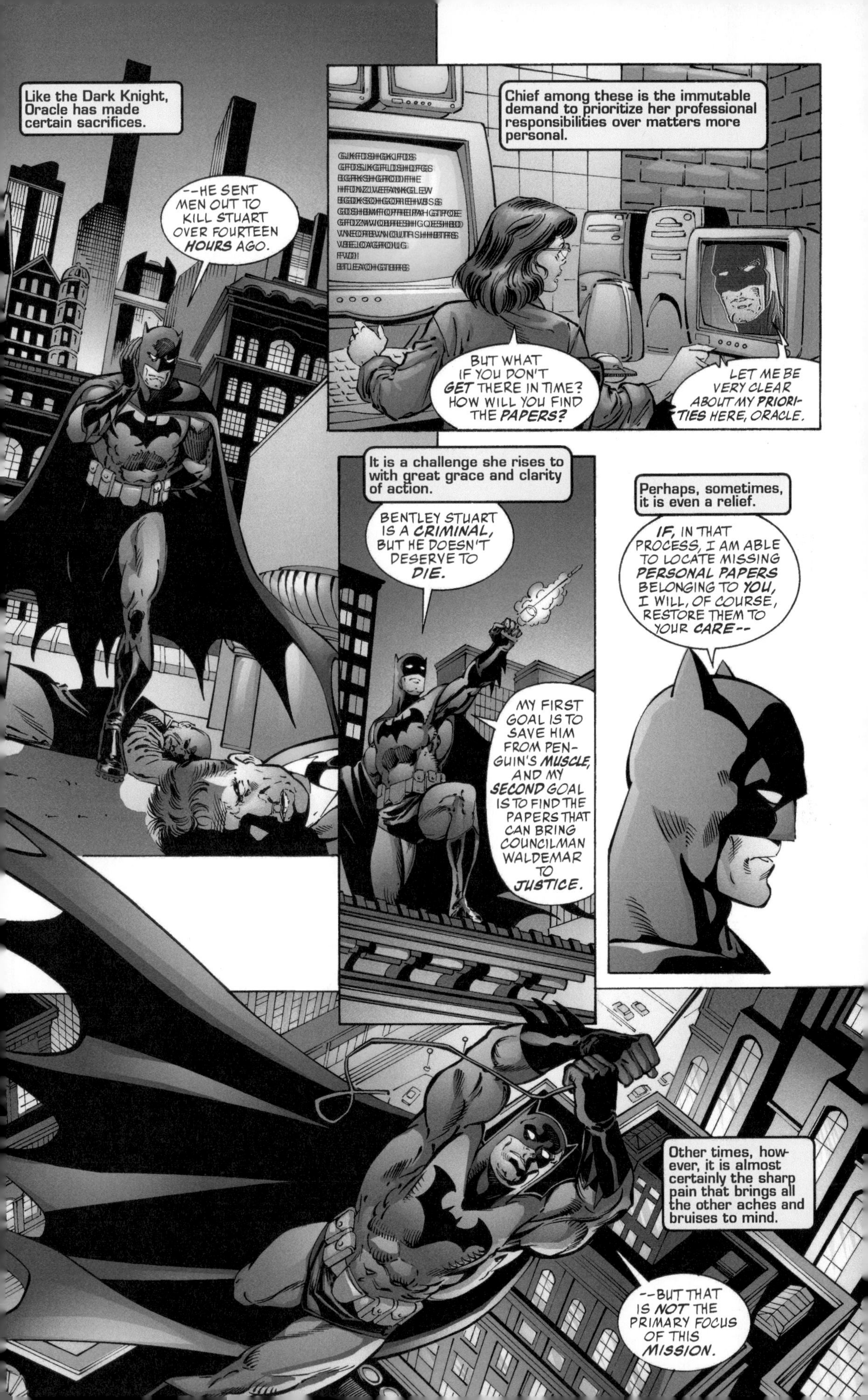
Like the Dark Knight, Oracle has made certain sacrifices.
--HE SENT MEN OUT TO KILL STUART OVER FOURTEEN HOURS AGO.
Chief among these is the immutable demand to prioritize her professional responsibilities over matters more personal.
BUT WHAT IF YOU DON'T GET THERE IN TIME? HOW WILL YOU FIND THE PAPERS?
LET ME BE VERY CLEAR ABOUT MY PRIORITIES HERE, ORACLE.
It is a challenge she rises to with great grace and clarity of action.
BENTLEY STUART IS A CRIMINAL, BUT HE DOESN'T DESERVE TO DIE.
MY FIRST GOAL IS TO SAVE HIM FROM PENGUIN'S MUSCLE, AND MY SECOND GOAL IS TO FIND THE PAPERS THAT CAN BRING COUNCILMAN WALDEMAR TO JUSTICE.
Perhaps, sometimes, it is even a relief.
IF, IN THAT PROCESS, I AM ABLE TO LOCATE MISSING PERSONAL PAPERS BELONGING TO YOU, I WILL, OF COURSE, RESTORE THEM TO YOUR CARE--
Other times, however, it is almost certainly the sharp pain that brings all the other aches and bruises to mind.
--BUT THAT IS NOT THE PRIMARY FOCUS OF THIS MISSION.

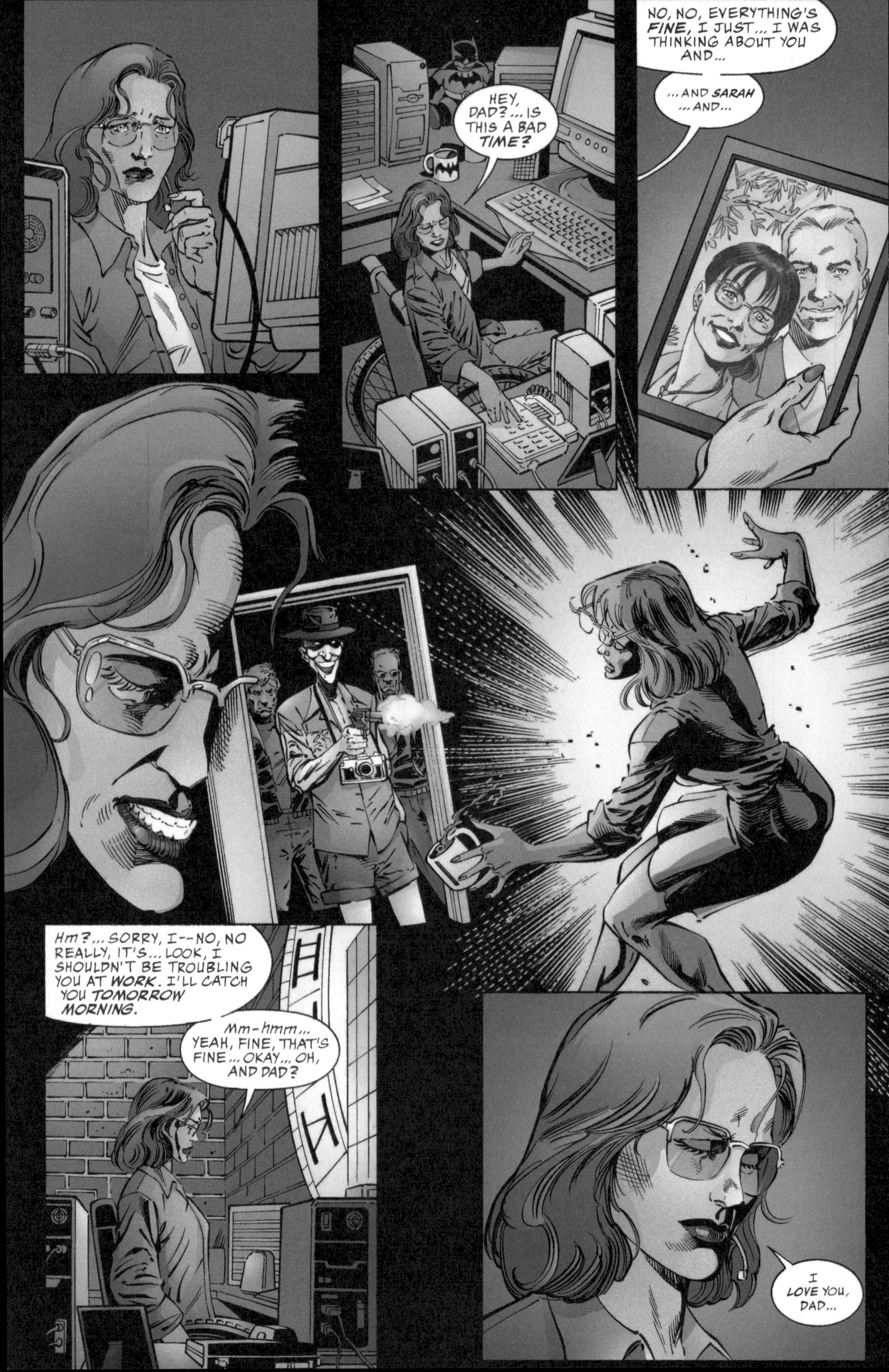

HEY, DAD?... IS THIS A BAD TIME?
NO, NO, EVERYTHING'S FINE, I JUST... I WAS THINKING ABOUT YOU AND...
...AND SARAH ...AND...
Hm?... SORRY, I--NO, NO REALLY, IT'S... LOOK, I SHOULDN'T BE TROUBLING YOU AT WORK. I'LL CATCH YOU TOMORROW MORNING.
Mm-hmm... YEAH, FINE, THAT'S FINE... OKAY... OH, AND DAD?
I LOVE YOU, DAD...

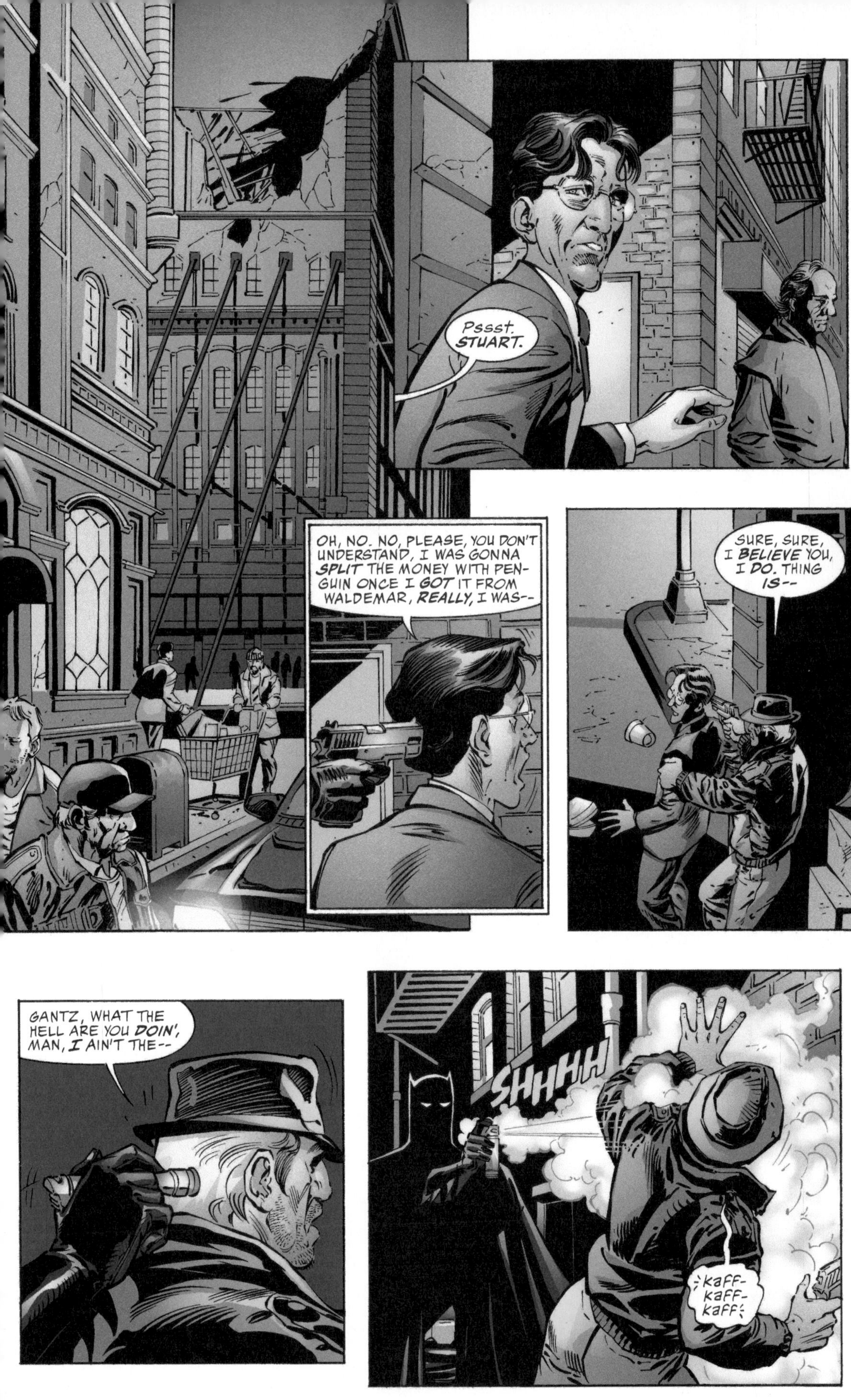
Pssst. STUART.
OH, NO. NO, PLEASE, YOU DON'T UNDERSTAND, I WAS GONNA SPLIT THE MONEY WITH PEN-GUIN ONCE I GOT IT FROM WALDEMAR, REALLY, I WAS--
SURE, SURE, I BELIEVE YOU, I DO. THING IS--
GANTZ, WHAT THE HELL ARE YOU DOIN', MAN, I AIN'T THE--
SHHHH
kaff-kaff-kaff

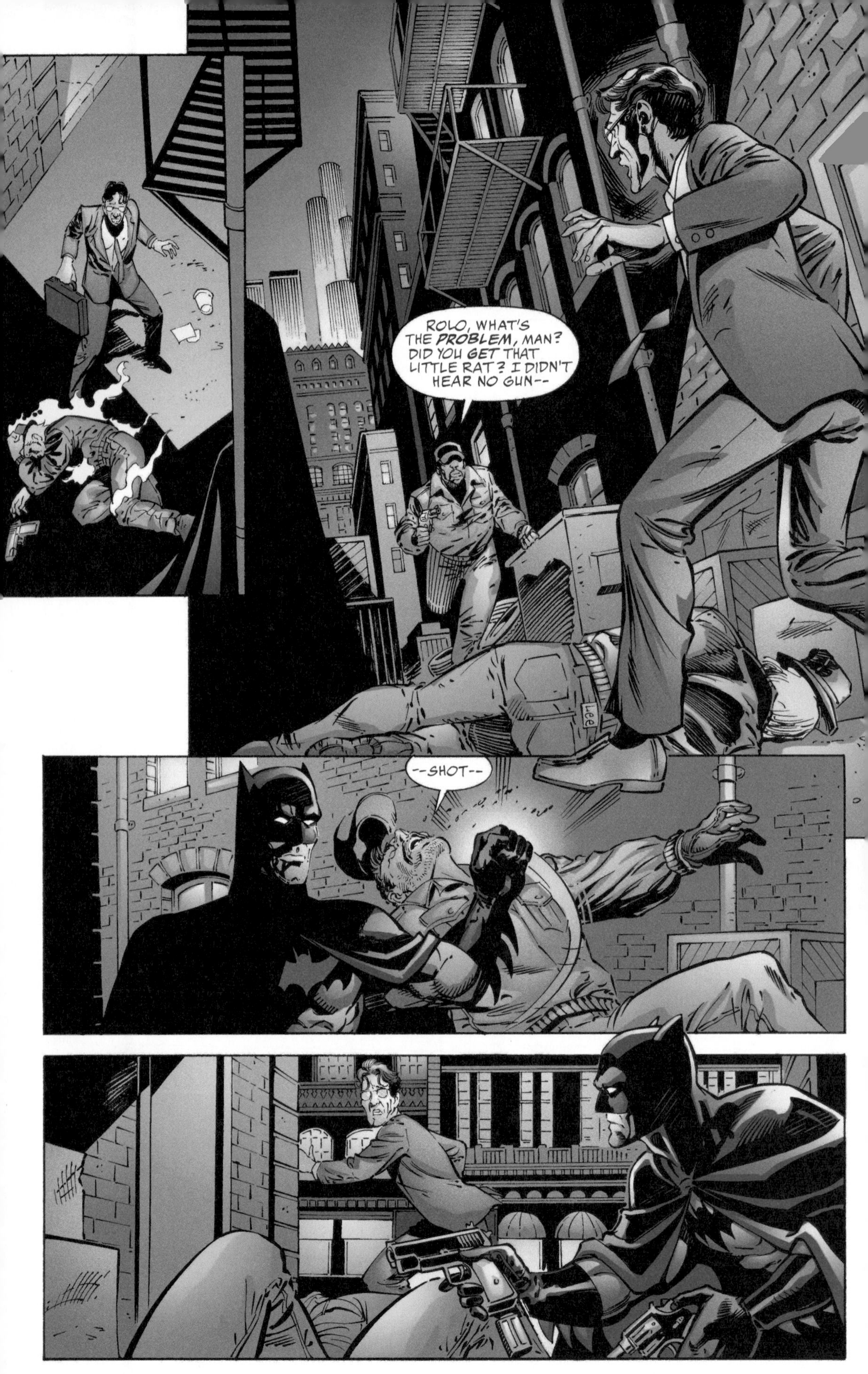
ROLO, WHAT'S THE PROBLEM, MAN? DID YOU GET THAT LITTLE RAT? I DIDN'T HEAR NO GUN--
--SHOT--

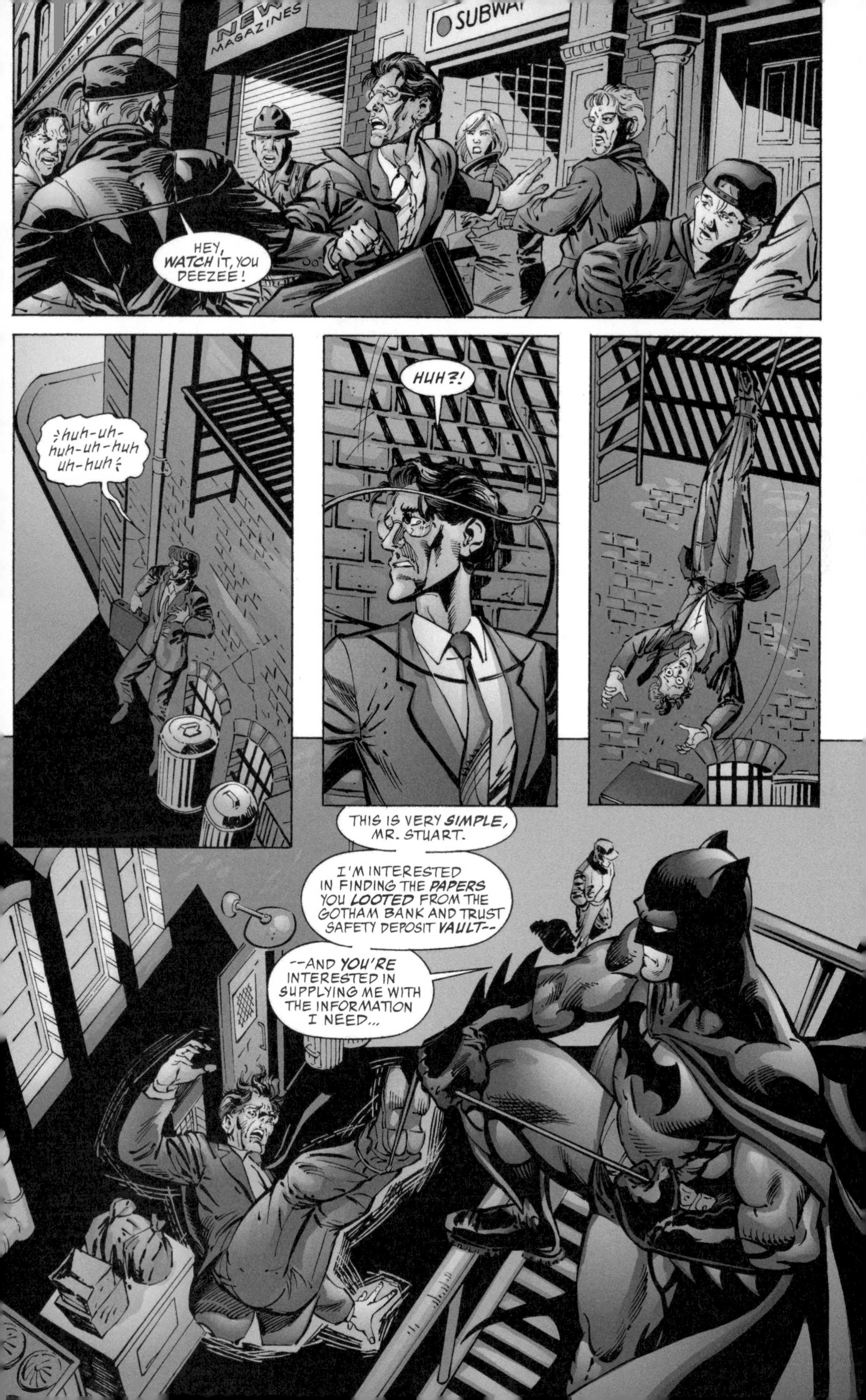

NEWS
MAGAZINES
SUBWAY
HEY, WATCH IT, YOU DEEZEE!
huh-uh-huh-uh-huh uh-huh
HUH?!
THIS IS VERY SIMPLE, MR. STUART.
I'M INTERESTED IN FINDING THE PAPERS YOU LOOTED FROM THE GOTHAM BANK AND TRUST SAFETY DEPOSIT VAULT--
--AND YOU'RE INTERESTED IN SUPPLYING ME WITH THE INFORMATION I NEED...

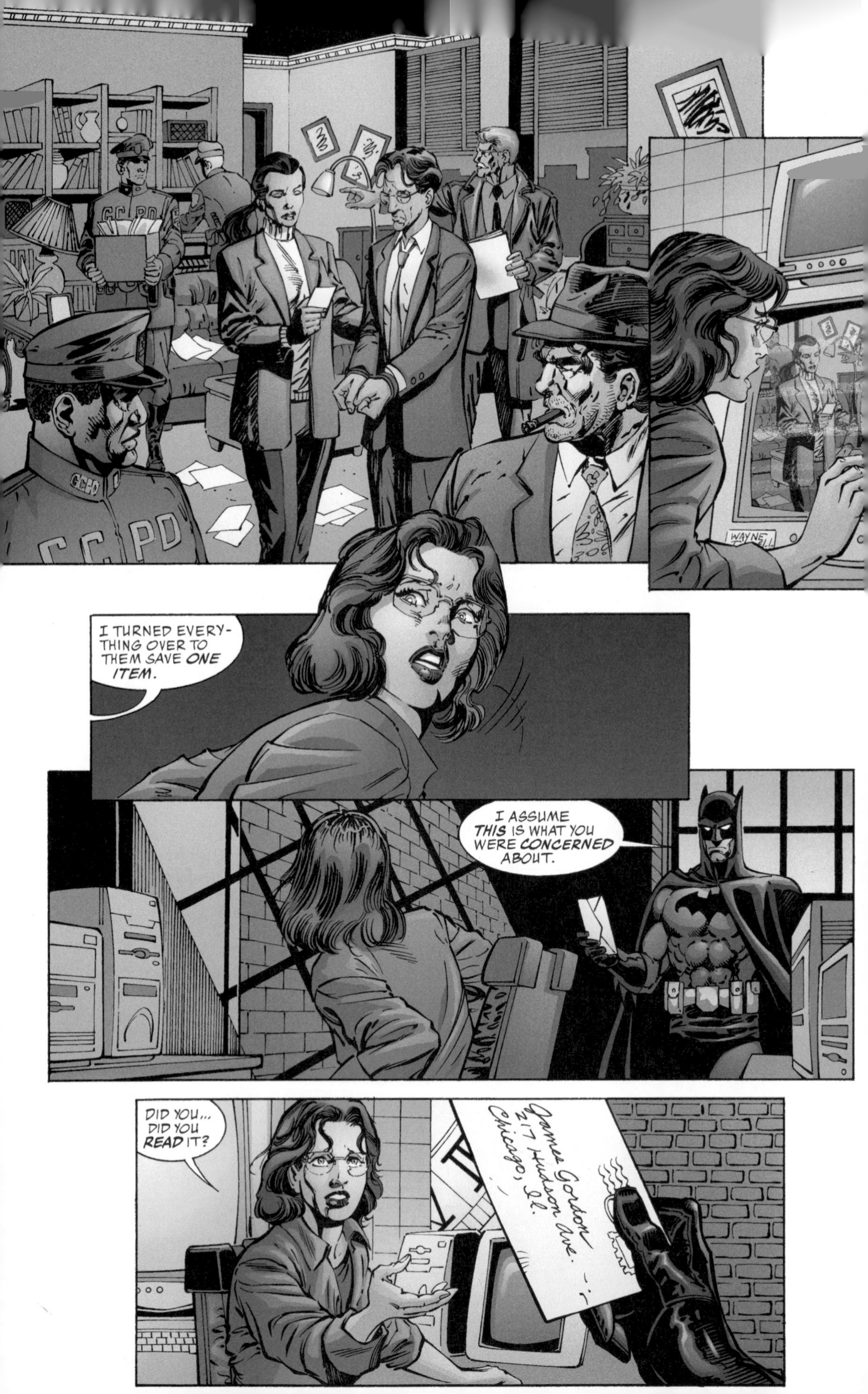
WAYNE
I TURNED EVERYTHING OVER TO THEM SAVE ONE ITEM.
I ASSUME THIS IS WHAT YOU WERE CONCERNED ABOUT.
DID YOU... DID YOU READ IT?
James Gordon
217 Hudson Ave.
Chicago, Il.

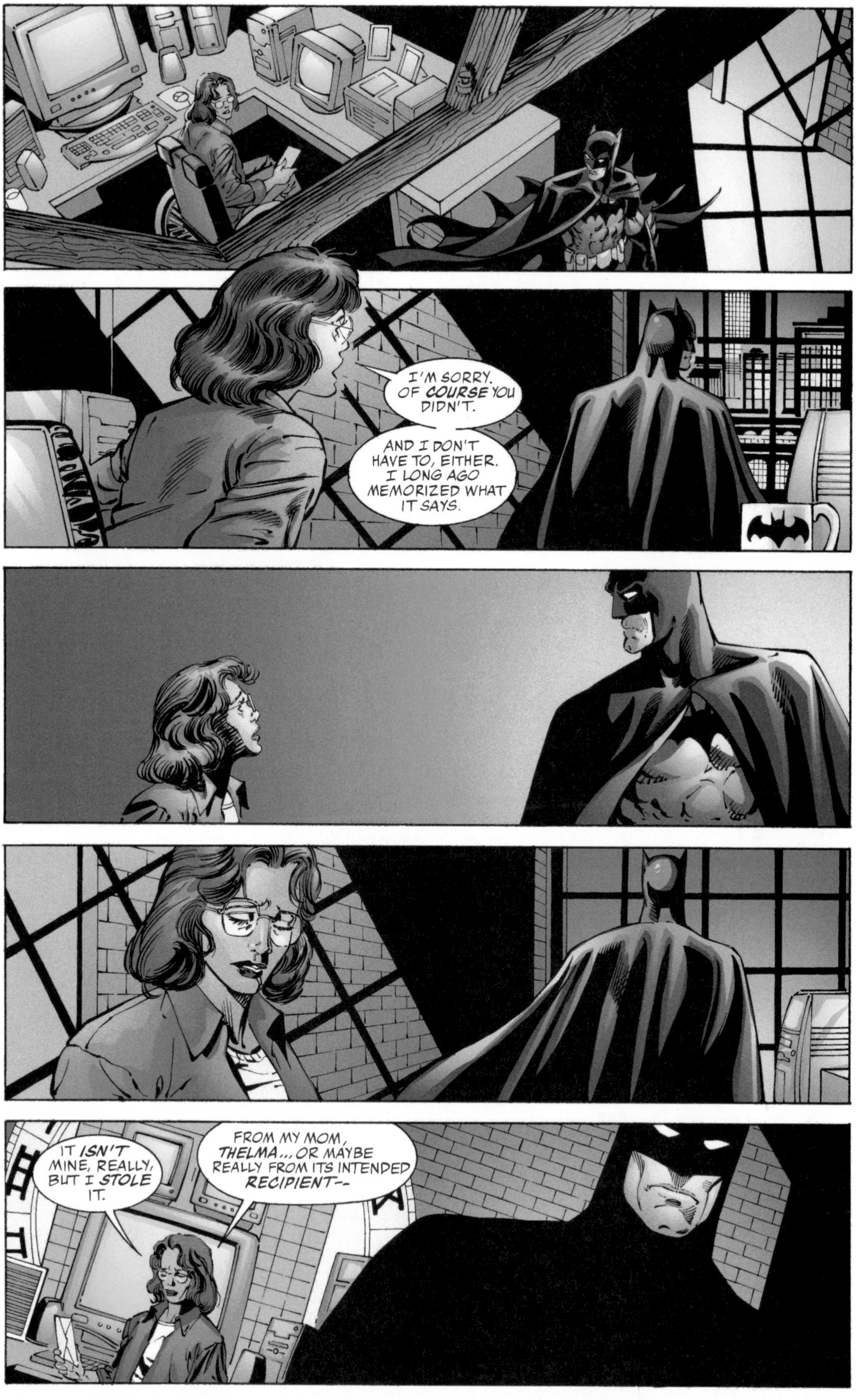
I'M SORRY. OF COURSE YOU DIDN'T.
AND I DON'T HAVE TO, EITHER. I LONG AGO MEMORIZED WHAT IT SAYS.
IT ISN'T MINE, REALLY, BUT I STOLE IT.
FROM MY MOM, THELMA... OR MAYBE REALLY FROM ITS INTENDED RECIPIENT--

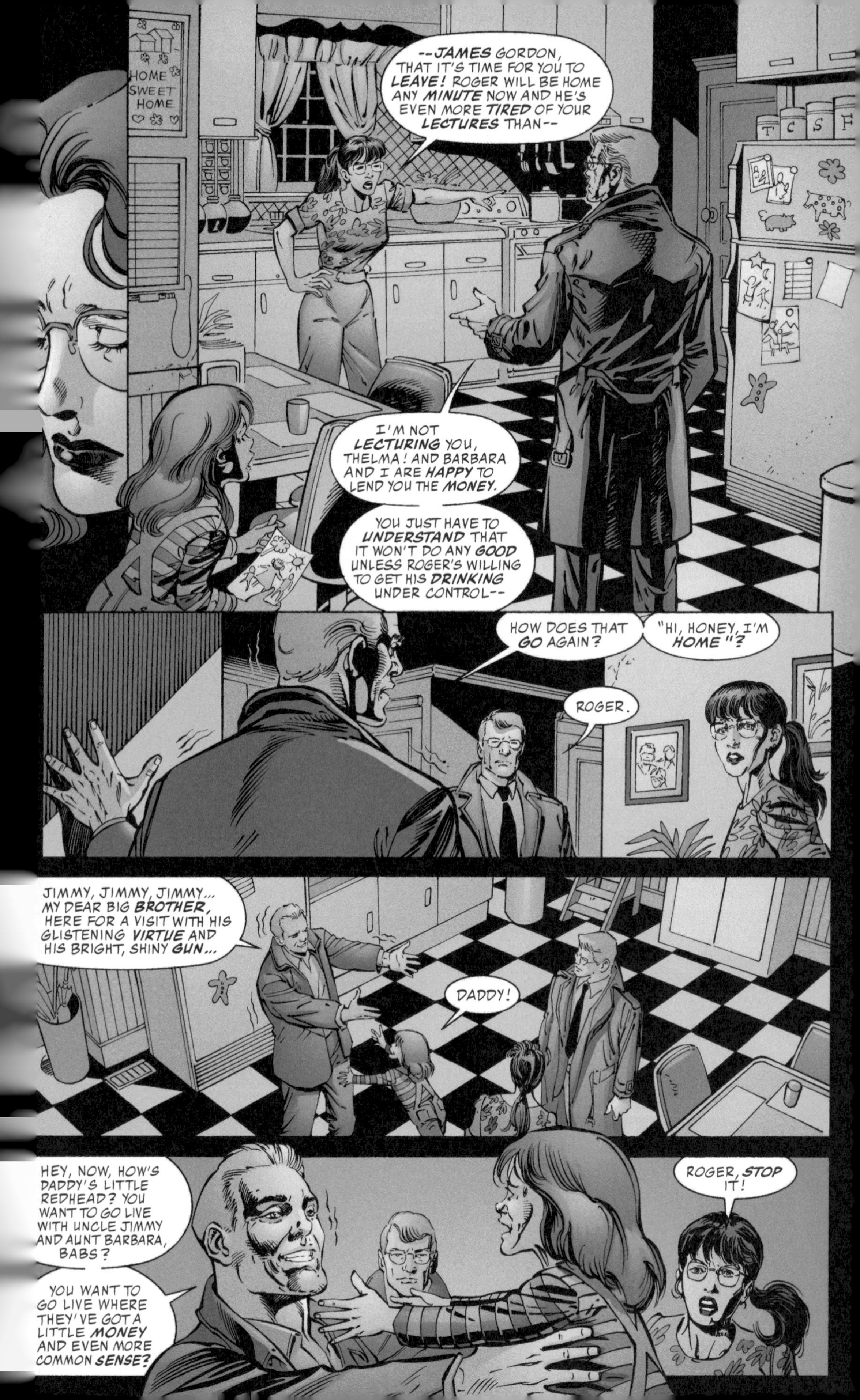
--JAMES GORDON, THAT IT'S TIME FOR YOU TO LEAVE! ROGER WILL BE HOME ANY MINUTE NOW AND HE'S EVEN MORE TIRED OF YOUR LECTURES THAN--
HOME SWEET HOME
T C S F
I'M NOT LECTURING YOU, THELMA! AND BARBARA AND I ARE HAPPY TO LEND YOU THE MONEY.
YOU JUST HAVE TO UNDERSTAND THAT IT WON'T DO ANY GOOD UNLESS ROGER'S WILLING TO GET HIS DRINKING UNDER CONTROL--
HOW DOES THAT GO AGAIN?
"HI, HONEY, I'M HOME"?
ROGER.
JIMMY, JIMMY, JIMMY... MY DEAR BIG BROTHER, HERE FOR A VISIT WITH HIS GLISTENING VIRTUE AND HIS BRIGHT, SHINY GUN...
DADDY!
HEY, NOW, HOW'S DADDY'S LITTLE REDHEAD? YOU WANT TO GO LIVE WITH UNCLE JIMMY AND AUNT BARBARA, BABS?
YOU WANT TO GO LIVE WHERE THEY'VE GOT A LITTLE MONEY AND EVEN MORE COMMON SENSE?
ROGER, STOP IT!

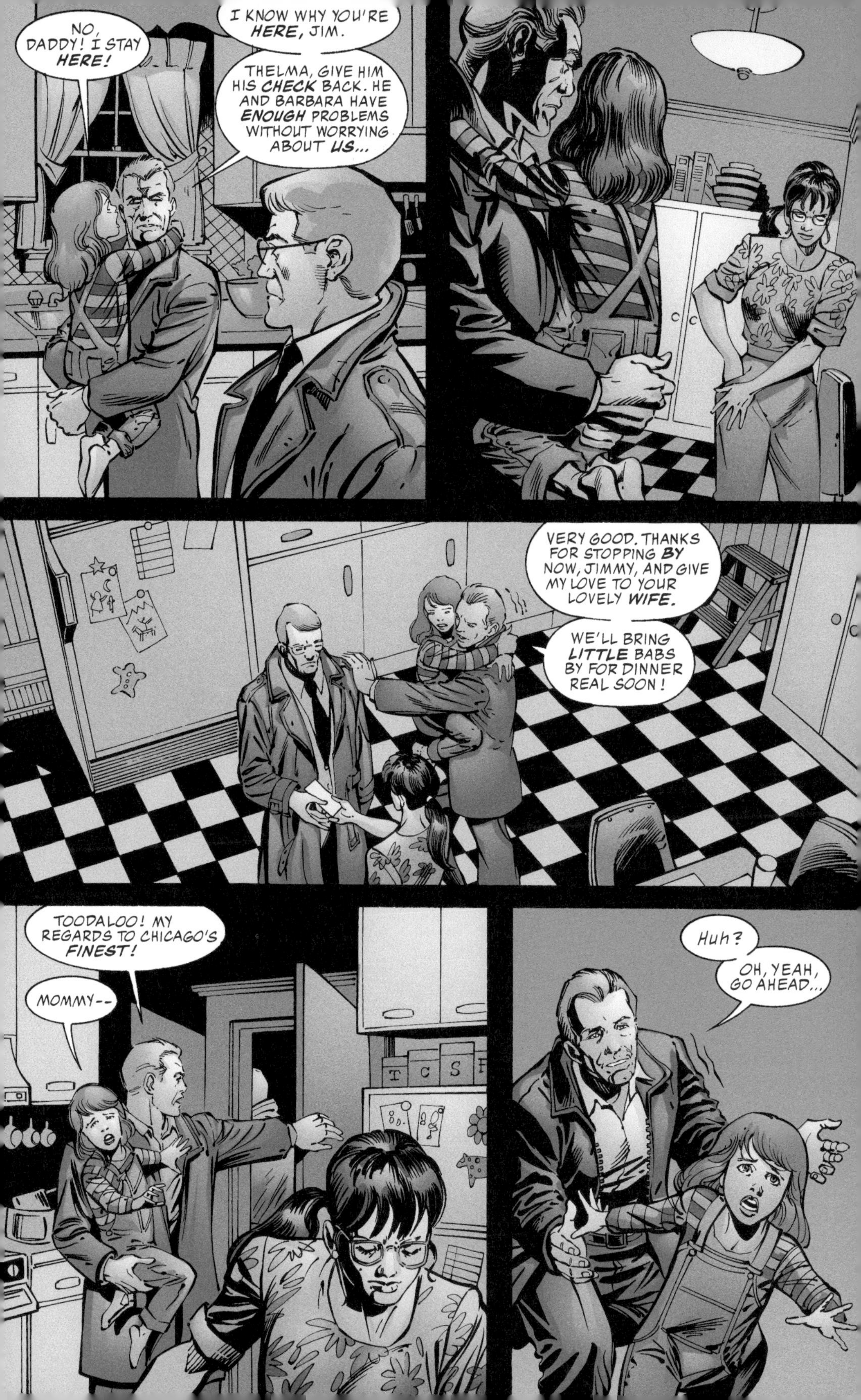
NO, DADDY! I STAY HERE!
I KNOW WHY YOU'RE HERE, JIM.
THELMA, GIVE HIM HIS CHECK BACK. HE AND BARBARA HAVE ENOUGH PROBLEMS WITHOUT WORRYING ABOUT US...
VERY GOOD. THANKS FOR STOPPING BY NOW, JIMMY, AND GIVE MY LOVE TO YOUR LOVELY WIFE.
WE'LL BRING LITTLE BABS BY FOR DINNER REAL SOON!
TOODALOO! MY REGARDS TO CHICAGO'S FINEST!
MOMMY--
Huh?
OH, YEAH, GO AHEAD...

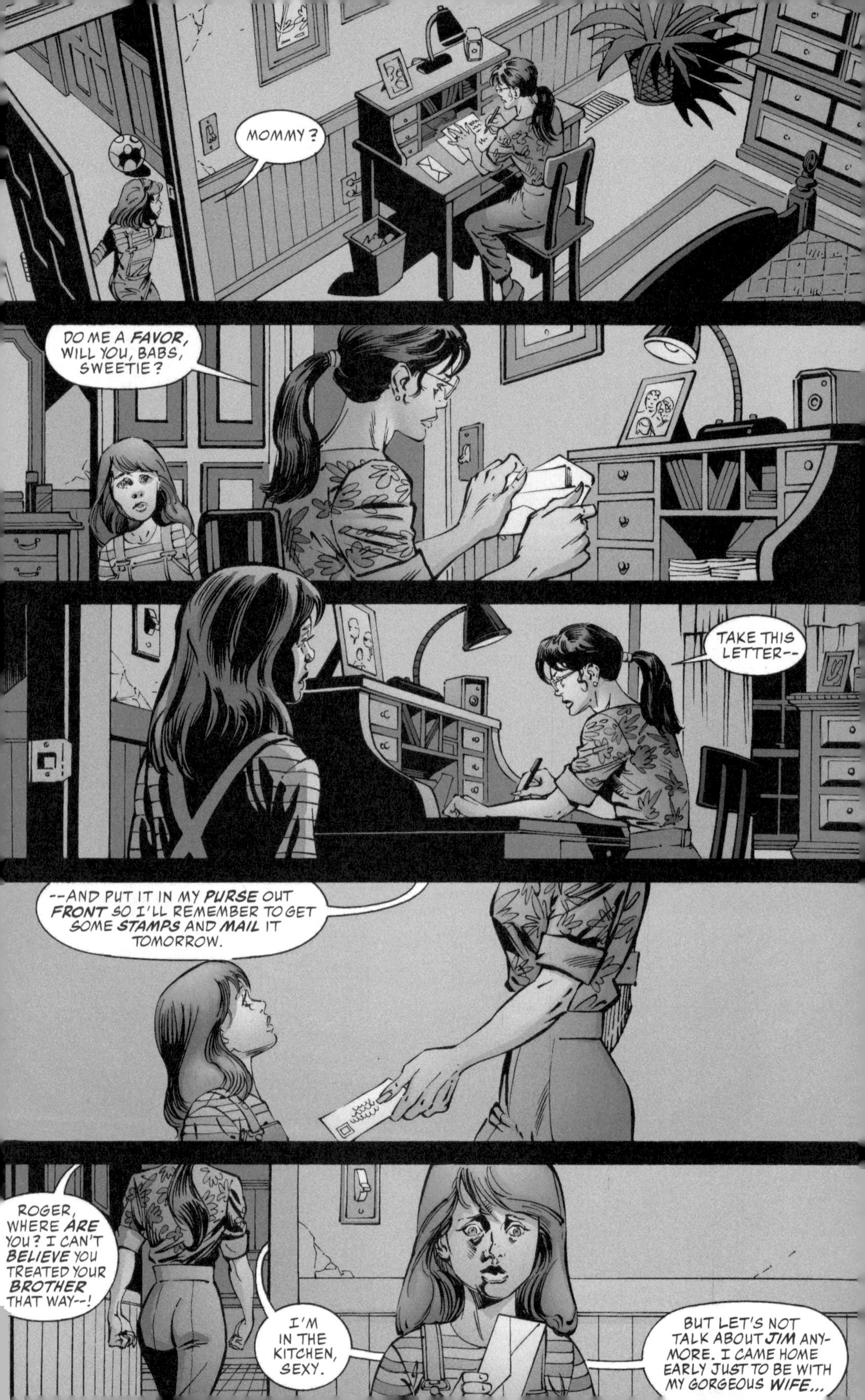
MOMMY?
DO ME A FAVOR, WILL YOU, BABS, SWEETIE?
TAKE THIS LETTER--
--AND PUT IT IN MY PURSE OUT FRONT SO I'LL REMEMBER TO GET SOME STAMPS AND MAIL IT TOMORROW.
ROGER, WHERE ARE YOU? I CAN'T BELIEVE YOU TREATED YOUR BROTHER THAT WAY--!
I'M IN THE KITCHEN, SEXY.
BUT LET'S NOT TALK ABOUT JIM ANYMORE. I CAME HOME EARLY JUST TO BE WITH MY GORGEOUS WIFE...

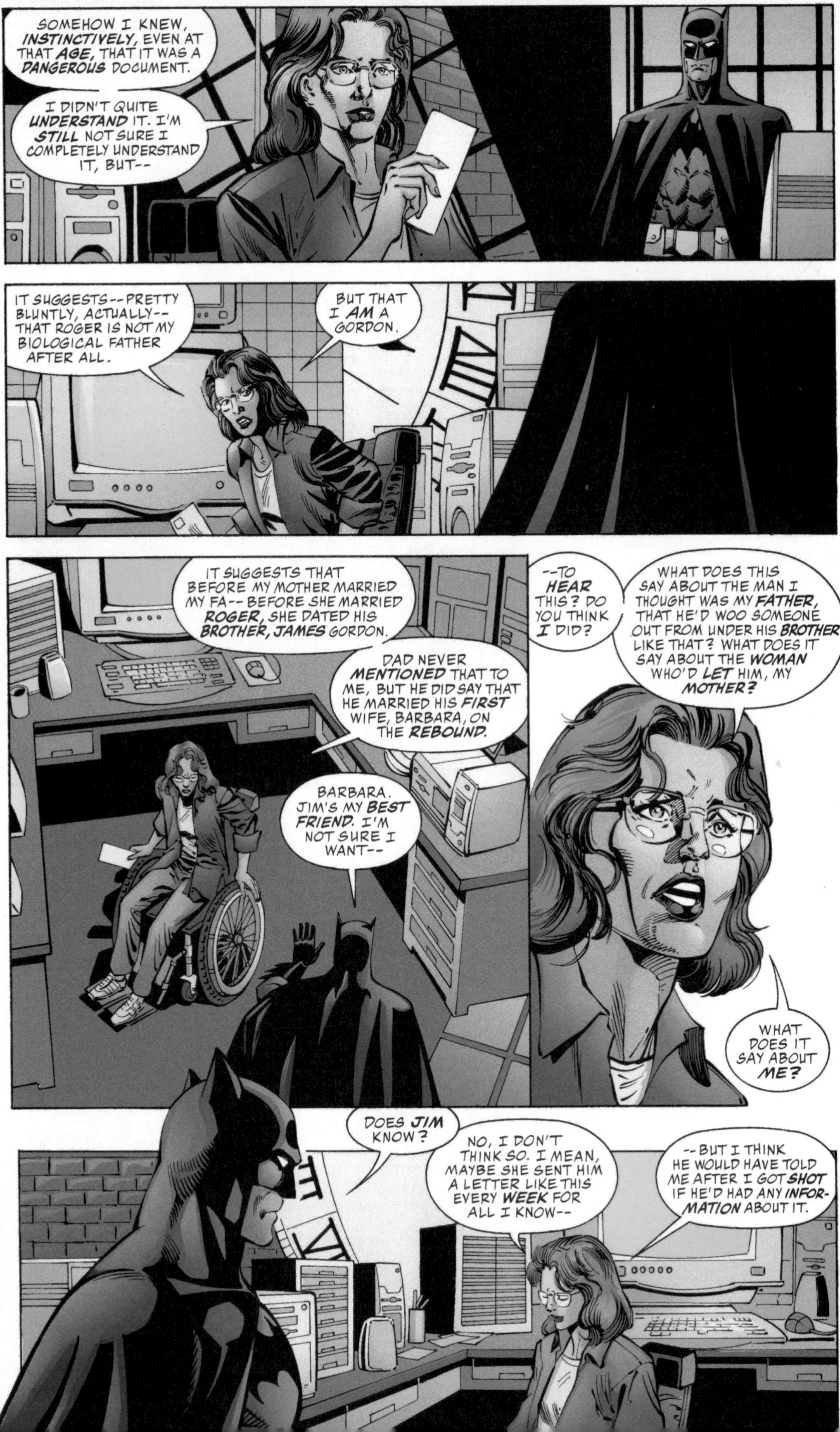
SOMEHOW I KNEW, INSTINCTIVELY, EVEN AT THAT AGE, THAT IT WAS A DANGEROUS DOCUMENT.
I DIDN'T QUITE UNDERSTAND IT. I'M STILL NOT SURE I COMPLETELY UNDERSTAND IT, BUT--
IT SUGGESTS--PRETTY BLUNTLY, ACTUALLY--THAT ROGER IS NOT MY BIOLOGICAL FATHER AFTER ALL.
BUT THAT I AM A GORDON.
IT SUGGESTS THAT BEFORE MY MOTHER MARRIED MY FA-- BEFORE SHE MARRIED ROGER, SHE DATED HIS BROTHER, JAMES GORDON.
DAD NEVER MENTIONED THAT TO ME, BUT HE DID SAY THAT HE MARRIED HIS FIRST WIFE, BARBARA, ON THE REBOUND.
BARBARA. JIM'S MY BEST FRIEND. I'M NOT SURE I WANT--
--TO HEAR THIS? DO YOU THINK I DID?
WHAT DOES THIS SAY ABOUT THE MAN I THOUGHT WAS MY FATHER, THAT HE'D WOO SOMEONE OUT FROM UNDER HIS BROTHER LIKE THAT? WHAT DOES IT SAY ABOUT THE WOMAN WHO'D LET HIM, MY MOTHER?
WHAT DOES IT SAY ABOUT ME?
DOES JIM KNOW?
NO, I DON'T THINK SO. I MEAN, MAYBE SHE SENT HIM A LETTER LIKE THIS EVERY WEEK FOR ALL I KNOW--
--BUT I THINK HE WOULD HAVE TOLD ME AFTER I GOT SHOT IF HE'D HAD ANY INFORMATION ABOUT IT.

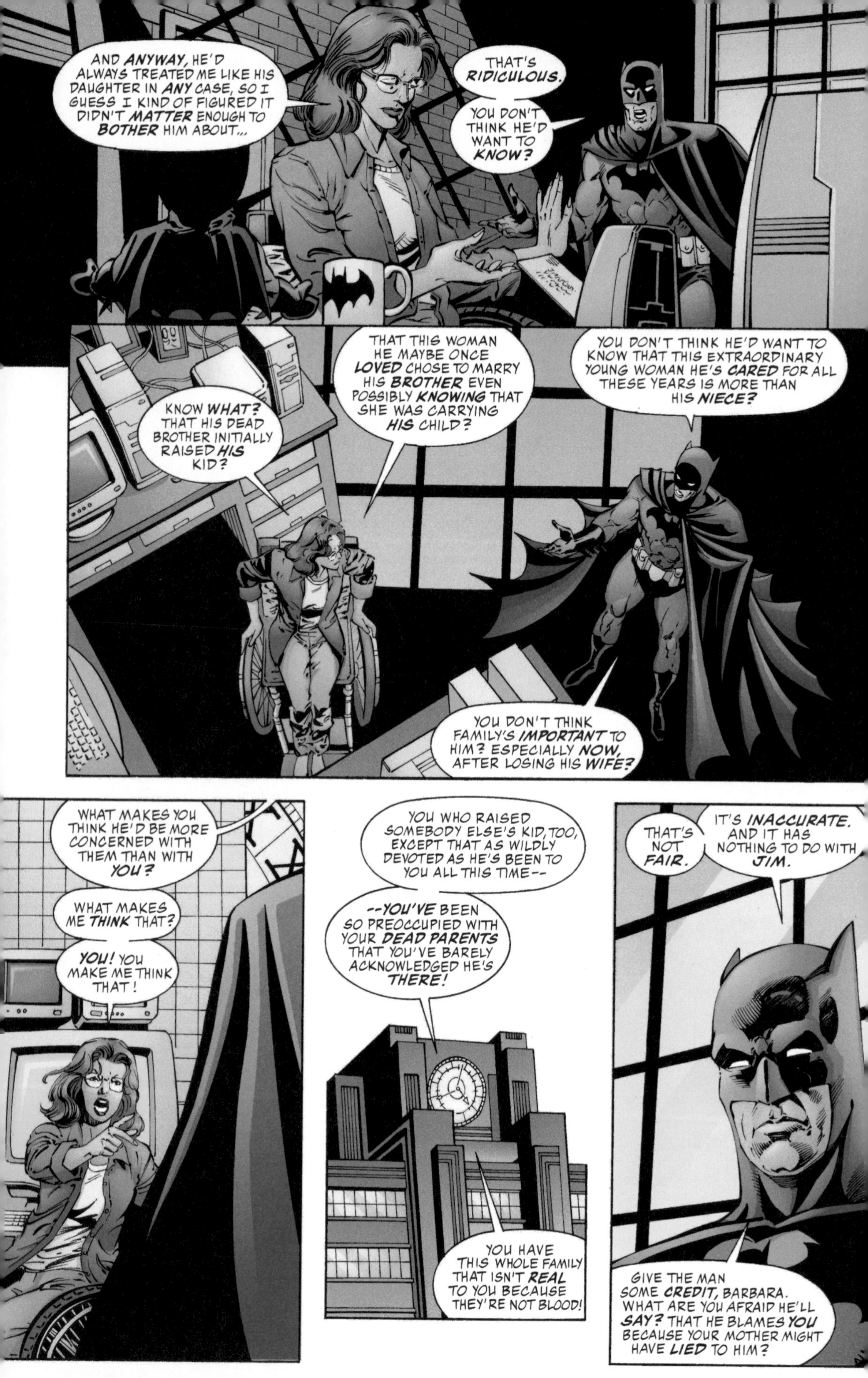
AND ANYWAY, HE'D ALWAYS TREATED ME LIKE HIS DAUGHTER IN ANY CASE, SO I GUESS I KIND OF FIGURED IT DIDN'T MATTER ENOUGH TO BOTHER HIM ABOUT...
THAT'S RIDICULOUS.
YOU DON'T THINK HE'D WANT TO KNOW?
KNOW WHAT? THAT HIS DEAD BROTHER INITIALLY RAISED HIS KID?
THAT THIS WOMAN HE MAYBE ONCE LOVED CHOSE TO MARRY HIS BROTHER EVEN POSSIBLY KNOWING THAT SHE WAS CARRYING HIS CHILD?
YOU DON'T THINK HE'D WANT TO KNOW THAT THIS EXTRAORDINARY YOUNG WOMAN HE'S CARED FOR ALL THESE YEARS IS MORE THAN HIS NIECE?
YOU DON'T THINK FAMILY'S IMPORTANT TO HIM? ESPECIALLY NOW, AFTER LOSING HIS WIFE?
WHAT MAKES YOU THINK HE'D BE MORE CONCERNED WITH THEM THAN WITH YOU?
WHAT MAKES ME THINK THAT?
YOU! YOU MAKE ME THINK THAT!
YOU WHO RAISED SOMEBODY ELSE'S KID, TOO, EXCEPT THAT AS WILDLY DEVOTED AS HE'S BEEN TO YOU ALL THIS TIME--
--YOU'VE BEEN SO PREOCCUPIED WITH YOUR DEAD PARENTS THAT YOU'VE BARELY ACKNOWLEDGED HE'S THERE!
YOU HAVE THIS WHOLE FAMILY THAT ISN'T REAL TO YOU BECAUSE THEY'RE NOT BLOOD!
THAT'S NOT FAIR.
IT'S INACCURATE. AND IT HAS NOTHING TO DO WITH JIM.
GIVE THE MAN SOME CREDIT, BARBARA. WHAT ARE YOU AFRAID HE'LL SAY? THAT HE BLAMES YOU BECAUSE YOUR MOTHER MIGHT HAVE LIED TO HIM?

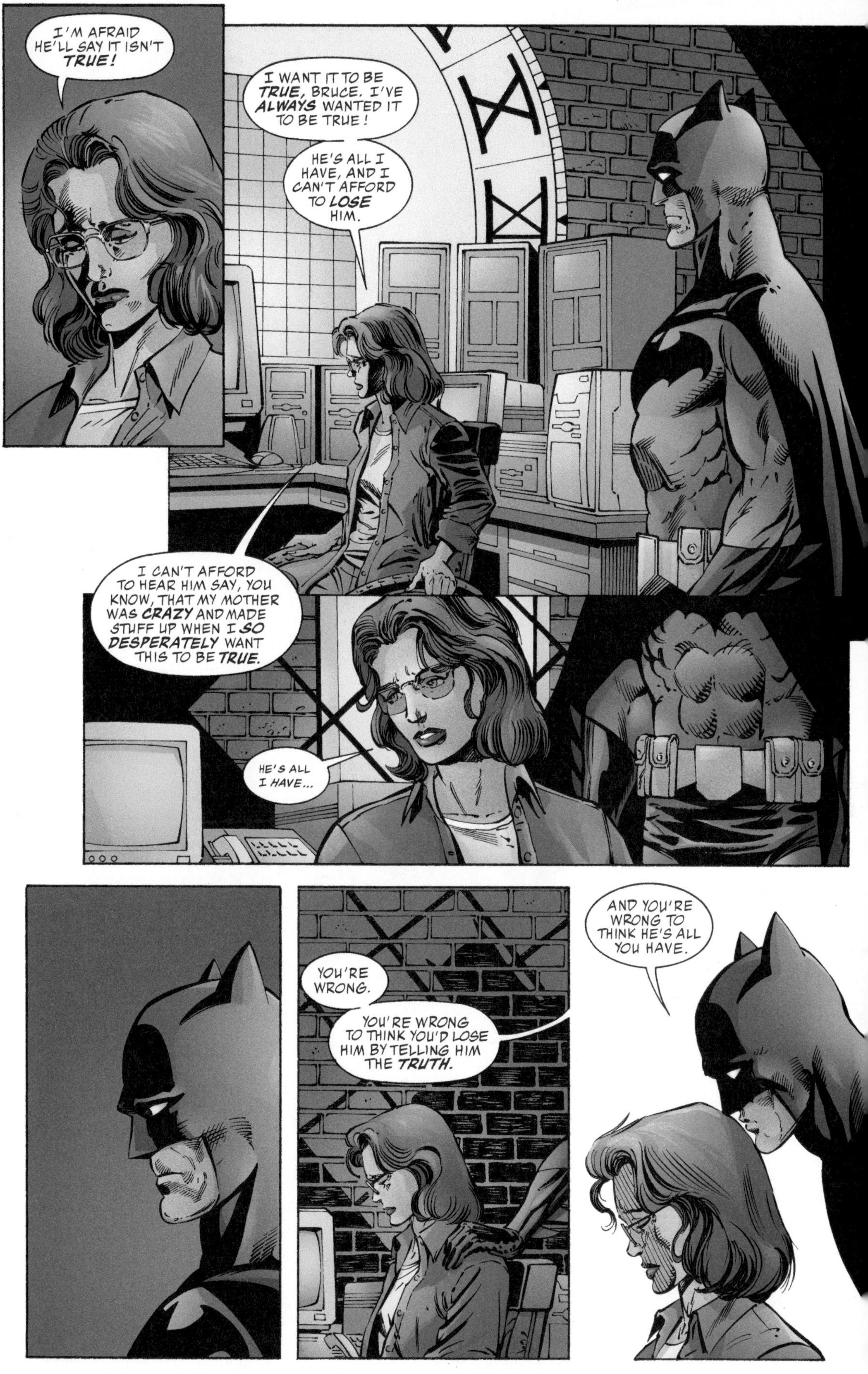
I'M AFRAID HE'LL SAY IT ISN'T **TRUE!**
I WANT IT TO BE **TRUE,** BRUCE. I'VE **ALWAYS** WANTED IT TO BE TRUE!
HE'S ALL I HAVE, AND I CAN'T AFFORD TO **LOSE** HIM.
I CAN'T AFFORD TO HEAR HIM SAY, YOU KNOW, THAT MY MOTHER WAS **CRAZY** AND MADE STUFF UP WHEN I **SO DESPERATELY** WANT THIS TO BE **TRUE.**
HE'S ALL *I HAVE...*
YOU'RE WRONG.
YOU'RE WRONG TO THINK YOU'D LOSE HIM BY TELLING HIM THE **TRUTH.**
AND YOU'RE WRONG TO THINK HE'S ALL YOU HAVE.

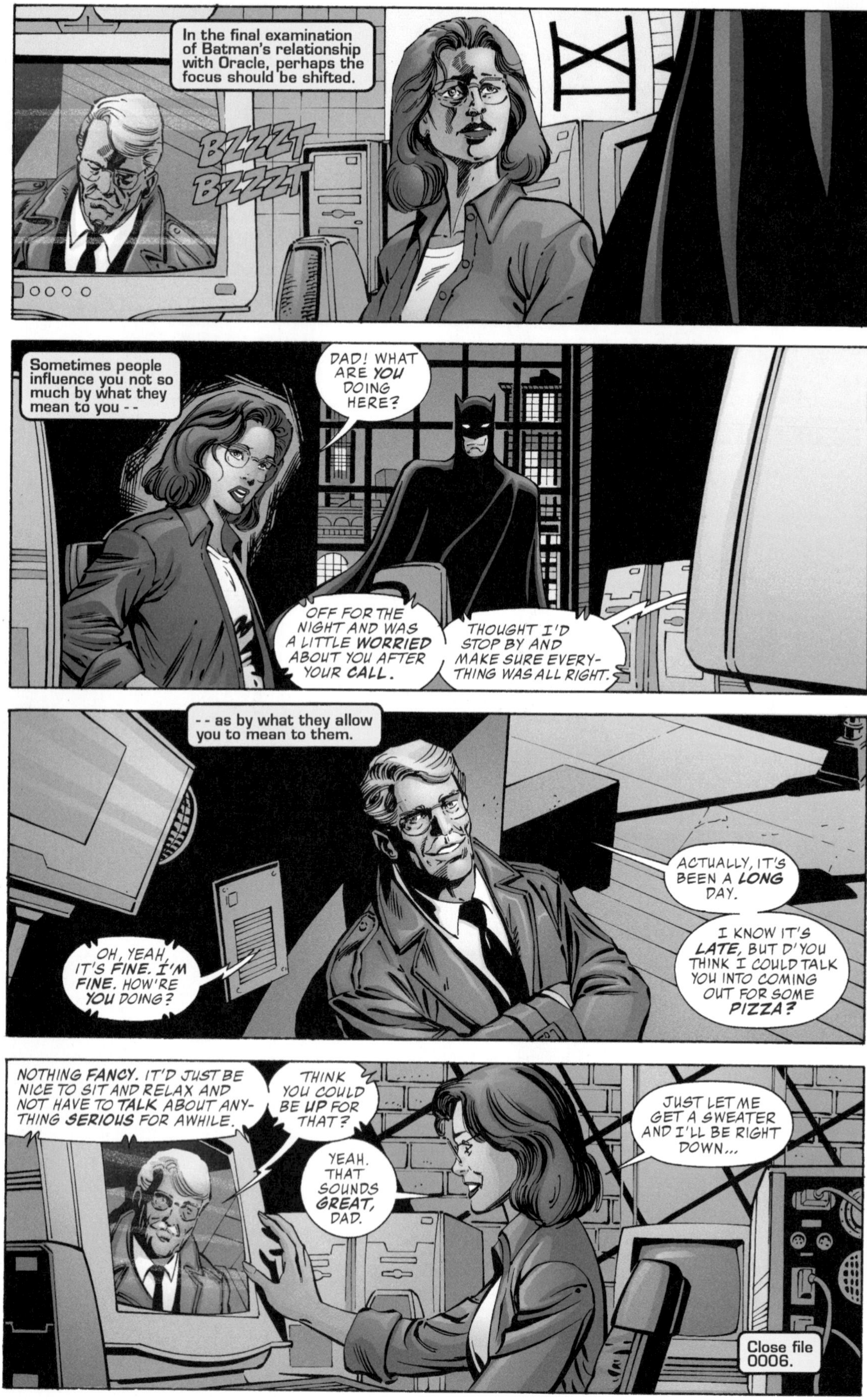
In the final examination of Batman's relationship with Oracle, perhaps the focus should be shifted.
BZZZT BZZZT
Sometimes people influence you not so much by what they mean to you - -
DAD! WHAT ARE YOU DOING HERE?
OFF FOR THE NIGHT AND WAS A LITTLE WORRIED ABOUT YOU AFTER YOUR CALL.
THOUGHT I'D STOP BY AND MAKE SURE EVERY-THING WAS ALL RIGHT.
- - as by what they allow you to mean to them.
OH, YEAH, IT'S FINE. I'M FINE. HOW'RE YOU DOING?
ACTUALLY, IT'S BEEN A LONG DAY.
I KNOW IT'S LATE, BUT D'YOU THINK I COULD TALK YOU INTO COMING OUT FOR SOME PIZZA?
NOTHING FANCY. IT'D JUST BE NICE TO SIT AND RELAX AND NOT HAVE TO TALK ABOUT ANY-THING SERIOUS FOR AWHILE.
THINK YOU COULD BE UP FOR THAT?
YEAH. THAT SOUNDS GREAT, DAD.
JUST LET ME GET A SWEATER AND I'LL BE RIGHT DOWN...
Close file 0006.

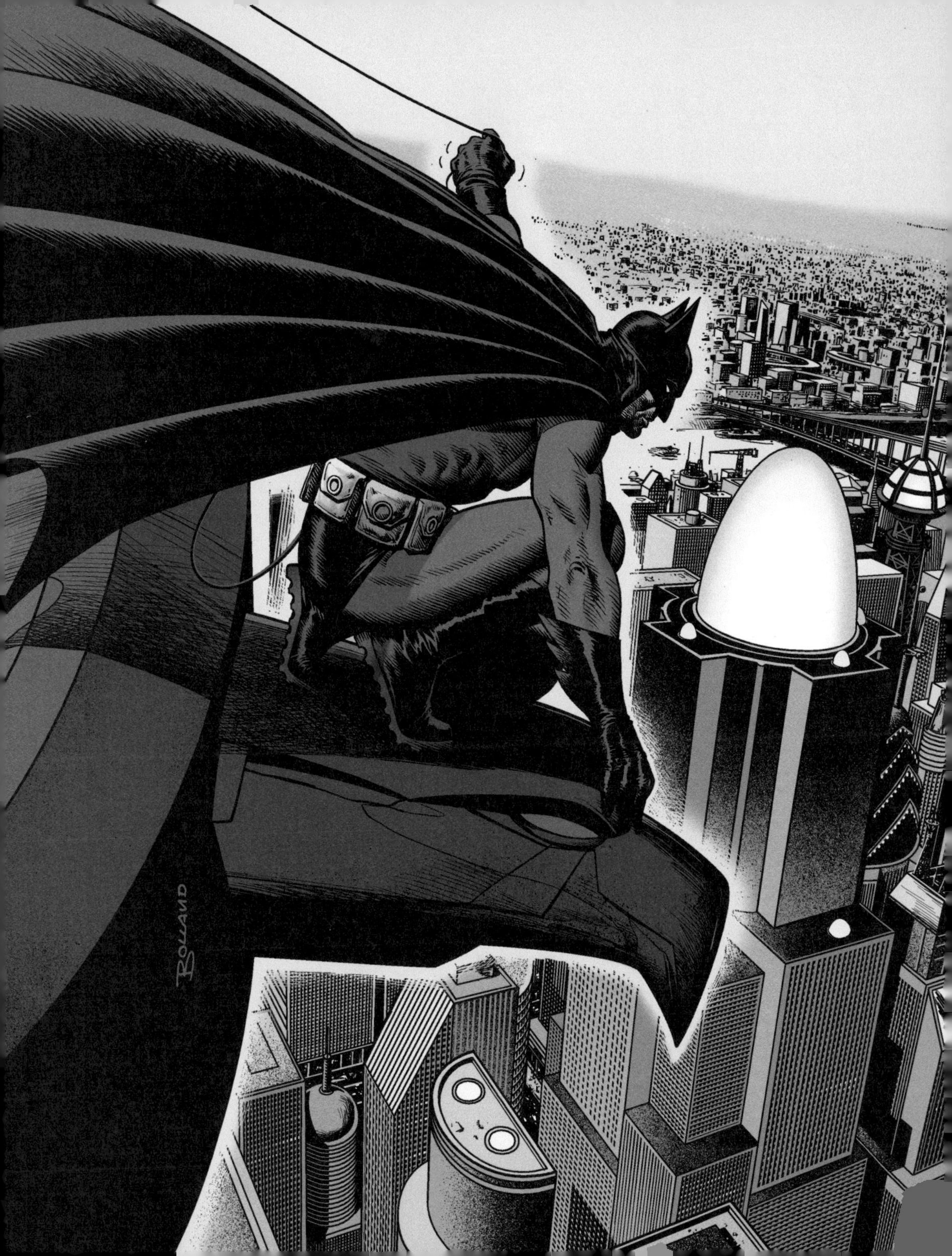

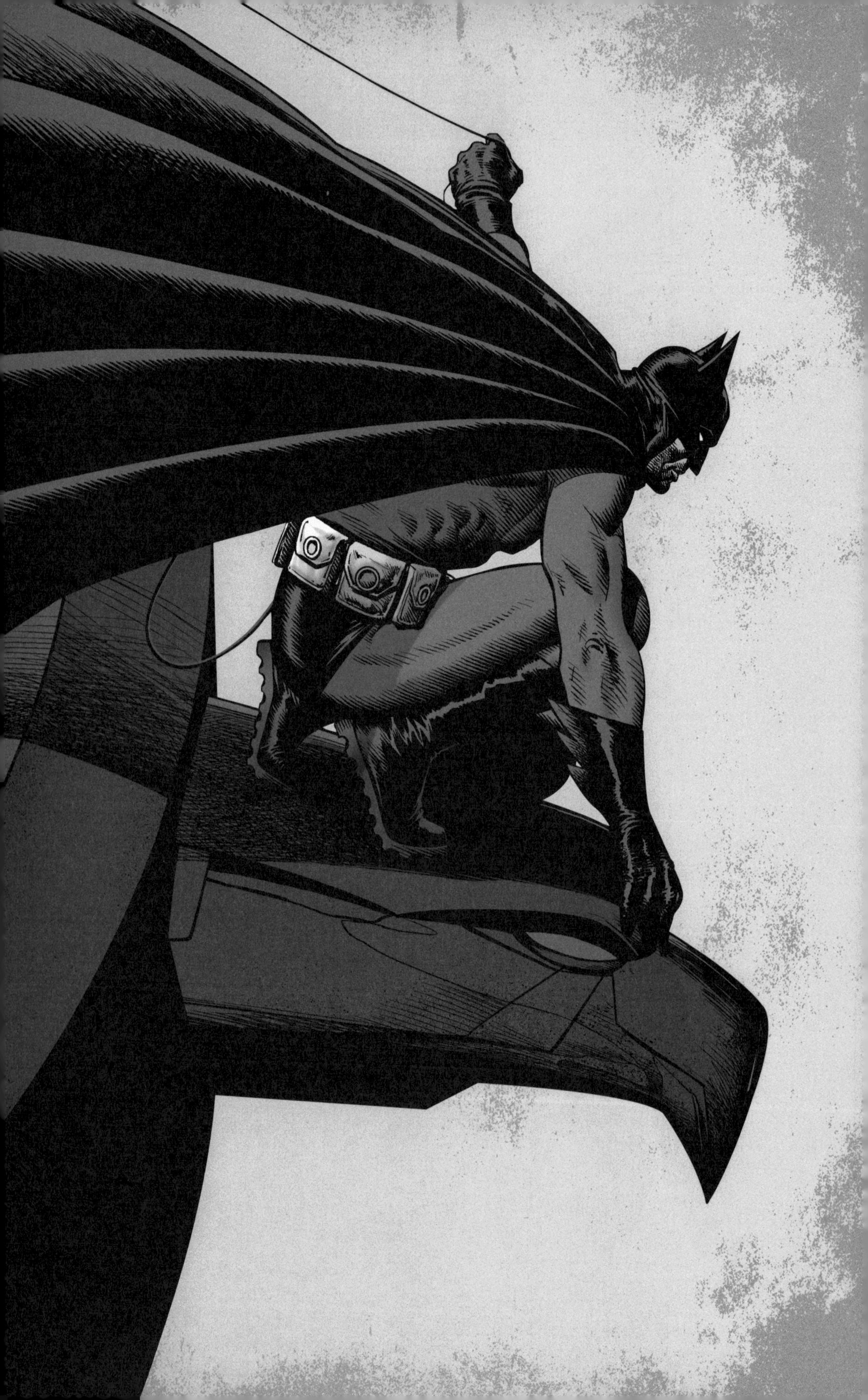

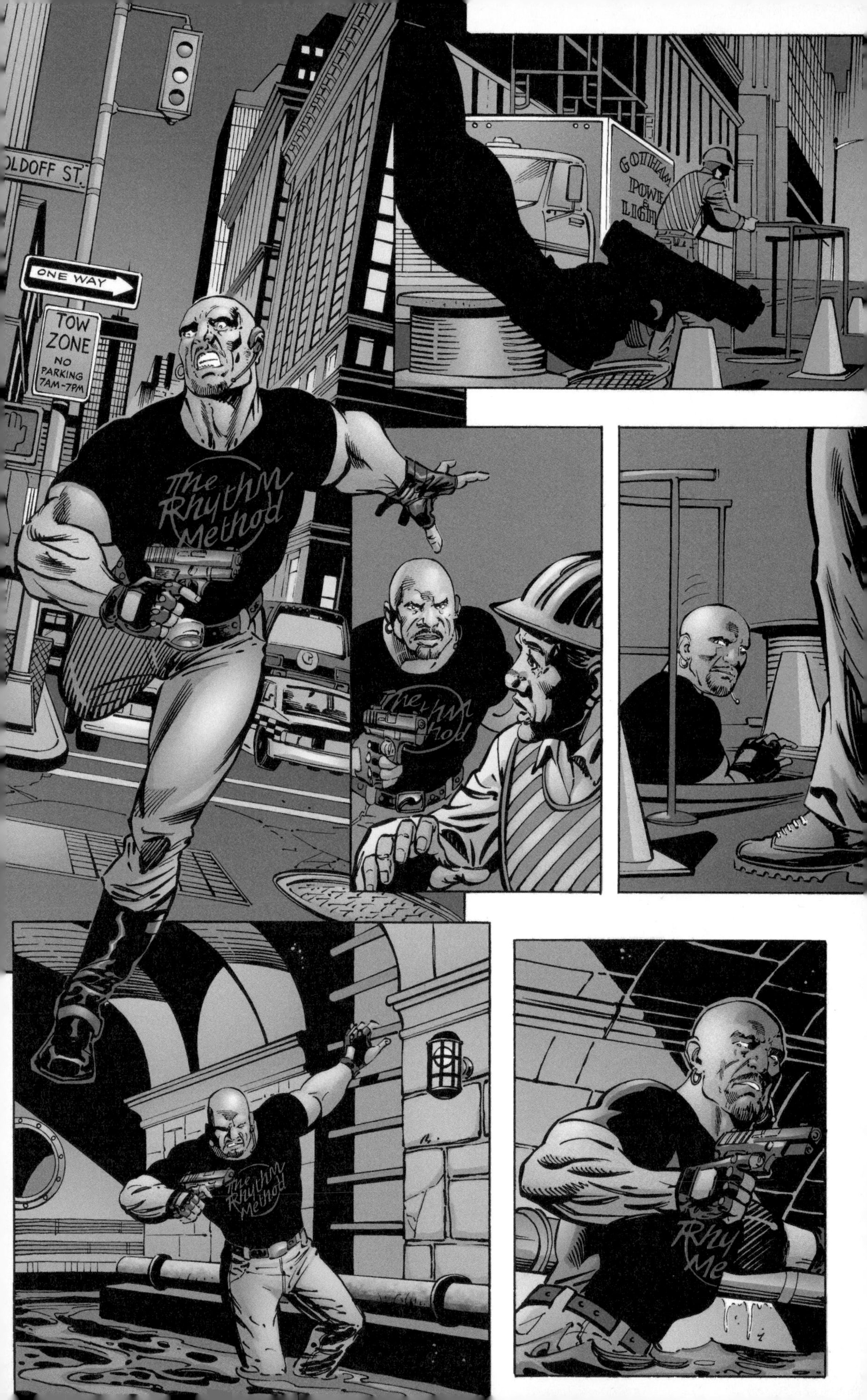
OLDOFF ST.
ONE WAY
TOW ZONE
NO PARKING
7AM-7PM
GOTHAM
The Rhythm Method

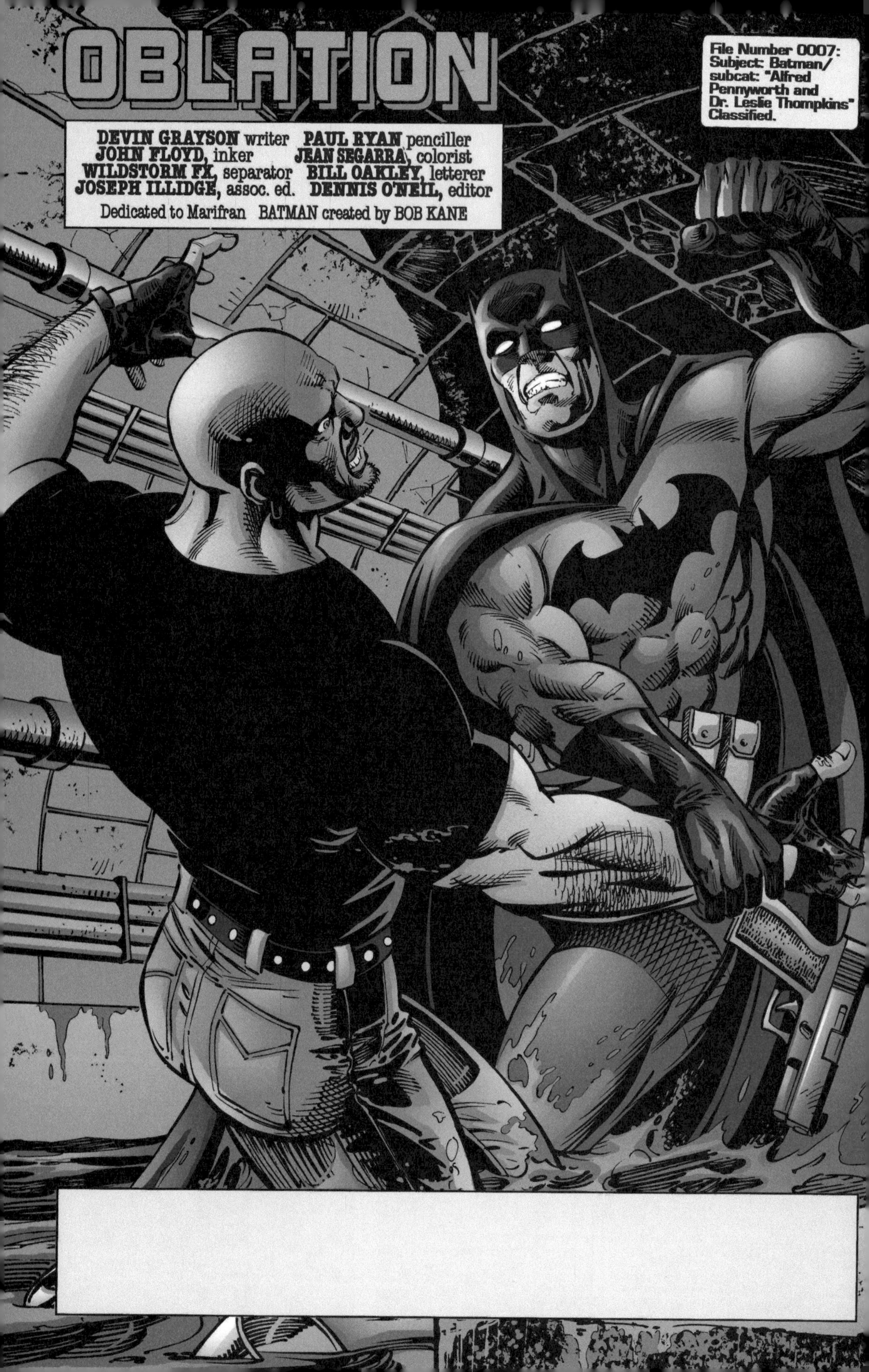
OBLATION
DEVIN GRAYSON writer PAUL RYAN penciller
JOHN FLOYD, inker JEAN SEGARRA, colorist
WILDSTORM FX, separator BILL OAKLEY, letterer
JOSEPH ILLIDGE, assoc. ed. DENNIS O'NEIL, editor
Dedicated to Marifran BATMAN created by BOB KANE
File Number 0007: Subject: Batman/ subcat: "Alfred Pennyworth and Dr. Leslie Thompkins" Classified.

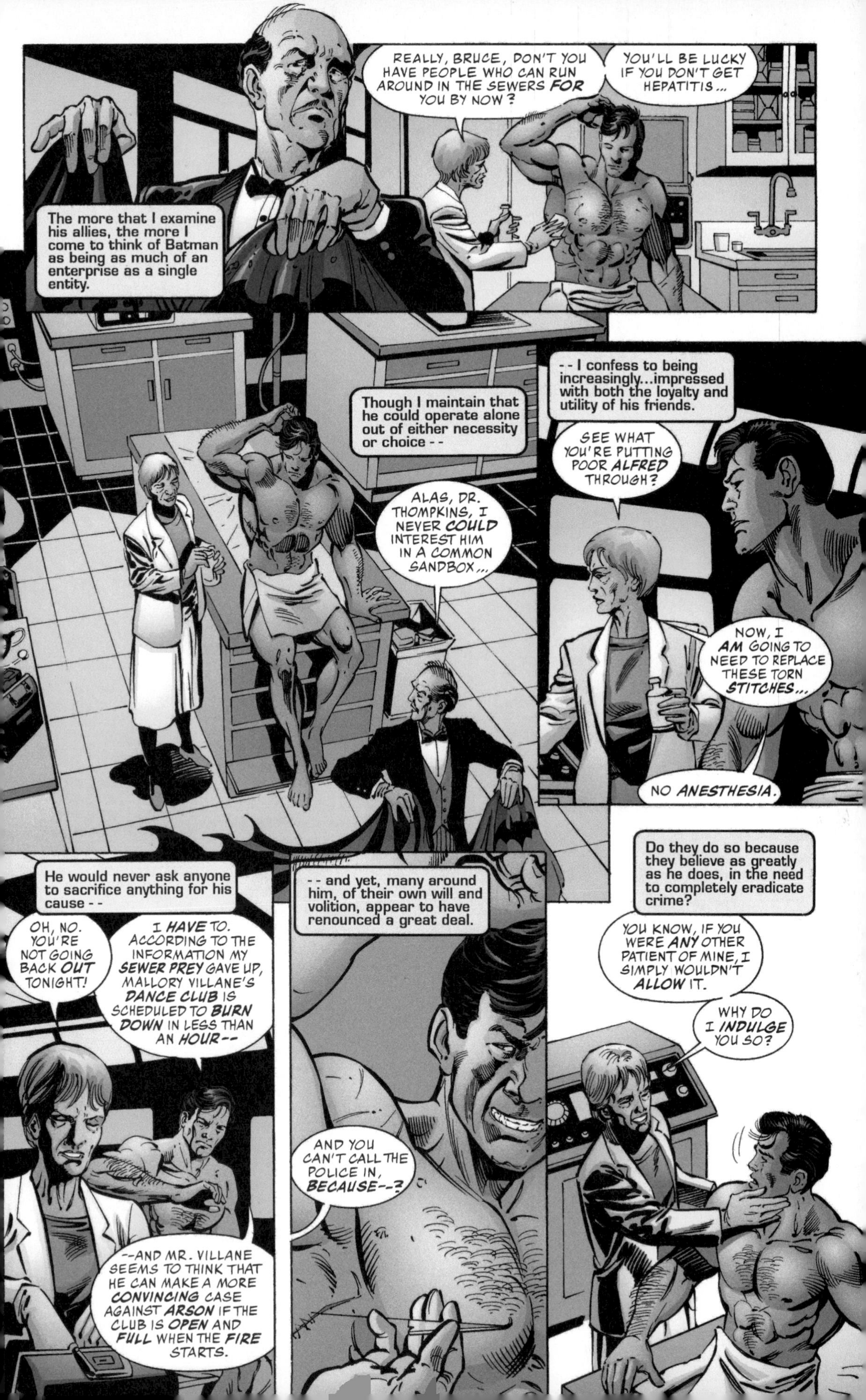
REALLY, BRUCE, DON'T YOU HAVE PEOPLE WHO CAN RUN AROUND IN THE SEWERS FOR YOU BY NOW?
YOU'LL BE LUCKY IF YOU DON'T GET HEPATITIS...
The more that I examine his allies, the more I come to think of Batman as being as much of an enterprise as a single entity.
Though I maintain that he could operate alone out of either necessity or choice --
ALAS, DR. THOMPKINS, I NEVER COULD INTEREST HIM IN A COMMON SANDBOX...
-- I confess to being increasingly...impressed with both the loyalty and utility of his friends.
SEE WHAT YOU'RE PUTTING POOR ALFRED THROUGH?
NOW, I AM GOING TO NEED TO REPLACE THESE TORN STITCHES...
NO ANESTHESIA.
He would never ask anyone to sacrifice anything for his cause --
OH, NO. YOU'RE NOT GOING BACK OUT TONIGHT!
I HAVE TO. ACCORDING TO THE INFORMATION MY SEWER PREY GAVE UP, MALLORY VILLANE'S DANCE CLUB IS SCHEDULED TO BURN DOWN IN LESS THAN AN HOUR--
--AND MR. VILLANE SEEMS TO THINK THAT HE CAN MAKE A MORE CONVINCING CASE AGAINST ARSON IF THE CLUB IS OPEN AND FULL WHEN THE FIRE STARTS.
-- and yet, many around him, of their own will and volition, appear to have renounced a great deal.
AND YOU CAN'T CALL THE POLICE IN, BECAUSE--?
Do they do so because they believe as greatly as he does, in the need to completely eradicate crime?
YOU KNOW, IF YOU WERE ANY OTHER PATIENT OF MINE, I SIMPLY WOULDN'T ALLOW IT.
WHY DO I INDULGE YOU SO?

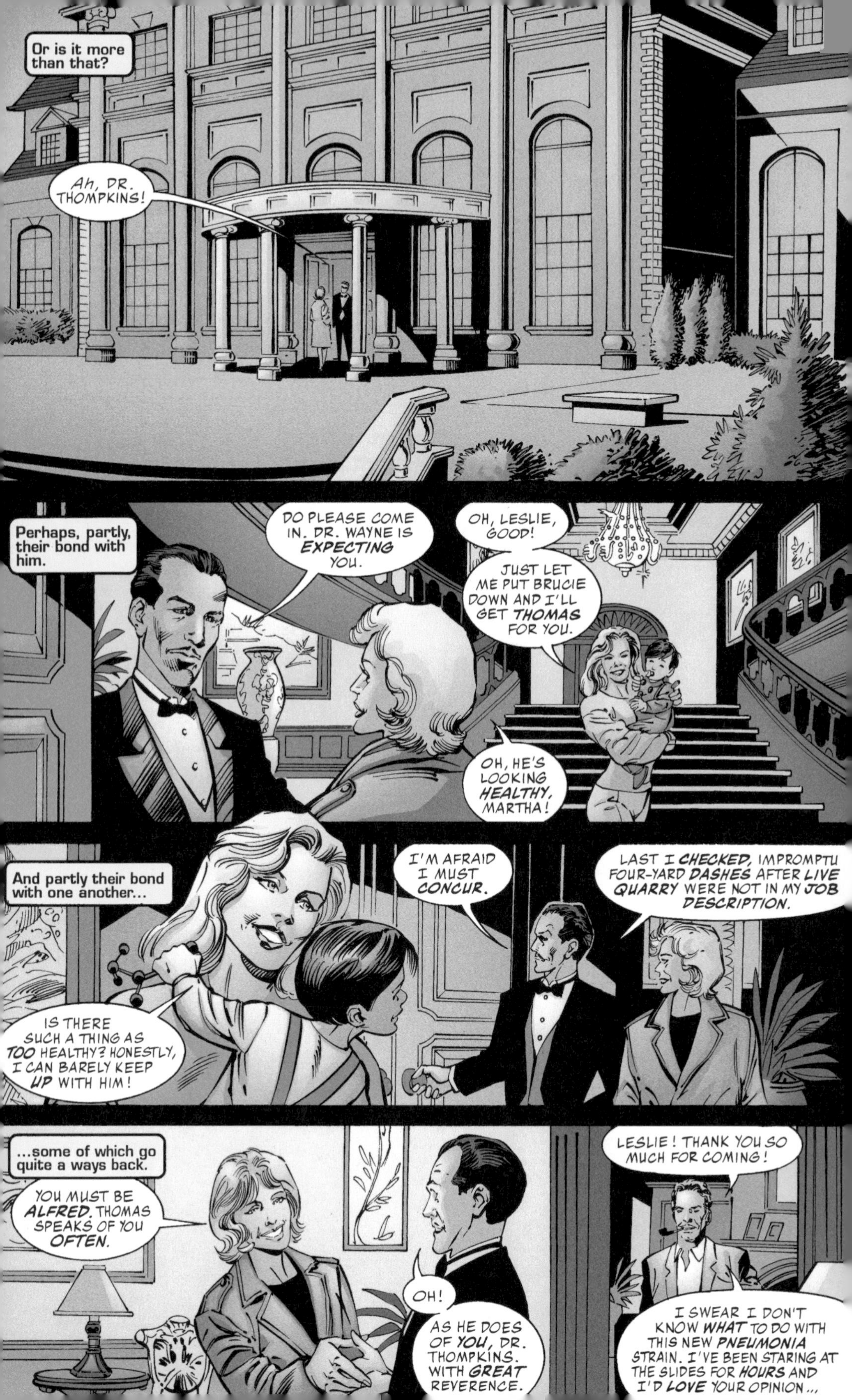
Or is it more than that?
Ah, DR. THOMPKINS!
Perhaps, partly, their bond with him.
DO PLEASE COME IN. DR. WAYNE IS EXPECTING YOU.
OH, LESLIE, GOOD!
JUST LET ME PUT BRUCIE DOWN AND I'LL GET THOMAS FOR YOU.
OH, HE'S LOOKING HEALTHY, MARTHA!
And partly their bond with one another...
IS THERE SUCH A THING AS TOO HEALTHY? HONESTLY, I CAN BARELY KEEP UP WITH HIM!
I'M AFRAID I MUST CONCUR.
LAST I CHECKED, IMPROMPTU FOUR-YARD DASHES AFTER LIVE QUARRY WERE NOT IN MY JOB DESCRIPTION.
...some of which go quite a ways back.
YOU MUST BE ALFRED. THOMAS SPEAKS OF YOU OFTEN.
OH!
AS HE DOES OF YOU, DR. THOMPKINS. WITH GREAT REVERENCE.
LESLIE! THANK YOU SO MUCH FOR COMING!
I SWEAR I DON'T KNOW WHAT TO DO WITH THIS NEW PNEUMONIA STRAIN. I'VE BEEN STARING AT THE SLIDES FOR HOURS AND I'D LOVE YOUR OPINION...

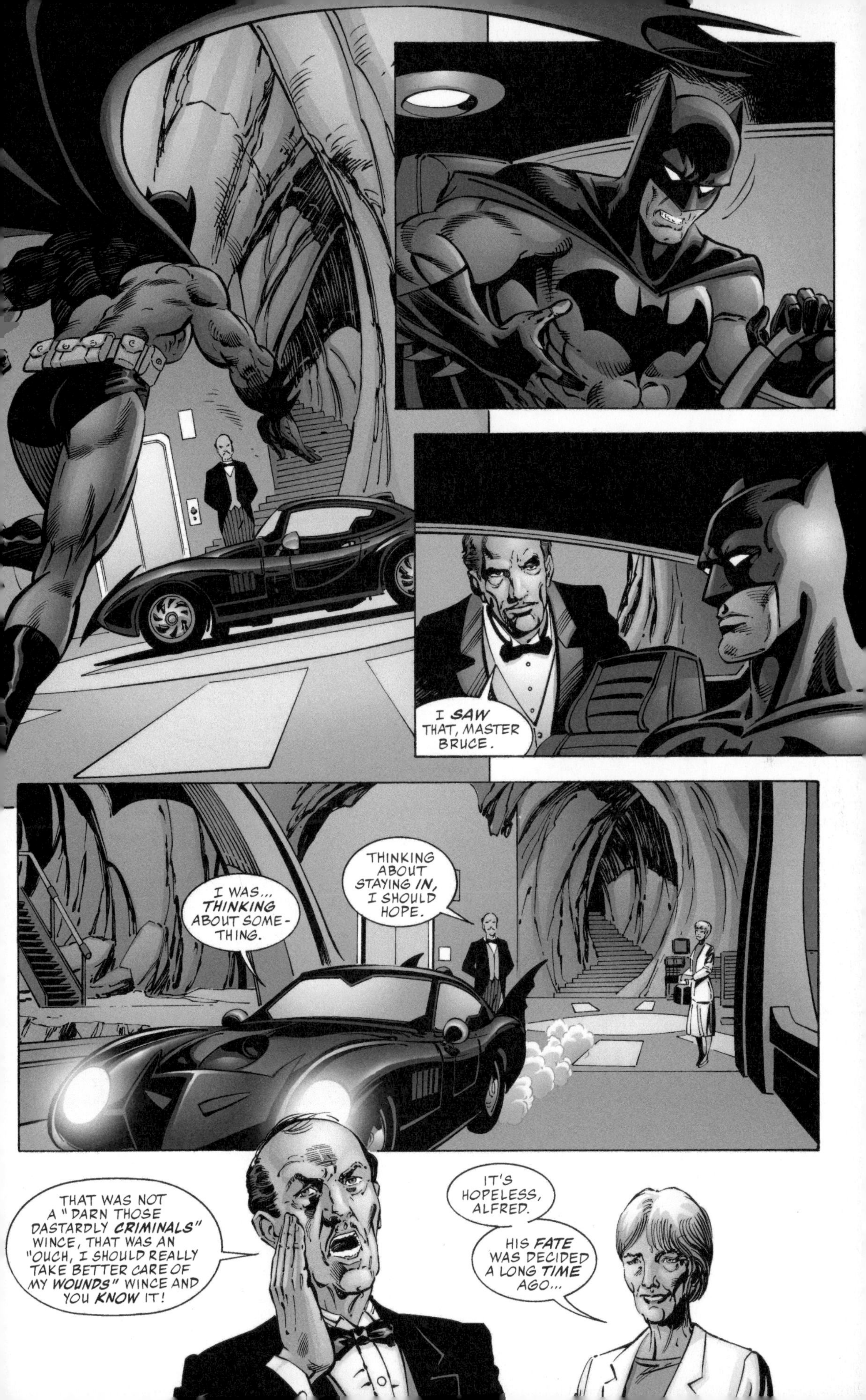

I SAW THAT, MASTER BRUCE.
I WAS... THINKING ABOUT SOME-THING.
THINKING ABOUT STAYING IN, I SHOULD HOPE.
THAT WAS NOT A "DARN THOSE DASTARDLY CRIMINALS" WINCE, THAT WAS AN "OUCH, I SHOULD REALLY TAKE BETTER CARE OF MY WOUNDS" WINCE AND YOU KNOW IT!
IT'S HOPELESS, ALFRED.
HIS FATE WAS DECIDED A LONG TIME AGO...

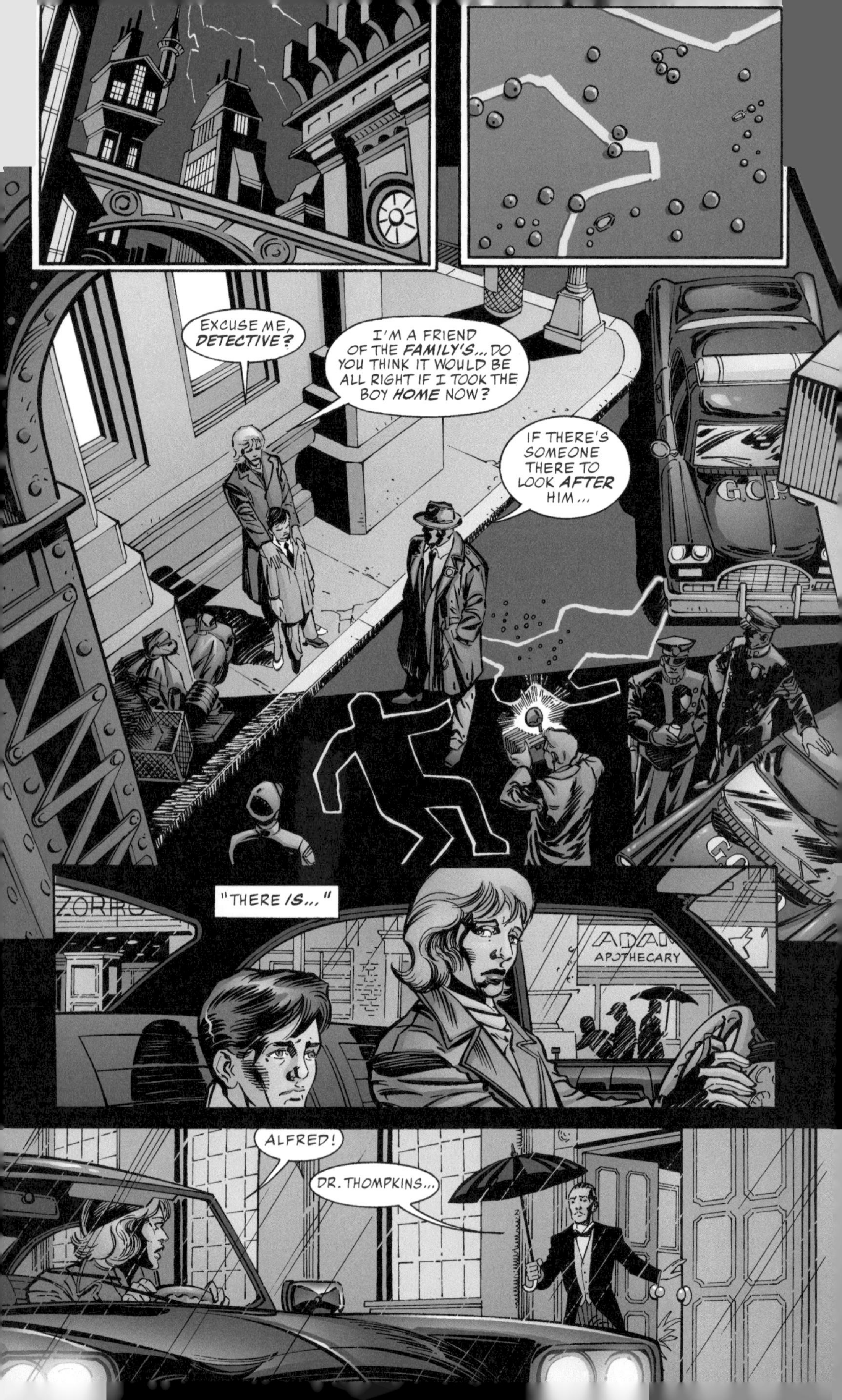

EXCUSE ME, DETECTIVE?
I'M A FRIEND OF THE FAMILY'S... DO YOU THINK IT WOULD BE ALL RIGHT IF I TOOK THE BOY HOME NOW?
IF THERE'S SOMEONE THERE TO LOOK AFTER HIM...
"THERE IS..."
APOTHECARY
ALFRED!
DR. THOMPKINS...

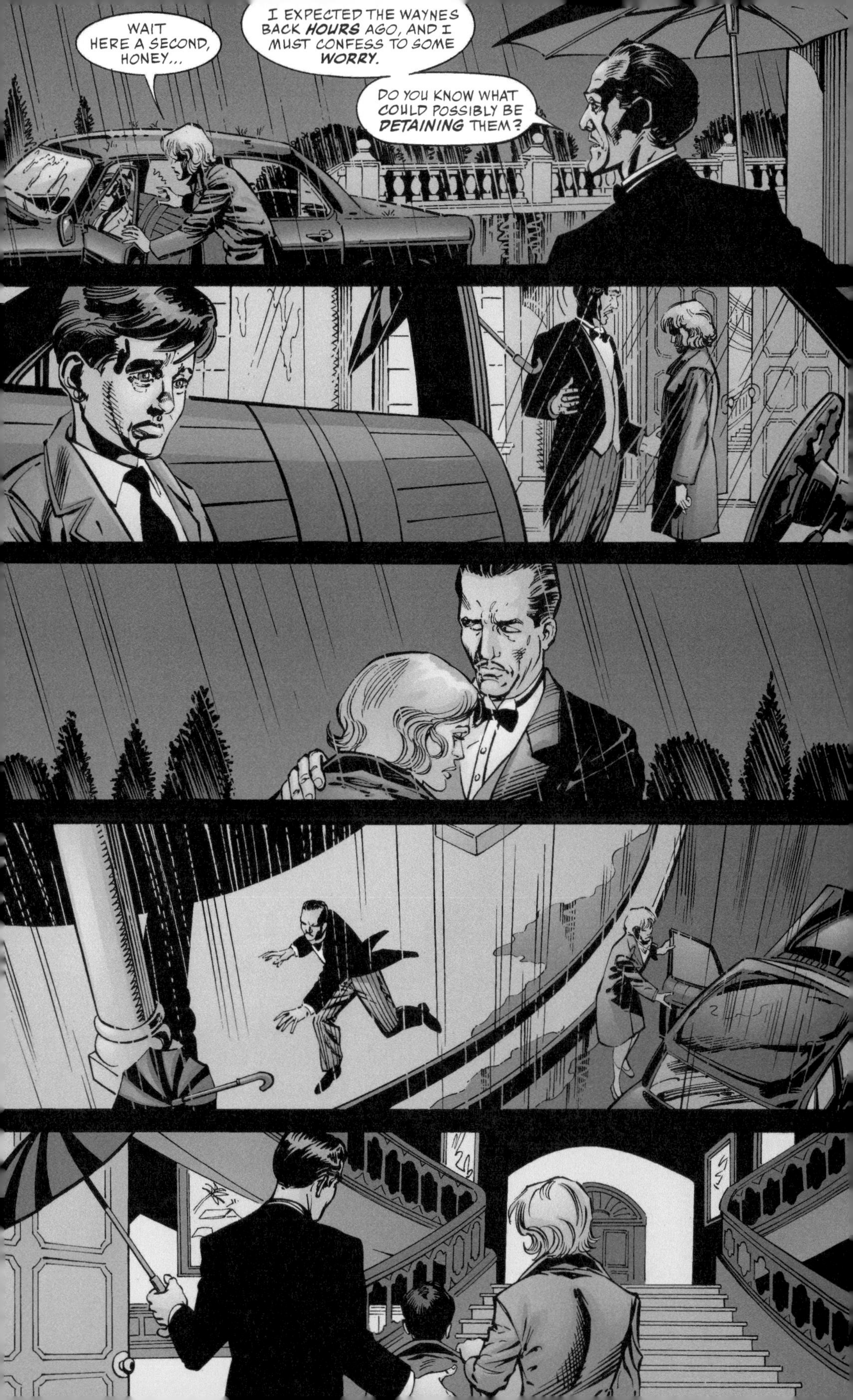
WAIT HERE A SECOND, HONEY...
I EXPECTED THE WAYNES BACK HOURS AGO, AND I MUST CONFESS TO SOME WORRY.
DO YOU KNOW WHAT COULD POSSIBLY BE DETAINING THEM?

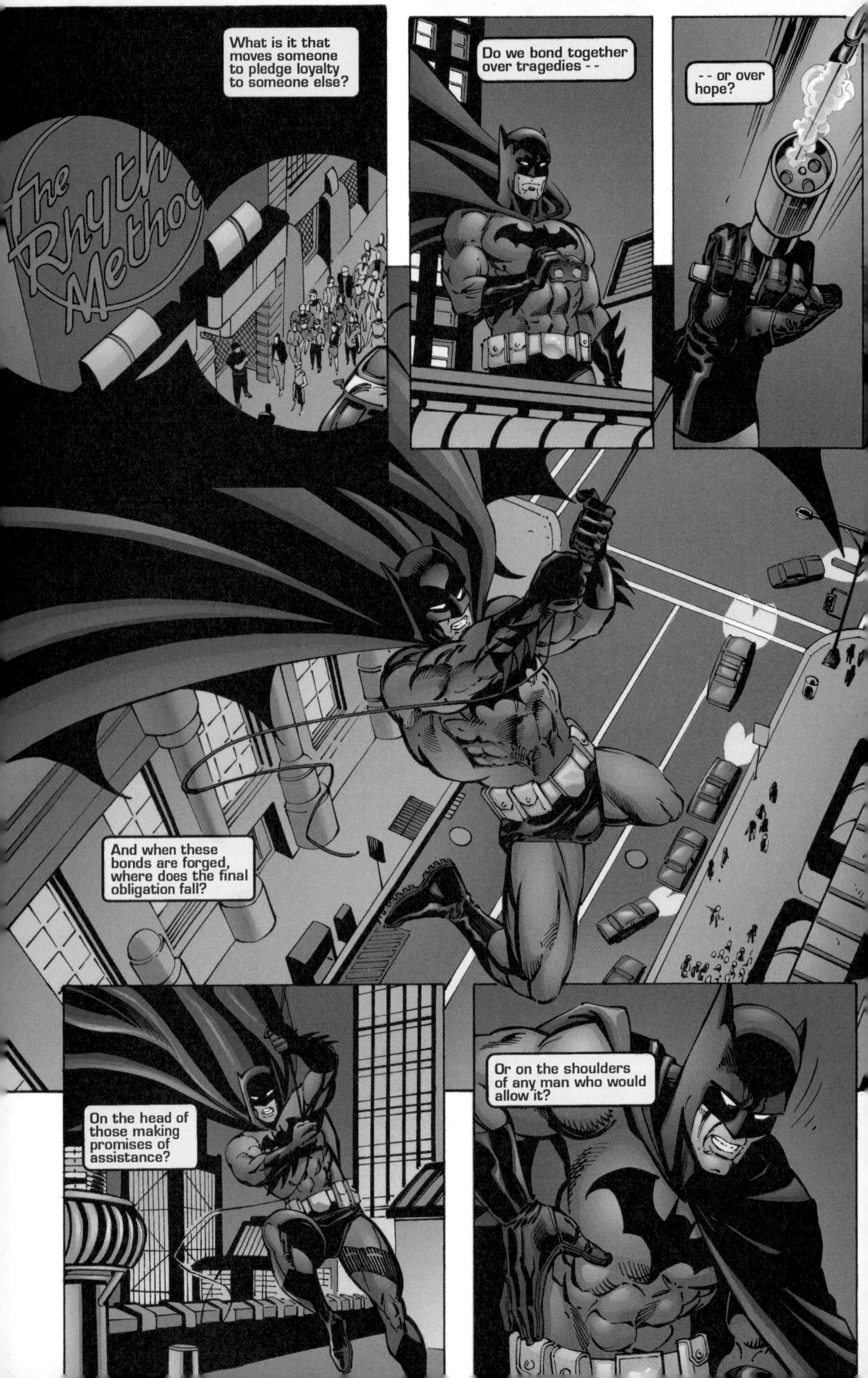
What is it that moves someone to pledge loyalty to someone else?
The Rhythm Method
Do we bond together over tragedies - -
- - or over hope?
And when these bonds are forged, where does the final obligation fall?
On the head of those making promises of assistance?
Or on the shoulders of any man who would allow it?

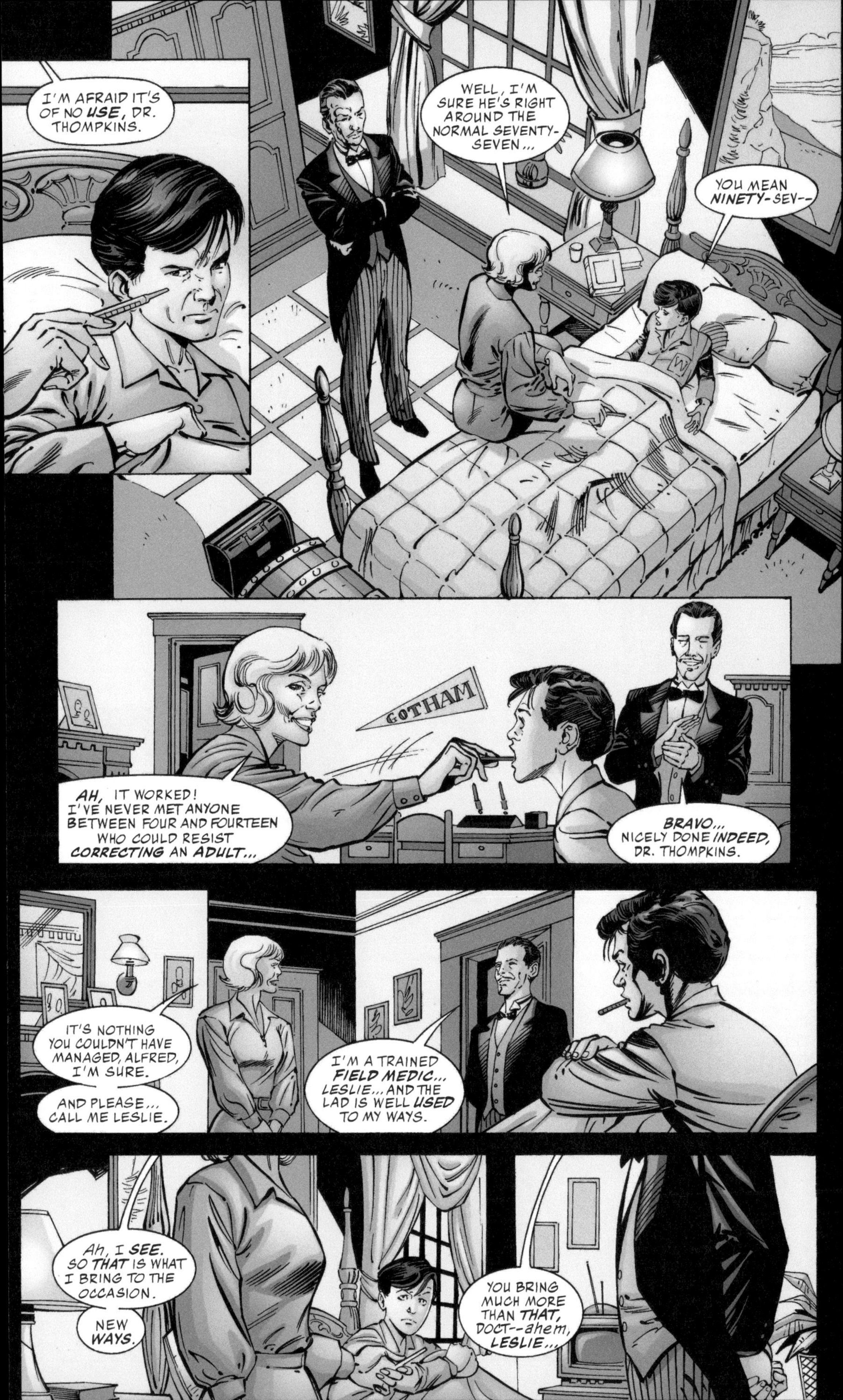
I'M AFRAID IT'S OF NO USE, DR. THOMPKINS.
WELL, I'M SURE HE'S RIGHT AROUND THE NORMAL SEVENTY-SEVEN...
YOU MEAN NINETY-SEV--
GOTHAM
AH, IT WORKED! I'VE NEVER MET ANYONE BETWEEN FOUR AND FOURTEEN WHO COULD RESIST CORRECTING AN ADULT...
BRAVO... NICELY DONE INDEED, DR. THOMPKINS.
IT'S NOTHING YOU COULDN'T HAVE MANAGED, ALFRED, I'M SURE.
AND PLEASE... CALL ME LESLIE.
I'M A TRAINED FIELD MEDIC... LESLIE... AND THE LAD IS WELL USED TO MY WAYS.
Ah, I SEE. SO THAT IS WHAT I BRING TO THE OCCASION.
NEW WAYS.
YOU BRING MUCH MORE THAN THAT, DOCT--ahem, LESLIE...

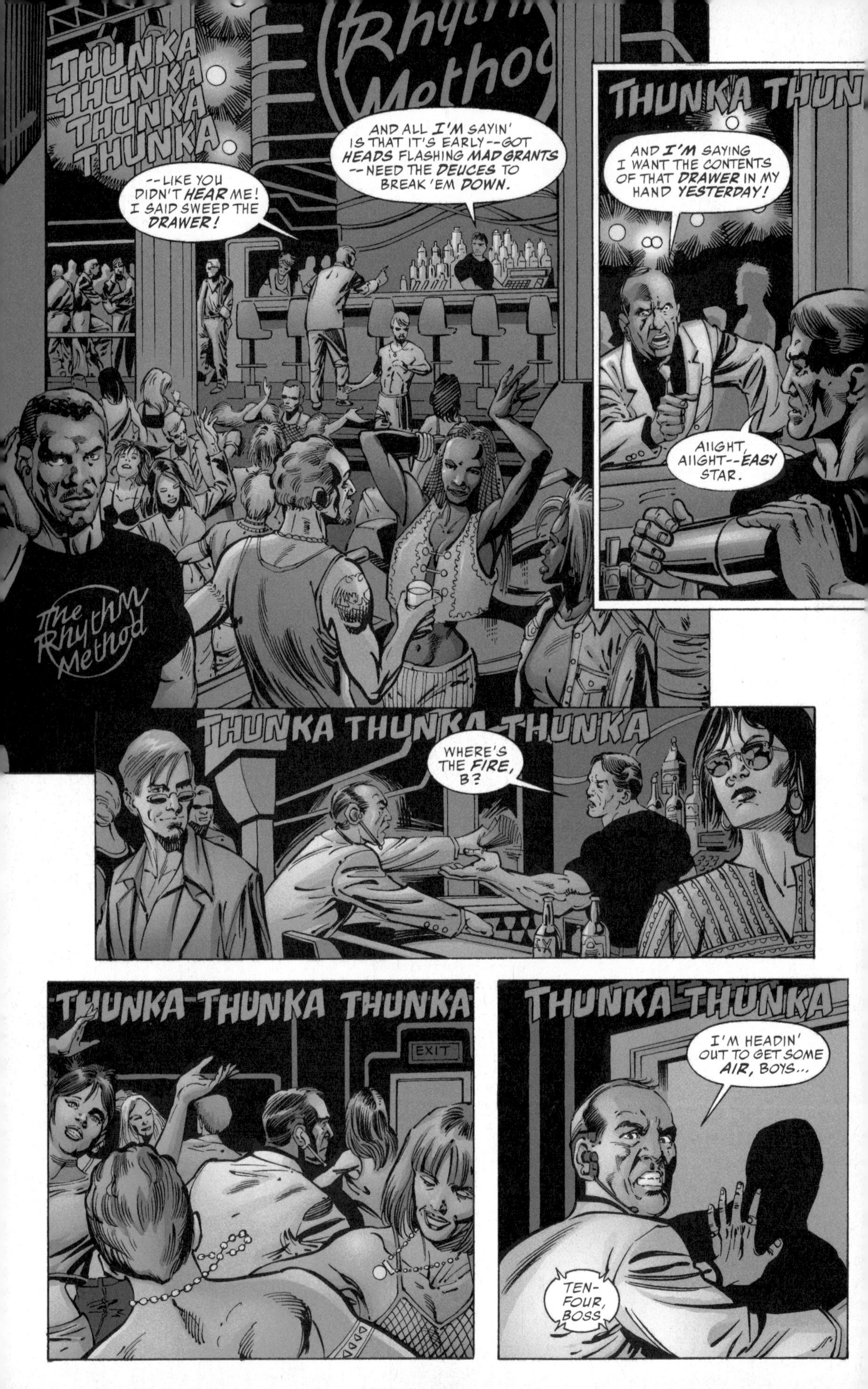
THUNKA THUNKA THUNKA THUNKA
Rhythm Method
--LIKE YOU DIDN'T HEAR ME! I SAID SWEEP THE DRAWER!
AND ALL I'M SAYIN' IS THAT IT'S EARLY--GOT HEADS FLASHING MAD GRANTS --NEED THE DEUCES TO BREAK 'EM DOWN.
The Rhythm Method
THUNKA THUN
AND I'M SAYING I WANT THE CONTENTS OF THAT DRAWER IN MY HAND YESTERDAY!
AIIGHT, AIIGHT--EASY STAR.
THUNKA THUNKA-THUNKA
WHERE'S THE FIRE, B?
THUNKA-THUNKA THUNKA
EXIT
THUNKA THUNKA
I'M HEADIN' OUT TO GET SOME AIR, BOYS...
TEN-FOUR, BOSS

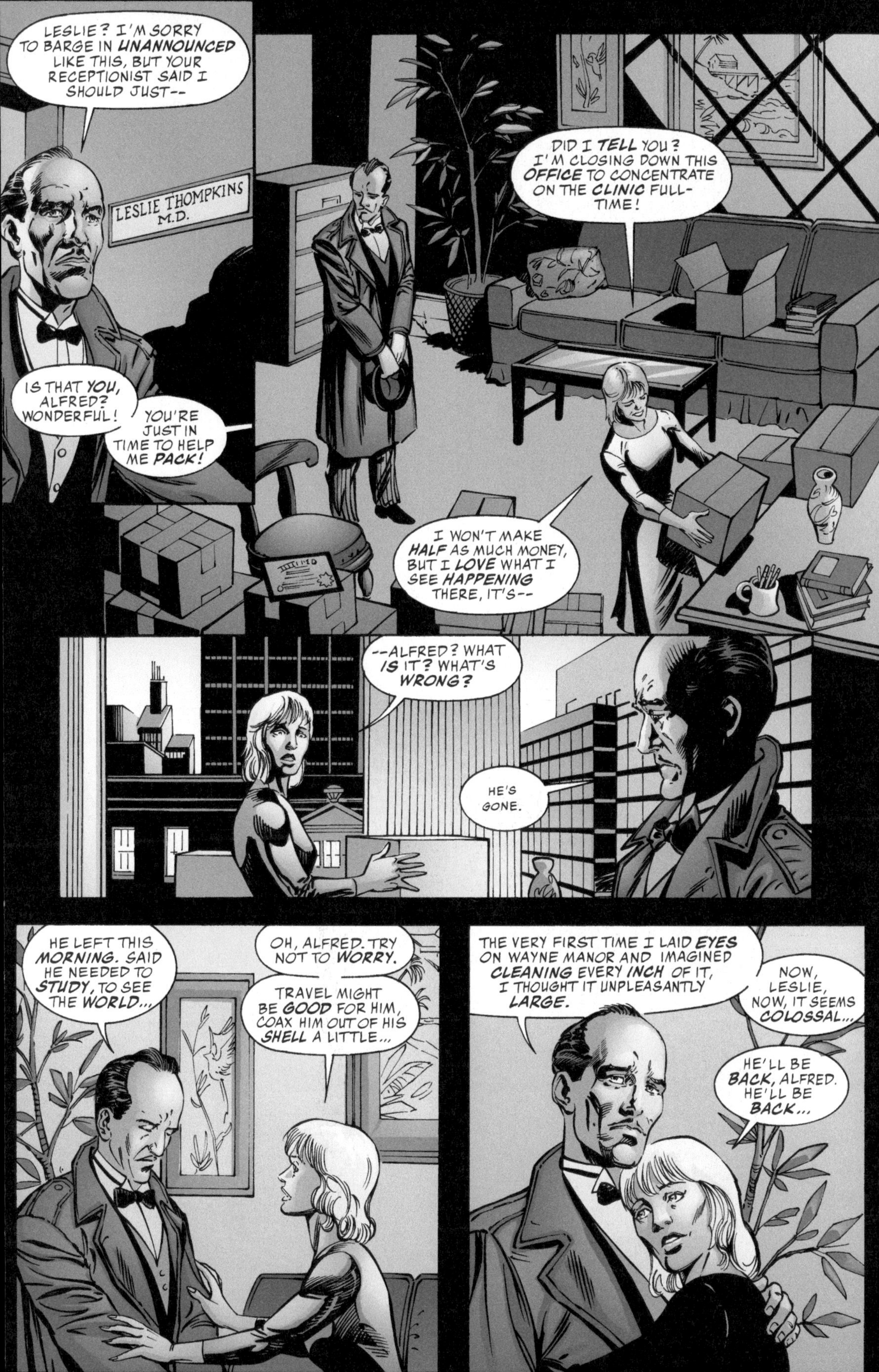
LESLIE? I'M SORRY TO BARGE IN UNANNOUNCED LIKE THIS, BUT YOUR RECEPTIONIST SAID I SHOULD JUST--
LESLIE THOMPKINS M.D.
IS THAT YOU, ALFRED? WONDERFUL!
YOU'RE JUST IN TIME TO HELP ME PACK!
DID I TELL YOU? I'M CLOSING DOWN THIS OFFICE TO CONCENTRATE ON THE CLINIC FULL-TIME!
I WON'T MAKE HALF AS MUCH MONEY, BUT I LOVE WHAT I SEE HAPPENING THERE, IT'S--
--ALFRED? WHAT IS IT? WHAT'S WRONG?
HE'S GONE.
HE LEFT THIS MORNING. SAID HE NEEDED TO STUDY, TO SEE THE WORLD...
OH, ALFRED. TRY NOT TO WORRY.
TRAVEL MIGHT BE GOOD FOR HIM, COAX HIM OUT OF HIS SHELL A LITTLE...
THE VERY FIRST TIME I LAID EYES ON WAYNE MANOR AND IMAGINED CLEANING EVERY INCH OF IT, I THOUGHT IT UNPLEASANTLY LARGE.
NOW, LESLIE, NOW, IT SEEMS COLOSSAL...
HE'LL BE BACK, ALFRED. HE'LL BE BACK...

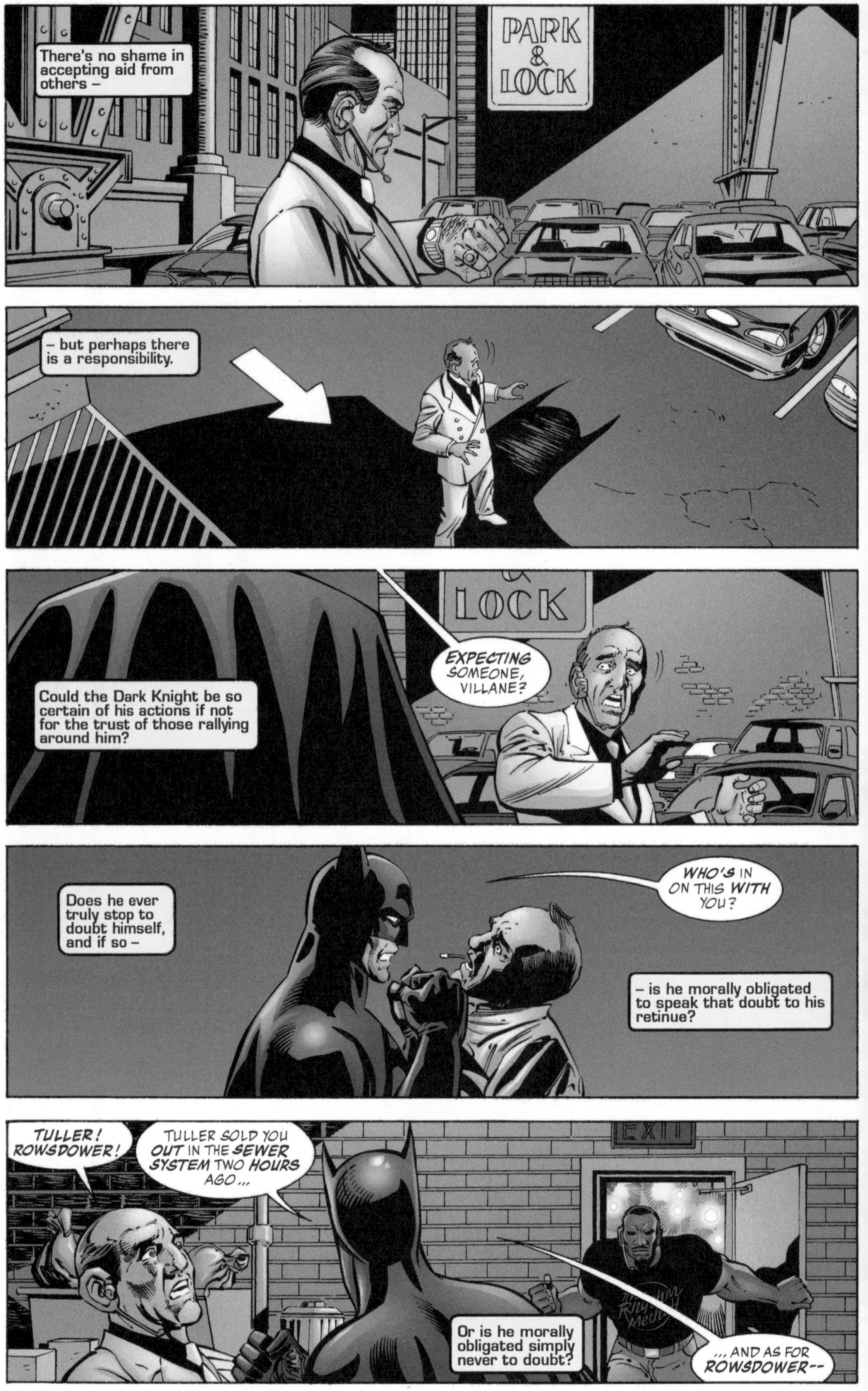
There's no shame in accepting aid from others –
PARK & LOCK
– but perhaps there is a responsibility.
LOCK
Could the Dark Knight be so certain of his actions if not for the trust of those rallying around him?
EXPECTING SOMEONE, VILLANE?
Does he ever truly stop to doubt himself, and if so –
WHO'S IN ON THIS WITH YOU?
– is he morally obligated to speak that doubt to his retinue?
TULLER! ROWSDOWER!
TULLER SOLD YOU OUT IN THE SEWER SYSTEM TWO HOURS AGO...
EXIT
Or is he morally obligated simply never to doubt?
...AND AS FOR ROWSDOWER--

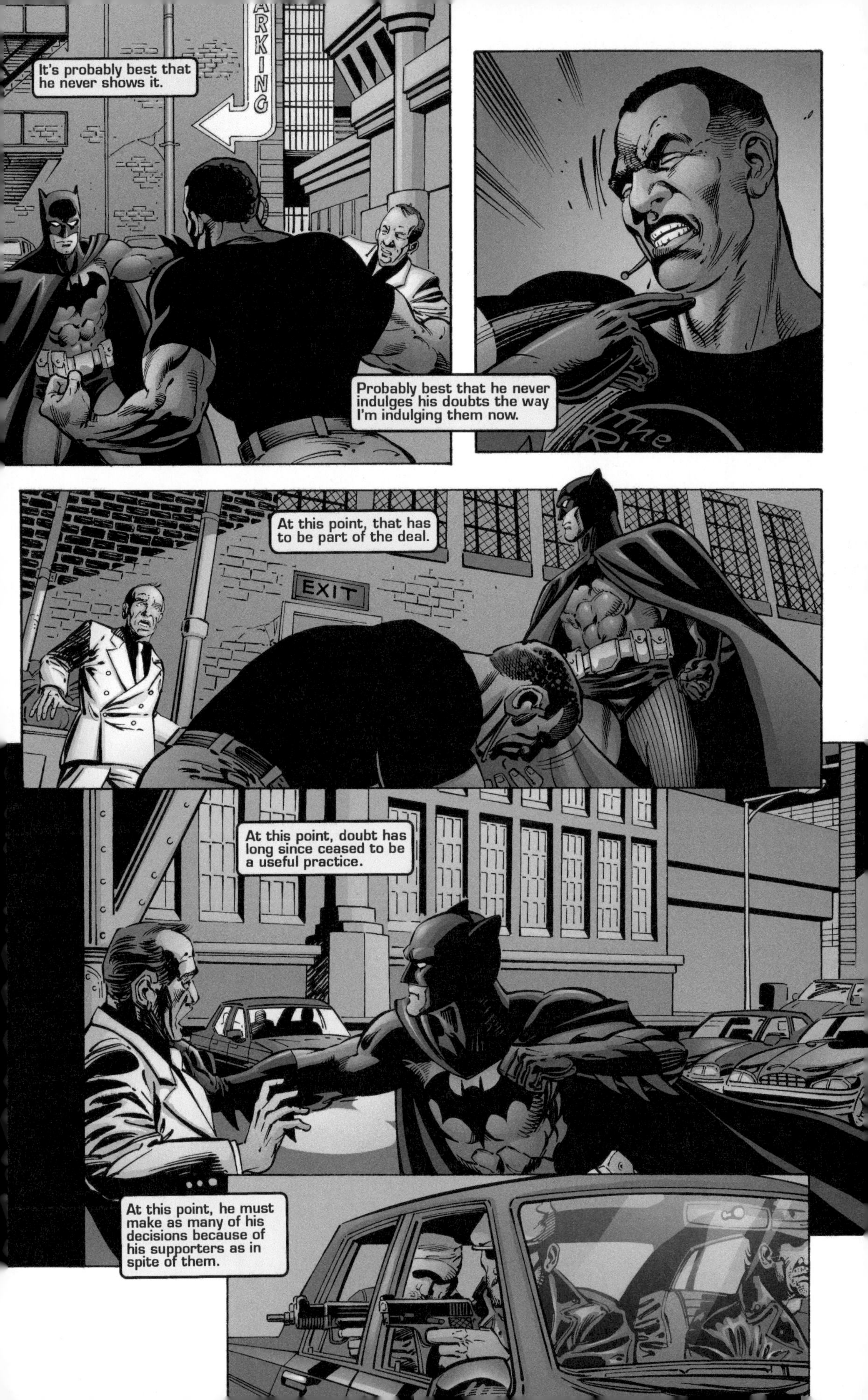
ARKING
It's probably best that he never shows it.
Probably best that he never indulges his doubts the way I'm indulging them now.
At this point, that has to be part of the deal.
EXIT
At this point, doubt has long since ceased to be a useful practice.
At this point, he must make as many of his decisions because of his supporters as in spite of them.

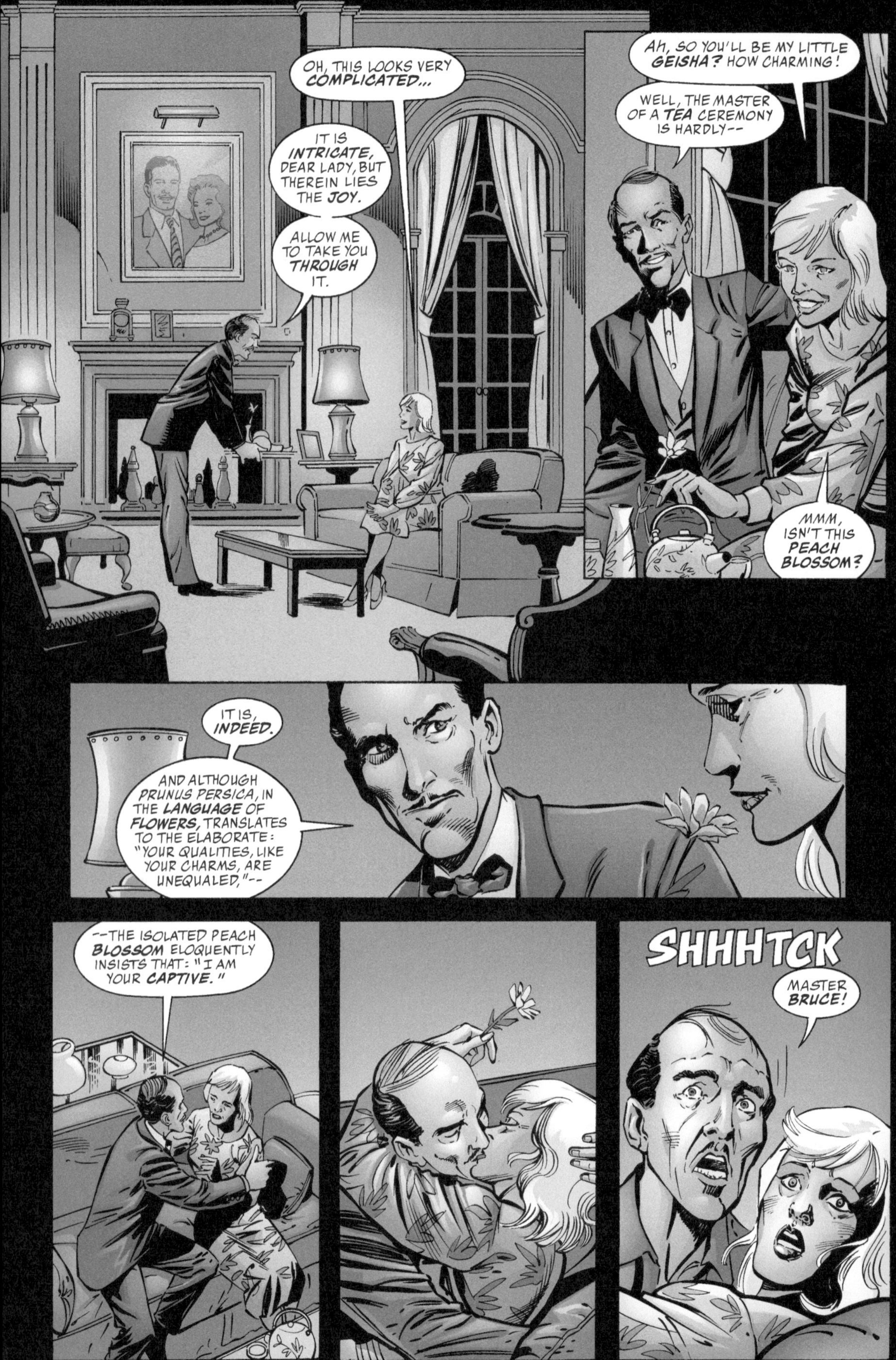
OH, THIS LOOKS VERY COMPLICATED...
IT IS INTRICATE, DEAR LADY, BUT THEREIN LIES THE JOY.
ALLOW ME TO TAKE YOU THROUGH IT.
Ah, SO YOU'LL BE MY LITTLE GEISHA? HOW CHARMING!
WELL, THE MASTER OF A TEA CEREMONY IS HARDLY--
MMM, ISN'T THIS PEACH BLOSSOM?
IT IS, INDEED.
AND ALTHOUGH PRUNUS PERSICA, IN THE LANGUAGE OF FLOWERS, TRANSLATES TO THE ELABORATE: "YOUR QUALITIES, LIKE YOUR CHARMS, ARE UNEQUALED,"--
--THE ISOLATED PEACH BLOSSOM ELOQUENTLY INSISTS THAT: "I AM YOUR CAPTIVE."
SHHHTCK
MASTER BRUCE!

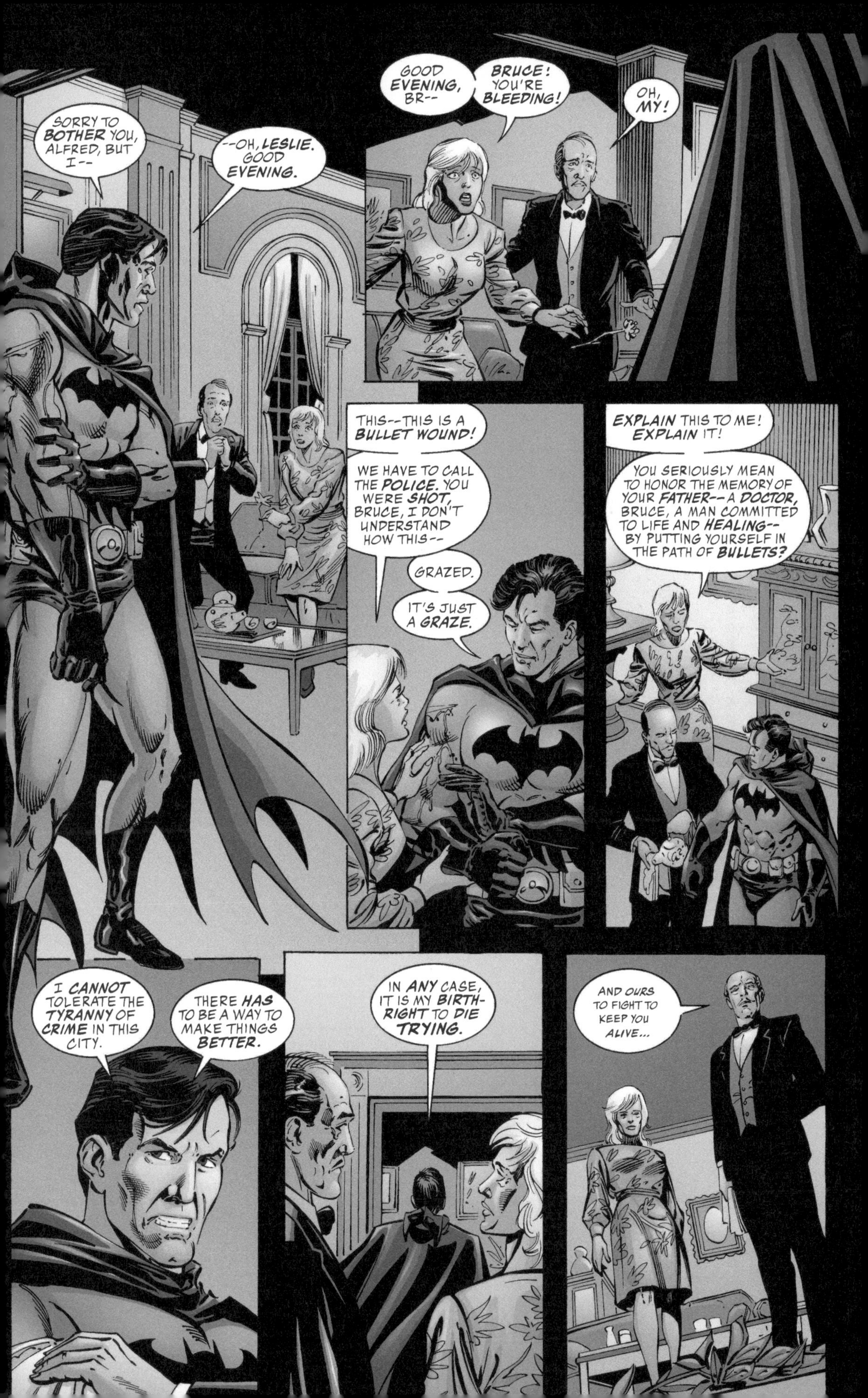
SORRY TO BOTHER YOU, ALFRED, BUT I--
--OH, LESLIE. GOOD EVENING.
GOOD EVENING, BR--
BRUCE! YOU'RE BLEEDING!
OH, MY!
THIS--THIS IS A BULLET WOUND!
WE HAVE TO CALL THE POLICE. YOU WERE SHOT, BRUCE, I DON'T UNDERSTAND HOW THIS--
GRAZED.
IT'S JUST A GRAZE.
EXPLAIN THIS TO ME! EXPLAIN IT!
YOU SERIOUSLY MEAN TO HONOR THE MEMORY OF YOUR FATHER--A DOCTOR, BRUCE, A MAN COMMITTED TO LIFE AND HEALING-- BY PUTTING YOURSELF IN THE PATH OF BULLETS?
I CANNOT TOLERATE THE TYRANNY OF CRIME IN THIS CITY.
THERE HAS TO BE A WAY TO MAKE THINGS BETTER.
IN ANY CASE, IT IS MY BIRTH-RIGHT TO DIE TRYING.
AND OURS TO FIGHT TO KEEP YOU ALIVE...

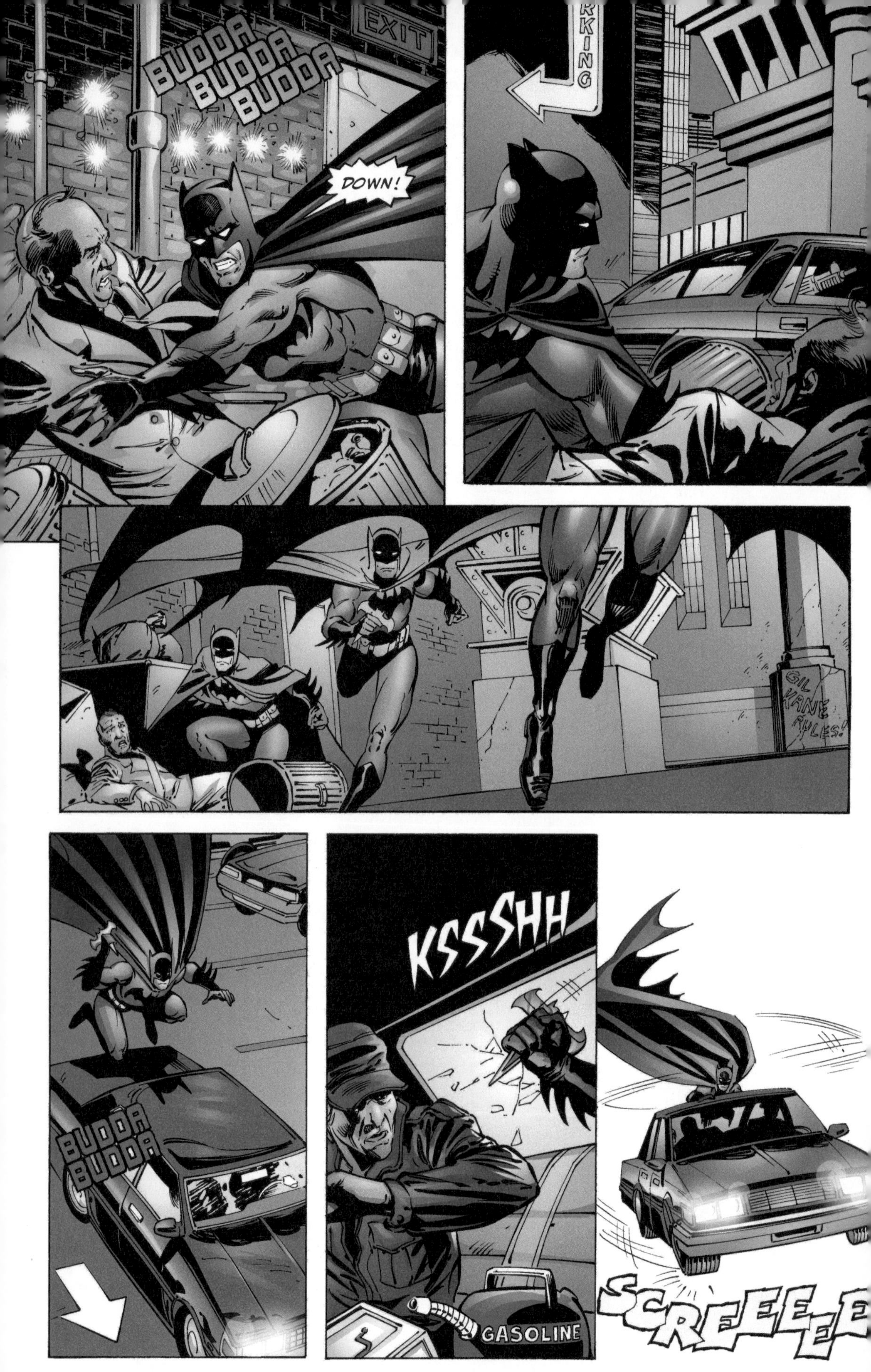
EXIT
BUDDA BUDDA BUDDA
DOWN!
RKING
GIL KANE RULES!
BUDDA BUDDA
KSSSHH
GASOLINE
SCREEEEE

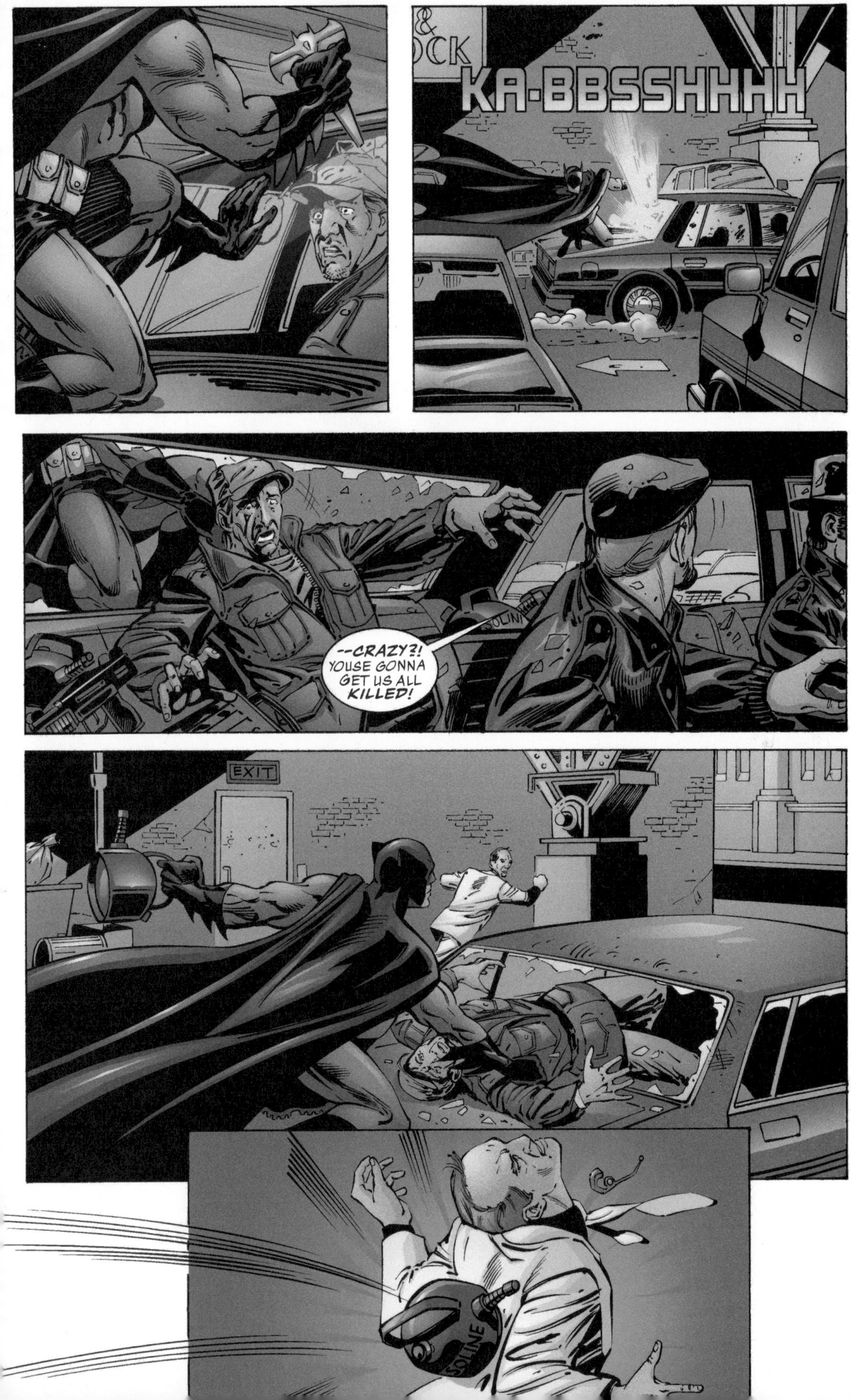
&
OCK
KA-BBSSHHHH
--CRAZY?! YOUSE GONNA GET US ALL KILLED!
EXIT
SOLINE

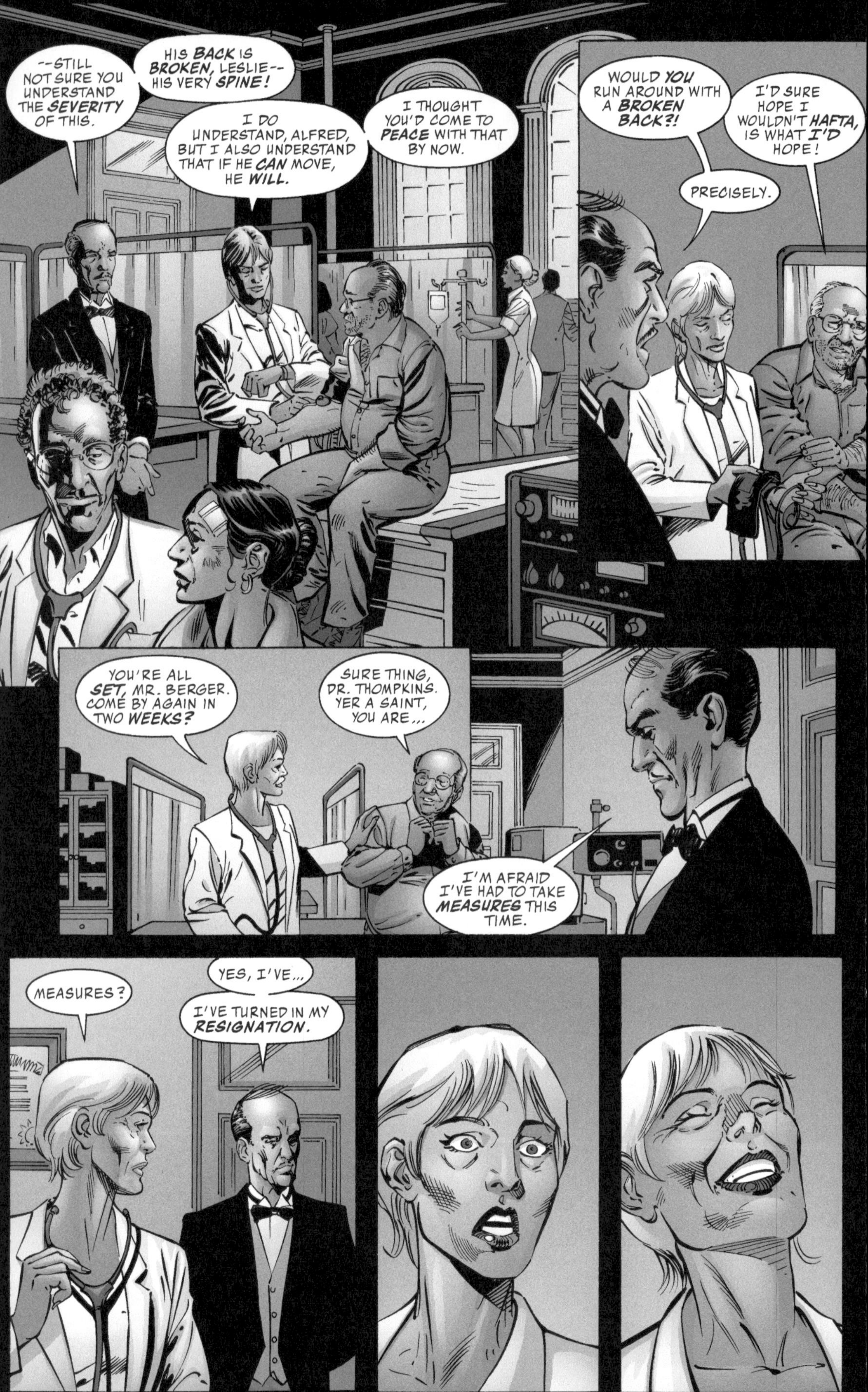
--STILL NOT SURE YOU UNDERSTAND THE SEVERITY OF THIS.
HIS BACK IS BROKEN, LESLIE--HIS VERY SPINE!
I DO UNDERSTAND, ALFRED, BUT I ALSO UNDERSTAND THAT IF HE CAN MOVE, HE WILL.
I THOUGHT YOU'D COME TO PEACE WITH THAT BY NOW.
WOULD YOU RUN AROUND WITH A BROKEN BACK?!
PRECISELY.
I'D SURE HOPE I WOULDN'T HAFTA, IS WHAT I'D HOPE!
YOU'RE ALL SET, MR. BERGER. COME BY AGAIN IN TWO WEEKS?
SURE THING, DR. THOMPKINS. YER A SAINT, YOU ARE...
I'M AFRAID I'VE HAD TO TAKE MEASURES THIS TIME.
MEASURES?
YES, I'VE...
I'VE TURNED IN MY RESIGNATION.

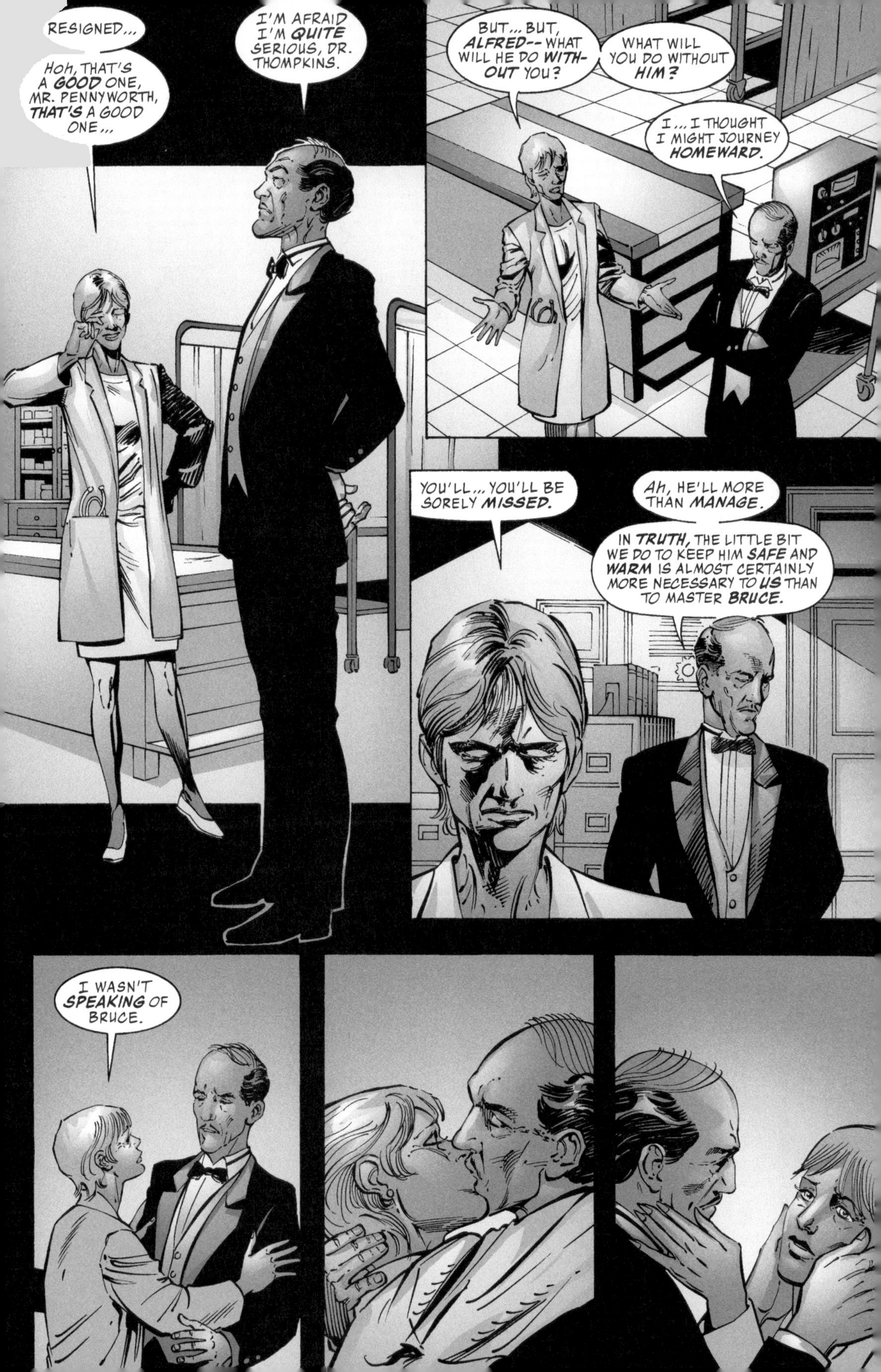
RESIGNED...
Hoh, THAT'S A GOOD ONE, MR. PENNYWORTH, THAT'S A GOOD ONE...
I'M AFRAID I'M QUITE SERIOUS, DR. THOMPKINS.
BUT... BUT, ALFRED-- WHAT WILL HE DO WITH-OUT YOU?
WHAT WILL YOU DO WITHOUT HIM?
I... I THOUGHT I MIGHT JOURNEY HOMEWARD.
YOU'LL... YOU'LL BE SORELY MISSED.
Ah, HE'LL MORE THAN MANAGE.
IN TRUTH, THE LITTLE BIT WE DO TO KEEP HIM SAFE AND WARM IS ALMOST CERTAINLY MORE NECESSARY TO US THAN TO MASTER BRUCE.
I WASN'T SPEAKING OF BRUCE.

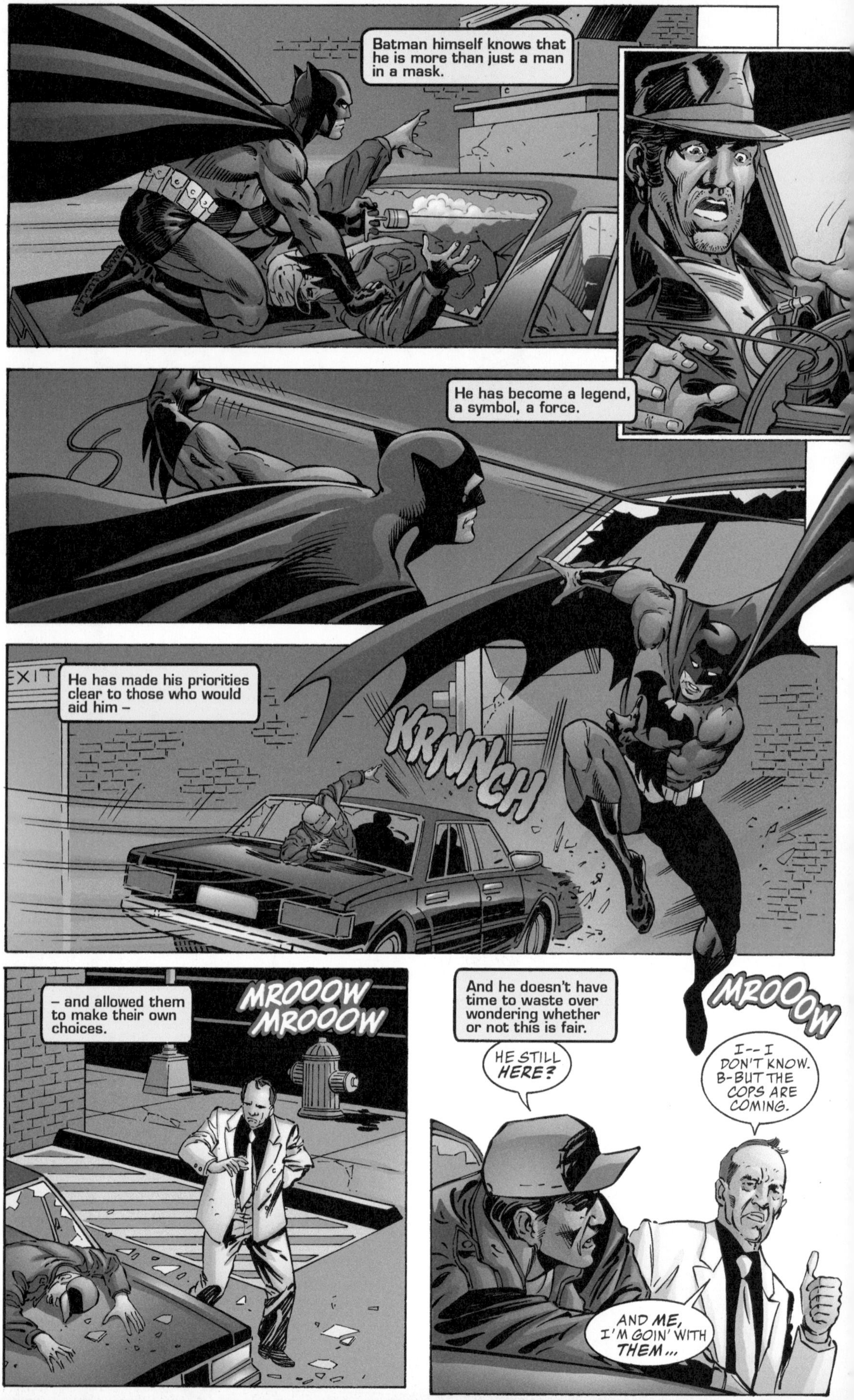

Batman himself knows that he is more than just a man in a mask.
He has become a legend, a symbol, a force.
EXIT
He has made his priorities clear to those who would aid him –
KRNNCH
– and allowed them to make their own choices.
MROOOW MROOOW
And he doesn't have time to waste over wondering whether or not this is fair.
MROOOW
HE STILL HERE?
I-- I DON'T KNOW. B-BUT THE COPS ARE COMING.
AND ME, I'M GOIN' WITH THEM...

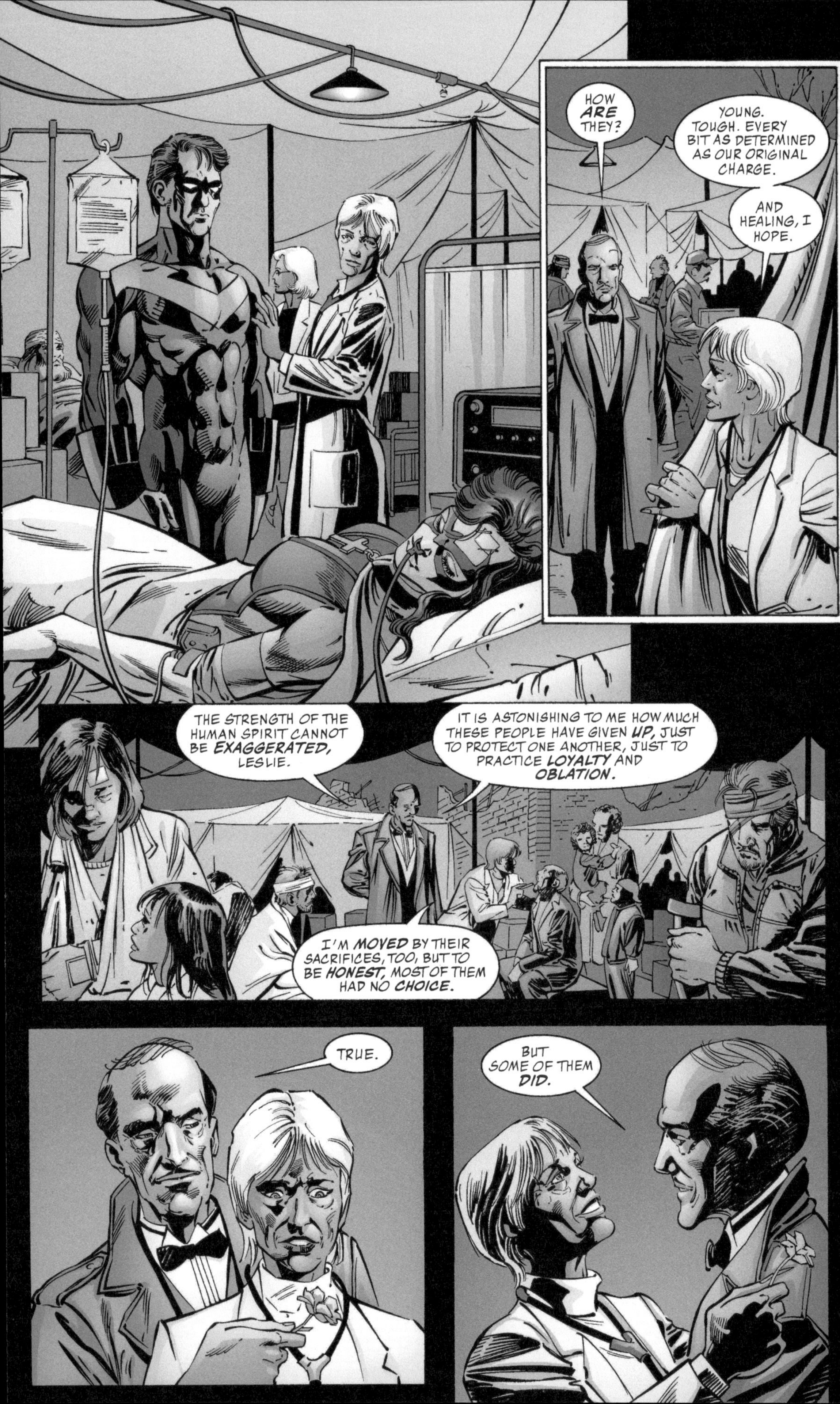

HOW ARE THEY?
YOUNG. TOUGH. EVERY BIT AS DETERMINED AS OUR ORIGINAL CHARGE.
AND HEALING, I HOPE.
THE STRENGTH OF THE HUMAN SPIRIT CANNOT BE EXAGGERATED, LESLIE.
IT IS ASTONISHING TO ME HOW MUCH THESE PEOPLE HAVE GIVEN UP, JUST TO PROTECT ONE ANOTHER, JUST TO PRACTICE LOYALTY AND OBLATION.
I'M MOVED BY THEIR SACRIFICES, TOO, BUT TO BE HONEST, MOST OF THEM HAD NO CHOICE.
TRUE.
BUT SOME OF THEM DID.

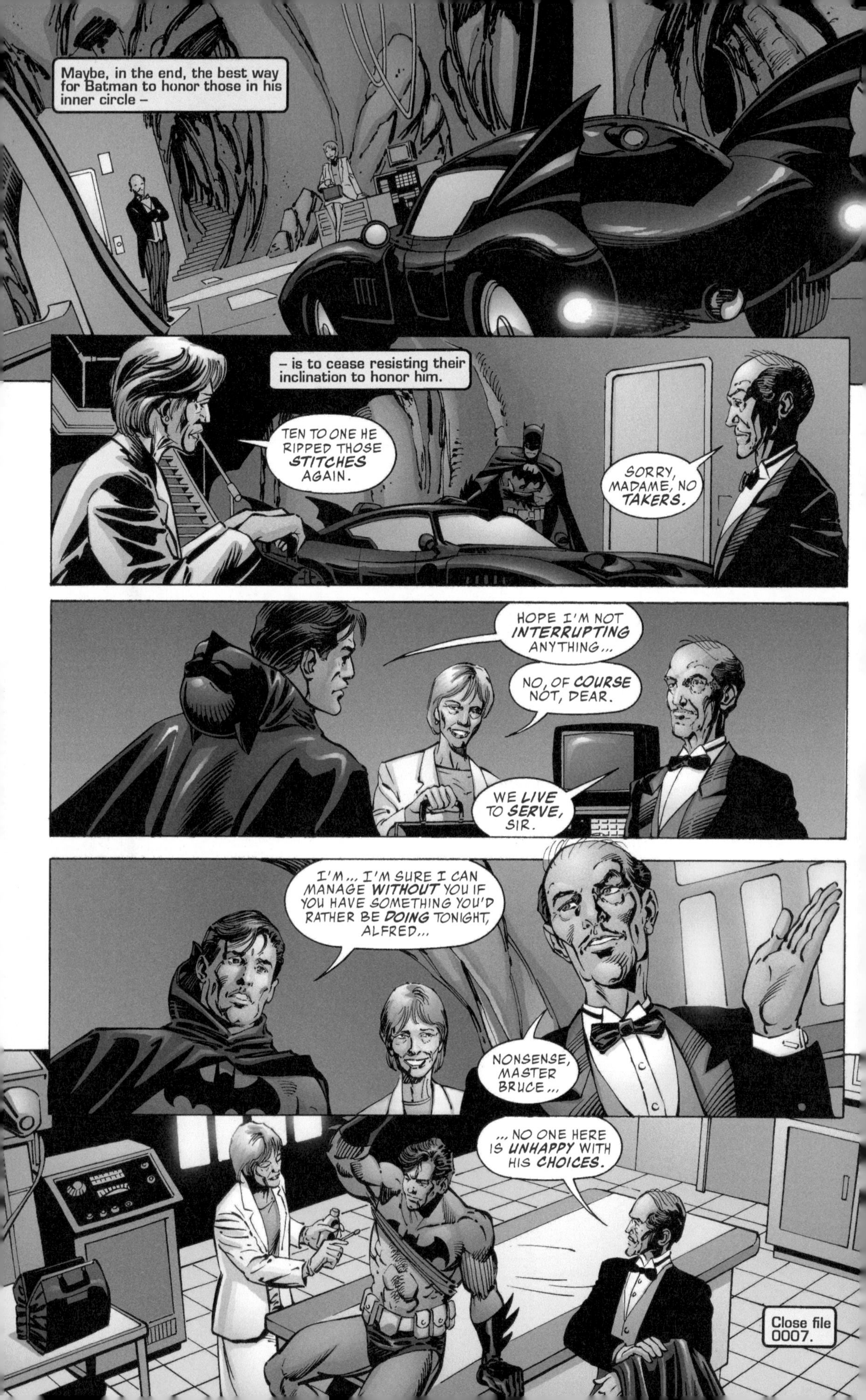
Maybe, in the end, the best way for Batman to honor those in his inner circle –
– is to cease resisting their inclination to honor him.
TEN TO ONE HE RIPPED THOSE STITCHES AGAIN.
SORRY, MADAME, NO TAKERS.
HOPE I'M NOT INTERRUPTING ANYTHING...
NO, OF COURSE NOT, DEAR.
WE LIVE TO SERVE, SIR.
I'M... I'M SURE I CAN MANAGE WITHOUT YOU IF YOU HAVE SOMETHING YOU'D RATHER BE DOING TONIGHT, ALFRED...
NONSENSE, MASTER BRUCE...
...NO ONE HERE IS UNHAPPY WITH HIS CHOICES.
Close file 0007.

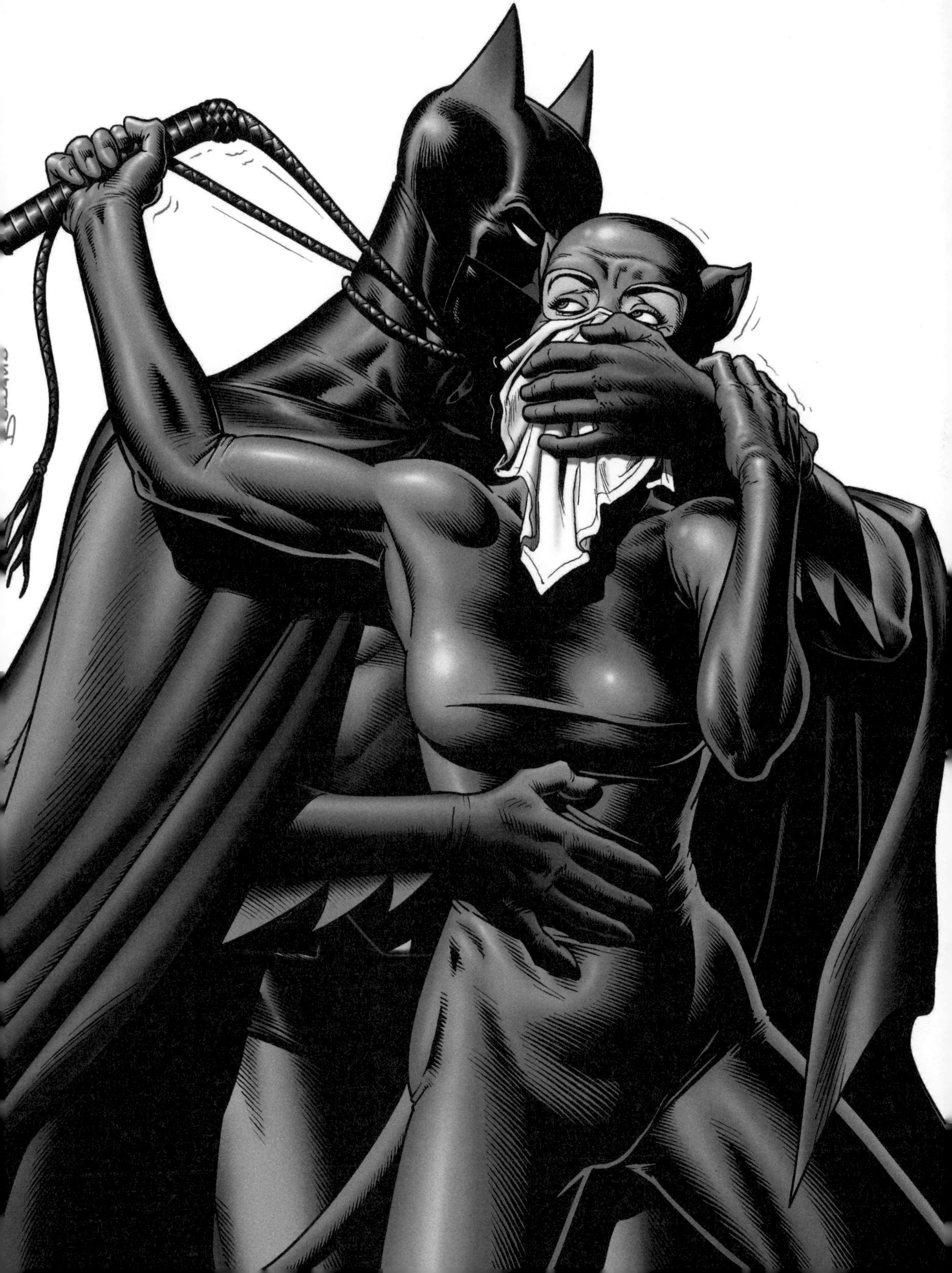

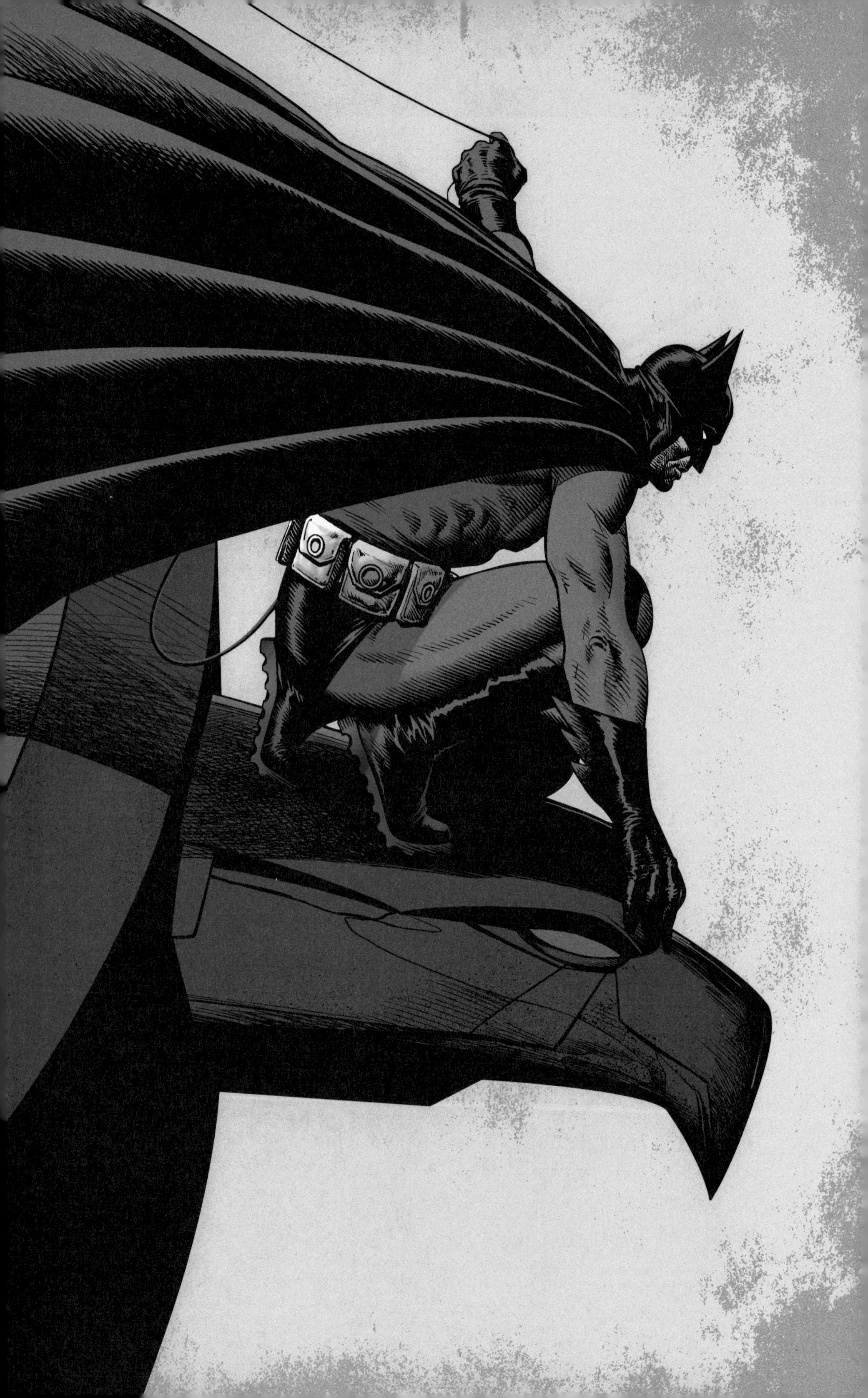

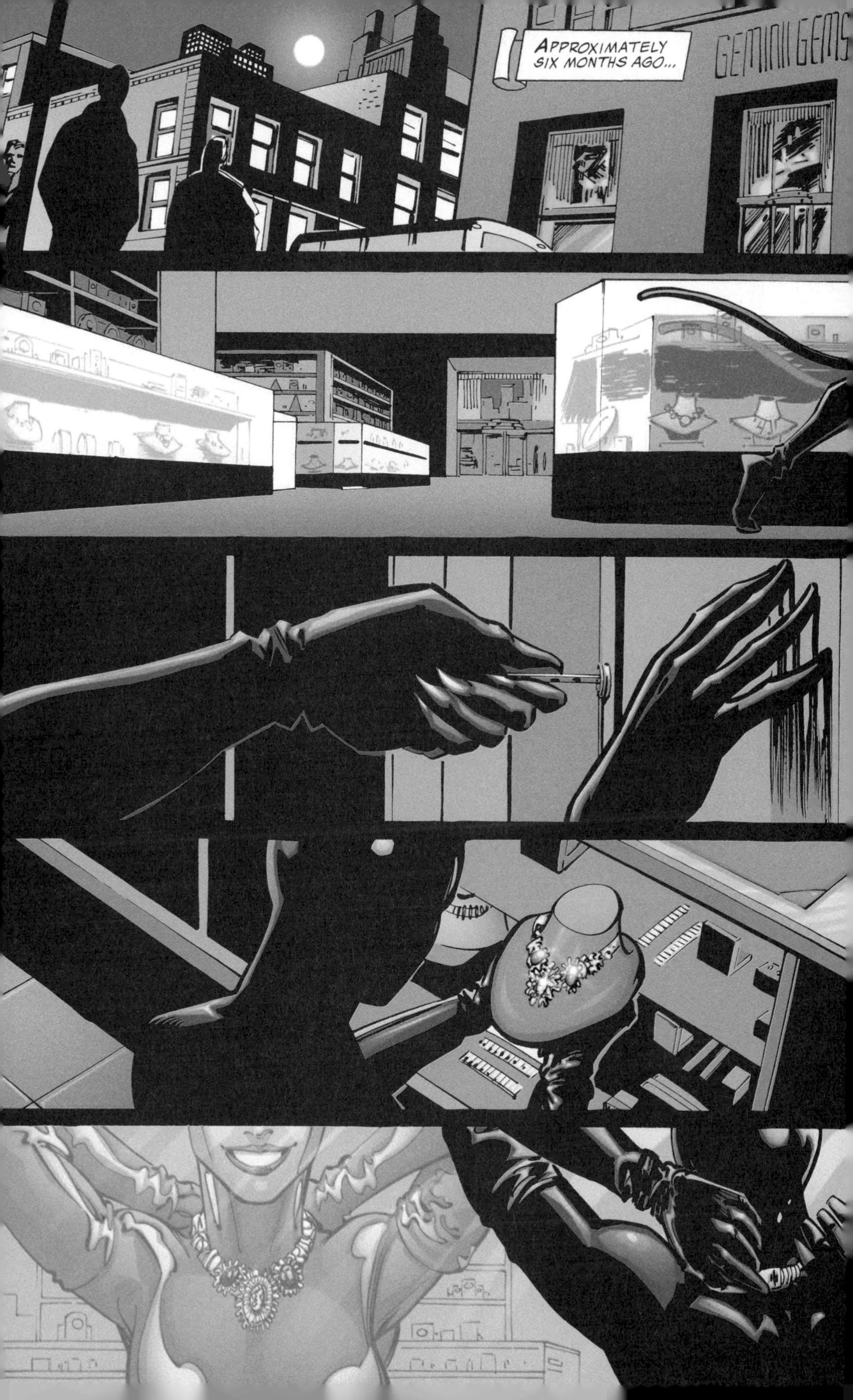
APPROXIMATELY SIX MONTHS AGO...
GEMINI GEMS

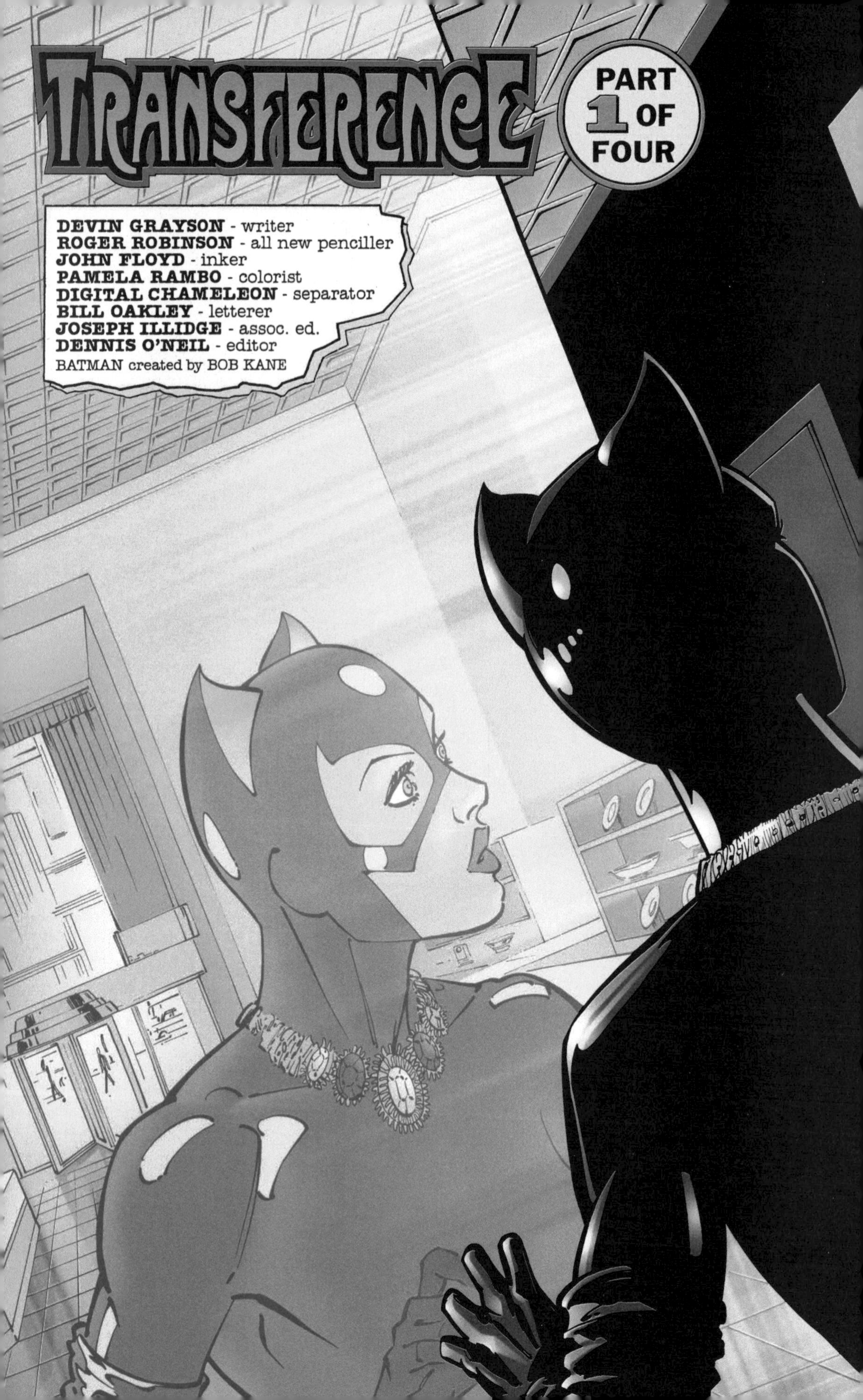
TRANSFERENCE
PART 1 OF FOUR
DEVIN GRAYSON - writer
ROGER ROBINSON - all new penciller
JOHN FLOYD - inker
PAMELA RAMBO - colorist
DIGITAL CHAMELEON - separator
BILL OAKLEY - letterer
JOSEPH ILLIDGE - assoc. ed.
DENNIS O'NEIL - editor
BATMAN created by BOB KANE

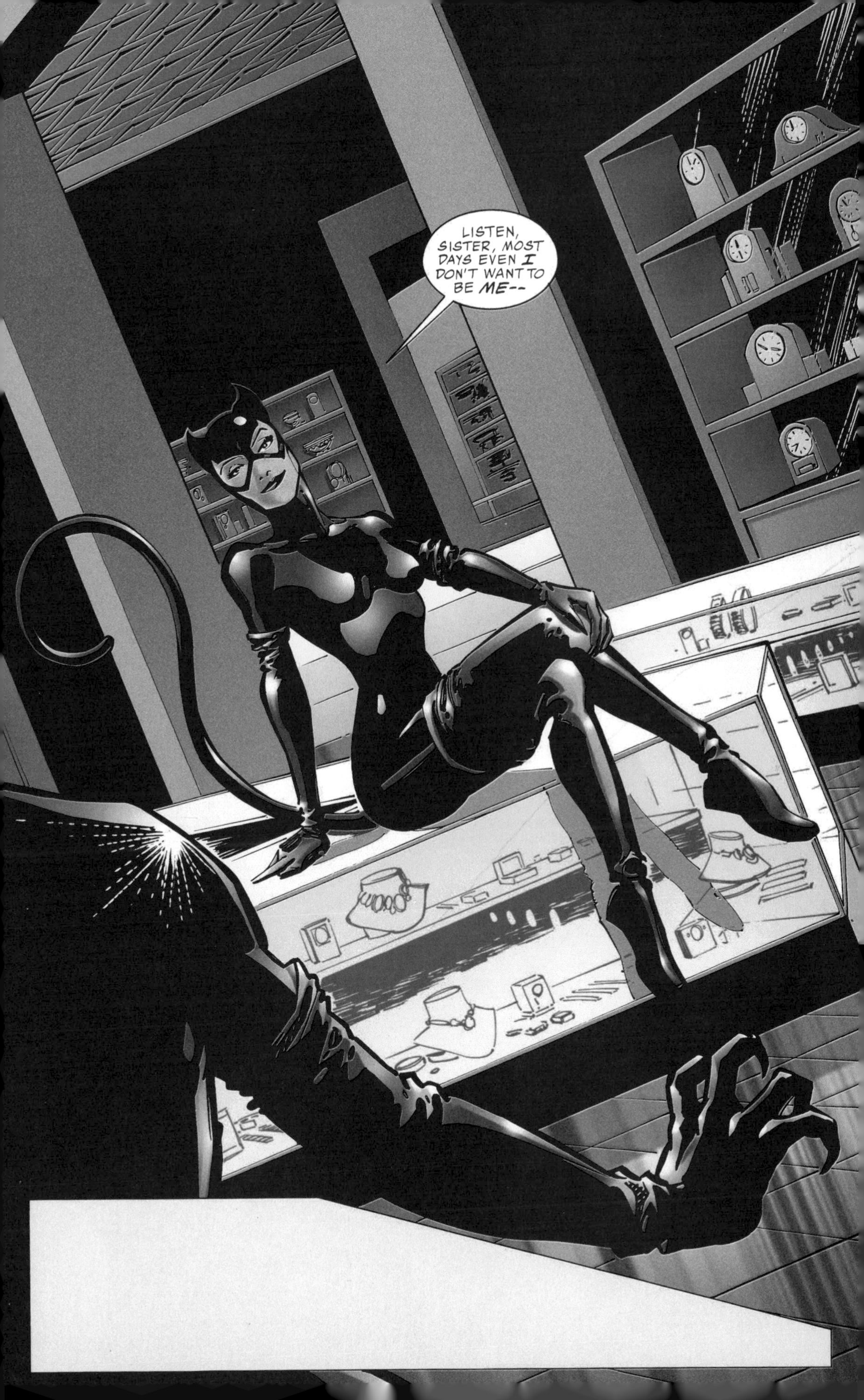
LISTEN, SISTER, MOST DAYS EVEN I DON'T WANT TO BE ME--

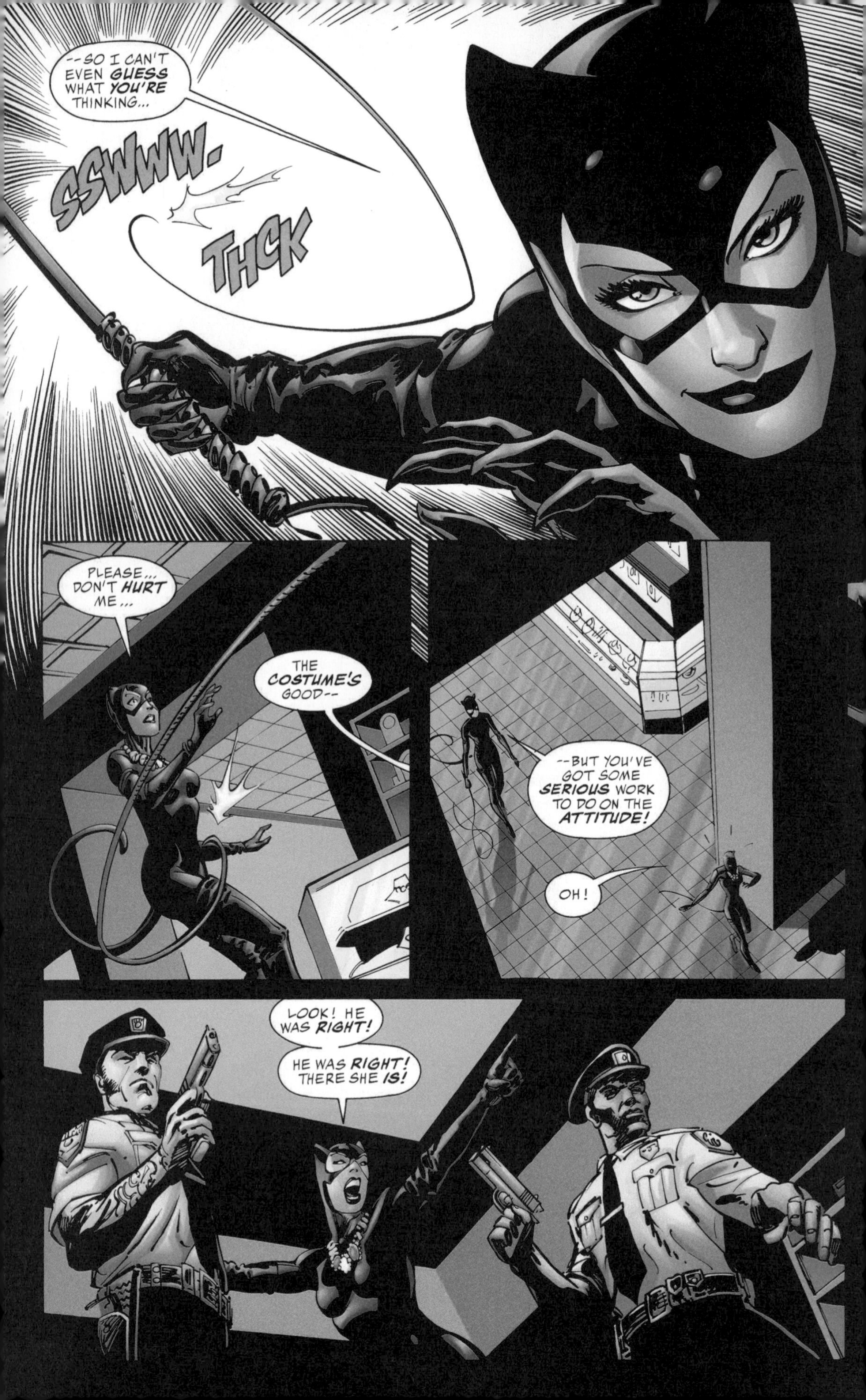
--SO I CAN'T EVEN GUESS WHAT YOU'RE THINKING...
SSWWW-
THCK
PLEASE... DON'T HURT ME...
THE COSTUME'S GOOD--
--BUT YOU'VE GOT SOME SERIOUS WORK TO DO ON THE ATTITUDE!
OH!
LOOK! HE WAS RIGHT!
HE WAS RIGHT! THERE SHE IS!

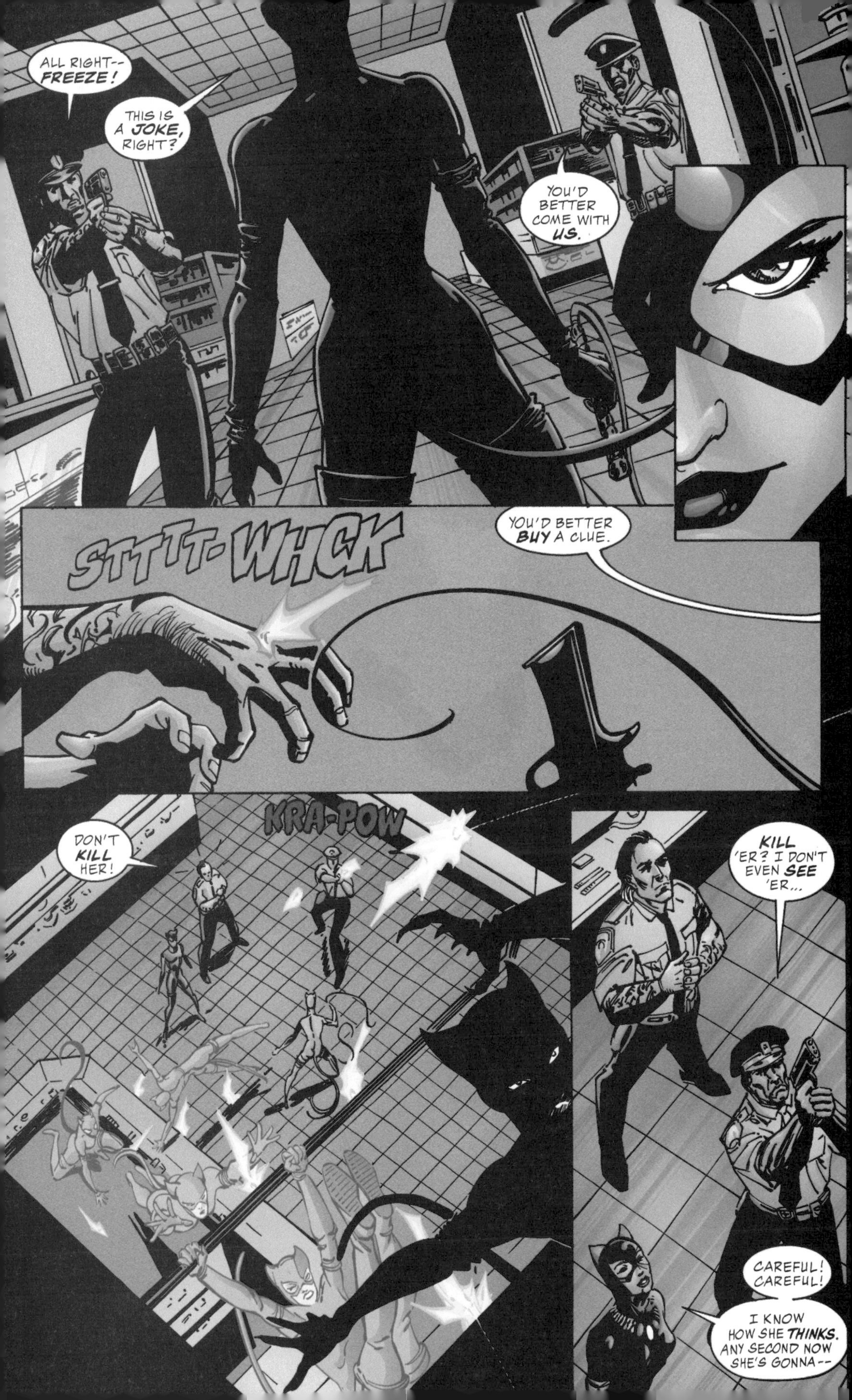
ALL RIGHT-- FREEZE!
THIS IS A JOKE, RIGHT?
YOU'D BETTER COME WITH US.
YOU'D BETTER BUY A CLUE.
STTTT-WHCK
KRA-POW
DON'T KILL HER!
KILL 'ER? I DON'T EVEN SEE 'ER...
CAREFUL! CAREFUL!
I KNOW HOW SHE THINKS. ANY SECOND NOW SHE'S GONNA--

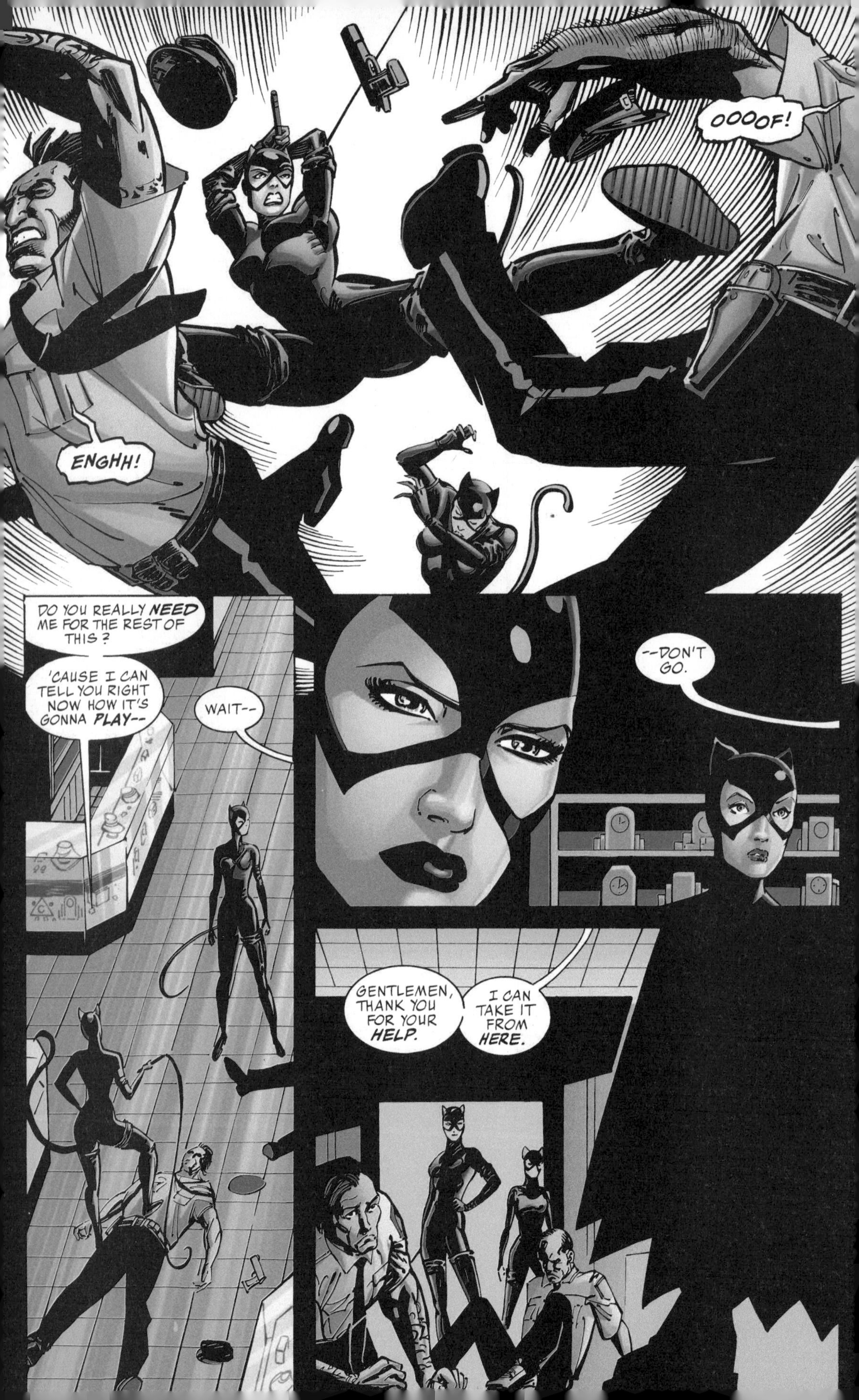

OOOOF!
ENGHH!
DO YOU REALLY NEED ME FOR THE REST OF THIS ?
'CAUSE I CAN TELL YOU RIGHT NOW HOW IT'S GONNA PLAY--
WAIT--
--DON'T GO.
GENTLEMEN, THANK YOU FOR YOUR HELP.
I CAN TAKE IT FROM HERE.

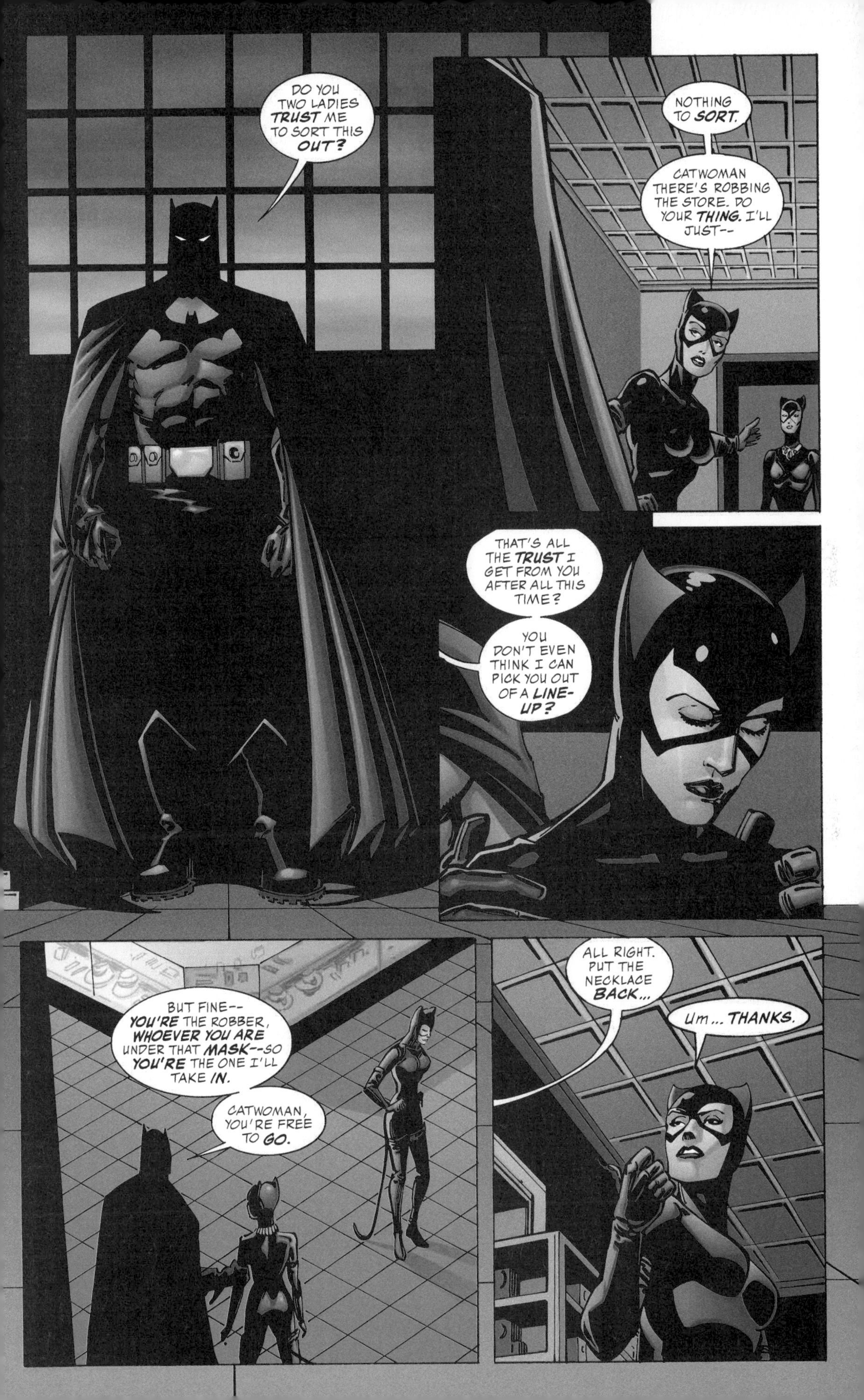

DO YOU TWO LADIES **TRUST** ME TO SORT THIS **OUT?**
NOTHING TO **SORT.**
CATWOMAN THERE'S ROBBING THE STORE. DO YOUR **THING.** I'LL JUST--
THAT'S ALL THE **TRUST** I GET FROM YOU AFTER ALL THIS TIME?
YOU DON'T EVEN THINK I CAN PICK YOU OUT OF A **LINE-UP?**
BUT FINE-- **YOU'RE** THE ROBBER, **WHOEVER YOU ARE** UNDER THAT **MASK**--SO **YOU'RE** THE ONE I'LL TAKE **IN.**
CATWOMAN, YOU'RE FREE TO **GO.**
ALL RIGHT. PUT THE NECKLACE **BACK...**
Um... **THANKS.**

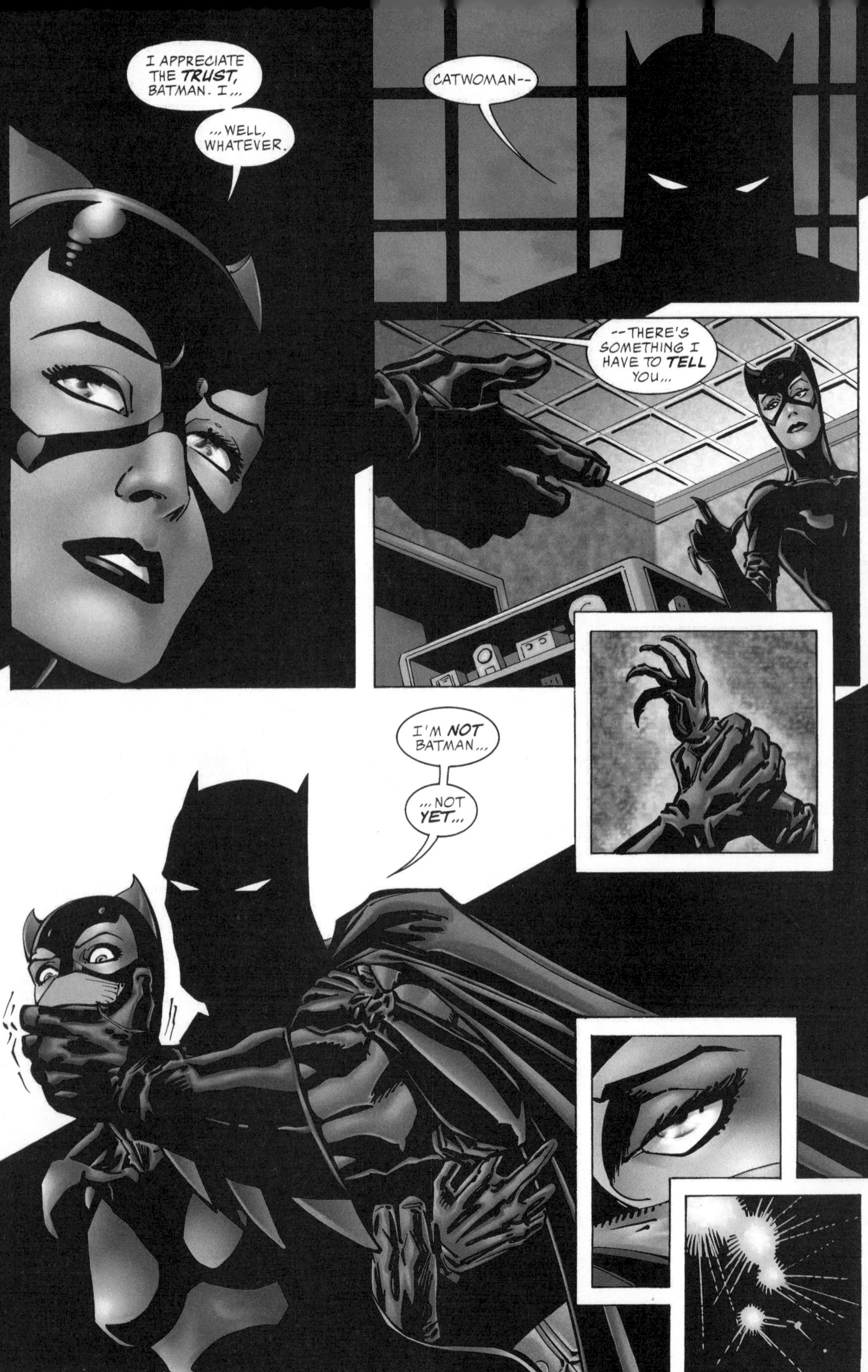
I APPRECIATE THE TRUST, BATMAN. I...
...WELL, WHATEVER.
CATWOMAN--
--THERE'S SOMETHING I HAVE TO TELL YOU...
I'M NOT BATMAN...
...NOT YET...

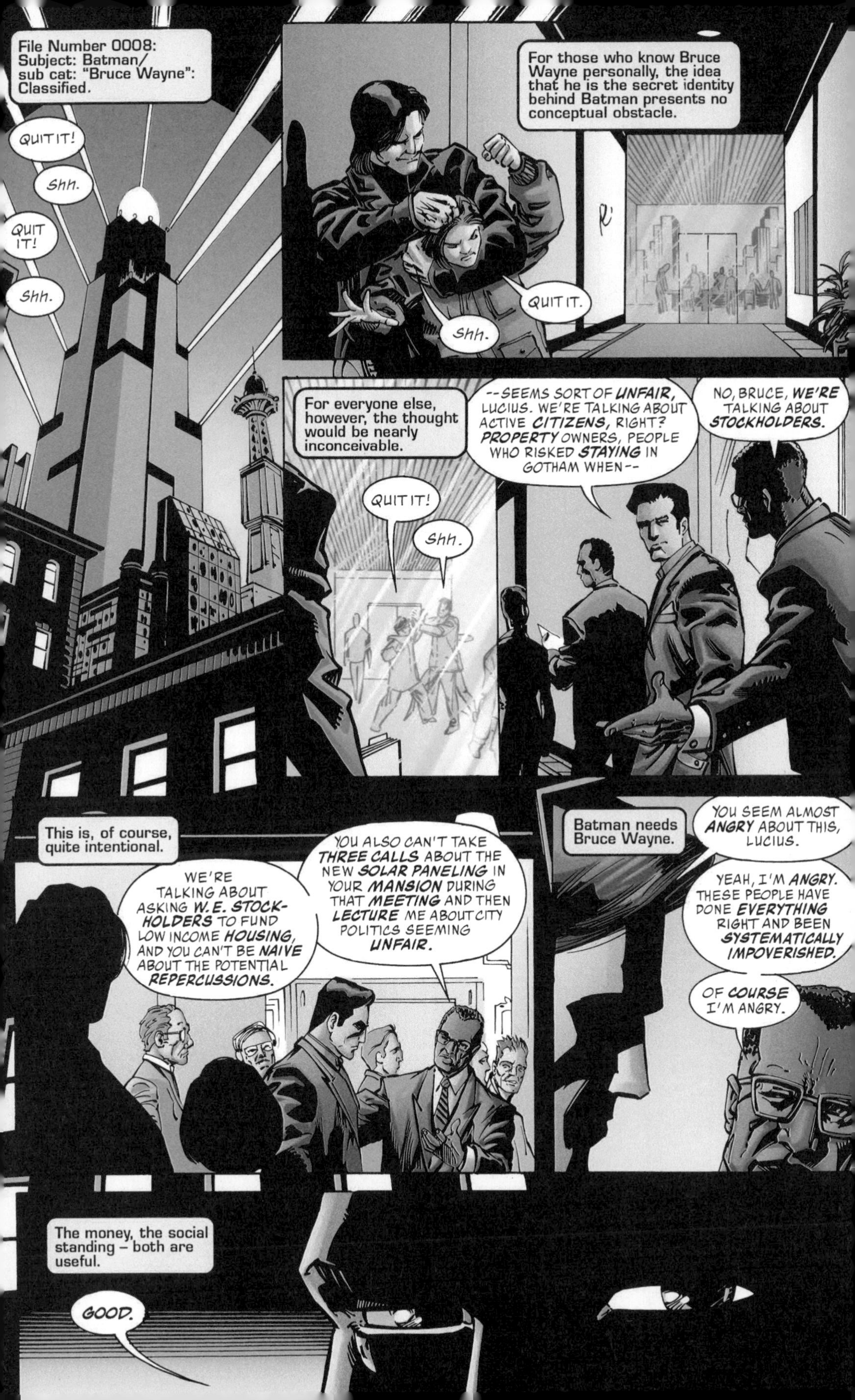

File Number 0008:
Subject: Batman/
sub cat: "Bruce Wayne":
Classified.
QUIT IT!
Shh.
QUIT IT!
Shh.
For those who know Bruce Wayne personally, the idea that he is the secret identity behind Batman presents no conceptual obstacle.
QUIT IT.
Shh.
For everyone else, however, the thought would be nearly inconceivable.
QUIT IT!
Shh.
--SEEMS SORT OF UNFAIR, LUCIUS. WE'RE TALKING ABOUT ACTIVE CITIZENS, RIGHT? PROPERTY OWNERS, PEOPLE WHO RISKED STAYING IN GOTHAM WHEN--
NO, BRUCE, WE'RE TALKING ABOUT STOCKHOLDERS.
This is, of course, quite intentional.
WE'RE TALKING ABOUT ASKING W.E. STOCKHOLDERS TO FUND LOW INCOME HOUSING, AND YOU CAN'T BE NAIVE ABOUT THE POTENTIAL REPERCUSSIONS.
YOU ALSO CAN'T TAKE THREE CALLS ABOUT THE NEW SOLAR PANELING IN YOUR MANSION DURING THAT MEETING AND THEN LECTURE ME ABOUT CITY POLITICS SEEMING UNFAIR.
Batman needs Bruce Wayne.
YOU SEEM ALMOST ANGRY ABOUT THIS, LUCIUS.
YEAH, I'M ANGRY. THESE PEOPLE HAVE DONE EVERYTHING RIGHT AND BEEN SYSTEMATICALLY IMPOVERISHED.
OF COURSE I'M ANGRY.
The money, the social standing – both are useful.
GOOD.

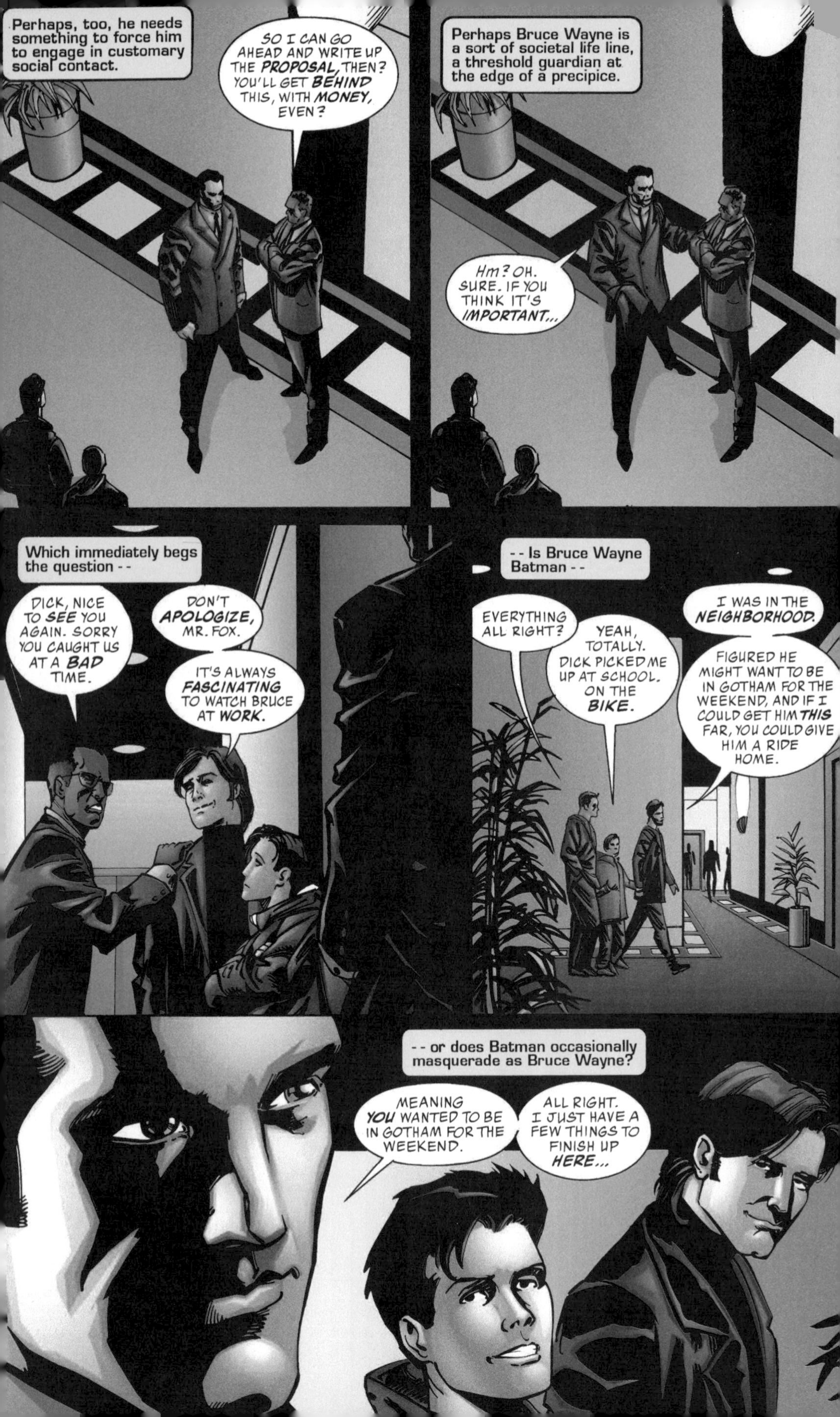
Perhaps, too, he needs something to force him to engage in customary social contact.
SO I CAN GO AHEAD AND WRITE UP THE PROPOSAL, THEN? YOU'LL GET BEHIND THIS, WITH MONEY, EVEN?
Perhaps Bruce Wayne is a sort of societal life line, a threshold guardian at the edge of a precipice.
Hm? OH. SURE. IF YOU THINK IT'S IMPORTANT...
Which immediately begs the question --
DICK, NICE TO SEE YOU AGAIN. SORRY YOU CAUGHT US AT A BAD TIME.
DON'T APOLOGIZE, MR. FOX.
IT'S ALWAYS FASCINATING TO WATCH BRUCE AT WORK.
-- Is Bruce Wayne Batman --
EVERYTHING ALL RIGHT?
YEAH, TOTALLY. DICK PICKED ME UP AT SCHOOL. ON THE BIKE.
I WAS IN THE NEIGHBORHOOD.
FIGURED HE MIGHT WANT TO BE IN GOTHAM FOR THE WEEKEND, AND IF I COULD GET HIM THIS FAR, YOU COULD GIVE HIM A RIDE HOME.
-- or does Batman occasionally masquerade as Bruce Wayne?
MEANING YOU WANTED TO BE IN GOTHAM FOR THE WEEKEND.
ALL RIGHT. I JUST HAVE A FEW THINGS TO FINISH UP HERE...

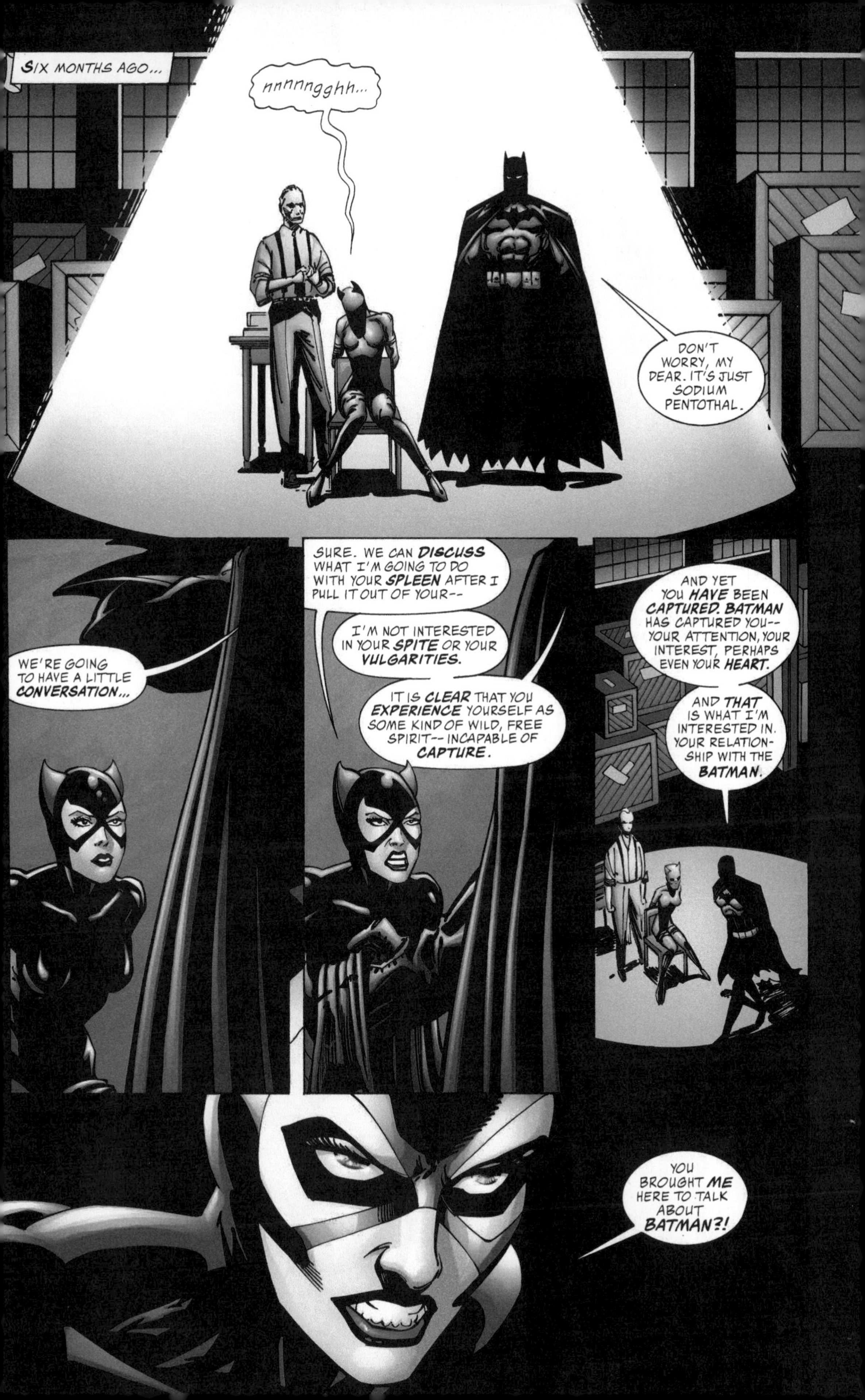
SIX MONTHS AGO...
nnnnngghh...
DON'T WORRY, MY DEAR. IT'S JUST SODIUM PENTOTHAL.
WE'RE GOING TO HAVE A LITTLE CONVERSATION...
SURE. WE CAN DISCUSS WHAT I'M GOING TO DO WITH YOUR SPLEEN AFTER I PULL IT OUT OF YOUR--
I'M NOT INTERESTED IN YOUR SPITE OR YOUR VULGARITIES.
IT IS CLEAR THAT YOU EXPERIENCE YOURSELF AS SOME KIND OF WILD, FREE SPIRIT-- INCAPABLE OF CAPTURE.
AND YET YOU HAVE BEEN CAPTURED. BATMAN HAS CAPTURED YOU-- YOUR ATTENTION, YOUR INTEREST, PERHAPS EVEN YOUR HEART.
AND THAT IS WHAT I'M INTERESTED IN. YOUR RELATIONSHIP WITH THE BATMAN.
YOU BROUGHT ME HERE TO TALK ABOUT BATMAN?!

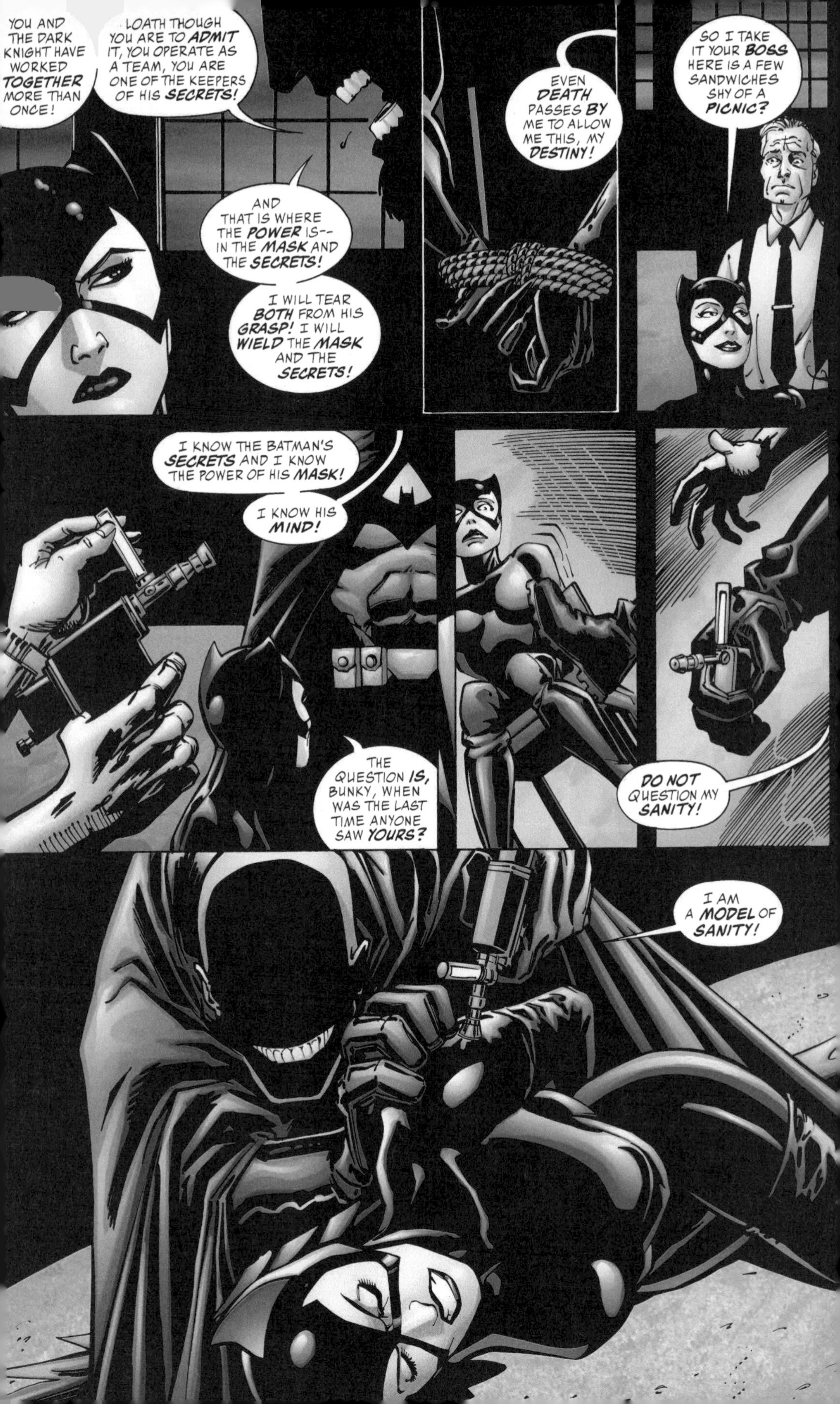

YOU AND THE DARK KNIGHT HAVE WORKED TOGETHER MORE THAN ONCE!
LOATH THOUGH YOU ARE TO ADMIT IT, YOU OPERATE AS A TEAM, YOU ARE ONE OF THE KEEPERS OF HIS SECRETS!
AND THAT IS WHERE THE POWER IS--IN THE MASK AND THE SECRETS!
I WILL TEAR BOTH FROM HIS GRASP! I WILL WIELD THE MASK AND THE SECRETS!
EVEN DEATH PASSES BY ME TO ALLOW ME THIS, MY DESTINY!
SO I TAKE IT YOUR BOSS HERE IS A FEW SANDWICHES SHY OF A PICNIC?
I KNOW THE BATMAN'S SECRETS AND I KNOW THE POWER OF HIS MASK!
I KNOW HIS MIND!
THE QUESTION IS, BUNKY, WHEN WAS THE LAST TIME ANYONE SAW YOURS?
DO NOT QUESTION MY SANITY!
I AM A MODEL OF SANITY!

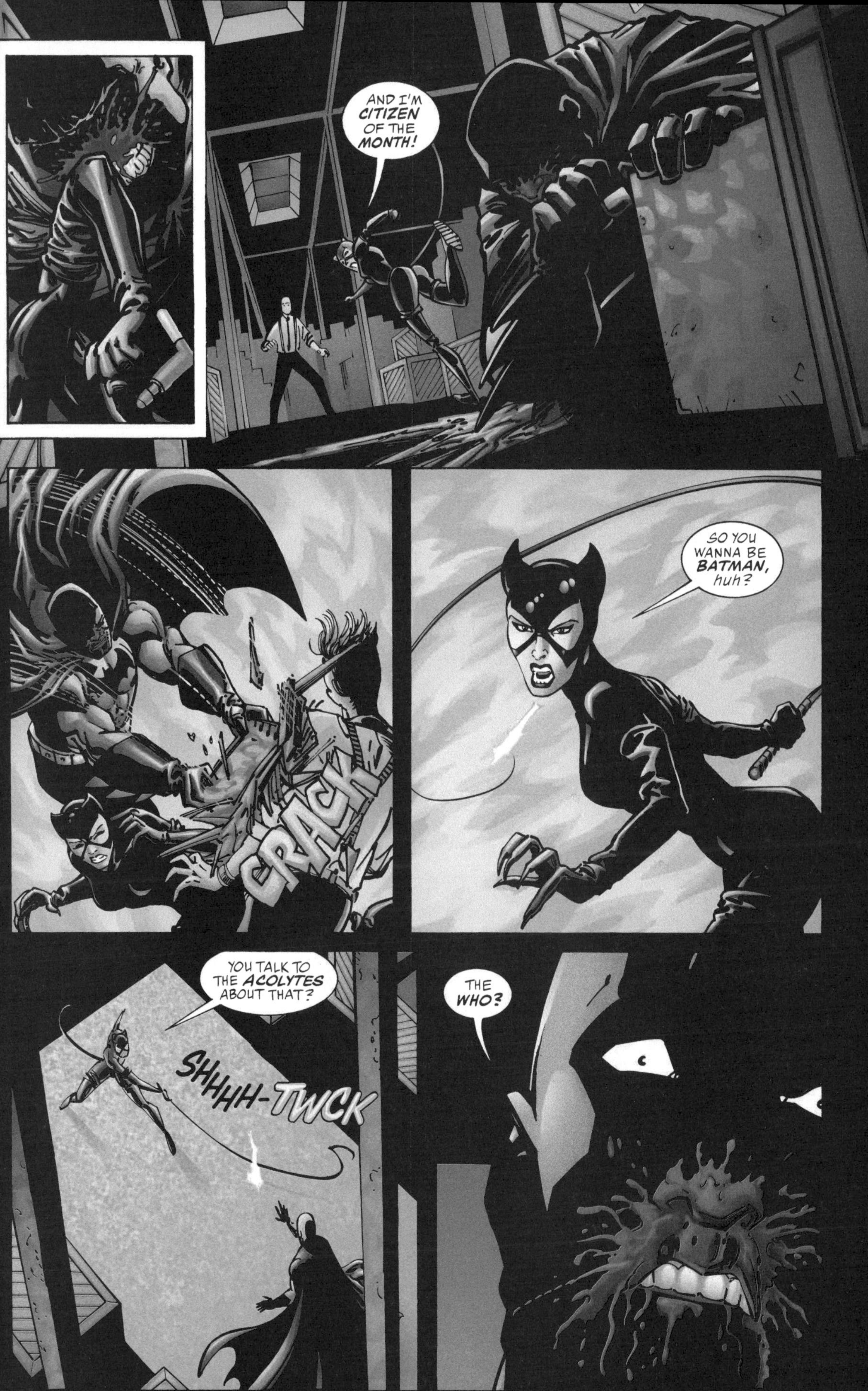
AND I'M CITIZEN OF THE MONTH!
CRACK
SO YOU WANNA BE BATMAN, huh?
YOU TALK TO THE ACOLYTES ABOUT THAT?
SHHHH-TWCK
THE WHO?

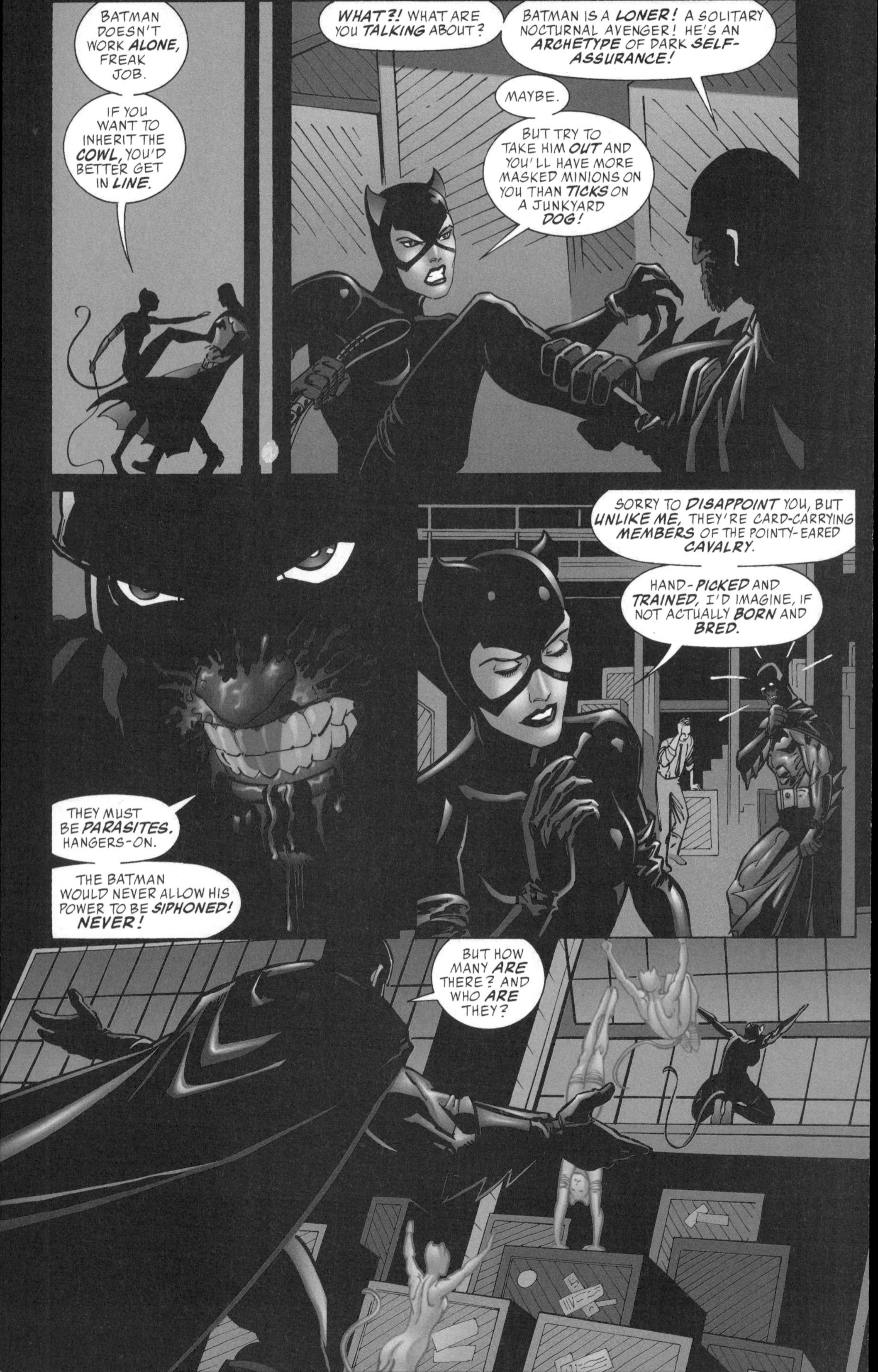
BATMAN DOESN'T WORK ALONE, FREAK JOB.
IF YOU WANT TO INHERIT THE COWL, YOU'D BETTER GET IN LINE.
WHAT?! WHAT ARE YOU TALKING ABOUT?
BATMAN IS A LONER! A SOLITARY NOCTURNAL AVENGER! HE'S AN ARCHETYPE OF DARK SELF-ASSURANCE!
MAYBE.
BUT TRY TO TAKE HIM OUT AND YOU'LL HAVE MORE MASKED MINIONS ON YOU THAN TICKS ON A JUNKYARD DOG!
SORRY TO DISAPPOINT YOU, BUT UNLIKE ME, THEY'RE CARD-CARRYING MEMBERS OF THE POINTY-EARED CAVALRY.
HAND-PICKED AND TRAINED, I'D IMAGINE, IF NOT ACTUALLY BORN AND BRED.
THEY MUST BE PARASITES. HANGERS-ON.
THE BATMAN WOULD NEVER ALLOW HIS POWER TO BE SIPHONED! NEVER!
BUT HOW MANY ARE THERE? AND WHO ARE THEY?

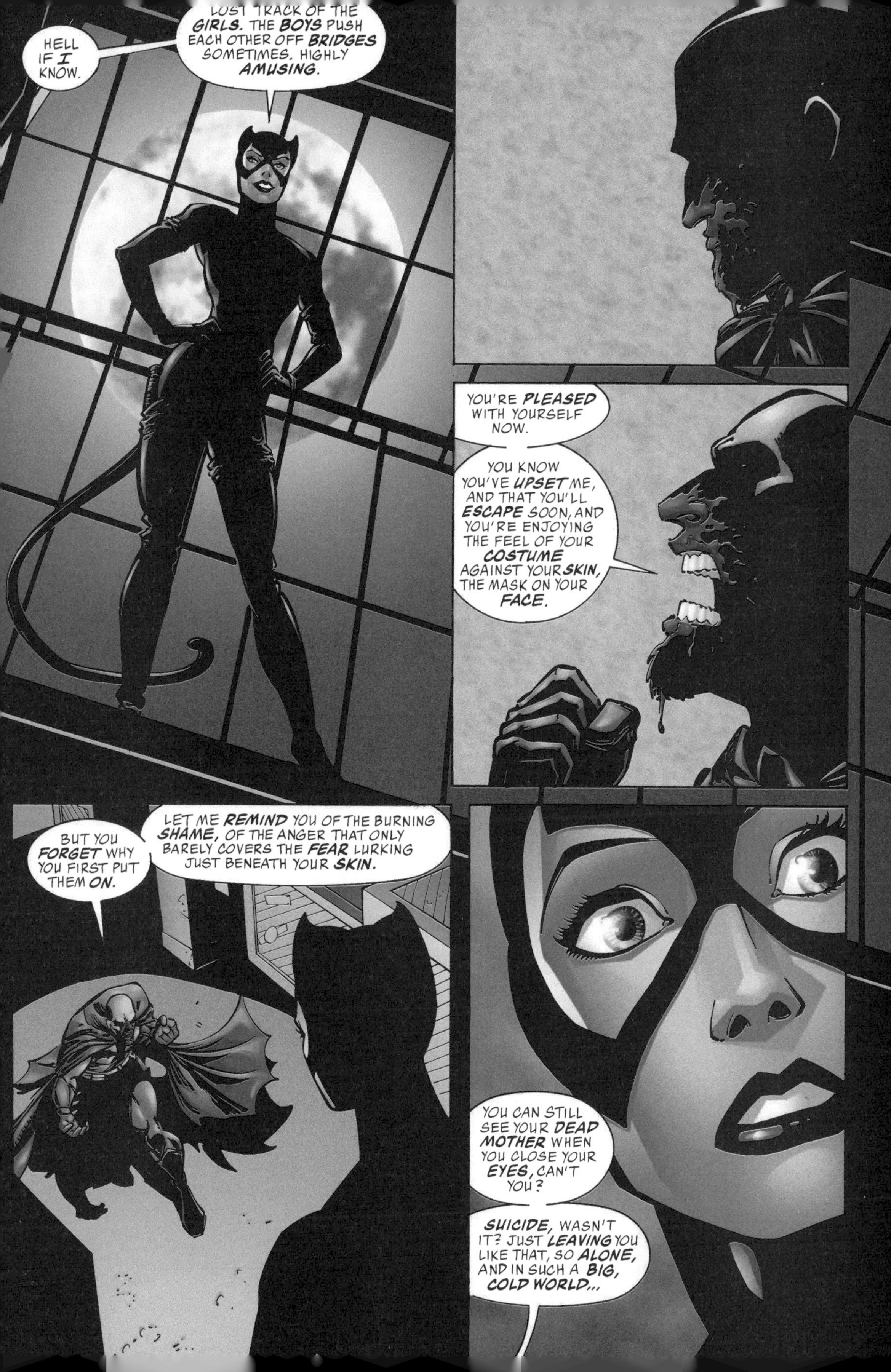
HELL IF I KNOW.
LOST TRACK OF THE GIRLS. THE BOYS PUSH EACH OTHER OFF BRIDGES SOMETIMES. HIGHLY AMUSING.
YOU'RE PLEASED WITH YOURSELF NOW.
YOU KNOW YOU'VE UPSET ME, AND THAT YOU'LL ESCAPE SOON, AND YOU'RE ENJOYING THE FEEL OF YOUR COSTUME AGAINST YOUR SKIN, THE MASK ON YOUR FACE.
BUT YOU FORGET WHY YOU FIRST PUT THEM ON.
LET ME REMIND YOU OF THE BURNING SHAME, OF THE ANGER THAT ONLY BARELY COVERS THE FEAR LURKING JUST BENEATH YOUR SKIN.
YOU CAN STILL SEE YOUR DEAD MOTHER WHEN YOU CLOSE YOUR EYES, CAN'T YOU?
SUICIDE, WASN'T IT? JUST LEAVING YOU LIKE THAT, SO ALONE, AND IN SUCH A BIG, COLD WORLD...

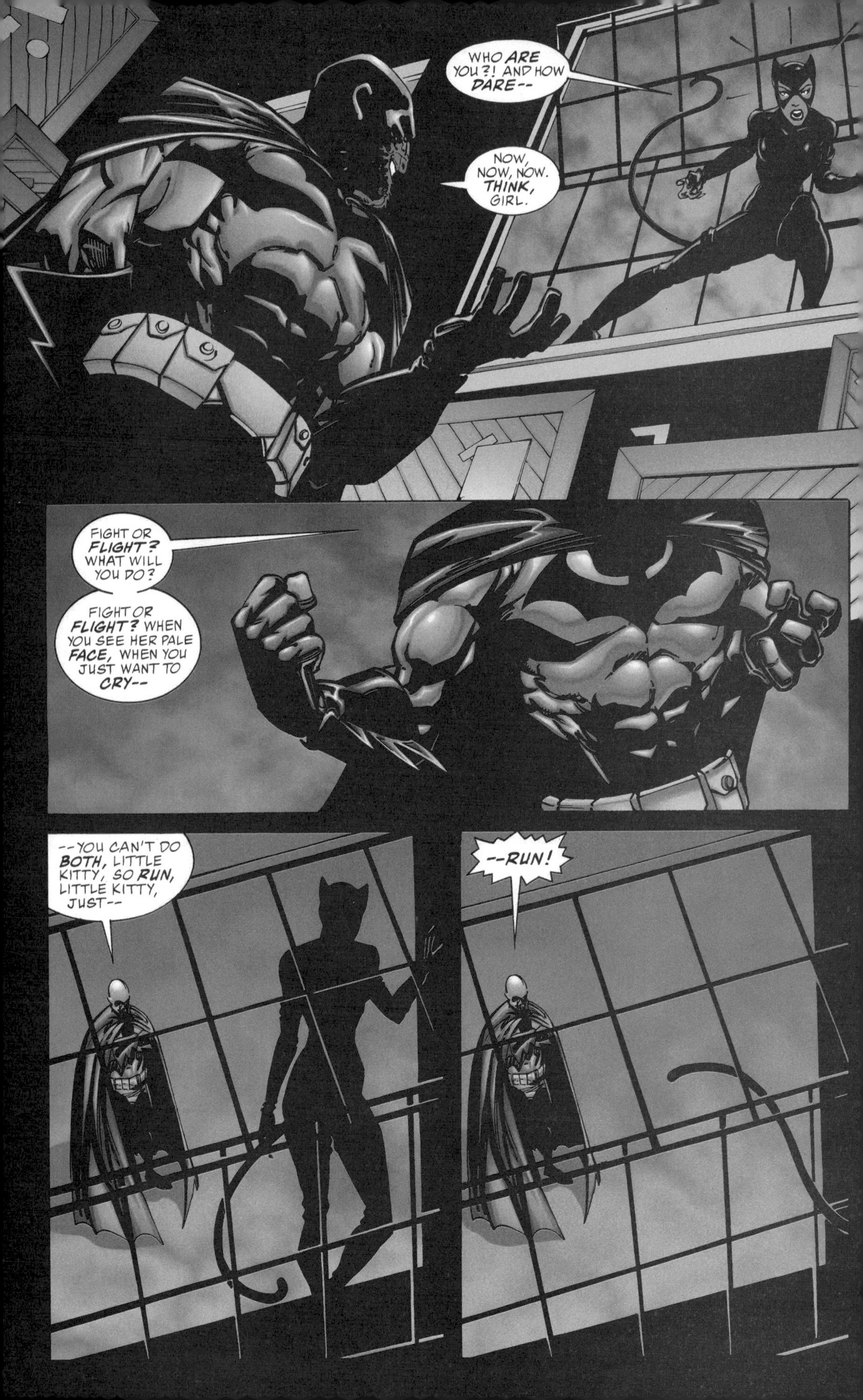
WHO ARE YOU?! AND HOW DARE--
NOW, NOW, NOW. THINK, GIRL.
FIGHT OR FLIGHT? WHAT WILL YOU DO?
FIGHT OR FLIGHT? WHEN YOU SEE HER PALE FACE, WHEN YOU JUST WANT TO CRY--
--YOU CAN'T DO BOTH, LITTLE KITTY, SO RUN, LITTLE KITTY, JUST--
--RUN!

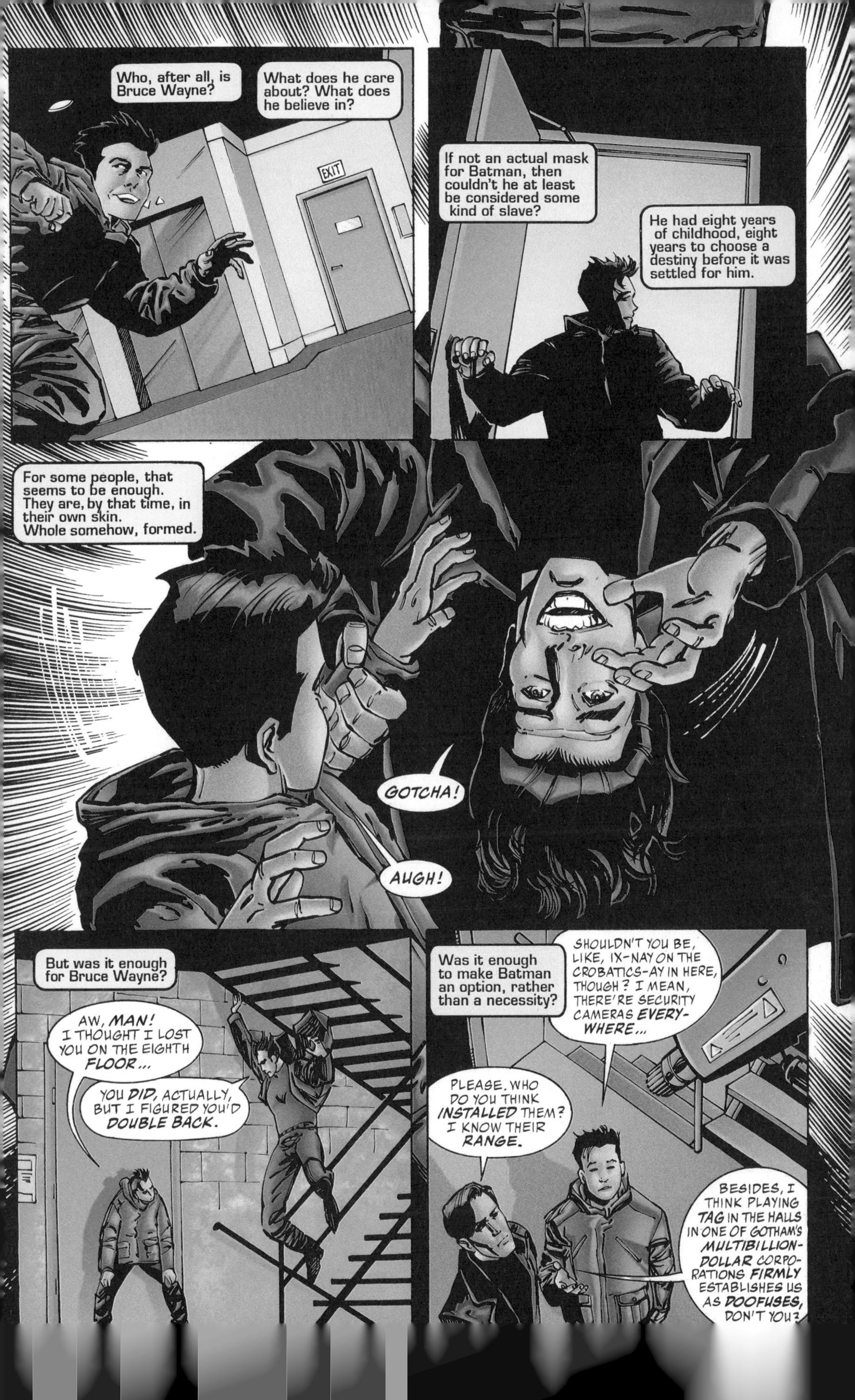
Who, after all, is Bruce Wayne?
What does he care about? What does he believe in?
EXIT
If not an actual mask for Batman, then couldn't he at least be considered some kind of slave?
He had eight years of childhood, eight years to choose a destiny before it was settled for him.
For some people, that seems to be enough. They are, by that time, in their own skin. Whole somehow, formed.
GOTCHA!
AUGH!
But was it enough for Bruce Wayne?
AW, MAN! I THOUGHT I LOST YOU ON THE EIGHTH FLOOR...
YOU DID, ACTUALLY, BUT I FIGURED YOU'D DOUBLE BACK.
Was it enough to make Batman an option, rather than a necessity?
SHOULDN'T YOU BE, LIKE, IX-NAY ON THE CROBATICS-AY IN HERE, THOUGH? I MEAN, THERE'RE SECURITY CAMERAS EVERY-WHERE...
PLEASE. WHO DO YOU THINK INSTALLED THEM? I KNOW THEIR RANGE.
BESIDES, I THINK PLAYING TAG IN THE HALLS IN ONE OF GOTHAM'S MULTIBILLION-DOLLAR CORPORATIONS FIRMLY ESTABLISHES US AS DOOFUSES, DON'T YOU?

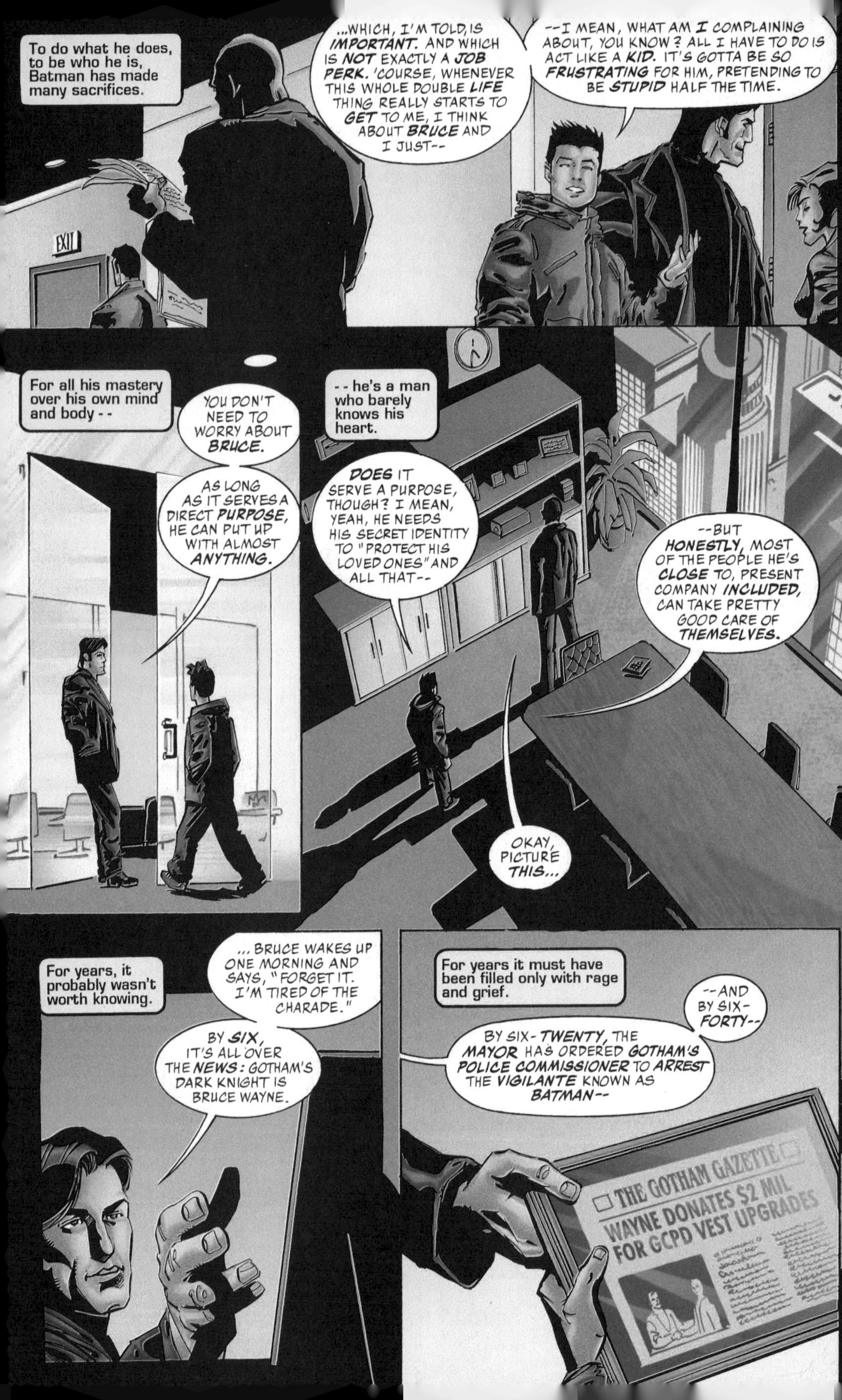
To do what he does, to be who he is, Batman has made many sacrifices.
...WHICH, I'M TOLD, IS IMPORTANT. AND WHICH IS NOT EXACTLY A JOB PERK. 'COURSE, WHENEVER THIS WHOLE DOUBLE LIFE THING REALLY STARTS TO GET TO ME, I THINK ABOUT BRUCE AND I JUST--
--I MEAN, WHAT AM I COMPLAINING ABOUT, YOU KNOW? ALL I HAVE TO DO IS ACT LIKE A KID. IT'S GOTTA BE SO FRUSTRATING FOR HIM, PRETENDING TO BE STUPID HALF THE TIME.
EXIT
For all his mastery over his own mind and body - -
YOU DON'T NEED TO WORRY ABOUT BRUCE.
AS LONG AS IT SERVES A DIRECT PURPOSE, HE CAN PUT UP WITH ALMOST ANYTHING.
- - he's a man who barely knows his heart.
DOES IT SERVE A PURPOSE, THOUGH? I MEAN, YEAH, HE NEEDS HIS SECRET IDENTITY TO "PROTECT HIS LOVED ONES" AND ALL THAT--
--BUT HONESTLY, MOST OF THE PEOPLE HE'S CLOSE TO, PRESENT COMPANY INCLUDED, CAN TAKE PRETTY GOOD CARE OF THEMSELVES.
OKAY, PICTURE THIS...
For years, it probably wasn't worth knowing.
...BRUCE WAKES UP ONE MORNING AND SAYS, "FORGET IT. I'M TIRED OF THE CHARADE."
BY SIX, IT'S ALL OVER THE NEWS: GOTHAM'S DARK KNIGHT IS BRUCE WAYNE.
For years it must have been filled only with rage and grief.
--AND BY SIX-FORTY--
BY SIX-TWENTY, THE MAYOR HAS ORDERED GOTHAM'S POLICE COMMISSIONER TO ARREST THE VIGILANTE KNOWN AS BATMAN--
THE GOTHAM GAZETTE
WAYNE DONATES $2 MIL FOR GCPD VEST UPGRADES

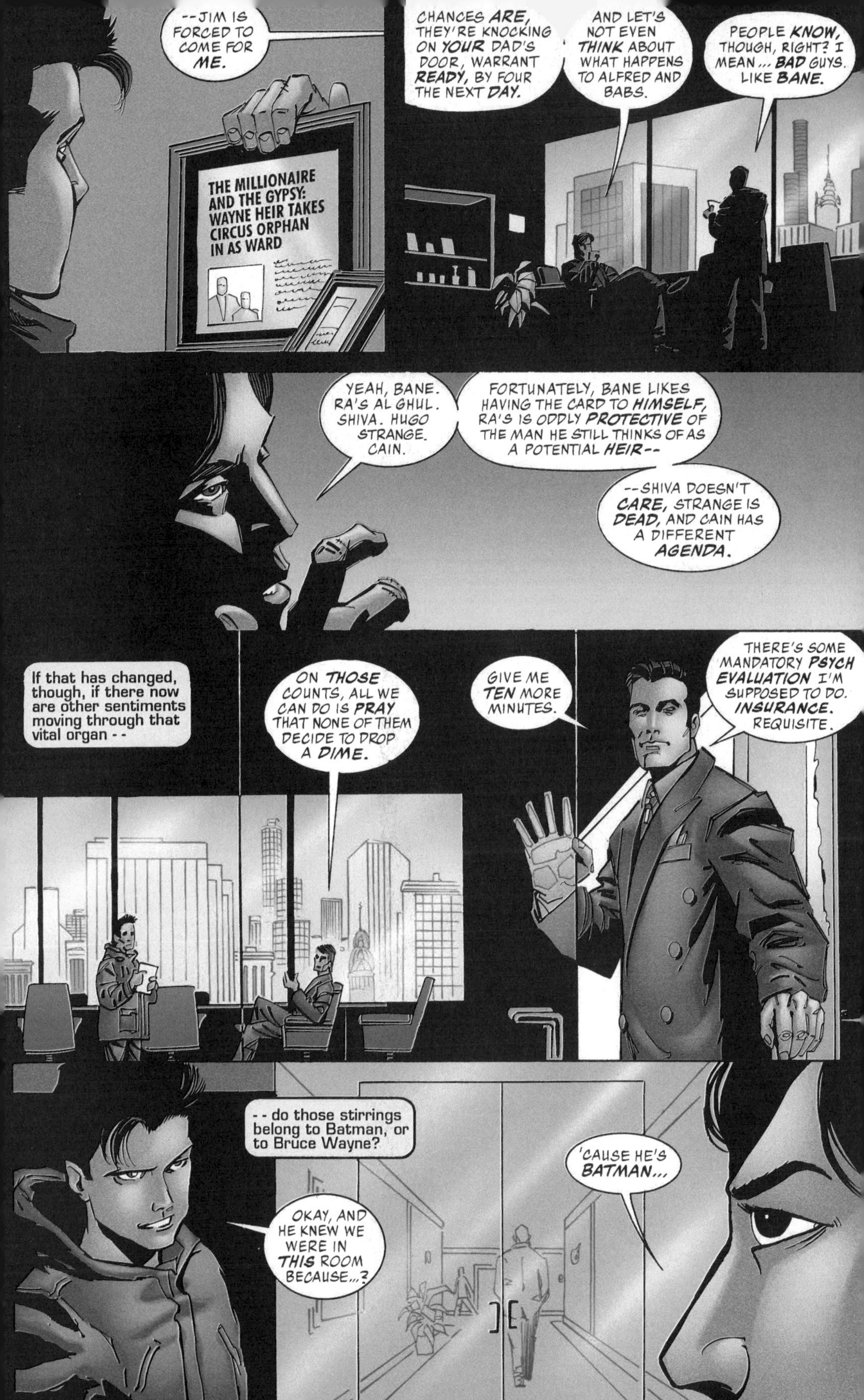
--JIM IS FORCED TO COME FOR ME.
THE MILLIONAIRE AND THE GYPSY: WAYNE HEIR TAKES CIRCUS ORPHAN IN AS WARD
CHANCES ARE, THEY'RE KNOCKING ON YOUR DAD'S DOOR, WARRANT READY, BY FOUR THE NEXT DAY.
AND LET'S NOT EVEN THINK ABOUT WHAT HAPPENS TO ALFRED AND BABS.
PEOPLE KNOW, THOUGH, RIGHT? I MEAN... BAD GUYS. LIKE BANE.
YEAH, BANE. RA'S AL GHUL. SHIVA. HUGO STRANGE. CAIN.
FORTUNATELY, BANE LIKES HAVING THE CARD TO HIMSELF, RA'S IS ODDLY PROTECTIVE OF THE MAN HE STILL THINKS OF AS A POTENTIAL HEIR--
--SHIVA DOESN'T CARE, STRANGE IS DEAD, AND CAIN HAS A DIFFERENT AGENDA.
If that has changed, though, if there now are other sentiments moving through that vital organ --
ON THOSE COUNTS, ALL WE CAN DO IS PRAY THAT NONE OF THEM DECIDE TO DROP A DIME.
GIVE ME TEN MORE MINUTES.
THERE'S SOME MANDATORY PSYCH EVALUATION I'M SUPPOSED TO DO. INSURANCE. REQUISITE.
-- do those stirrings belong to Batman, or to Bruce Wayne?
OKAY, AND HE KNEW WE WERE IN THIS ROOM BECAUSE...?
'CAUSE HE'S BATMAN...

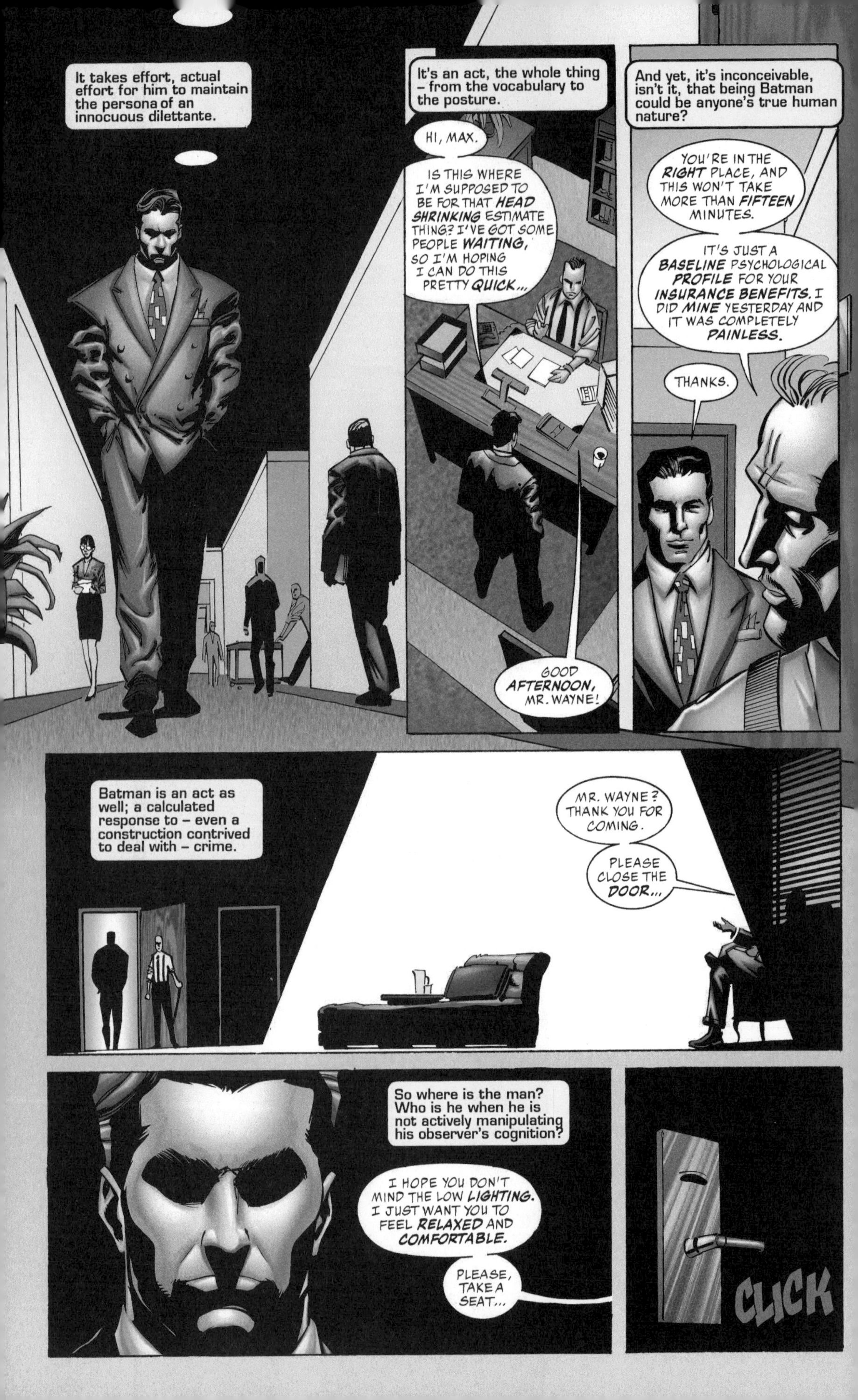

It takes effort, actual effort for him to maintain the persona of an innocuous dilettante.
It's an act, the whole thing – from the vocabulary to the posture.
HI, MAX.
IS THIS WHERE I'M SUPPOSED TO BE FOR THAT HEAD SHRINKING ESTIMATE THING? I'VE GOT SOME PEOPLE WAITING, SO I'M HOPING I CAN DO THIS PRETTY QUICK...
GOOD AFTERNOON, MR. WAYNE!
And yet, it's inconceivable, isn't it, that being Batman could be anyone's true human nature?
YOU'RE IN THE RIGHT PLACE, AND THIS WON'T TAKE MORE THAN FIFTEEN MINUTES.
IT'S JUST A BASELINE PSYCHOLOGICAL PROFILE FOR YOUR INSURANCE BENEFITS. I DID MINE YESTERDAY AND IT WAS COMPLETELY PAINLESS.
THANKS.
Batman is an act as well; a calculated response to – even a construction contrived to deal with – crime.
MR. WAYNE? THANK YOU FOR COMING.
PLEASE CLOSE THE DOOR...
So where is the man? Who is he when he is not actively manipulating his observer's cognition?
I HOPE YOU DON'T MIND THE LOW LIGHTING. I JUST WANT YOU TO FEEL RELAXED AND COMFORTABLE.
PLEASE, TAKE A SEAT...
CLICK

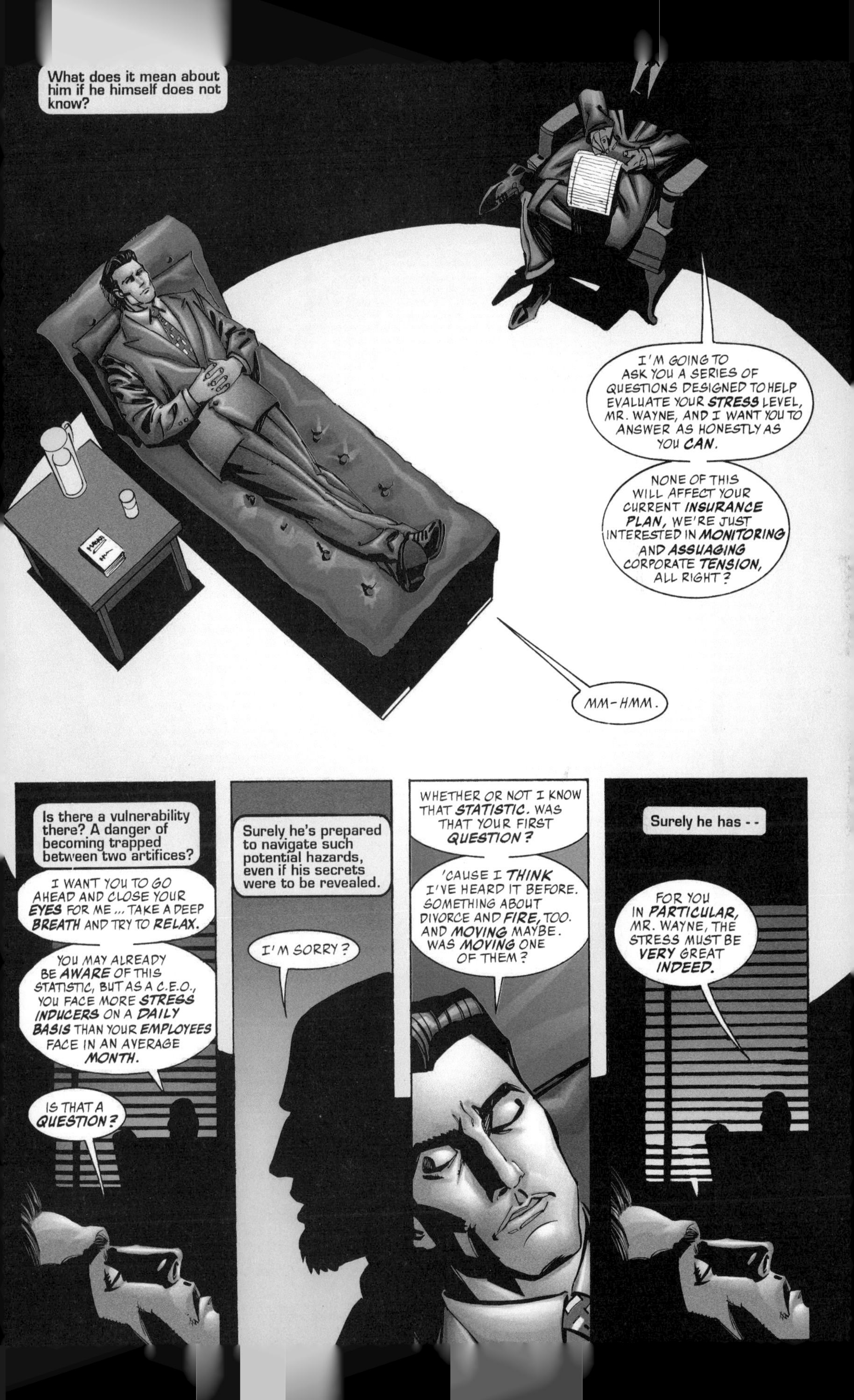
What does it mean about him if he himself does not know?
I'M GOING TO ASK YOU A SERIES OF QUESTIONS DESIGNED TO HELP EVALUATE YOUR STRESS LEVEL, MR. WAYNE, AND I WANT YOU TO ANSWER AS HONESTLY AS YOU CAN.
NONE OF THIS WILL AFFECT YOUR CURRENT INSURANCE PLAN, WE'RE JUST INTERESTED IN MONITORING AND ASSUAGING CORPORATE TENSION, ALL RIGHT?
MM-HMM.
Is there a vulnerability there? A danger of becoming trapped between two artifices?
I WANT YOU TO GO AHEAD AND CLOSE YOUR EYES FOR ME... TAKE A DEEP BREATH AND TRY TO RELAX.
YOU MAY ALREADY BE AWARE OF THIS STATISTIC, BUT AS A C.E.O., YOU FACE MORE STRESS INDUCERS ON A DAILY BASIS THAN YOUR EMPLOYEES FACE IN AN AVERAGE MONTH.
IS THAT A QUESTION?
Surely he's prepared to navigate such potential hazards, even if his secrets were to be revealed.
I'M SORRY?
WHETHER OR NOT I KNOW THAT STATISTIC. WAS THAT YOUR FIRST QUESTION?
'CAUSE I THINK I'VE HEARD IT BEFORE. SOMETHING ABOUT DIVORCE AND FIRE, TOO. AND MOVING MAYBE. WAS MOVING ONE OF THEM?
Surely he has --
FOR YOU IN PARTICULAR, MR. WAYNE, THE STRESS MUST BE VERY GREAT INDEED.

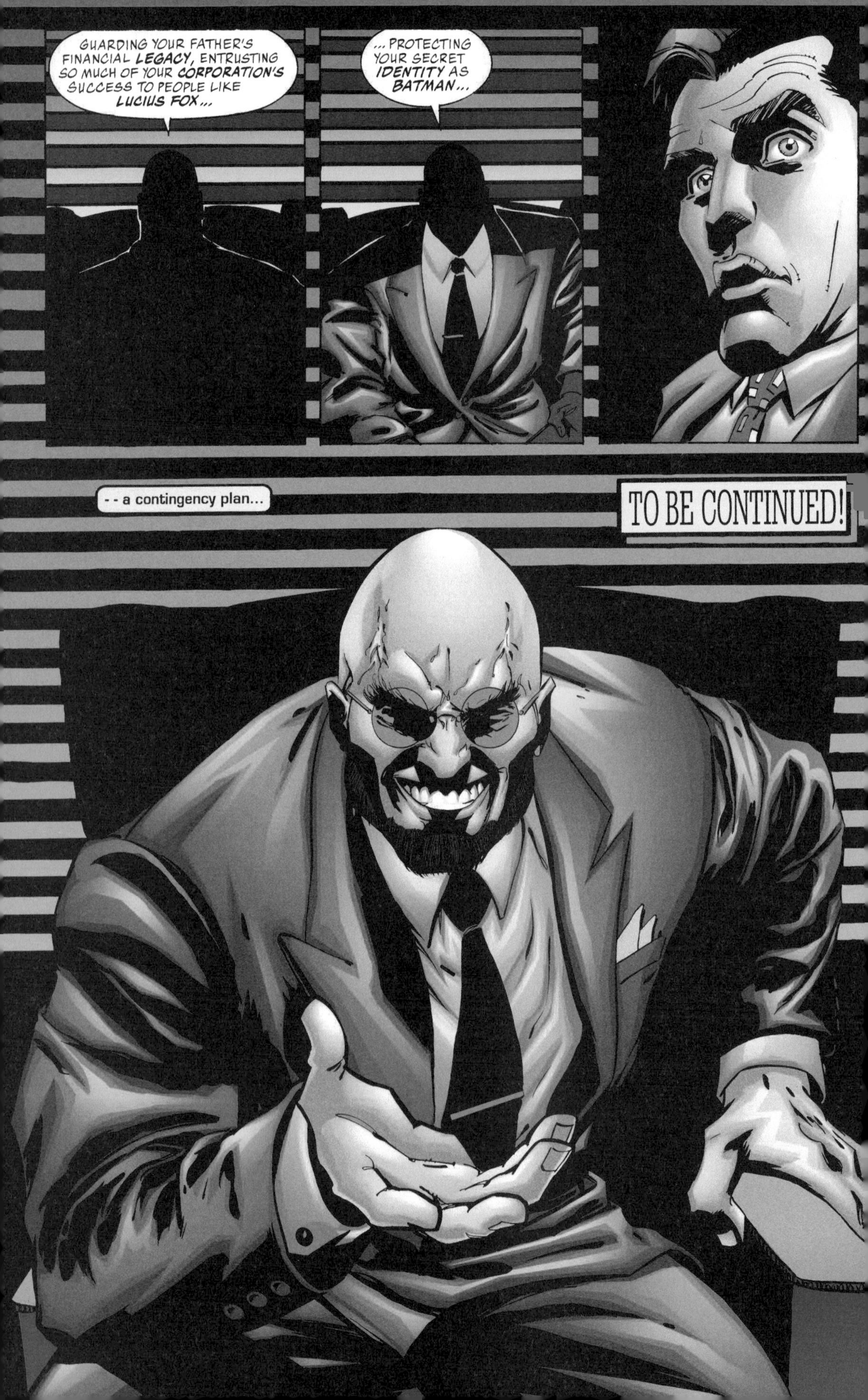
GUARDING YOUR FATHER'S FINANCIAL LEGACY, ENTRUSTING SO MUCH OF YOUR CORPORATION'S SUCCESS TO PEOPLE LIKE LUCIUS FOX...
...PROTECTING YOUR SECRET IDENTITY AS BATMAN...
--a contingency plan...
TO BE CONTINUED!

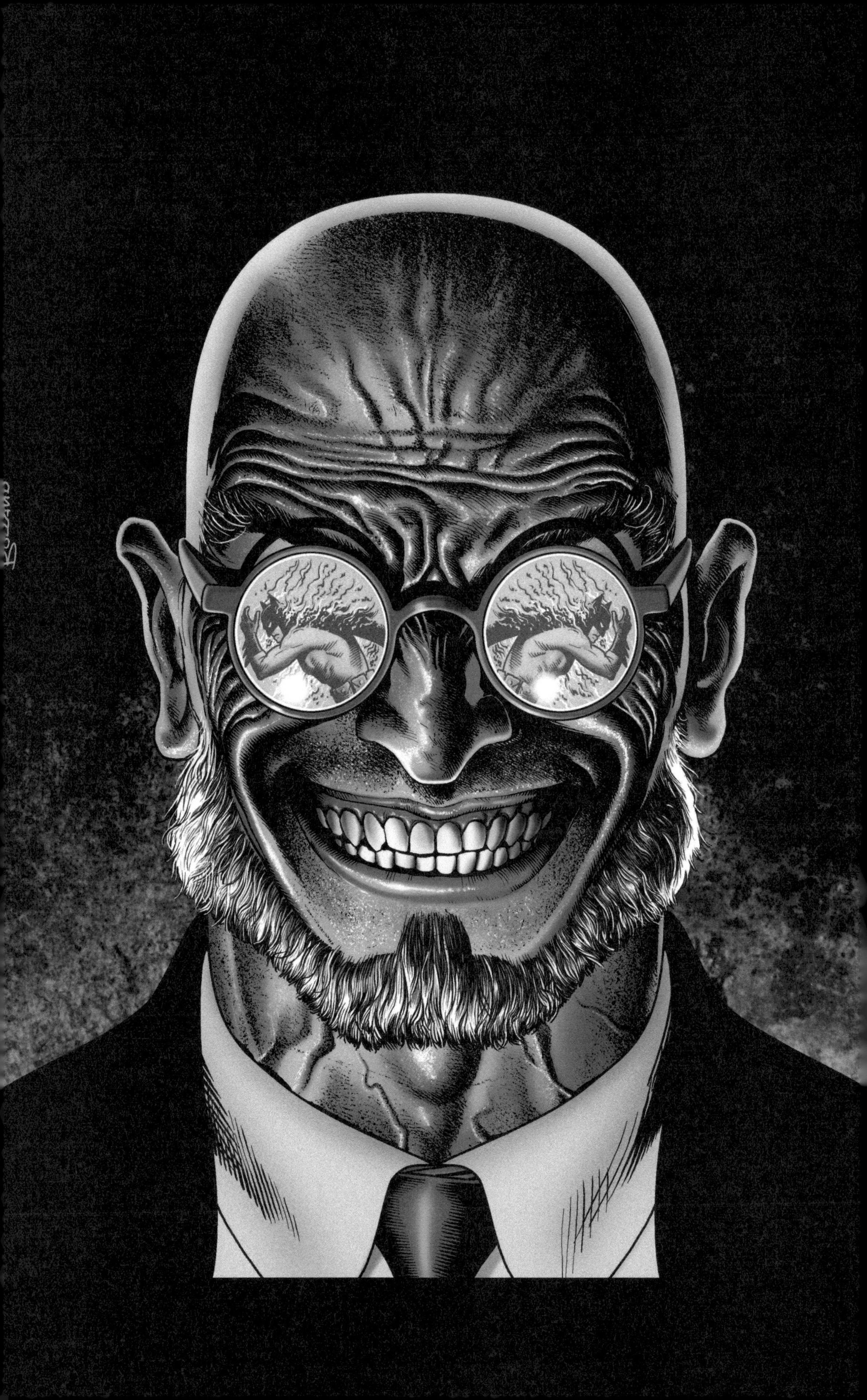

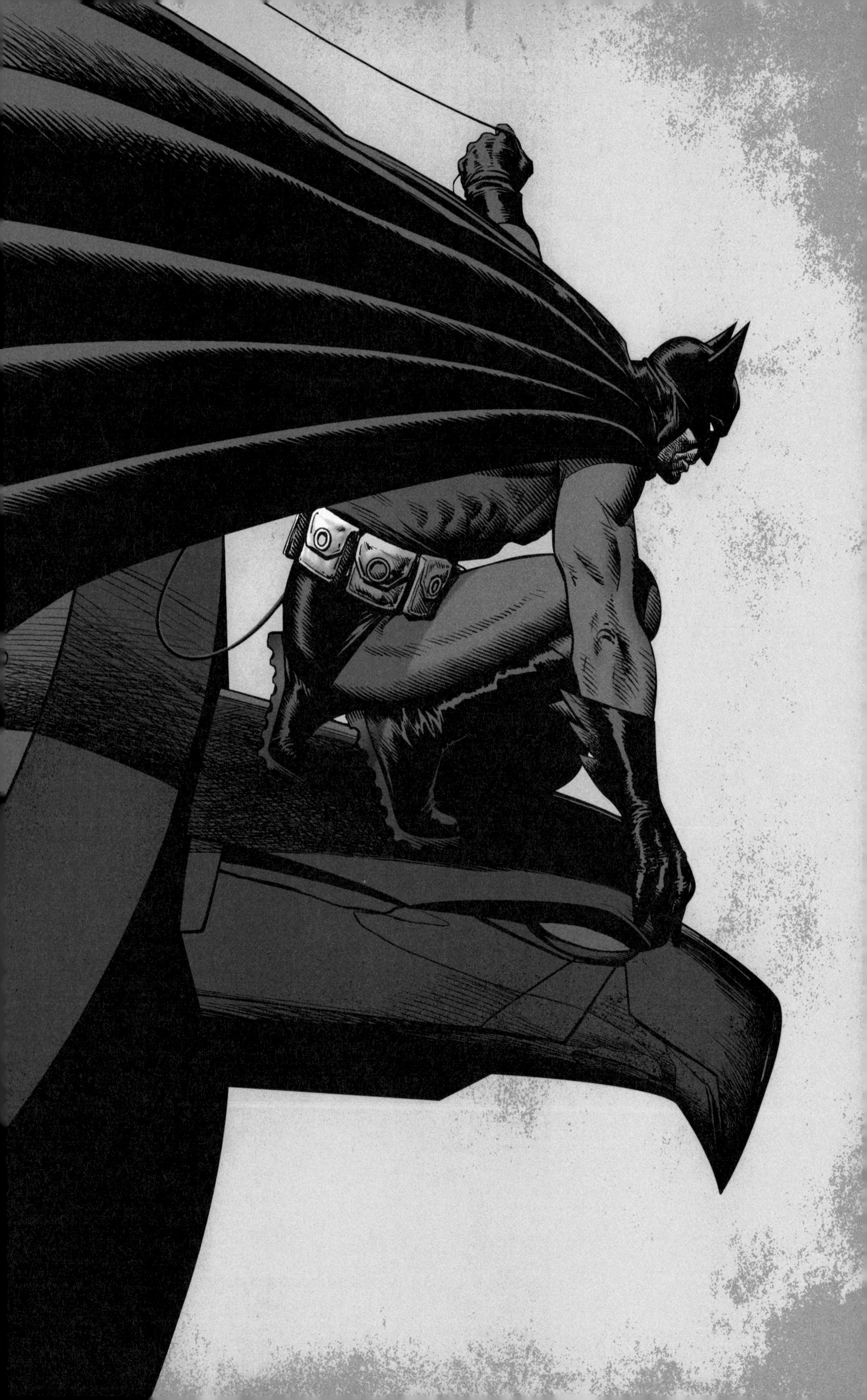

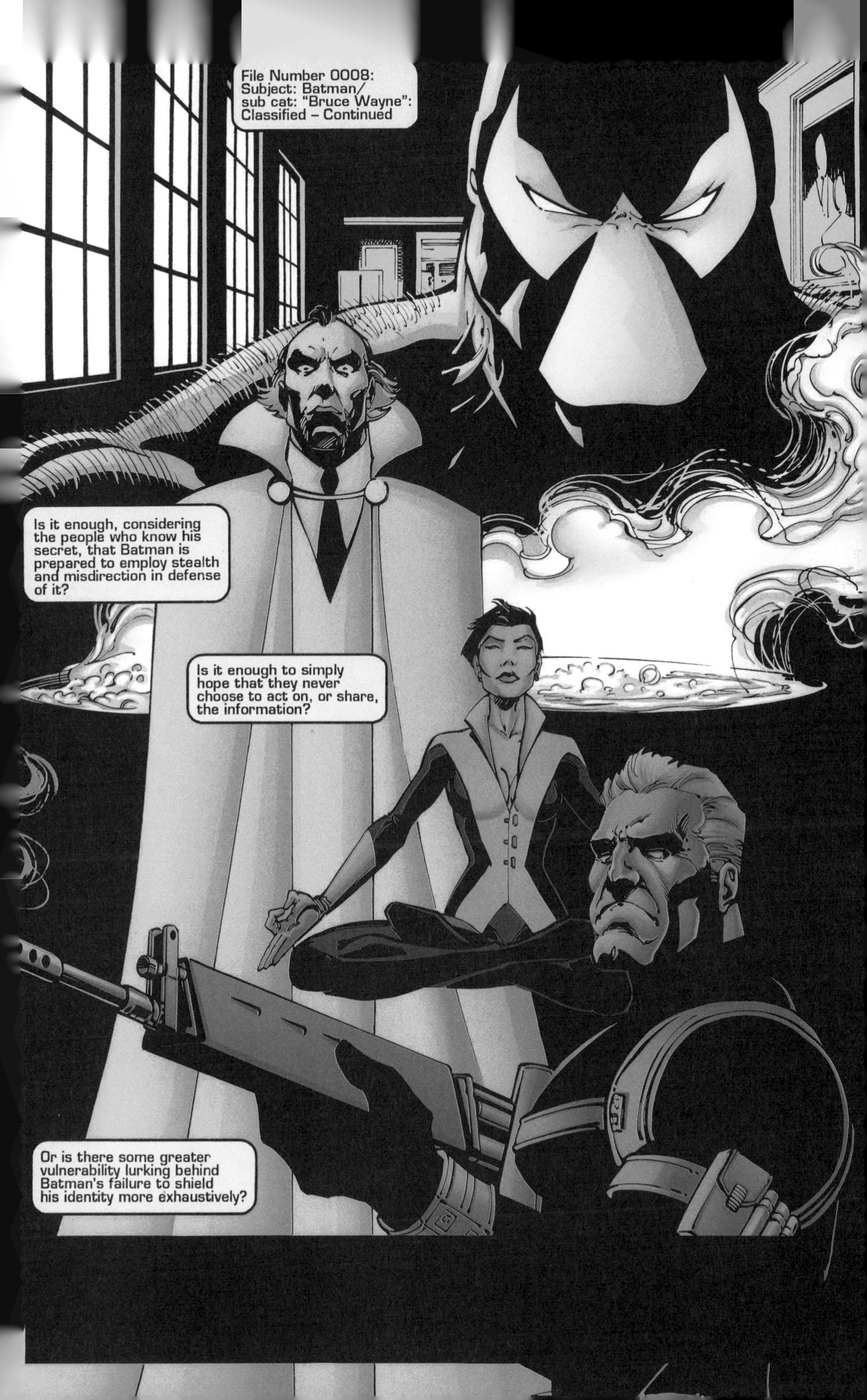
File Number 0008:
Subject: Batman/
sub cat: "Bruce Wayne":
Classified – Continued
Is it enough, considering the people who know his secret, that Batman is prepared to employ stealth and misdirection in defense of it?
Is it enough to simply hope that they never choose to act on, or share, the information?
Or is there some greater vulnerability lurking behind Batman's failure to shield his identity more exhaustively?

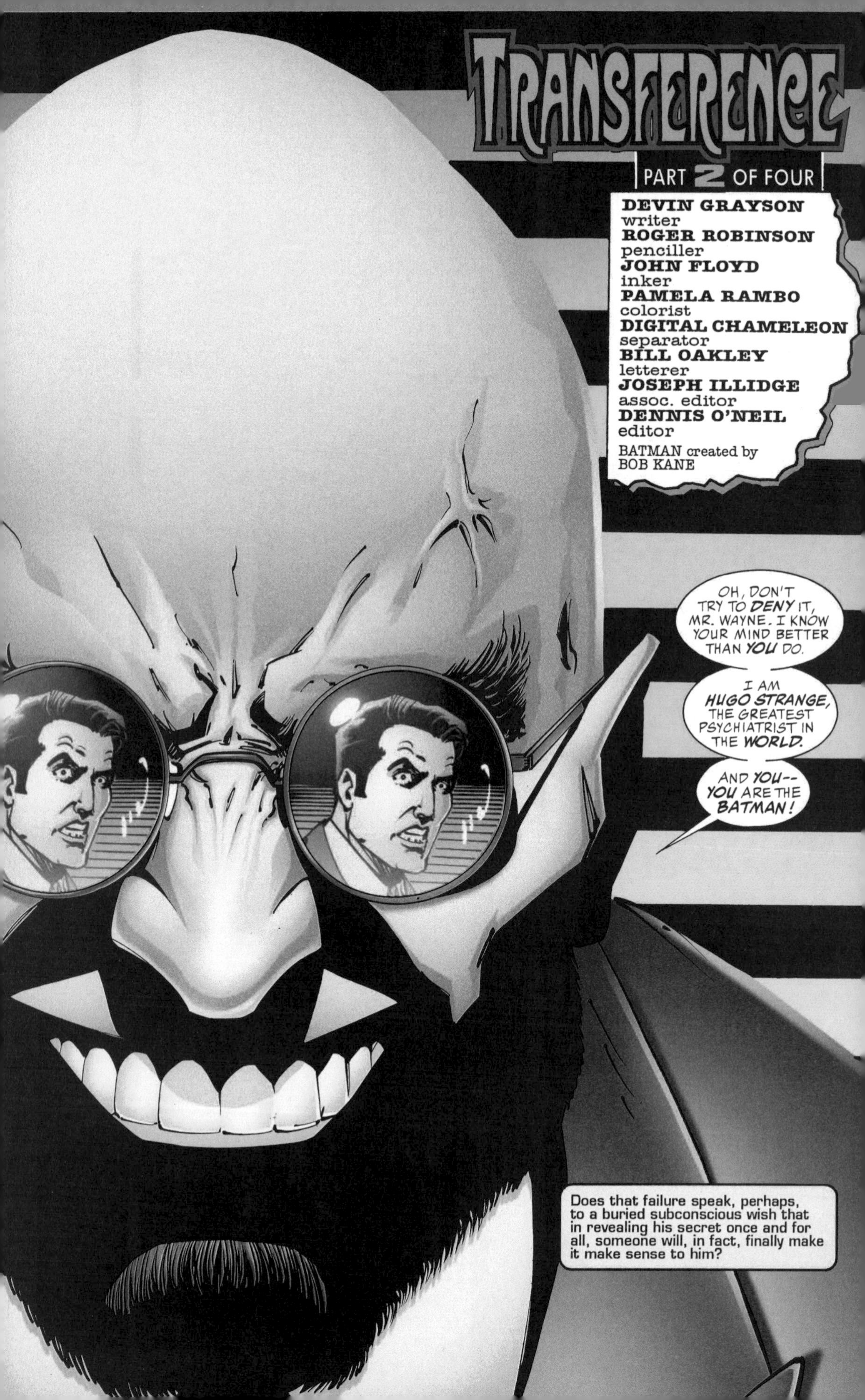
TRANSFERENCE
PART 2 OF FOUR
DEVIN GRAYSON writer
ROGER ROBINSON penciller
JOHN FLOYD inker
PAMELA RAMBO colorist
DIGITAL CHAMELEON separator
BILL OAKLEY letterer
JOSEPH ILLIDGE assoc. editor
DENNIS O'NEIL editor
BATMAN created by BOB KANE
OH, DON'T TRY TO DENY IT, MR. WAYNE. I KNOW YOUR MIND BETTER THAN YOU DO.
I AM HUGO STRANGE, THE GREATEST PSYCHIATRIST IN THE WORLD.
AND YOU-- YOU ARE THE BATMAN!
Does that failure speak, perhaps, to a buried subconscious wish that in revealing his secret once and for all, someone will, in fact, finally make it make sense to him?

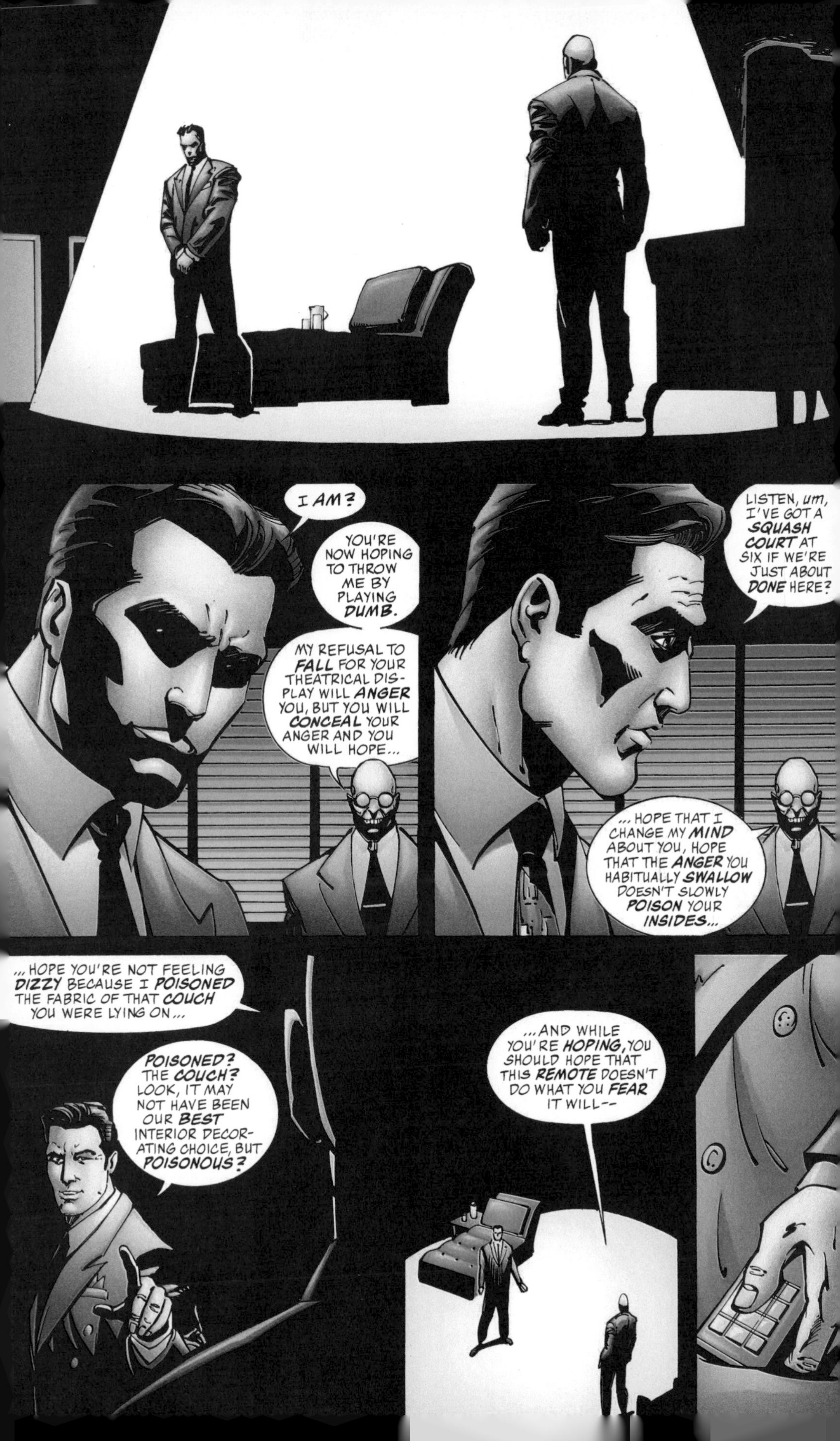
I AM?
YOU'RE NOW HOPING TO THROW ME BY PLAYING DUMB.
MY REFUSAL TO FALL FOR YOUR THEATRICAL DISPLAY WILL ANGER YOU, BUT YOU WILL CONCEAL YOUR ANGER AND YOU WILL HOPE...
LISTEN, um, I'VE GOT A SQUASH COURT AT SIX IF WE'RE JUST ABOUT DONE HERE?
...HOPE THAT I CHANGE MY MIND ABOUT YOU, HOPE THAT THE ANGER YOU HABITUALLY SWALLOW DOESN'T SLOWLY POISON YOUR INSIDES...
...HOPE YOU'RE NOT FEELING DIZZY BECAUSE I POISONED THE FABRIC OF THAT COUCH YOU WERE LYING ON...
POISONED? THE COUCH? LOOK, IT MAY NOT HAVE BEEN OUR BEST INTERIOR DECORATING CHOICE, BUT POISONOUS?
...AND WHILE YOU'RE HOPING, YOU SHOULD HOPE THAT THIS REMOTE DOESN'T DO WHAT YOU FEAR IT WILL--

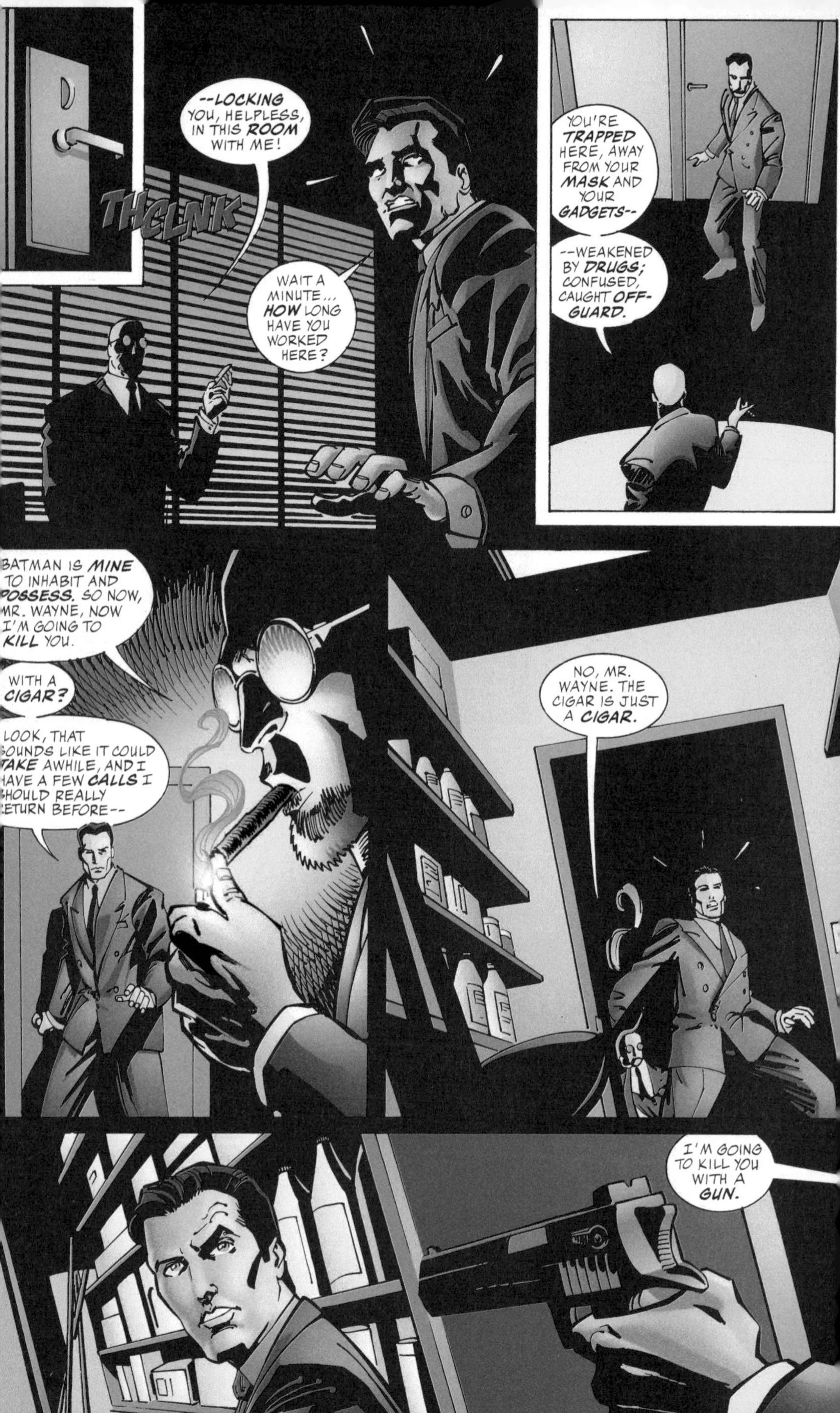
THCLNK
--LOCKING YOU, HELPLESS, IN THIS ROOM WITH ME!
WAIT A MINUTE... HOW LONG HAVE YOU WORKED HERE?
YOU'RE TRAPPED HERE, AWAY FROM YOUR MASK AND YOUR GADGETS--
--WEAKENED BY DRUGS; CONFUSED, CAUGHT OFF-GUARD.
BATMAN IS MINE TO INHABIT AND POSSESS. SO NOW, MR. WAYNE, NOW I'M GOING TO KILL YOU.
WITH A CIGAR?
LOOK, THAT SOUNDS LIKE IT COULD TAKE AWHILE, AND I HAVE A FEW CALLS I SHOULD REALLY RETURN BEFORE--
NO, MR. WAYNE. THE CIGAR IS JUST A CIGAR.
I'M GOING TO KILL YOU WITH A GUN.

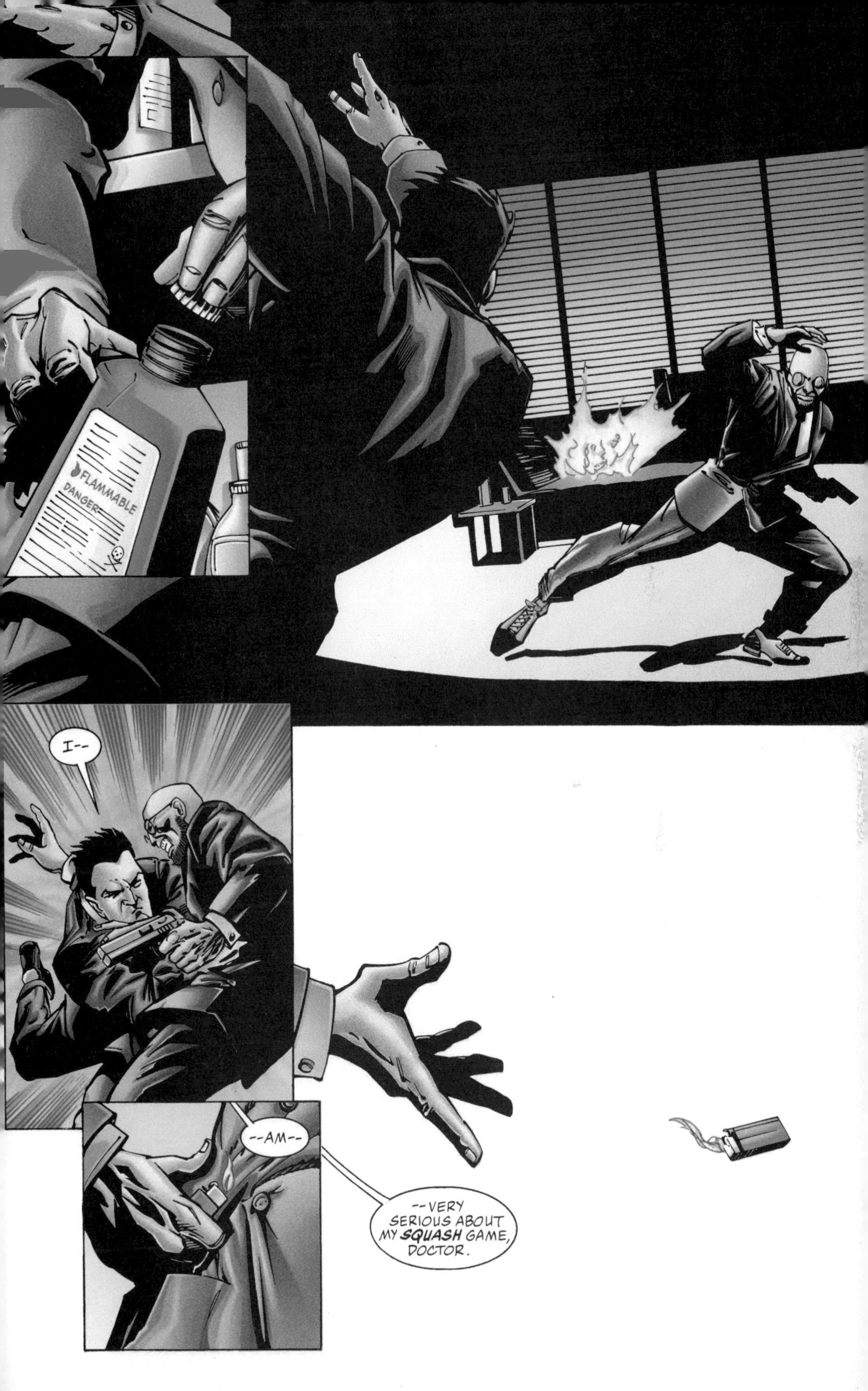

FLAMMABLE
DANGER
I--
--AM--
--VERY SERIOUS ABOUT MY SQUASH GAME, DOCTOR.

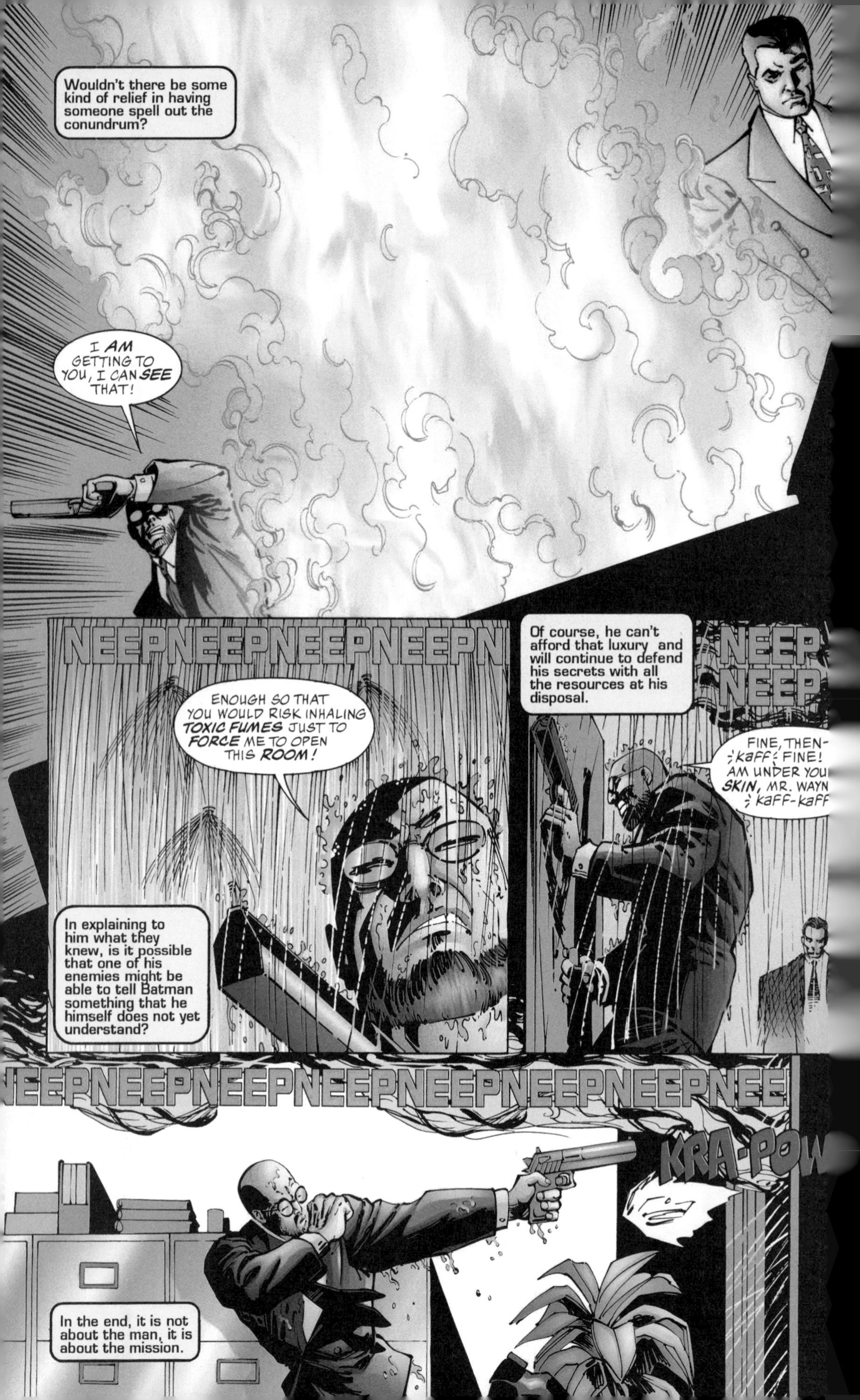

Wouldn't there be some kind of relief in having someone spell out the conundrum?
I AM GETTING TO YOU, I CAN SEE THAT!
NEEPNEEPNEEPNEEPN
ENOUGH SO THAT YOU WOULD RISK INHALING TOXIC FUMES JUST TO FORCE ME TO OPEN THIS ROOM!
In explaining to him what they knew, is it possible that one of his enemies might be able to tell Batman something that he himself does not yet understand?
Of course, he can't afford that luxury and will continue to defend his secrets with all the resources at his disposal.
NEEP
NEEP
FINE, THEN- kaff FINE! AM UNDER YOU SKIN, MR. WAYN kaff-kaff
NEEPNEEPNEEPNEEPNEEPNEEPNEE
KRA-POW
In the end, it is not about the man, it is about the mission.

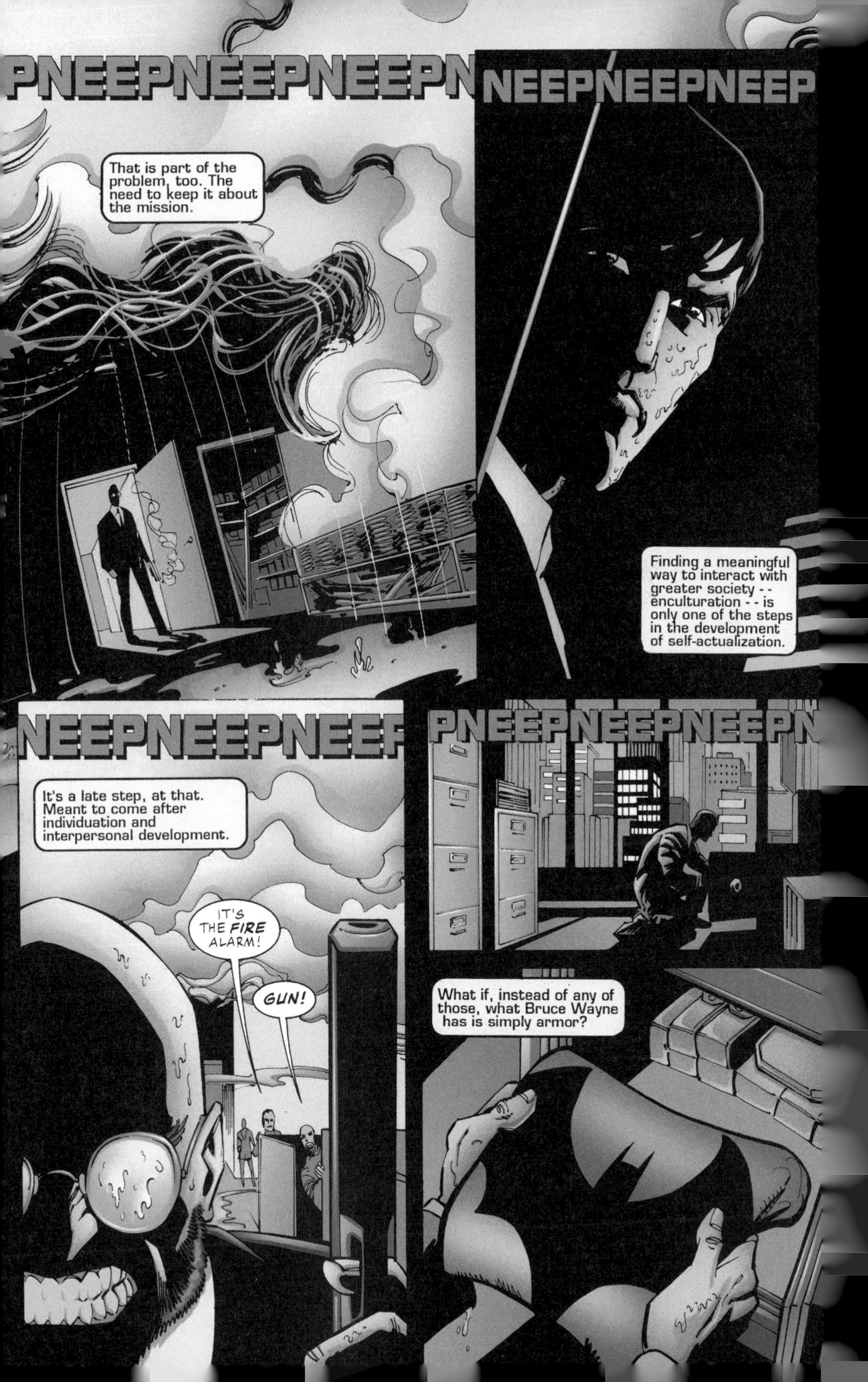
PNEEPNEEPNEEPN
NEEPNEEPNEEP
That is part of the problem, too. The need to keep it about the mission.
Finding a meaningful way to interact with greater society - - enculturation - - is only one of the steps in the development of self-actualization.
NEEPNEEPNEEP
It's a late step, at that. Meant to come after individuation and interpersonal development.
IT'S THE FIRE ALARM!
GUN!
PNEEPNEEPNEEPN
What if, instead of any of those, what Bruce Wayne has is simply armor?

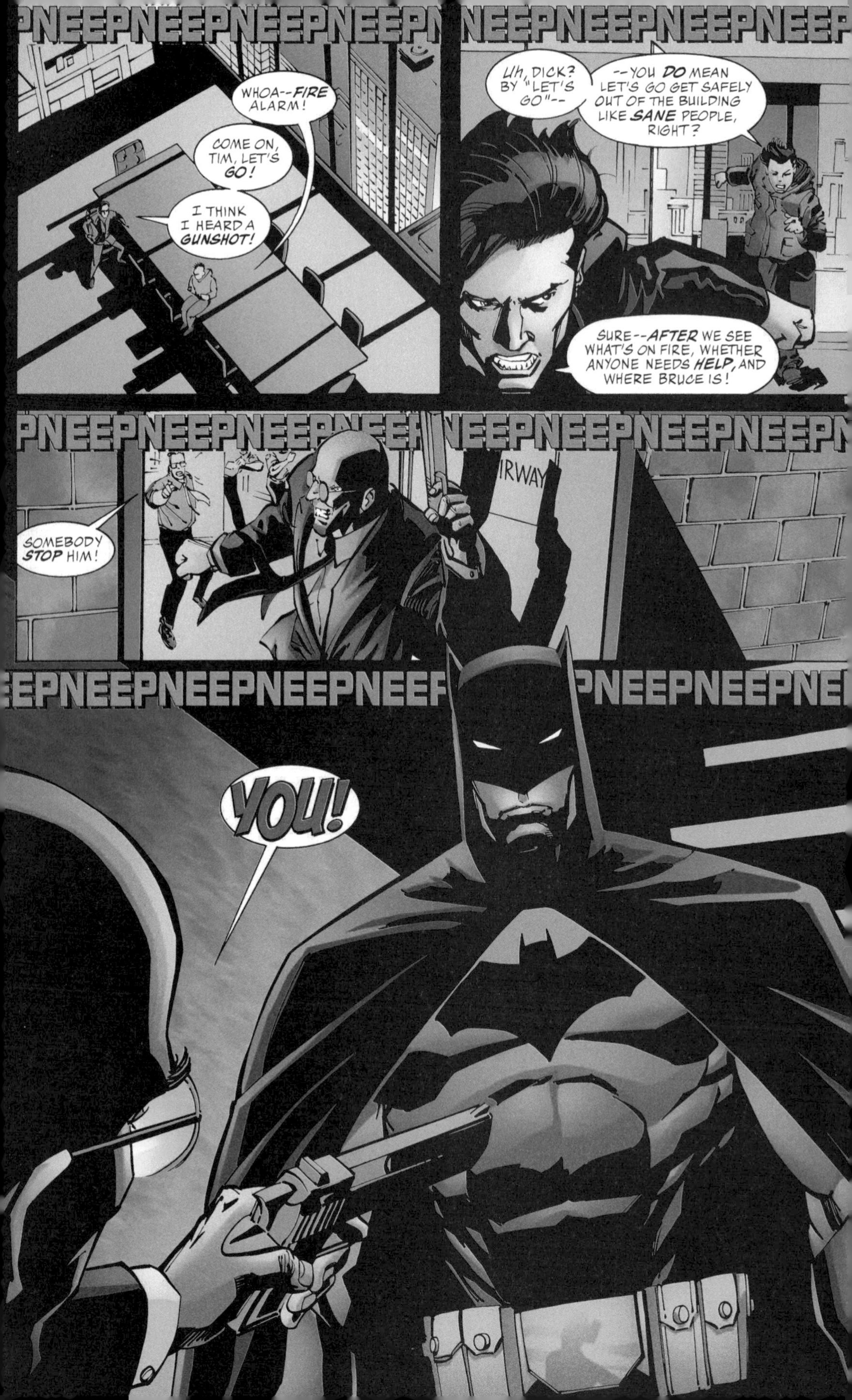
PNEEPNEEPNEEPNEEPNEEPNEEPNEEPNEEP
WHOA--FIRE ALARM!
COME ON, TIM, LET'S GO!
I THINK I HEARD A GUNSHOT!
UH, DICK? BY "LET'S GO"--
--YOU DO MEAN LET'S GO GET SAFELY OUT OF THE BUILDING LIKE SANE PEOPLE, RIGHT?
SURE--AFTER WE SEE WHAT'S ON FIRE, WHETHER ANYONE NEEDS HELP, AND WHERE BRUCE IS!
PNEEPNEEPNEEPNEEPNEEPNEEPNEEPNEEP
SOMEBODY STOP HIM!
EPNEEPNEEPNEEPNEEPNEEPNEEP
YOU!

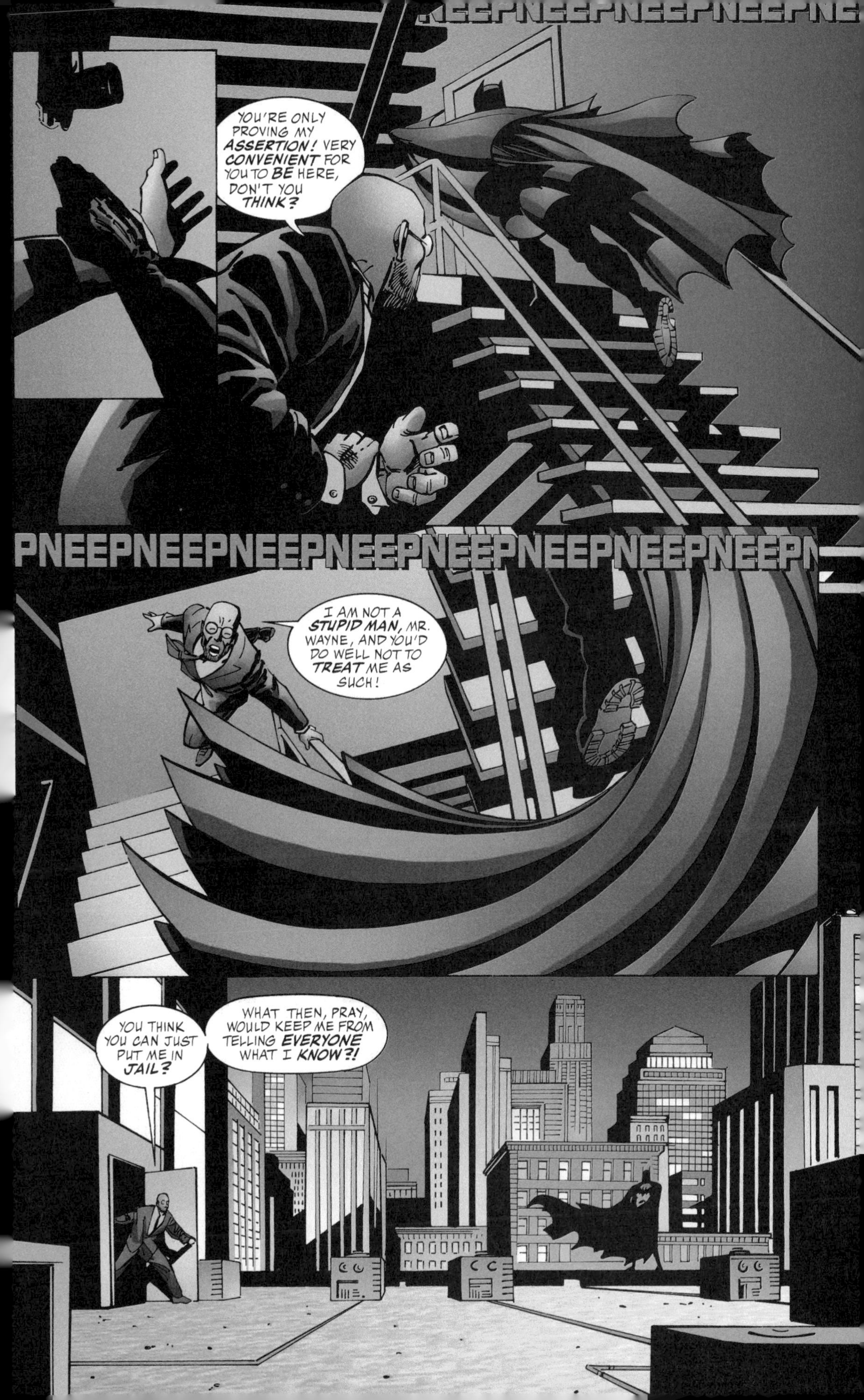
NEEPNEEPNEEPNEEPNE
YOU'RE ONLY PROVING MY ASSERTION! VERY CONVENIENT FOR YOU TO BE HERE, DON'T YOU THINK?
PNEEPNEEPNEEPNEEPNEEPNEEPNEEPNEEPN
I AM NOT A STUPID MAN, MR. WAYNE, AND YOU'D DO WELL NOT TO TREAT ME AS SUCH!
YOU THINK YOU CAN JUST PUT ME IN JAIL?
WHAT THEN, PRAY, WOULD KEEP ME FROM TELLING EVERYONE WHAT I KNOW?!

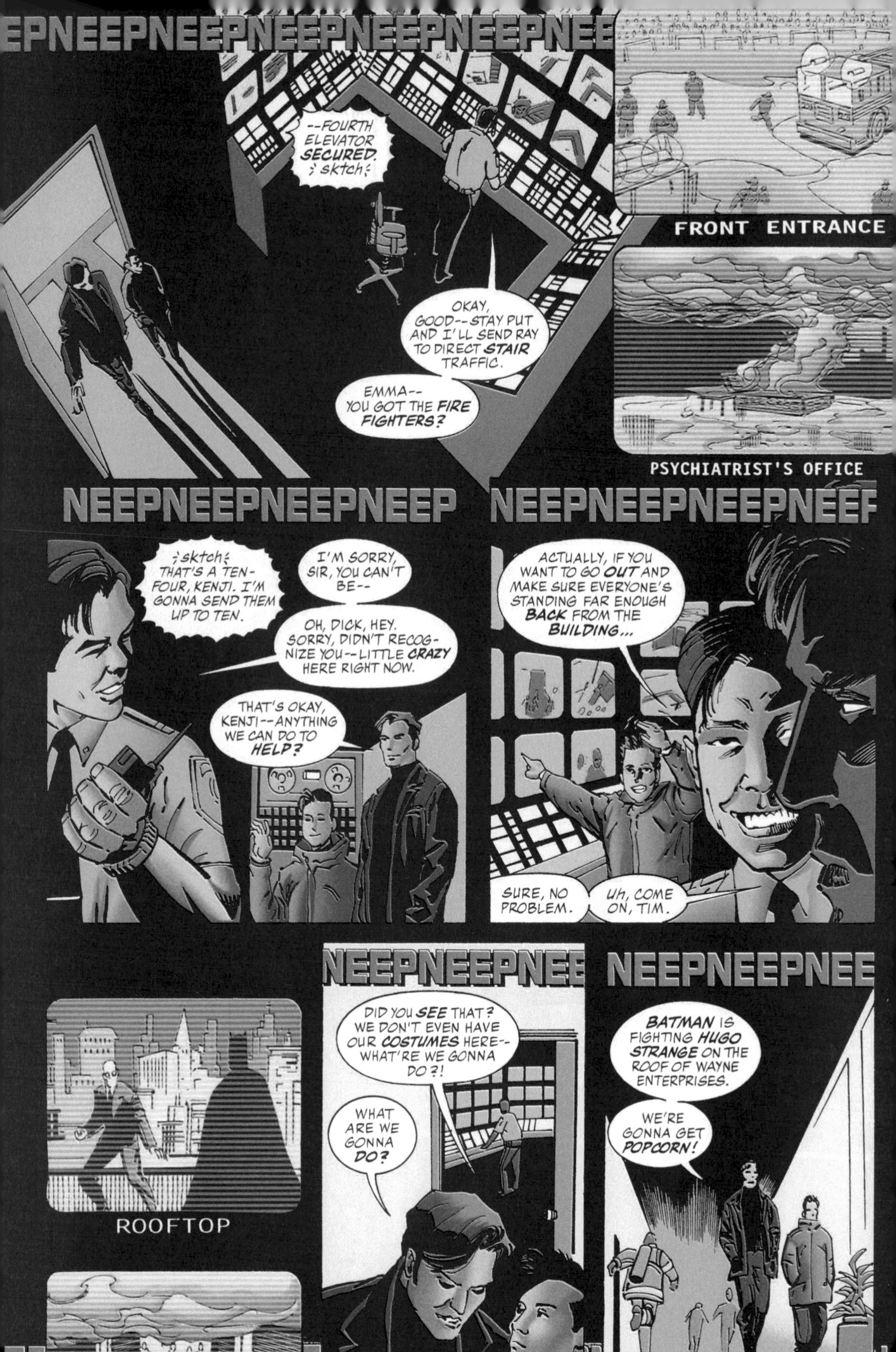
EPNEEPNEEPNEEPNEEPNEEPNEEPNEE
--FOURTH ELEVATOR SECURED. ⁏sktch⁏
OKAY, GOOD--STAY PUT AND I'LL SEND RAY TO DIRECT STAIR TRAFFIC.
EMMA-- YOU GOT THE FIRE FIGHTERS?
FRONT ENTRANCE
PSYCHIATRIST'S OFFICE
NEEPNEEPNEEPNEEP
NEEPNEEPNEEPNEEF
⁏sktch⁏ THAT'S A TEN-FOUR, KENJI. I'M GONNA SEND THEM UP TO TEN.
I'M SORRY, SIR, YOU CAN'T BE--
OH, DICK, HEY. SORRY, DIDN'T RECOGNIZE YOU--LITTLE CRAZY HERE RIGHT NOW.
THAT'S OKAY, KENJI--ANYTHING WE CAN DO TO HELP?
ACTUALLY, IF YOU WANT TO GO OUT AND MAKE SURE EVERYONE'S STANDING FAR ENOUGH BACK FROM THE BUILDING...
SURE, NO PROBLEM.
UH, COME ON, TIM.
ROOFTOP
NEEPNEEPNEE
DID YOU SEE THAT? WE DON'T EVEN HAVE OUR COSTUMES HERE--WHAT'RE WE GONNA DO?!
WHAT ARE WE GONNA DO?
NEEPNEEPNEE
BATMAN IS FIGHTING HUGO STRANGE ON THE ROOF OF WAYNE ENTERPRISES.
WE'RE GONNA GET POPCORN!

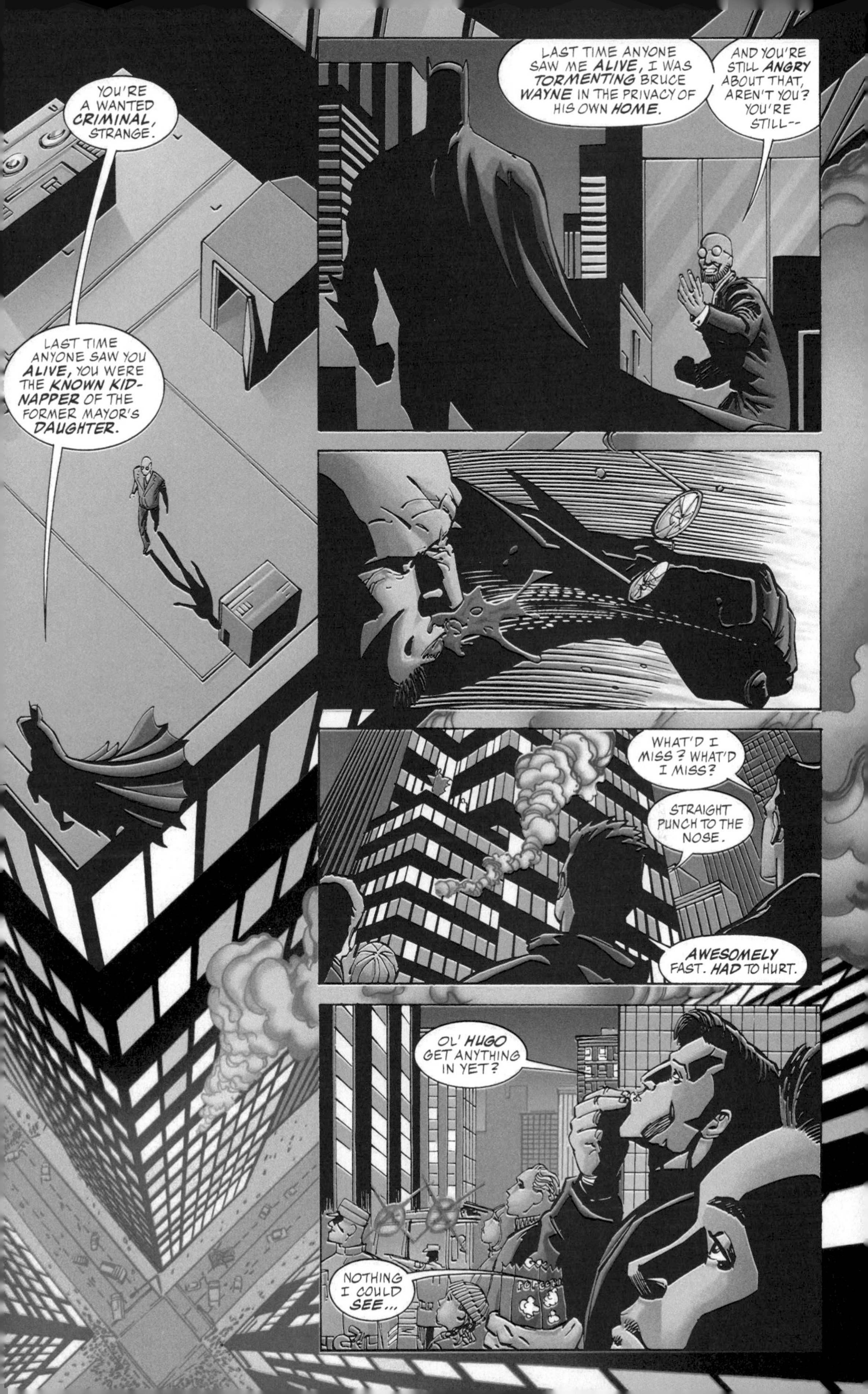
YOU'RE A WANTED CRIMINAL, STRANGE.
LAST TIME ANYONE SAW YOU ALIVE, YOU WERE THE KNOWN KID-NAPPER OF THE FORMER MAYOR'S DAUGHTER.
LAST TIME ANYONE SAW ME ALIVE, I WAS TORMENTING BRUCE WAYNE IN THE PRIVACY OF HIS OWN HOME.
AND YOU'RE STILL ANGRY ABOUT THAT, AREN'T YOU? YOU'RE STILL--
WHAT'D I MISS? WHAT'D I MISS?
STRAIGHT PUNCH TO THE NOSE.
AWESOMELY FAST. HAD TO HURT.
OL' HUGO GET ANYTHING IN YET?
NOTHING I COULD SEE...

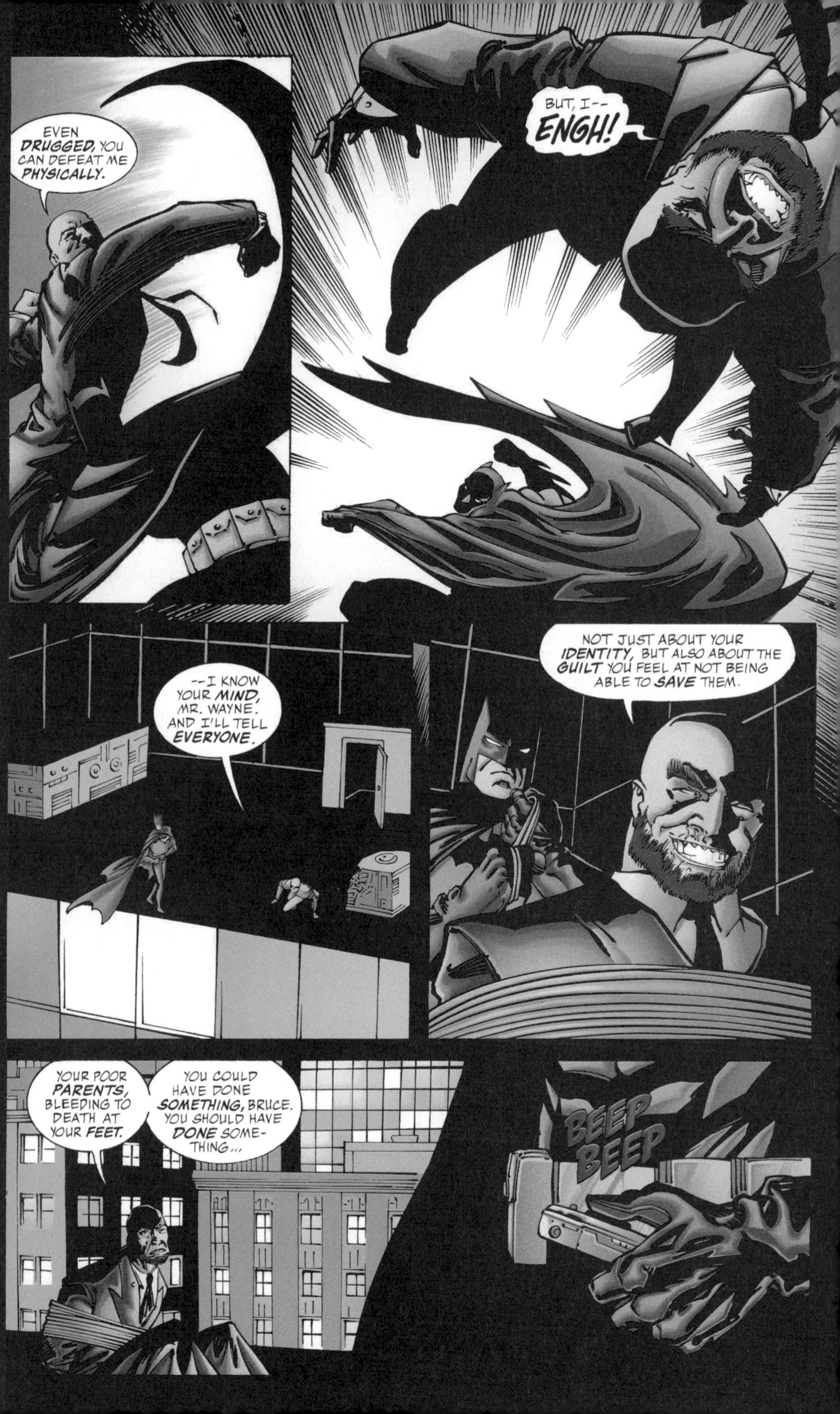
EVEN DRUGGED, YOU CAN DEFEAT ME PHYSICALLY.
BUT, I-- ENGH!
--I KNOW YOUR MIND, MR. WAYNE. AND I'LL TELL EVERYONE.
NOT JUST ABOUT YOUR IDENTITY, BUT ALSO ABOUT THE GUILT YOU FEEL AT NOT BEING ABLE TO SAVE THEM.
YOUR POOR PARENTS, BLEEDING TO DEATH AT YOUR FEET.
YOU COULD HAVE DONE SOMETHING, BRUCE. YOU SHOULD HAVE DONE SOME-THING...
BEEP BEEP

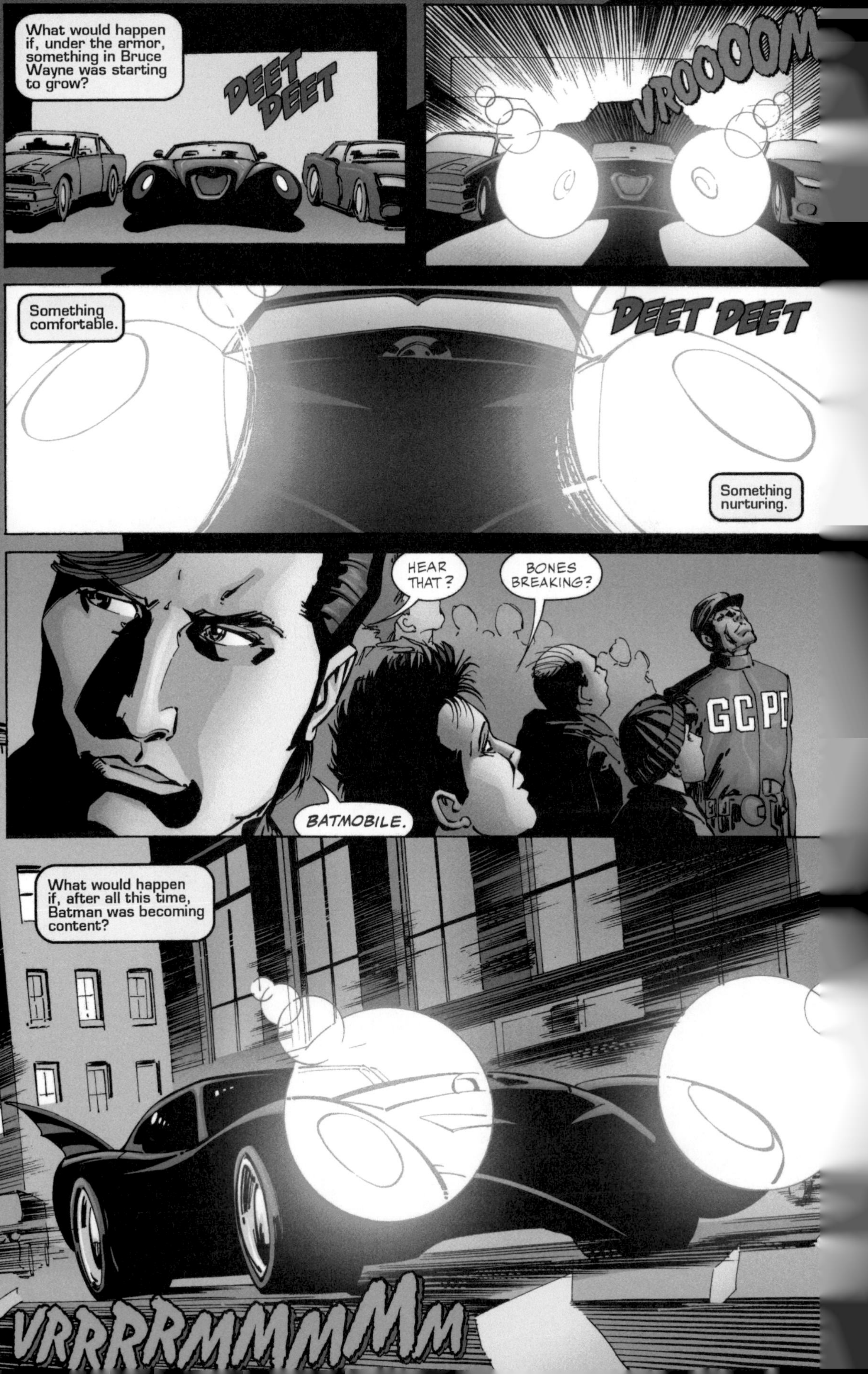
What would happen if, under the armor, something in Bruce Wayne was starting to grow?
DEET DEET
VROOOOM
Something comfortable.
DEET DEET
Something nurturing.
HEAR THAT?
BONES BREAKING?
GCPD
BATMOBILE.
What would happen if, after all this time, Batman was becoming content?
VRRRRMMMMMm

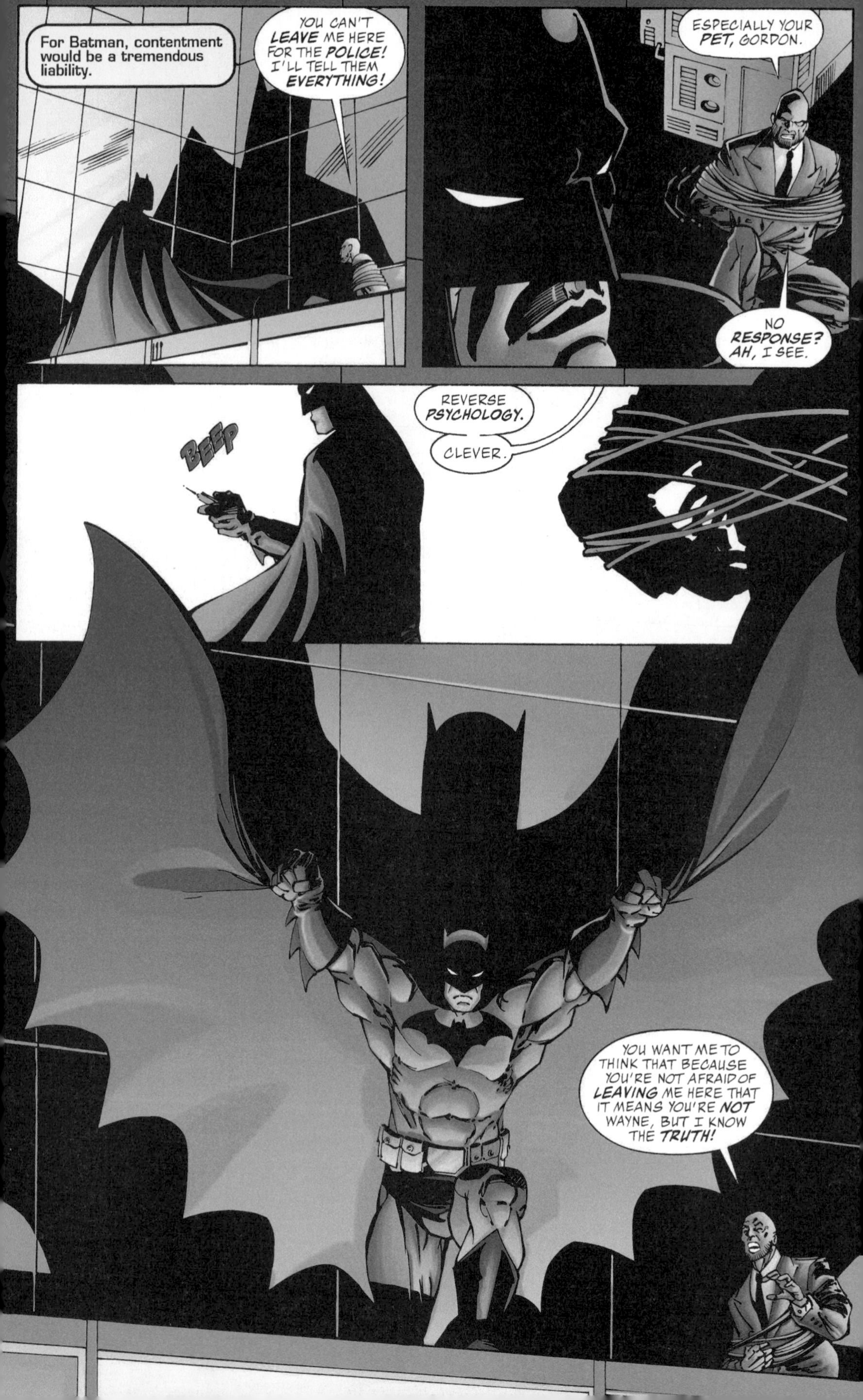
For Batman, contentment would be a tremendous liability.
YOU CAN'T LEAVE ME HERE FOR THE POLICE! I'LL TELL THEM EVERYTHING!
ESPECIALLY YOUR PET, GORDON.
NO RESPONSE? AH, I SEE.
REVERSE PSYCHOLOGY.
CLEVER.
BEEP
YOU WANT ME TO THINK THAT BECAUSE YOU'RE NOT AFRAID OF LEAVING ME HERE THAT IT MEANS YOU'RE NOT WAYNE, BUT I KNOW THE TRUTH!

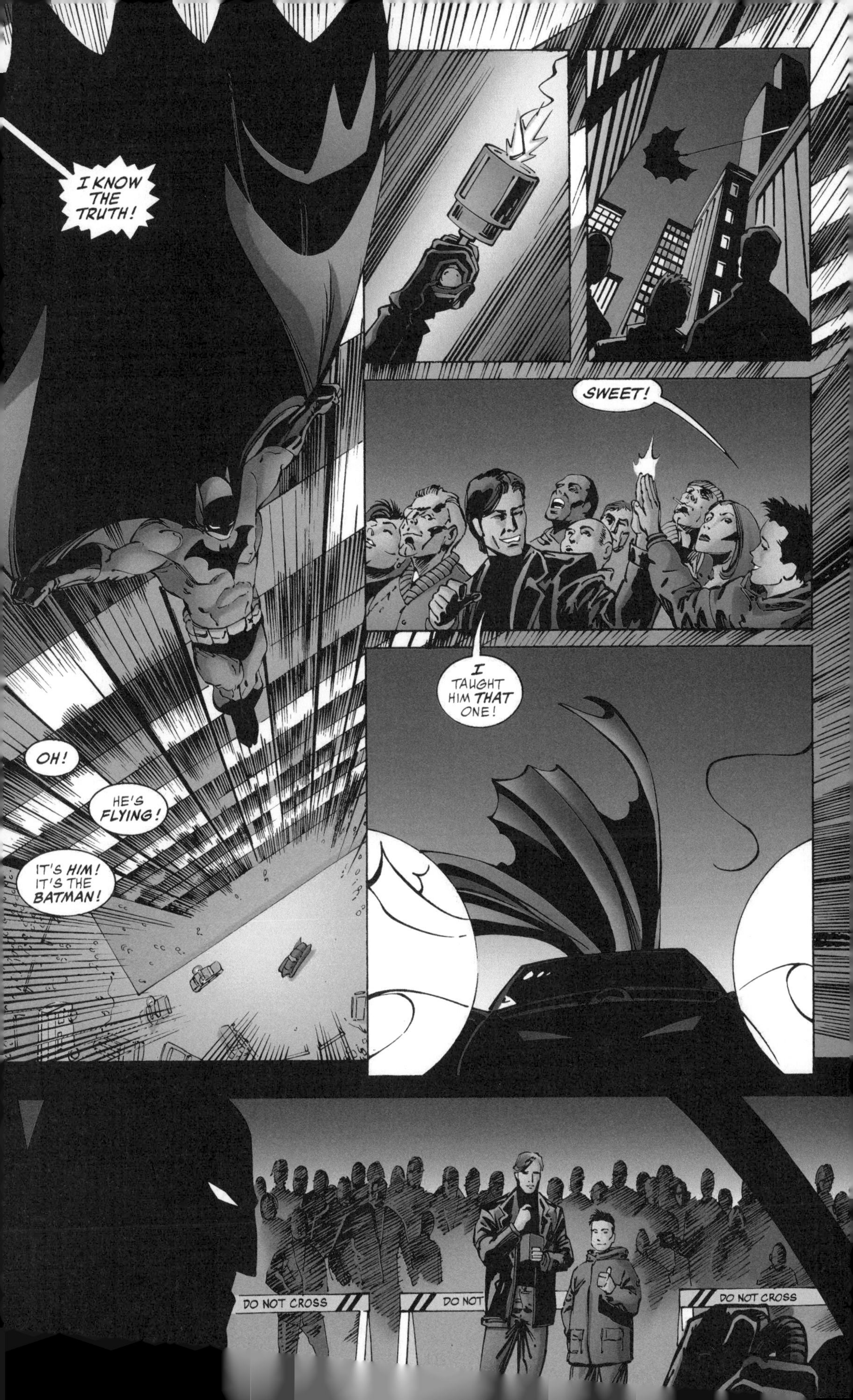
I KNOW THE TRUTH!
OH!
HE'S FLYING!
IT'S HIM! IT'S THE BATMAN!
SWEET!
I TAUGHT HIM THAT ONE!
DO NOT CROSS
DO NOT
DO NOT CROSS

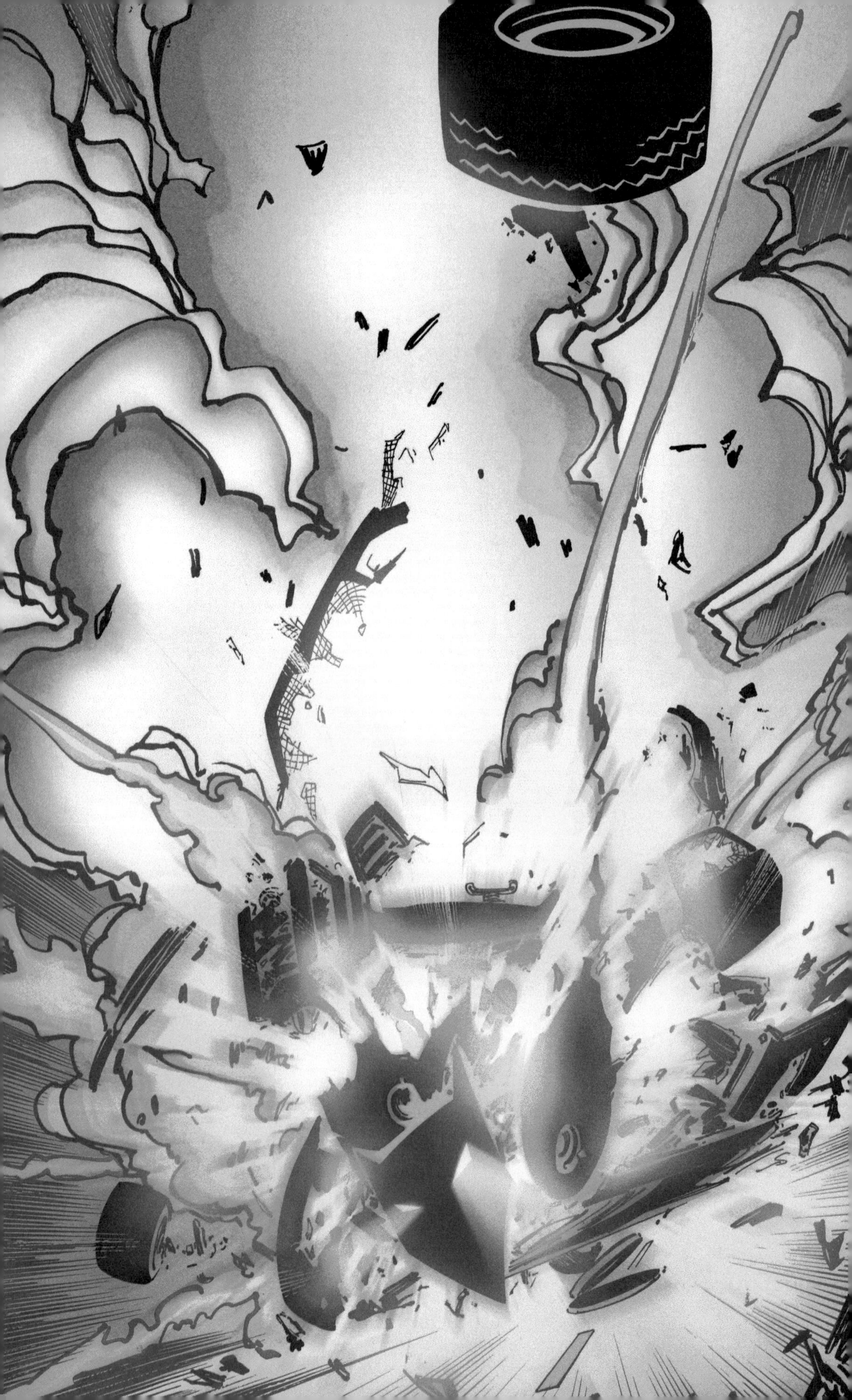

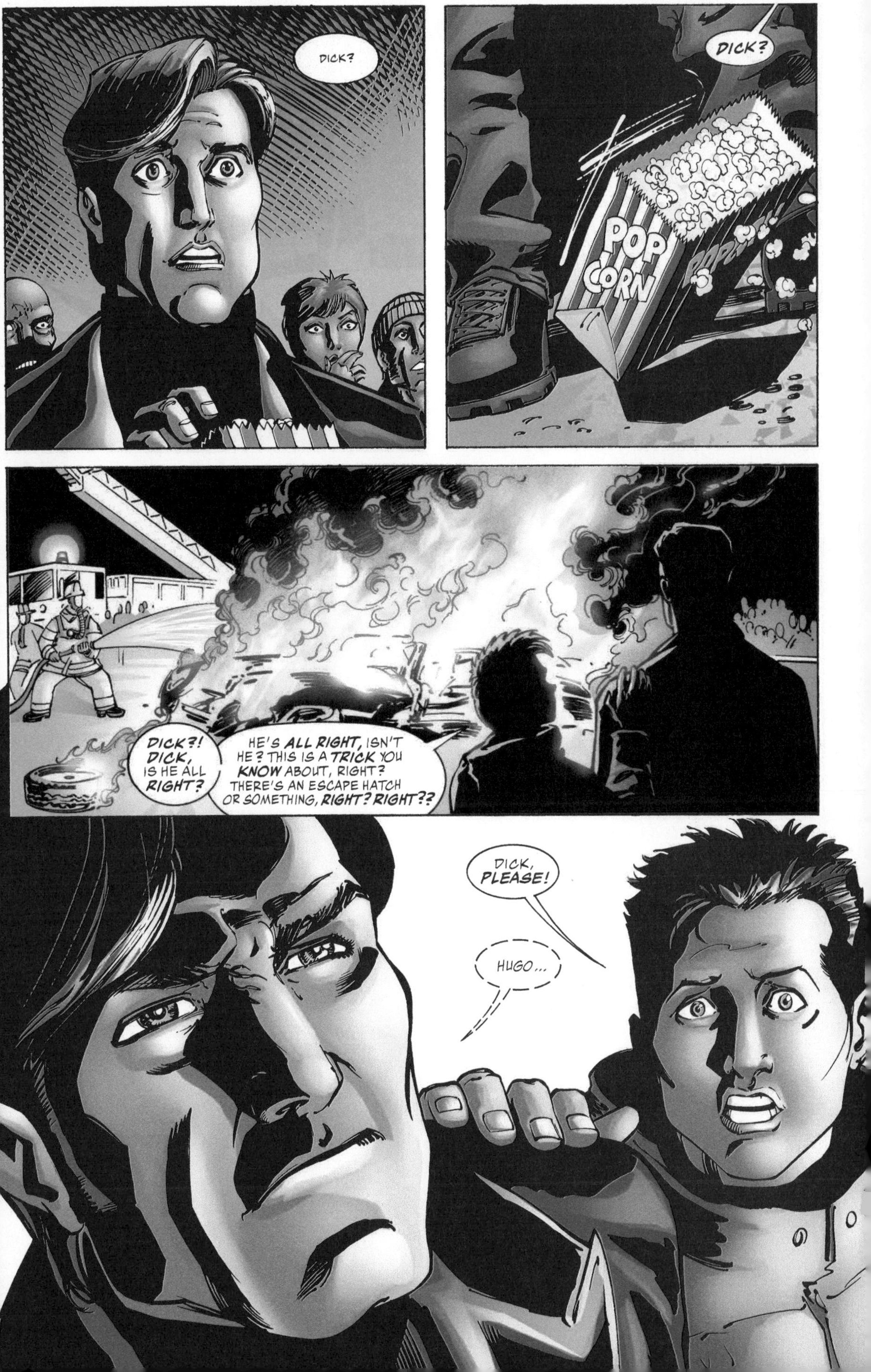
DICK?
DICK?
DICK?! DICK, IS HE ALL RIGHT?
HE'S ALL RIGHT, ISN'T HE? THIS IS A TRICK YOU KNOW ABOUT, RIGHT? THERE'S AN ESCAPE HATCH OR SOMETHING, RIGHT? RIGHT??
DICK, PLEASE!
HUGO...

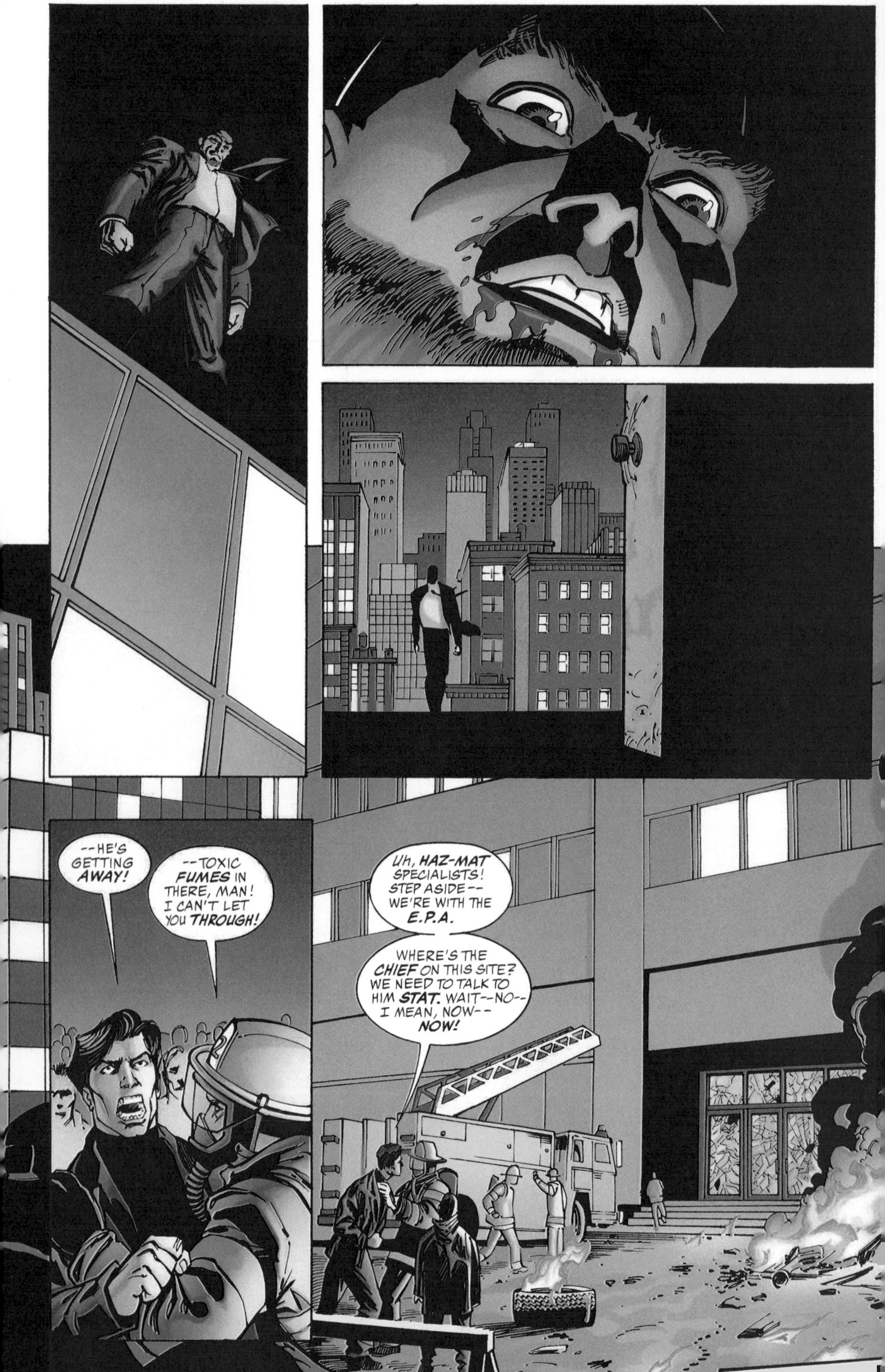
--HE'S GETTING AWAY!
--TOXIC FUMES IN THERE, MAN! I CAN'T LET YOU THROUGH!
Uh, HAZ-MAT SPECIALISTS! STEP ASIDE--WE'RE WITH THE E.P.A.
WHERE'S THE CHIEF ON THIS SITE? WE NEED TO TALK TO HIM STAT. WAIT--NO--I MEAN, NOW--NOW!

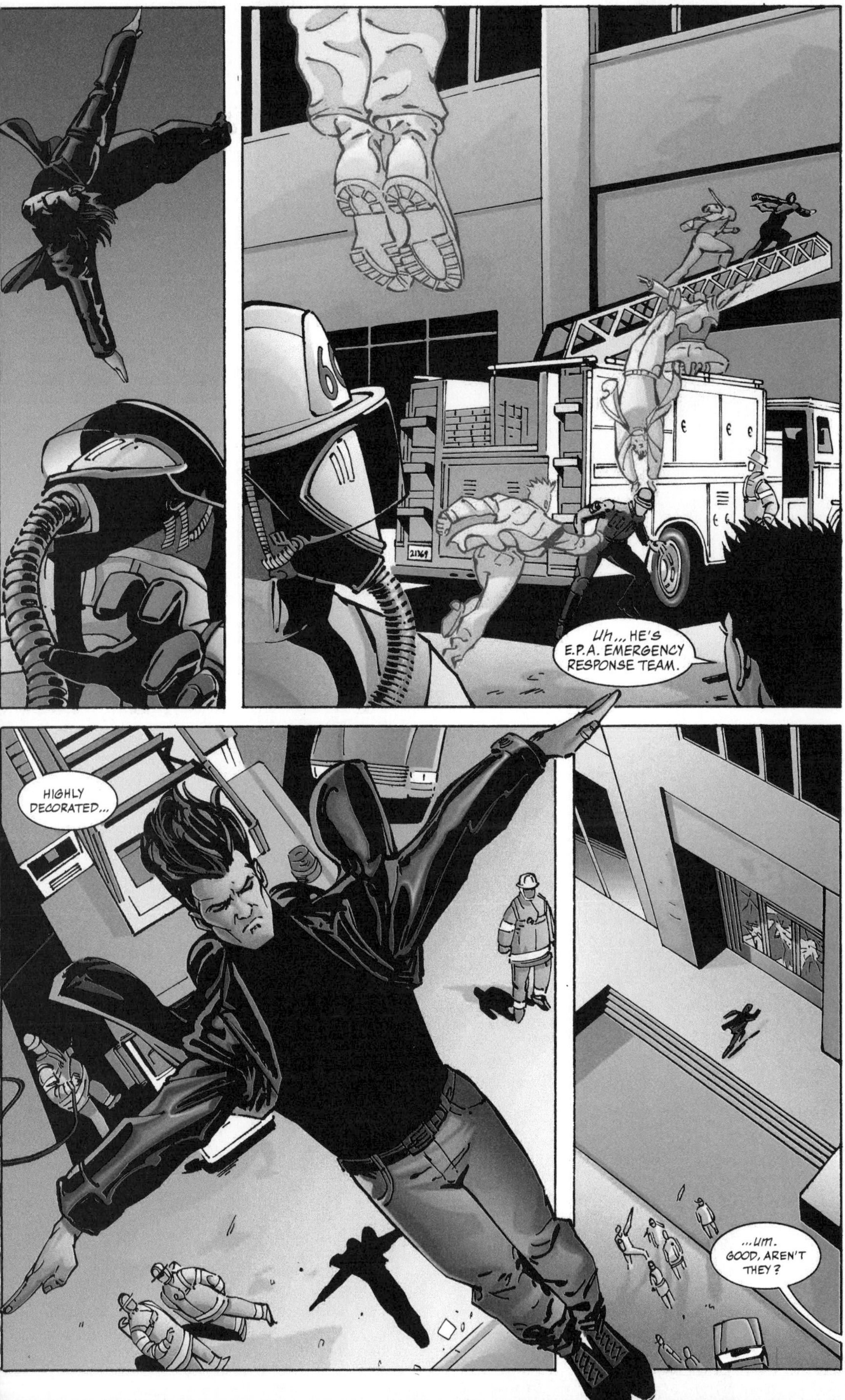
UH... HE'S E.P.A. EMERGENCY RESPONSE TEAM.
HIGHLY DECORATED...
...UM. GOOD, AREN'T THEY?

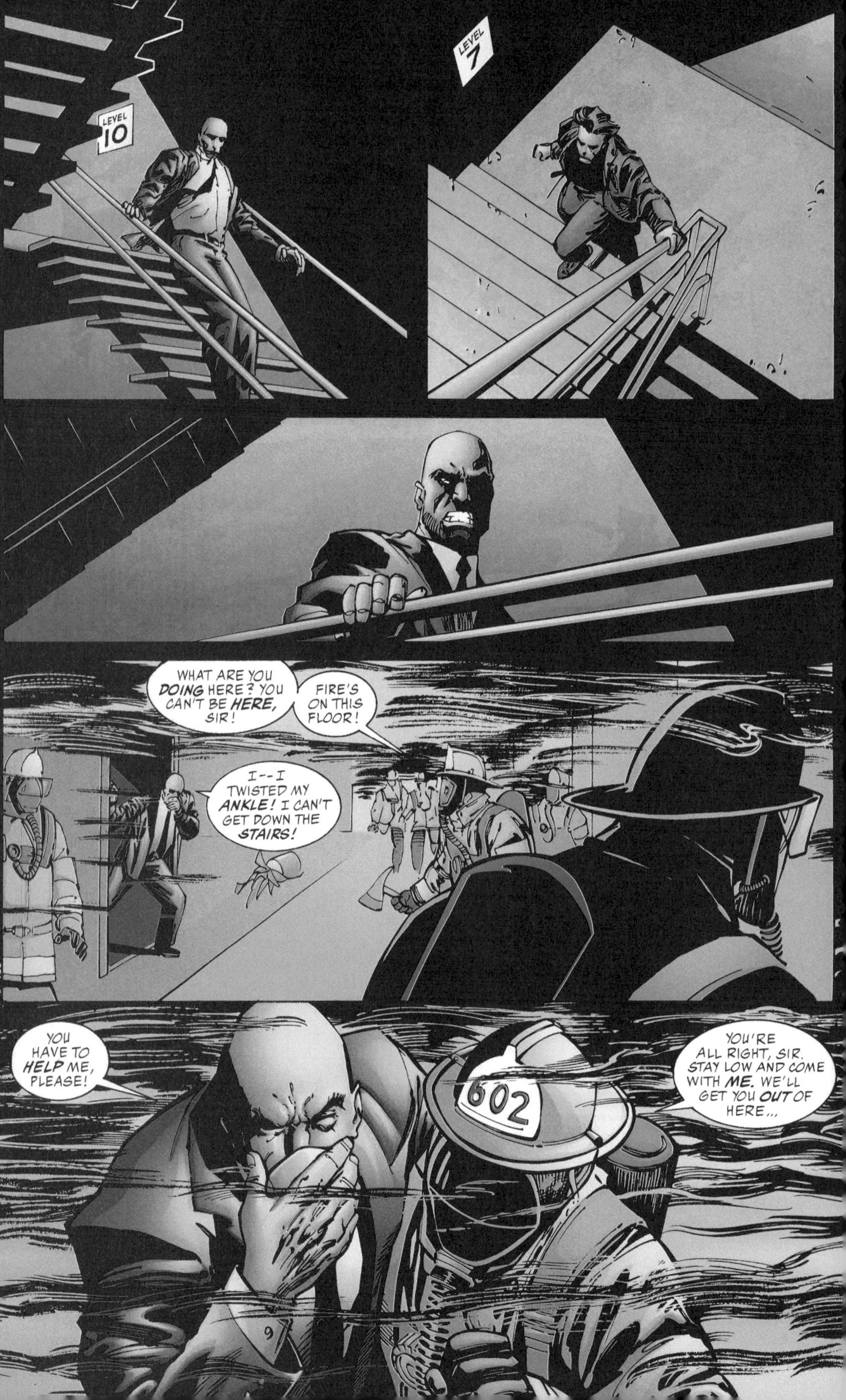
LEVEL 10
LEVEL 7
WHAT ARE YOU DOING HERE? YOU CAN'T BE HERE, SIR!
FIRE'S ON THIS FLOOR!
I--I TWISTED MY ANKLE! I CAN'T GET DOWN THE STAIRS!
YOU HAVE TO HELP ME, PLEASE!
YOU'RE ALL RIGHT, SIR. STAY LOW AND COME WITH ME. WE'LL GET YOU OUT OF HERE...
602

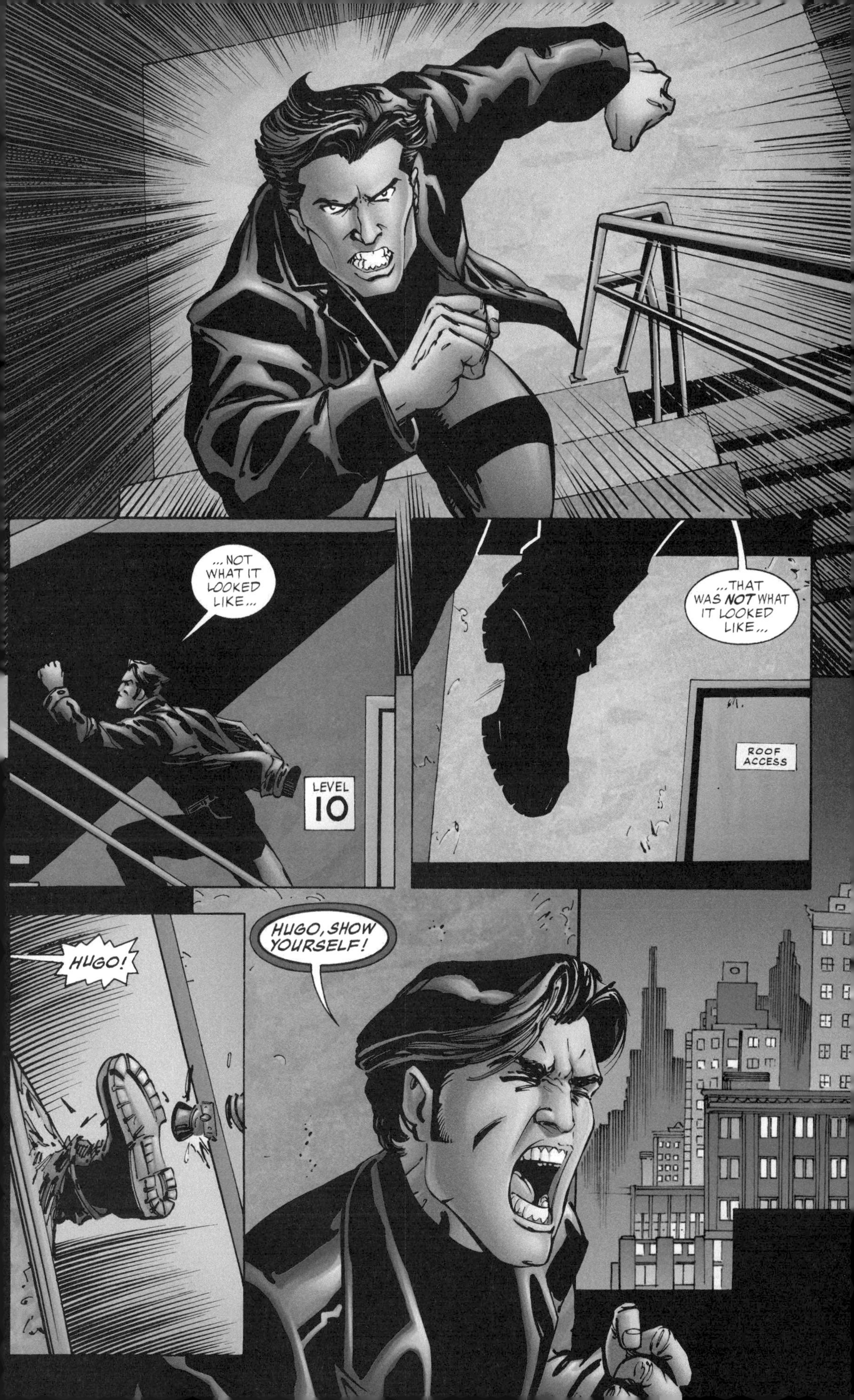
...NOT WHAT IT LOOKED LIKE...
LEVEL 10
...THAT WAS NOT WHAT IT LOOKED LIKE...
ROOF ACCESS
HUGO!
HUGO, SHOW YOURSELF!

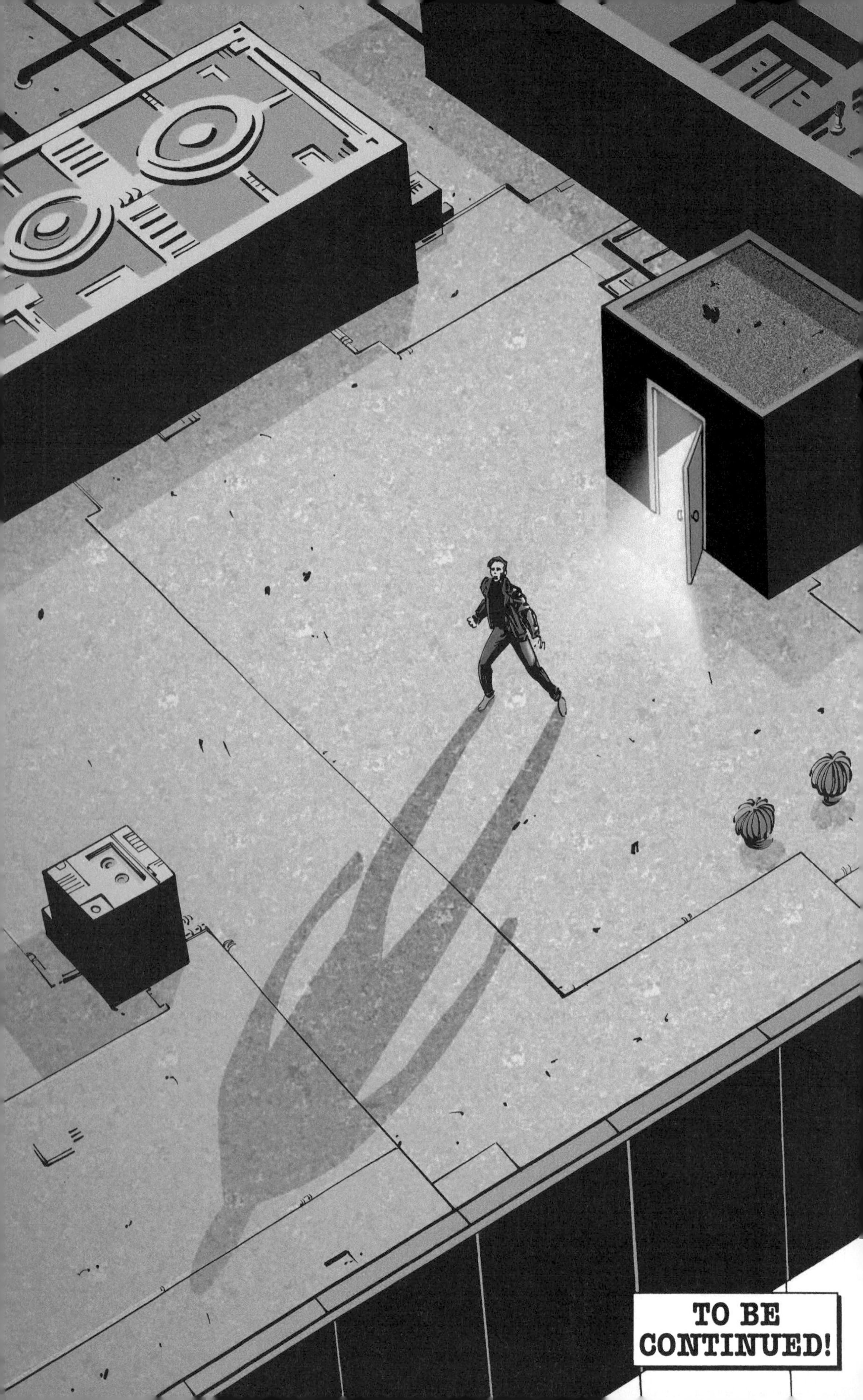
TO BE CONTINUED!

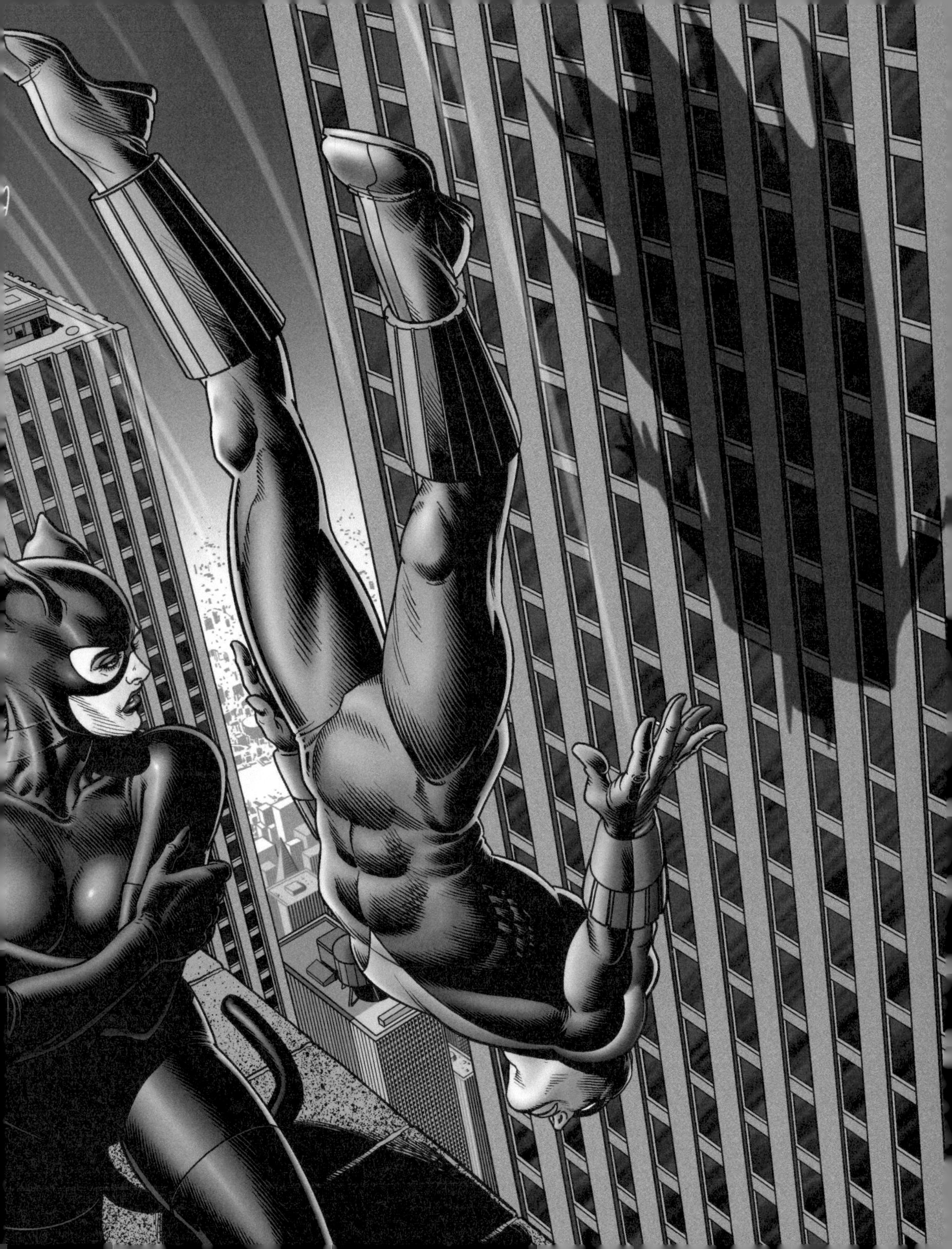

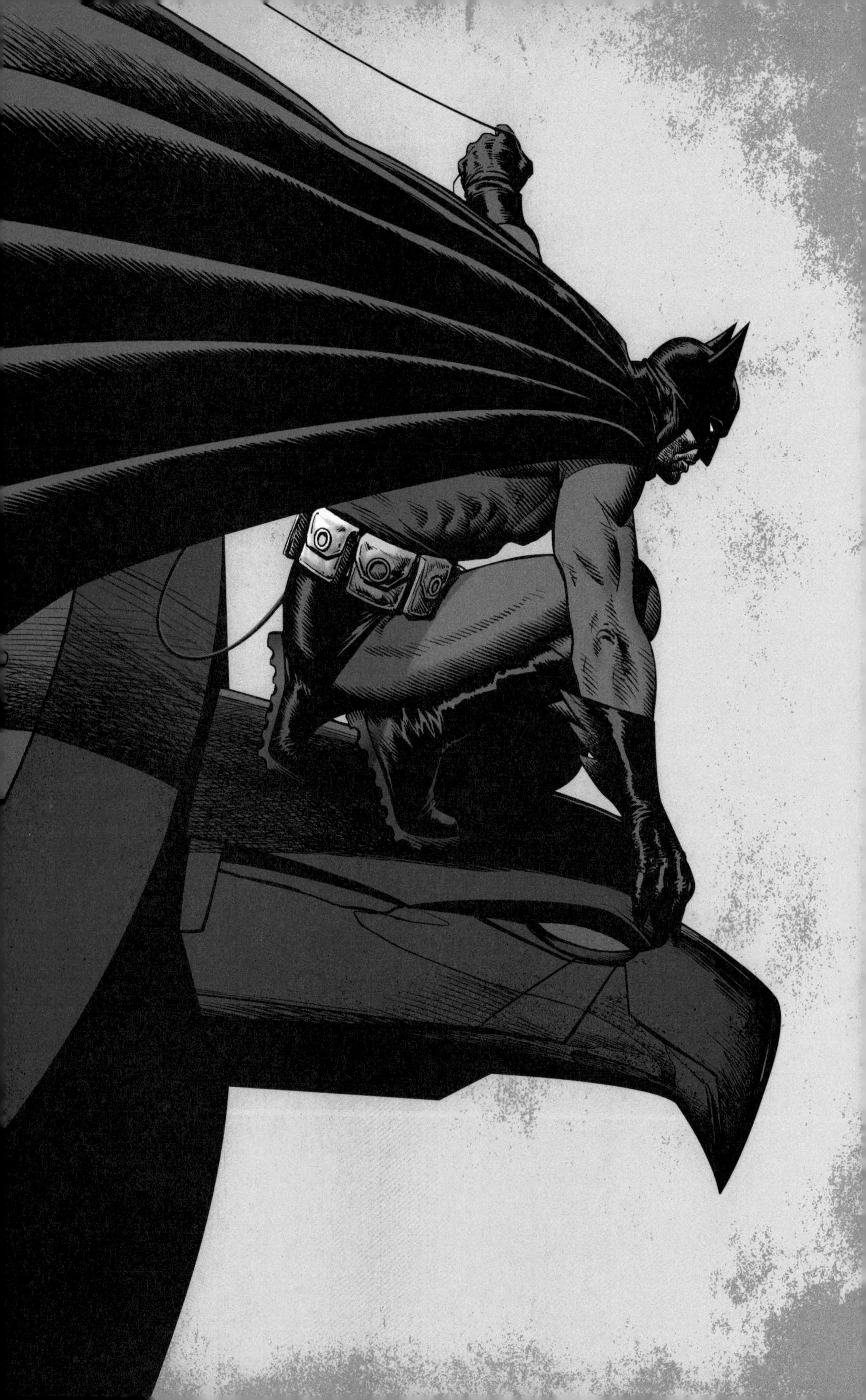

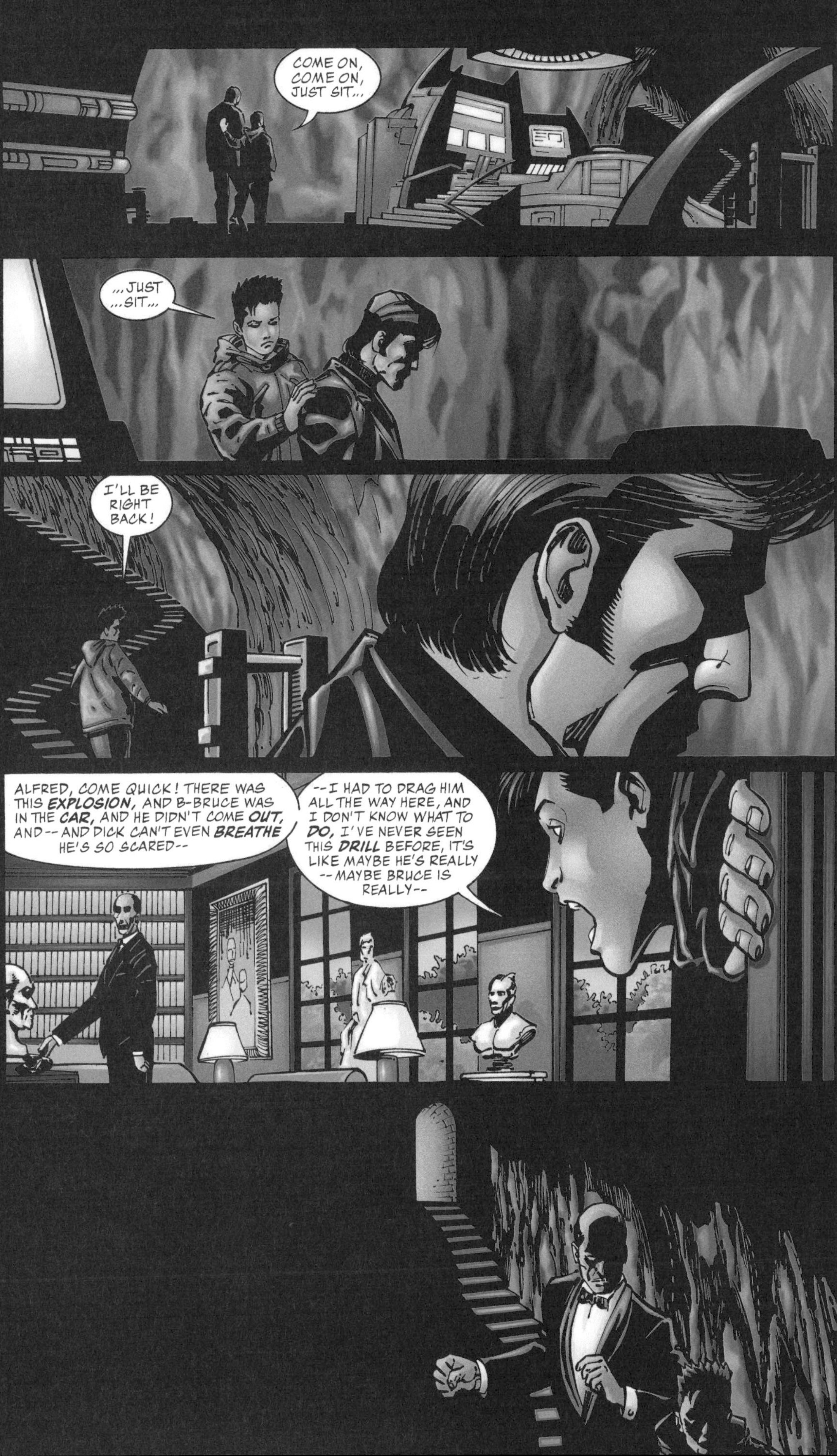
COME ON, COME ON, JUST SIT...
...JUST ...SIT...
I'LL BE RIGHT BACK!
ALFRED, COME QUICK! THERE WAS THIS **EXPLOSION**, AND B-BRUCE WAS IN THE **CAR**, AND HE DIDN'T COME **OUT**, AND-- AND DICK CAN'T EVEN **BREATHE** HE'S SO SCARED--
--I HAD TO DRAG HIM ALL THE WAY HERE, AND I DON'T KNOW WHAT TO **DO**, I'VE NEVER SEEN THIS **DRILL** BEFORE, IT'S LIKE MAYBE HE'S REALLY --MAYBE BRUCE IS REALLY--

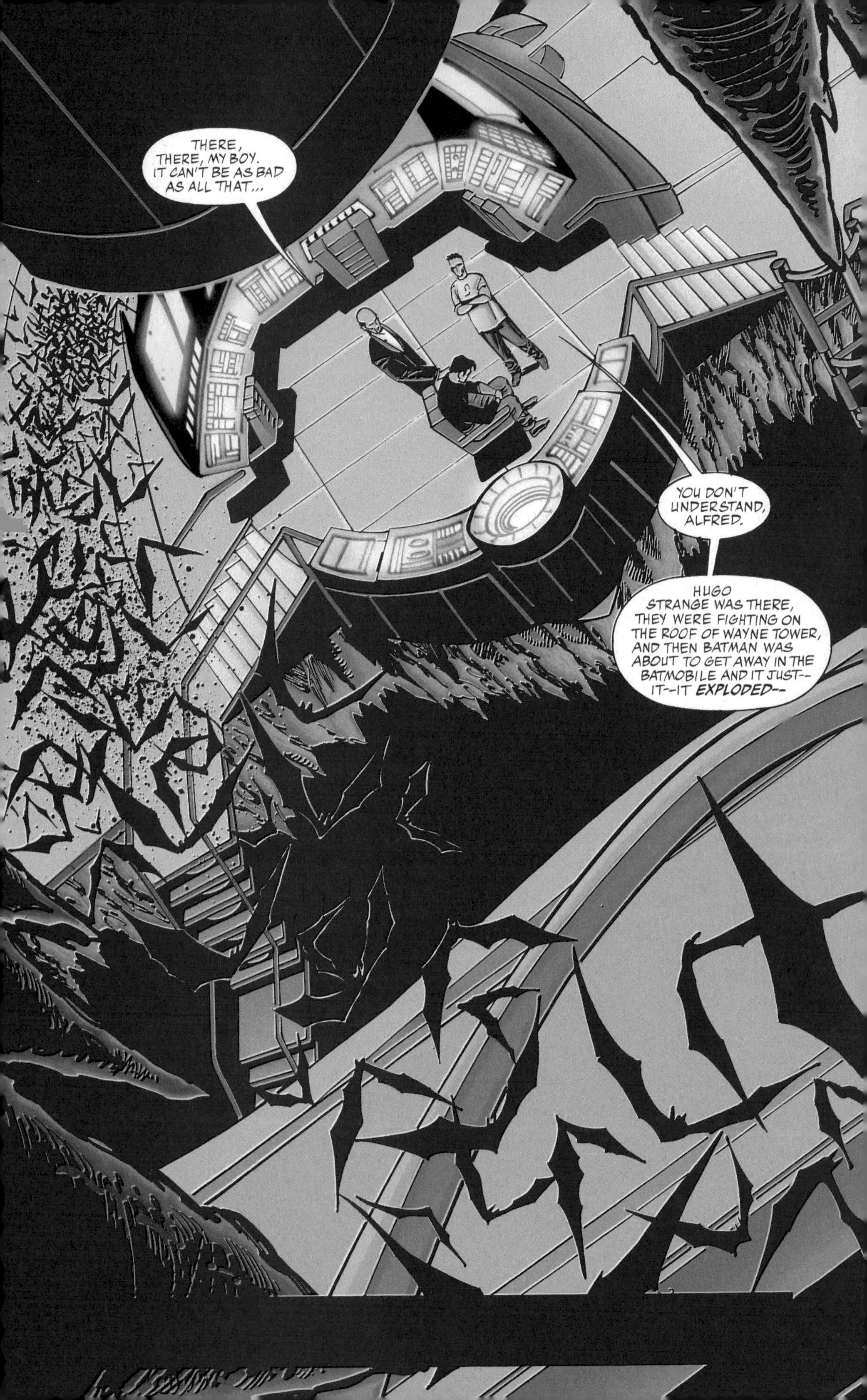
THERE, THERE, MY BOY. IT CAN'T BE AS BAD AS ALL THAT...
YOU DON'T UNDERSTAND, ALFRED.
HUGO STRANGE WAS THERE, THEY WERE FIGHTING ON THE ROOF OF WAYNE TOWER, AND THEN BATMAN WAS ABOUT TO GET AWAY IN THE BATMOBILE AND IT JUST-- IT--IT EXPLODED--

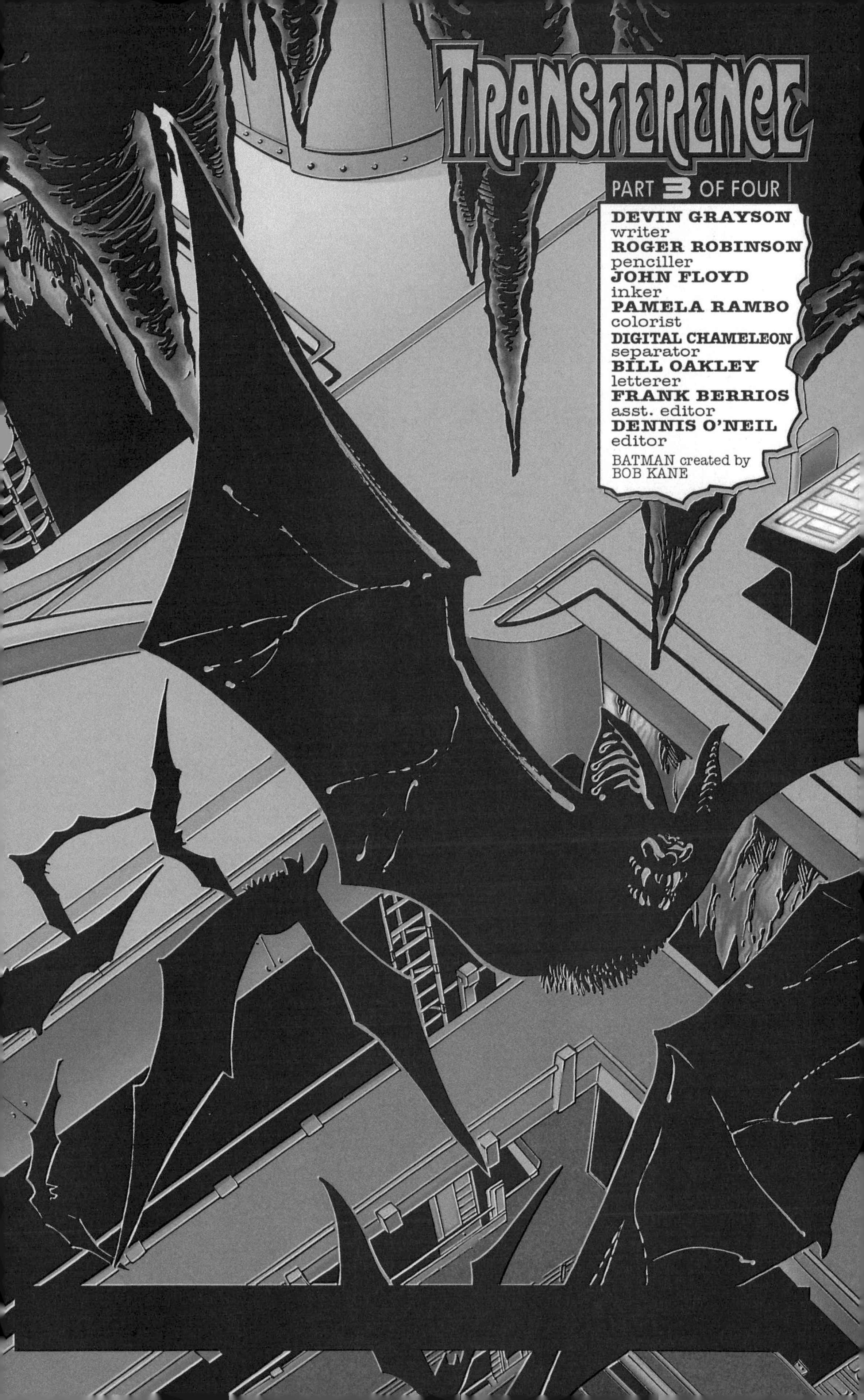
TRANSFERENCE
PART 3 OF FOUR
DEVIN GRAYSON writer
ROGER ROBINSON penciller
JOHN FLOYD inker
PAMELA RAMBO colorist
DIGITAL CHAMELEON separator
BILL OAKLEY letterer
FRANK BERRIOS asst. editor
DENNIS O'NEIL editor
BATMAN created by BOB KANE

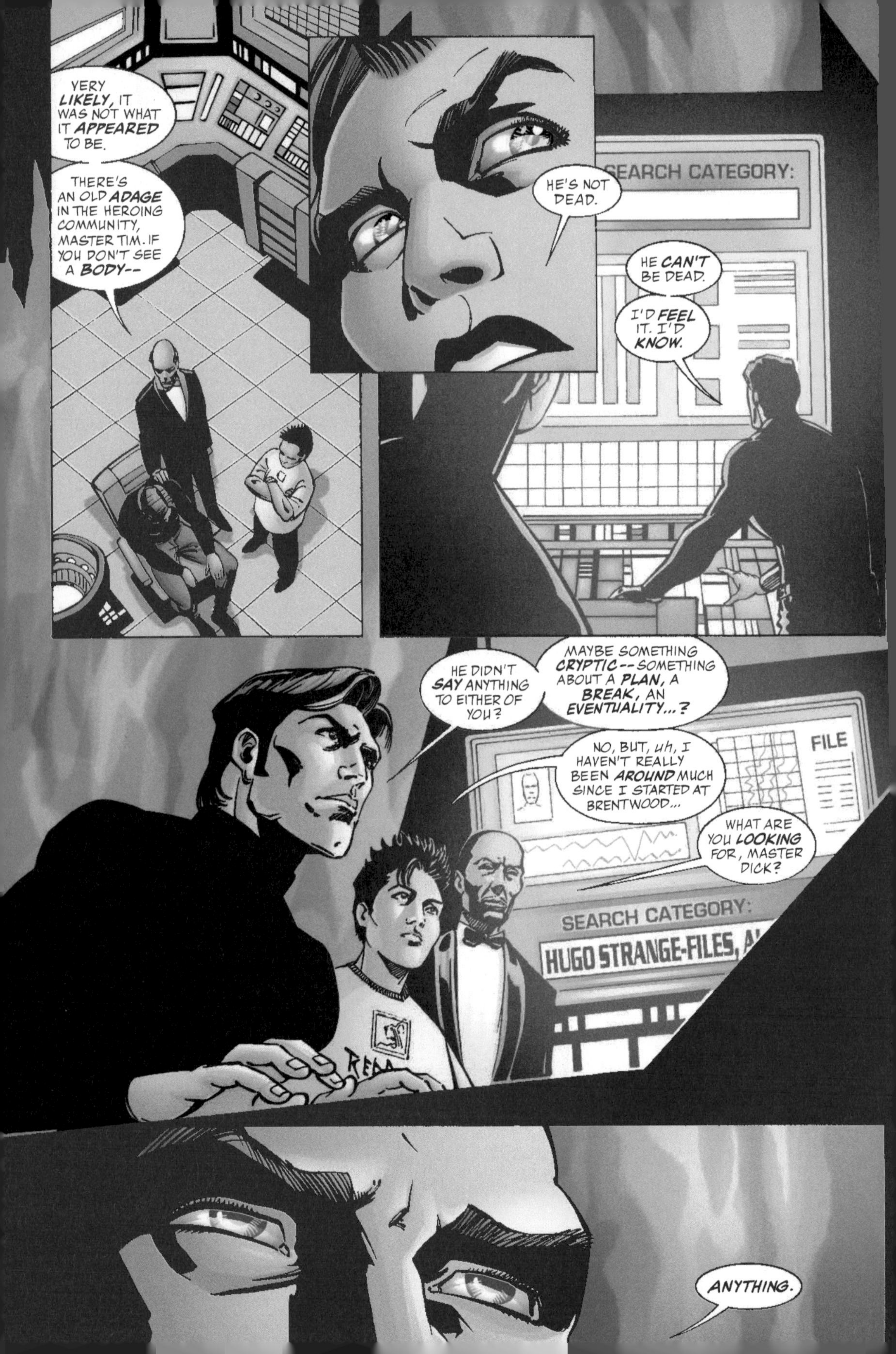

VERY LIKELY, IT WAS NOT WHAT IT APPEARED TO BE.
THERE'S AN OLD ADAGE IN THE HEROING COMMUNITY, MASTER TIM. IF YOU DON'T SEE A BODY--
HE'S NOT DEAD.
SEARCH CATEGORY:
HE CAN'T BE DEAD.
I'D FEEL IT. I'D KNOW.
HE DIDN'T SAY ANYTHING TO EITHER OF YOU?
MAYBE SOMETHING CRYPTIC--SOMETHING ABOUT A PLAN, A BREAK, AN EVENTUALITY...?
FILE
NO, BUT, uh, I HAVEN'T REALLY BEEN AROUND MUCH SINCE I STARTED AT BRENTWOOD...
WHAT ARE YOU LOOKING FOR, MASTER DICK?
SEARCH CATEGORY:
HUGO STRANGE-FILES, A
ANYTHING.

YEAH, GOOD. I DON'T HAVE THE *PATIENCE* FOR THIS.

NO *KIDDING*...

CALL IN *BABS* IF YOU NEED TO.

AND IF *HUGO* DOESN'T YIELD ANYTHING, CHECK ANY FILES WITH YOUR OR MY *NAME* IN THEM -- MAYBE HE LEFT US A *MESSAGE* SOMEWHERE.

AND WHERE ARE *YOU* GOING, MASTER DICK?

SEARCH CATEGORY:

HUGO STRANGE-FILES, ALL

YIELDS 472 MATCHES
ENTER SORT PARAMETER?

AH, BRUCE, FOR CRYING OUT LOUD, YOU DON'T NEED TO WRITE DOWN *EVERYTHING*...

I CAN LOOK THROUGH THOSE *FOR* YOU IF YOU WANT...?

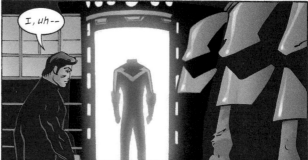

I, *UH*--

I'M GONNA GO CHECK THE *CRIME SCENE* AGAIN...

...MAYBE GET A CLUE AS TO WHERE BRUCE OR HUGO MIGHT HAVE *GONE*...

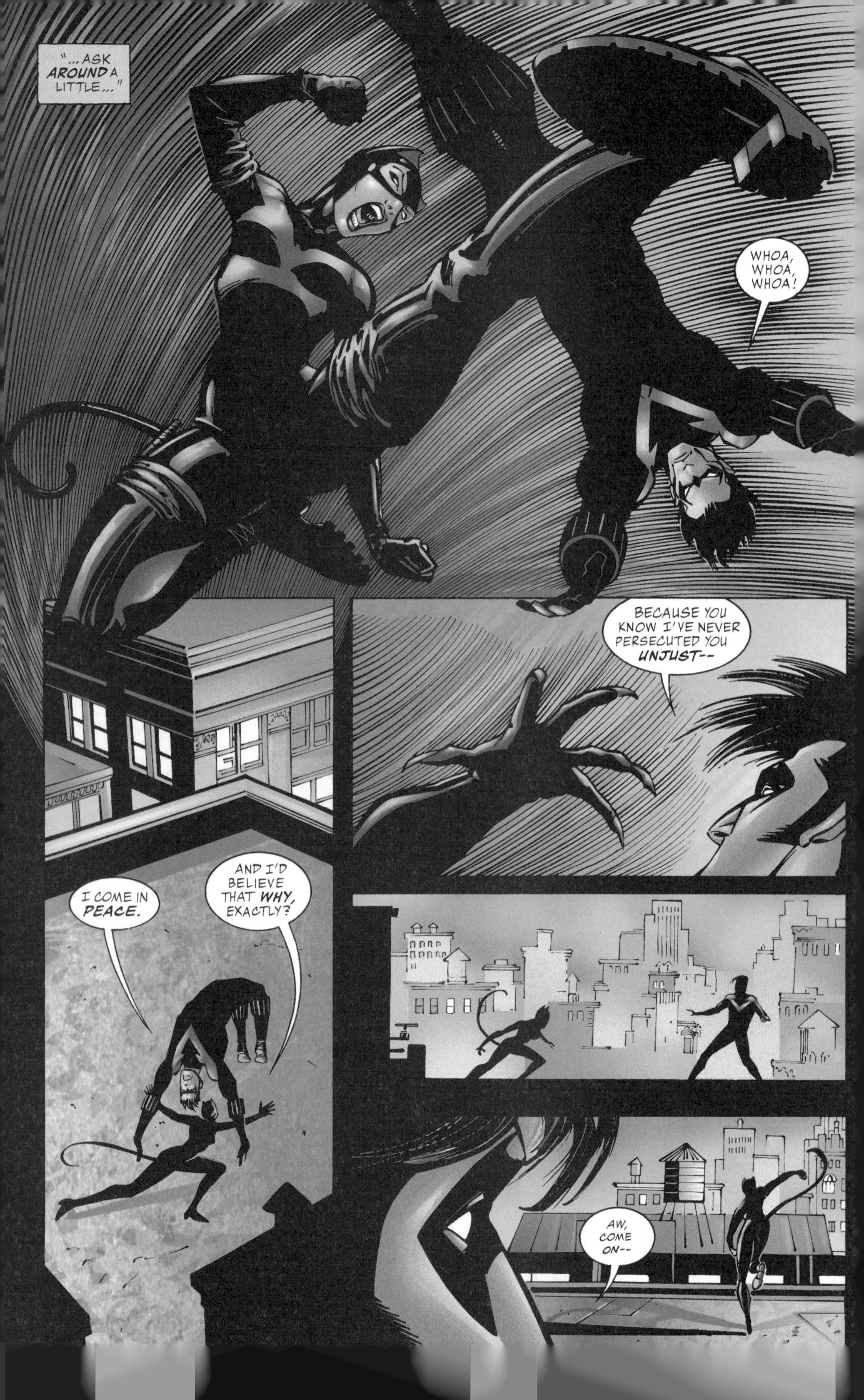
"...ASK AROUND A LITTLE..."
WHOA, WHOA, WHOA!
BECAUSE YOU KNOW I'VE NEVER PERSECUTED YOU UNJUST--
I COME IN PEACE.
AND I'D BELIEVE THAT WHY, EXACTLY?
AW, COME ON--

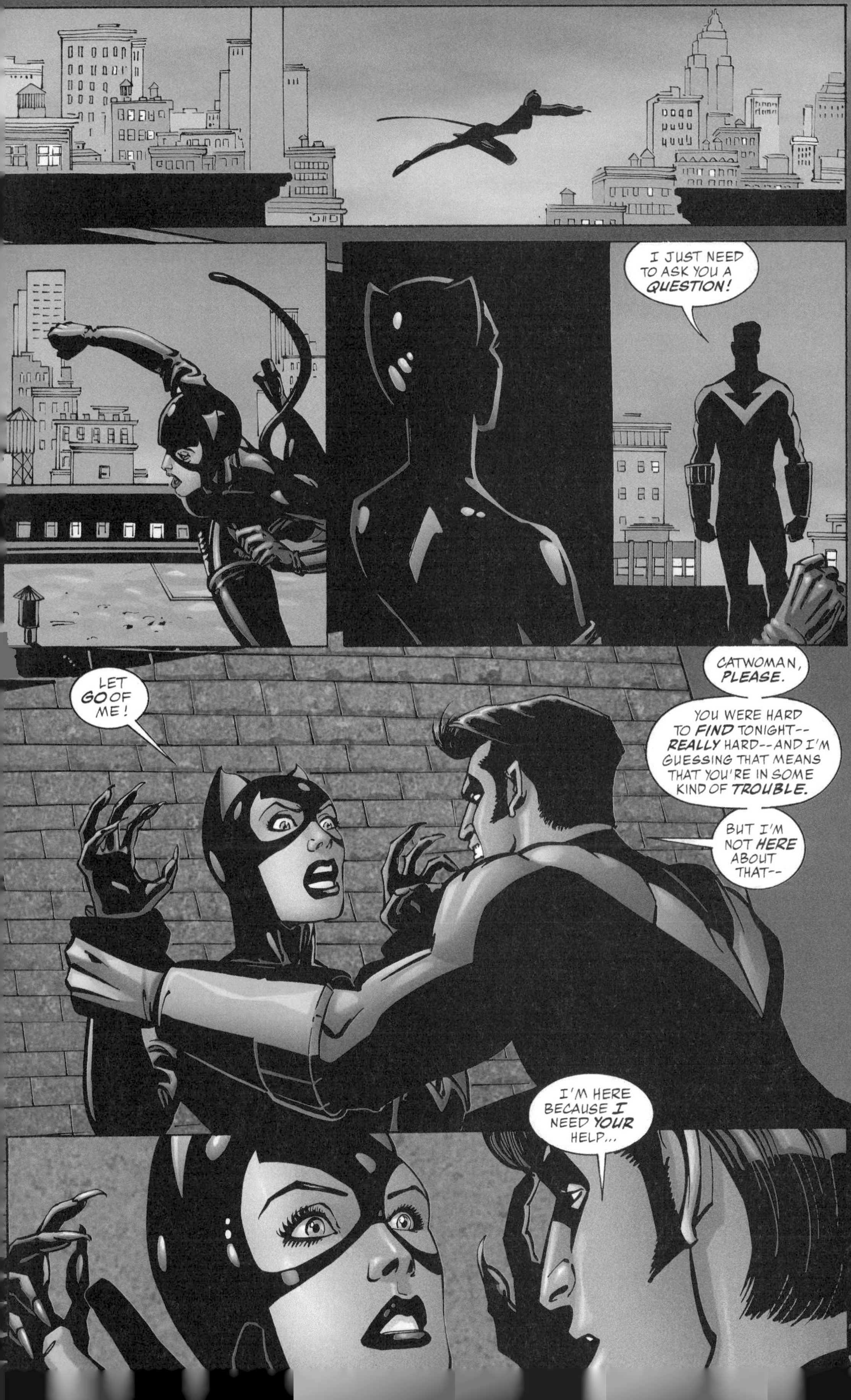
I JUST NEED TO ASK YOU A QUESTION!
LET GO OF ME!
CATWOMAN, PLEASE.
YOU WERE HARD TO FIND TONIGHT-- REALLY HARD--AND I'M GUESSING THAT MEANS THAT YOU'RE IN SOME KIND OF TROUBLE.
BUT I'M NOT HERE ABOUT THAT--
I'M HERE BECAUSE I NEED YOUR HELP...

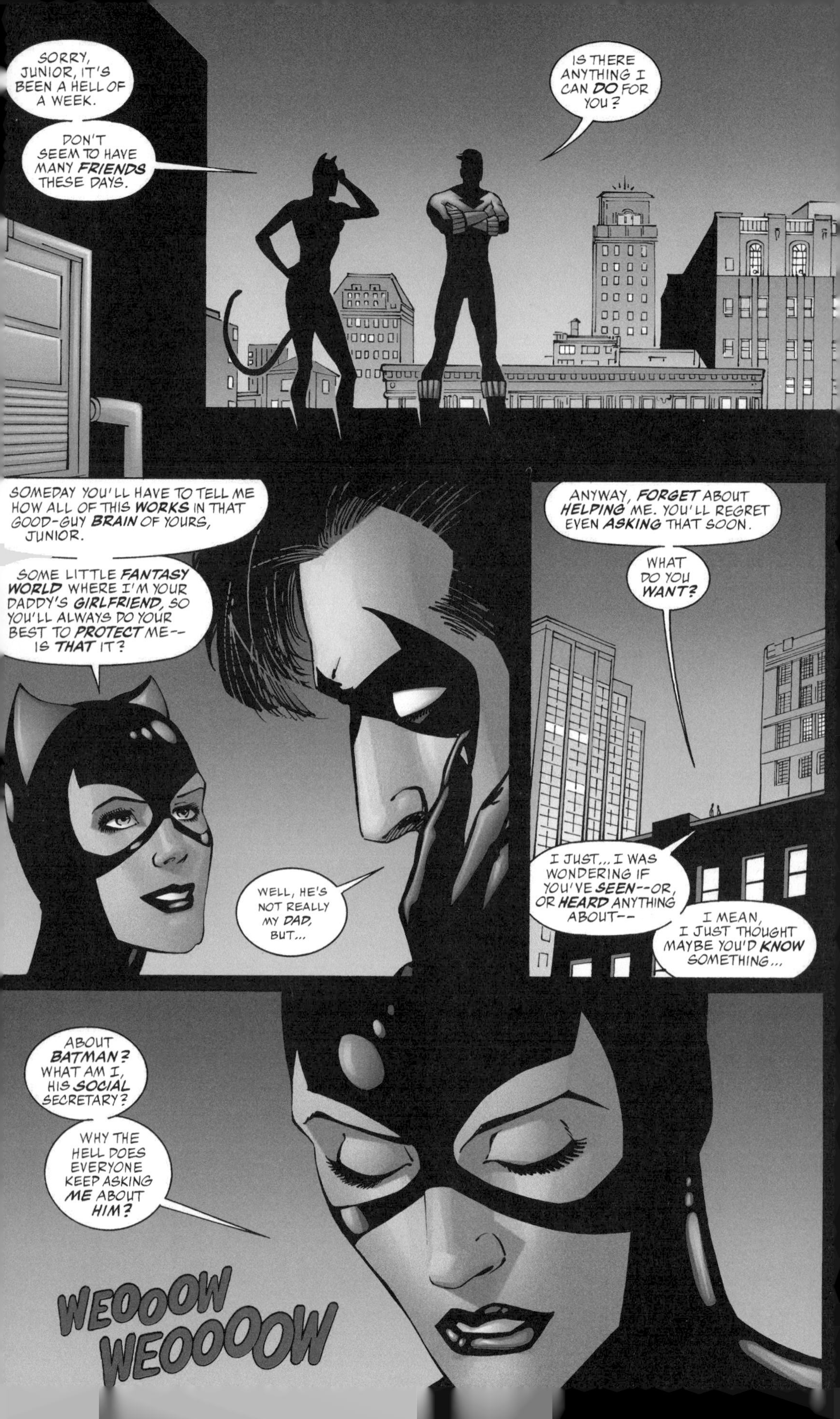
SORRY, JUNIOR, IT'S BEEN A HELL OF A WEEK.
DON'T SEEM TO HAVE MANY FRIENDS THESE DAYS.
IS THERE ANYTHING I CAN DO FOR YOU?
SOMEDAY YOU'LL HAVE TO TELL ME HOW ALL OF THIS WORKS IN THAT GOOD-GUY BRAIN OF YOURS, JUNIOR.
SOME LITTLE FANTASY WORLD WHERE I'M YOUR DADDY'S GIRLFRIEND, SO YOU'LL ALWAYS DO YOUR BEST TO PROTECT ME--IS THAT IT?
WELL, HE'S NOT REALLY MY DAD, BUT...
ANYWAY, FORGET ABOUT HELPING ME. YOU'LL REGRET EVEN ASKING THAT SOON.
WHAT DO YOU WANT?
I JUST... I WAS WONDERING IF YOU'VE SEEN--OR, OR HEARD ANYTHING ABOUT--
I MEAN, I JUST THOUGHT MAYBE YOU'D KNOW SOMETHING...
ABOUT BATMAN? WHAT AM I, HIS SOCIAL SECRETARY?
WHY THE HELL DOES EVERYONE KEEP ASKING ME ABOUT HIM?
WEOOOW WEOOOOW

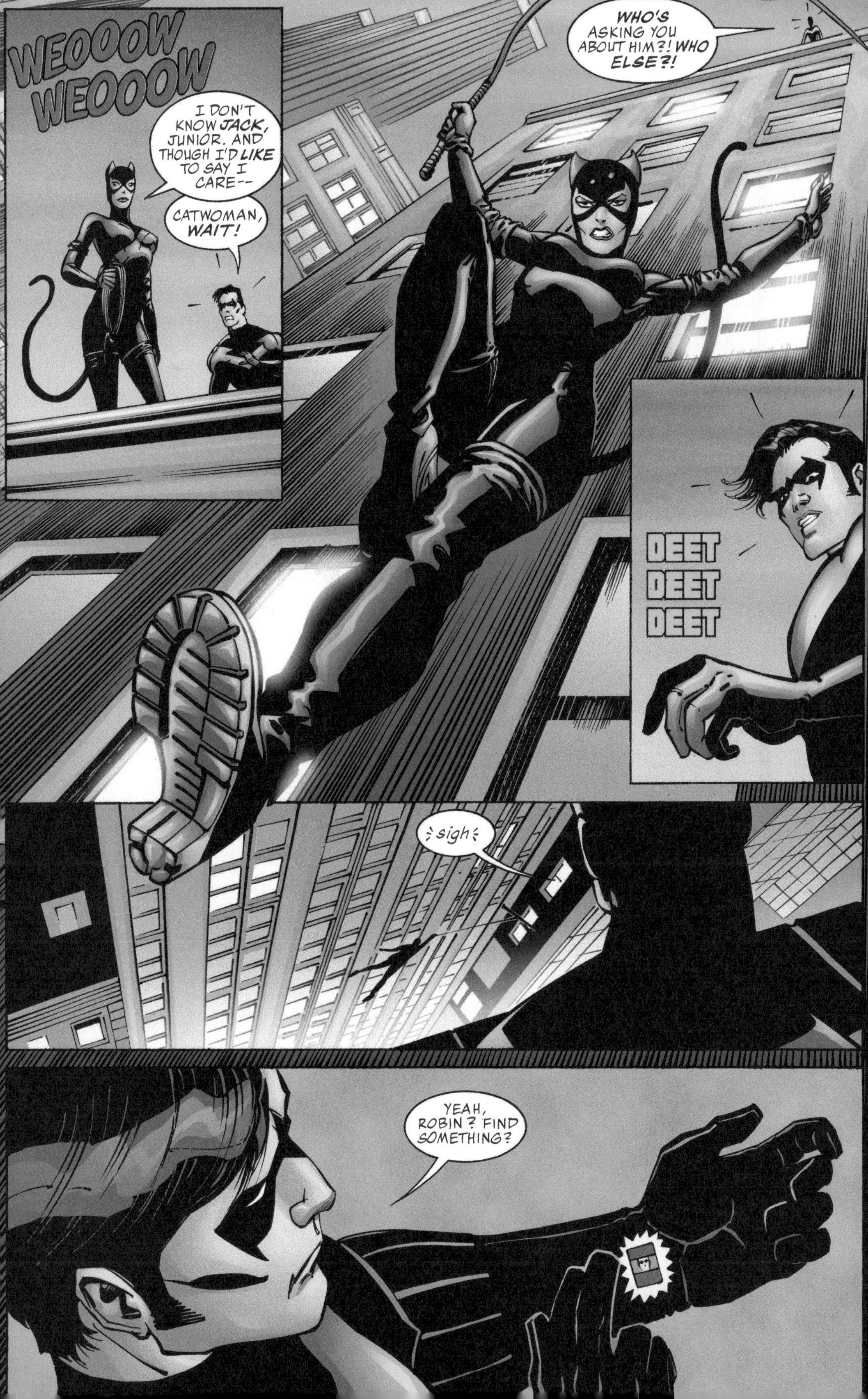
WEOOOW WEOOOW
I DON'T KNOW JACK, JUNIOR. AND THOUGH I'D LIKE TO SAY I CARE--
CATWOMAN, WAIT!
WHO'S ASKING YOU ABOUT HIM?! WHO ELSE?!
DEET DEET DEET
sigh
YEAH, ROBIN? FIND SOMETHING?

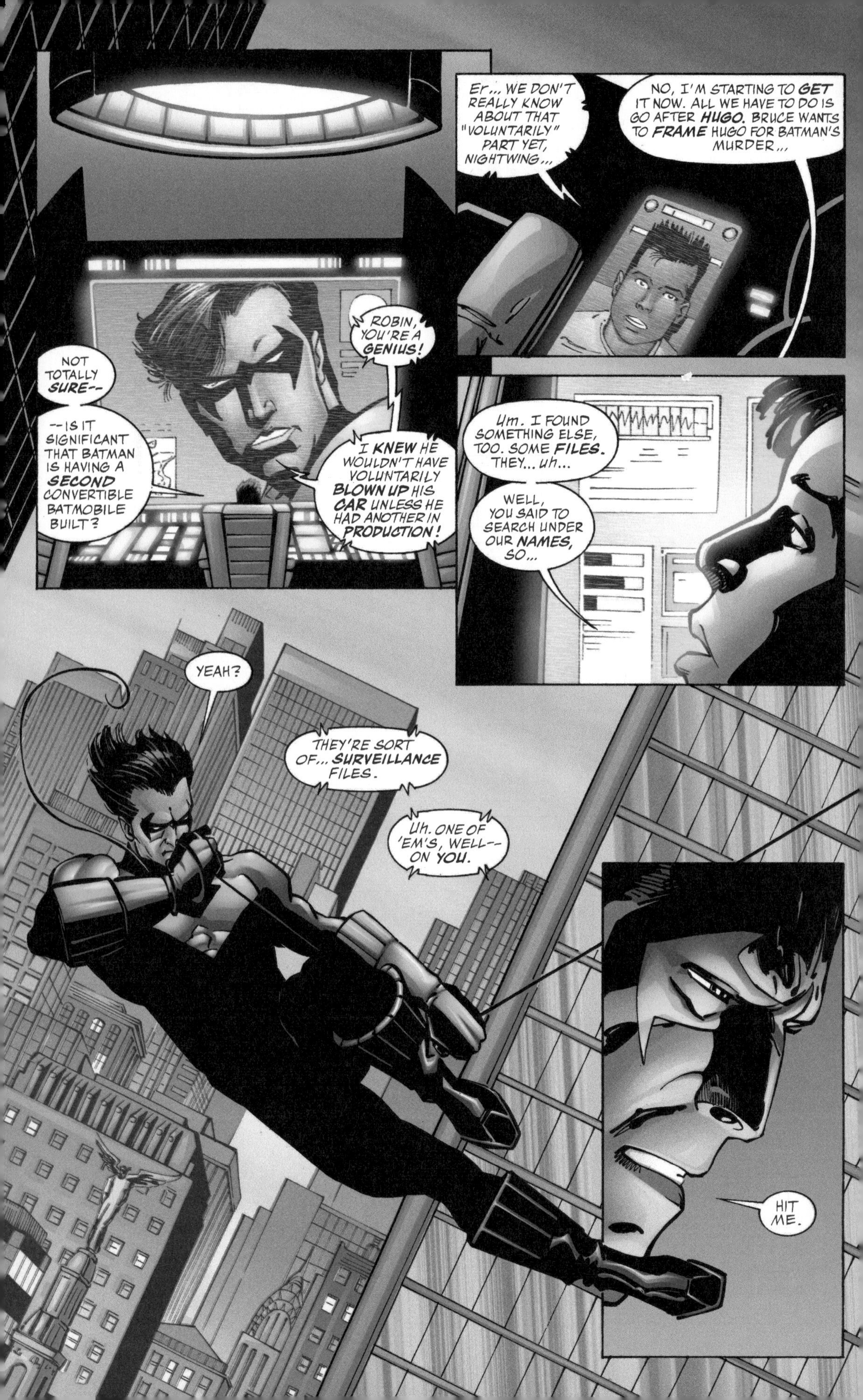
ROBIN, YOU'RE A GENIUS!
NOT TOTALLY SURE--
--IS IT SIGNIFICANT THAT BATMAN IS HAVING A SECOND CONVERTIBLE BATMOBILE BUILT?
I KNEW HE WOULDN'T HAVE VOLUNTARILY BLOWN UP HIS CAR UNLESS HE HAD ANOTHER IN PRODUCTION!
Er... WE DON'T REALLY KNOW ABOUT THAT "VOLUNTARILY" PART YET, NIGHTWING...
NO, I'M STARTING TO GET IT NOW. ALL WE HAVE TO DO IS GO AFTER HUGO. BRUCE WANTS TO FRAME HUGO FOR BATMAN'S MURDER...
Um. I FOUND SOMETHING ELSE, TOO. SOME FILES. THEY... uh...
WELL, YOU SAID TO SEARCH UNDER OUR NAMES, SO...
YEAH?
THEY'RE SORT OF... SURVEILLANCE FILES.
Uh. ONE OF 'EM'S, WELL-- ON YOU.
HIT ME.

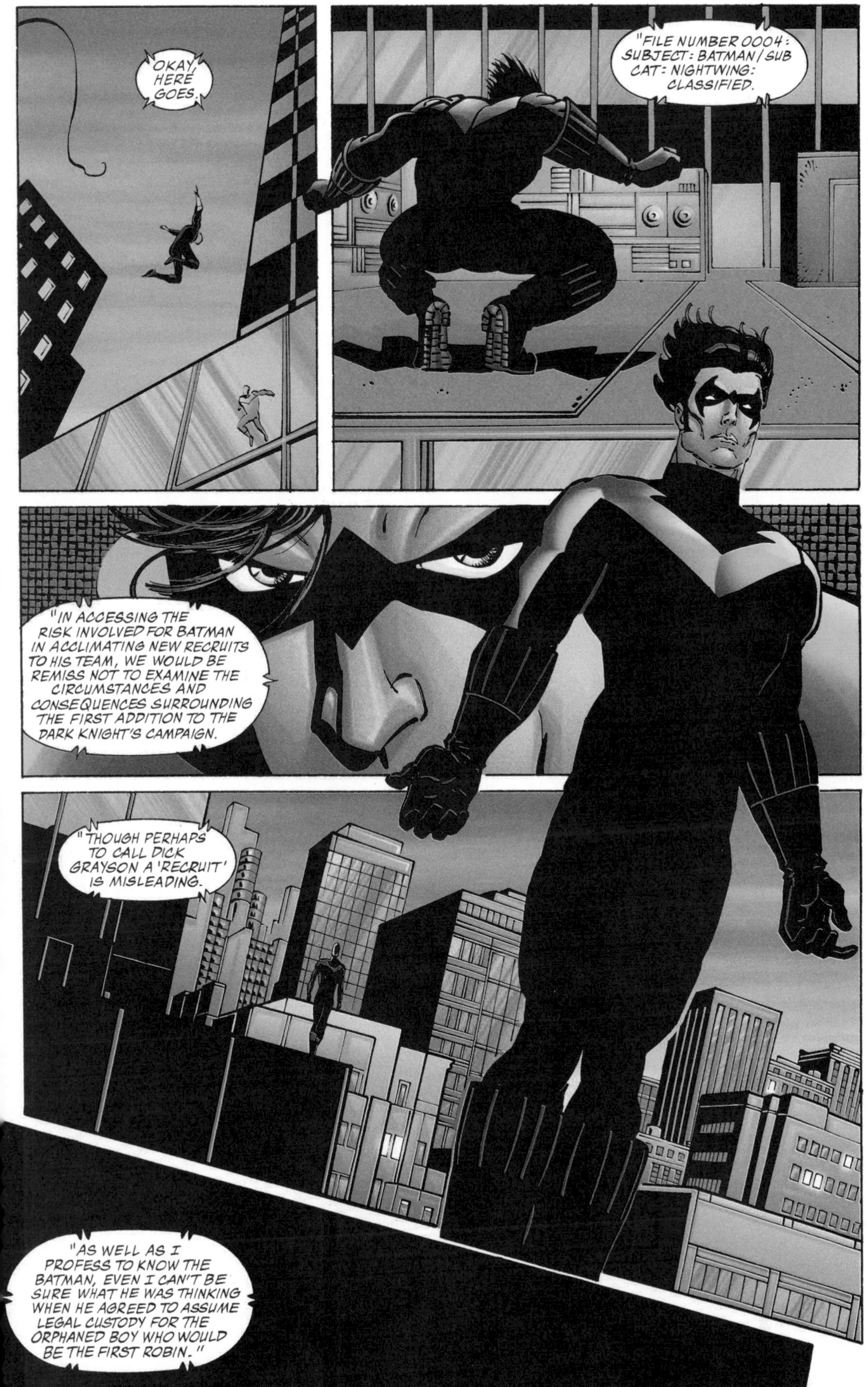
OKAY, HERE GOES.
"FILE NUMBER 0004: SUBJECT: BATMAN / SUB CAT: NIGHTWING: CLASSIFIED.
"IN ACCESSING THE RISK INVOLVED FOR BATMAN IN ACCLIMATING NEW RECRUITS TO HIS TEAM, WE WOULD BE REMISS NOT TO EXAMINE THE CIRCUMSTANCES AND CONSEQUENCES SURROUNDING THE FIRST ADDITION TO THE DARK KNIGHT'S CAMPAIGN.
"THOUGH PERHAPS TO CALL DICK GRAYSON A 'RECRUIT' IS MISLEADING.
"AS WELL AS I PROFESS TO KNOW THE BATMAN, EVEN I CAN'T BE SURE WHAT HE WAS THINKING WHEN HE AGREED TO ASSUME LEGAL CUSTODY FOR THE ORPHANED BOY WHO WOULD BE THE FIRST ROBIN."

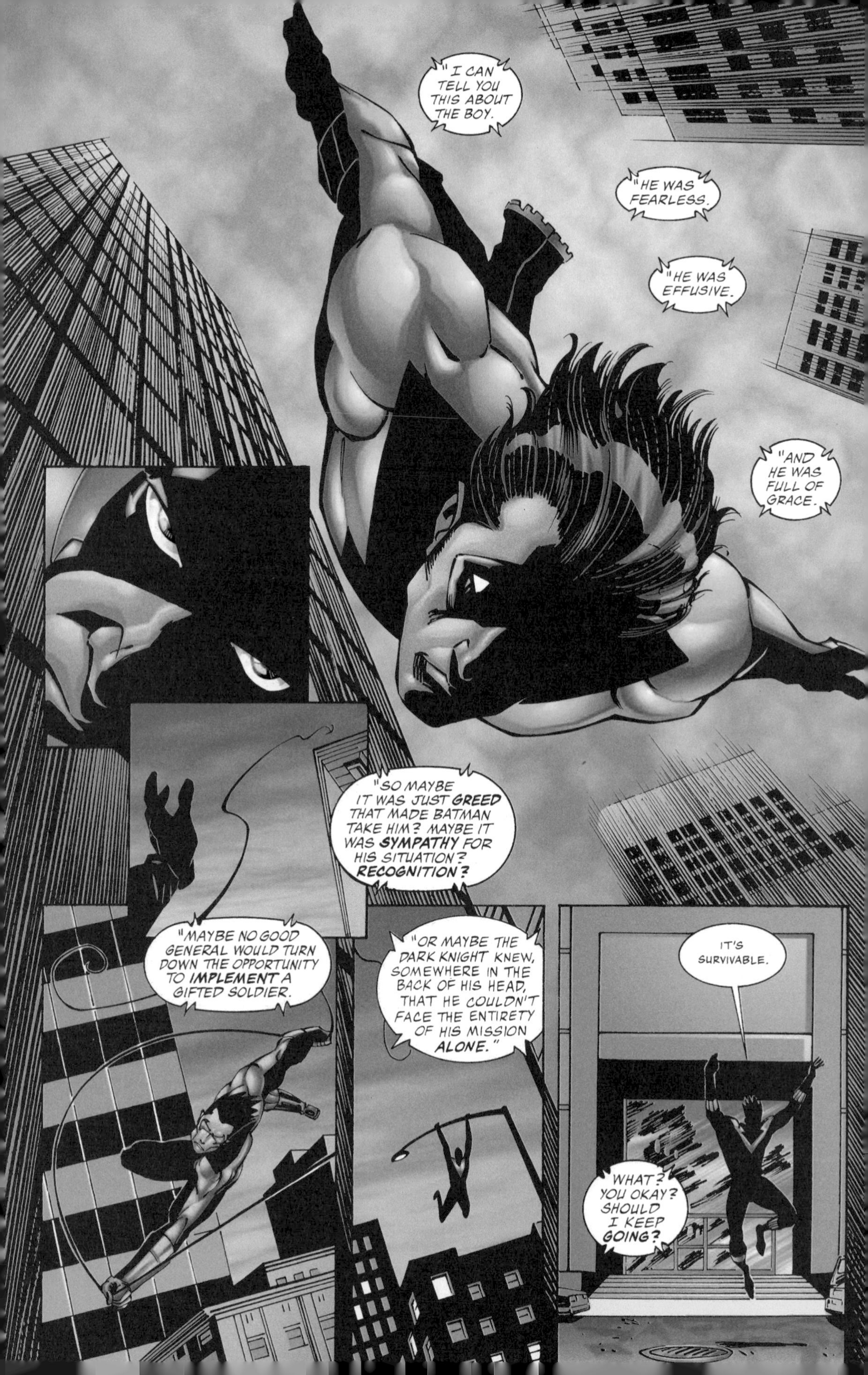
"I CAN TELL YOU THIS ABOUT THE BOY.
"HE WAS FEARLESS.
"HE WAS EFFUSIVE.
"AND HE WAS FULL OF GRACE.
"SO MAYBE IT WAS JUST GREED THAT MADE BATMAN TAKE HIM? MAYBE IT WAS SYMPATHY FOR HIS SITUATION? RECOGNITION?
"MAYBE NO GOOD GENERAL WOULD TURN DOWN THE OPPORTUNITY TO IMPLEMENT A GIFTED SOLDIER.
"OR MAYBE THE DARK KNIGHT KNEW, SOMEWHERE IN THE BACK OF HIS HEAD, THAT HE COULDN'T FACE THE ENTIRETY OF HIS MISSION ALONE."
IT'S SURVIVABLE.
WHAT? YOU OKAY? SHOULD I KEEP GOING?

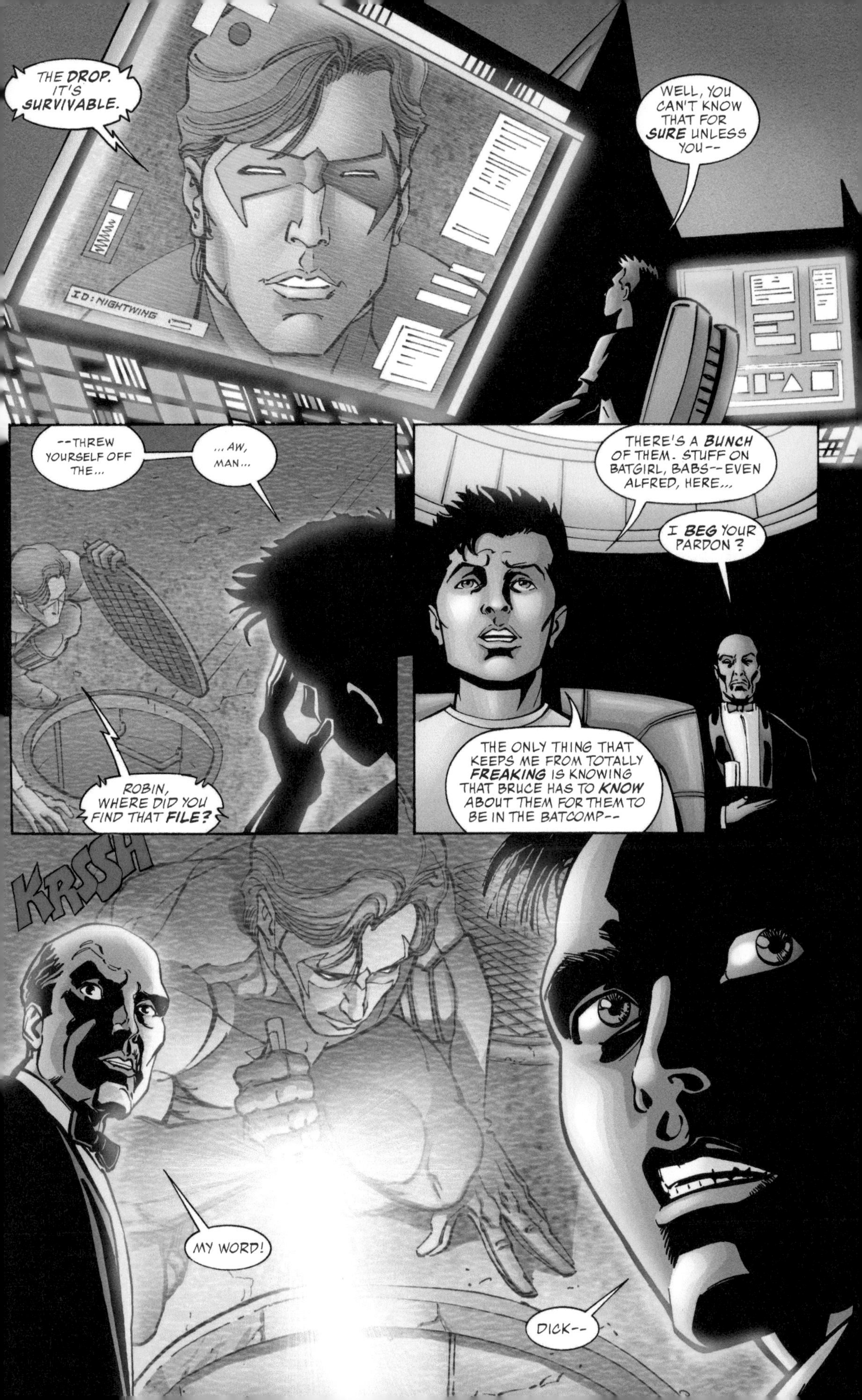
THE DROP. IT'S SURVIVABLE.
WELL, YOU CAN'T KNOW THAT FOR SURE UNLESS YOU--
ID: NIGHTWING
--THREW YOURSELF OFF THE...
...AW, MAN...
ROBIN, WHERE DID YOU FIND THAT FILE?
THERE'S A BUNCH OF THEM. STUFF ON BATGIRL, BABS--EVEN ALFRED, HERE...
I BEG YOUR PARDON?
THE ONLY THING THAT KEEPS ME FROM TOTALLY FREAKING IS KNOWING THAT BRUCE HAS TO KNOW ABOUT THEM FOR THEM TO BE IN THE BATCOMP--
KRSSH
MY WORD!
DICK--

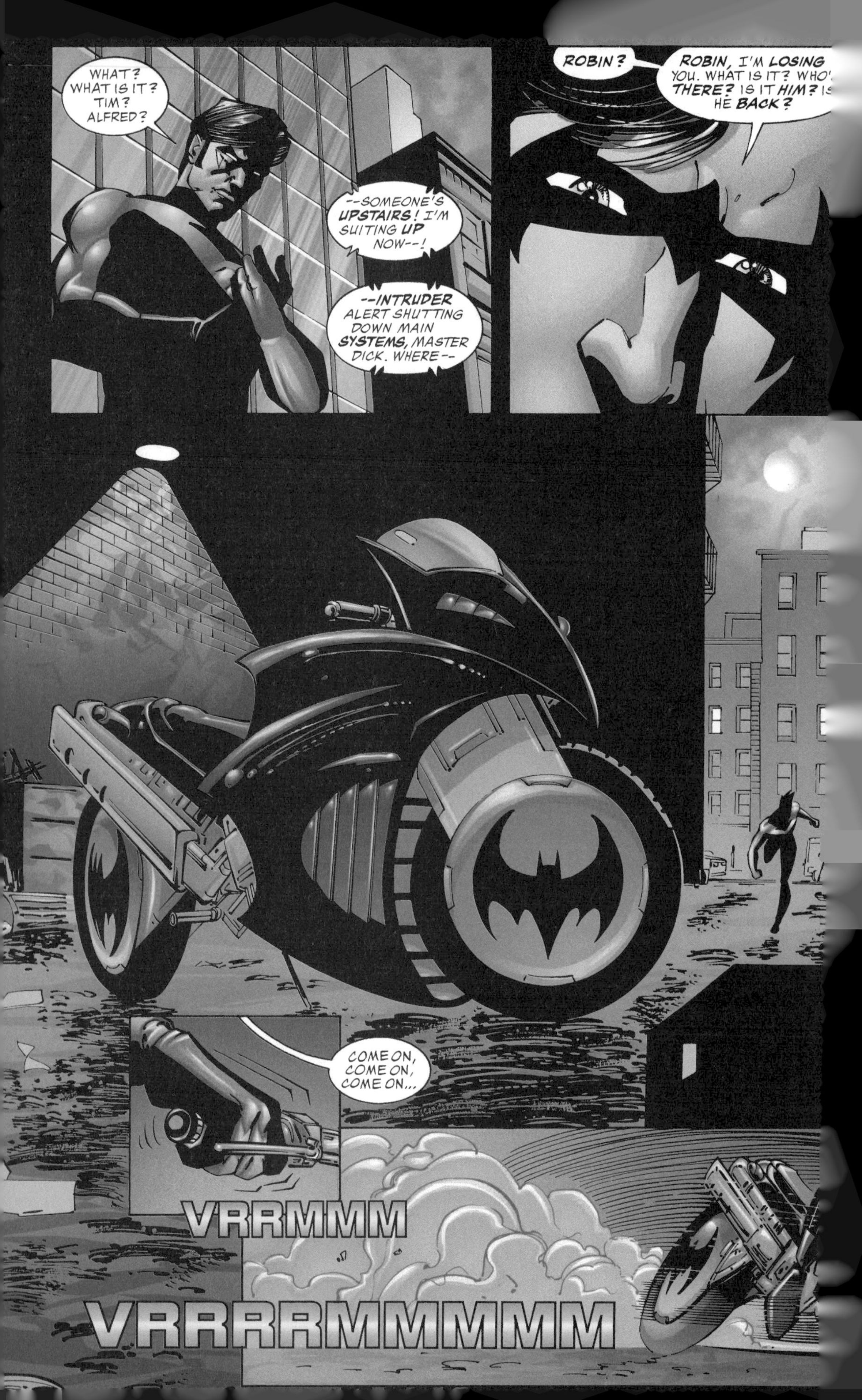
WHAT? WHAT IS IT? TIM? ALFRED?
--SOMEONE'S UPSTAIRS! I'M SUITING UP NOW--!
--INTRUDER ALERT SHUTTING DOWN MAIN SYSTEMS, MASTER DICK. WHERE--
ROBIN?
ROBIN, I'M LOSING YOU. WHAT IS IT? WHO'S THERE? IS IT HIM? IS HE BACK?
COME ON, COME ON, COME ON...
VRRMMM
VRRRRMMMMMM

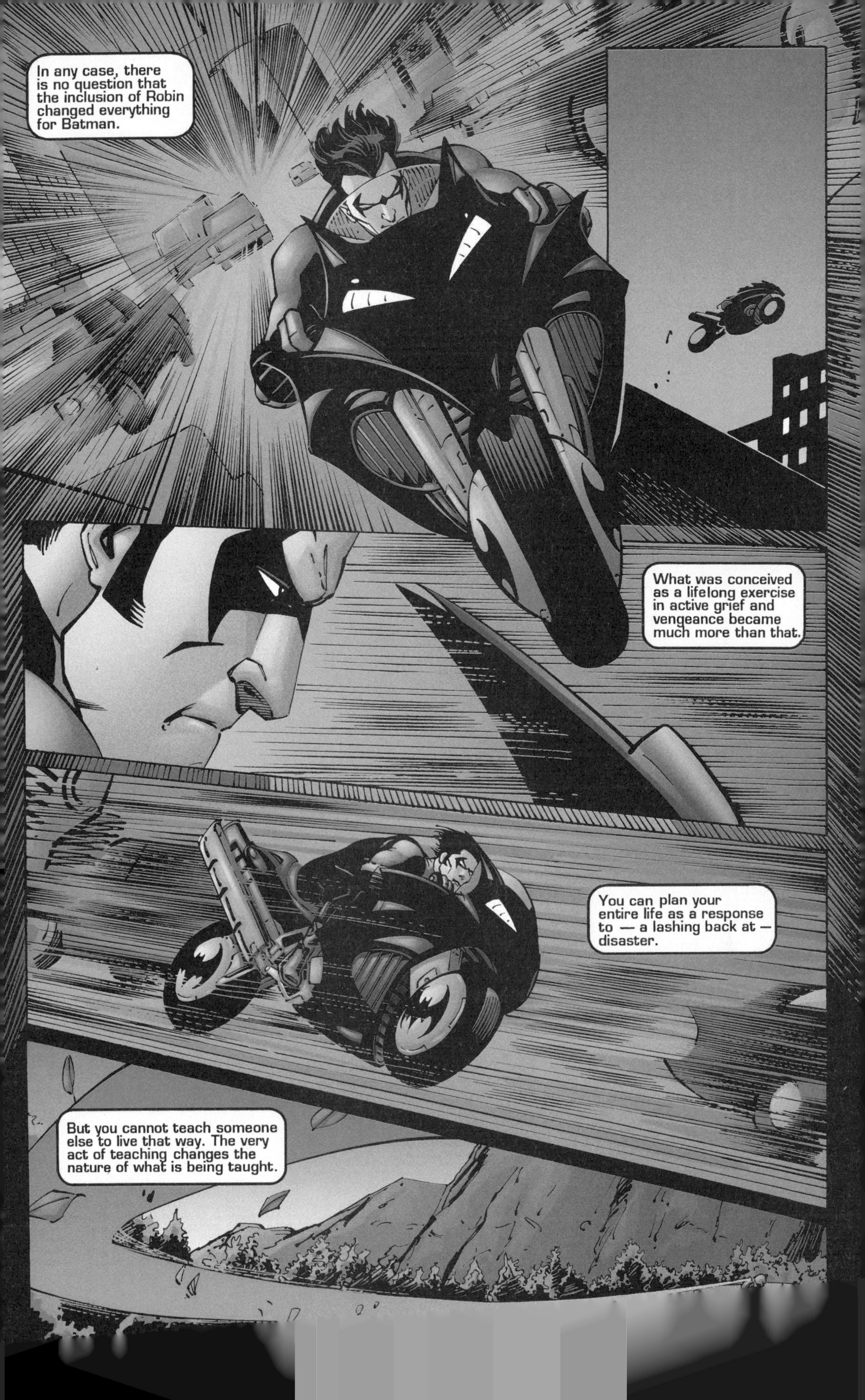
In any case, there is no question that the inclusion of Robin changed everything for Batman.
What was conceived as a lifelong exercise in active grief and vengeance became much more than that.
You can plan your entire life as a response to — a lashing back at — disaster.
But you cannot teach someone else to live that way. The very act of teaching changes the nature of what is being taught.

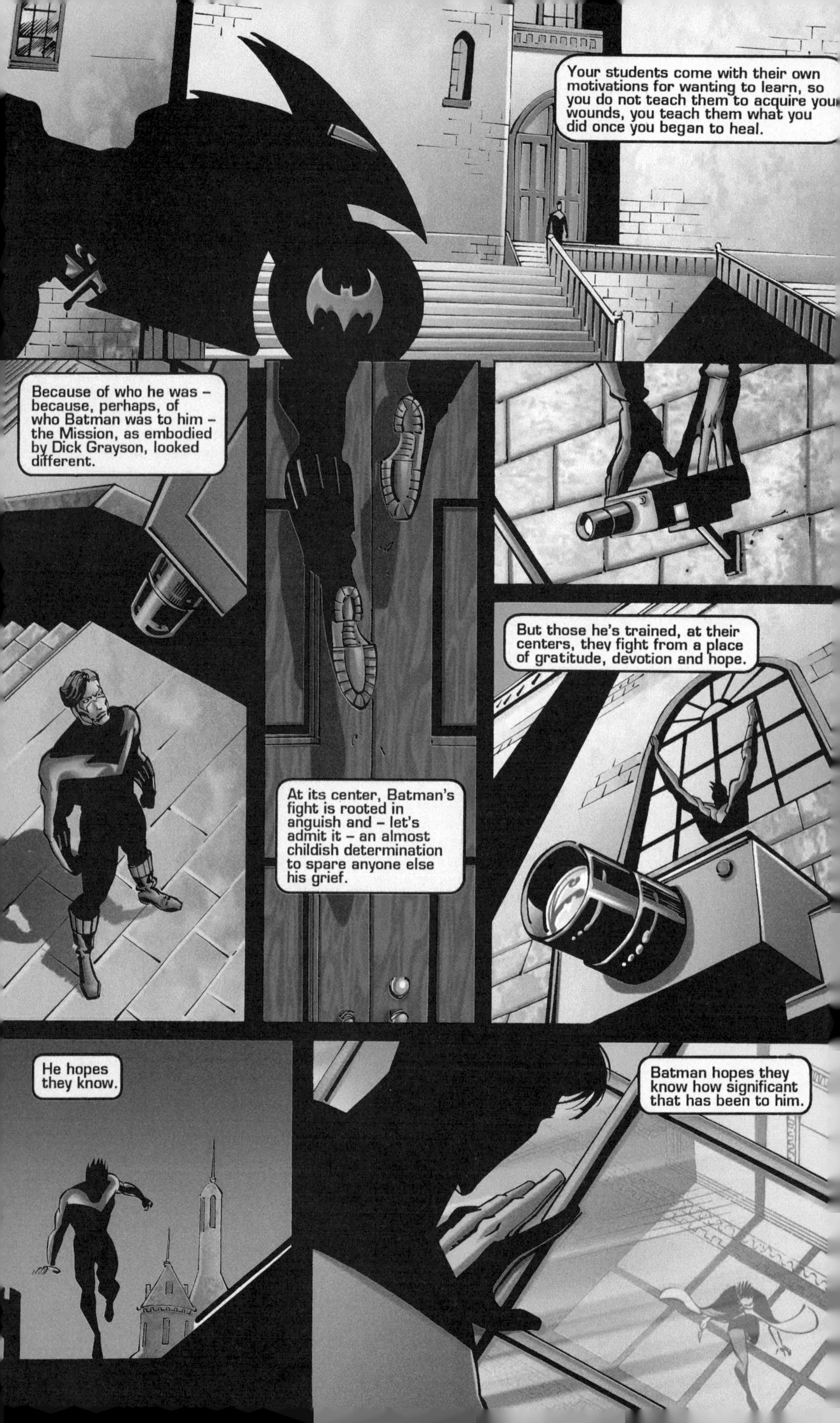
Your students come with their own motivations for wanting to learn, so you do not teach them to acquire your wounds, you teach them what you did once you began to heal.
Because of who he was – because, perhaps, of who Batman was to him – the Mission, as embodied by Dick Grayson, looked different.
At its center, Batman's fight is rooted in anguish and – let's admit it – an almost childish determination to spare anyone else his grief.
But those he's trained, at their centers, they fight from a place of gratitude, devotion and hope.
He hopes they know.
Batman hopes they know how significant that has been to him.

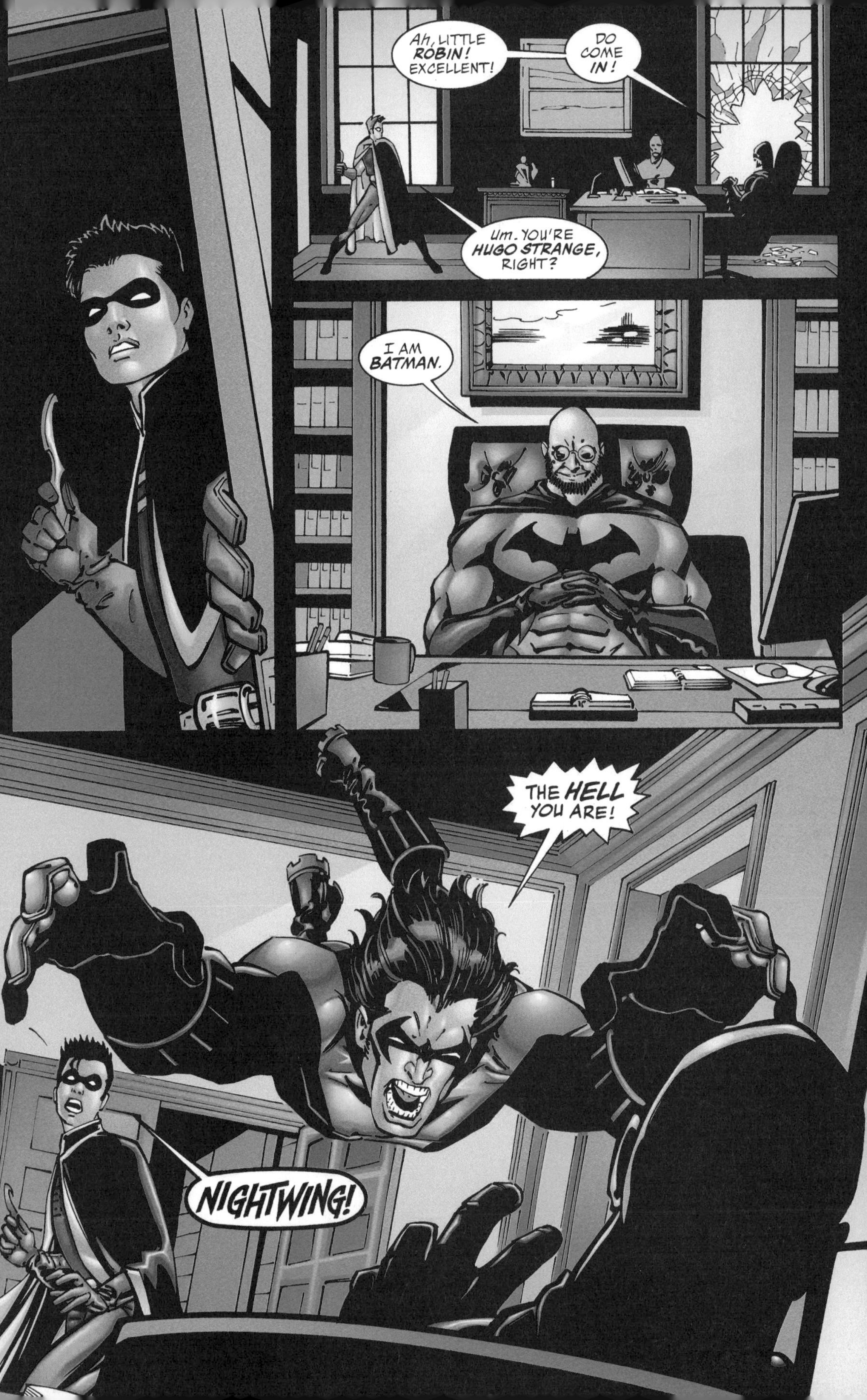
AH, LITTLE ROBIN! EXCELLENT!
DO COME IN!
UM. YOU'RE HUGO STRANGE, RIGHT?
I AM BATMAN.
THE HELL YOU ARE!
NIGHTWING!

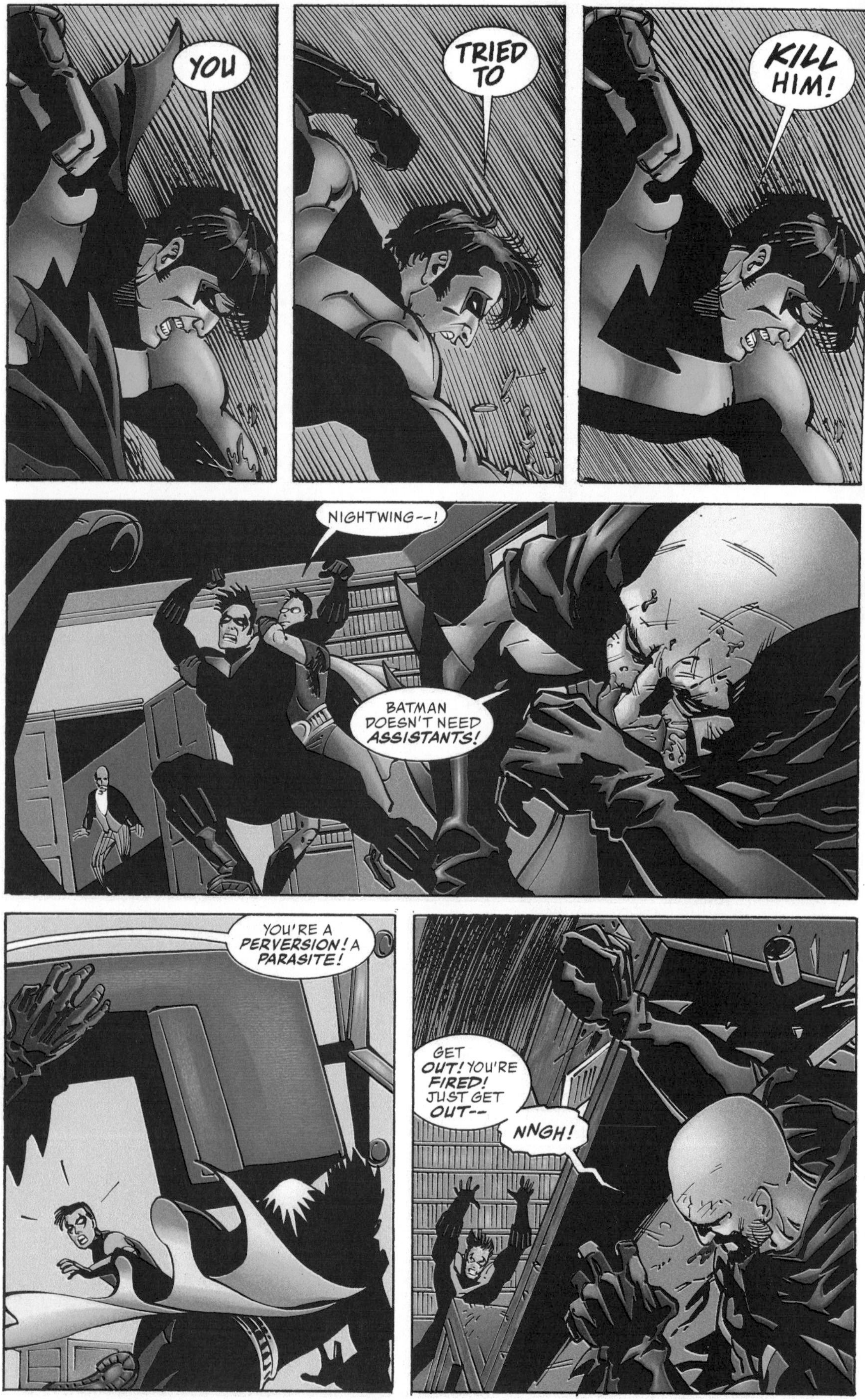
YOU
TRIED TO
KILL HIM!
NIGHTWING--!
BATMAN DOESN'T NEED ASSISTANTS!
YOU'RE A PERVERSION! A PARASITE!
GET OUT! YOU'RE FIRED! JUST GET OUT--
NNGH!

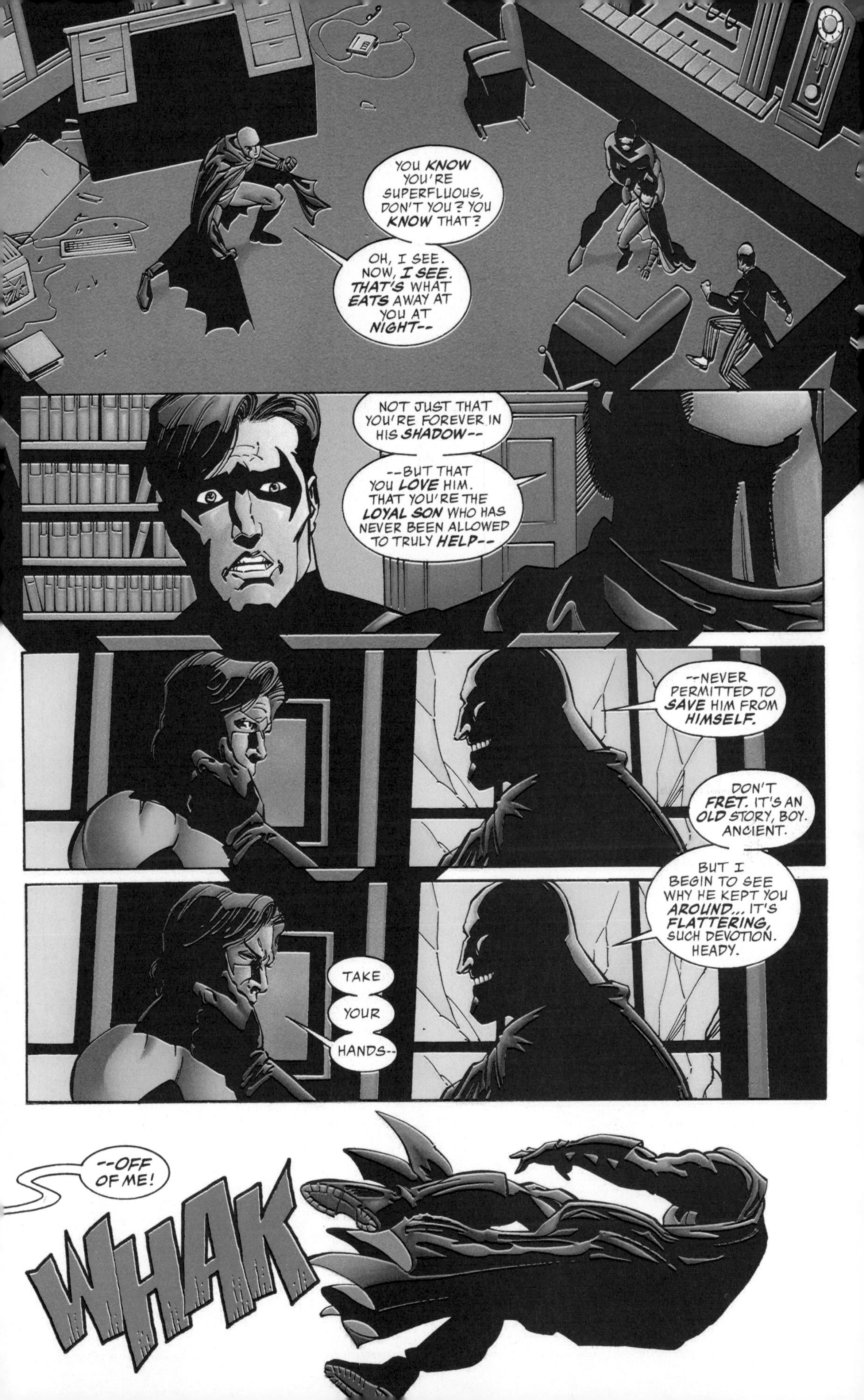
YOU KNOW YOU'RE SUPERFLUOUS, DON'T YOU? YOU KNOW THAT?
OH, I SEE. NOW, I SEE. THAT'S WHAT EATS AWAY AT YOU AT NIGHT--
NOT JUST THAT YOU'RE FOREVER IN HIS SHADOW--
--BUT THAT YOU LOVE HIM. THAT YOU'RE THE LOYAL SON WHO HAS NEVER BEEN ALLOWED TO TRULY HELP--
--NEVER PERMITTED TO SAVE HIM FROM HIMSELF.
DON'T FRET. IT'S AN OLD STORY, BOY. ANCIENT.
BUT I BEGIN TO SEE WHY HE KEPT YOU AROUND... IT'S FLATTERING, SUCH DEVOTION. HEADY.
TAKE
YOUR
HANDS--
--OFF OF ME!
WHAK

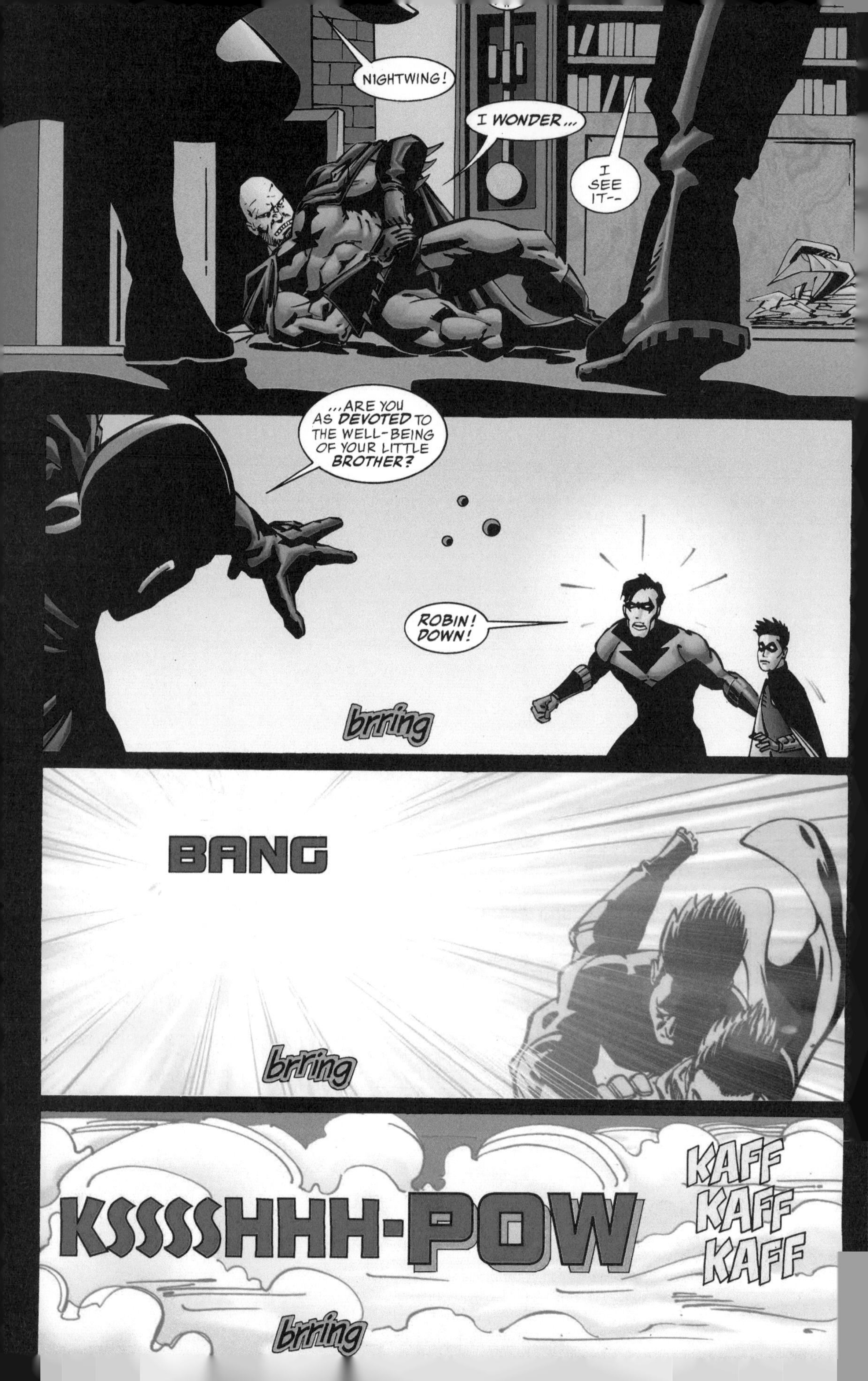
NIGHTWING!
I WONDER...
I SEE IT--
...ARE YOU AS DEVOTED TO THE WELL-BEING OF YOUR LITTLE BROTHER?
ROBIN! DOWN!
brrring
BANG
brrring
KSSSSHHH-POW
KAFF KAFF KAFF
brrring

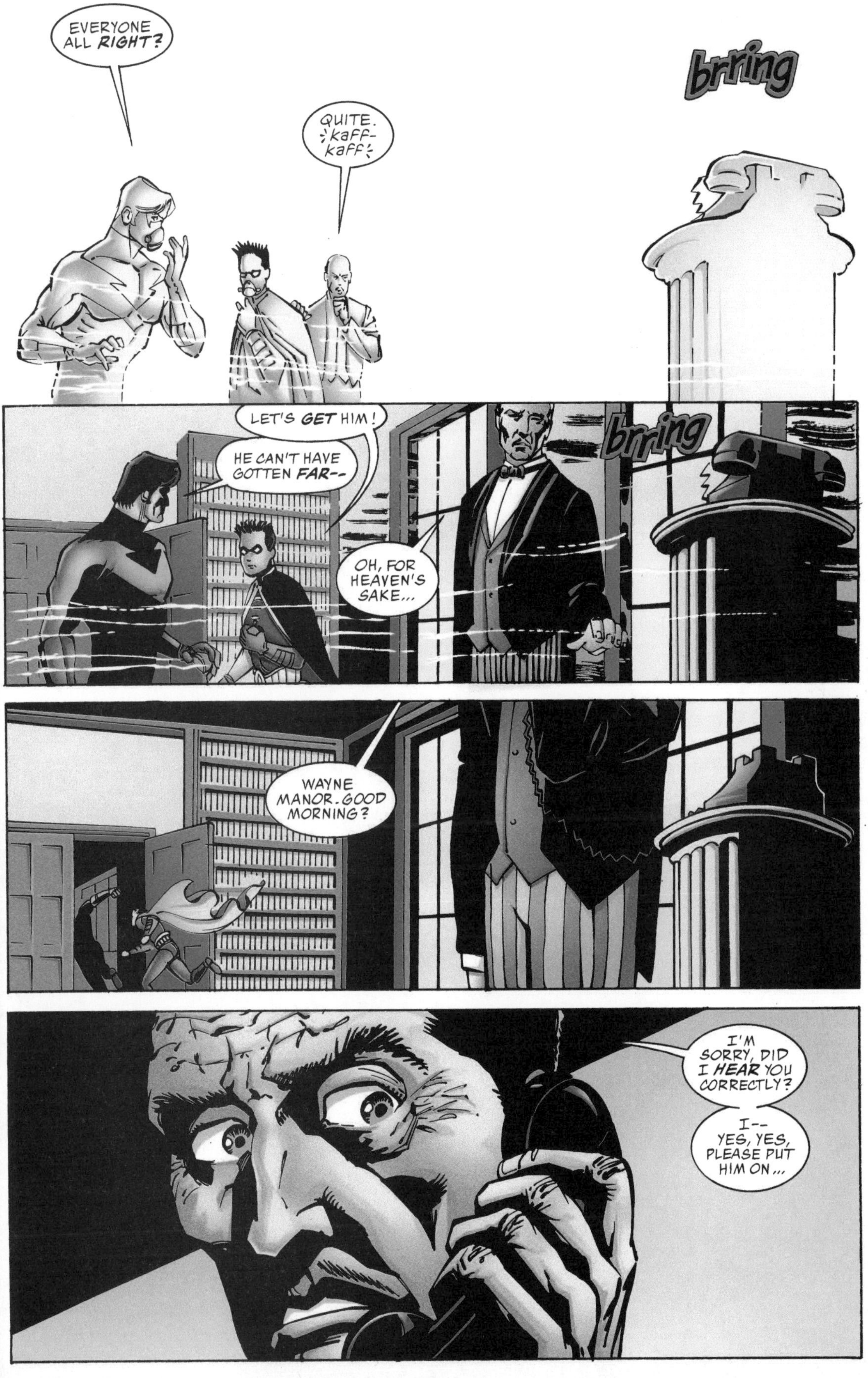
EVERYONE ALL RIGHT?
QUITE. kaff-kaff
brring
LET'S GET HIM!
HE CAN'T HAVE GOTTEN FAR--
brring
OH, FOR HEAVEN'S SAKE...
WAYNE MANOR. GOOD MORNING?
I'M SORRY, DID I HEAR YOU CORRECTLY?
I-- YES, YES, PLEASE PUT HIM ON...

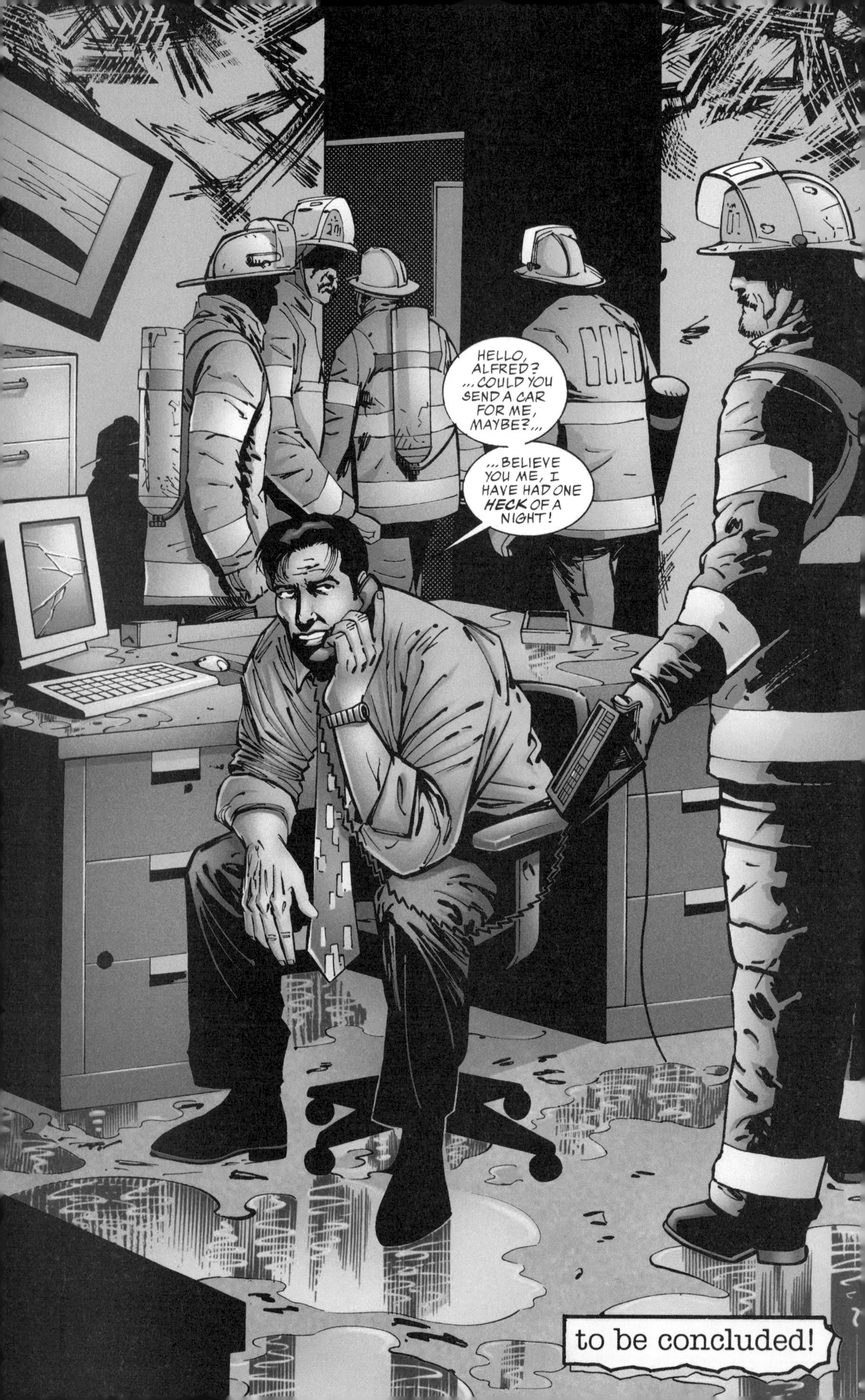
HELLO, ALFRED? ...COULD YOU SEND A CAR FOR ME, MAYBE?...
...BELIEVE YOU ME, I HAVE HAD ONE HECK OF A NIGHT!
to be concluded!

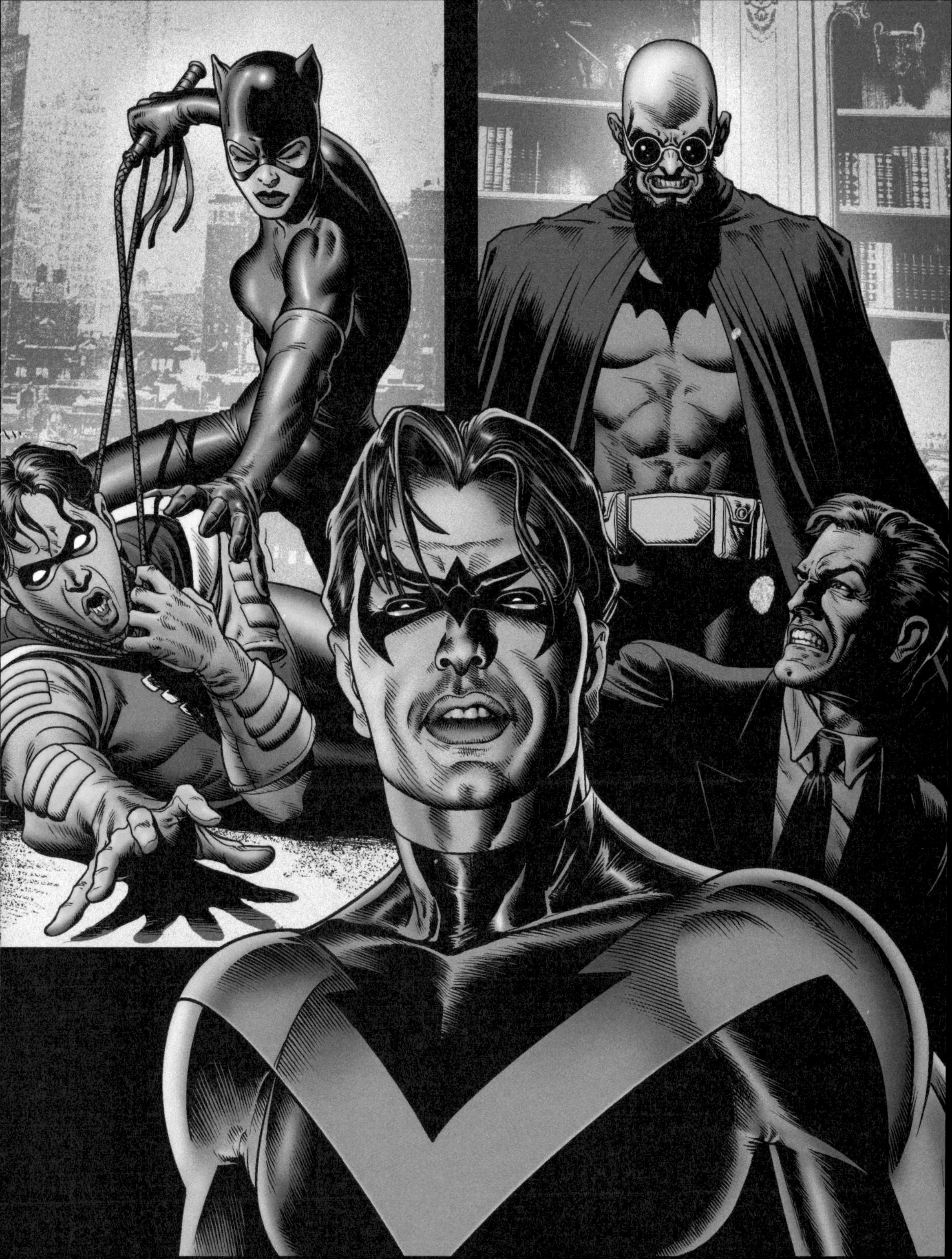

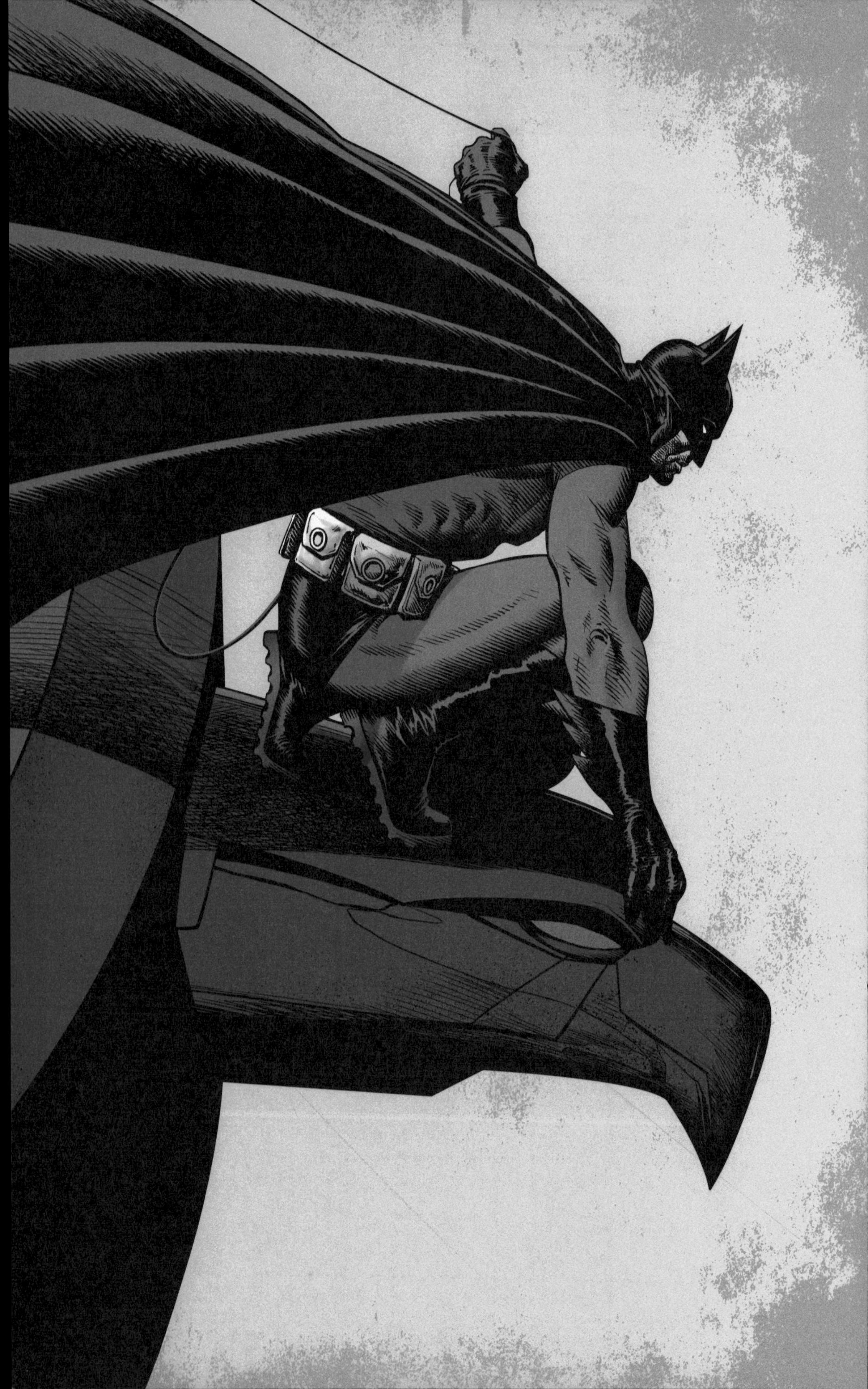

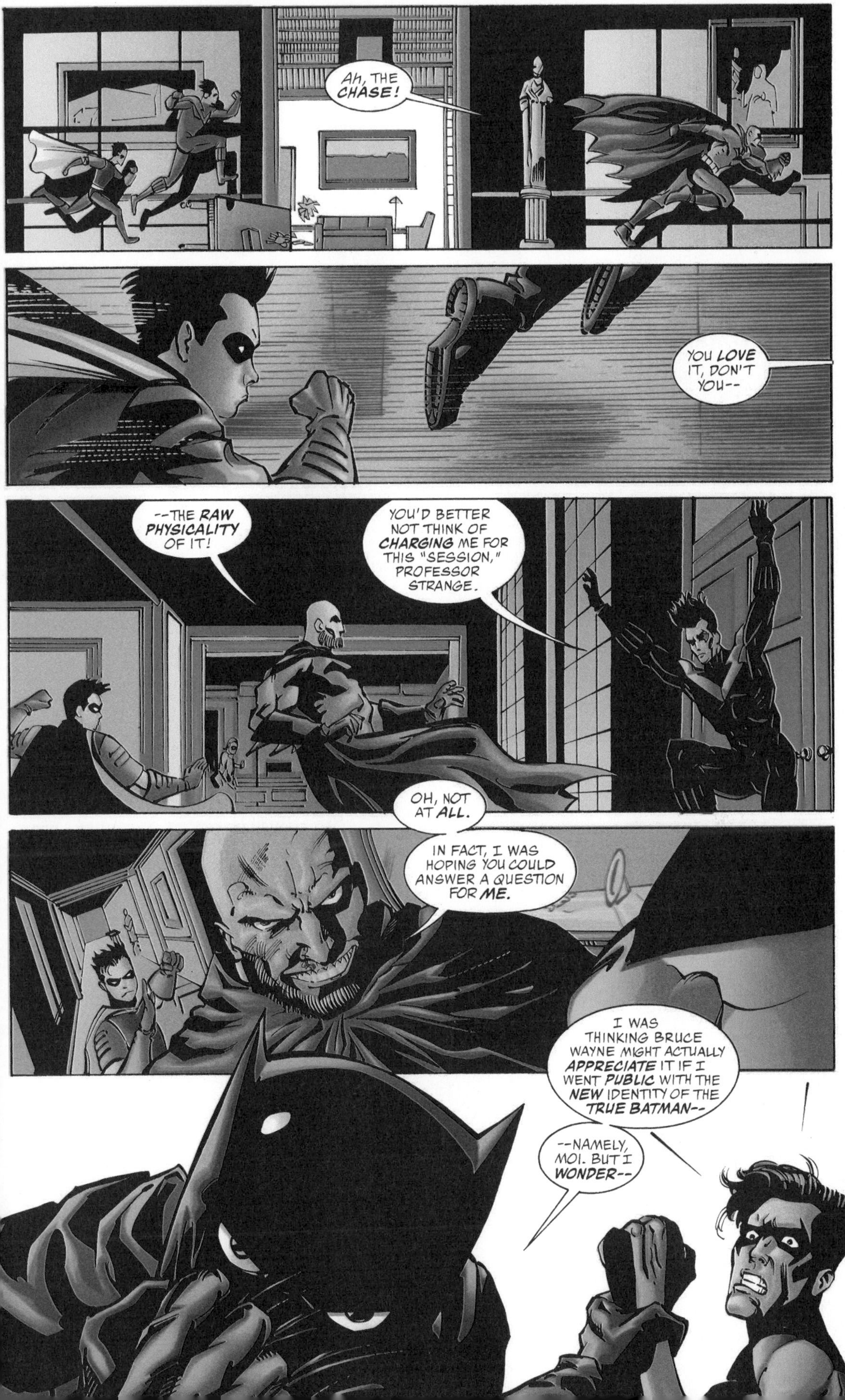
Ah, THE CHASE!
YOU LOVE IT, DON'T YOU--
--THE RAW PHYSICALITY OF IT!
YOU'D BETTER NOT THINK OF CHARGING ME FOR THIS "SESSION," PROFESSOR STRANGE.
OH, NOT AT ALL.
IN FACT, I WAS HOPING YOU COULD ANSWER A QUESTION FOR ME.
I WAS THINKING BRUCE WAYNE MIGHT ACTUALLY APPRECIATE IT IF I WENT PUBLIC WITH THE NEW IDENTITY OF THE TRUE BATMAN--
--NAMELY, MOI. BUT I WONDER--

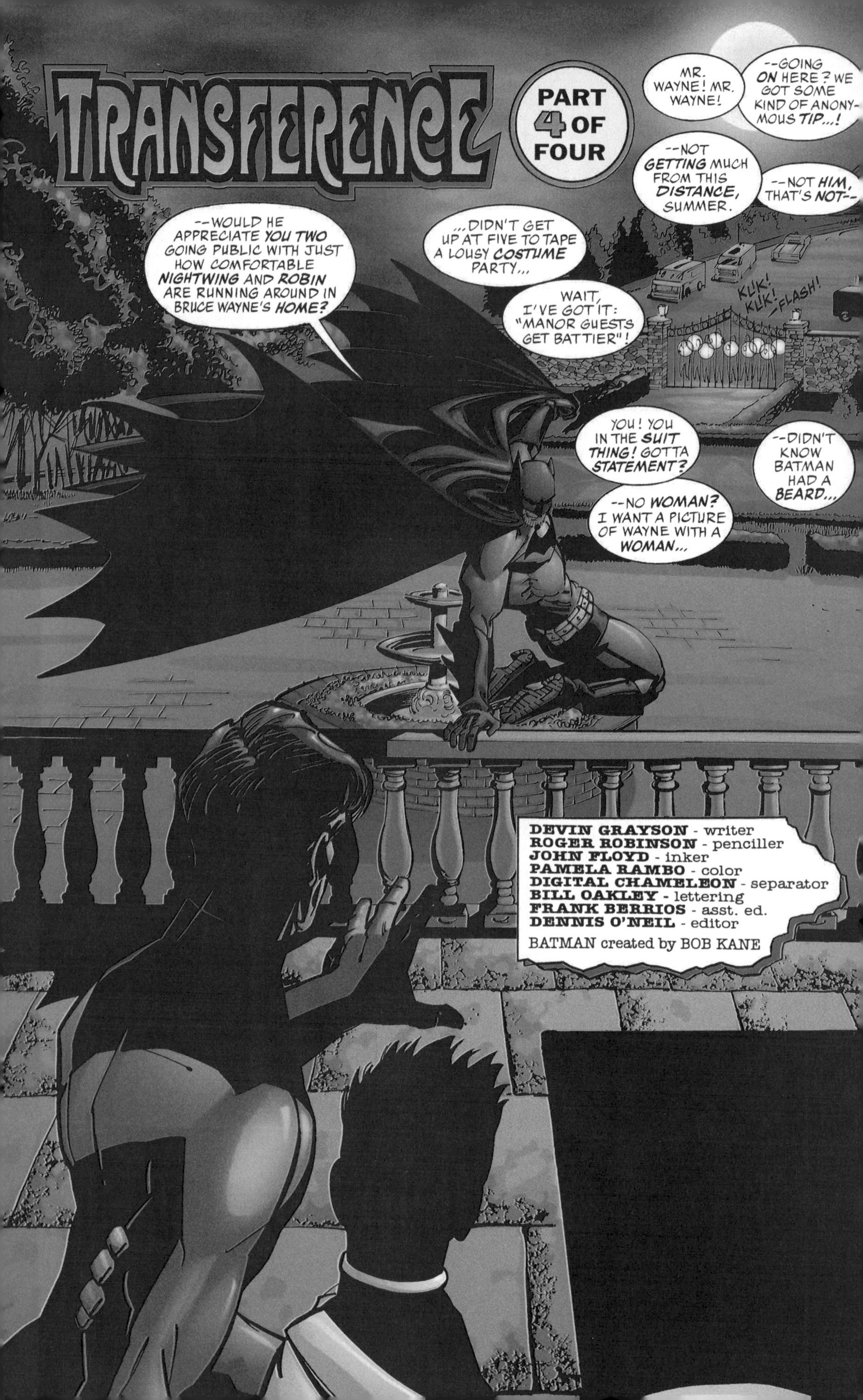
TRANSFERENCE
PART 4 OF FOUR
MR. WAYNE! MR. WAYNE!
--GOING ON HERE? WE GOT SOME KIND OF ANONYMOUS TIP...!
--NOT GETTING MUCH FROM THIS DISTANCE, SUMMER.
--NOT HIM, THAT'S NOT--
--WOULD HE APPRECIATE YOU TWO GOING PUBLIC WITH JUST HOW COMFORTABLE NIGHTWING AND ROBIN ARE RUNNING AROUND IN BRUCE WAYNE'S HOME?
...DIDN'T GET UP AT FIVE TO TAPE A LOUSY COSTUME PARTY...
WAIT, I'VE GOT IT: "MANOR GUESTS GET BATTIER"!
KLIK! KLIK! -FLASH!
YOU! YOU IN THE SUIT THING! GOTTA STATEMENT?
--DIDN'T KNOW BATMAN HAD A BEARD...
--NO WOMAN? I WANT A PICTURE OF WAYNE WITH A WOMAN...
DEVIN GRAYSON - writer
ROGER ROBINSON - penciller
JOHN FLOYD - inker
PAMELA RAMBO - color
DIGITAL CHAMELEON - separator
BILL OAKLEY - lettering
FRANK BERRIOS - asst. ed.
DENNIS O'NEIL - editor
BATMAN created by BOB KANE

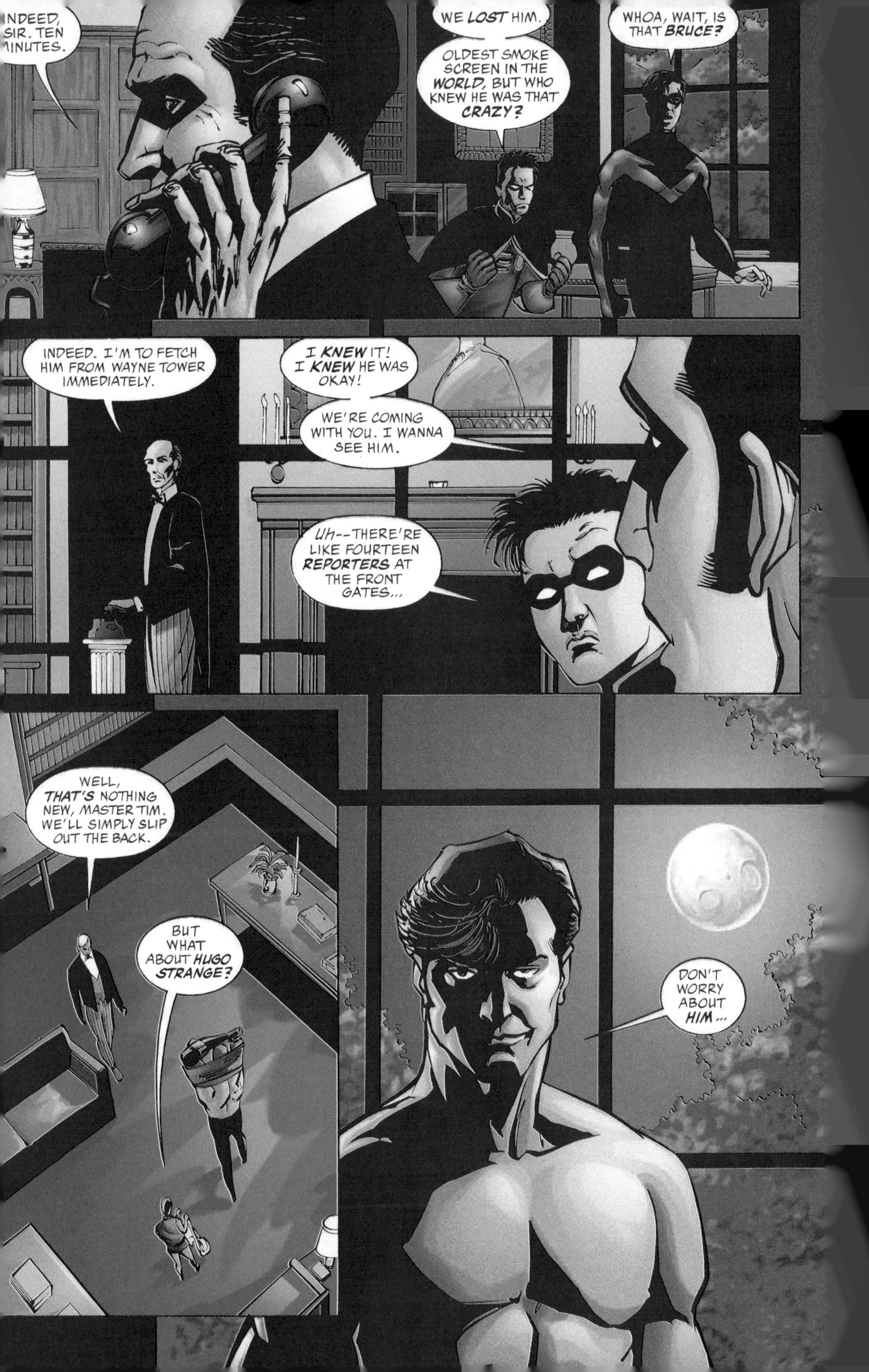

INDEED, SIR. TEN MINUTES.
WE LOST HIM.
OLDEST SMOKE SCREEN IN THE WORLD, BUT WHO KNEW HE WAS THAT CRAZY?
WHOA, WAIT, IS THAT BRUCE?
INDEED. I'M TO FETCH HIM FROM WAYNE TOWER IMMEDIATELY.
I KNEW IT! I KNEW HE WAS OKAY!
WE'RE COMING WITH YOU. I WANNA SEE HIM.
Uh--THERE'RE LIKE FOURTEEN REPORTERS AT THE FRONT GATES...
WELL, THAT'S NOTHING NEW, MASTER TIM. WE'LL SIMPLY SLIP OUT THE BACK.
BUT WHAT ABOUT HUGO STRANGE?
DON'T WORRY ABOUT HIM...

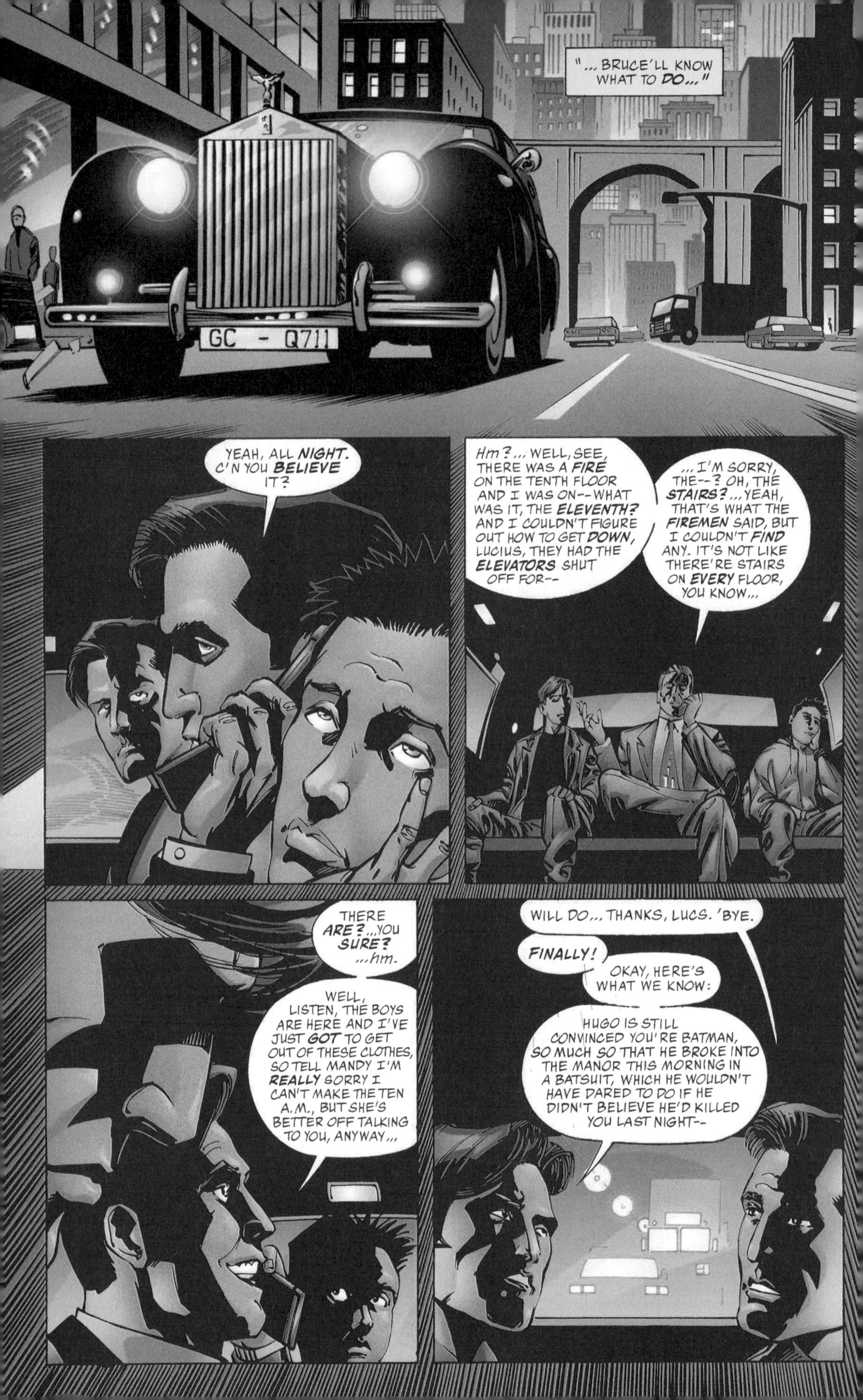
"... BRUCE'LL KNOW WHAT TO DO..."
GC - Q711
YEAH, ALL NIGHT. C'N YOU BELIEVE IT?
Hm?... WELL, SEE, THERE WAS A FIRE ON THE TENTH FLOOR AND I WAS ON--WHAT WAS IT, THE ELEVENTH? AND I COULDN'T FIGURE OUT HOW TO GET DOWN, LUCIUS, THEY HAD THE ELEVATORS SHUT OFF FOR--
... I'M SORRY, THE--? OH, THE STAIRS?... YEAH, THAT'S WHAT THE FIREMEN SAID, BUT I COULDN'T FIND ANY. IT'S NOT LIKE THERE'RE STAIRS ON EVERY FLOOR, YOU KNOW...
THERE ARE?...YOU SURE? ...hm.
WELL, LISTEN, THE BOYS ARE HERE AND I'VE JUST GOT TO GET OUT OF THESE CLOTHES, SO TELL MANDY I'M REALLY SORRY I CAN'T MAKE THE TEN A.M., BUT SHE'S BETTER OFF TALKING TO YOU, ANYWAY...
WILL DO... THANKS, LUCS. 'BYE.
FINALLY!
OKAY, HERE'S WHAT WE KNOW:
HUGO IS STILL CONVINCED YOU'RE BATMAN, SO MUCH SO THAT HE BROKE INTO THE MANOR THIS MORNING IN A BATSUIT, WHICH HE WOULDN'T HAVE DARED TO DO IF HE DIDN'T BELIEVE HE'D KILLED YOU LAST NIGHT--

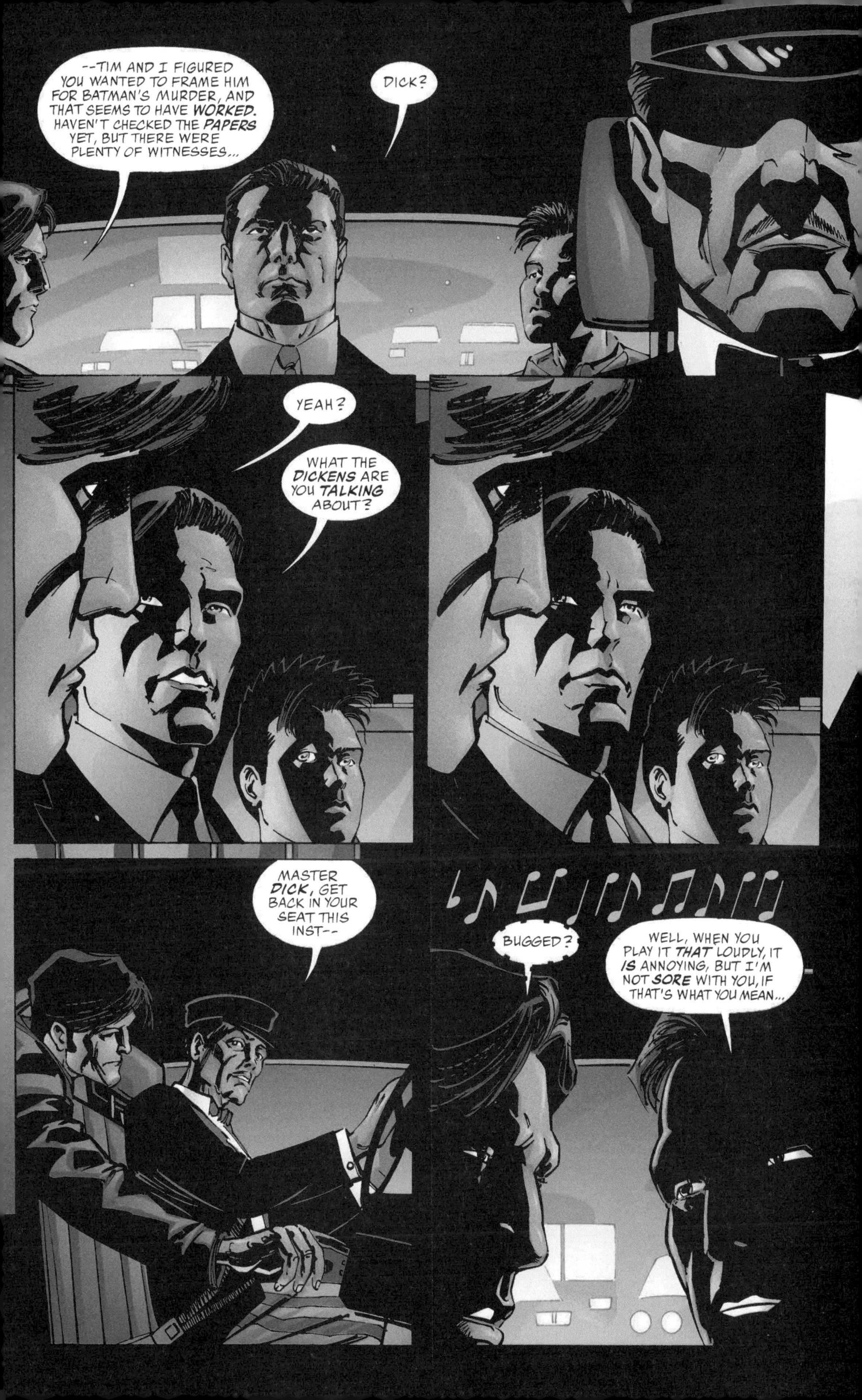
--TIM AND I FIGURED YOU WANTED TO FRAME HIM FOR BATMAN'S MURDER, AND THAT SEEMS TO HAVE WORKED. HAVEN'T CHECKED THE PAPERS YET, BUT THERE WERE PLENTY OF WITNESSES...
DICK?
YEAH?
WHAT THE DICKENS ARE YOU TALKING ABOUT?
MASTER DICK, GET BACK IN YOUR SEAT THIS INST--
BUGGED?
WELL, WHEN YOU PLAY IT THAT LOUDLY, IT IS ANNOYING, BUT I'M NOT SORE WITH YOU, IF THAT'S WHAT YOU MEAN...

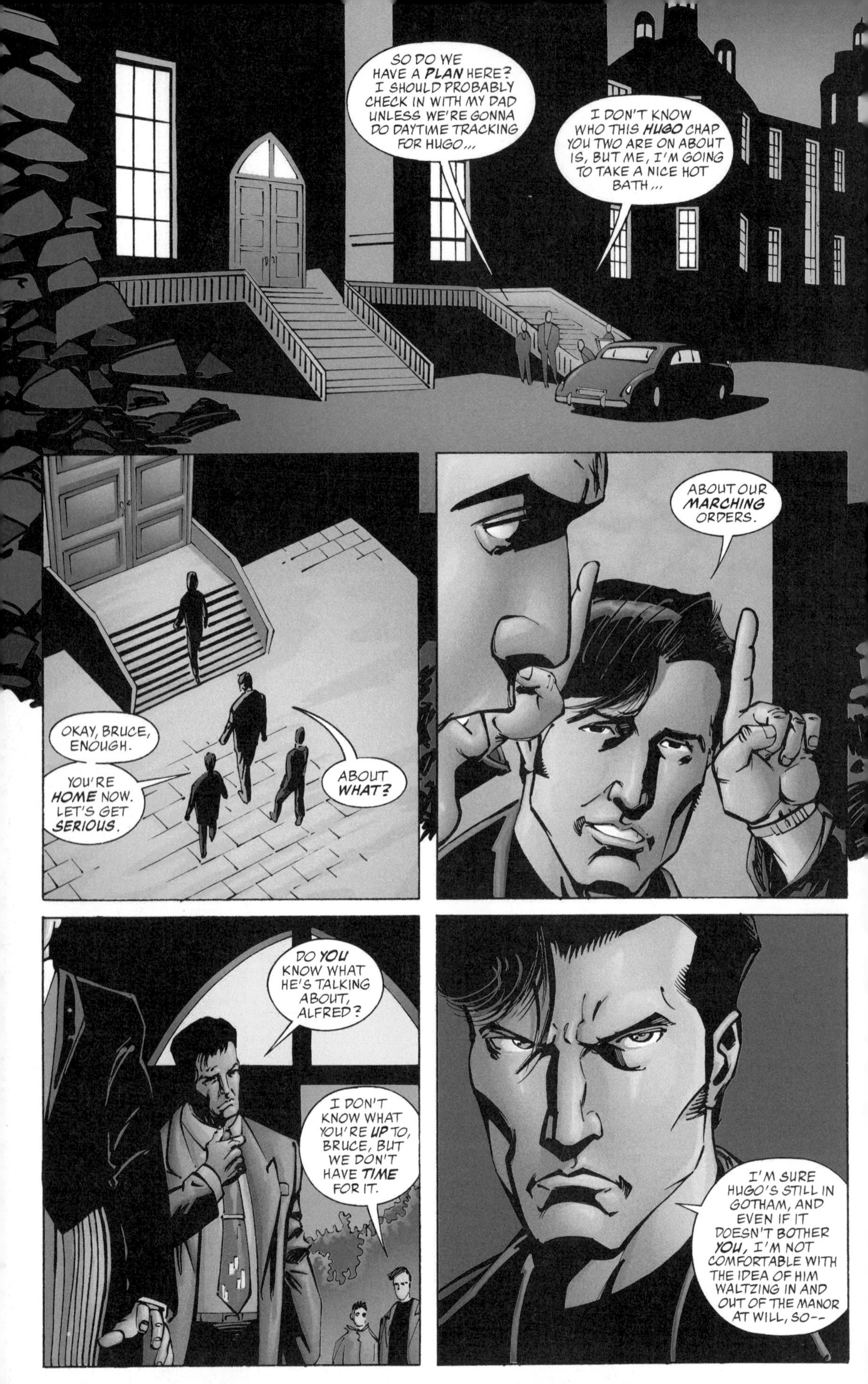
SO DO WE HAVE A PLAN HERE? I SHOULD PROBABLY CHECK IN WITH MY DAD UNLESS WE'RE GONNA DO DAYTIME TRACKING FOR HUGO...
I DON'T KNOW WHO THIS HUGO CHAP YOU TWO ARE ON ABOUT IS, BUT ME, I'M GOING TO TAKE A NICE HOT BATH...
OKAY, BRUCE, ENOUGH.
YOU'RE HOME NOW. LET'S GET SERIOUS.
ABOUT WHAT?
ABOUT OUR MARCHING ORDERS.
DO YOU KNOW WHAT HE'S TALKING ABOUT, ALFRED?
I DON'T KNOW WHAT YOU'RE UP TO, BRUCE, BUT WE DON'T HAVE TIME FOR IT.
I'M SURE HUGO'S STILL IN GOTHAM, AND EVEN IF IT DOESN'T BOTHER YOU, I'M NOT COMFORTABLE WITH THE IDEA OF HIM WALTZING IN AND OUT OF THE MANOR AT WILL, SO--

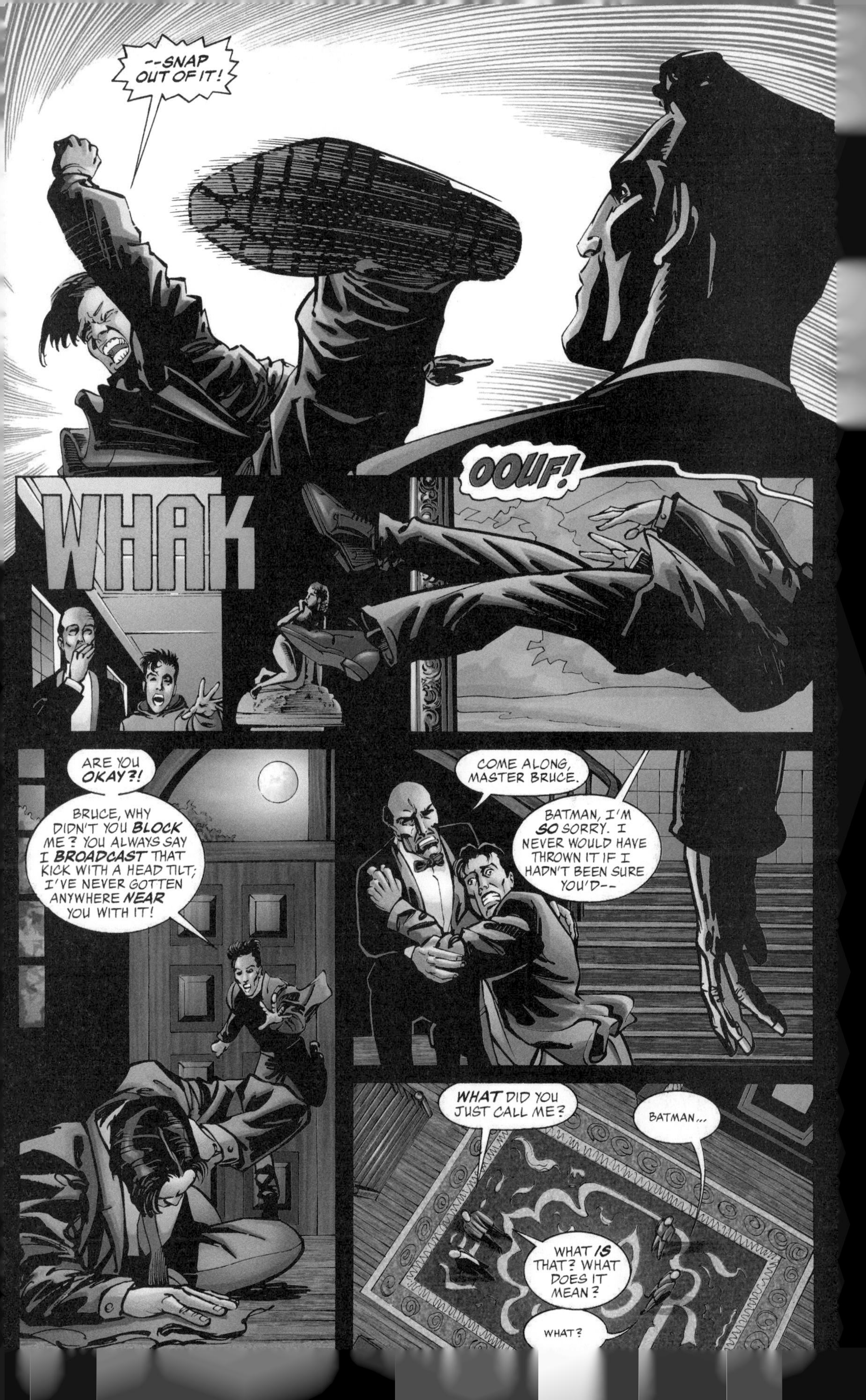
--SNAP OUT OF IT!
WHAK
OOUF!
ARE YOU OKAY?!
BRUCE, WHY DIDN'T YOU BLOCK ME? YOU ALWAYS SAY I BROADCAST THAT KICK WITH A HEAD TILT; I'VE NEVER GOTTEN ANYWHERE NEAR YOU WITH IT!
COME ALONG, MASTER BRUCE.
BATMAN, I'M SO SORRY. I NEVER WOULD HAVE THROWN IT IF I HADN'T BEEN SURE YOU'D--
WHAT DID YOU JUST CALL ME?
BATMAN...
WHAT IS THAT? WHAT DOES IT MEAN?
WHAT?

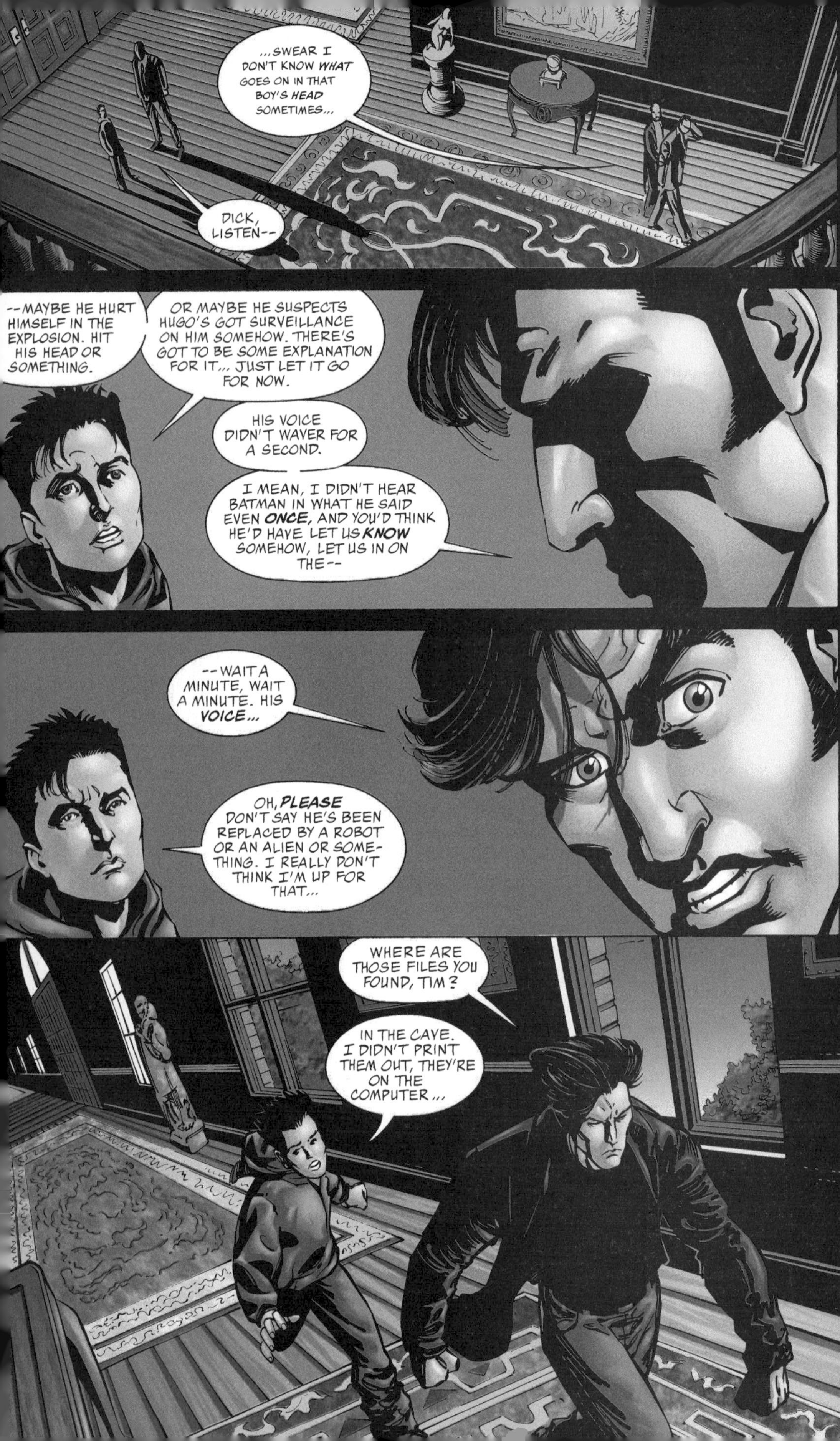
...SWEAR I DON'T KNOW WHAT GOES ON IN THAT BOY'S HEAD SOMETIMES...
DICK, LISTEN--
--MAYBE HE HURT HIMSELF IN THE EXPLOSION. HIT HIS HEAD OR SOMETHING.
OR MAYBE HE SUSPECTS HUGO'S GOT SURVEILLANCE ON HIM SOMEHOW. THERE'S GOT TO BE SOME EXPLANATION FOR IT... JUST LET IT GO FOR NOW.
HIS VOICE DIDN'T WAVER FOR A SECOND.
I MEAN, I DIDN'T HEAR BATMAN IN WHAT HE SAID EVEN ONCE, AND YOU'D THINK HE'D HAVE LET US KNOW SOMEHOW, LET US IN ON THE--
--WAIT A MINUTE, WAIT A MINUTE. HIS VOICE...
OH, PLEASE DON'T SAY HE'S BEEN REPLACED BY A ROBOT OR AN ALIEN OR SOME-THING. I REALLY DON'T THINK I'M UP FOR THAT...
WHERE ARE THOSE FILES YOU FOUND, TIM?
IN THE CAVE. I DIDN'T PRINT THEM OUT, THEY'RE ON THE COMPUTER...

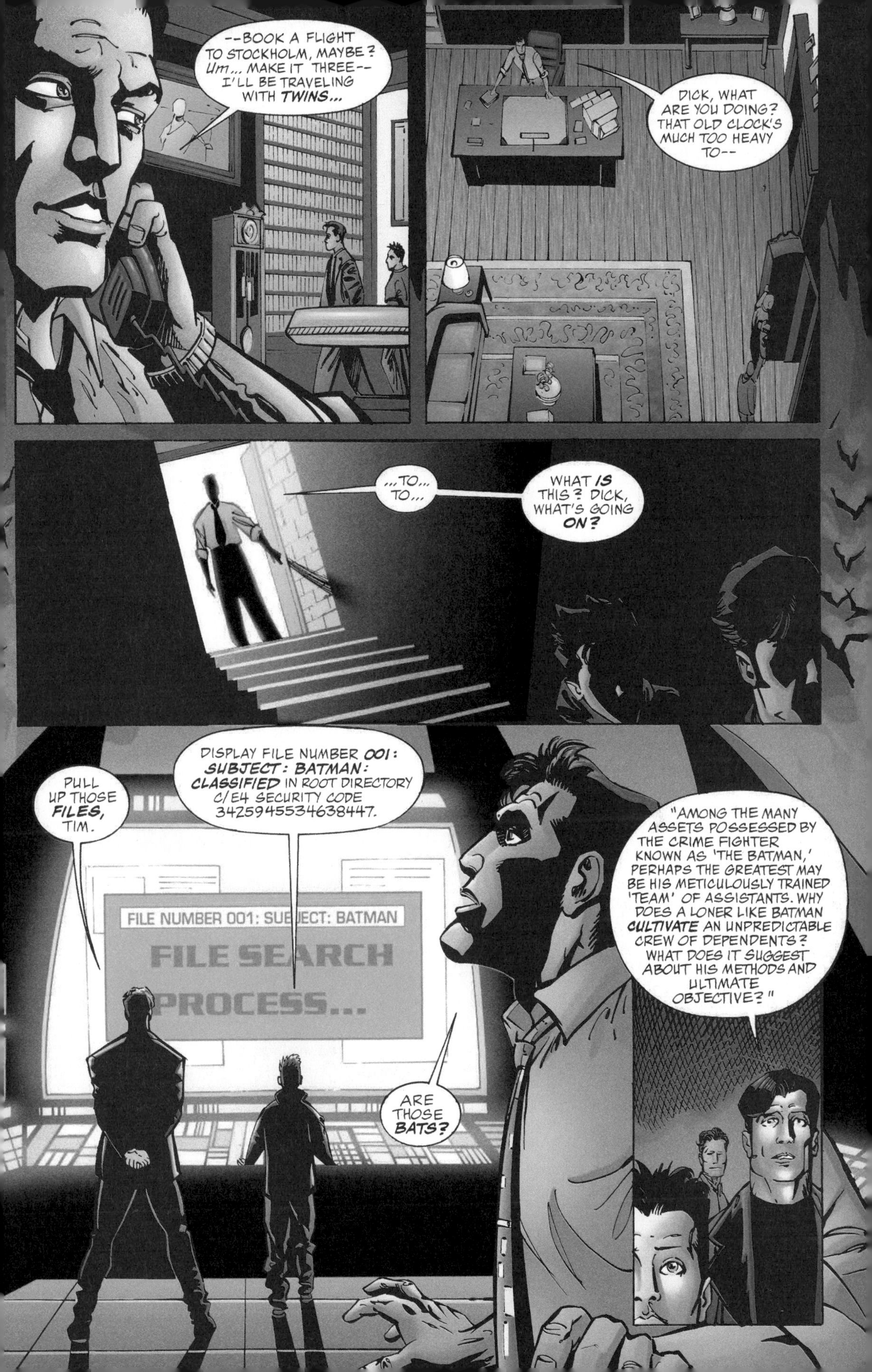
--BOOK A FLIGHT TO STOCKHOLM, MAYBE? Um... MAKE IT THREE-- I'LL BE TRAVELING WITH TWINS...
DICK, WHAT ARE YOU DOING? THAT OLD CLOCK'S MUCH TOO HEAVY TO--
...TO... TO...
WHAT IS THIS? DICK, WHAT'S GOING ON?
PULL UP THOSE FILES, TIM.
DISPLAY FILE NUMBER 001: SUBJECT: BATMAN: CLASSIFIED IN ROOT DIRECTORY C/E4 SECURITY CODE 3425945534638447.
FILE NUMBER 001: SUBJECT: BATMAN
FILE SEARCH PROCESS...
ARE THOSE BATS?
"AMONG THE MANY ASSETS POSSESSED BY THE CRIME FIGHTER KNOWN AS 'THE BATMAN,' PERHAPS THE GREATEST MAY BE HIS METICULOUSLY TRAINED 'TEAM' OF ASSISTANTS. WHY DOES A LONER LIKE BATMAN CULTIVATE AN UNPREDICTABLE CREW OF DEPENDENTS? WHAT DOES IT SUGGEST ABOUT HIS METHODS AND ULTIMATE OBJECTIVE?"

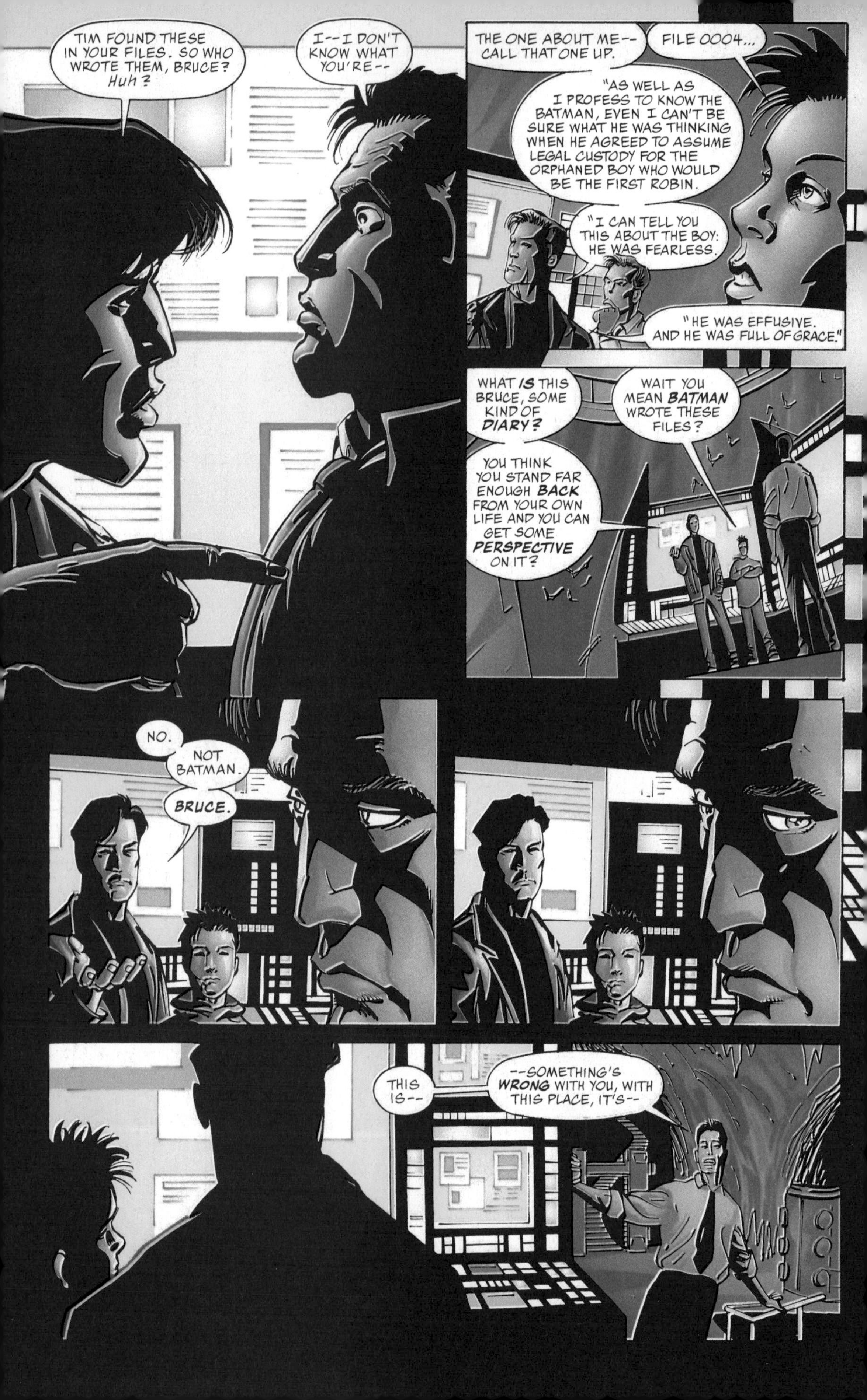
TIM FOUND THESE IN YOUR FILES. SO WHO WROTE THEM, BRUCE? *Huh?*
I--I DON'T KNOW WHAT YOU'RE--
THE ONE ABOUT ME--CALL THAT ONE UP.
FILE 0004...
"AS WELL AS I PROFESS TO KNOW THE BATMAN, EVEN I CAN'T BE SURE WHAT HE WAS THINKING WHEN HE AGREED TO ASSUME LEGAL CUSTODY FOR THE ORPHANED BOY WHO WOULD BE THE FIRST ROBIN.
"I CAN TELL YOU THIS ABOUT THE BOY: HE WAS FEARLESS.
"HE WAS EFFUSIVE. AND HE WAS FULL OF GRACE."
WHAT ***IS*** THIS BRUCE, SOME KIND OF ***DIARY?***
WAIT YOU MEAN ***BATMAN*** WROTE THESE FILES?
YOU THINK YOU STAND FAR ENOUGH ***BACK*** FROM YOUR OWN LIFE AND YOU CAN GET SOME ***PERSPECTIVE*** ON IT?
NO.
NOT BATMAN.
BRUCE.
THIS IS--
--SOMETHING'S ***WRONG*** WITH YOU, WITH THIS PLACE, IT'S--

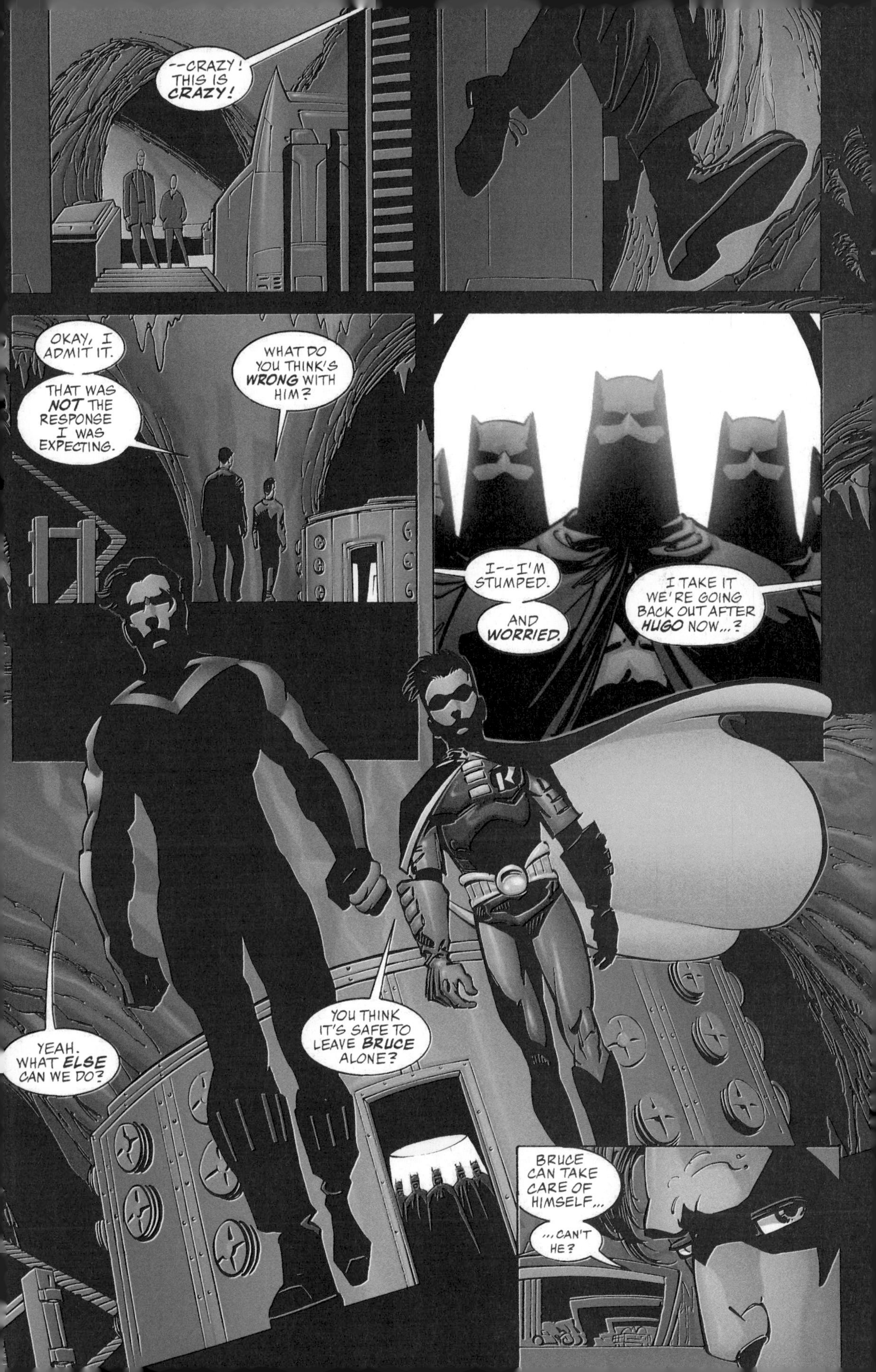
--CRAZY! THIS IS CRAZY!
OKAY, I ADMIT IT.
THAT WAS NOT THE RESPONSE I WAS EXPECTING.
WHAT DO YOU THINK'S WRONG WITH HIM?
I--I'M STUMPED.
AND WORRIED.
I TAKE IT WE'RE GOING BACK OUT AFTER HUGO NOW...?
YEAH. WHAT ELSE CAN WE DO?
YOU THINK IT'S SAFE TO LEAVE BRUCE ALONE?
BRUCE CAN TAKE CARE OF HIMSELF...
...CAN'T HE?

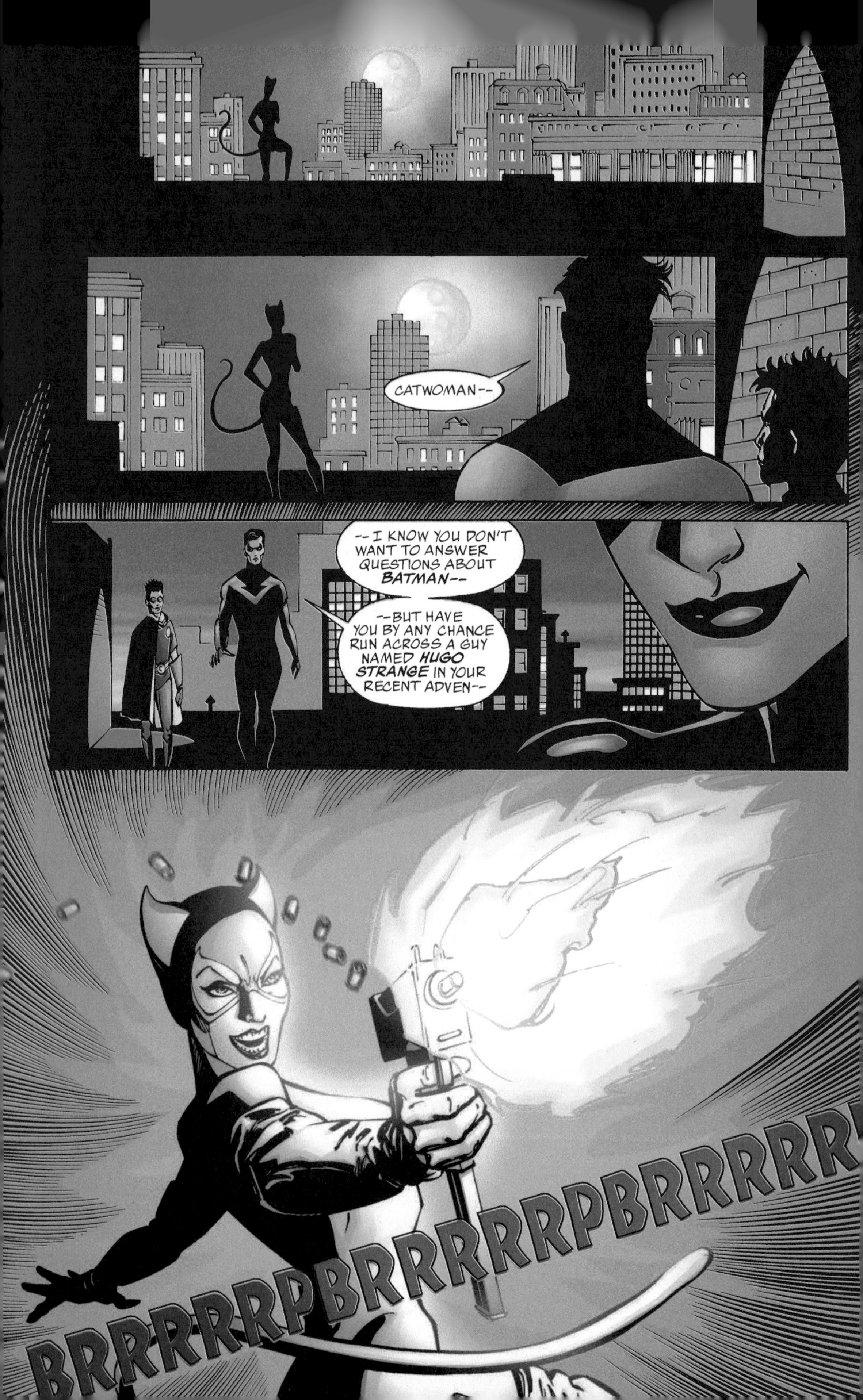
CATWOMAN--
--I KNOW YOU DON'T WANT TO ANSWER QUESTIONS ABOUT BATMAN--
--BUT HAVE YOU BY ANY CHANCE RUN ACROSS A GUY NAMED HUGO STRANGE IN YOUR RECENT ADVEN--
BRRRRRPBRRRRRRRPBRRRRRR

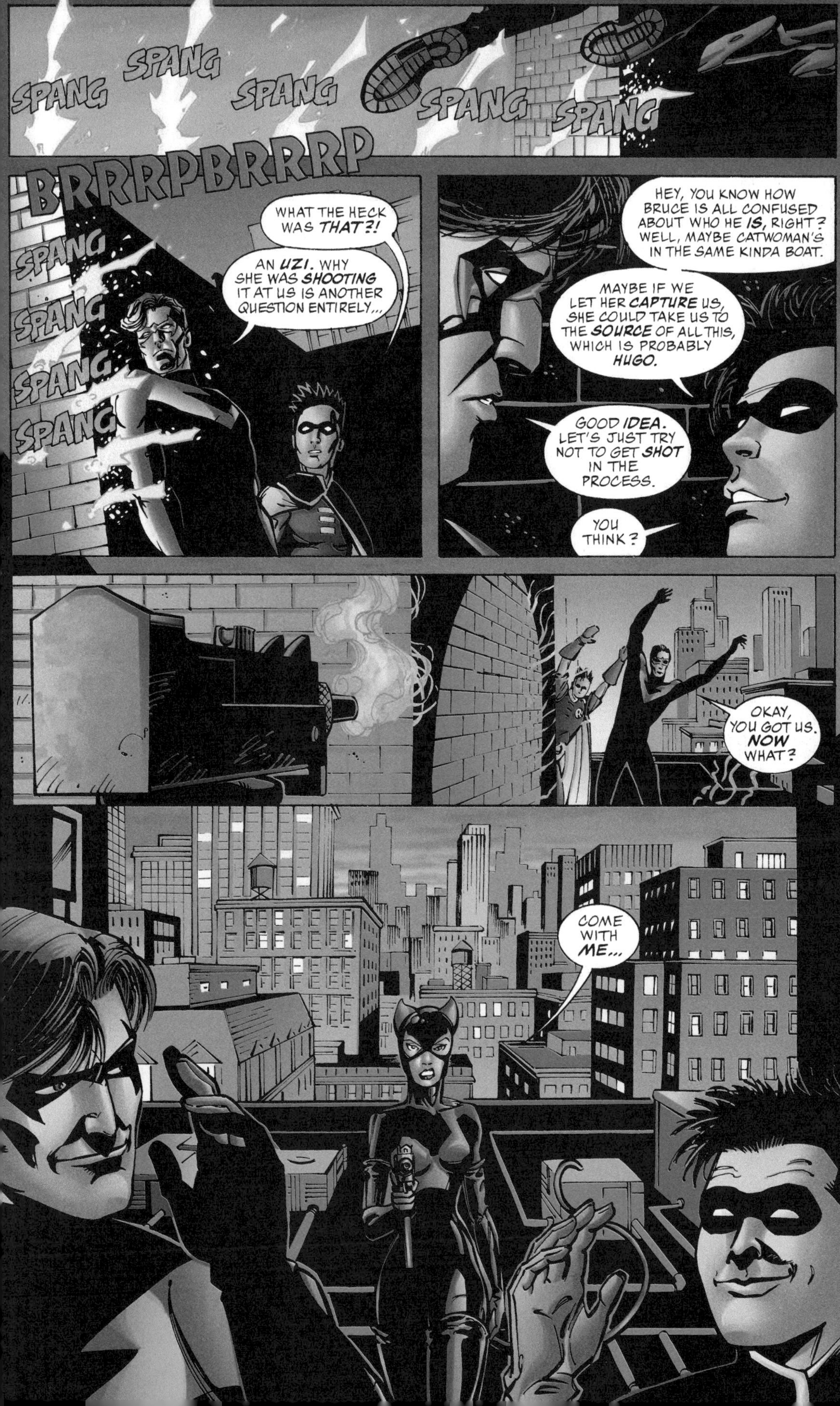
SPANG
SPANG
SPANG
SPANG
SPANG
BRRRPBRRRP
SPANG
SPANG
SPANG
SPANG
WHAT THE HECK WAS THAT?!
AN UZI. WHY SHE WAS SHOOTING IT AT US IS ANOTHER QUESTION ENTIRELY...
HEY, YOU KNOW HOW BRUCE IS ALL CONFUSED ABOUT WHO HE IS, RIGHT? WELL, MAYBE CATWOMAN'S IN THE SAME KINDA BOAT.
MAYBE IF WE LET HER CAPTURE US, SHE COULD TAKE US TO THE SOURCE OF ALL THIS, WHICH IS PROBABLY HUGO.
GOOD IDEA. LET'S JUST TRY NOT TO GET SHOT IN THE PROCESS.
YOU THINK?
OKAY, YOU GOT US. NOW WHAT?
COME WITH ME...

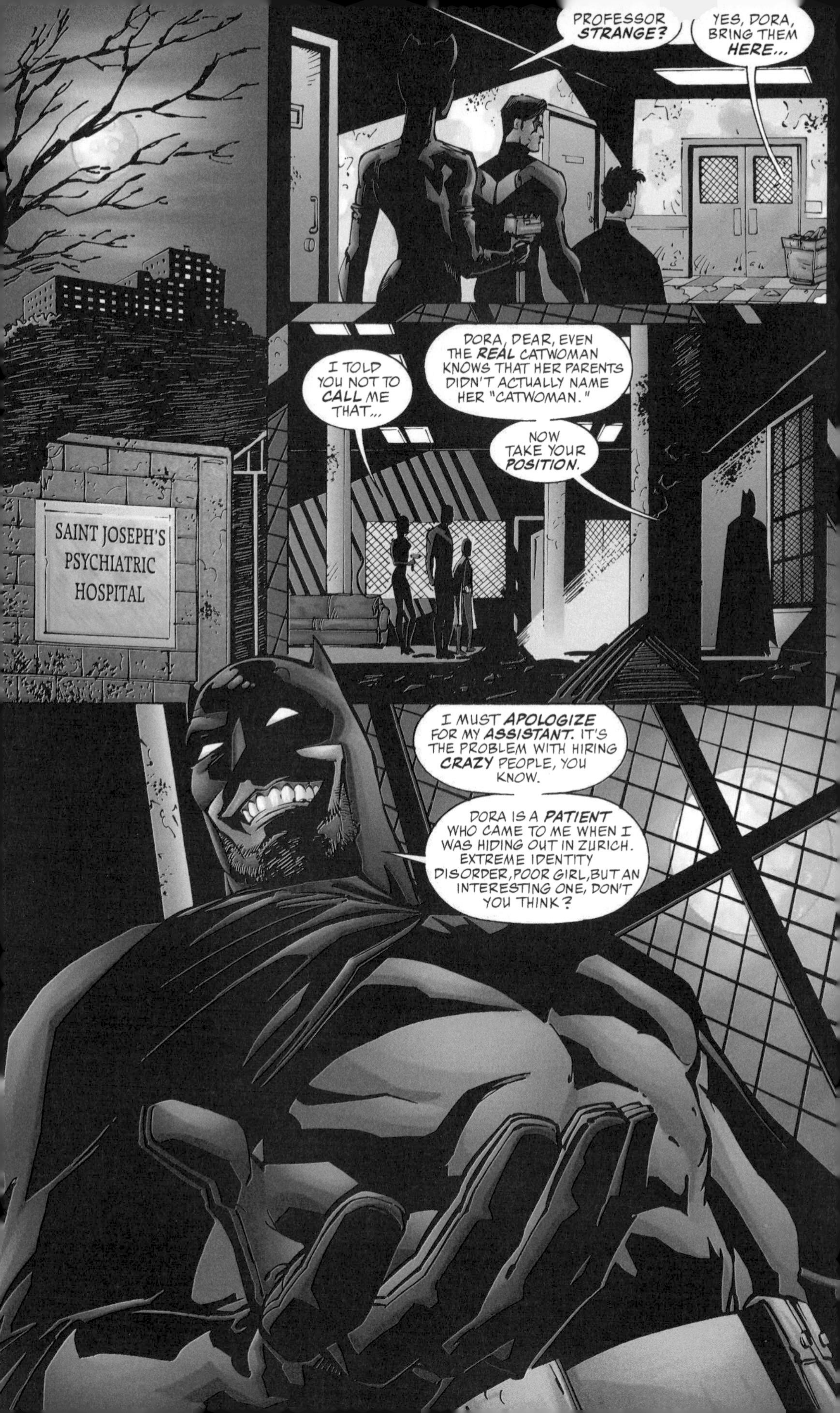
SAINT JOSEPH'S PSYCHIATRIC HOSPITAL
PROFESSOR STRANGE?
YES, DORA, BRING THEM HERE...
I TOLD YOU NOT TO CALL ME THAT...
DORA, DEAR, EVEN THE REAL CATWOMAN KNOWS THAT HER PARENTS DIDN'T ACTUALLY NAME HER "CATWOMAN."
NOW TAKE YOUR POSITION.
I MUST APOLOGIZE FOR MY ASSISTANT. IT'S THE PROBLEM WITH HIRING CRAZY PEOPLE, YOU KNOW.
DORA IS A PATIENT WHO CAME TO ME WHEN I WAS HIDING OUT IN ZURICH. EXTREME IDENTITY DISORDER, POOR GIRL, BUT AN INTERESTING ONE, DON'T YOU THINK?

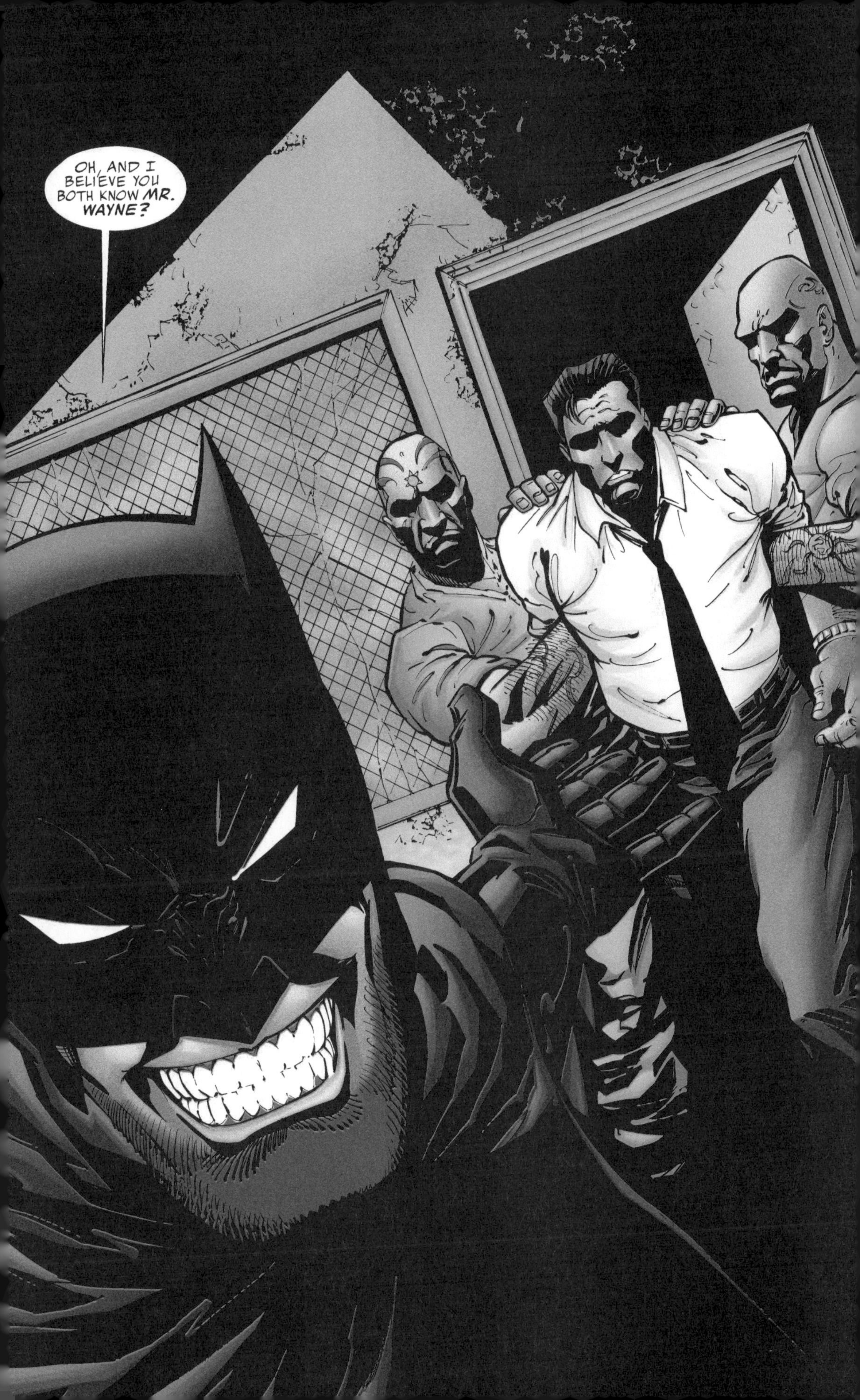
OH, AND I BELIEVE YOU BOTH KNOW MR. WAYNE?

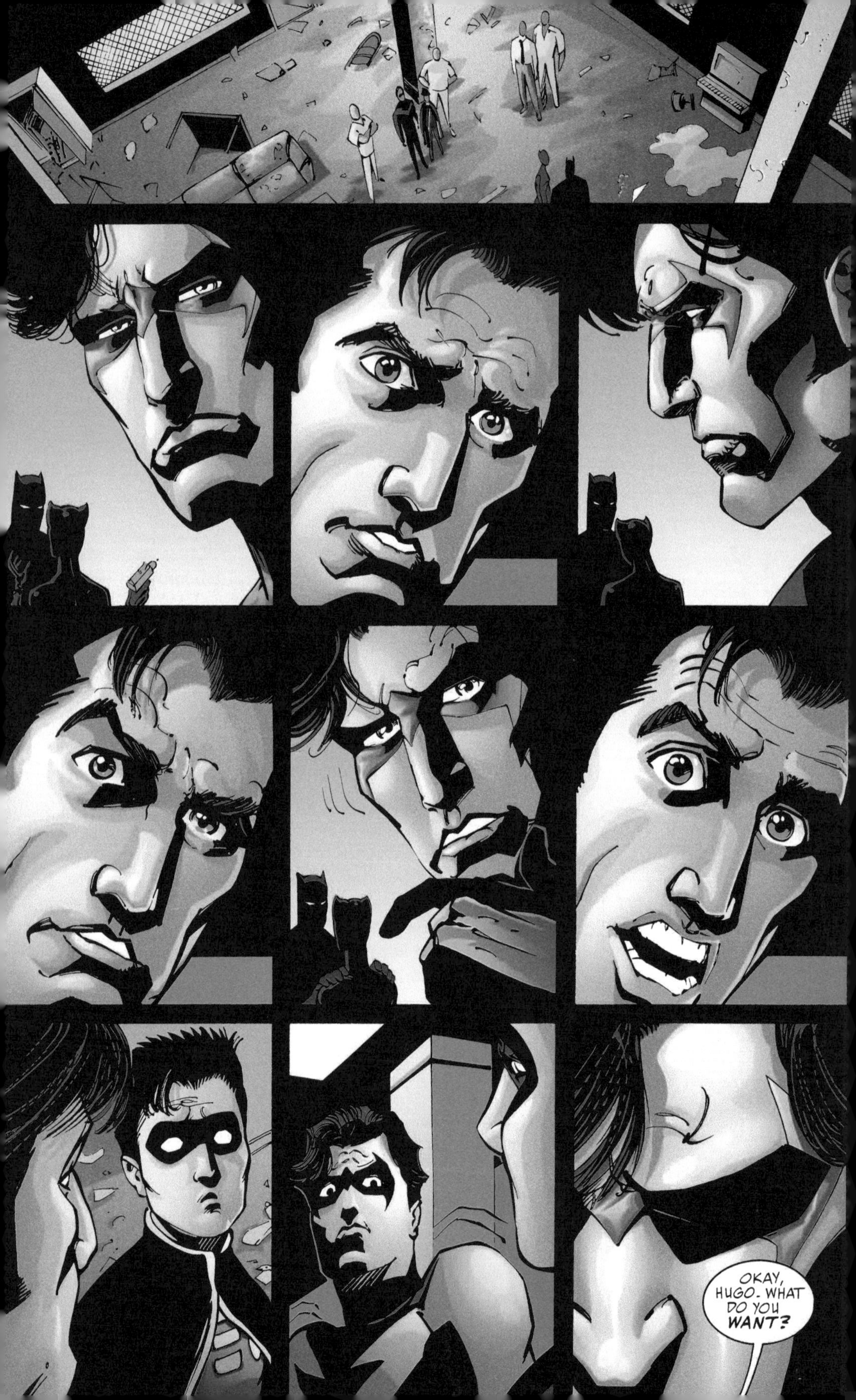
OKAY, HUGO. WHAT DO YOU WANT?

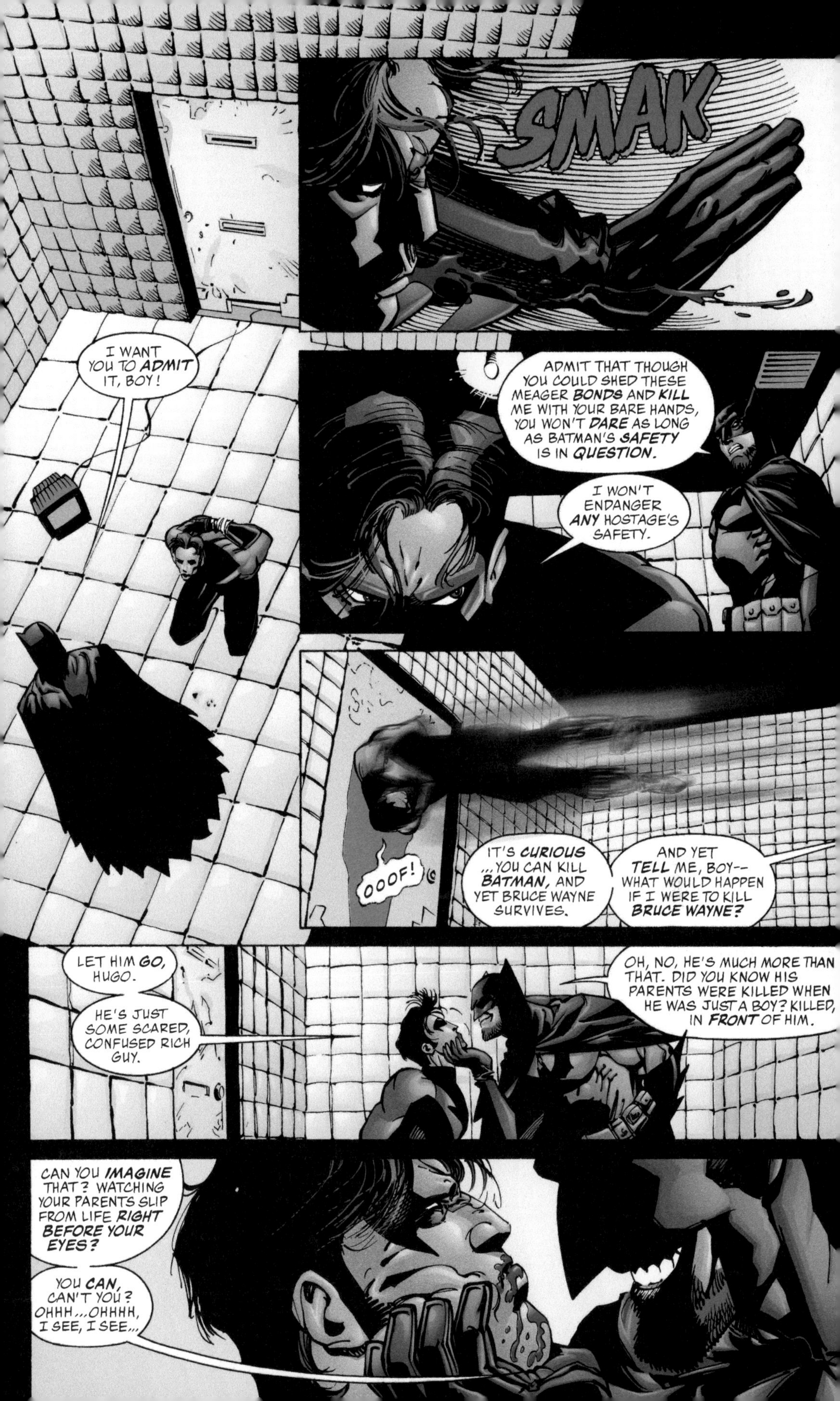

SMAK
I WANT YOU TO ADMIT IT, BOY!
ADMIT THAT THOUGH YOU COULD SHED THESE MEAGER BONDS AND KILL ME WITH YOUR BARE HANDS, YOU WON'T DARE AS LONG AS BATMAN'S SAFETY IS IN QUESTION.
I WON'T ENDANGER ANY HOSTAGE'S SAFETY.
OOOF!
IT'S CURIOUS ...YOU CAN KILL BATMAN, AND YET BRUCE WAYNE SURVIVES.
AND YET TELL ME, BOY-- WHAT WOULD HAPPEN IF I WERE TO KILL BRUCE WAYNE?
LET HIM GO, HUGO.
HE'S JUST SOME SCARED, CONFUSED RICH GUY.
OH, NO, HE'S MUCH MORE THAN THAT. DID YOU KNOW HIS PARENTS WERE KILLED WHEN HE WAS JUST A BOY? KILLED, IN FRONT OF HIM.
CAN YOU IMAGINE THAT? WATCHING YOUR PARENTS SLIP FROM LIFE RIGHT BEFORE YOUR EYES?
YOU CAN, CAN'T YOU? OHHH...OHHHH, I SEE, I SEE...

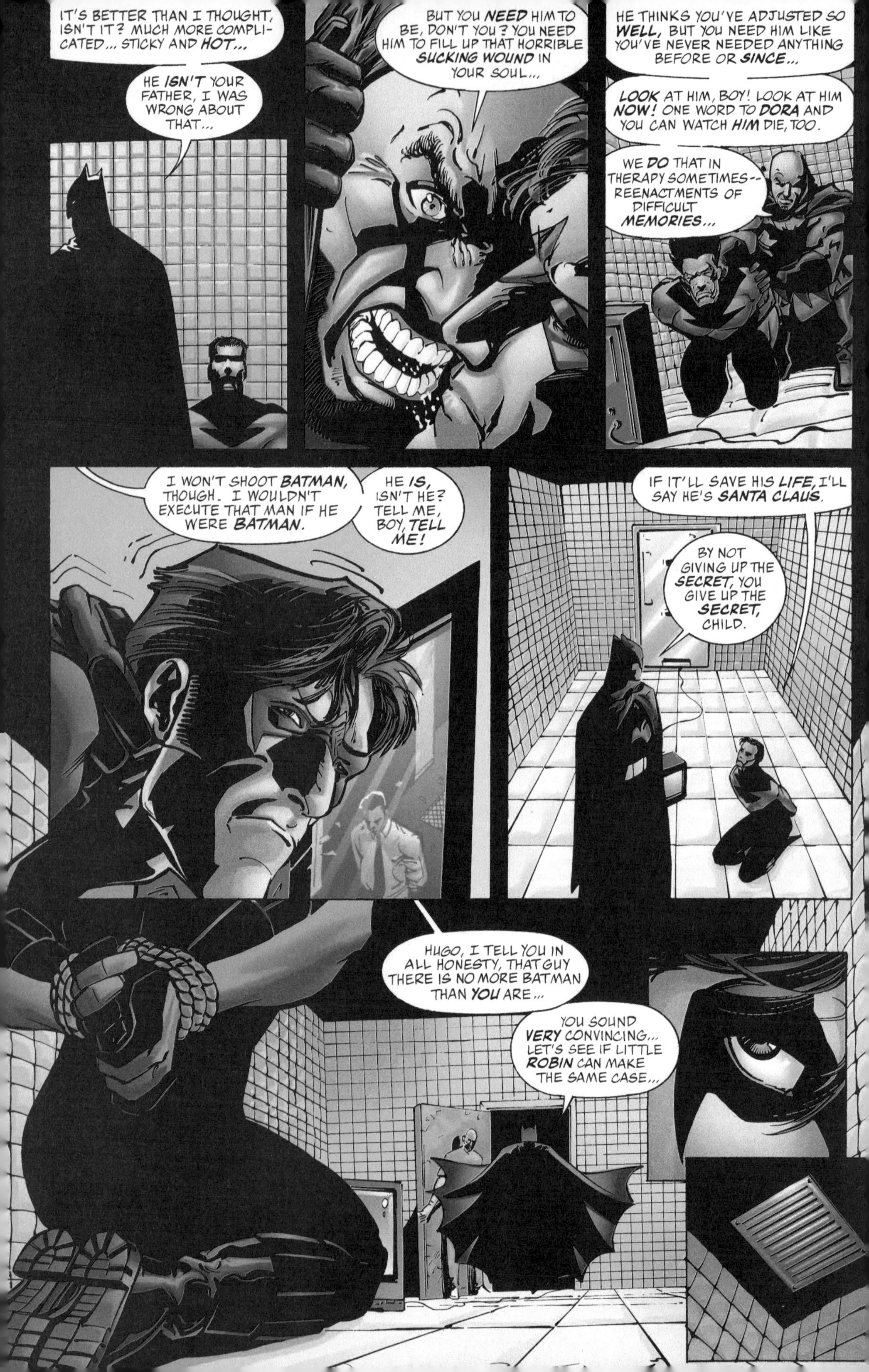
IT'S BETTER THAN I THOUGHT, ISN'T IT? MUCH MORE COMPLICATED... STICKY AND HOT...
HE ISN'T YOUR FATHER, I WAS WRONG ABOUT THAT...
BUT YOU NEED HIM TO BE, DON'T YOU? YOU NEED HIM TO FILL UP THAT HORRIBLE SUCKING WOUND IN YOUR SOUL...
HE THINKS YOU'VE ADJUSTED SO WELL, BUT YOU NEED HIM LIKE YOU'VE NEVER NEEDED ANYTHING BEFORE OR SINCE...
LOOK AT HIM, BOY! LOOK AT HIM NOW! ONE WORD TO DORA AND YOU CAN WATCH HIM DIE, TOO.
WE DO THAT IN THERAPY SOMETIMES-- REENACTMENTS OF DIFFICULT MEMORIES...
I WON'T SHOOT BATMAN, THOUGH. I WOULDN'T EXECUTE THAT MAN IF HE WERE BATMAN.
HE IS, ISN'T HE? TELL ME, BOY, TELL ME!
IF IT'LL SAVE HIS LIFE, I'LL SAY HE'S SANTA CLAUS.
BY NOT GIVING UP THE SECRET, YOU GIVE UP THE SECRET, CHILD.
HUGO, I TELL YOU IN ALL HONESTY, THAT GUY THERE IS NO MORE BATMAN THAN YOU ARE...
YOU SOUND VERY CONVINCING... LET'S SEE IF LITTLE ROBIN CAN MAKE THE SAME CASE...

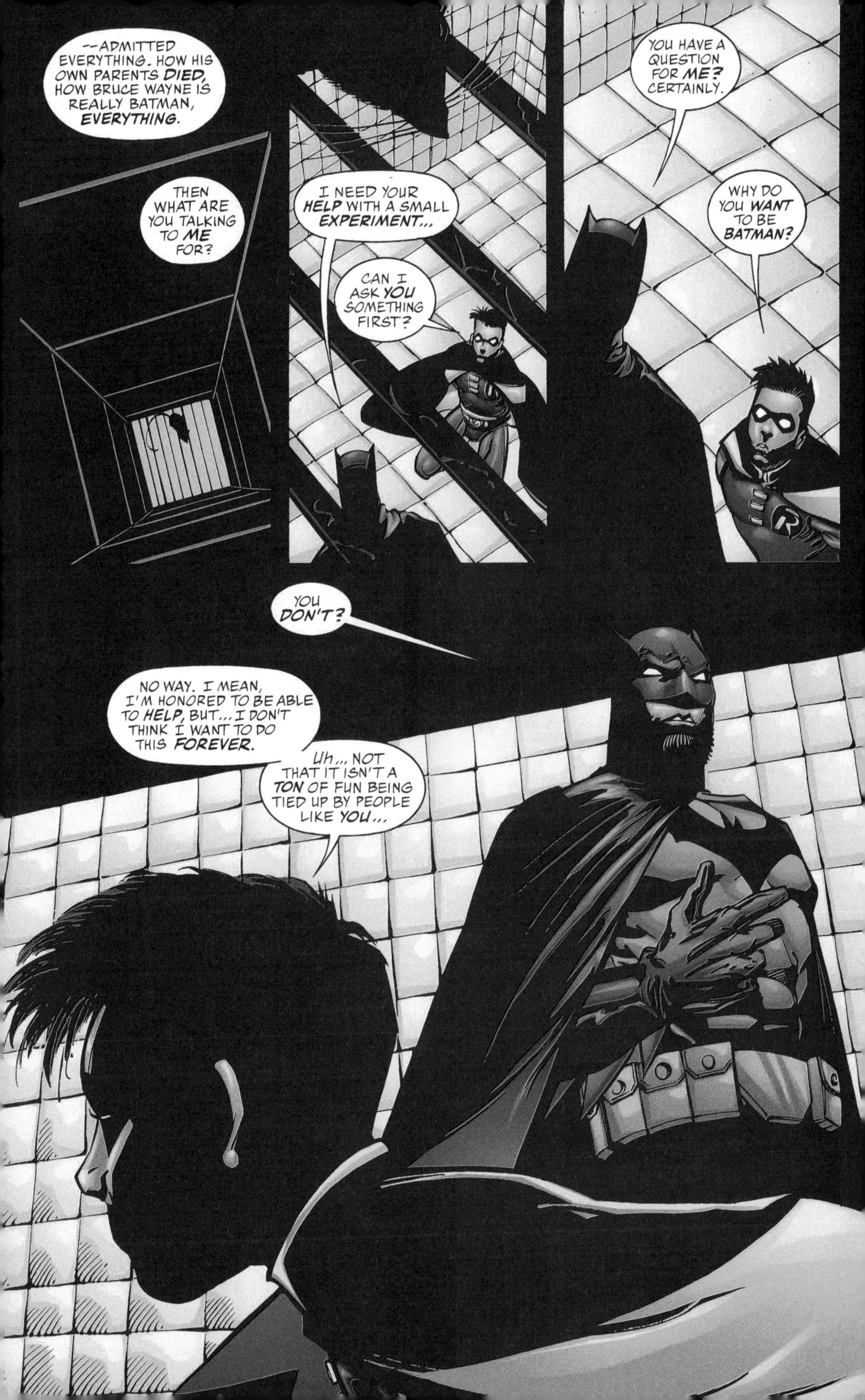
--ADMITTED EVERYTHING. HOW HIS OWN PARENTS DIED, HOW BRUCE WAYNE IS REALLY BATMAN, EVERYTHING.
THEN WHAT ARE YOU TALKING TO ME FOR?
I NEED YOUR HELP WITH A SMALL EXPERIMENT...
CAN I ASK YOU SOMETHING FIRST?
YOU HAVE A QUESTION FOR ME? CERTAINLY.
WHY DO YOU WANT TO BE BATMAN?
YOU DON'T?
NO WAY. I MEAN, I'M HONORED TO BE ABLE TO HELP, BUT... I DON'T THINK I WANT TO DO THIS FOREVER.
UH... NOT THAT IT ISN'T A TON OF FUN BEING TIED UP BY PEOPLE LIKE YOU...

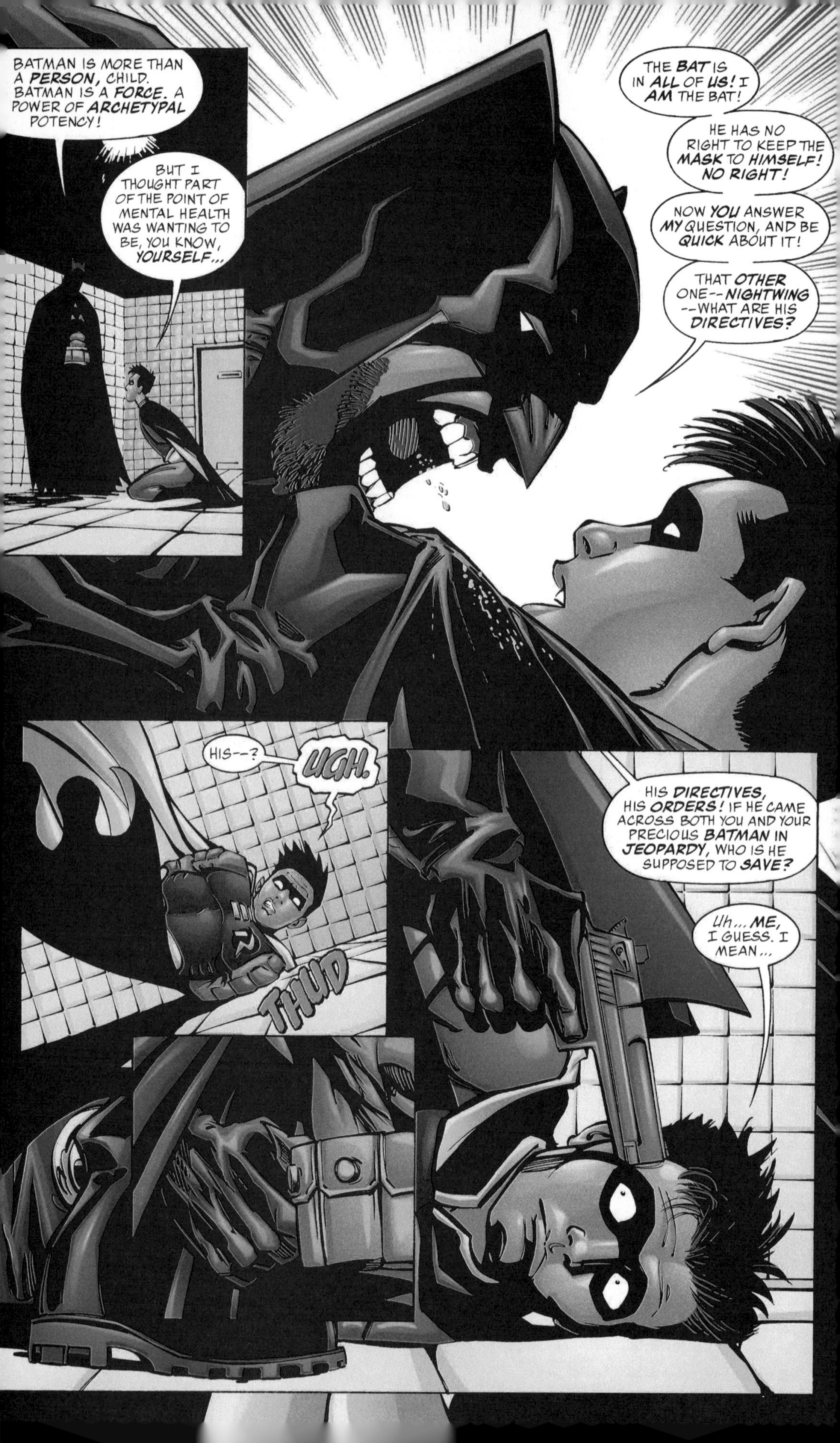
BATMAN IS MORE THAN A PERSON, CHILD. BATMAN IS A FORCE. A POWER OF ARCHETYPAL POTENCY!
BUT I THOUGHT PART OF THE POINT OF MENTAL HEALTH WAS WANTING TO BE, YOU KNOW, YOURSELF...
THE BAT IS IN ALL OF US! I AM THE BAT!
HE HAS NO RIGHT TO KEEP THE MASK TO HIMSELF! NO RIGHT!
NOW YOU ANSWER MY QUESTION, AND BE QUICK ABOUT IT!
THAT OTHER ONE--NIGHTWING--WHAT ARE HIS DIRECTIVES?
HIS--?
UGH.
THUD
HIS DIRECTIVES, HIS ORDERS! IF HE CAME ACROSS BOTH YOU AND YOUR PRECIOUS BATMAN IN JEOPARDY, WHO IS HE SUPPOSED TO SAVE?
Uh... ME, I GUESS. I MEAN...

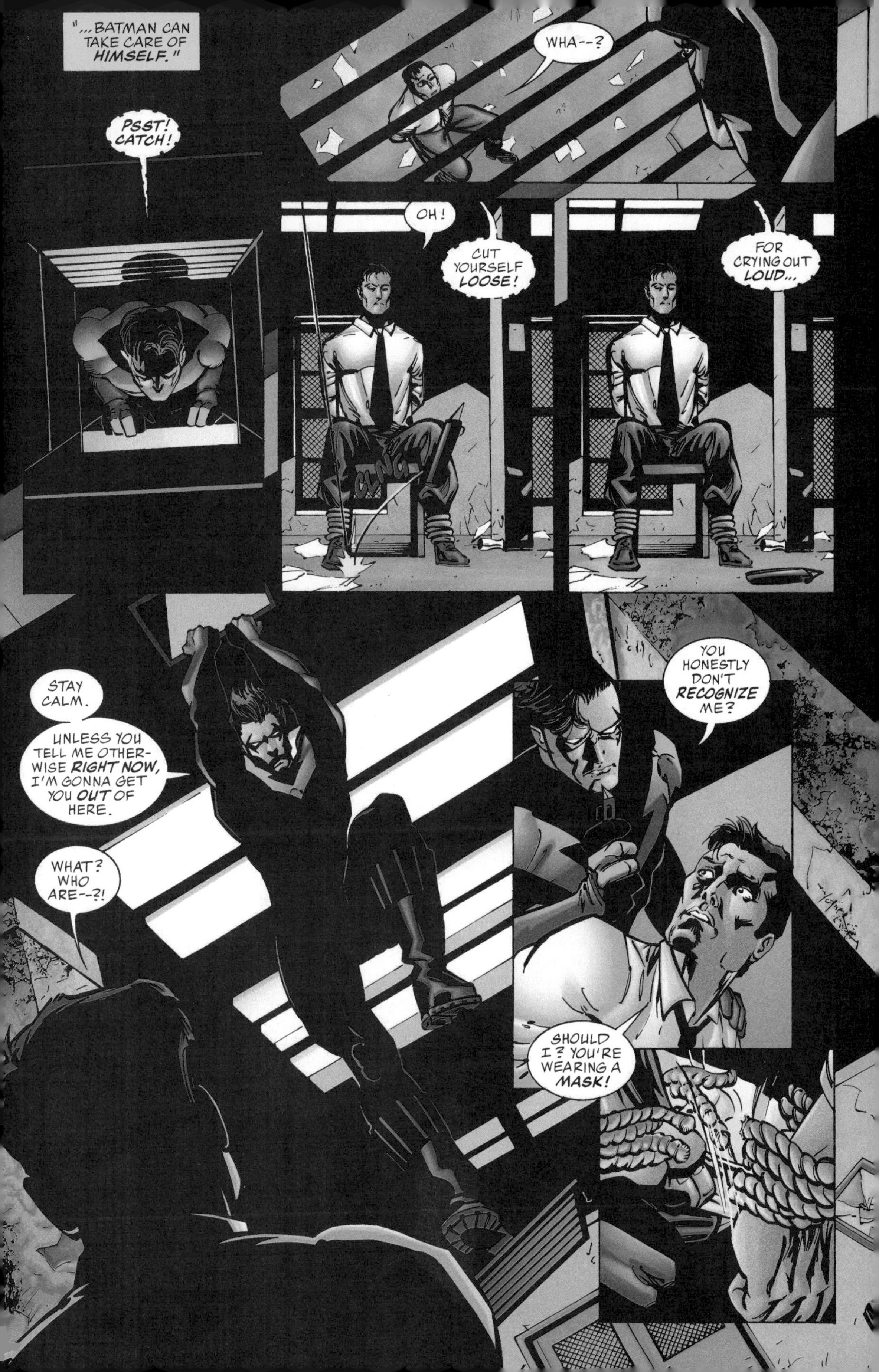

"...BATMAN CAN TAKE CARE OF HIMSELF."
WHA--?
PSST! CATCH!
OH!
CUT YOURSELF LOOSE!
CLNG
FOR CRYING OUT LOUD...
STAY CALM.
UNLESS YOU TELL ME OTHER-WISE RIGHT NOW, I'M GONNA GET YOU OUT OF HERE.
WHAT? WHO ARE--?!
YOU HONESTLY DON'T RECOGNIZE ME?
SHOULD I? YOU'RE WEARING A MASK!

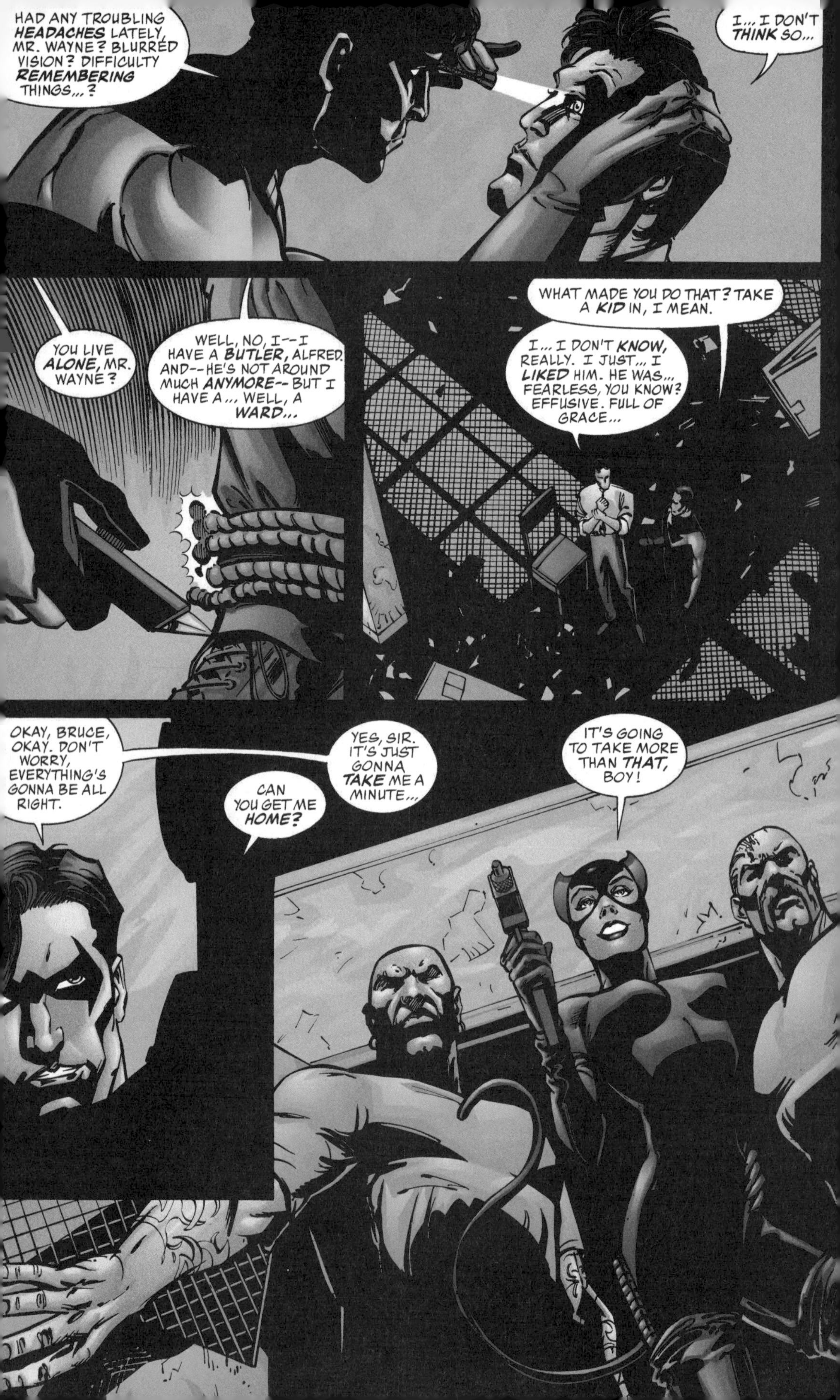
HAD ANY TROUBLING HEADACHES LATELY, MR. WAYNE? BLURRED VISION? DIFFICULTY REMEMBERING THINGS...?
I... I DON'T THINK SO...
YOU LIVE ALONE, MR. WAYNE?
WELL, NO, I--I HAVE A BUTLER, ALFRED. AND--HE'S NOT AROUND MUCH ANYMORE--BUT I HAVE A... WELL, A WARD...
WHAT MADE YOU DO THAT? TAKE A KID IN, I MEAN.
I... I DON'T KNOW, REALLY. I JUST... I LIKED HIM. HE WAS... FEARLESS, YOU KNOW? EFFUSIVE. FULL OF GRACE...
OKAY, BRUCE, OKAY. DON'T WORRY, EVERYTHING'S GONNA BE ALL RIGHT.
CAN YOU GET ME HOME?
YES, SIR. IT'S JUST GONNA TAKE ME A MINUTE...
IT'S GOING TO TAKE MORE THAN THAT, BOY!

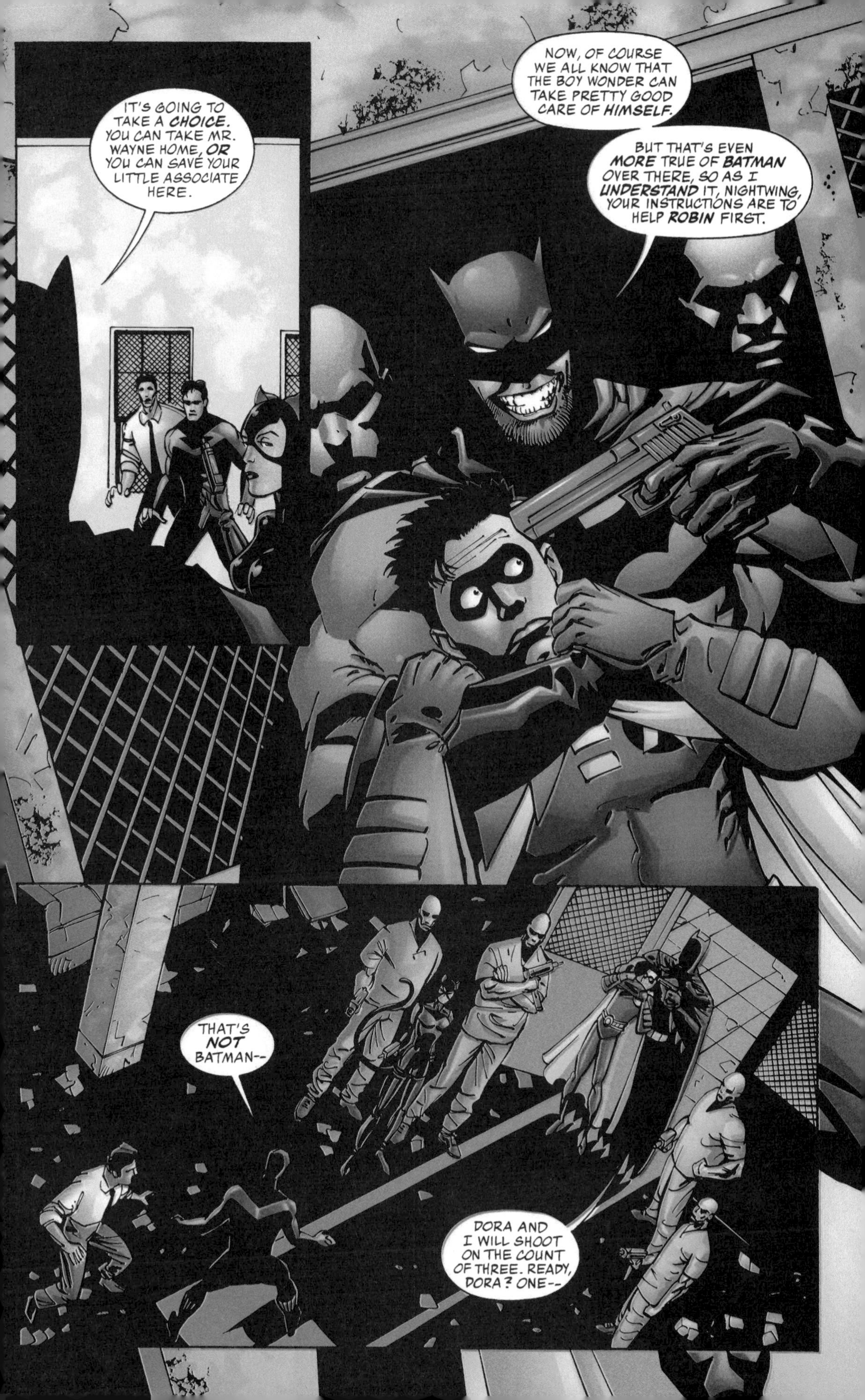

IT'S GOING TO TAKE A CHOICE. YOU CAN TAKE MR. WAYNE HOME, OR YOU CAN SAVE YOUR LITTLE ASSOCIATE HERE.
NOW, OF COURSE WE ALL KNOW THAT THE BOY WONDER CAN TAKE PRETTY GOOD CARE OF HIMSELF.
BUT THAT'S EVEN MORE TRUE OF BATMAN OVER THERE, SO AS I UNDERSTAND IT, NIGHTWING, YOUR INSTRUCTIONS ARE TO HELP ROBIN FIRST.
THAT'S NOT BATMAN--
DORA AND I WILL SHOOT ON THE COUNT OF THREE. READY, DORA? ONE--

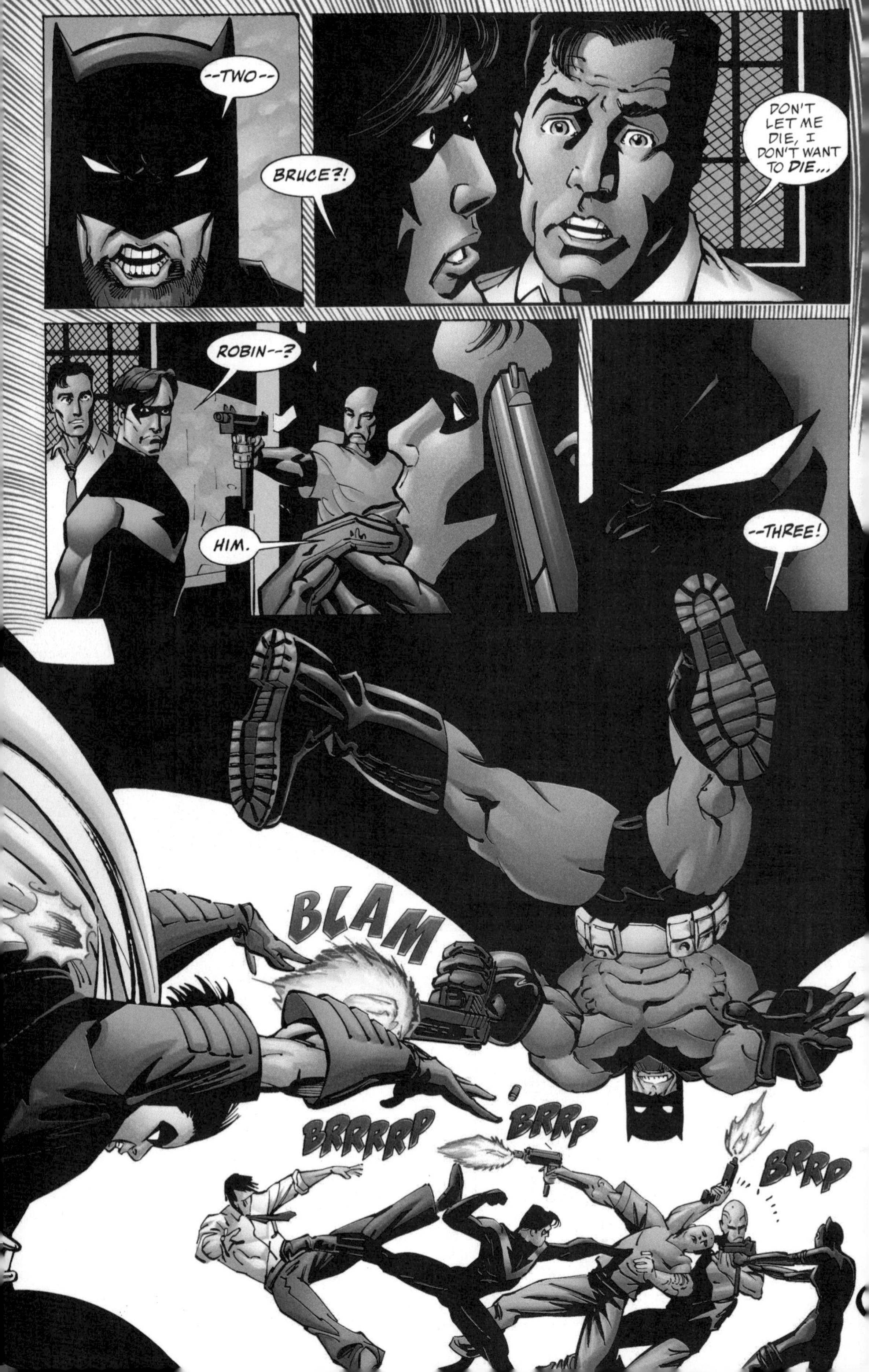
--TWO--
BRUCE?!
DON'T LET ME DIE, I DON'T WANT TO DIE...
ROBIN--?
HIM.
--THREE!
BLAM
BRRRRRP
BRRP
BRRP

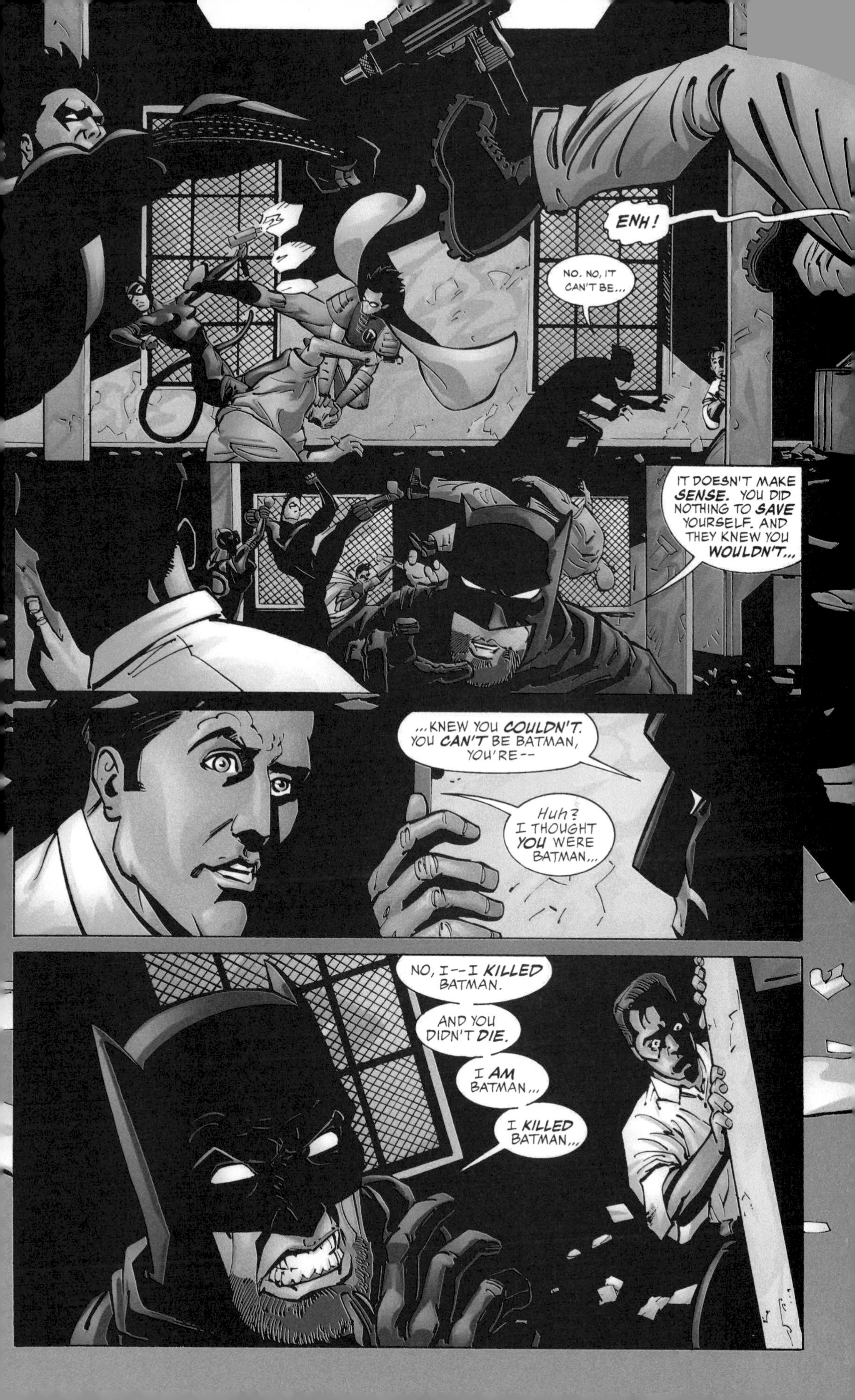
ENH!
NO. NO, IT CAN'T BE...
IT DOESN'T MAKE SENSE. YOU DID NOTHING TO SAVE YOURSELF. AND THEY KNEW YOU WOULDN'T...
...KNEW YOU COULDN'T. YOU CAN'T BE BATMAN, YOU'RE--
Huh? I THOUGHT YOU WERE BATMAN...
NO, I--I KILLED BATMAN.
AND YOU DIDN'T DIE.
I AM BATMAN...
I KILLED BATMAN...

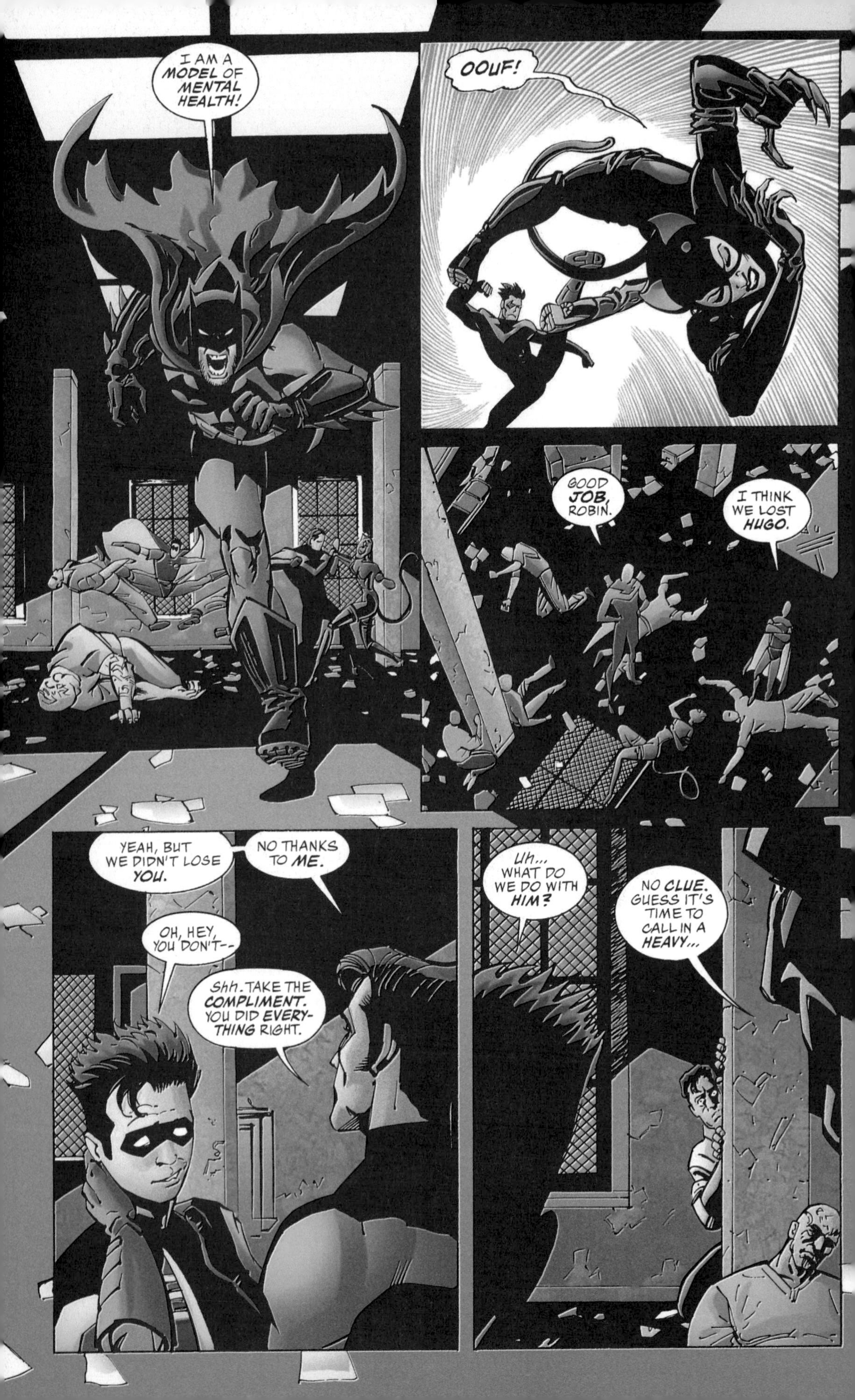
I AM A MODEL OF MENTAL HEALTH!
OOUF!
GOOD JOB, ROBIN.
I THINK WE LOST HUGO.
YEAH, BUT WE DIDN'T LOSE YOU.
NO THANKS TO ME.
OH, HEY, YOU DON'T--
Shh. TAKE THE COMPLIMENT. YOU DID EVERYTHING RIGHT.
Uh... WHAT DO WE DO WITH HIM?
NO CLUE. GUESS IT'S TIME TO CALL IN A HEAVY...

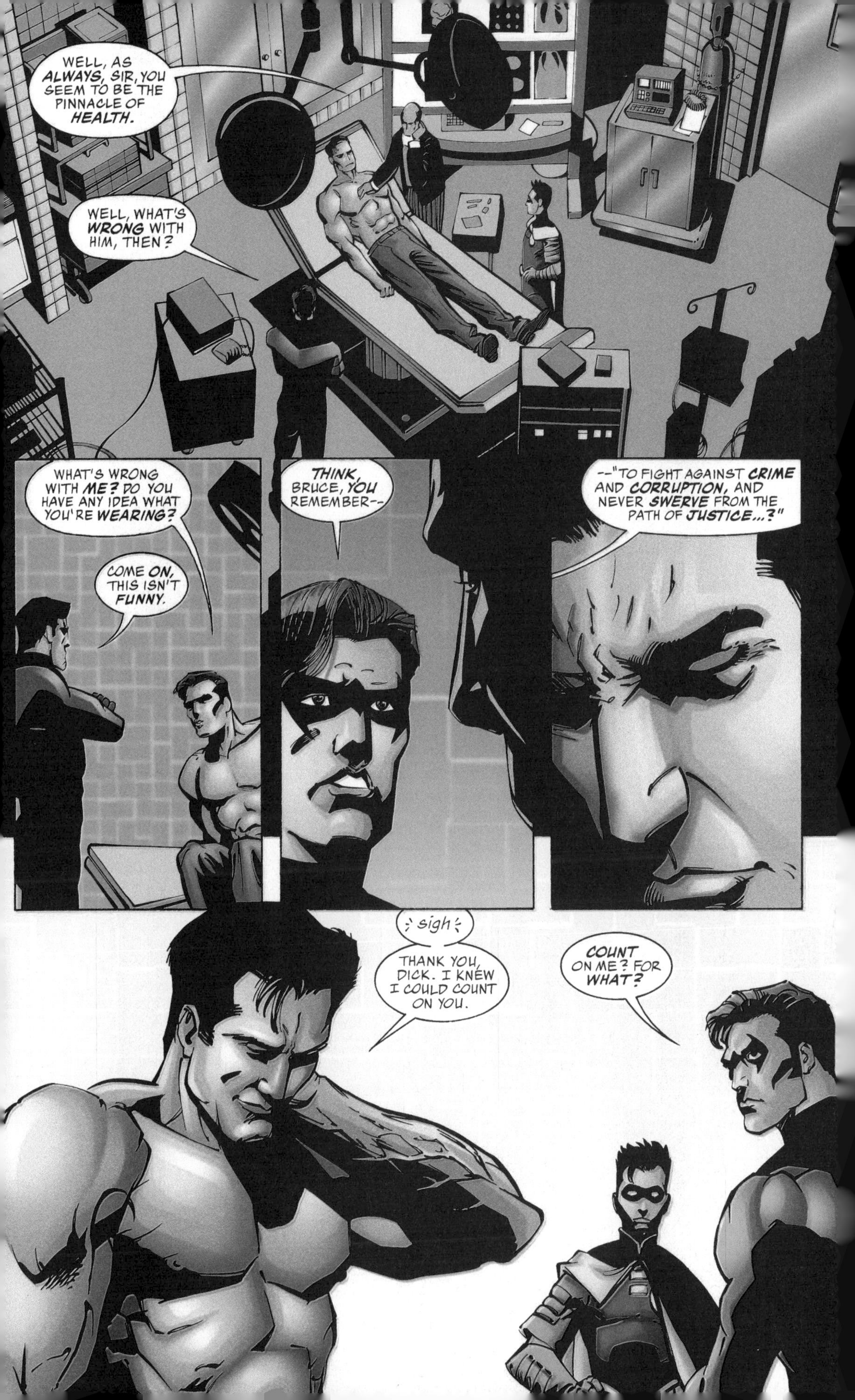
WELL, AS ALWAYS, SIR, YOU SEEM TO BE THE PINNACLE OF HEALTH.
WELL, WHAT'S WRONG WITH HIM, THEN?
WHAT'S WRONG WITH ME? DO YOU HAVE ANY IDEA WHAT YOU'RE WEARING?
COME ON, THIS ISN'T FUNNY.
THINK, BRUCE, YOU REMEMBER--
--"TO FIGHT AGAINST CRIME AND CORRUPTION, AND NEVER SWERVE FROM THE PATH OF JUSTICE...?"
sigh
THANK YOU, DICK. I KNEW I COULD COUNT ON YOU.
COUNT ON ME? FOR WHAT?

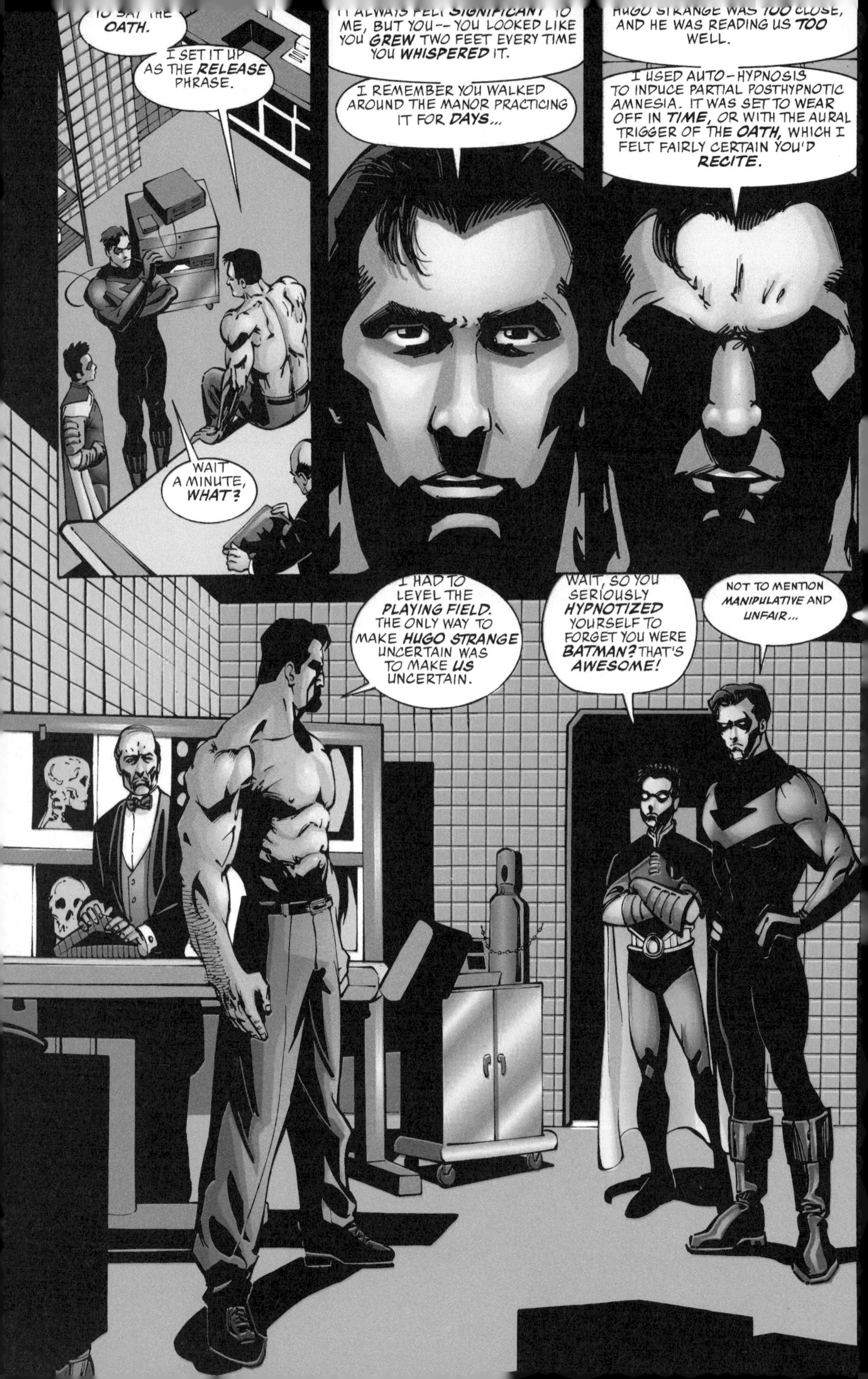
TO SAY THE OATH.
I SET IT UP AS THE RELEASE PHRASE.
WAIT A MINUTE, WHAT?
IT ALWAYS FELT SIGNIFICANT TO ME, BUT YOU-- YOU LOOKED LIKE YOU GREW TWO FEET EVERY TIME YOU WHISPERED IT.
I REMEMBER YOU WALKED AROUND THE MANOR PRACTICING IT FOR DAYS...
HUGO STRANGE WAS TOO CLOSE, AND HE WAS READING US TOO WELL.
I USED AUTO-HYPNOSIS TO INDUCE PARTIAL POSTHYPNOTIC AMNESIA. IT WAS SET TO WEAR OFF IN TIME, OR WITH THE AURAL TRIGGER OF THE OATH, WHICH I FELT FAIRLY CERTAIN YOU'D RECITE.
I HAD TO LEVEL THE PLAYING FIELD. THE ONLY WAY TO MAKE HUGO STRANGE UNCERTAIN WAS TO MAKE US UNCERTAIN.
WAIT, SO YOU SERIOUSLY HYPNOTIZED YOURSELF TO FORGET YOU WERE BATMAN? THAT'S AWESOME!
NOT TO MENTION MANIPULATIVE AND UNFAIR...

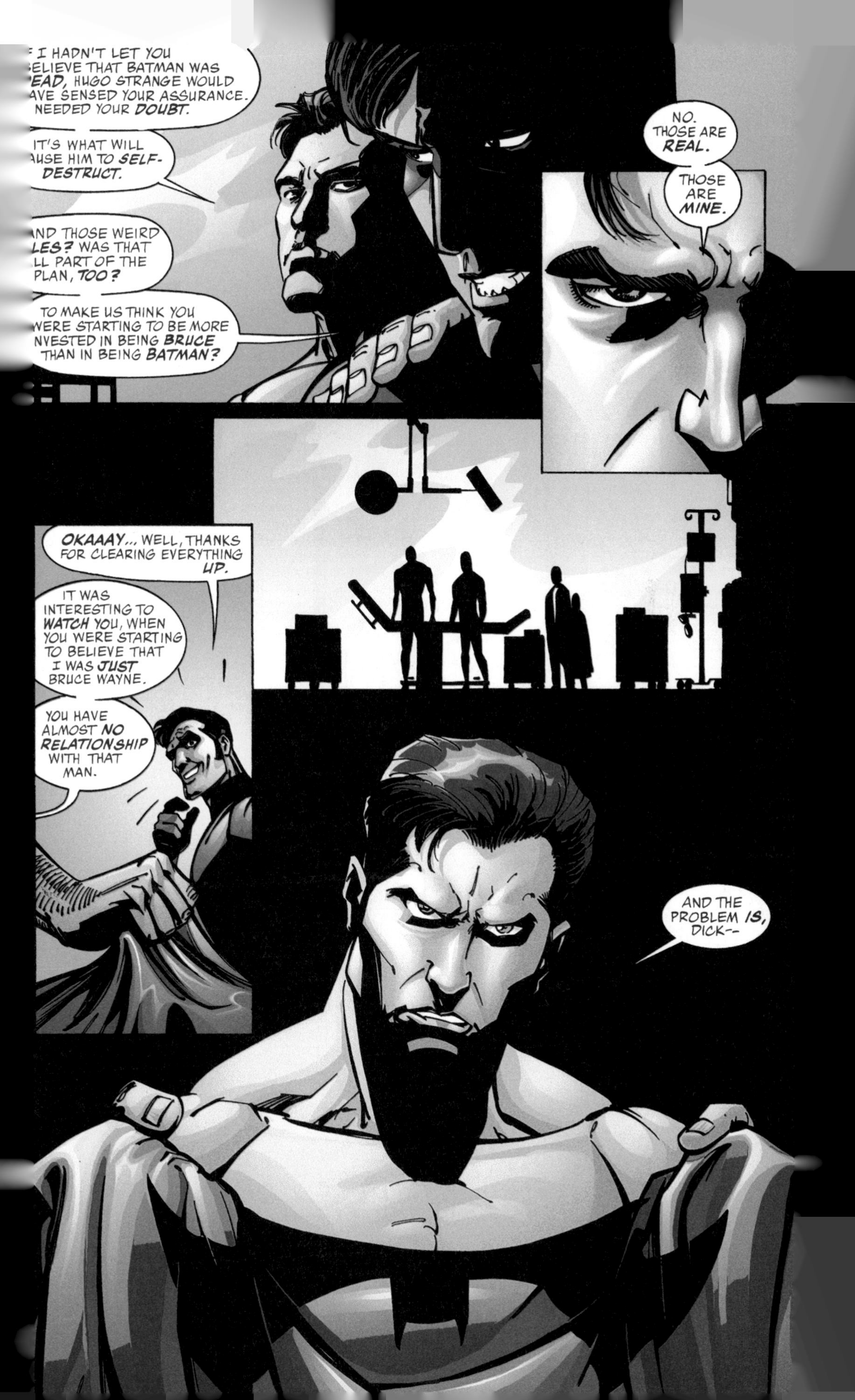

F I HADN'T LET YOU BELIEVE THAT BATMAN WAS DEAD, HUGO STRANGE WOULD AVE SENSED YOUR ASSURANCE. NEEDED YOUR DOUBT.
IT'S WHAT WILL AUSE HIM TO SELF-DESTRUCT.
AND THOSE WEIRD LES? WAS THAT LL PART OF THE PLAN, TOO?
TO MAKE US THINK YOU WERE STARTING TO BE MORE NVESTED IN BEING BRUCE THAN IN BEING BATMAN?
NO. THOSE ARE REAL.
THOSE ARE MINE.
OKAAAY... WELL, THANKS FOR CLEARING EVERYTHING UP.
IT WAS INTERESTING TO WATCH YOU, WHEN YOU WERE STARTING TO BELIEVE THAT I WAS JUST BRUCE WAYNE.
YOU HAVE ALMOST NO RELATIONSHIP WITH THAT MAN.
AND THE PROBLEM IS, DICK--

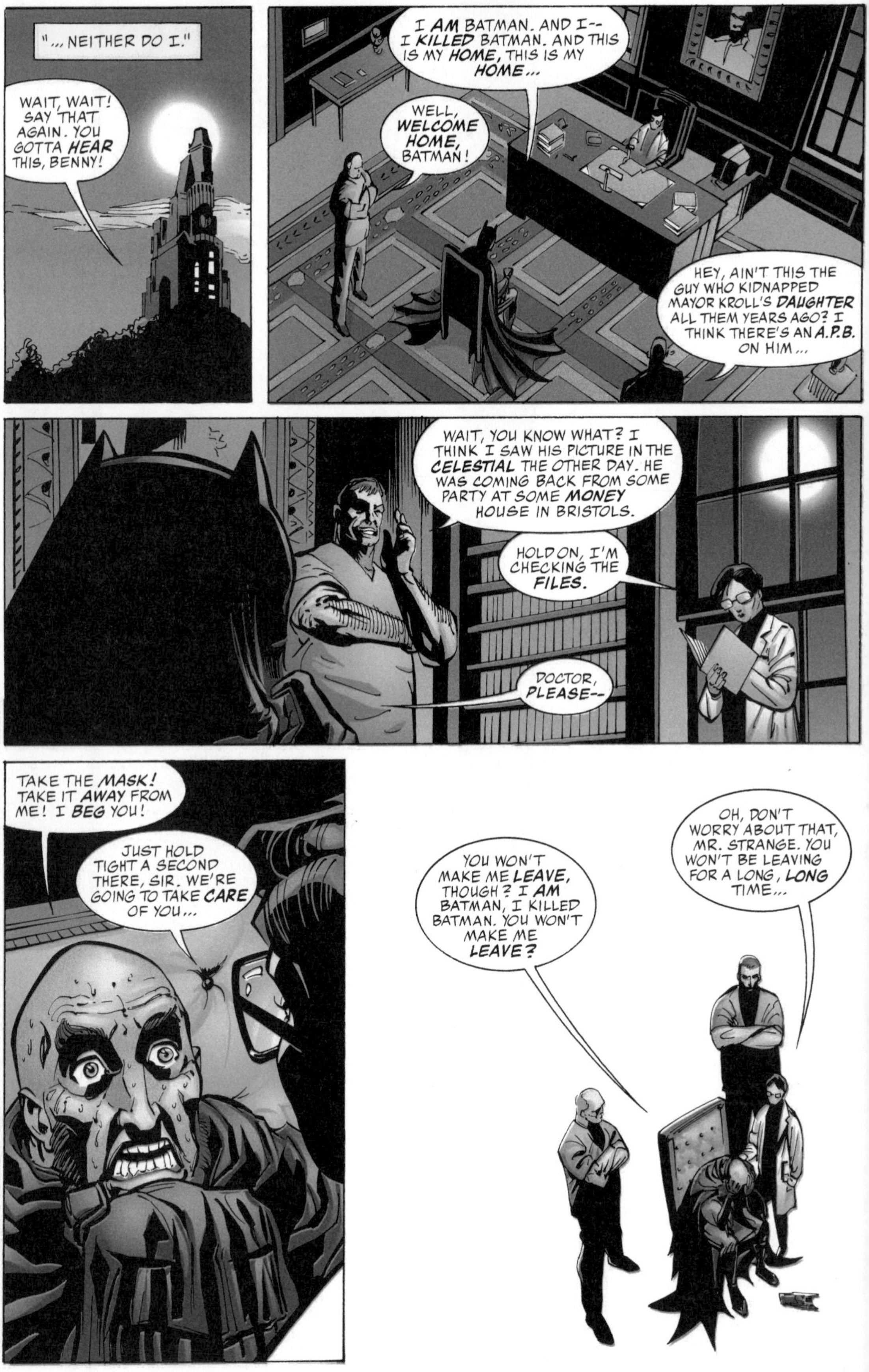
"... NEITHER DO I."
WAIT, WAIT! SAY THAT AGAIN. YOU GOTTA HEAR THIS, BENNY!
I AM BATMAN. AND I-- I KILLED BATMAN. AND THIS IS MY HOME, THIS IS MY HOME...
WELL, WELCOME HOME, BATMAN!
HEY, AIN'T THIS THE GUY WHO KIDNAPPED MAYOR KROLL'S DAUGHTER ALL THEM YEARS AGO? I THINK THERE'S AN A.P.B. ON HIM...
WAIT, YOU KNOW WHAT? I THINK I SAW HIS PICTURE IN THE CELESTIAL THE OTHER DAY. HE WAS COMING BACK FROM SOME PARTY AT SOME MONEY HOUSE IN BRISTOLS.
HOLD ON, I'M CHECKING THE FILES.
DOCTOR, PLEASE--
TAKE THE MASK! TAKE IT AWAY FROM ME! I BEG YOU!
JUST HOLD TIGHT A SECOND THERE, SIR. WE'RE GOING TO TAKE CARE OF YOU...
YOU WON'T MAKE ME LEAVE, THOUGH? I AM BATMAN, I KILLED BATMAN. YOU WON'T MAKE ME LEAVE?
OH, DON'T WORRY ABOUT THAT, MR. STRANGE. YOU WON'T BE LEAVING FOR A LONG, LONG TIME...

the end.

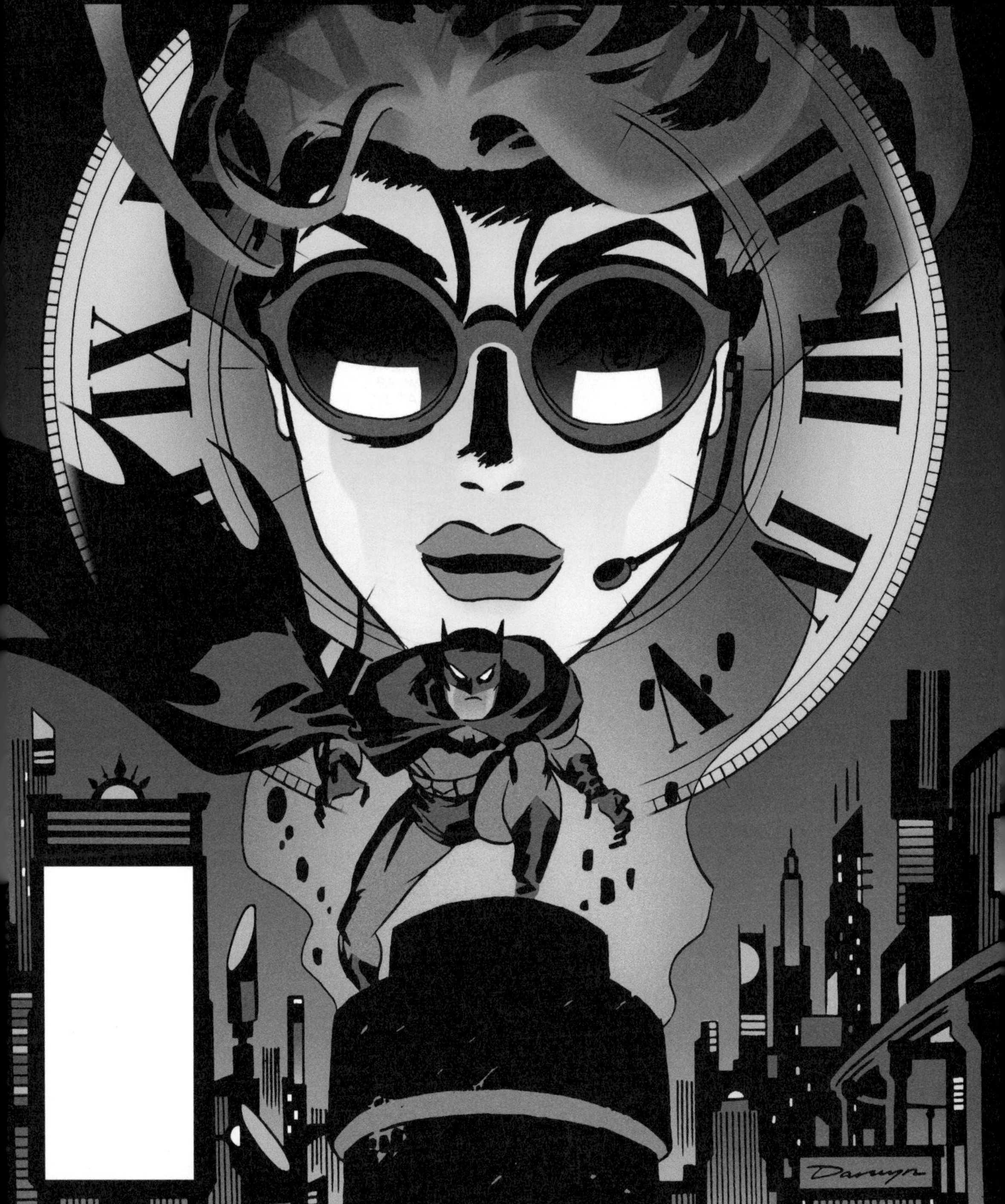
Darwyn

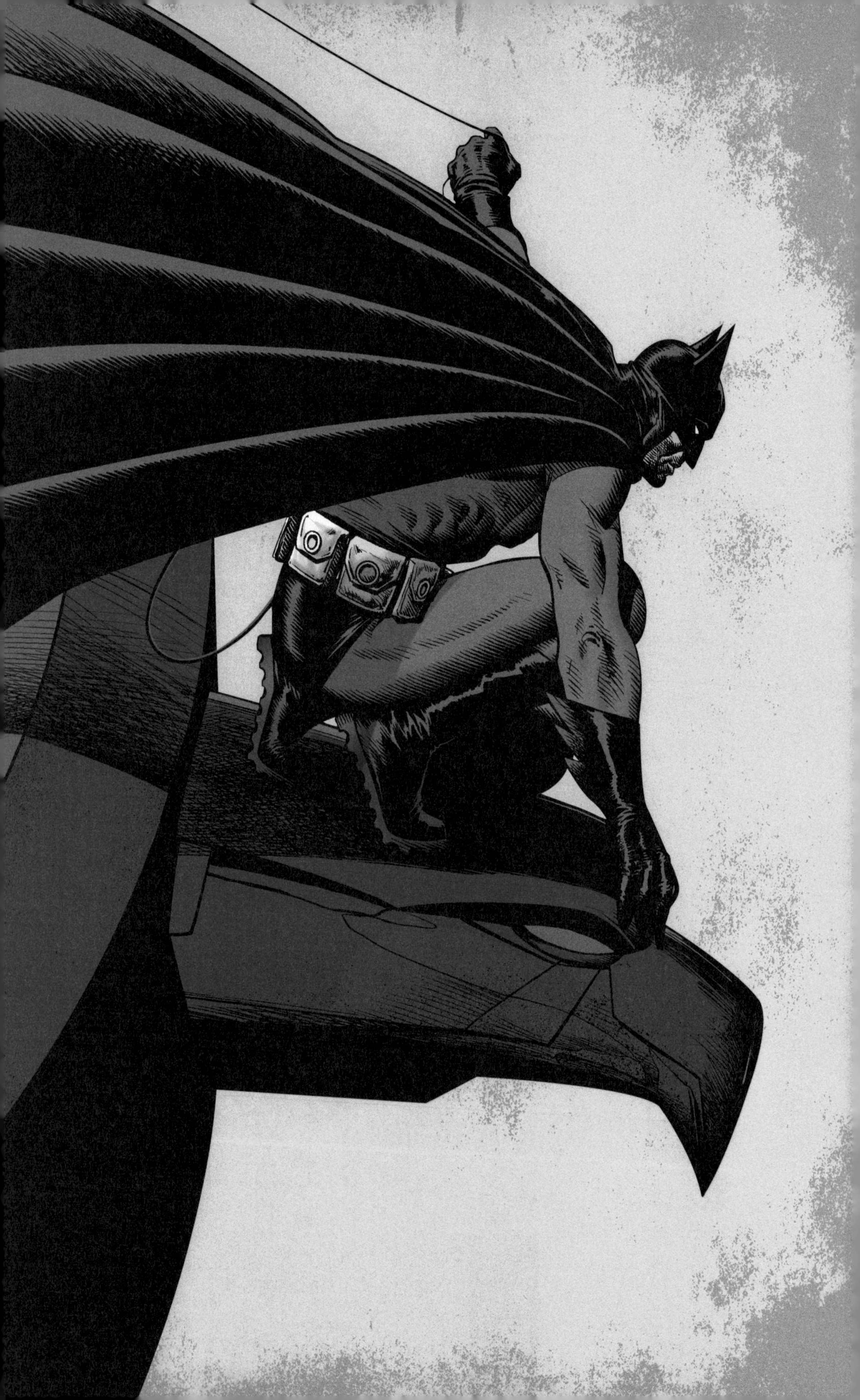

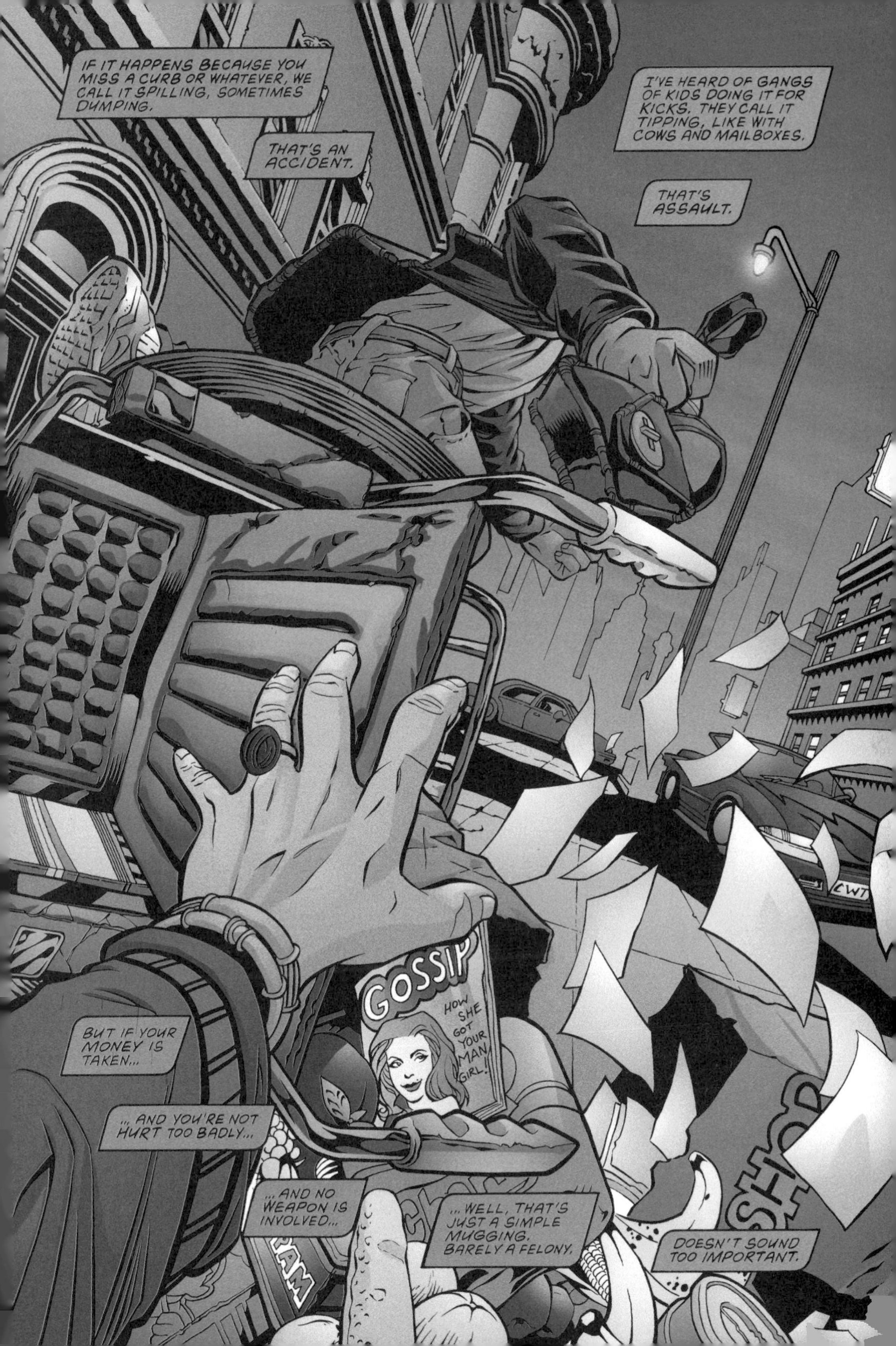
IF IT HAPPENS BECAUSE YOU MISS A CURB OR WHATEVER, WE CALL IT SPILLING, SOMETIMES DUMPING.
THAT'S AN ACCIDENT.
I'VE HEARD OF GANGS OF KIDS DOING IT FOR KICKS. THEY CALL IT TIPPING, LIKE WITH COWS AND MAILBOXES.
THAT'S ASSAULT.
GOSSIP
HOW SHE GOT YOUR MAN GIRL!
BUT IF YOUR MONEY IS TAKEN...
...AND YOU'RE NOT HURT TOO BADLY...
...AND NO WEAPON IS INVOLVED...
...WELL, THAT'S JUST A SIMPLE MUGGING. BARELY A FELONY.
DOESN'T SOUND TOO IMPORTANT.

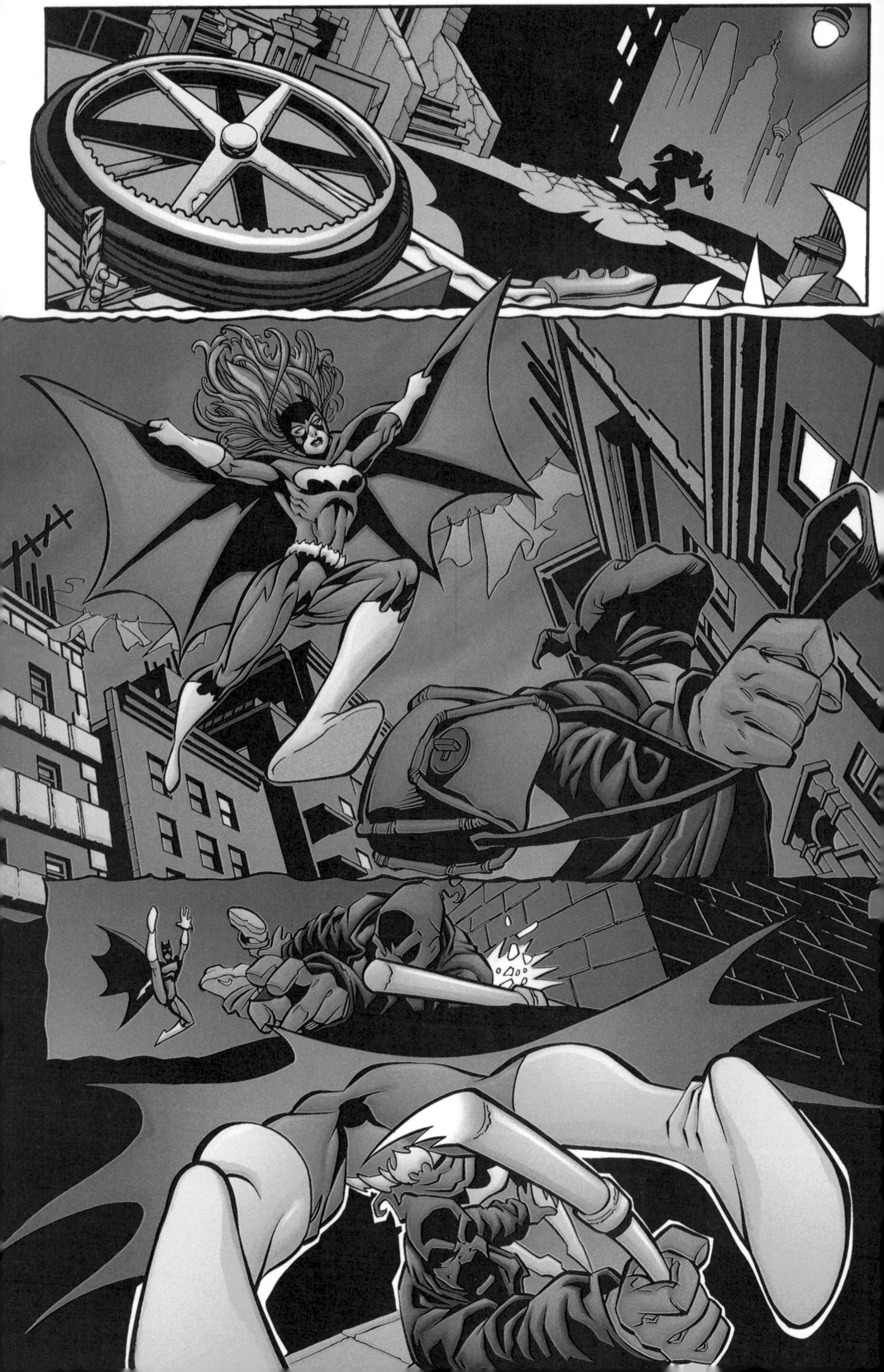

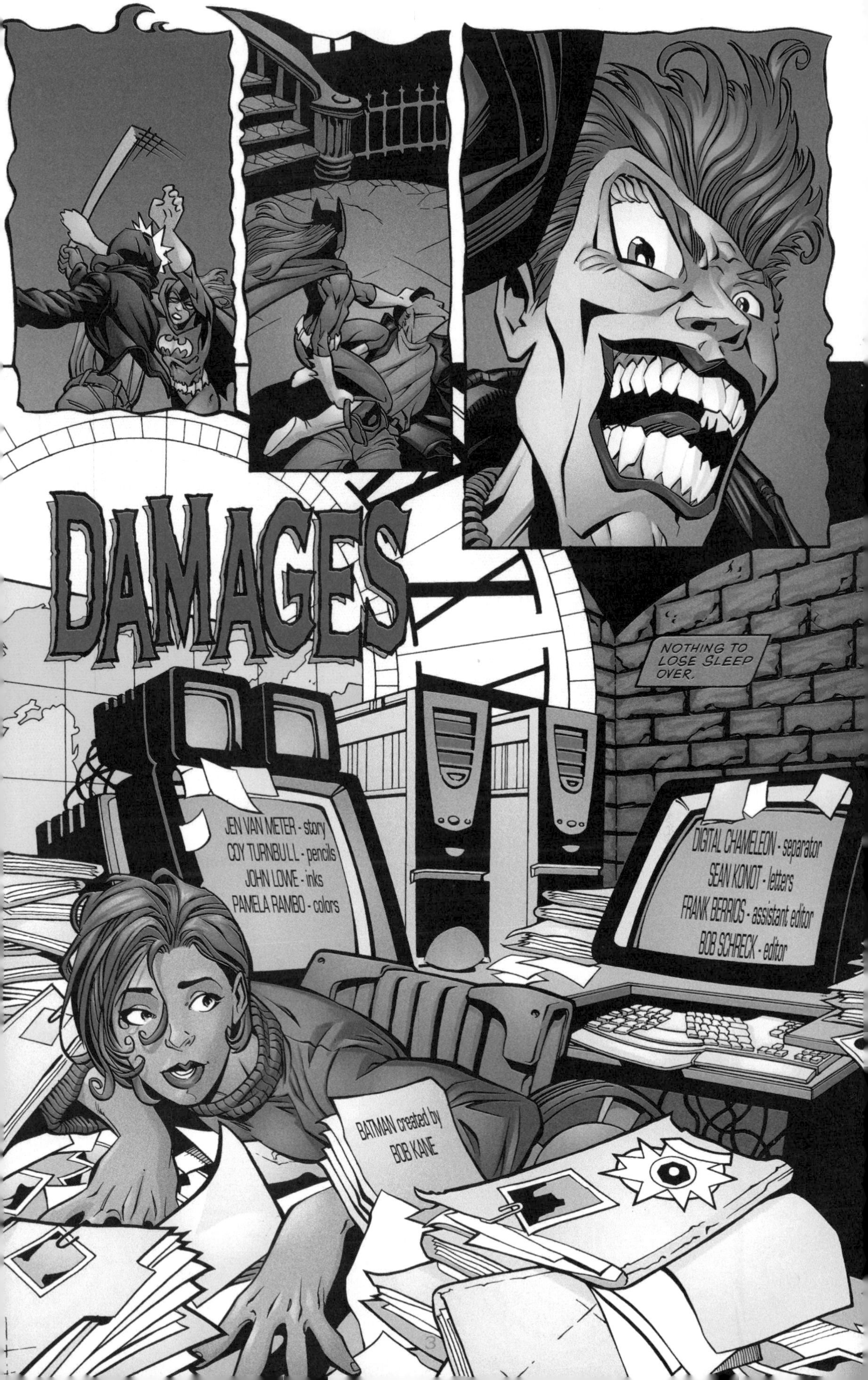
DAMAGES
NOTHING TO LOSE SLEEP OVER.
JEN VAN METER - story
COY TURNBULL - pencils
JOHN LOWE - inks
PAMELA RAMBO - colors
DIGITAL CHAMELEON - separator
SEAN KONOT - letters
FRANK BERRIOS - assistant editor
BOB SCHRECK - editor
BATMAN created by
BOB KANE

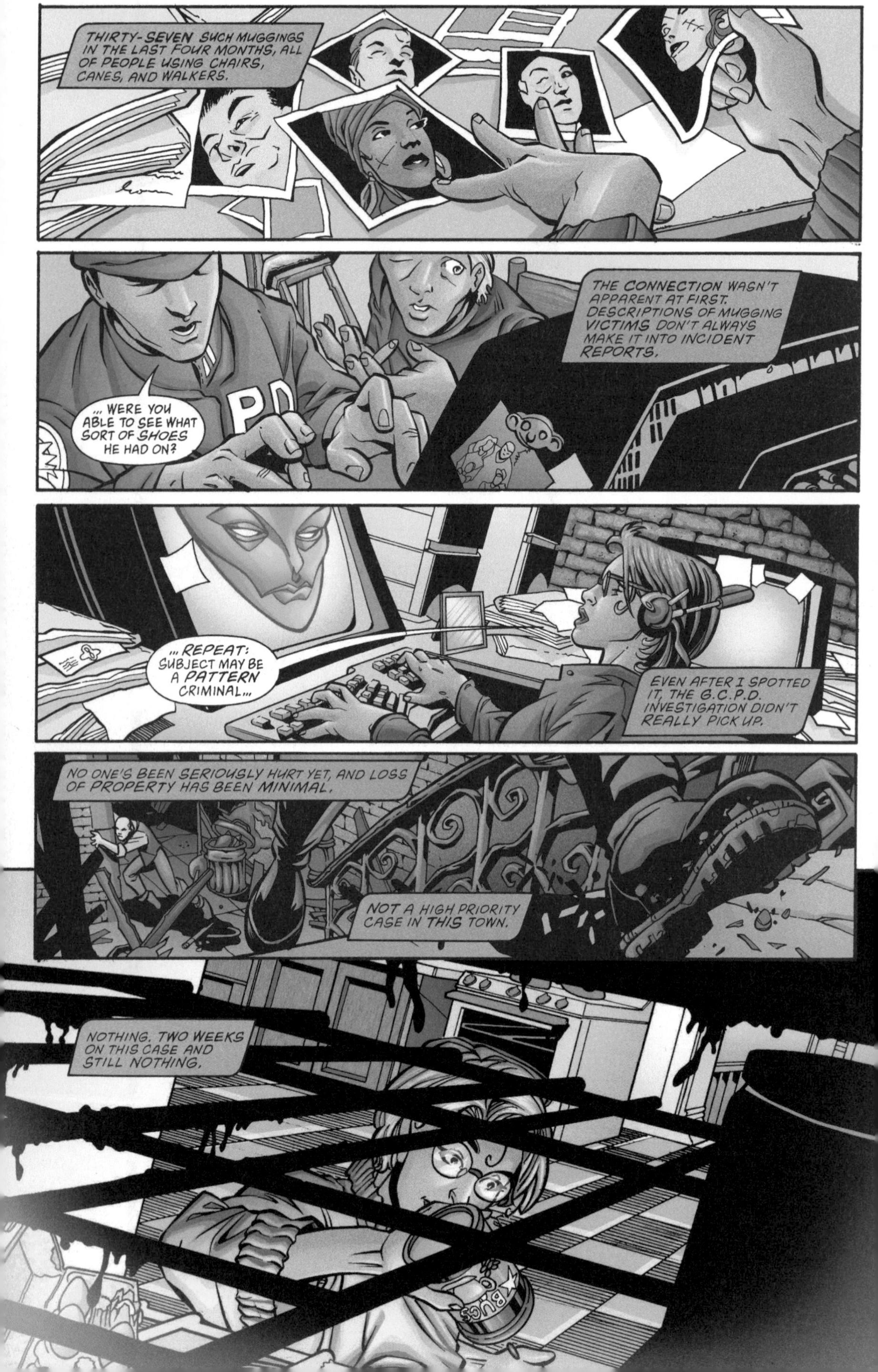
THIRTY-SEVEN SUCH MUGGINGS IN THE LAST FOUR MONTHS, ALL OF PEOPLE USING CHAIRS, CANES, AND WALKERS.
THE CONNECTION WASN'T APPARENT AT FIRST. DESCRIPTIONS OF MUGGING VICTIMS DON'T ALWAYS MAKE IT INTO INCIDENT REPORTS.
...WERE YOU ABLE TO SEE WHAT SORT OF SHOES HE HAD ON?
PD
...REPEAT: SUBJECT MAY BE A PATTERN CRIMINAL...
EVEN AFTER I SPOTTED IT, THE G.C.P.D. INVESTIGATION DIDN'T REALLY PICK UP.
NO ONE'S BEEN SERIOUSLY HURT YET, AND LOSS OF PROPERTY HAS BEEN MINIMAL.
NOT A HIGH PRIORITY CASE IN THIS TOWN.
NOTHING. TWO WEEKS ON THIS CASE AND STILL NOTHING.
BUGS

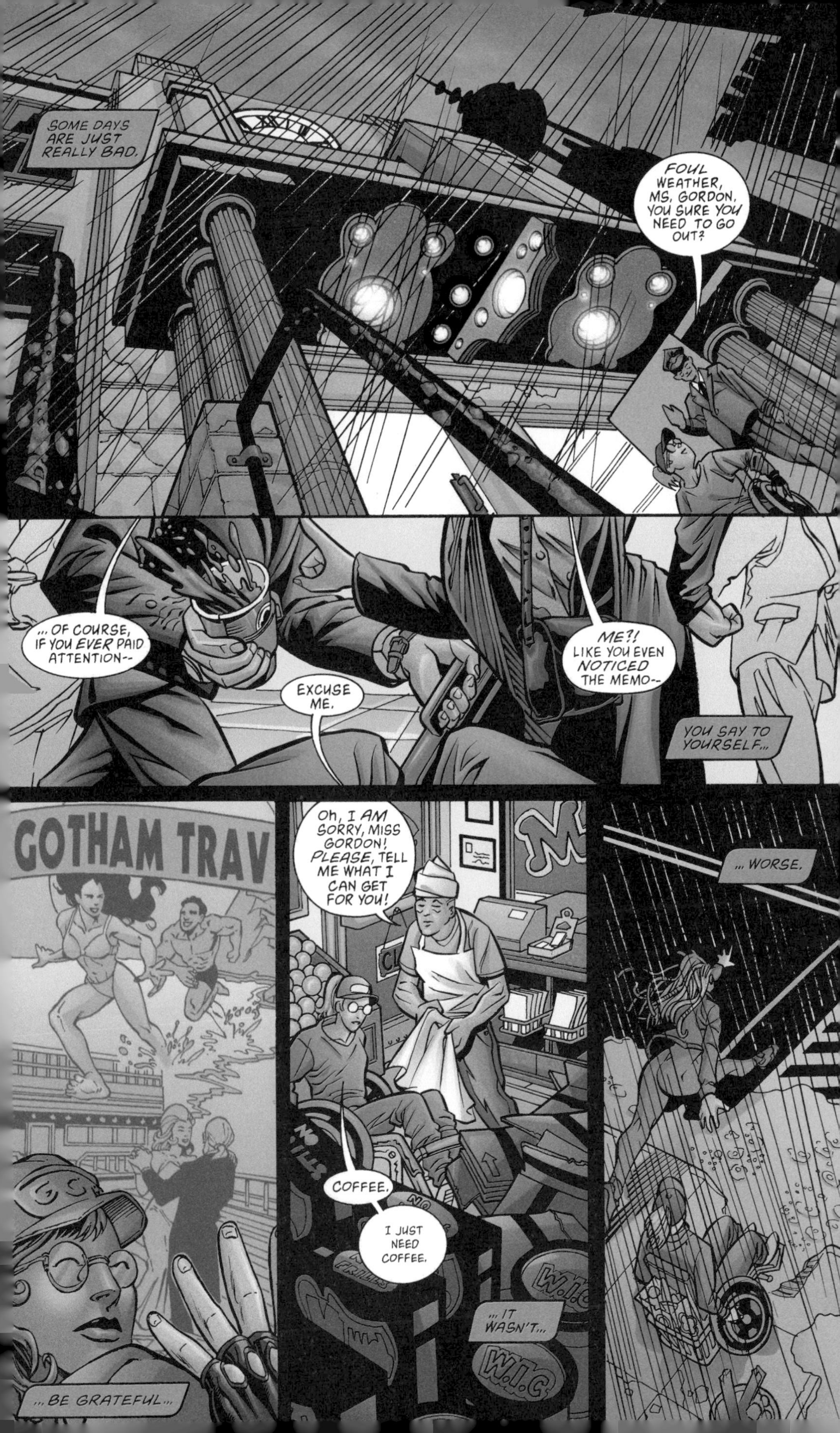
SOME DAYS ARE JUST REALLY BAD.
FOUL WEATHER, MS. GORDON. YOU SURE YOU NEED TO GO OUT?
...OF COURSE, IF YOU EVER PAID ATTENTION--
EXCUSE ME.
ME?! LIKE YOU EVEN NOTICED THE MEMO--
YOU SAY TO YOURSELF...
GOTHAM TRAV
...BE GRATEFUL...
Oh, I AM SORRY, MISS GORDON! PLEASE, TELL ME WHAT I CAN GET FOR YOU!
COFFEE.
I JUST NEED COFFEE.
...IT WASN'T...
...WORSE.

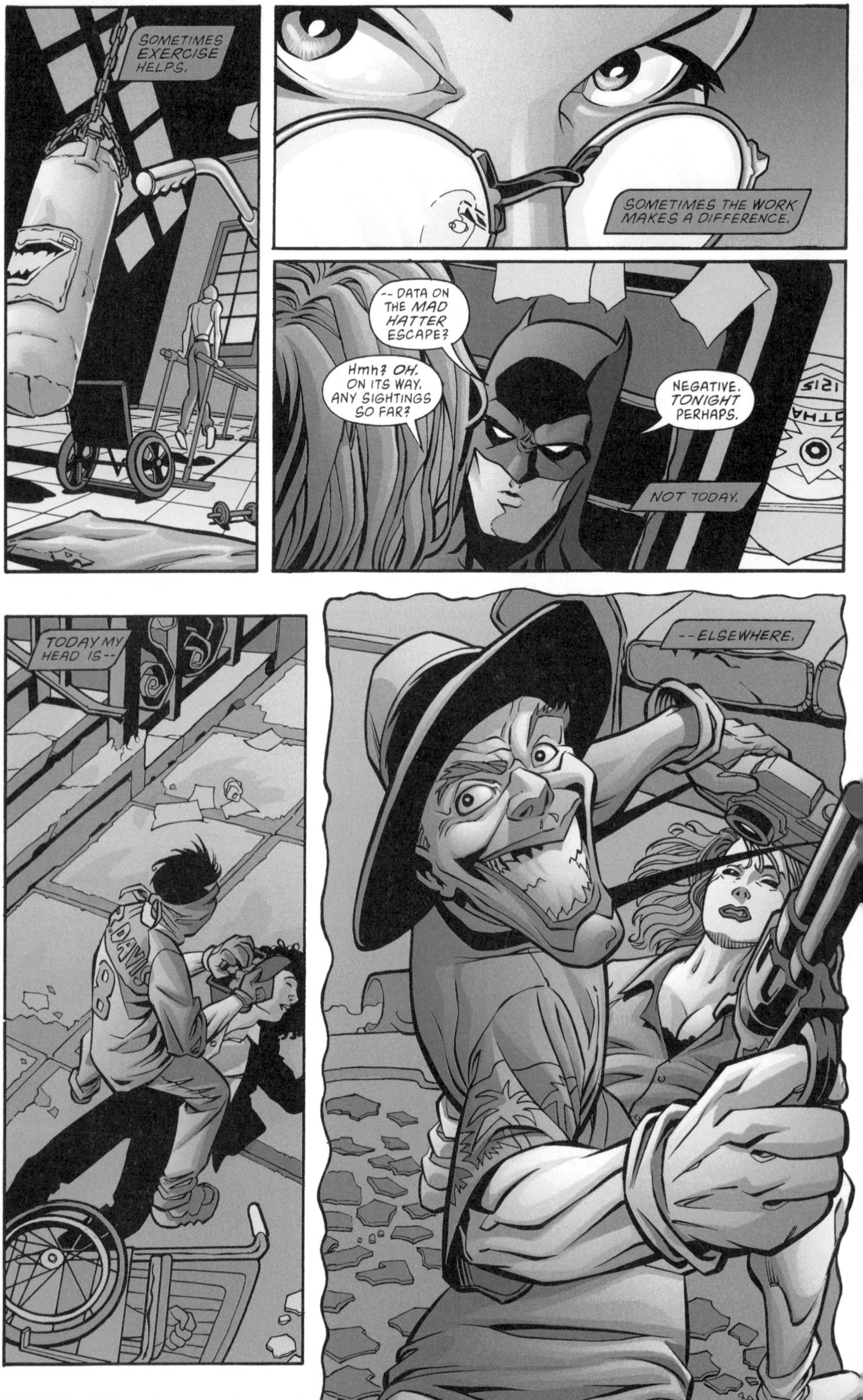
SOMETIMES EXERCISE HELPS.
SOMETIMES THE WORK MAKES A DIFFERENCE.
-- DATA ON THE MAD HATTER ESCAPE?
Hmh? OH. ON ITS WAY. ANY SIGHTINGS SO FAR?
NEGATIVE. TONIGHT PERHAPS.
NOT TODAY.
TODAY MY HEAD IS--
--ELSEWHERE.

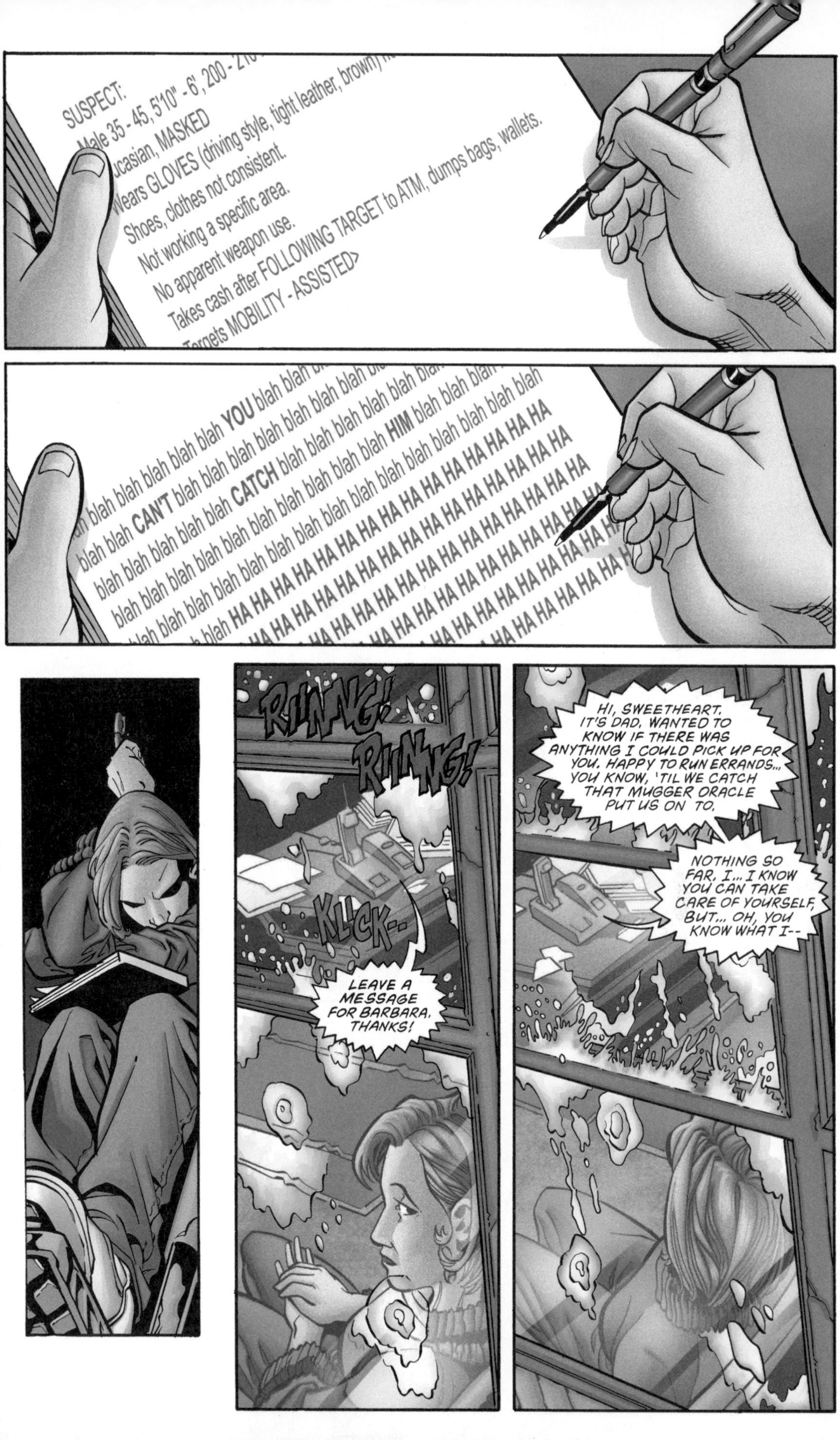
SUSPECT:
Male 35 - 45, 5'10" - 6', 200 -
ucasian, MASKED
Wears GLOVES (driving style, tight leather, brown)
Shoes, clothes not consistent.
Not working a specific area.
No apparent weapon use.
Takes cash after FOLLOWING TARGET to ATM, dumps bags, wallets.
Targets MOBILITY - ASSISTED>
blah blah blah blah blah YOU blah blah
blah blah CAN'T blah blah blah blah blah blah blah
blah blah blah blah blah CATCH blah blah blah blah blah blah
blah blah blah blah blah blah blah blah blah HIM blah blah blah
blah blah blah blah blah blah blah blah blah blah blah blah blah blah
blah HA HA HA HA HA HA HA HA HA HA HA HA HA HA HA HA HA
HA HA HA HA HA HA HA HA HA HA HA HA HA HA HA HA HA
HA HA HA HA HA HA HA HA HA HA HA HA HA HA HA HA
HA HA HA HA HA HA HA HA HA HA HA HA HA HA HA
RIIINNG!
RIIINNG!
KLICK--
LEAVE A MESSAGE FOR BARBARA. THANKS!
HI, SWEETHEART. IT'S DAD. WANTED TO KNOW IF THERE WAS ANYTHING I COULD PICK UP FOR YOU. HAPPY TO RUN ERRANDS... YOU KNOW, 'TIL WE CATCH THAT MUGGER ORACLE PUT US ON TO.
NOTHING SO FAR. I... I KNOW YOU CAN TAKE CARE OF YOURSELF, BUT... OH, YOU KNOW WHAT I--

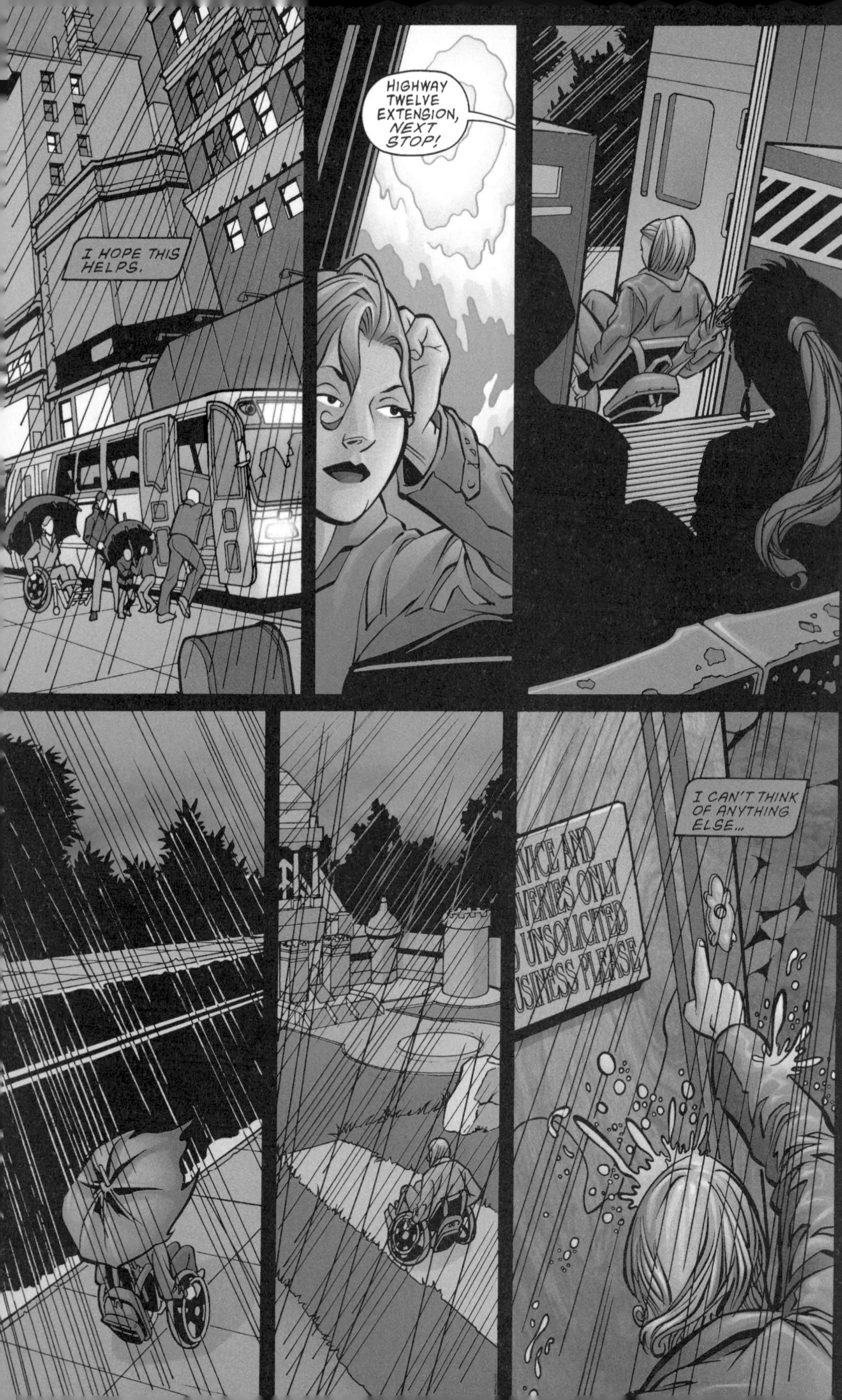
I HOPE THIS HELPS.
HIGHWAY TWELVE EXTENSION, NEXT STOP!
VICE AND
VERIES ONLY
UNSOLICITED
USINESS PLEASE
I CAN'T THINK OF ANYTHING ELSE...

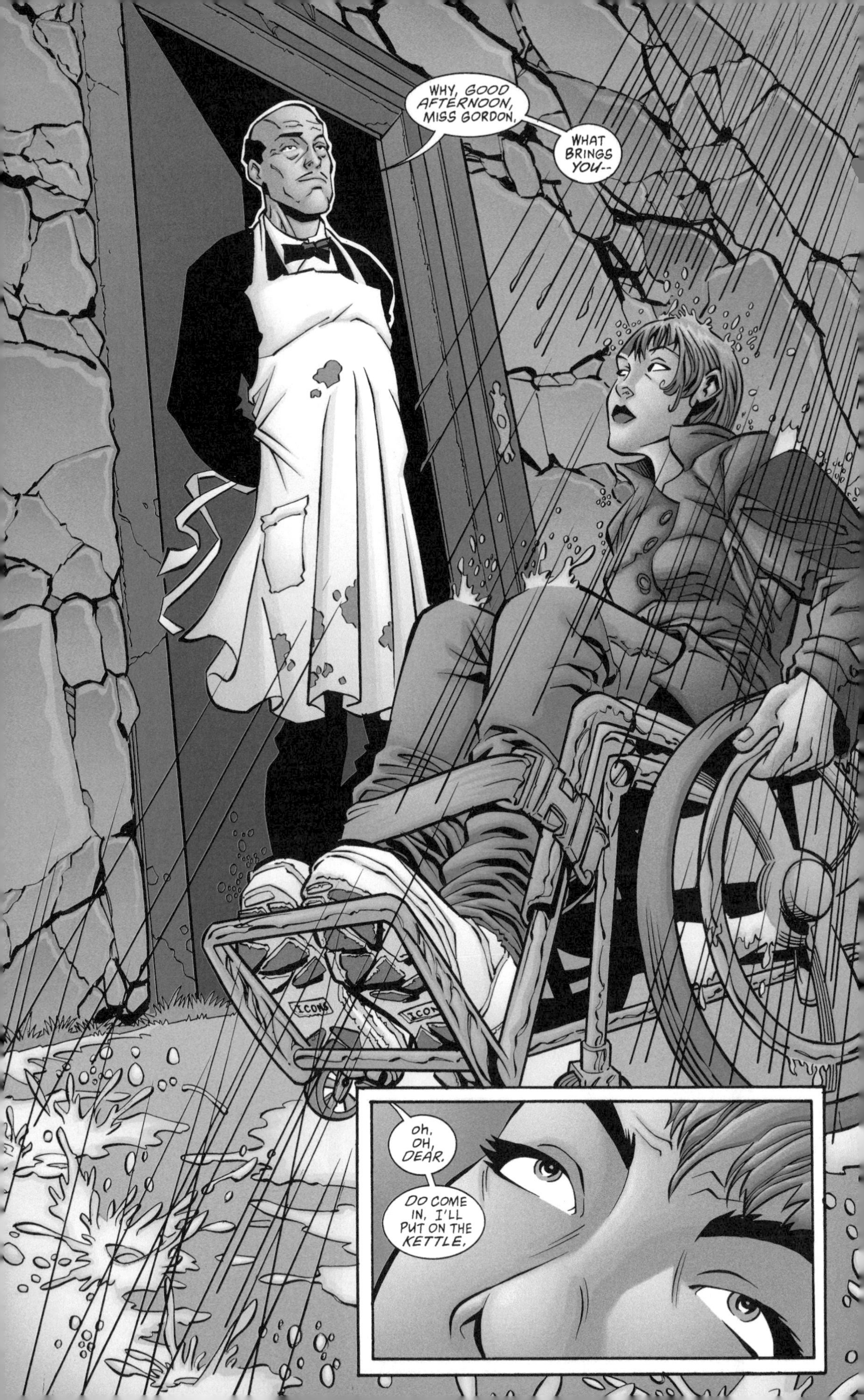
WHY, GOOD AFTERNOON, MISS GORDON.
WHAT BRINGS YOU--
ICONS
ICONS
oh. OH, DEAR.
DO COME IN. I'LL PUT ON THE KETTLE.

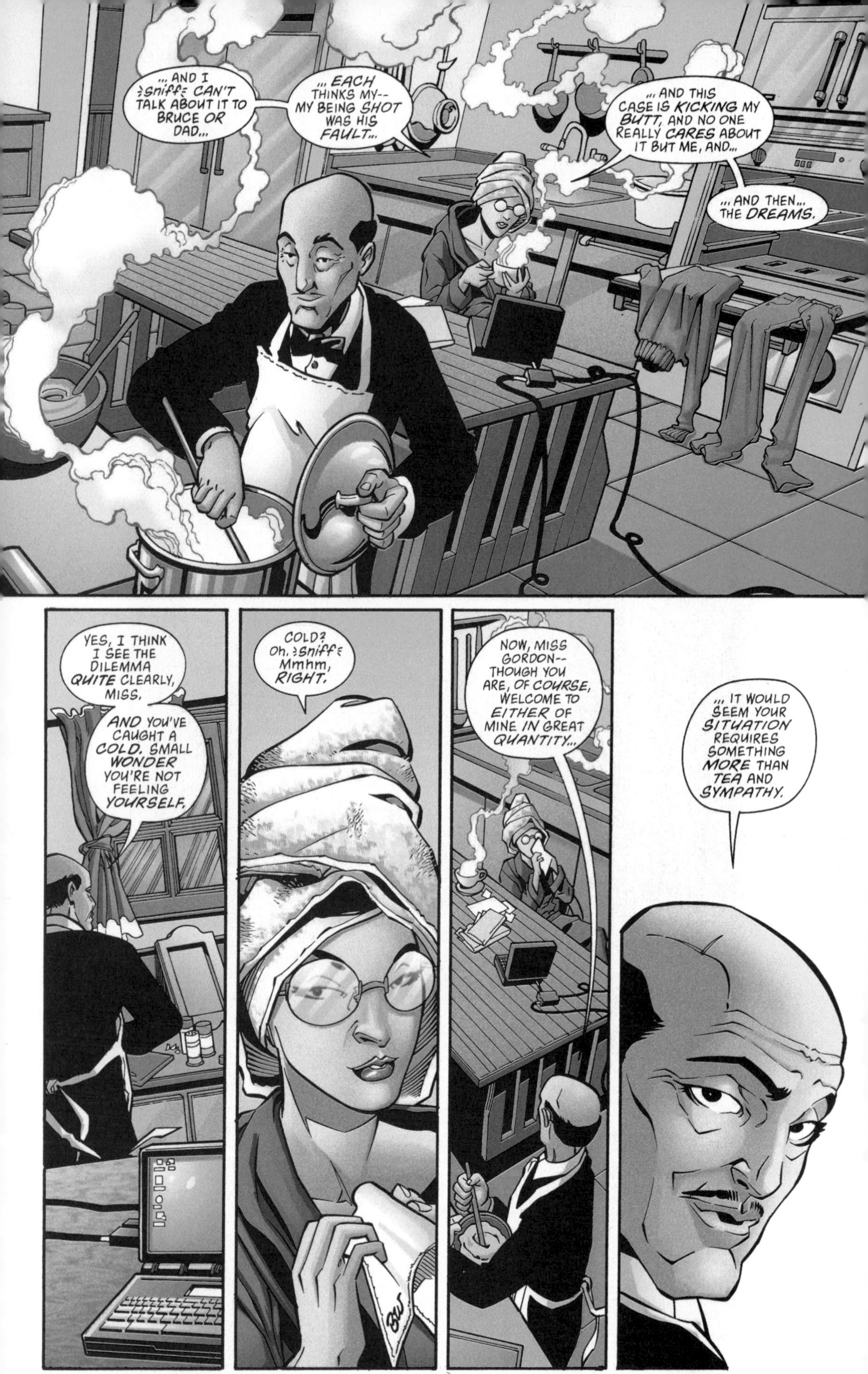
...AND I ≷sniff≶ CAN'T TALK ABOUT IT TO BRUCE OR DAD...
...EACH THINKS MY-- MY BEING SHOT WAS HIS FAULT...
...AND THIS CASE IS KICKING MY BUTT, AND NO ONE REALLY CARES ABOUT IT BUT ME, AND...
...AND THEN... THE DREAMS.
YES, I THINK I SEE THE DILEMMA QUITE CLEARLY, MISS.
AND YOU'VE CAUGHT A COLD. SMALL WONDER YOU'RE NOT FEELING YOURSELF.
COLD? Oh. ≷sniff≶ Mmhm, RIGHT.
NOW, MISS GORDON-- THOUGH YOU ARE, OF COURSE, WELCOME TO EITHER OF MINE IN GREAT QUANTITY...
...IT WOULD SEEM YOUR SITUATION REQUIRES SOMETHING MORE THAN TEA AND SYMPATHY.

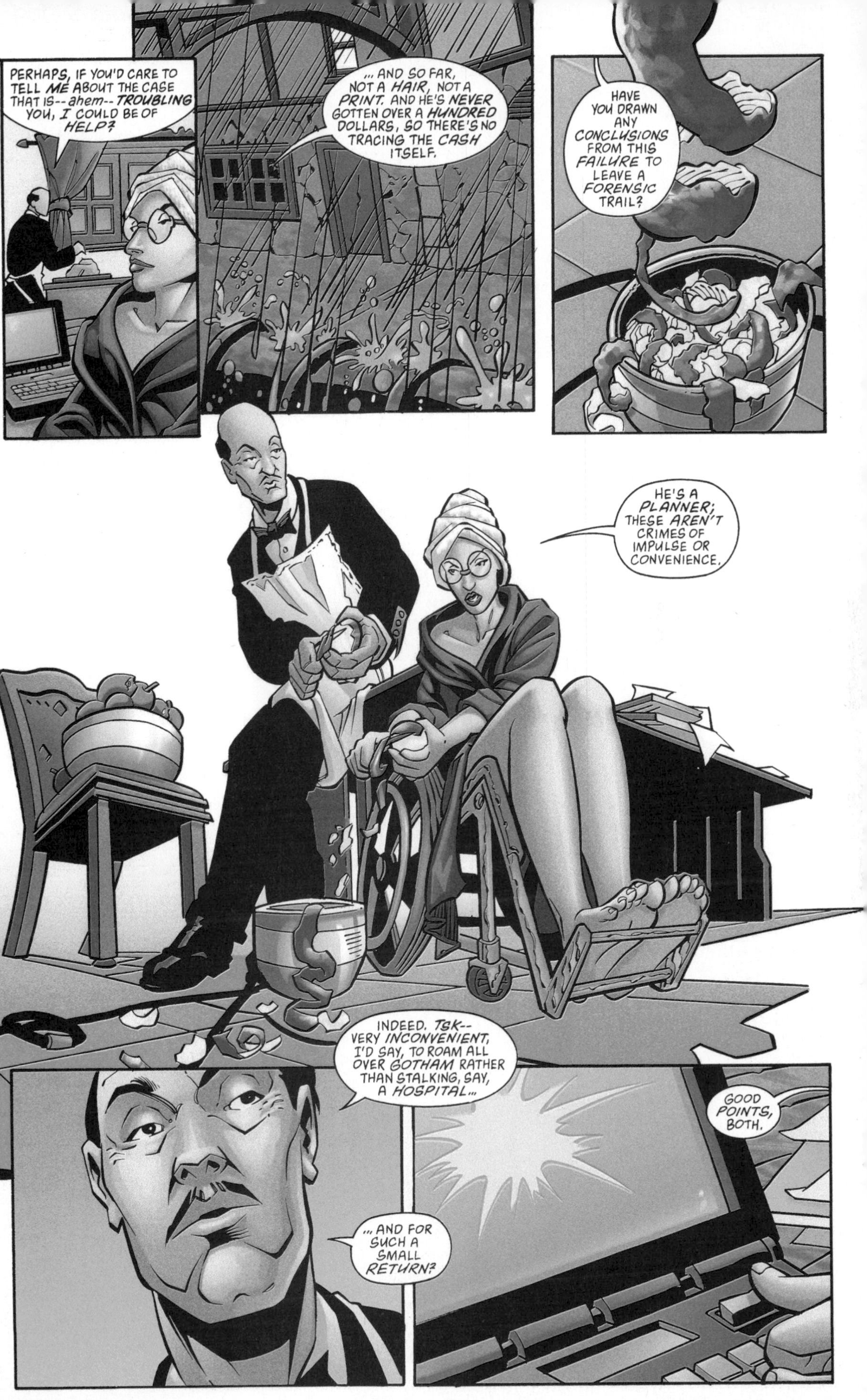
PERHAPS, IF YOU'D CARE TO TELL ME ABOUT THE CASE THAT IS-- ahem-- TROUBLING YOU, I COULD BE OF HELP?
... AND SO FAR, NOT A HAIR, NOT A PRINT. AND HE'S NEVER GOTTEN OVER A HUNDRED DOLLARS, SO THERE'S NO TRACING THE CASH ITSELF.
HAVE YOU DRAWN ANY CONCLUSIONS FROM THIS FAILURE TO LEAVE A FORENSIC TRAIL?
HE'S A PLANNER; THESE AREN'T CRIMES OF IMPULSE OR CONVENIENCE.
INDEED. TSK-- VERY INCONVENIENT, I'D SAY, TO ROAM ALL OVER GOTHAM RATHER THAN STALKING, SAY, A HOSPITAL...
... AND FOR SUCH A SMALL RETURN?
GOOD POINTS, BOTH.

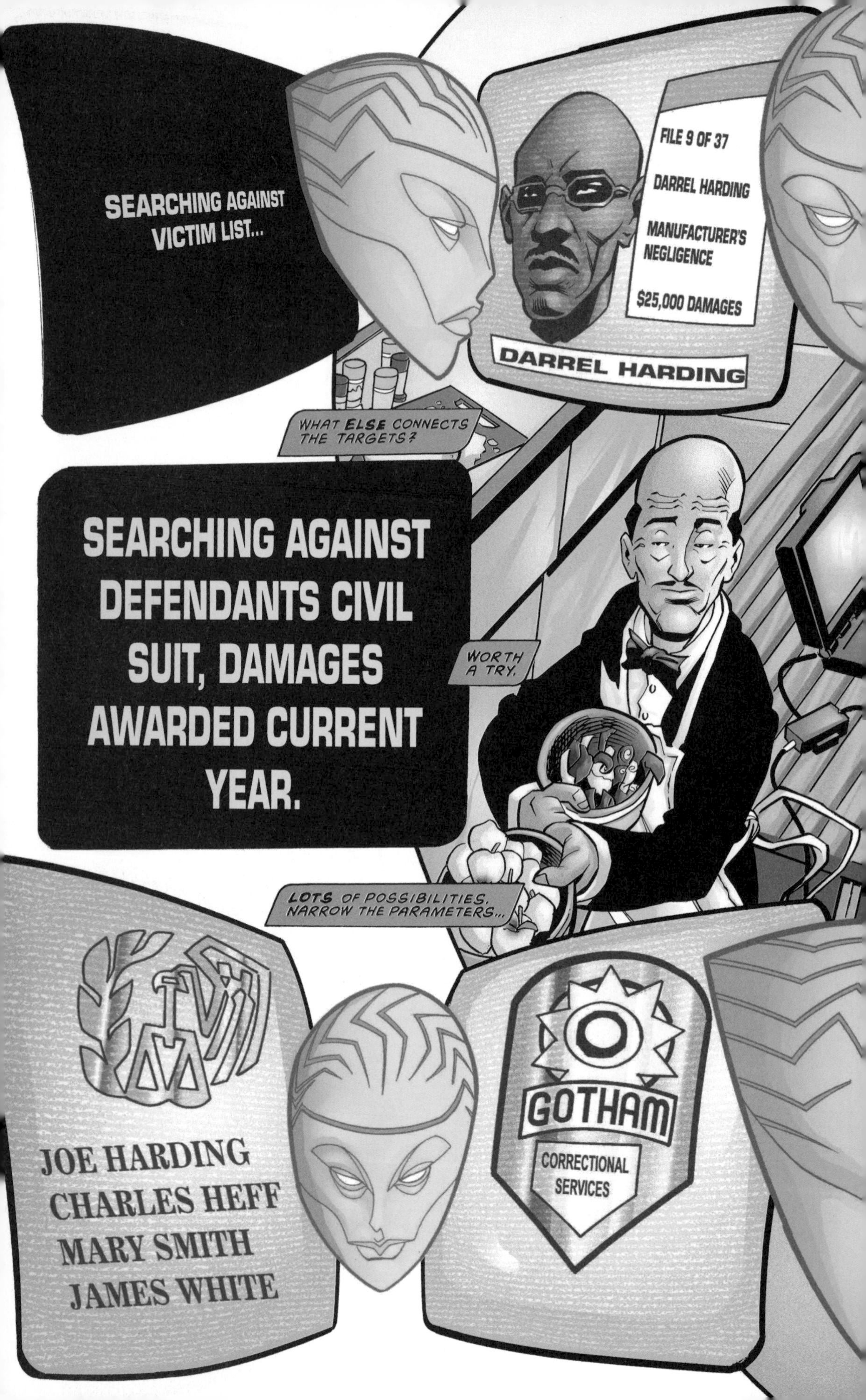
SEARCHING AGAINST VICTIM LIST...
FILE 9 OF 37
DARREL HARDING
MANUFACTURER'S NEGLIGENCE
$25,000 DAMAGES
DARREL HARDING
WHAT ELSE CONNECTS THE TARGETS?
SEARCHING AGAINST DEFENDANTS CIVIL SUIT, DAMAGES AWARDED CURRENT YEAR.
WORTH A TRY.
LOTS OF POSSIBILITIES. NARROW THE PARAMETERS...
JOE HARDING
CHARLES HEFF
MARY SMITH
JAMES WHITE
GOTHAM
CORRECTIONAL SERVICES

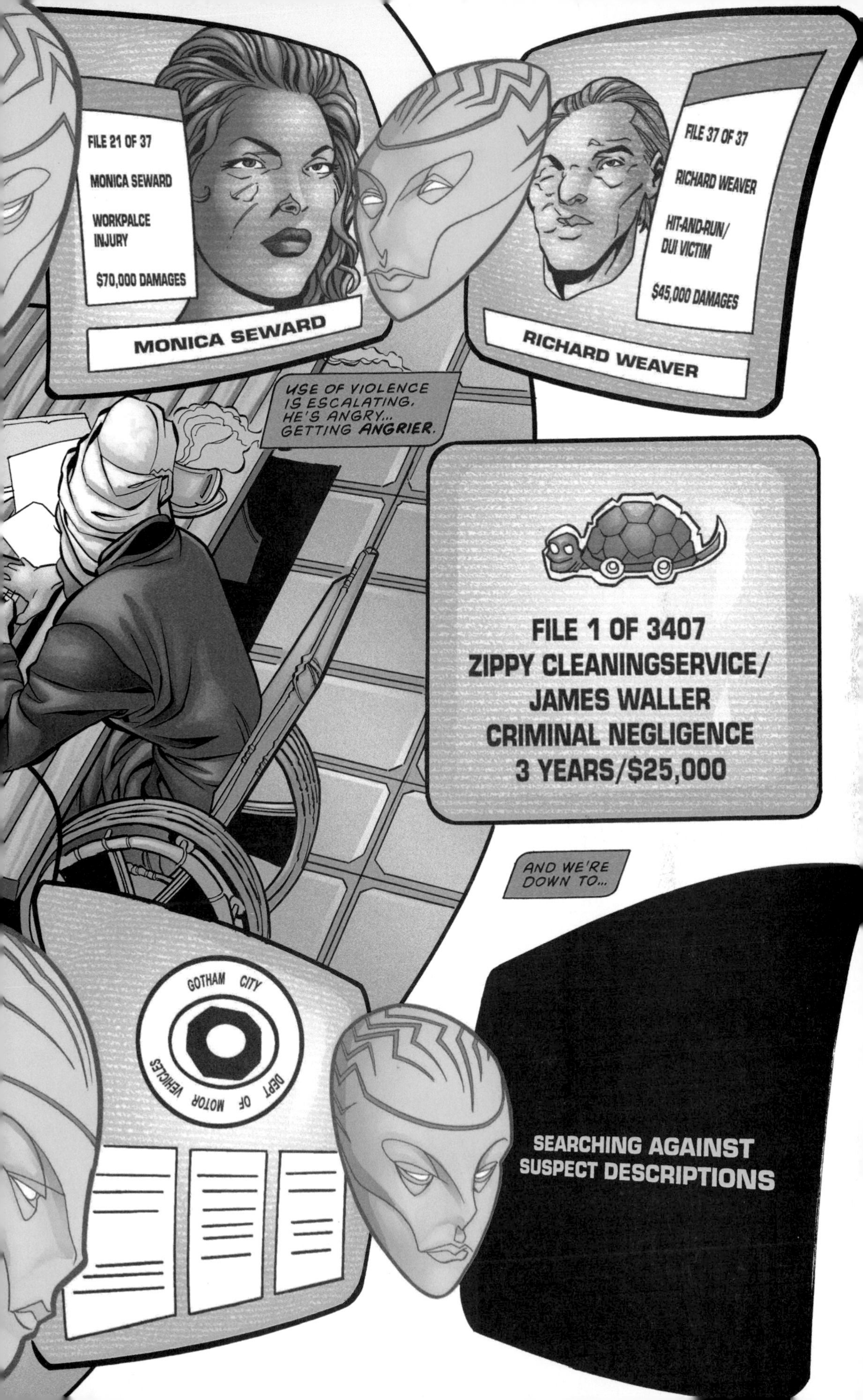
FILE 21 OF 37
MONICA SEWARD
WORKPALCE INJURY
$70,000 DAMAGES
MONICA SEWARD
FILE 37 OF 37
RICHARD WEAVER
HIT-AND-RUN/ DUI VICTIM
$45,000 DAMAGES
RICHARD WEAVER
USE OF VIOLENCE IS ESCALATING. HE'S ANGRY... GETTING ANGRIER.
FILE 1 OF 3407
ZIPPY CLEANINGSERVICE/
JAMES WALLER
CRIMINAL NEGLIGENCE
3 YEARS/$25,000
AND WE'RE DOWN TO...
GOTHAM CITY DEPT OF MOTOR VEHICLES
SEARCHING AGAINST SUSPECT DESCRIPTIONS

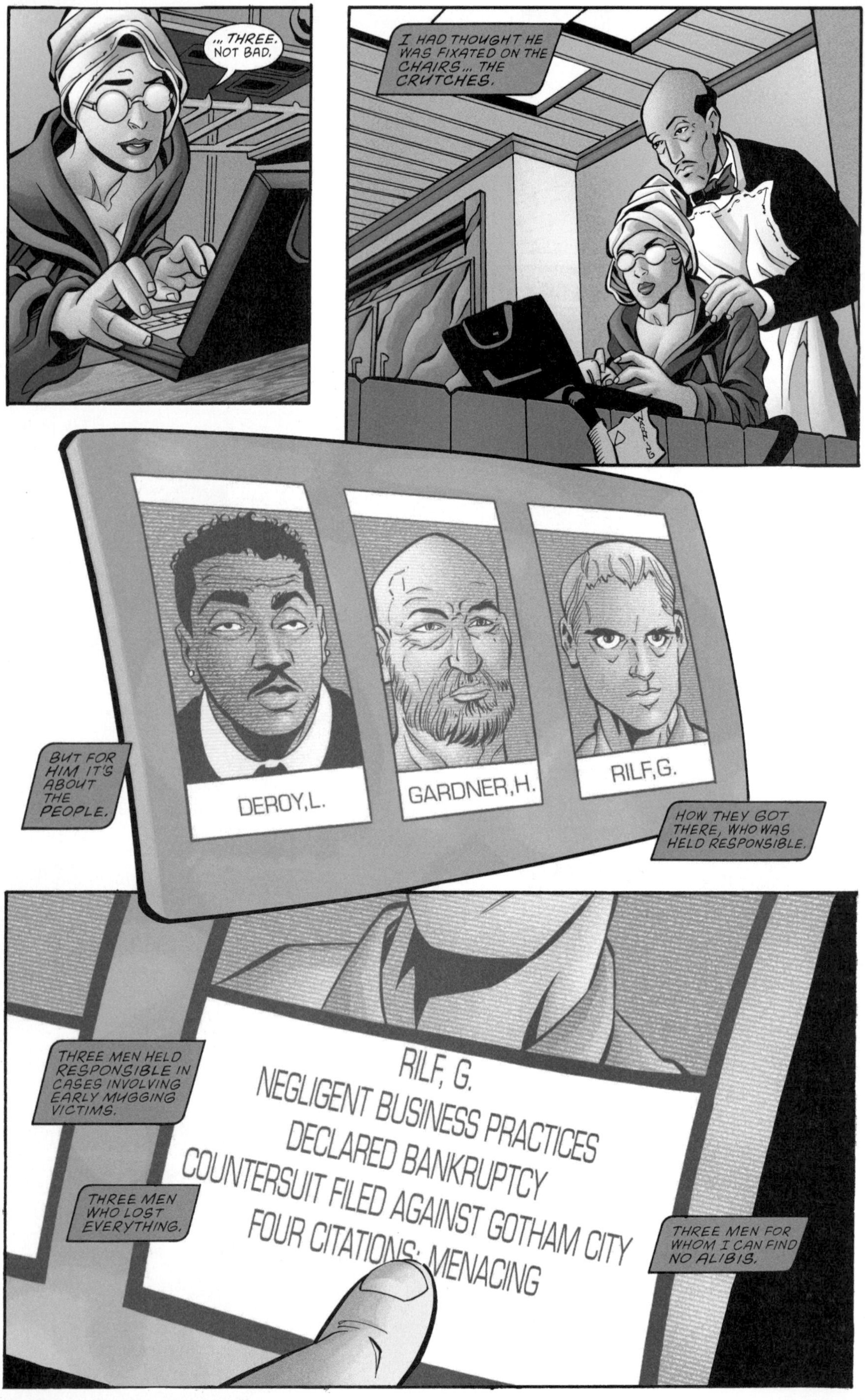

...THREE. NOT BAD.
I HAD THOUGHT HE WAS FIXATED ON THE CHAIRS... THE CRUTCHES.
BUT FOR HIM IT'S ABOUT THE PEOPLE.
DEROY, L.
GARDNER, H.
RILF, G.
HOW THEY GOT THERE, WHO WAS HELD RESPONSIBLE.
THREE MEN HELD RESPONSIBLE IN CASES INVOLVING EARLY MUGGING VICTIMS.
RILF, G.
NEGLIGENT BUSINESS PRACTICES
DECLARED BANKRUPTCY
COUNTERSUIT FILED AGAINST GOTHAM CITY
FOUR CITATIONS: MENACING
THREE MEN WHO LOST EVERYTHING.
THREE MEN FOR WHOM I CAN FIND NO ALIBIS.

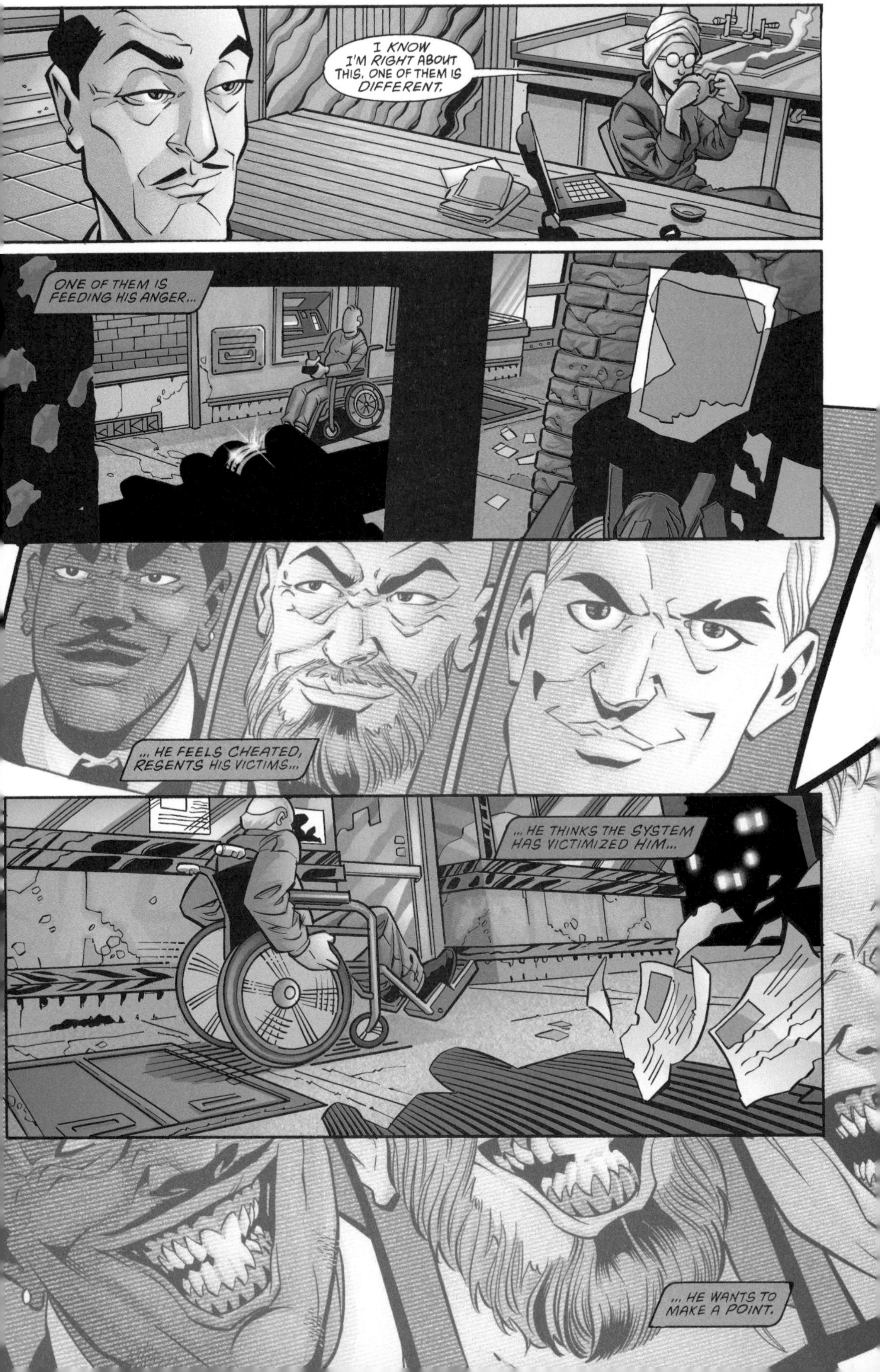
I KNOW I'M RIGHT ABOUT THIS. ONE OF THEM IS DIFFERENT.
ONE OF THEM IS FEEDING HIS ANGER...
...HE FEELS CHEATED, RESENTS HIS VICTIMS...
...HE THINKS THE SYSTEM HAS VICTIMIZED HIM...
...HE WANTS TO MAKE A POINT.

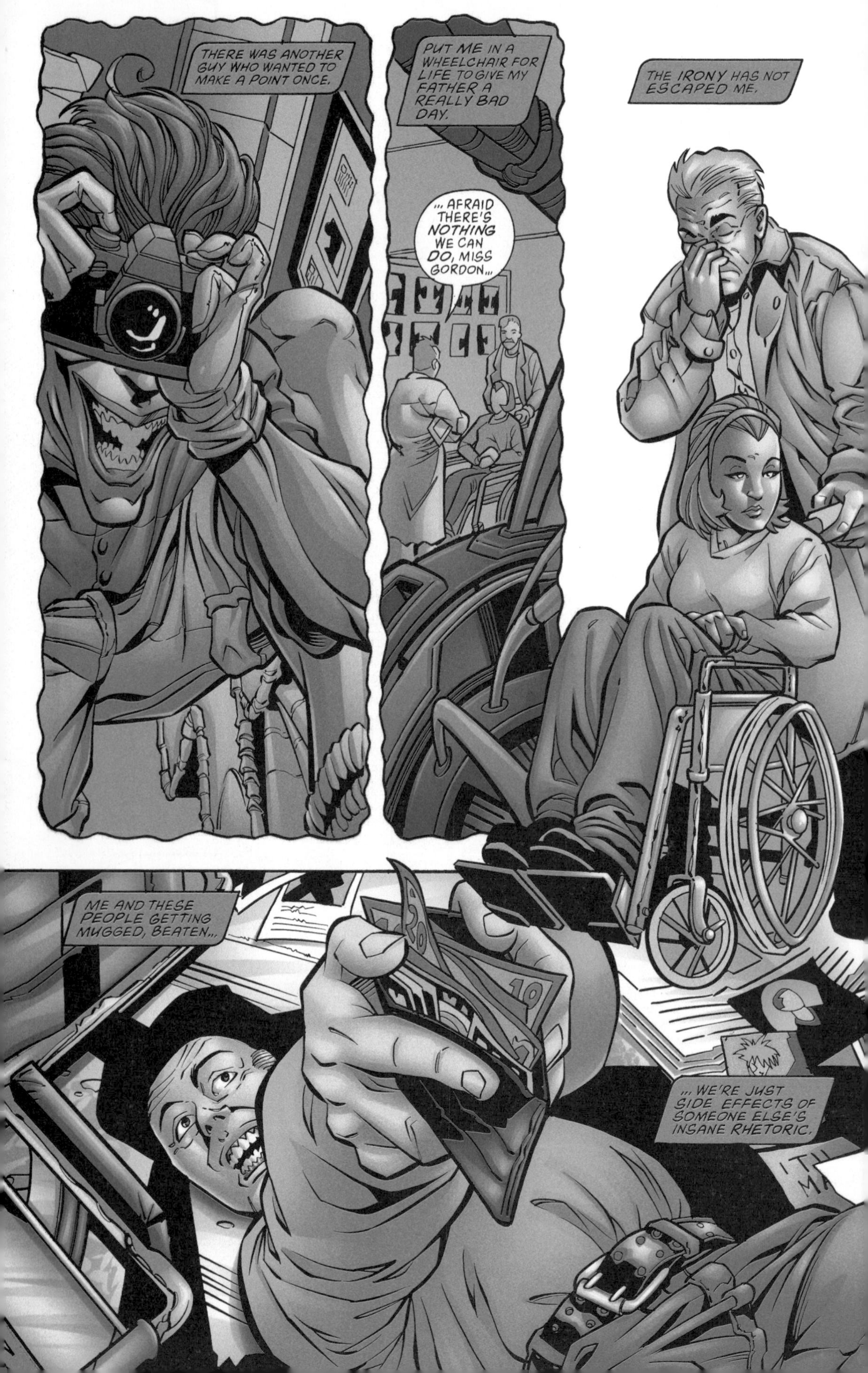
THERE WAS ANOTHER GUY WHO WANTED TO MAKE A POINT ONCE.
PUT ME IN A WHEELCHAIR FOR LIFE TO GIVE MY FATHER A REALLY BAD DAY.
...AFRAID THERE'S NOTHING WE CAN DO, MISS GORDON...
THE IRONY HAS NOT ESCAPED ME.
ME AND THESE PEOPLE GETTING MUGGED, BEATEN...
...WE'RE JUST SIDE EFFECTS OF SOMEONE ELSE'S INSANE RHETORIC.

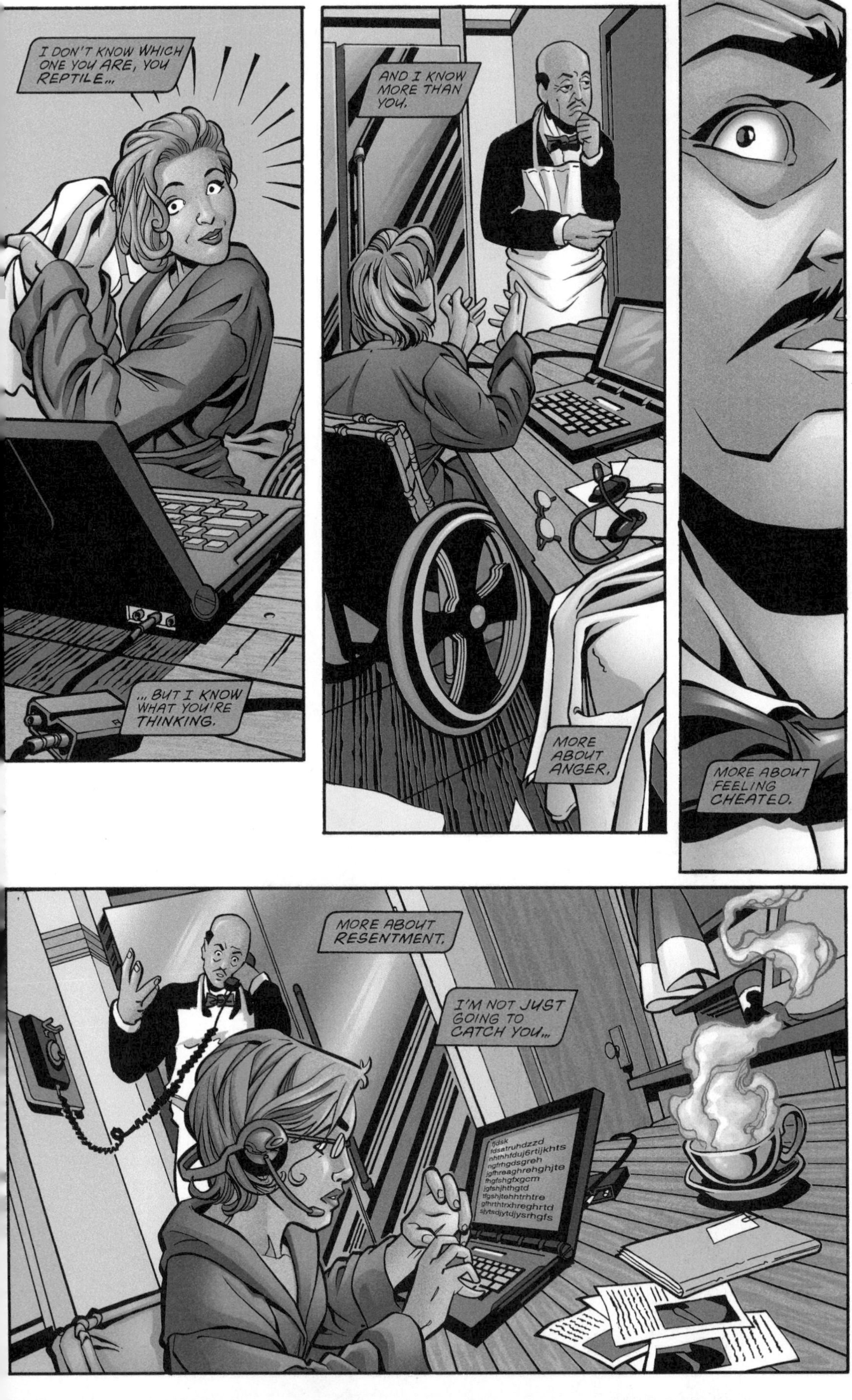
I DON'T KNOW WHICH ONE YOU ARE, YOU REPTILE...
...BUT I KNOW WHAT YOU'RE THINKING.
AND I KNOW MORE THAN YOU.
MORE ABOUT ANGER.
MORE ABOUT FEELING CHEATED.
MORE ABOUT RESENTMENT.
I'M NOT JUST GOING TO CATCH YOU...

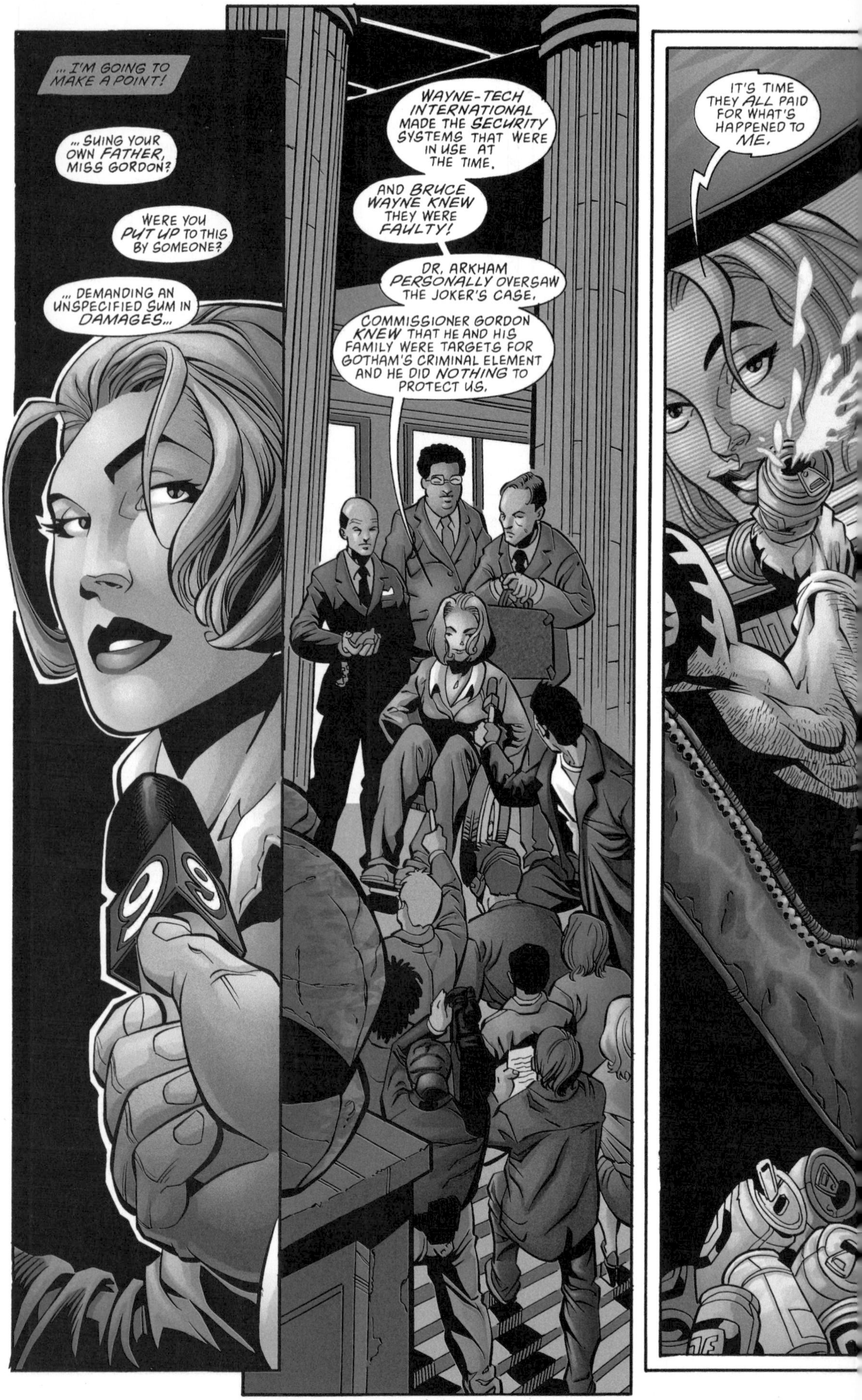
...I'M GOING TO MAKE A POINT!
...SUING YOUR OWN FATHER, MISS GORDON?
WERE YOU PUT UP TO THIS BY SOMEONE?
...DEMANDING AN UNSPECIFIED SUM IN DAMAGES...
WAYNE-TECH INTERNATIONAL MADE THE SECURITY SYSTEMS THAT WERE IN USE AT THE TIME.
AND BRUCE WAYNE KNEW THEY WERE FAULTY!
DR. ARKHAM PERSONALLY OVERSAW THE JOKER'S CASE.
COMMISSIONER GORDON KNEW THAT HE AND HIS FAMILY WERE TARGETS FOR GOTHAM'S CRIMINAL ELEMENT AND HE DID NOTHING TO PROTECT US.
IT'S TIME THEY ALL PAID FOR WHAT'S HAPPENED TO ME.

Y'SEE? SHTINKIN' **MALINGERERS!**

LOOKIN' TO **DESTROY** A GUY...

GOTHAM HERALD

25 CENTS

Gordon's daughter sues, ...with only weeks before the statute of limitations would make suit ...ossible, Barbara Gordon, aided ...histle-blowing testimony ...family employee, charges ...e naming Bruce ...ersonally as well

Um, NO COMMENT?

NO COMMENT.

...MISTAKES IS MISTAKES, LADY...

WAYNE'S JUST A **WORKIN'** MAN, TRYIN' TO GET SOME HOUSES BUILT FAST.

SOME **FOREIGN** KID WANTS **SAFETY** EQUIPMENT, THAS'IS **OWN** LOOKOUT.

THAT STUFF COSTS **MONEY!** SLOWS DOWN THE JOB!

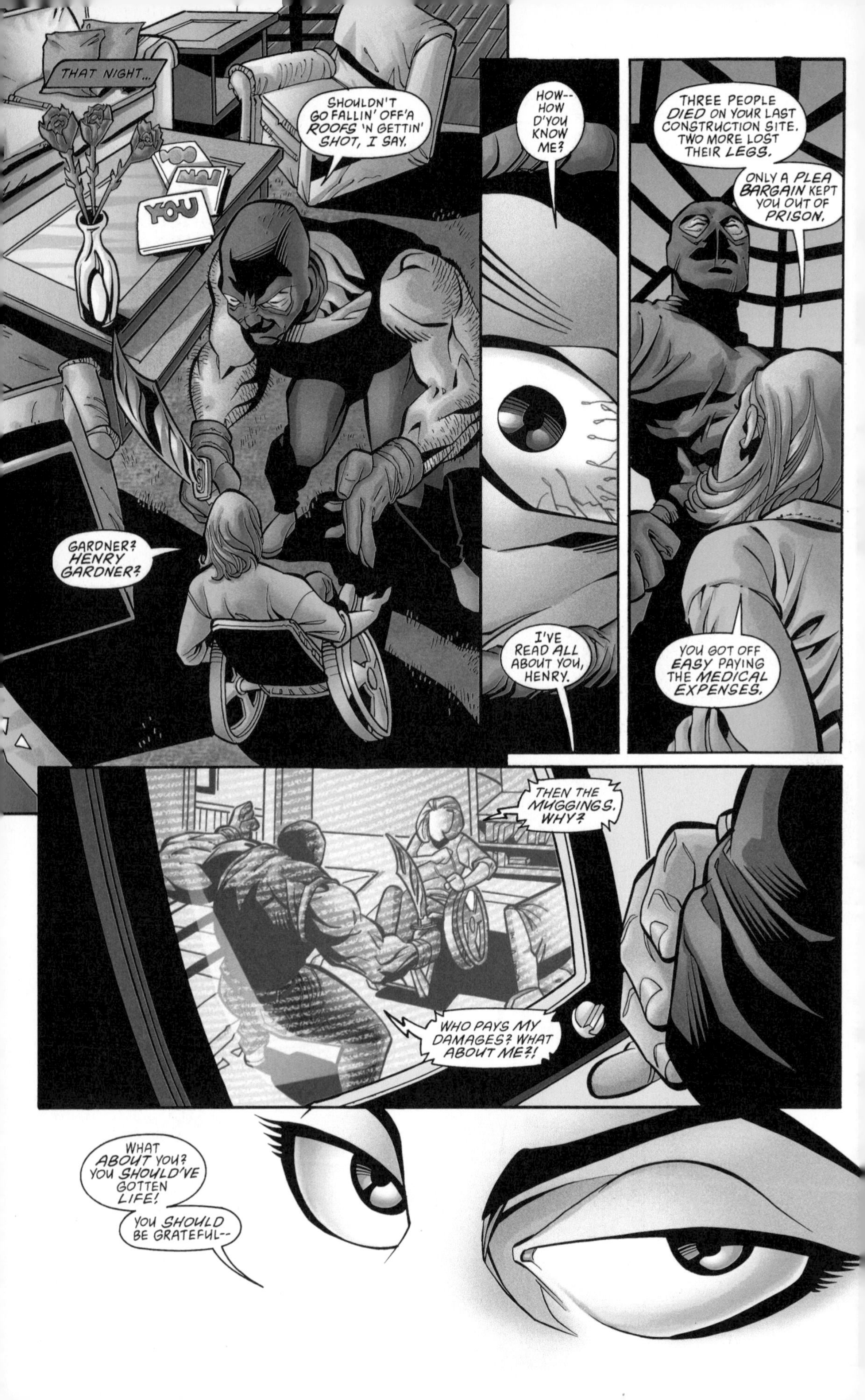
THAT NIGHT...
SHOULDN'T GO FALLIN' OFF'A ROOFS 'N GETTIN' SHOT, I SAY.
GARDNER? HENRY GARDNER?
HOW-- HOW D'YOU KNOW ME?
I'VE READ ALL ABOUT YOU, HENRY.
THREE PEOPLE DIED ON YOUR LAST CONSTRUCTION SITE. TWO MORE LOST THEIR LEGS.
ONLY A PLEA BARGAIN KEPT YOU OUT OF PRISON.
YOU GOT OFF EASY PAYING THE MEDICAL EXPENSES.
THEN THE MUGGINGS. WHY?
WHO PAYS MY DAMAGES? WHAT ABOUT ME?!
WHAT ABOUT YOU? YOU SHOULD'VE GOTTEN LIFE!
YOU SHOULD BE GRATEFUL--

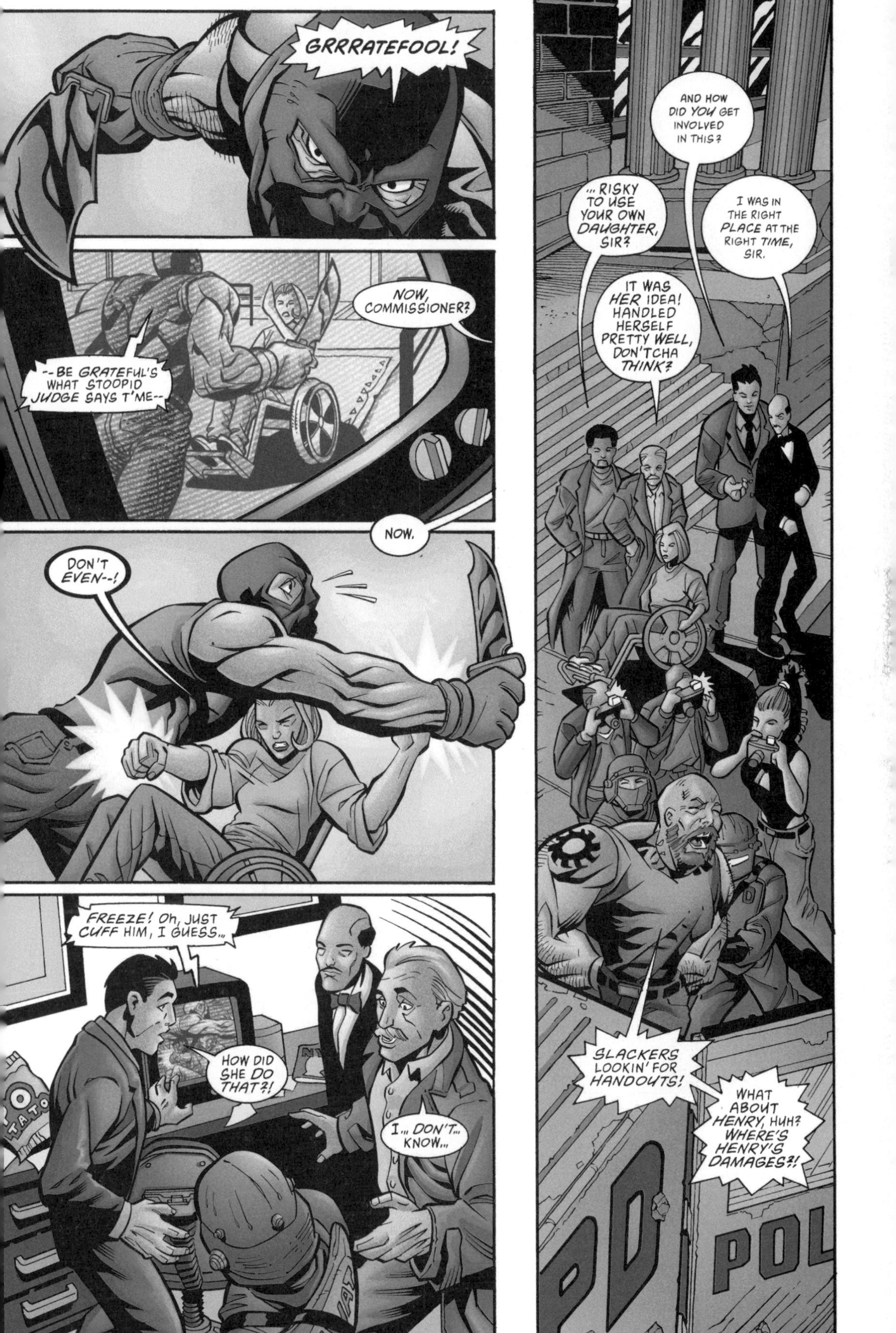
GRRRATEFOOL!
NOW, COMMISSIONER?
--BE GRATEFUL'S WHAT STOOPID JUDGE SAYS T'ME--
NOW.
DON'T EVEN--!
FREEZE! Oh, JUST CUFF HIM, I GUESS...
HOW DID SHE DO THAT?!
I... DON'T... KNOW...
AND HOW DID YOU GET INVOLVED IN THIS?
...RISKY TO USE YOUR OWN DAUGHTER, SIR?
I WAS IN THE RIGHT PLACE AT THE RIGHT TIME, SIR.
IT WAS HER IDEA! HANDLED HERSELF PRETTY WELL, DON'TCHA THINK?
SLACKERS LOOKIN' FOR HANDOUTS!
WHAT ABOUT HENRY, HUH? WHERE'S HENRY'S DAMAGES?!
PD
POL

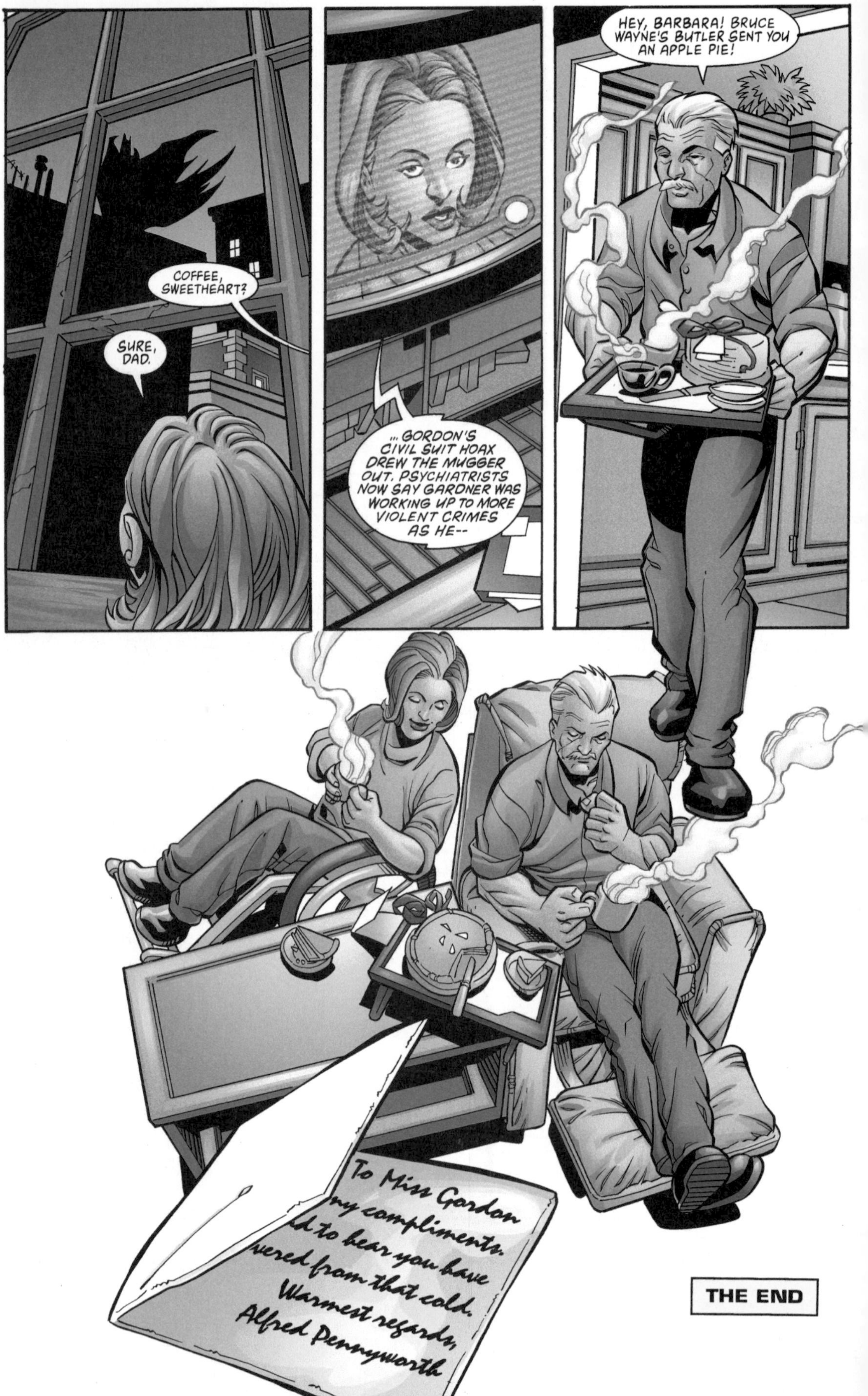
COFFEE, SWEETHEART?
SURE, DAD.
...GORDON'S CIVIL SUIT HOAX DREW THE MUGGER OUT. PSYCHIATRISTS NOW SAY GARDNER WAS WORKING UP TO MORE VIOLENT CRIMES AS HE--
HEY, BARBARA! BRUCE WAYNE'S BUTLER SENT YOU AN APPLE PIE!
To Miss Gordon
my compliments.
to hear you have
from that cold.
Warmest regards,
Alfred Pennyworth
THE END

"Batman is getting a brand-new voice."
– USA TODAY

"A great showcase for the new team as well as offering a taste of the new flavor they'll be bringing to Gotham City." **– IGN**

DC UNIVERSE REBIRTH

BATMAN

VOL. 1: I AM GOTHAM
TOM KING
with DAVID FINCH

VOL. 1 I AM GOTHAM
TOM KING · DAVID FINCH

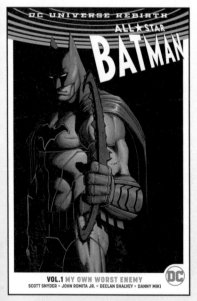

ALL-STAR BATMAN VOL. 1:
MY OWN WORST ENEMY

NIGHTWING VOL. 1:
BETTER THAN BATMAN

DETECTIVE COMICS VOL. 1:
RISE OF THE BATMEN

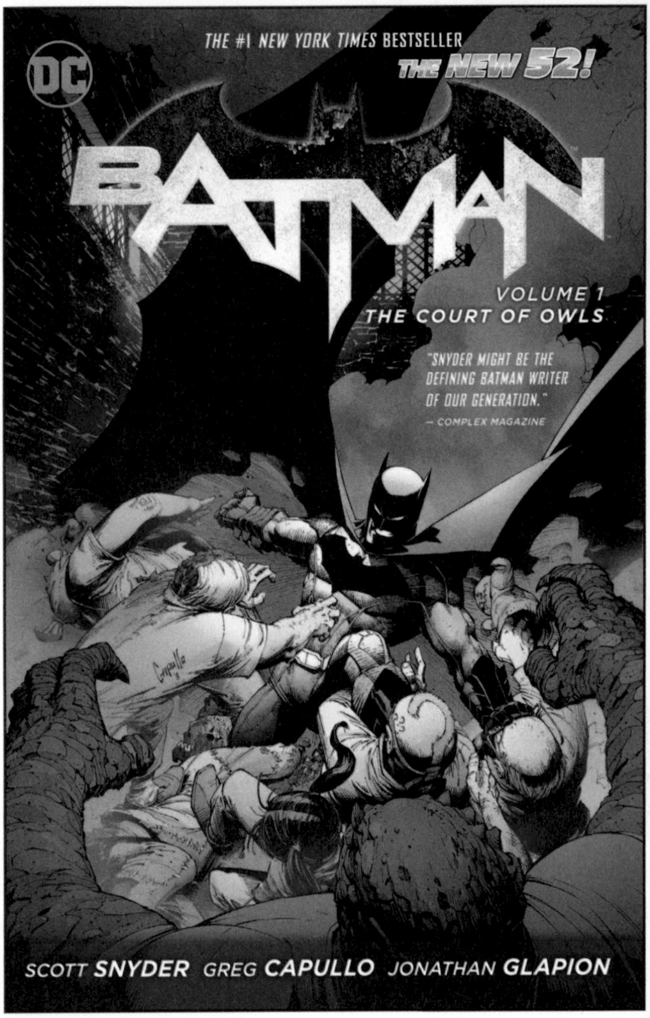
THE #1 NEW YORK TIMES BESTSELLER
THE NEW 52!
BATMAN
VOLUME 1
THE COURT OF OWLS
"SNYDER MIGHT BE THE DEFINING BATMAN WRITER OF OUR GENERATION."
— COMPLEX MAGAZINE
SCOTT SNYDER GREG CAPULLO JONATHAN GLAPION

"[Writer Scott Snyder] pulls from the oldest aspects of the Batman myth, combines it with sinister-comic elements from the series' best period, and gives the whole thing terrific forward-spin."
– ENTERTAINMENT WEEKLY

START AT THE BEGINNING!

BATMAN

VOL. 1: THE COURT OF OWLS

SCOTT SNYDER with GREG CAPULLO

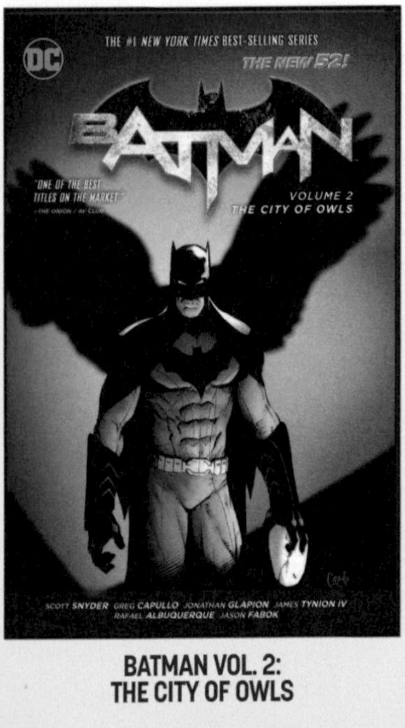
THE #1 NEW YORK TIMES BEST-SELLING SERIES
THE NEW 52!
BATMAN
VOLUME 2
THE CITY OF OWLS
SCOTT SNYDER GREG CAPULLO JONATHAN GLAPION JAMES TYNION IV
RAFAEL ALBUQUERQUE JASON FABOK

BATMAN VOL. 2: THE CITY OF OWLS

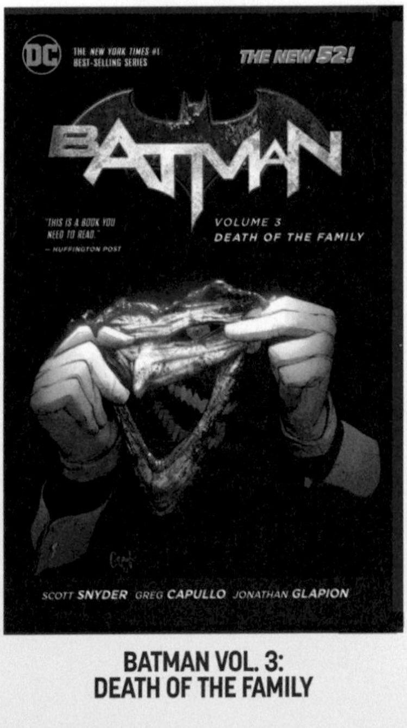
THE NEW 52!
BATMAN
VOLUME 3
DEATH OF THE FAMILY
SCOTT SNYDER GREG CAPULLO JONATHAN GLAPION

BATMAN VOL. 3: DEATH OF THE FAMILY

READ THE ENTIRE EPIC!

BATMAN VOL. 4: ZERO YEAR – SECRET CITY

BATMAN VOL. 5: ZERO YEAR – DARK CITY

BATMAN VOL. 6: GRAVEYARD SHIFT

BATMAN VOL. 7: ENDGAME

BATMAN VOL. 8: SUPERHEAVY

BATMAN VOL. 9: BLOOM

BATMAN VOL. 10: EPILOGUE

Get more DC graphic novels wherever comics and books are sold!

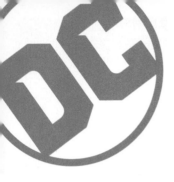

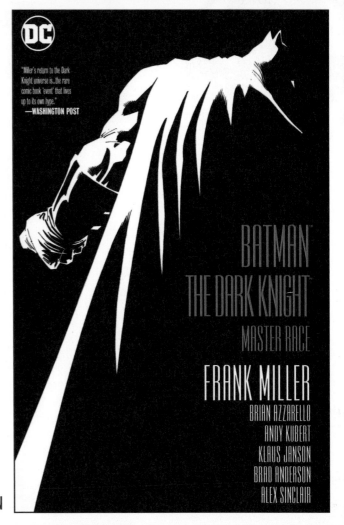

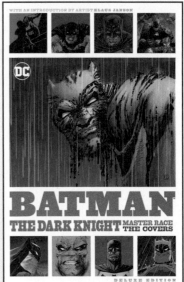

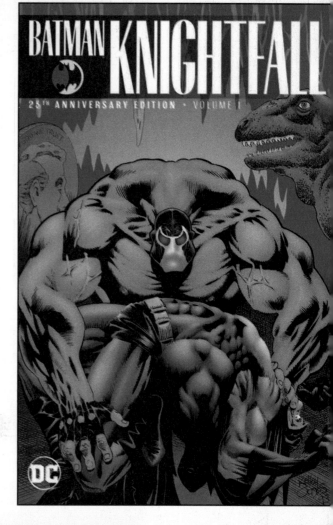